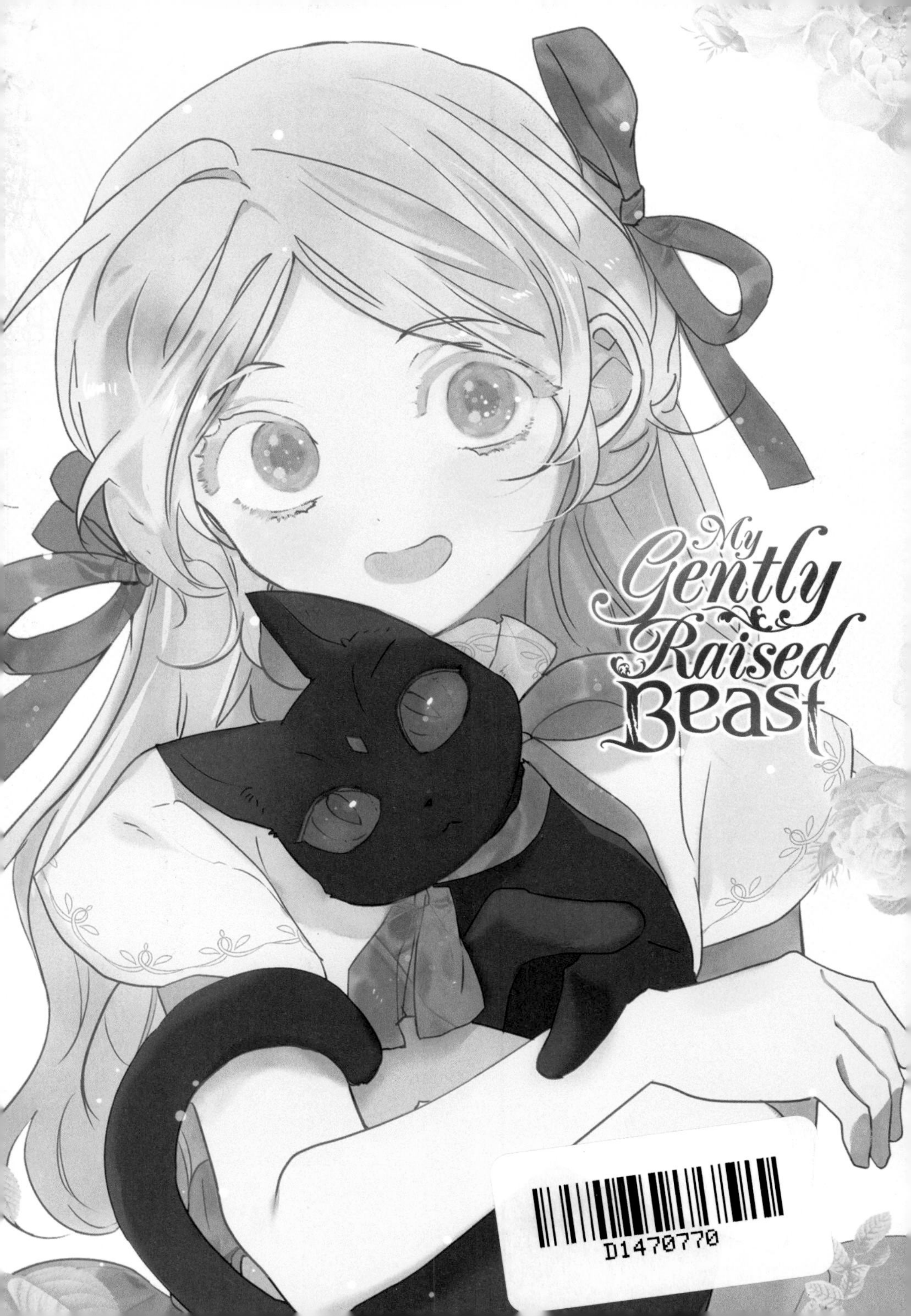
My
Gently
Raised
Beast

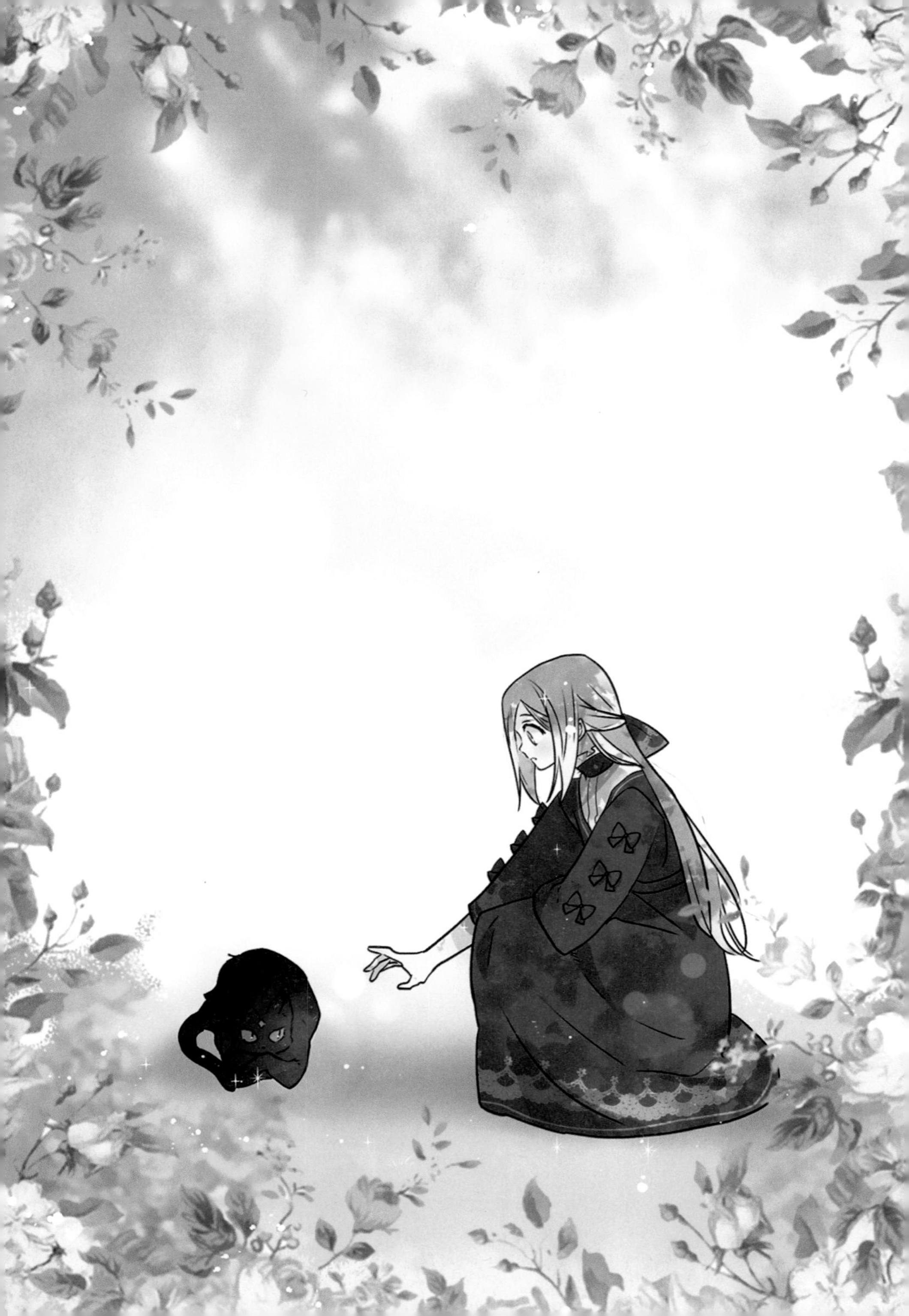

CONTENTS

PART
1

My
Gently
Raised
Beast

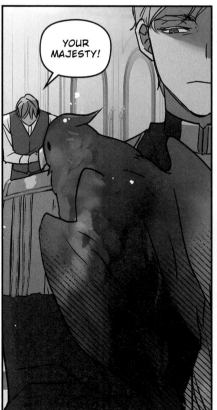

YOUR MAJESTY!

I HAVE AN URGENT MESSAGE!

FLAP

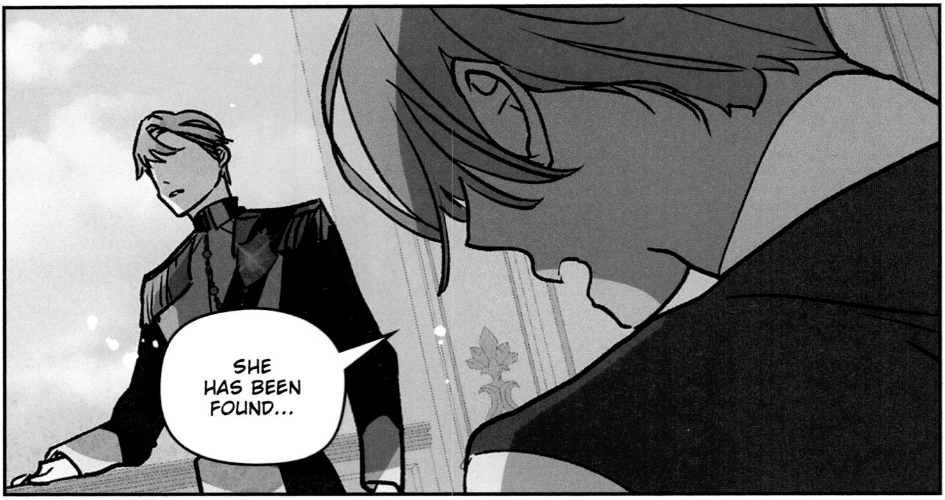
SHE HAS BEEN FOUND...

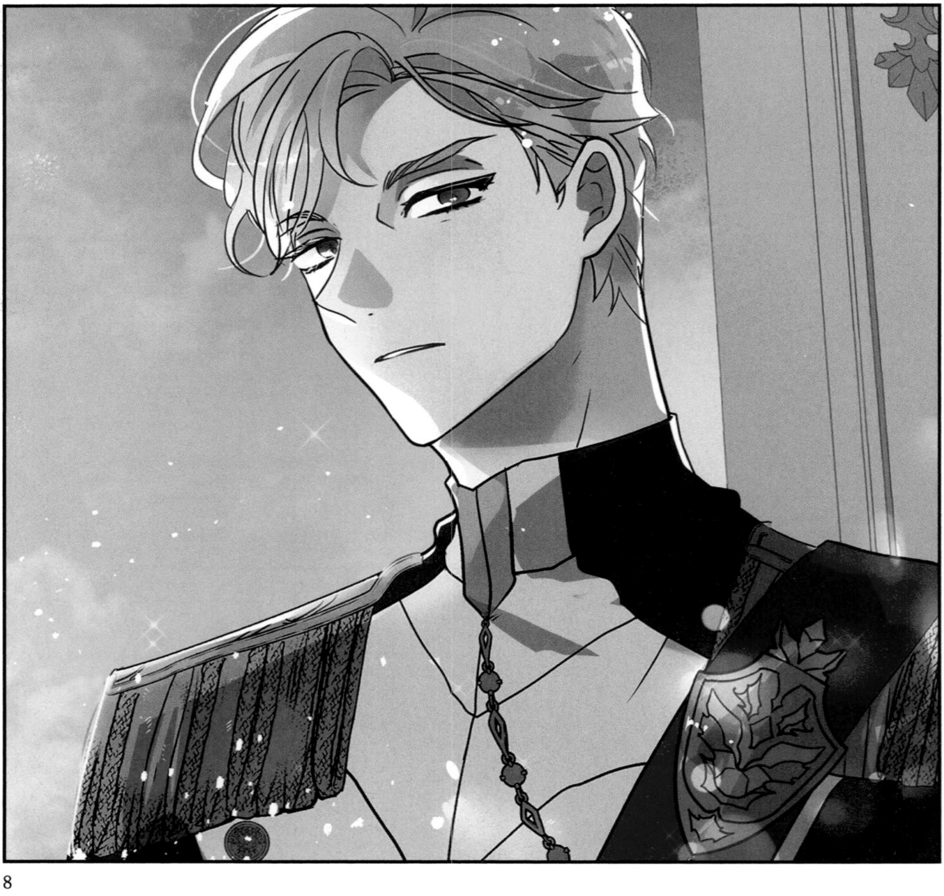

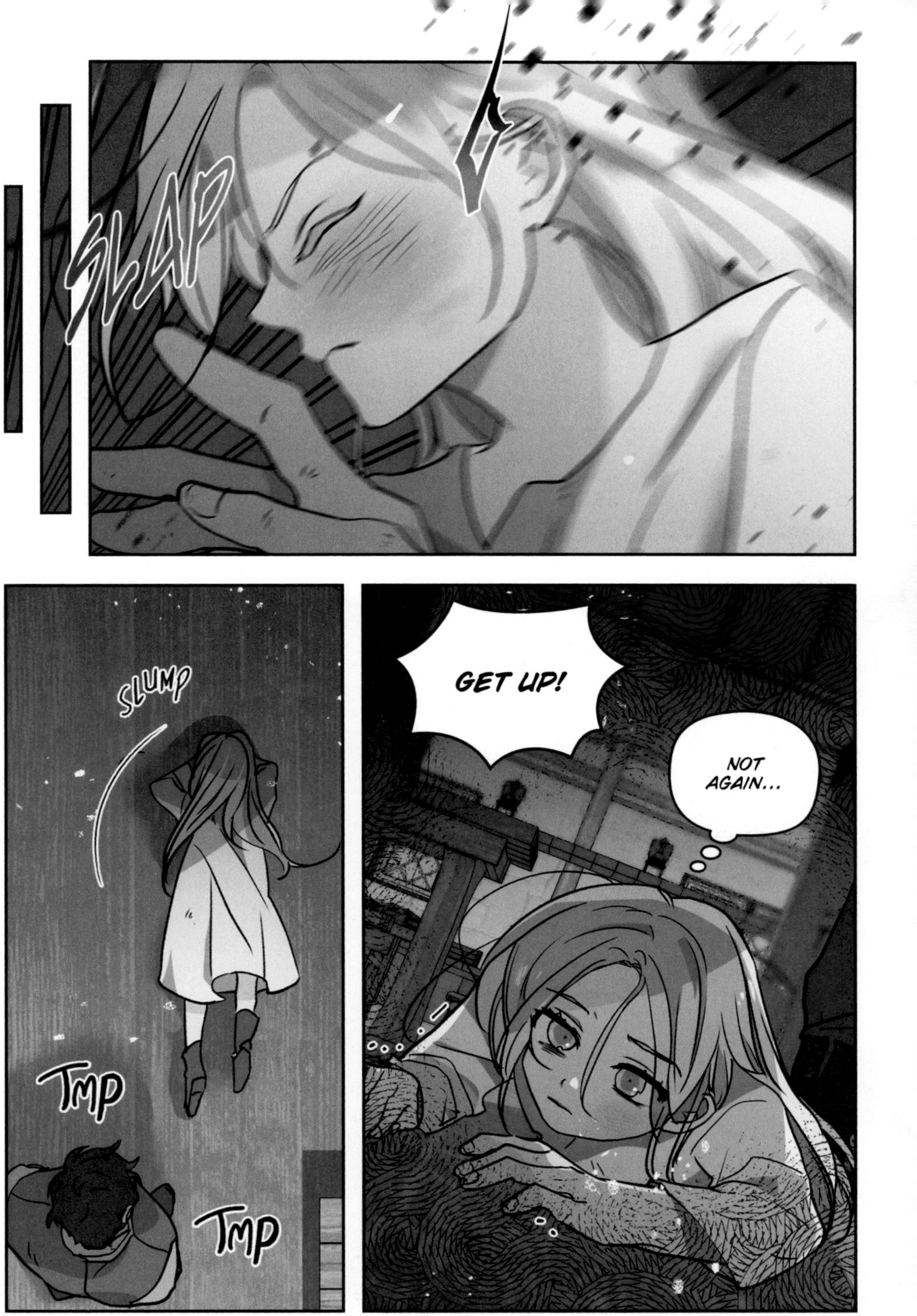
SLAP
SLUMP
TMP
TMP
GET UP!
NOT AGAIN...

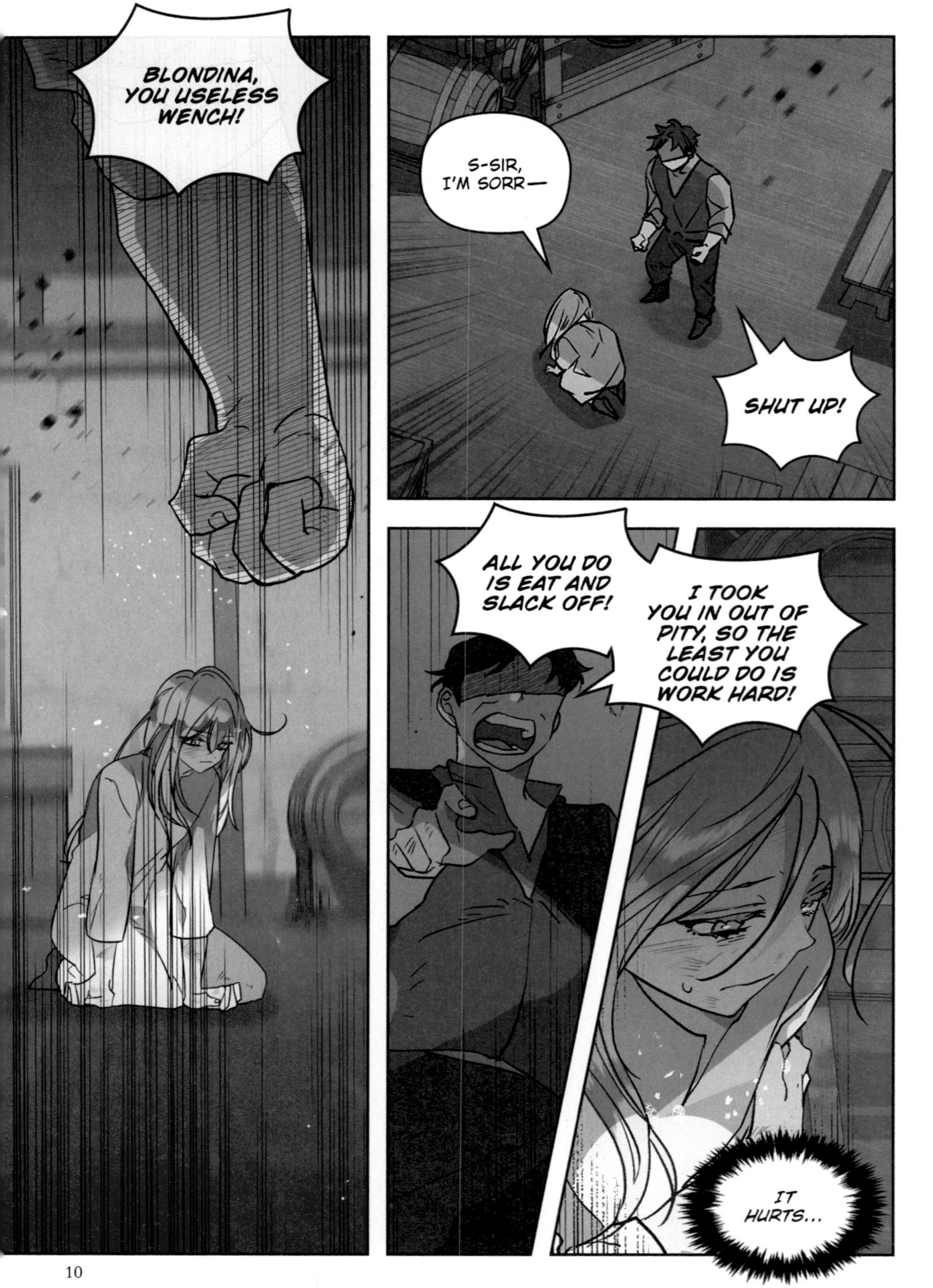
BLONDINA, YOU USELESS WENCH!
S-SIR, I'M SORR—
SHUT UP!
ALL YOU DO IS EAT AND SLACK OFF!
I TOOK YOU IN OUT OF PITY, SO THE LEAST YOU COULD DO IS WORK HARD!
IT HURTS...

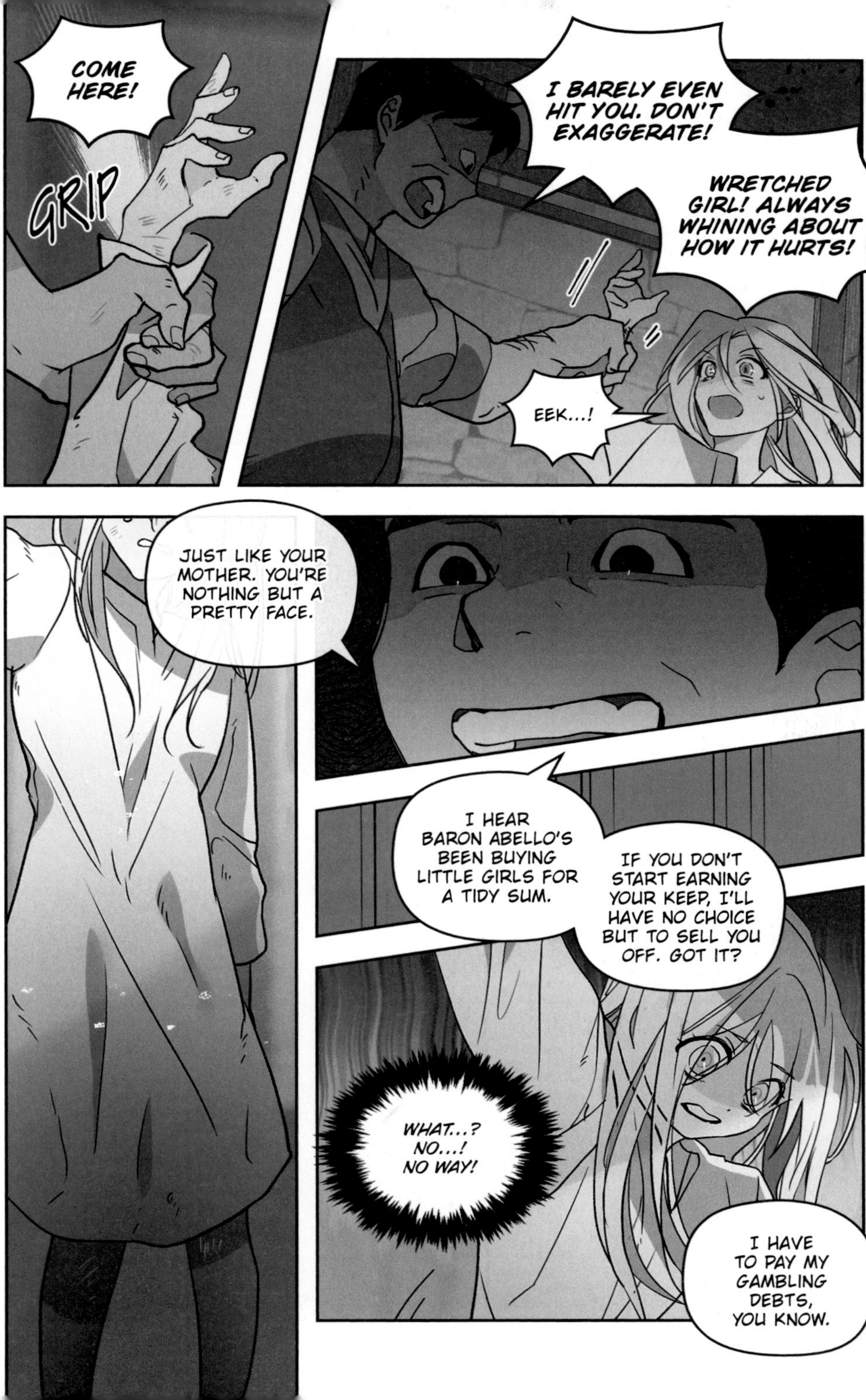
COME HERE!
GRIP
I BARELY EVEN HIT YOU. DON'T EXAGGERATE!
WRETCHED GIRL! ALWAYS WHINING ABOUT HOW IT HURTS!
EEK...!
JUST LIKE YOUR MOTHER. YOU'RE NOTHING BUT A PRETTY FACE.
I HEAR BARON ABELLO'S BEEN BUYING LITTLE GIRLS FOR A TIDY SUM.
IF YOU DON'T START EARNING YOUR KEEP, I'LL HAVE NO CHOICE BUT TO SELL YOU OFF. GOT IT?
WHAT...? NO...! NO WAY!
I HAVE TO PAY MY GAMBLING DEBTS, YOU KNOW.

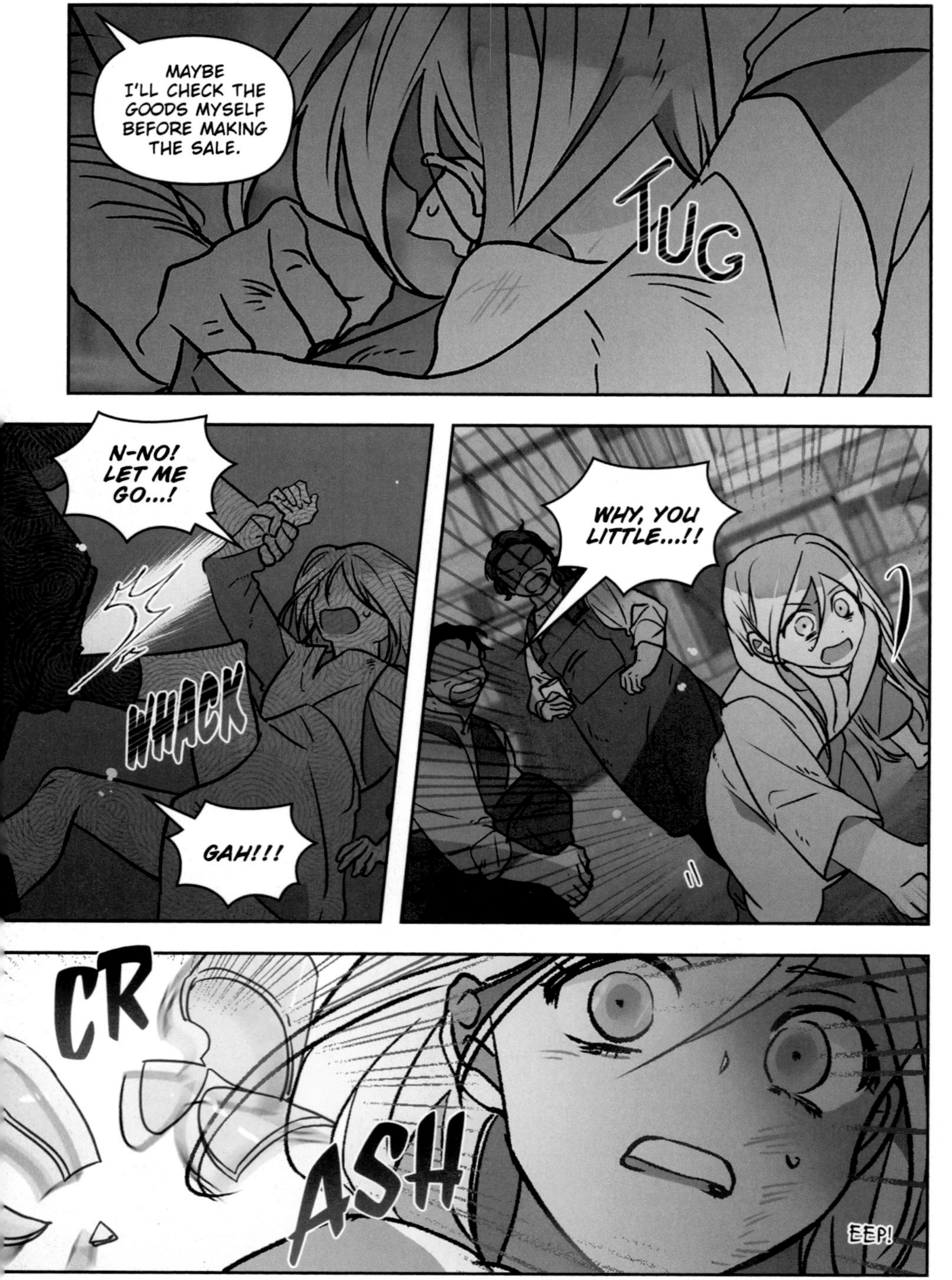
MAYBE I'LL CHECK THE GOODS MYSELF BEFORE MAKING THE SALE.
TUG
N-NO! LET ME GO...!
WHACK
GAH!!!
WHY, YOU LITTLE...!!
CR
ASH
EEP!

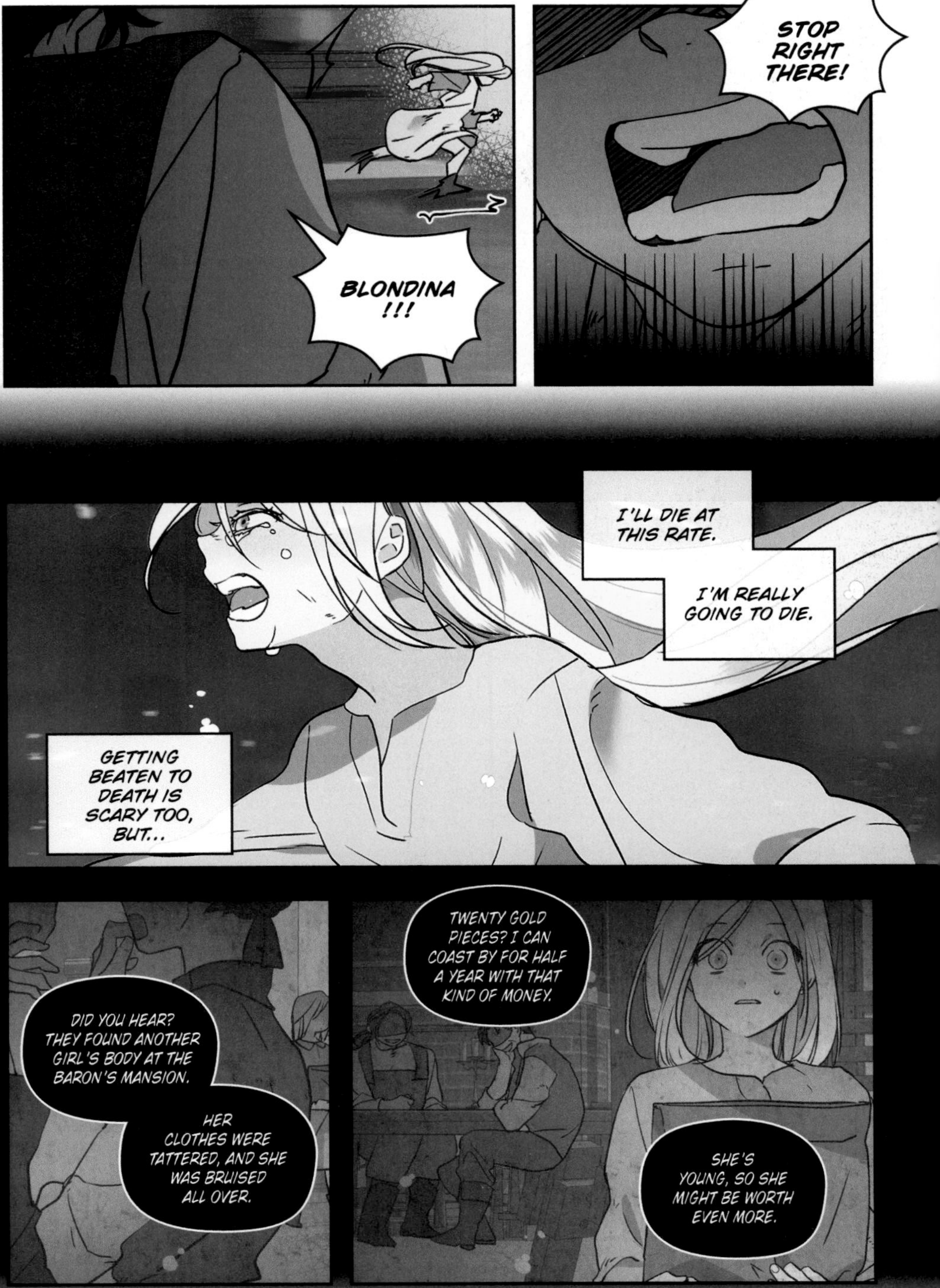
BLONDINA !!!
STOP RIGHT THERE!
I'LL DIE AT THIS RATE.
I'M REALLY GOING TO DIE.
GETTING BEATEN TO DEATH IS SCARY TOO, BUT...
DID YOU HEAR? THEY FOUND ANOTHER GIRL'S BODY AT THE BARON'S MANSION.
HER CLOTHES WERE TATTERED, AND SHE WAS BRUISED ALL OVER.
TWENTY GOLD PIECES? I CAN COAST BY FOR HALF A YEAR WITH THAT KIND OF MONEY.
SHE'S YOUNG, SO SHE MIGHT BE WORTH EVEN MORE.

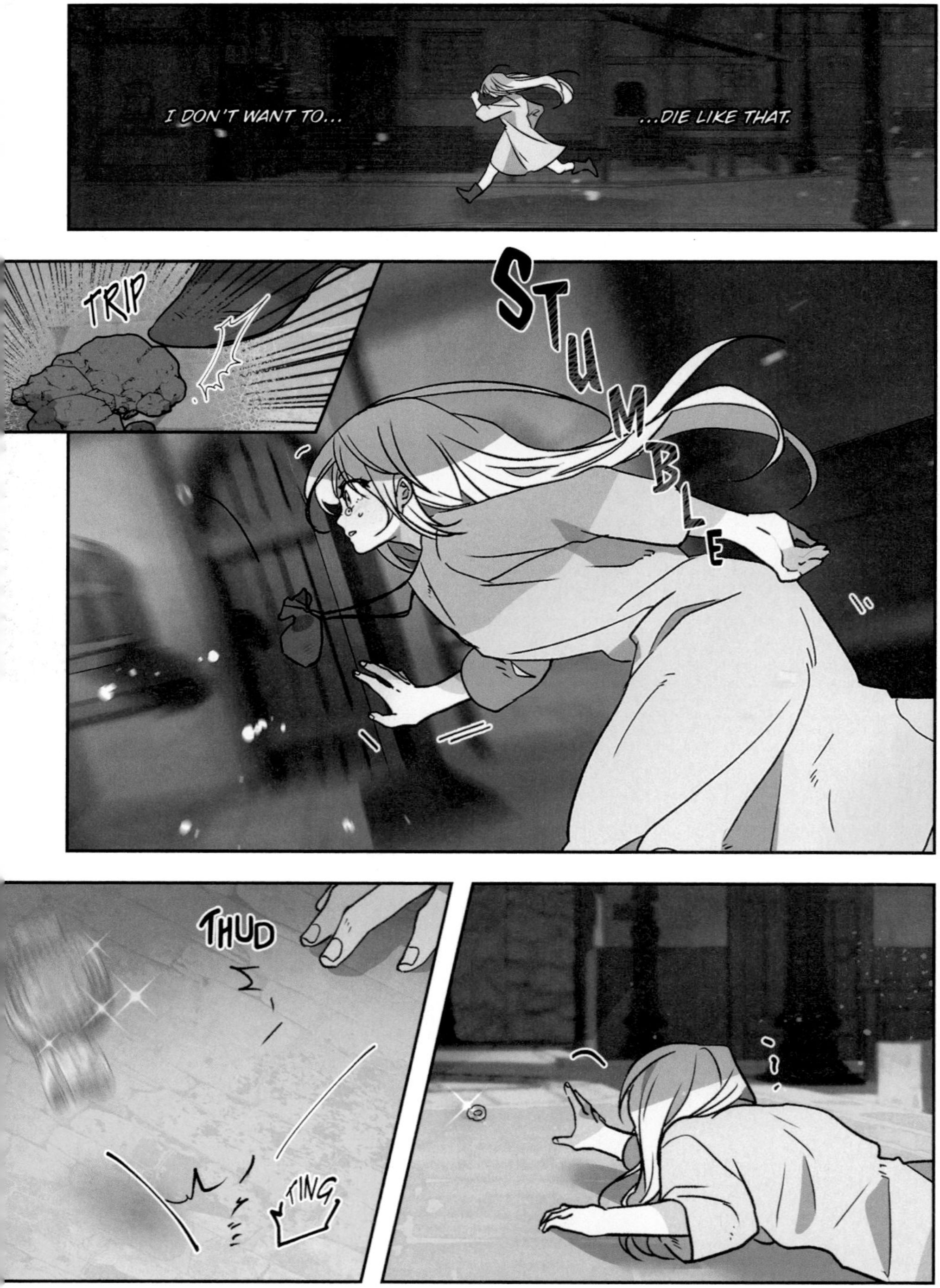
I DON'T WANT TO...
...DIE LIKE THAT.
TRIP
STUMBLE
THUD
TING

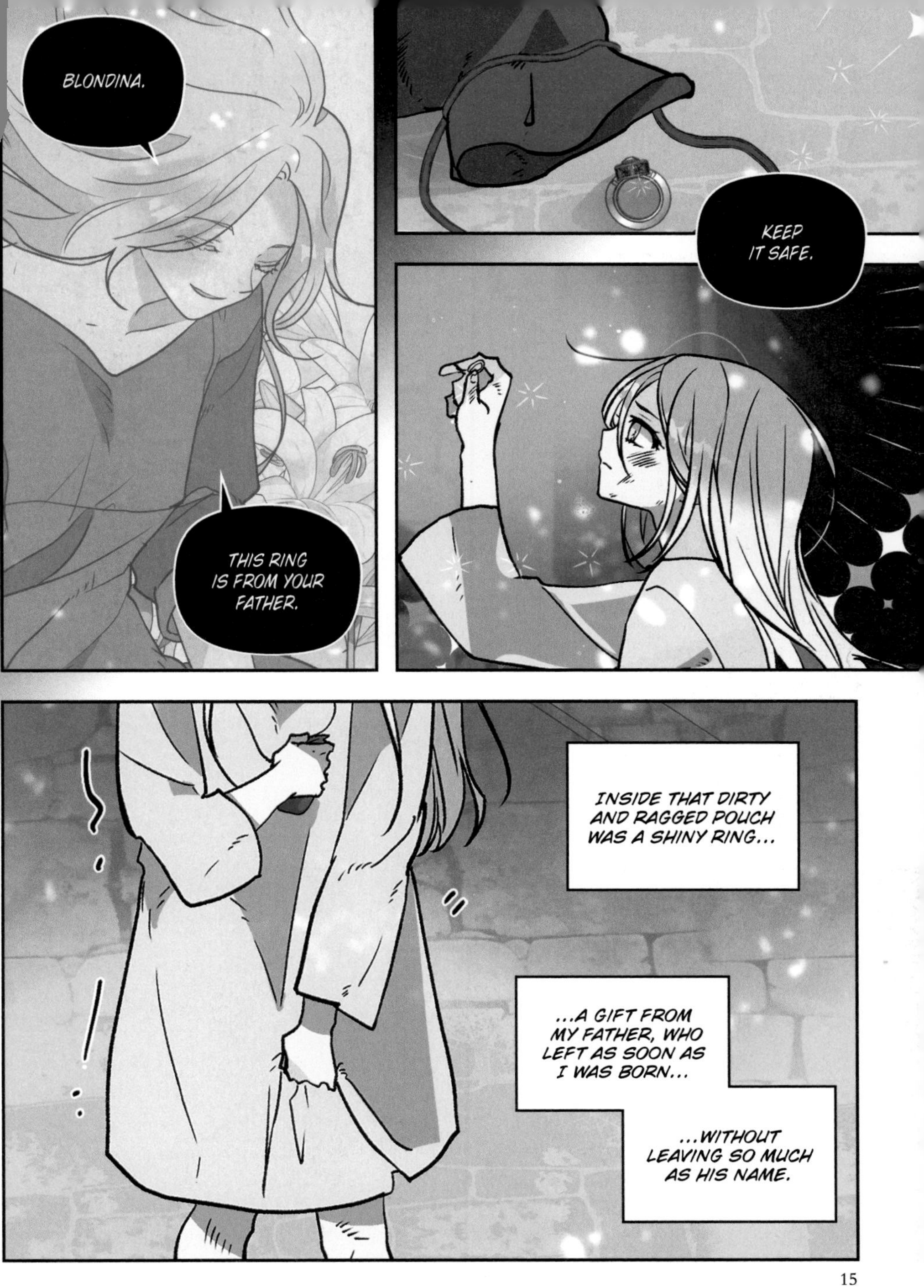
BLONDINA.
THIS RING IS FROM YOUR FATHER.
KEEP IT SAFE.
INSIDE THAT DIRTY AND RAGGED POUCH WAS A SHINY RING...
...A GIFT FROM MY FATHER, WHO LEFT AS SOON AS I WAS BORN...
...WITHOUT LEAVING SO MUCH AS HIS NAME.

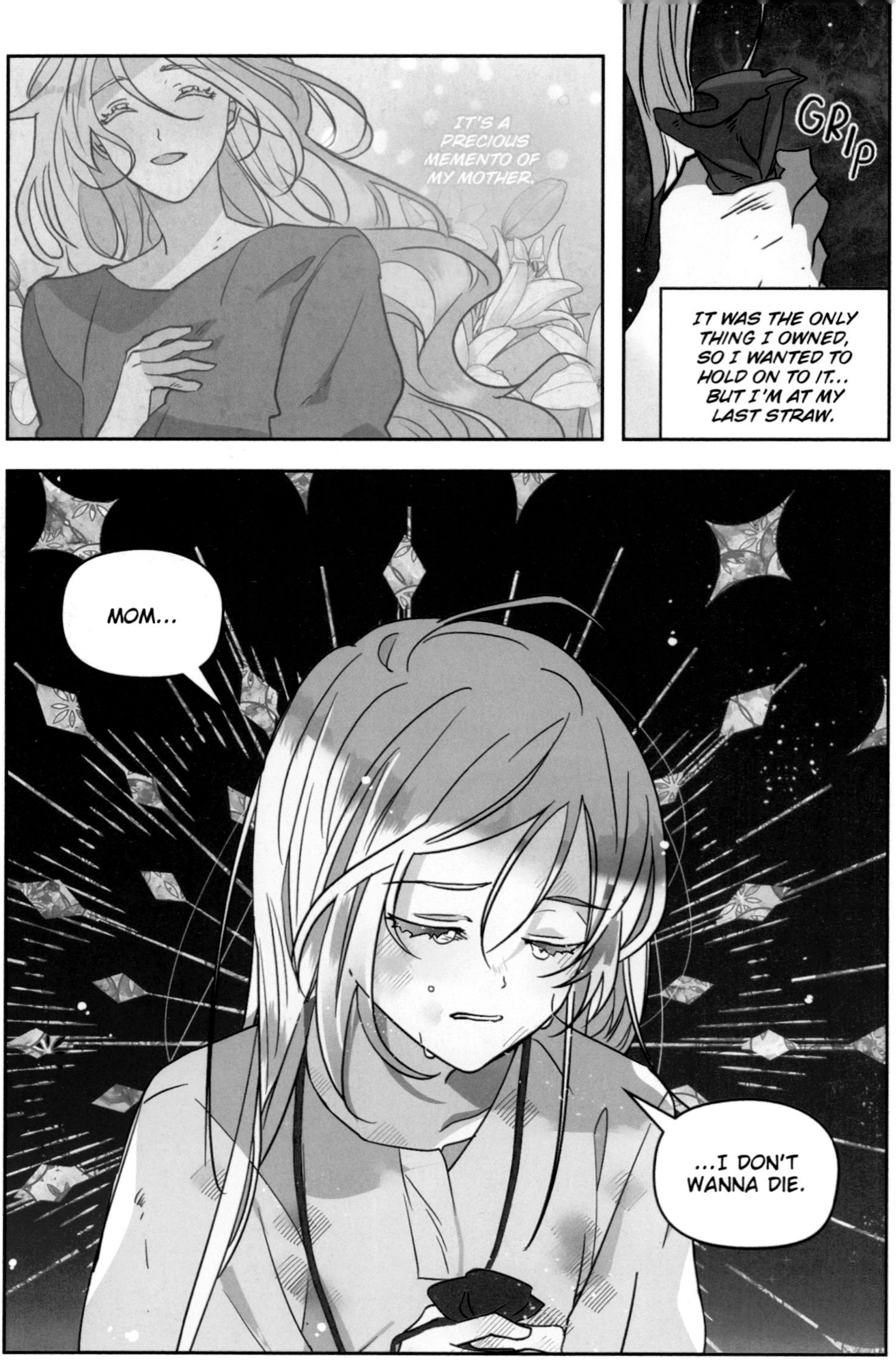
IT'S A PRECIOUS MEMENTO OF MY MOTHER.
GRIP
IT WAS THE ONLY THING I OWNED, SO I WANTED TO HOLD ON TO IT... BUT I'M AT MY LAST STRAW.
MOM...
...I DON'T WANNA DIE.

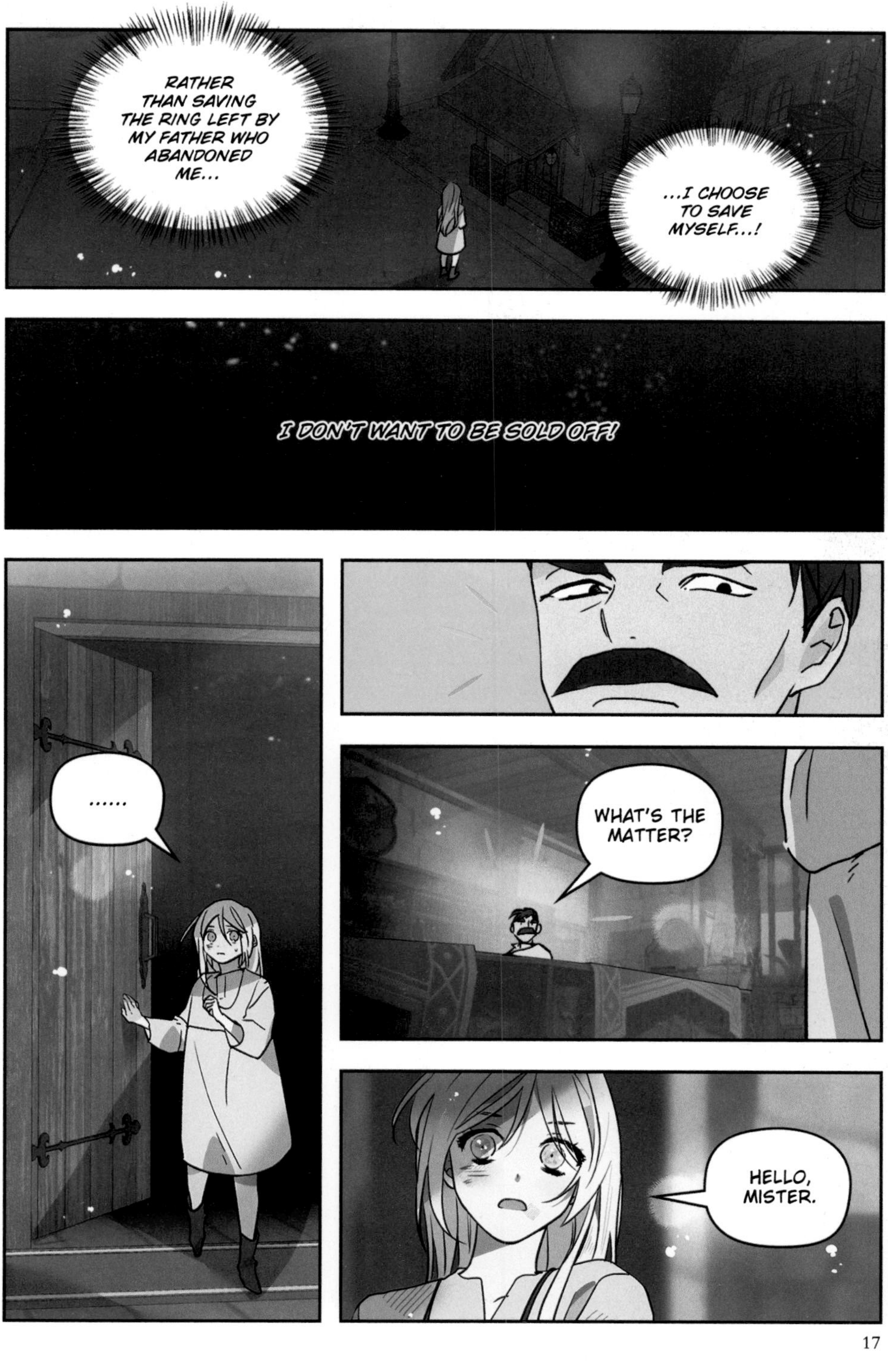
RATHER THAN SAVING THE RING LEFT BY MY FATHER WHO ABANDONED ME...
...I CHOOSE TO SAVE MYSELF...!
I DON'T WANT TO BE SOLD OFF!
......
WHAT'S THE MATTER?
HELLO, MISTER.

SO THAT NORDI SENT YOU TO PAWN SOMETHING OFF AGAIN, EH?

I SWEAR, THAT FOOL WON'T QUIT GAMBLING UNTIL HIS HANDS ARE CHOPPED OFF.

UM, ACTUALLY I'M HERE TO SELL SOMETHING OF MY OWN TODAY.

YOURS?

YES, IT'S MY MOM'S KEEPSAKE...

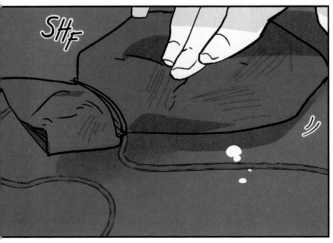

SHF

STINKY~

HMM...

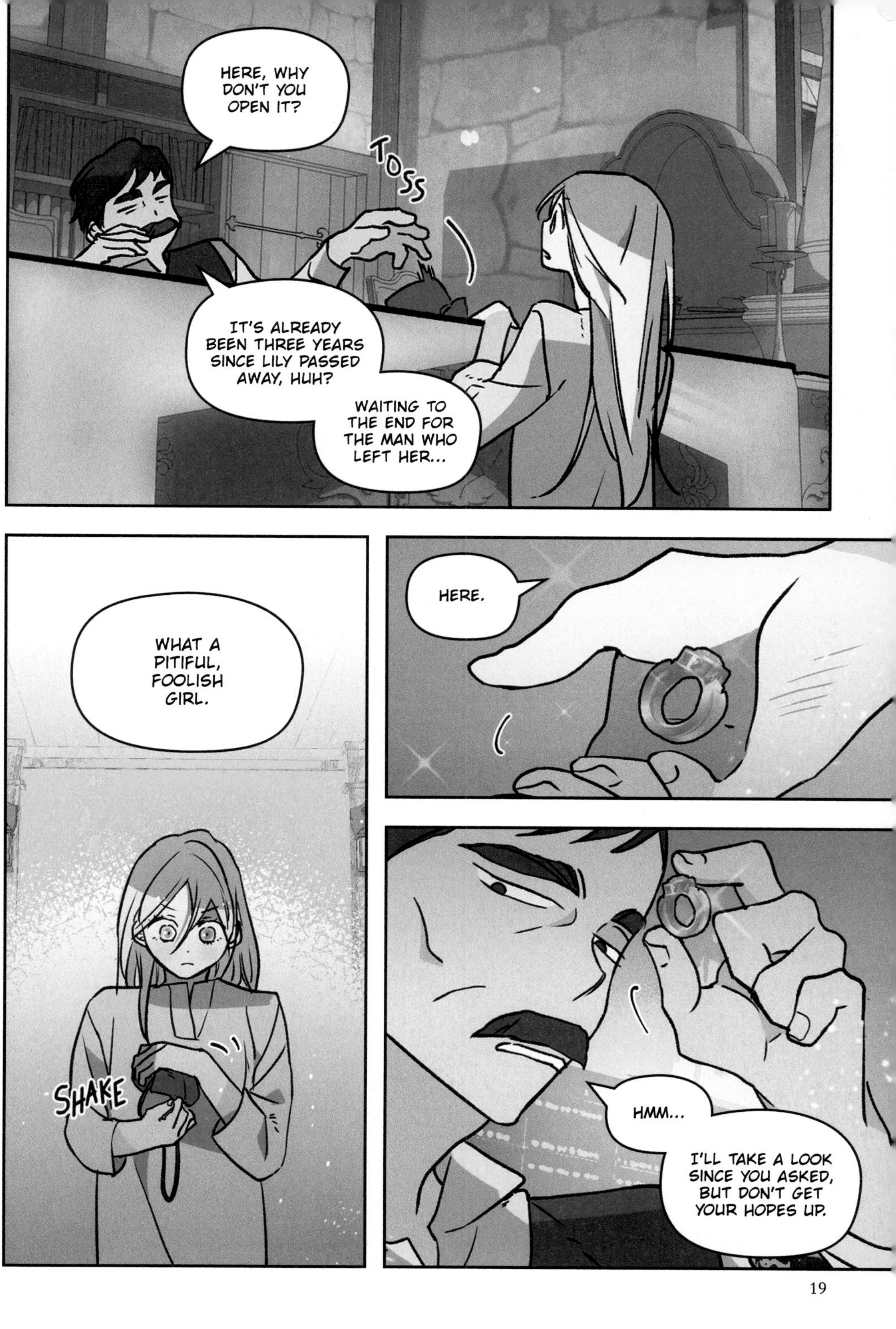
HERE, WHY DON'T YOU OPEN IT?
TOSS
IT'S ALREADY BEEN THREE YEARS SINCE LILY PASSED AWAY, HUH?
WAITING TO THE END FOR THE MAN WHO LEFT HER...
WHAT A PITIFUL, FOOLISH GIRL.
SHAKE
HERE.
HMM...
I'LL TAKE A LOOK SINCE YOU ASKED, BUT DON'T GET YOUR HOPES UP.

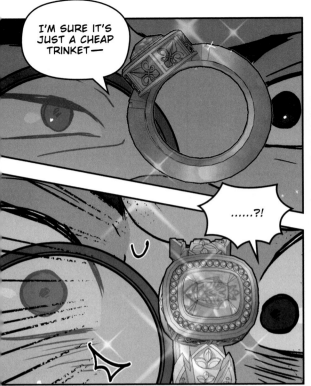

I'M SURE IT'S JUST A CHEAP TRINKET—

......?!

WH-WHERE DID YOU STEAL THIS?

YOU SNEAKY LITTLE RAT!

I DIDN'T STEAL IT!

TH-THEN HOW COULD YOU HAVE SOMETHING LIKE THIS...?!!

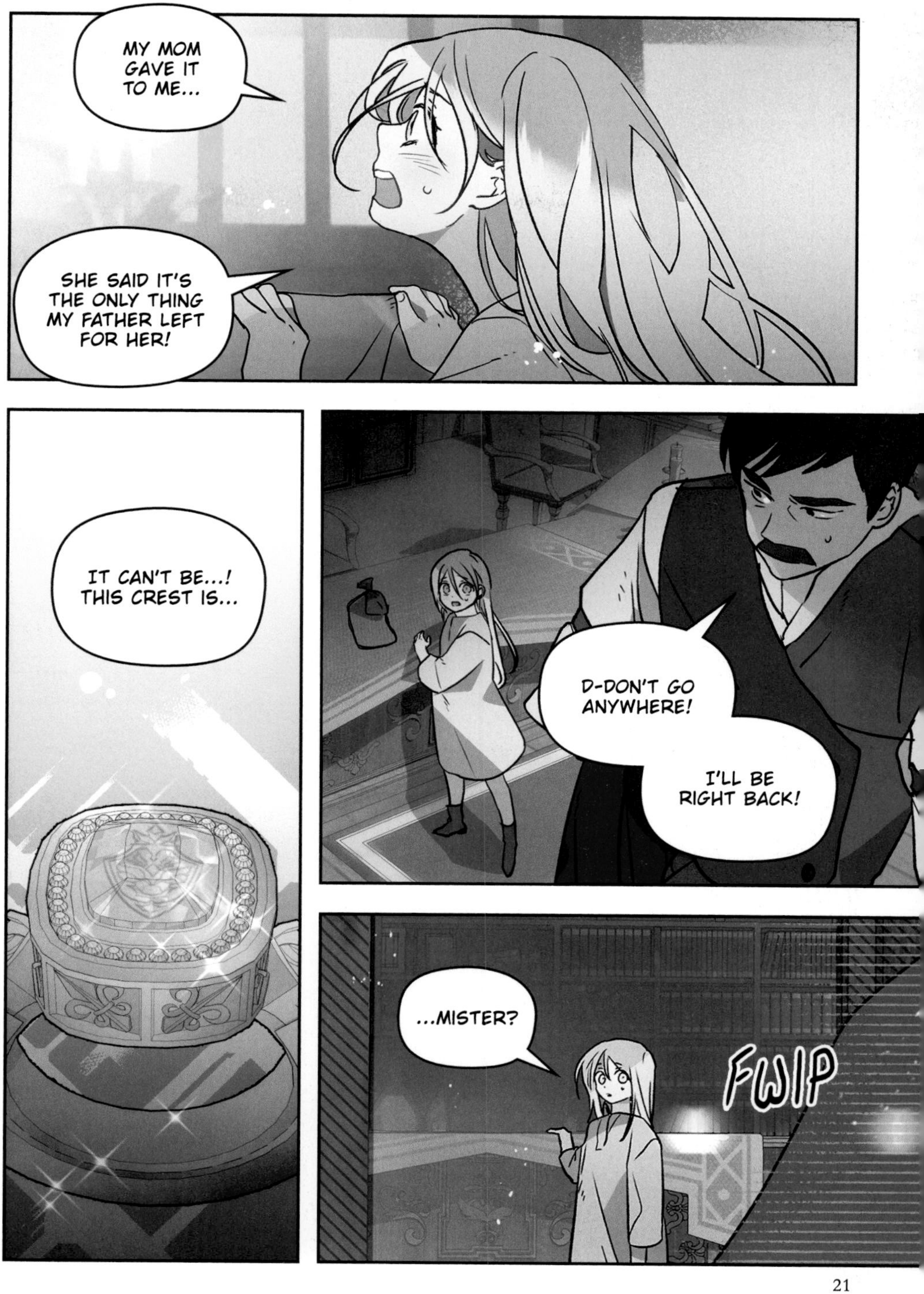
MY MOM GAVE IT TO ME...
SHE SAID IT'S THE ONLY THING MY FATHER LEFT FOR HER!
IT CAN'T BE...! THIS CREST IS...
D-DON'T GO ANYWHERE!
I'LL BE RIGHT BACK!
...MISTER?
FWIP

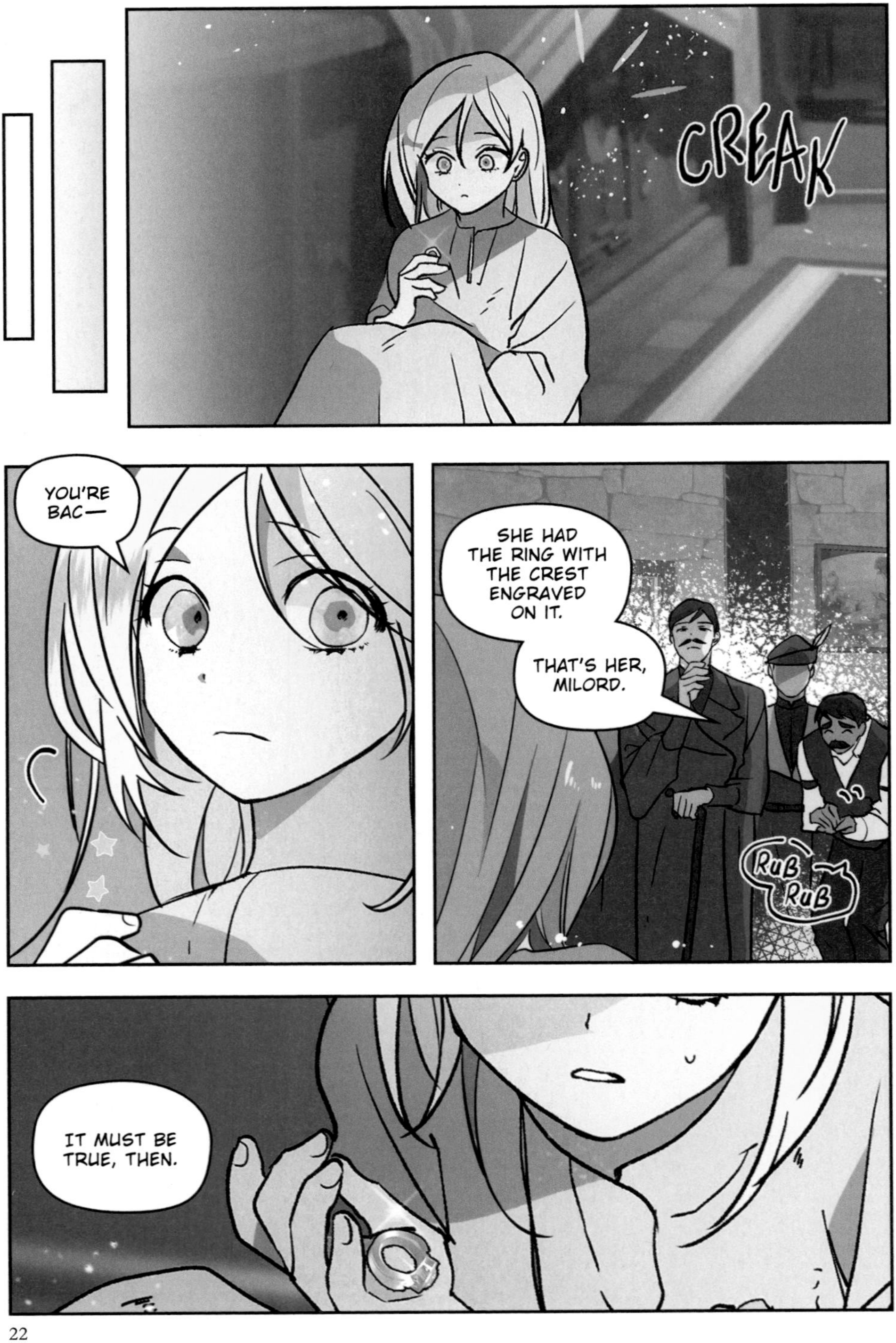
CREAK
YOU'RE BAC—
SHE HAD THE RING WITH THE CREST ENGRAVED ON IT.
THAT'S HER, MILORD.
RUB RUB
IT MUST BE TRUE, THEN.

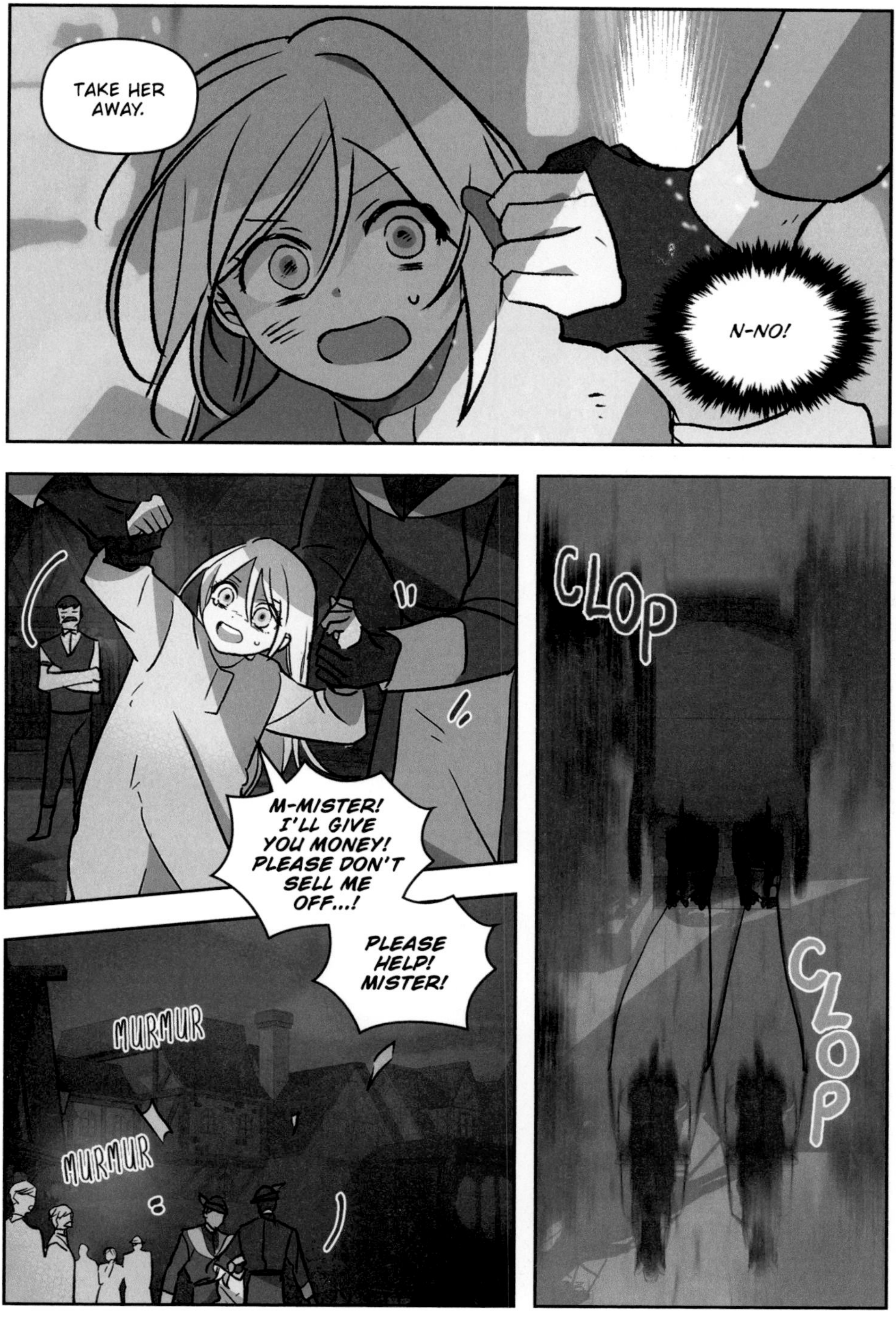
TAKE HER AWAY.
N-NO!
M-MISTER! I'LL GIVE YOU MONEY! PLEASE DON'T SELL ME OFF...!
PLEASE HELP! MISTER!
MURMUR
MURMUR
CLOP
CLOP

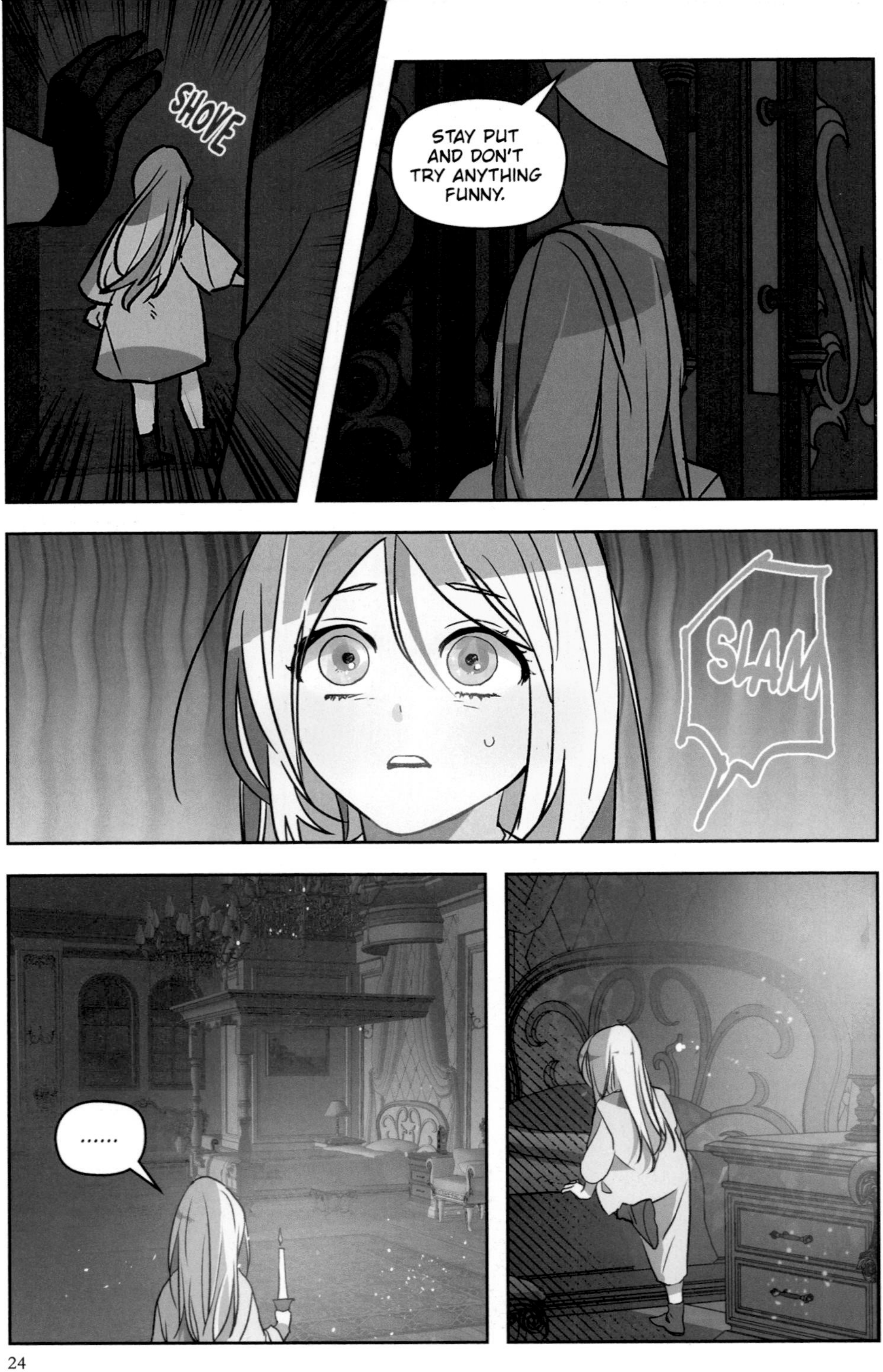
SHOVE
STAY PUT AND DON'T TRY ANYTHING FUNNY.
SLAM
......

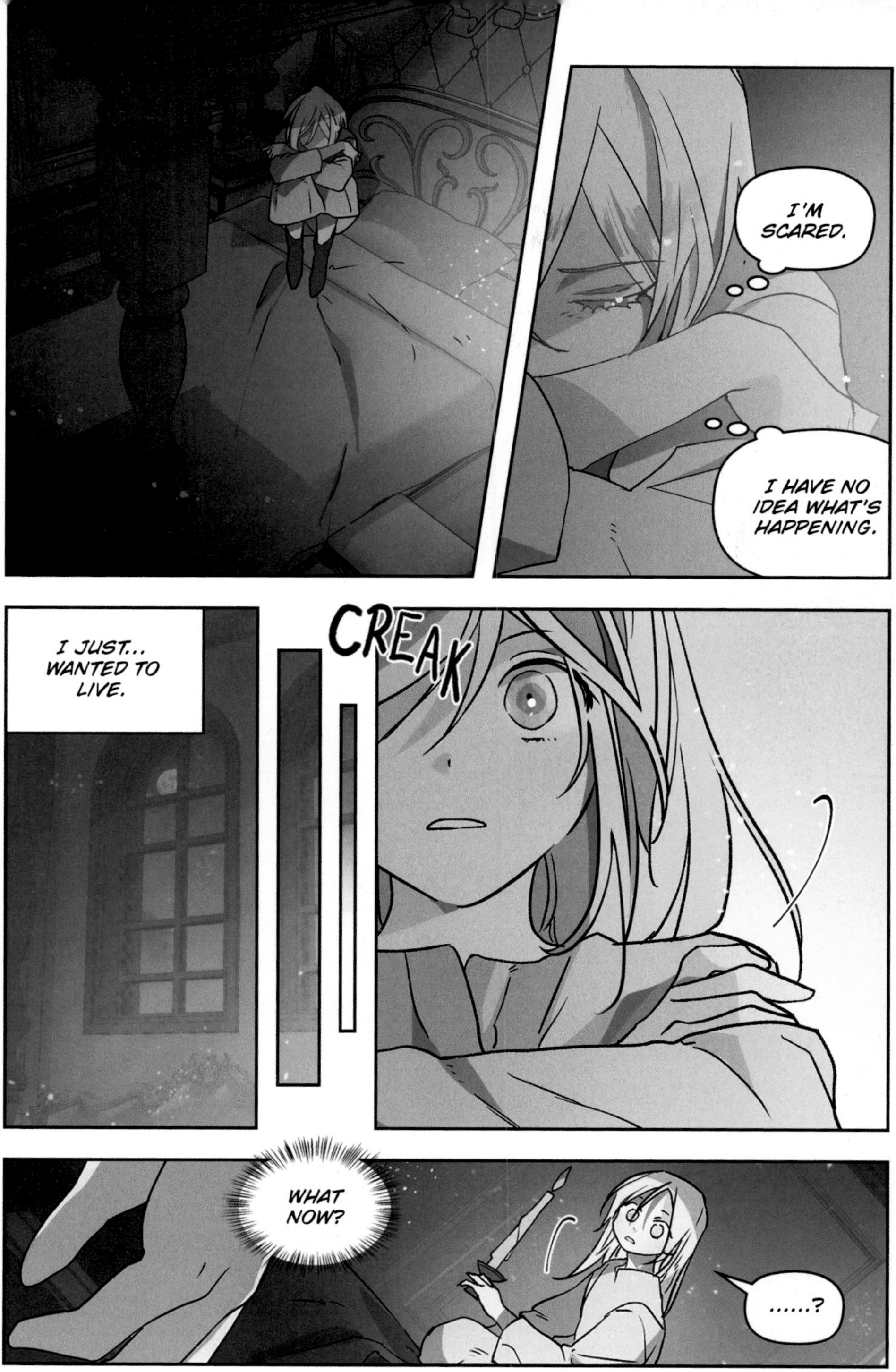
I'M SCARED.
I HAVE NO IDEA WHAT'S HAPPENING.
I JUST... WANTED TO LIVE.
CREAK
WHAT NOW?
......?

WHO...?

IS BARON ABELLO HERE TO TAKE ME?

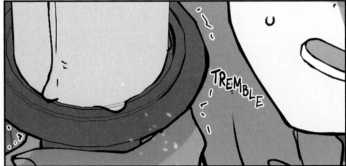

TREMBLE

TMP

TMP

TMP

TMP

26

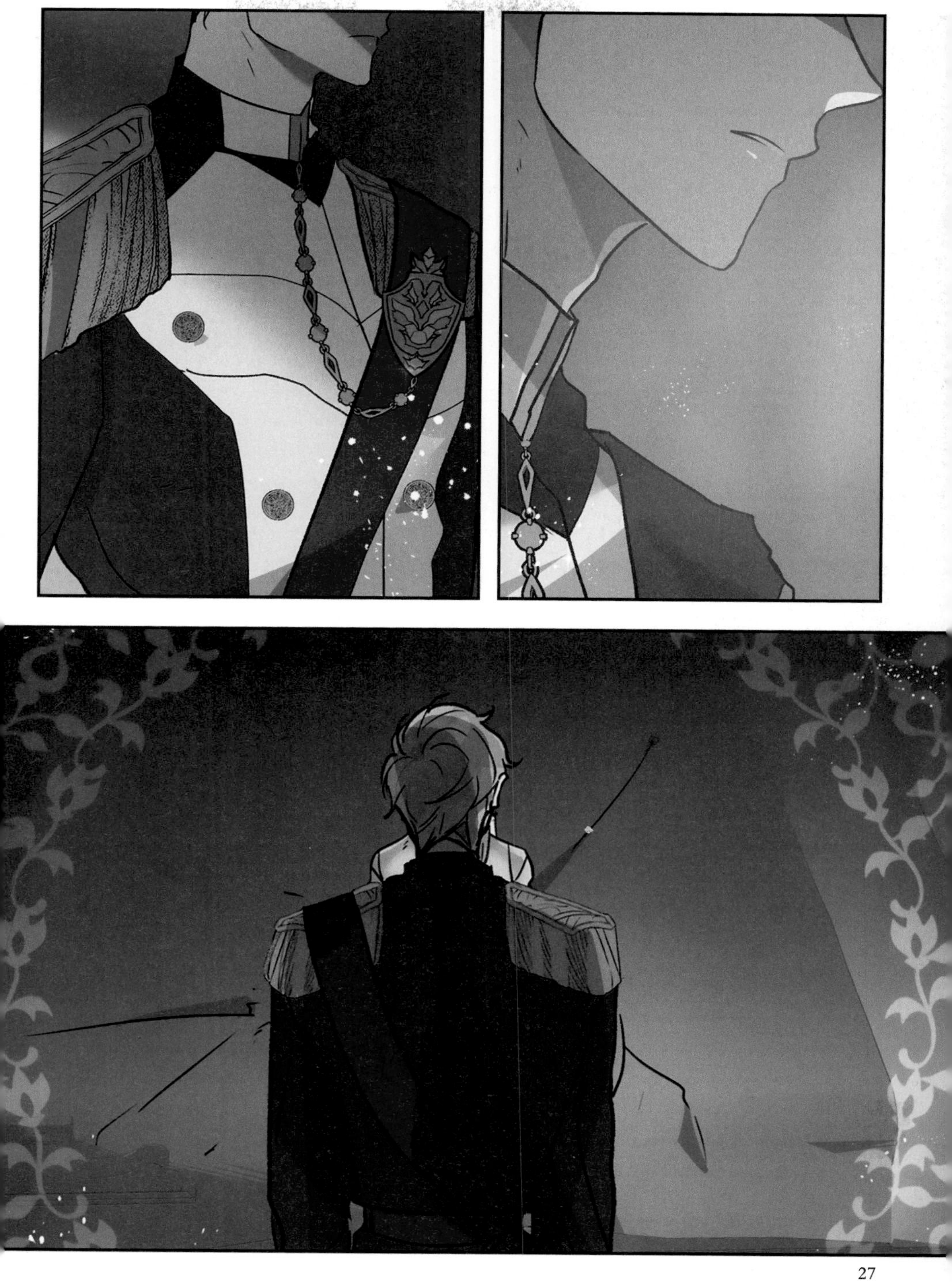

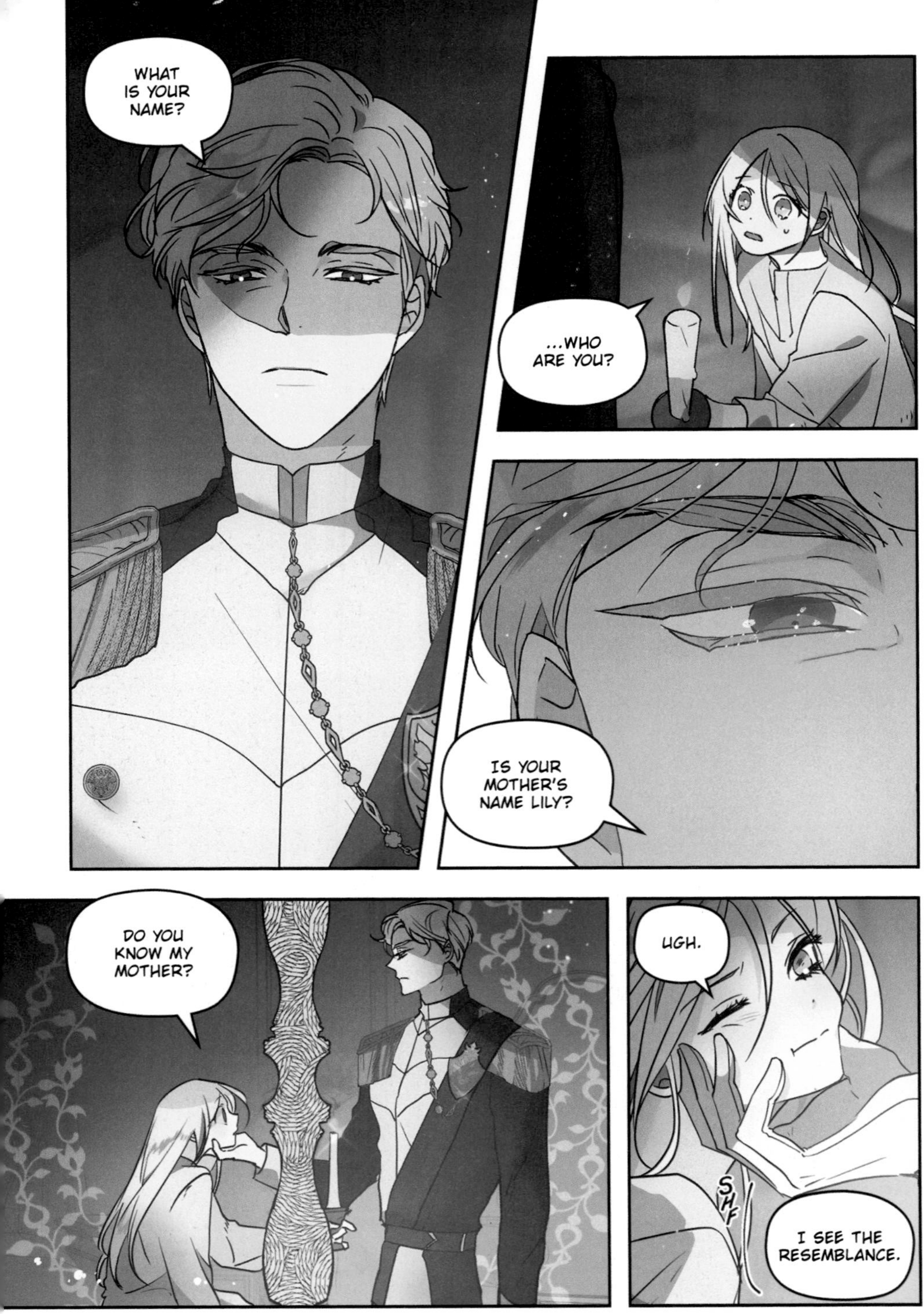
WHAT IS YOUR NAME?
...WHO ARE YOU?
IS YOUR MOTHER'S NAME LILY?
DO YOU KNOW MY MOTHER?
UGH.
SHF
I SEE THE RESEMBLANCE.

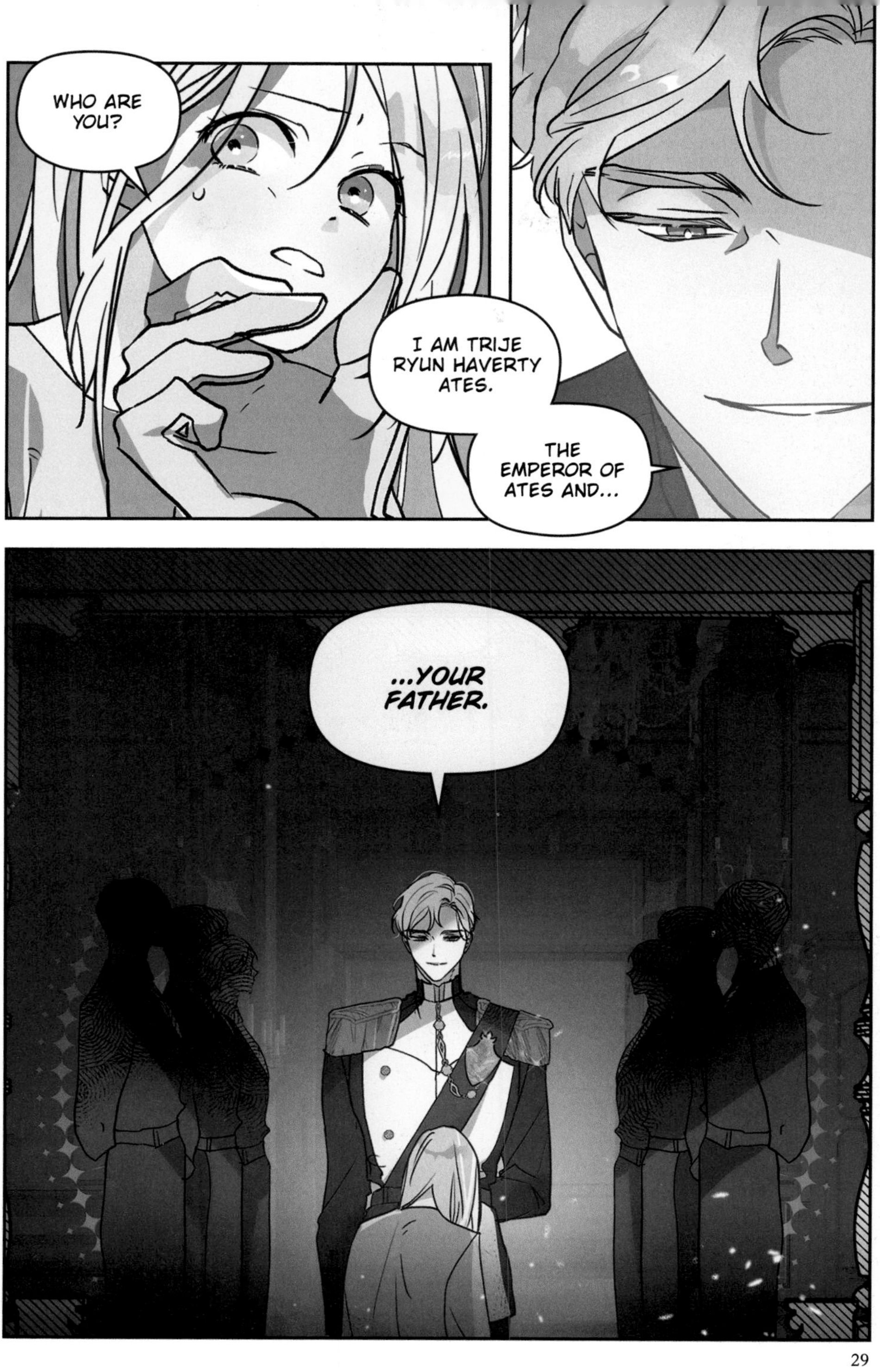
WHO ARE YOU?
I AM TRIJE RYUN HAVERTY ATES.
THE EMPEROR OF ATES AND...
...YOUR FATHER.

My Gently Raised Beast

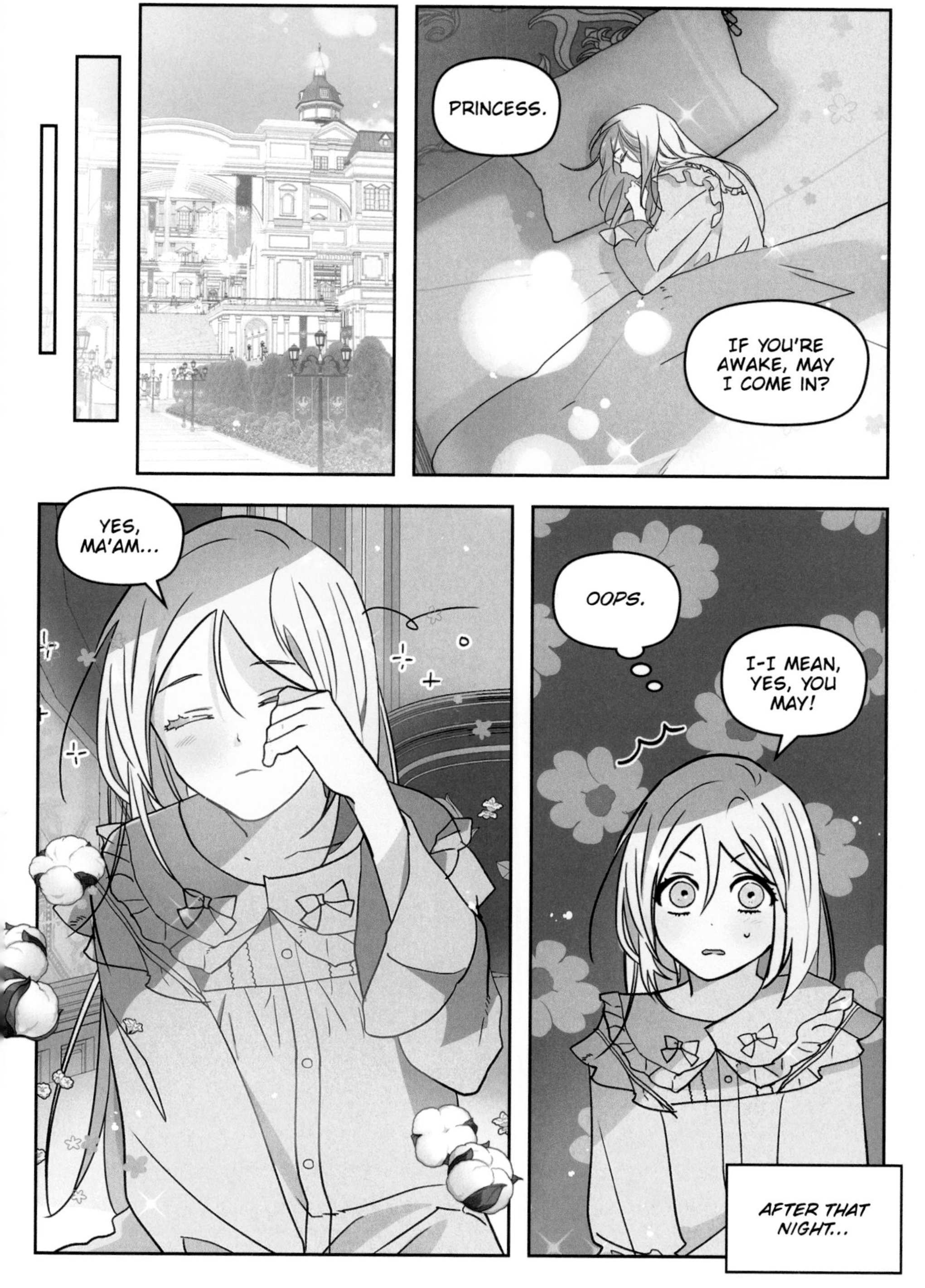
PRINCESS.
IF YOU'RE AWAKE, MAY I COME IN?
YES, MA'AM...
OOPS.
I-I MEAN, YES, YOU MAY!
AFTER THAT NIGHT...

...I FOLLOWED THE MAN WHO CALLED HIMSELF MY FATHER TO THE PALACE.

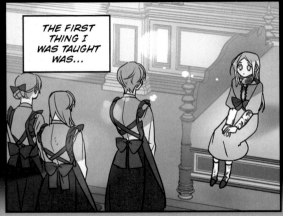

THE FIRST THING I WAS TAUGHT WAS...

...ROYAL ETIQUETTE.

32

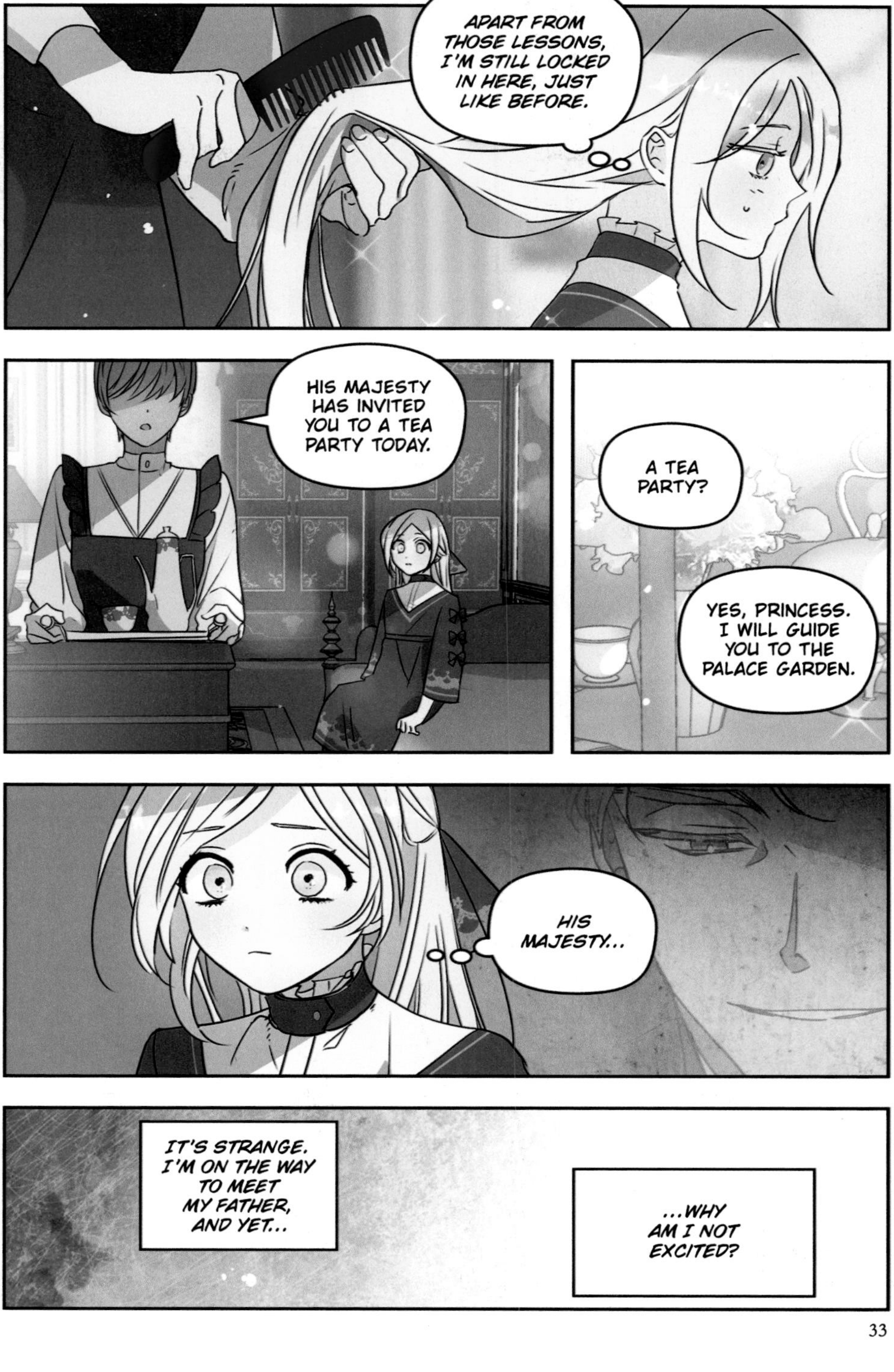
APART FROM THOSE LESSONS, I'M STILL LOCKED IN HERE, JUST LIKE BEFORE.
HIS MAJESTY HAS INVITED YOU TO A TEA PARTY TODAY.
A TEA PARTY?
YES, PRINCESS. I WILL GUIDE YOU TO THE PALACE GARDEN.
HIS MAJESTY...
IT'S STRANGE. I'M ON THE WAY TO MEET MY FATHER, AND YET...
...WHY AM I NOT EXCITED?

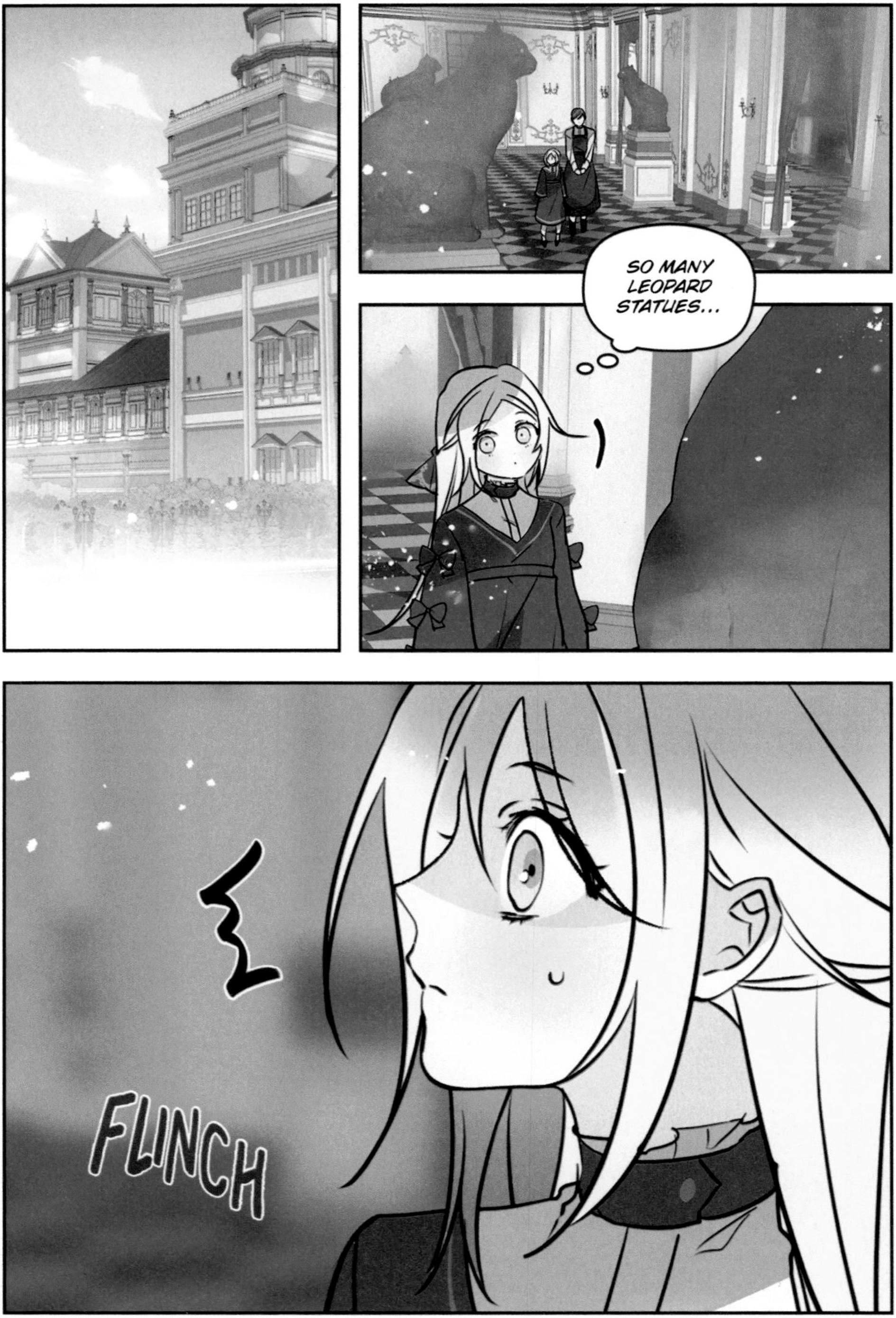
SO MANY LEOPARD STATUES...
FLINCH

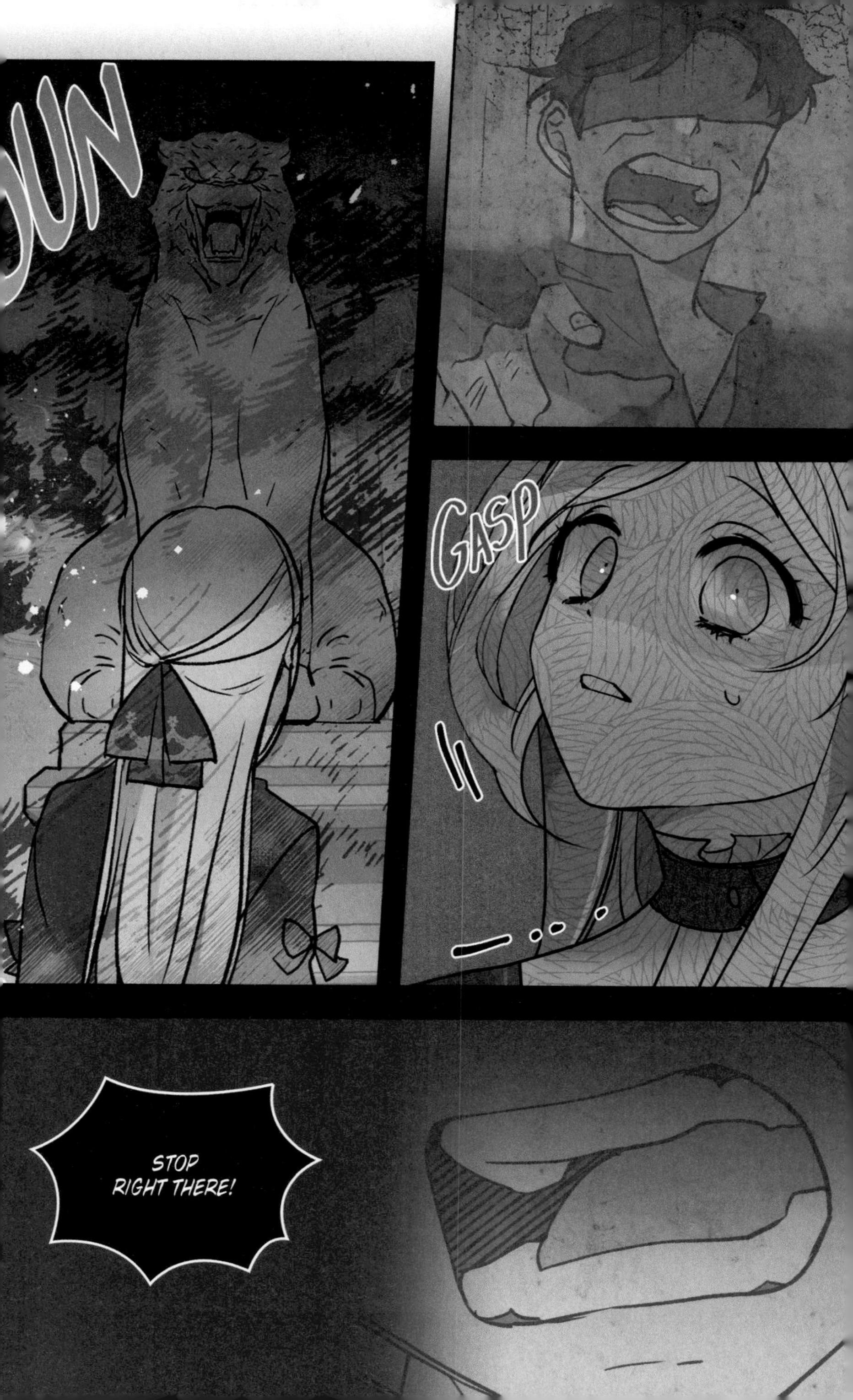

JUN
GASP
—...
STOP RIGHT THERE!

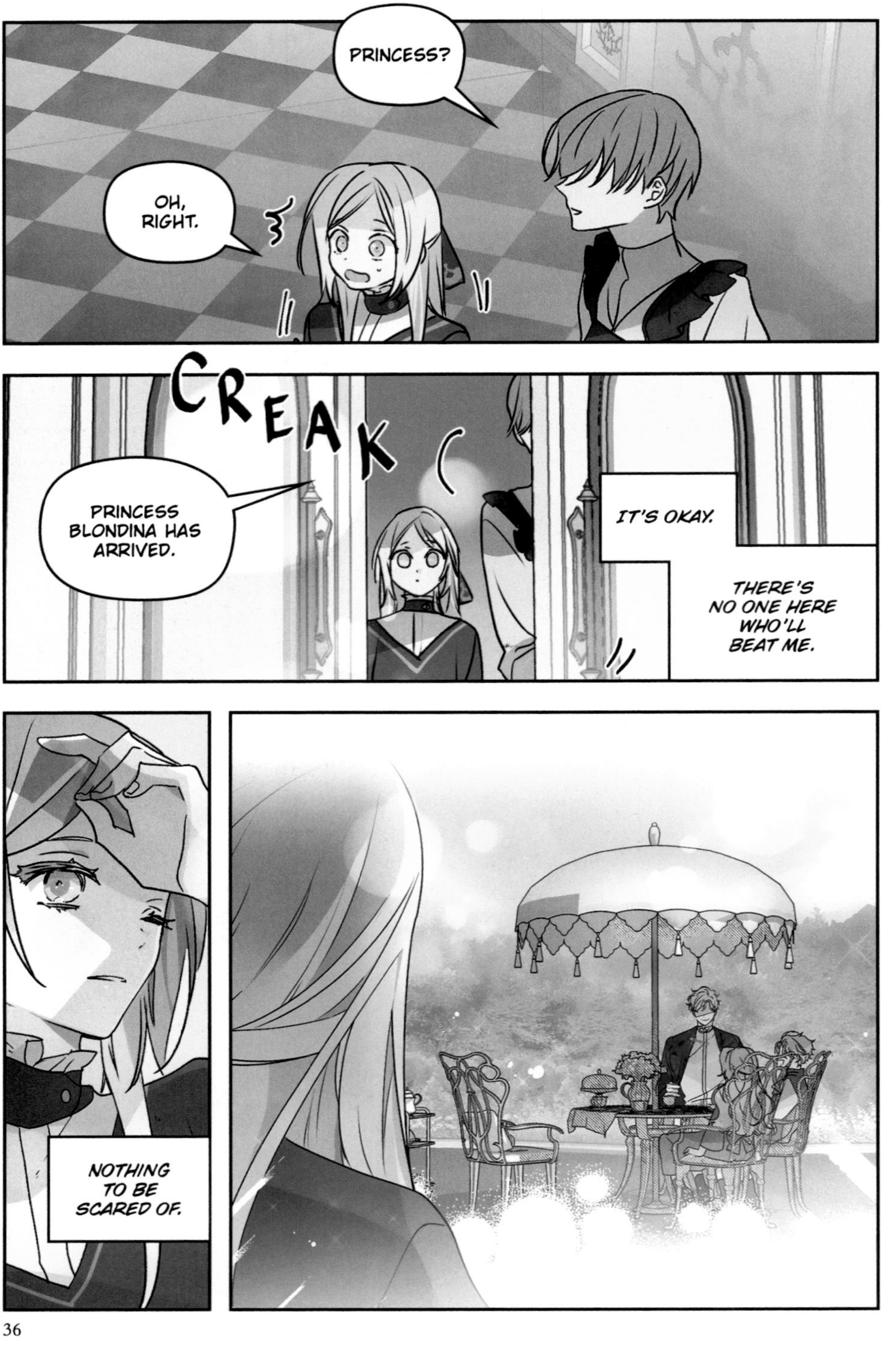
PRINCESS?
OH, RIGHT.
CREAK
PRINCESS BLONDINA HAS ARRIVED.
IT'S OKAY.
THERE'S NO ONE HERE WHO'LL BEAT ME.
NOTHING TO BE SCARED OF.

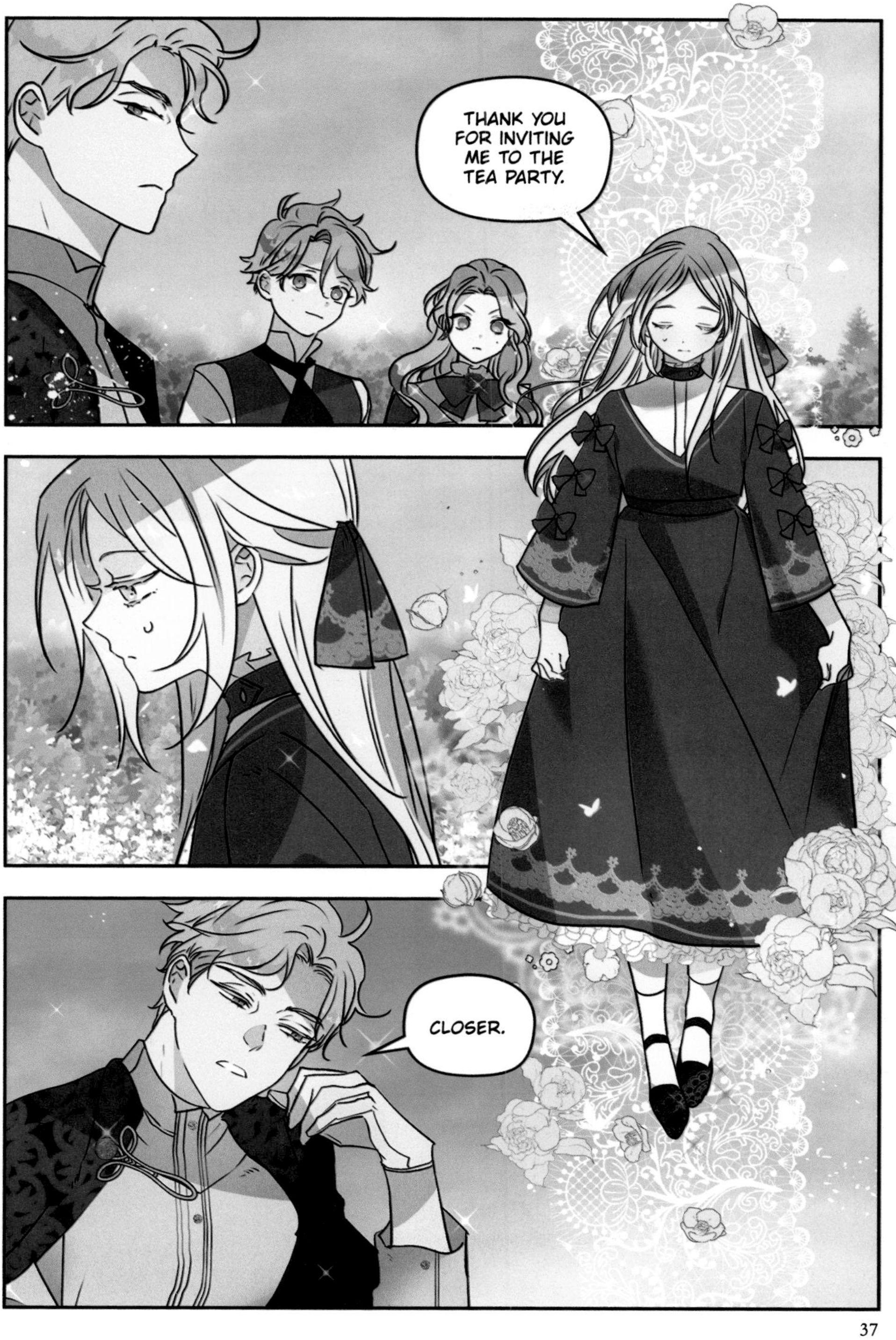
THANK YOU FOR INVITING ME TO THE TEA PARTY.
CLOSER.

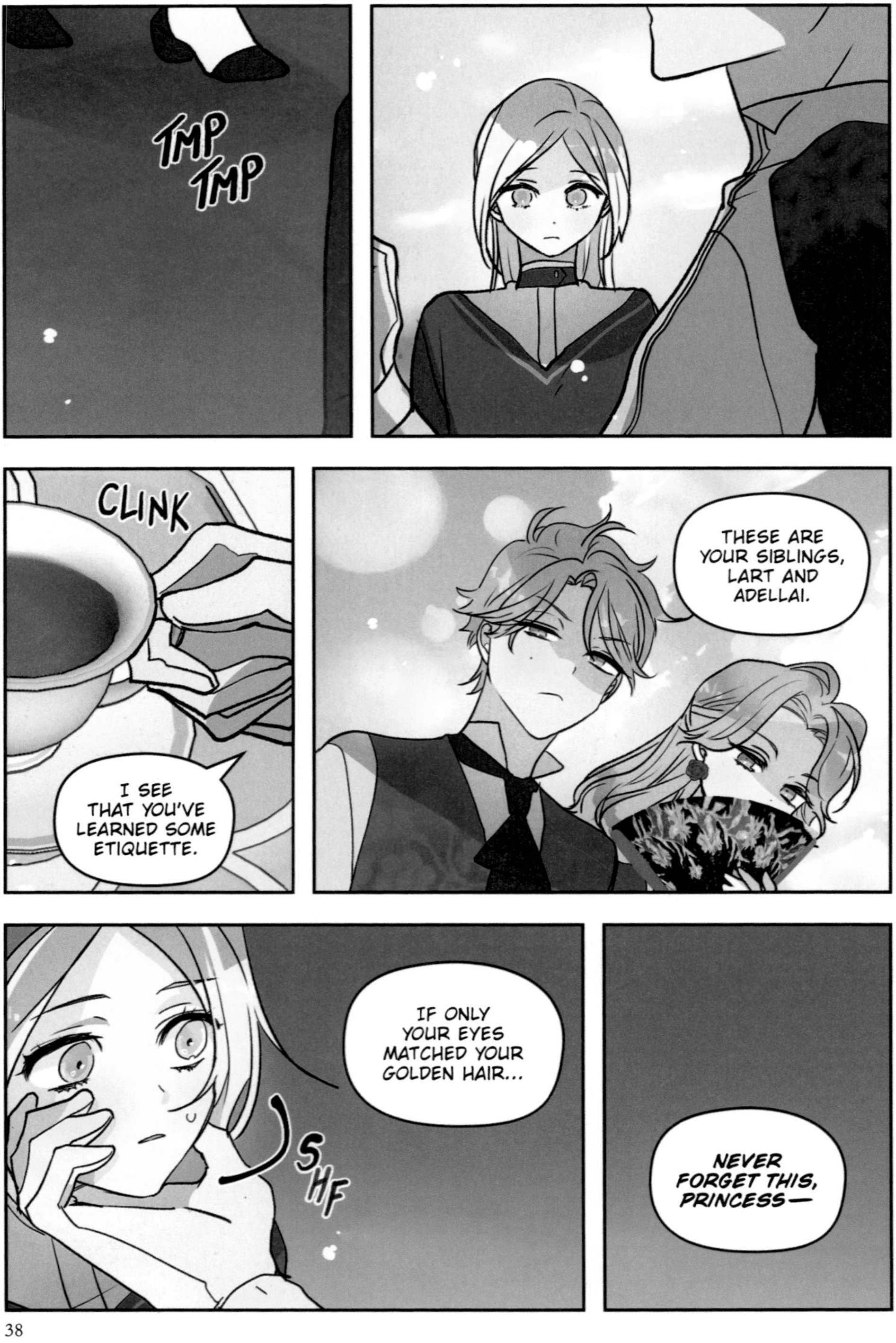
TMP TMP
CLINK
I SEE THAT YOU'VE LEARNED SOME ETIQUETTE.
THESE ARE YOUR SIBLINGS, LART AND ADELLAI.
IF ONLY YOUR EYES MATCHED YOUR GOLDEN HAIR...
SHF
NEVER FORGET THIS, PRINCESS—

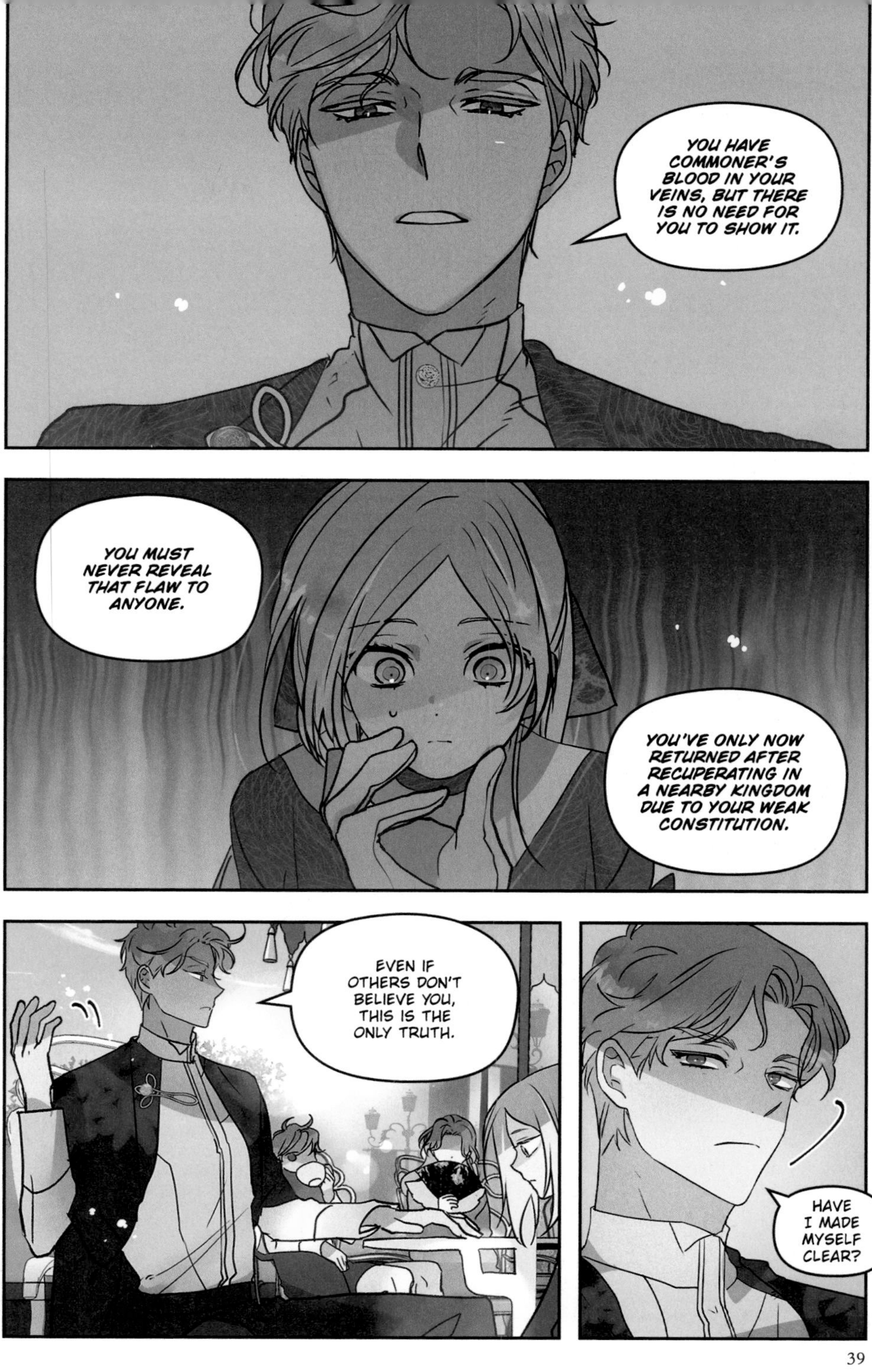
YOU HAVE COMMONER'S BLOOD IN YOUR VEINS, BUT THERE IS NO NEED FOR YOU TO SHOW IT.
YOU MUST NEVER REVEAL THAT FLAW TO ANYONE.
YOU'VE ONLY NOW RETURNED AFTER RECUPERATING IN A NEARBY KINGDOM DUE TO YOUR WEAK CONSTITUTION.
EVEN IF OTHERS DON'T BELIEVE YOU, THIS IS THE ONLY TRUTH.
HAVE I MADE MYSELF CLEAR?

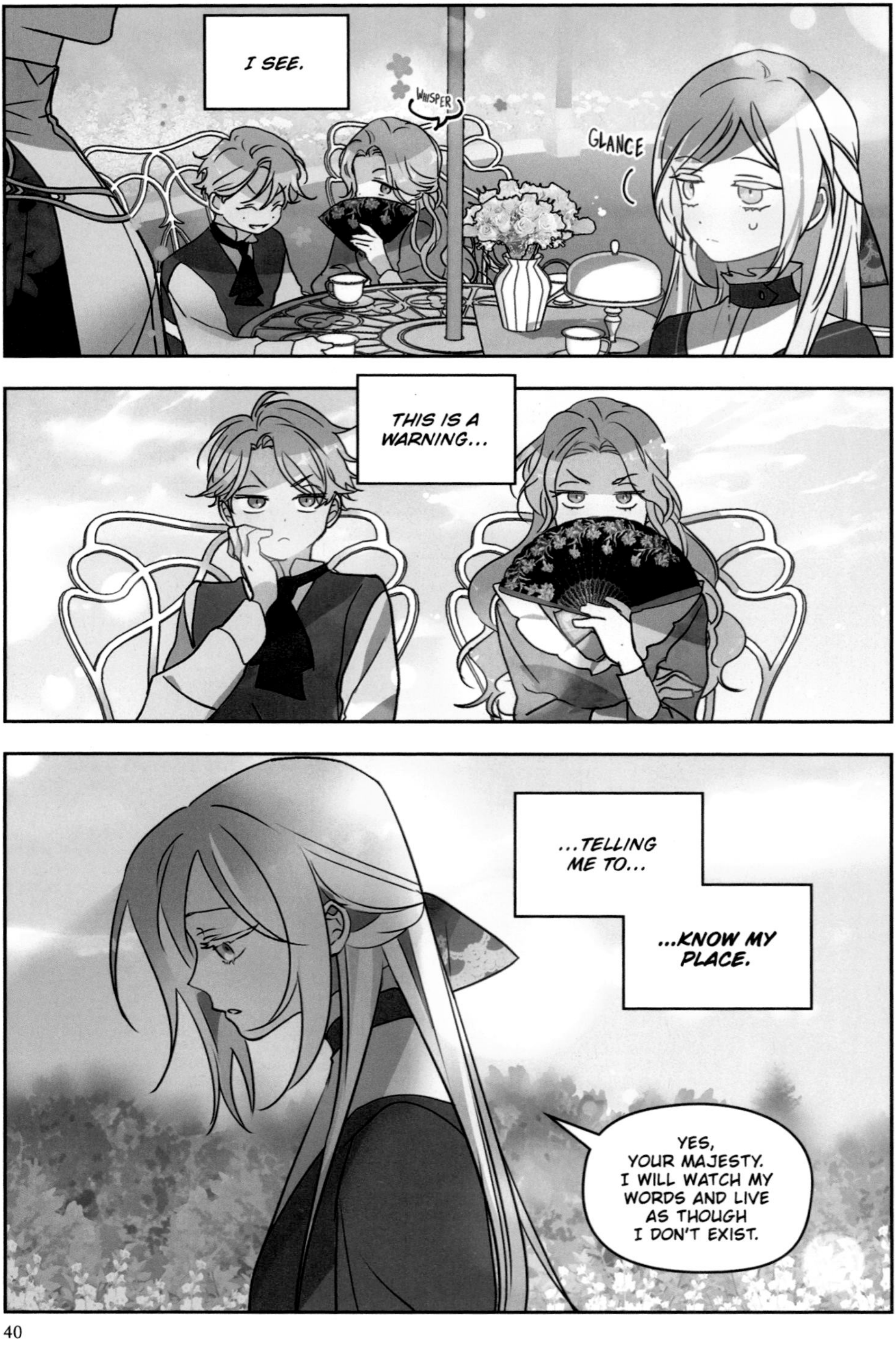
I SEE.
WHISPER
GLANCE
THIS IS A WARNING...
...TELLING ME TO...
...KNOW MY PLACE.
YES, YOUR MAJESTY. I WILL WATCH MY WORDS AND LIVE AS THOUGH I DON'T EXIST.

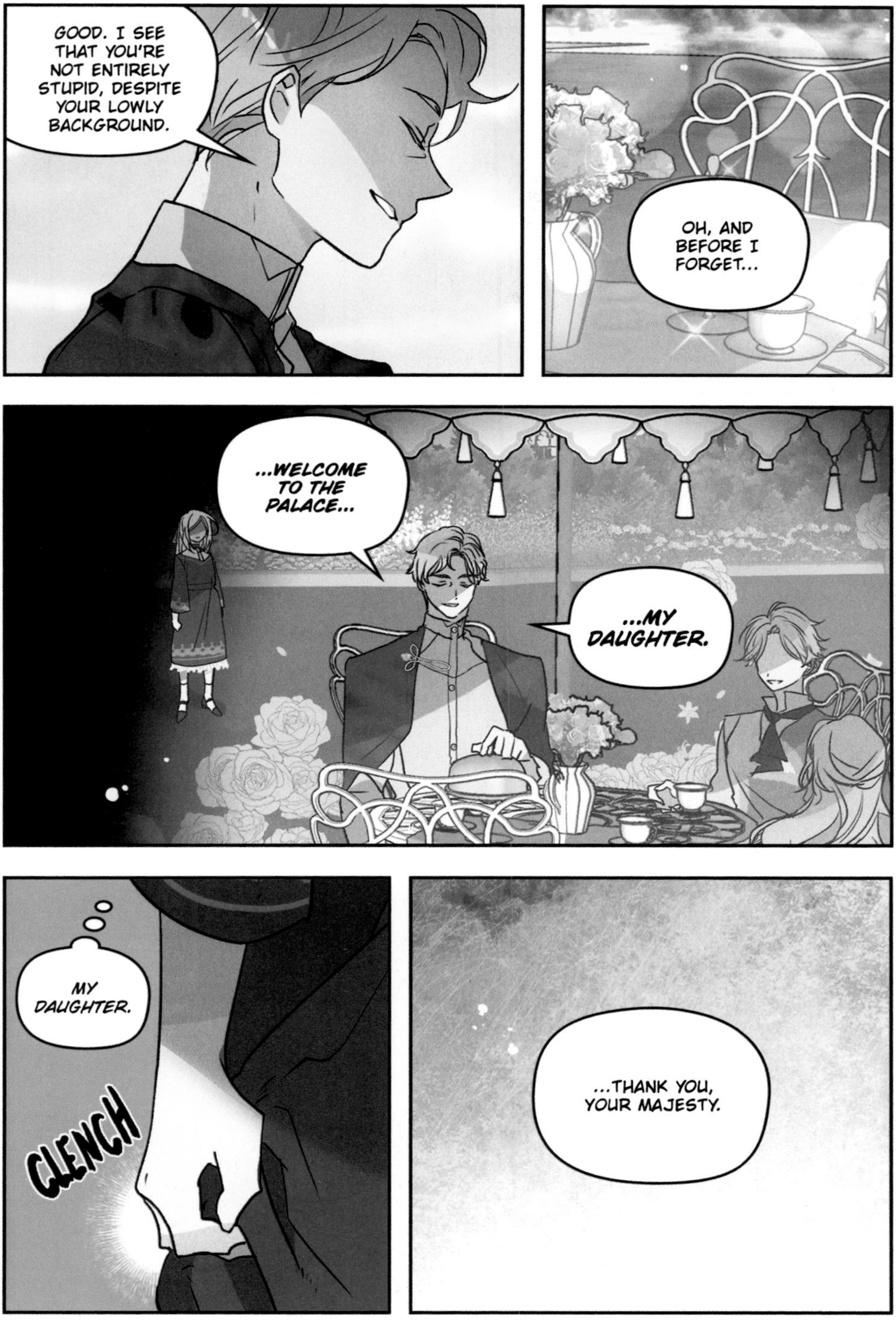
GOOD. I SEE THAT YOU'RE NOT ENTIRELY STUPID, DESPITE YOUR LOWLY BACKGROUND.
OH, AND BEFORE I FORGET...
...WELCOME TO THE PALACE...
...MY DAUGHTER.
MY DAUGHTER.
CLENCH
...THANK YOU, YOUR MAJESTY.

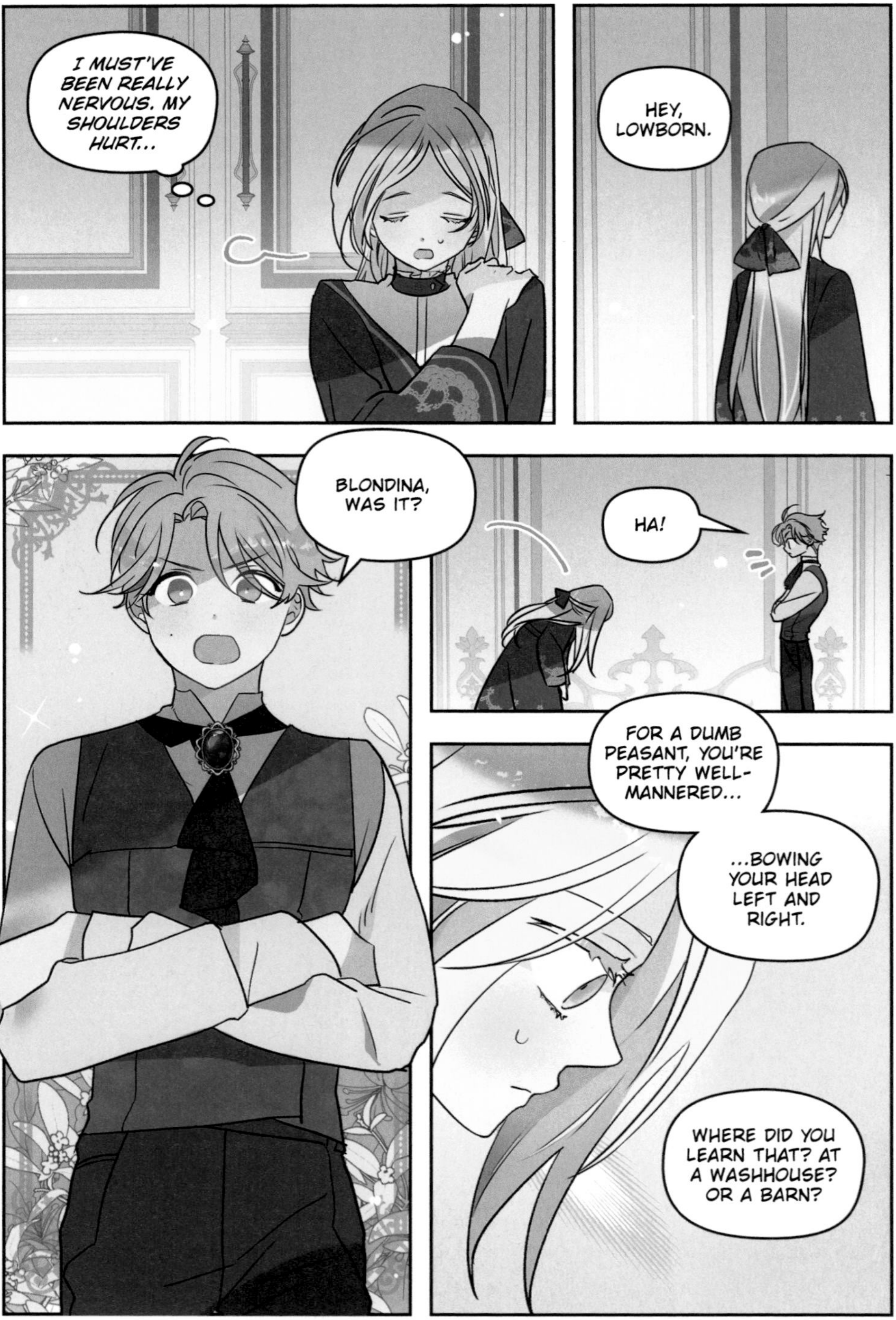
I MUST'VE BEEN REALLY NERVOUS. MY SHOULDERS HURT...
HEY, LOWBORN.
BLONDINA, WAS IT?
HA!
FOR A DUMB PEASANT, YOU'RE PRETTY WELL-MANNERED...
...BOWING YOUR HEAD LEFT AND RIGHT.
WHERE DID YOU LEARN THAT? AT A WASHHOUSE? OR A BARN?

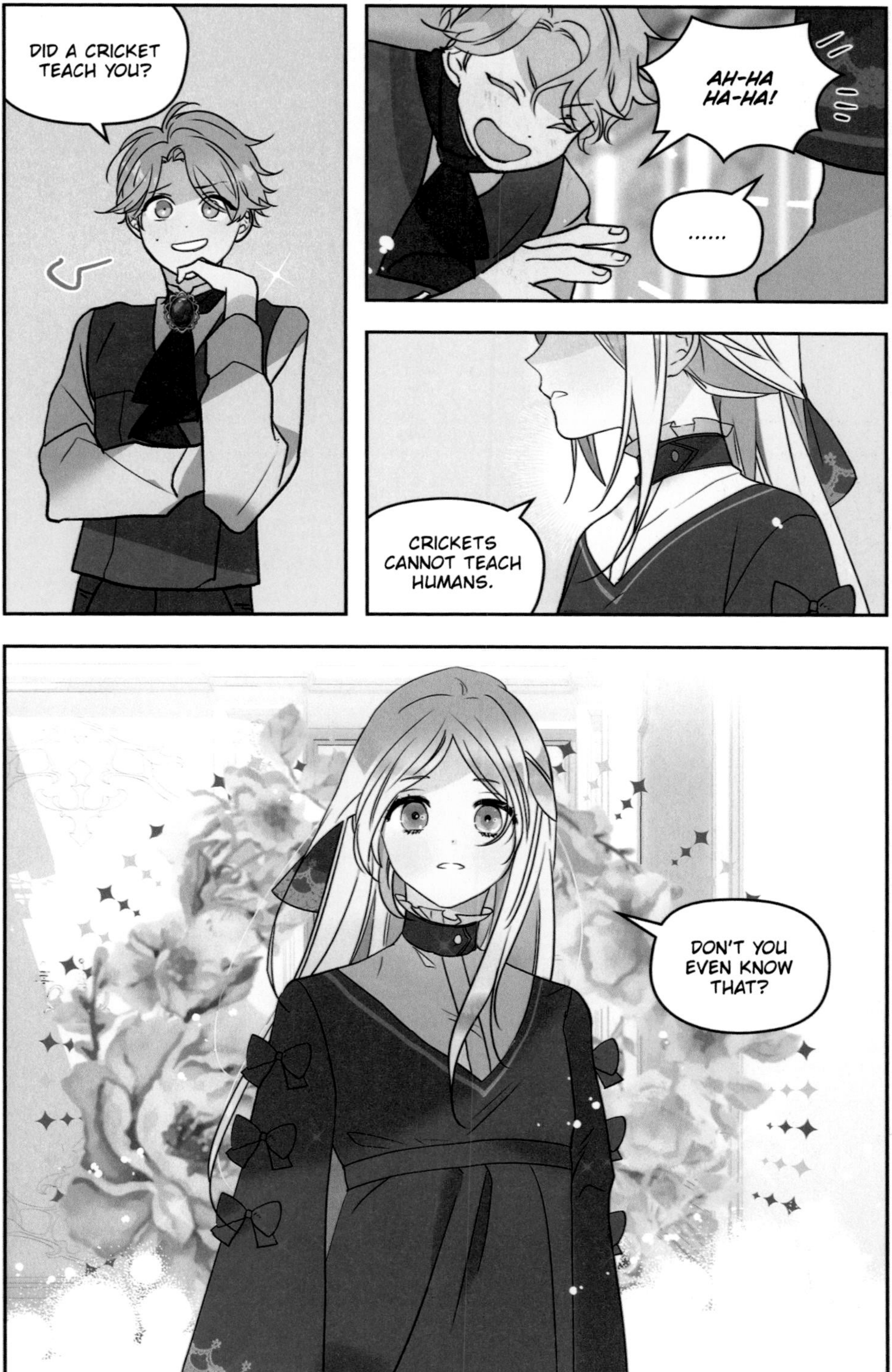
DID A CRICKET TEACH YOU?
AH-HA HA-HA!
......
CRICKETS CANNOT TEACH HUMANS.
DON'T YOU EVEN KNOW THAT?

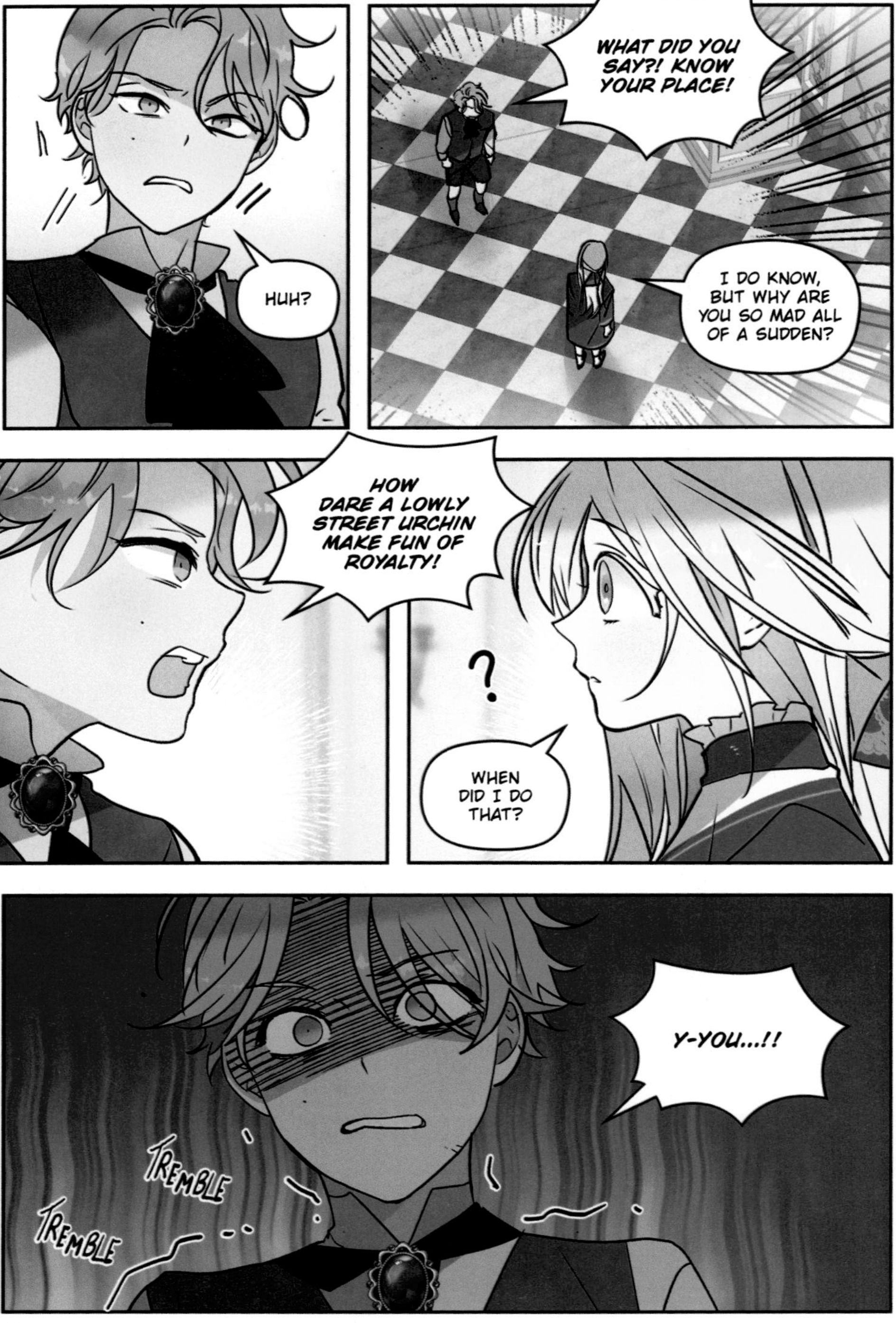
HUH?
WHAT DID YOU SAY?! KNOW YOUR PLACE!
I DO KNOW, BUT WHY ARE YOU SO MAD ALL OF A SUDDEN?
HOW DARE A LOWLY STREET URCHIN MAKE FUN OF ROYALTY!
?
WHEN DID I DO THAT?
Y-YOU...!!
TREMBLE
TREMBLE

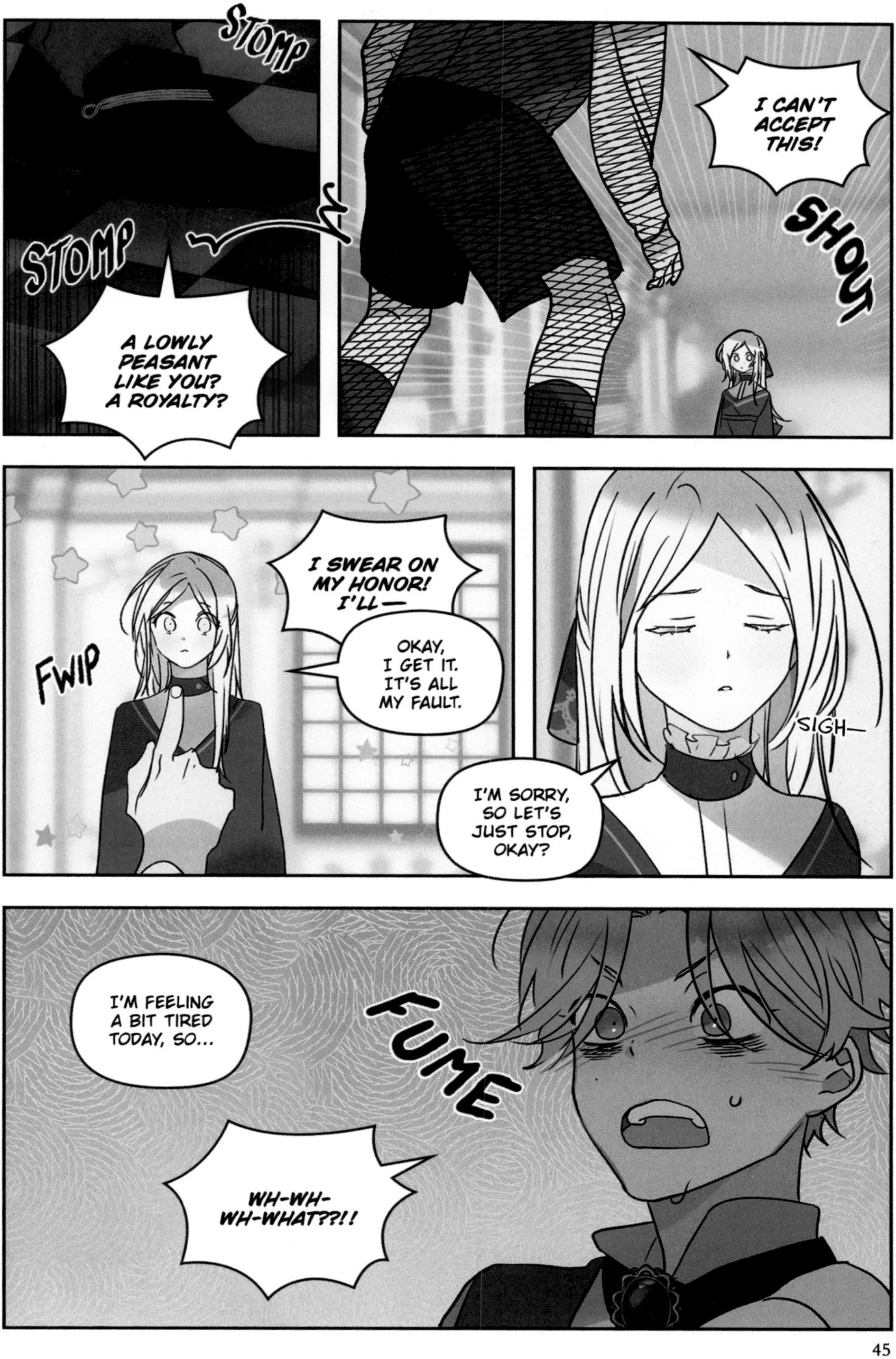
STOMP
STOMP
A LOWLY PEASANT LIKE YOU? A ROYALTY?
I CAN'T ACCEPT THIS!
SHOUT
I SWEAR ON MY HONOR! I'LL—
FWIP
OKAY, I GET IT. IT'S ALL MY FAULT.
SIGH—
I'M SORRY, SO LET'S JUST STOP, OKAY?
I'M FEELING A BIT TIRED TODAY, SO...
FUME
WH-WH-WH-WHAT??!!

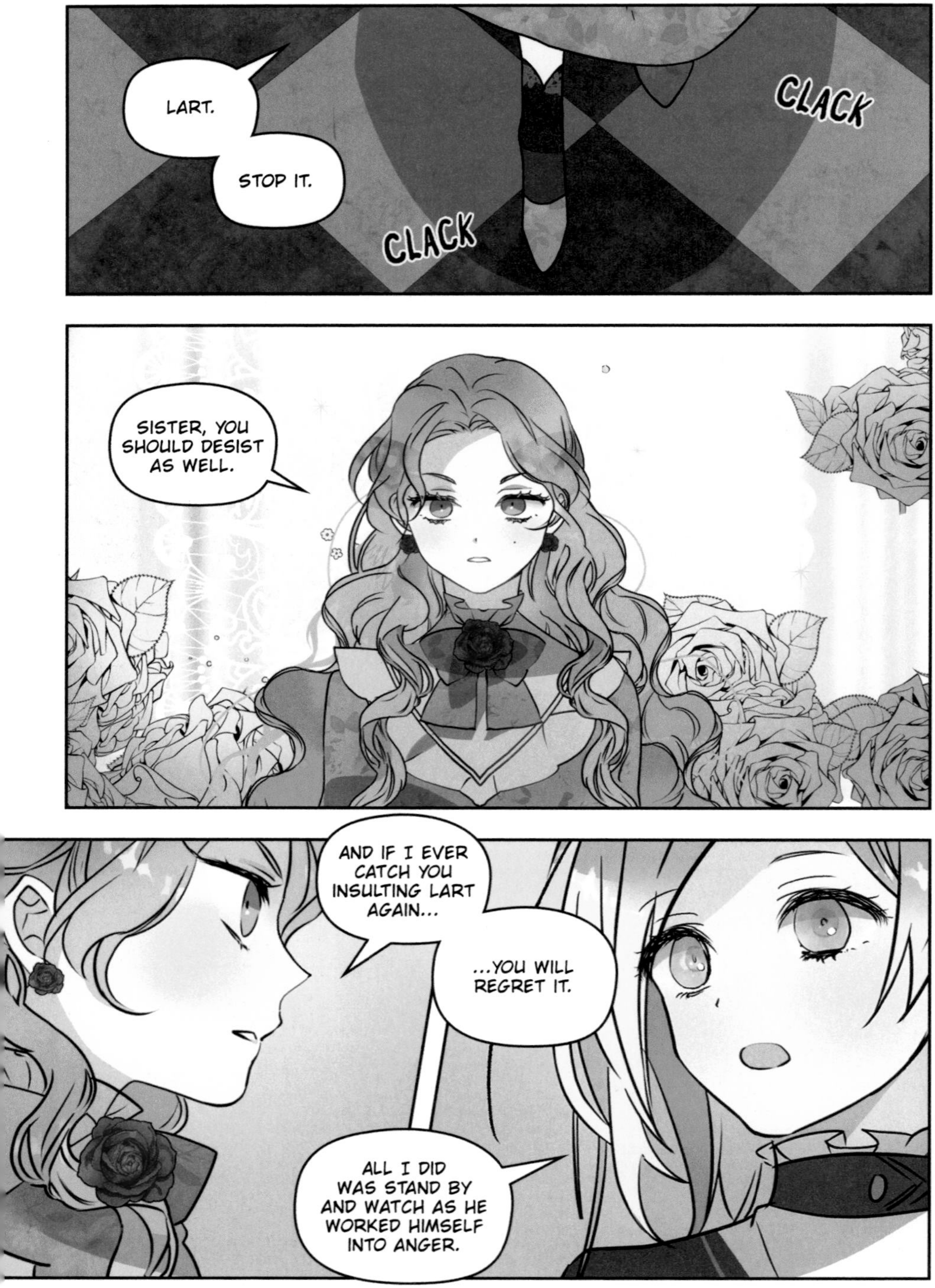
LART.
STOP IT.
CLACK
CLACK
SISTER, YOU SHOULD DESIST AS WELL.
AND IF I EVER CATCH YOU INSULTING LART AGAIN...
...YOU WILL REGRET IT.
ALL I DID WAS STAND BY AND WATCH AS HE WORKED HIMSELF INTO ANGER.

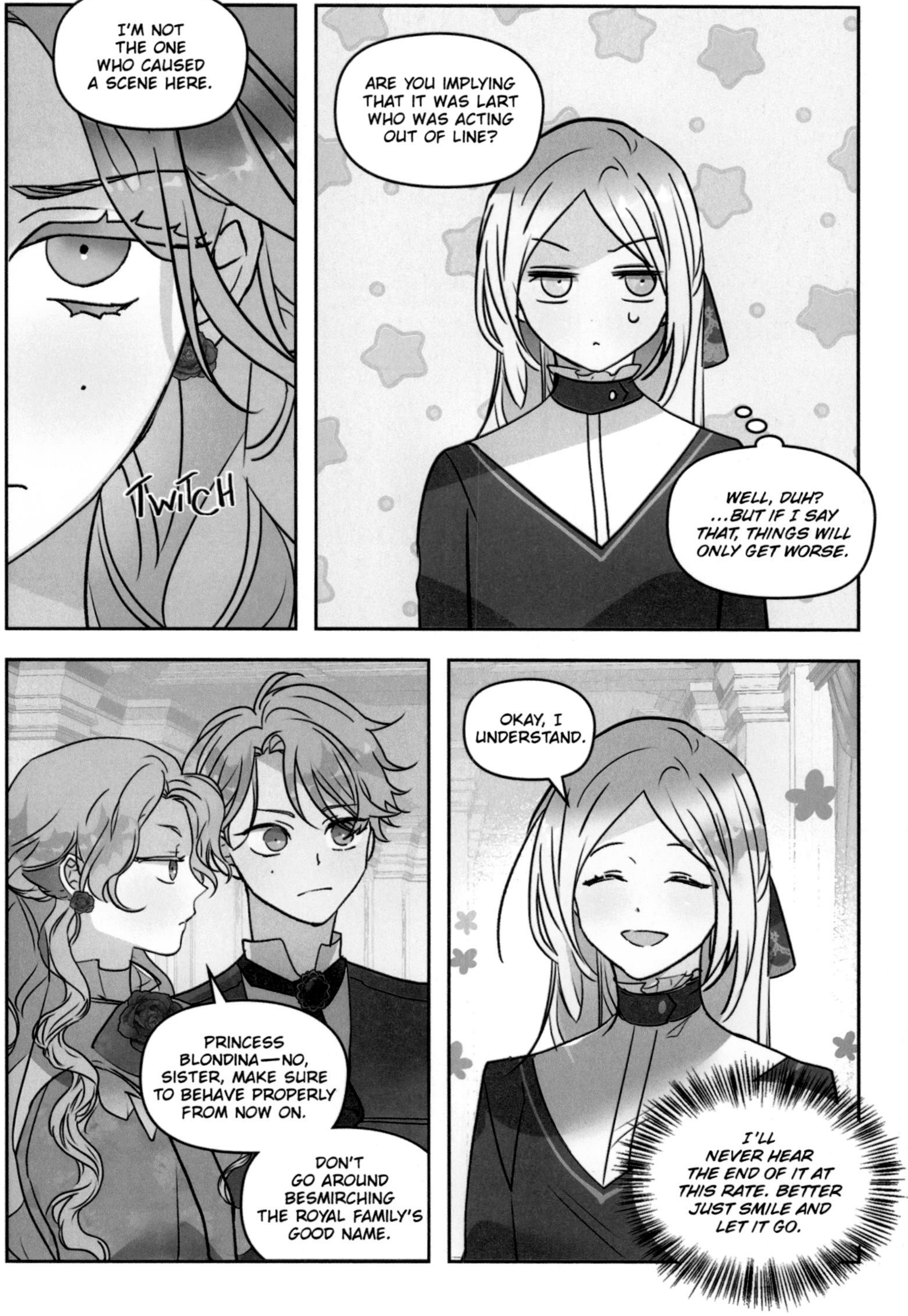
I'M NOT THE ONE WHO CAUSED A SCENE HERE.
TWITCH
ARE YOU IMPLYING THAT IT WAS LART WHO WAS ACTING OUT OF LINE?
WELL, DUH? ...BUT IF I SAY THAT, THINGS WILL ONLY GET WORSE.
PRINCESS BLONDINA—NO, SISTER, MAKE SURE TO BEHAVE PROPERLY FROM NOW ON.
DON'T GO AROUND BESMIRCHING THE ROYAL FAMILY'S GOOD NAME.
OKAY, I UNDERSTAND.
I'LL NEVER HEAR THE END OF IT AT THIS RATE. BETTER JUST SMILE AND LET IT GO.

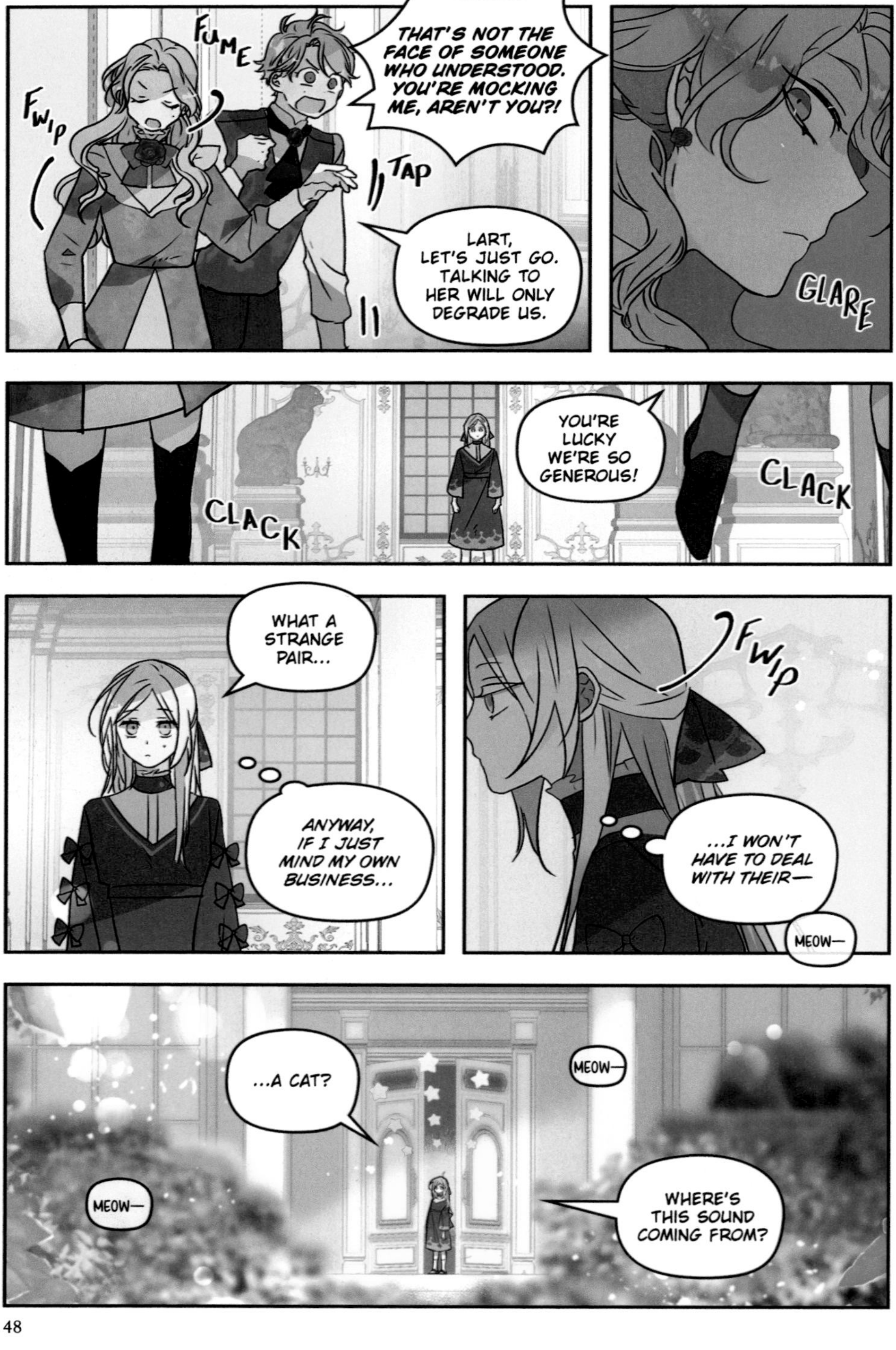
FUME
FWIP
THAT'S NOT THE FACE OF SOMEONE WHO UNDERSTOOD. YOU'RE MOCKING ME, AREN'T YOU?!
TAP
LART, LET'S JUST GO. TALKING TO HER WILL ONLY DEGRADE US.
GLARE
CLACK
YOU'RE LUCKY WE'RE SO GENEROUS!
CLACK
WHAT A STRANGE PAIR...
ANYWAY, IF I JUST MIND MY OWN BUSINESS...
FWIP
...I WON'T HAVE TO DEAL WITH THEIR—
MEOW—
...A CAT?
MEOW—
MEOW—
WHERE'S THIS SOUND COMING FROM?

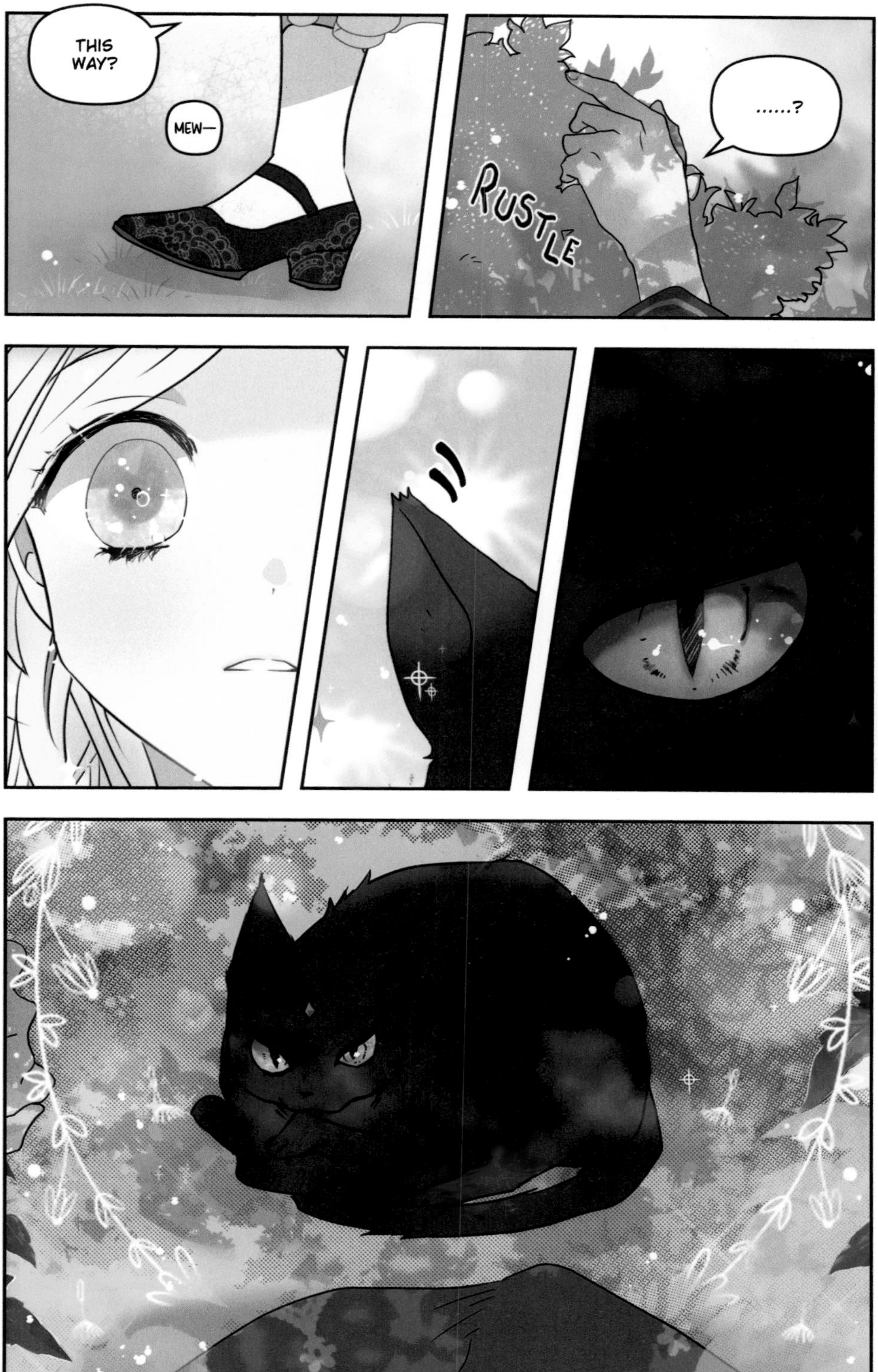
THIS WAY?
MEW—
RUSTLE
......?

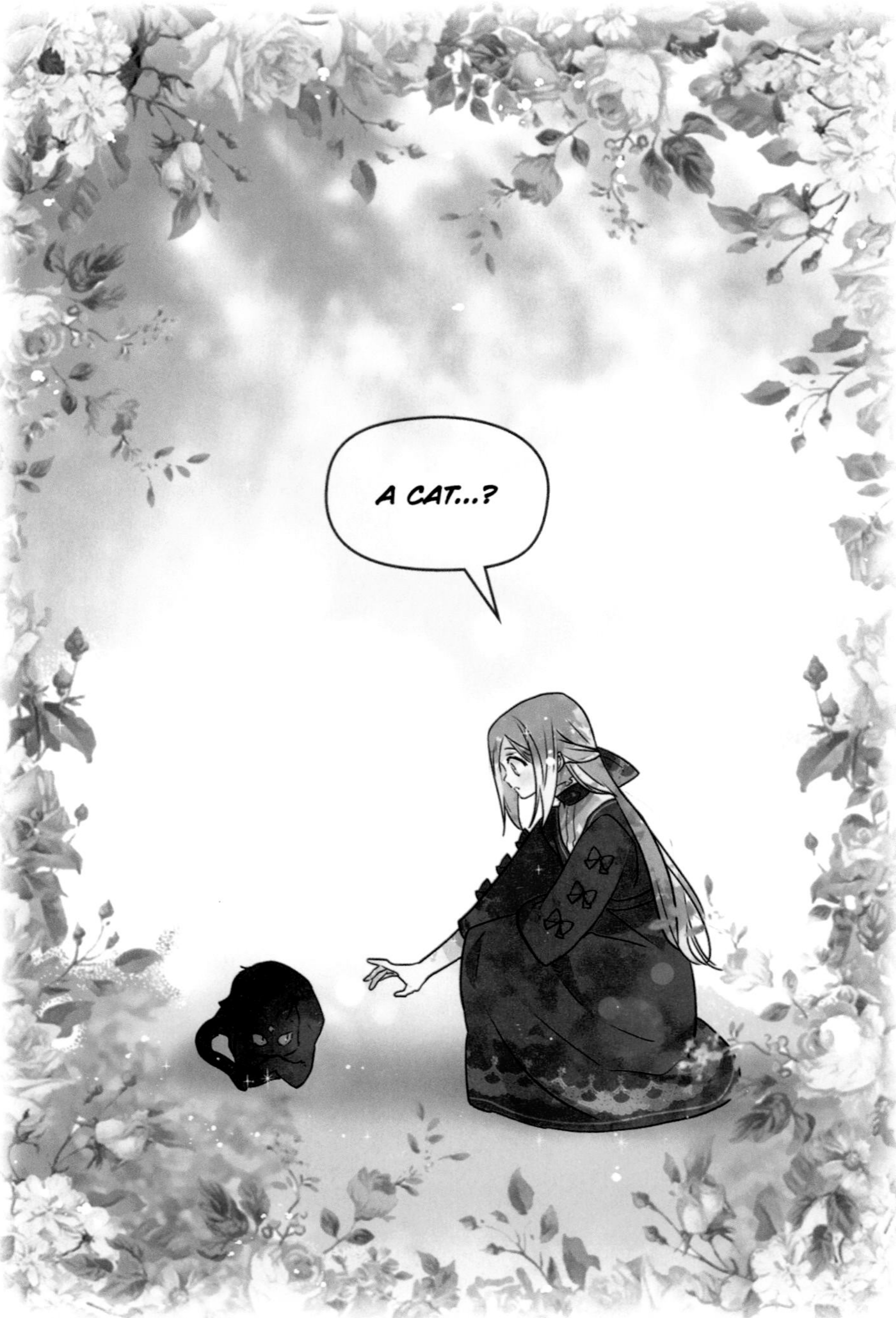
A CAT...?

My Gently Raised Beast

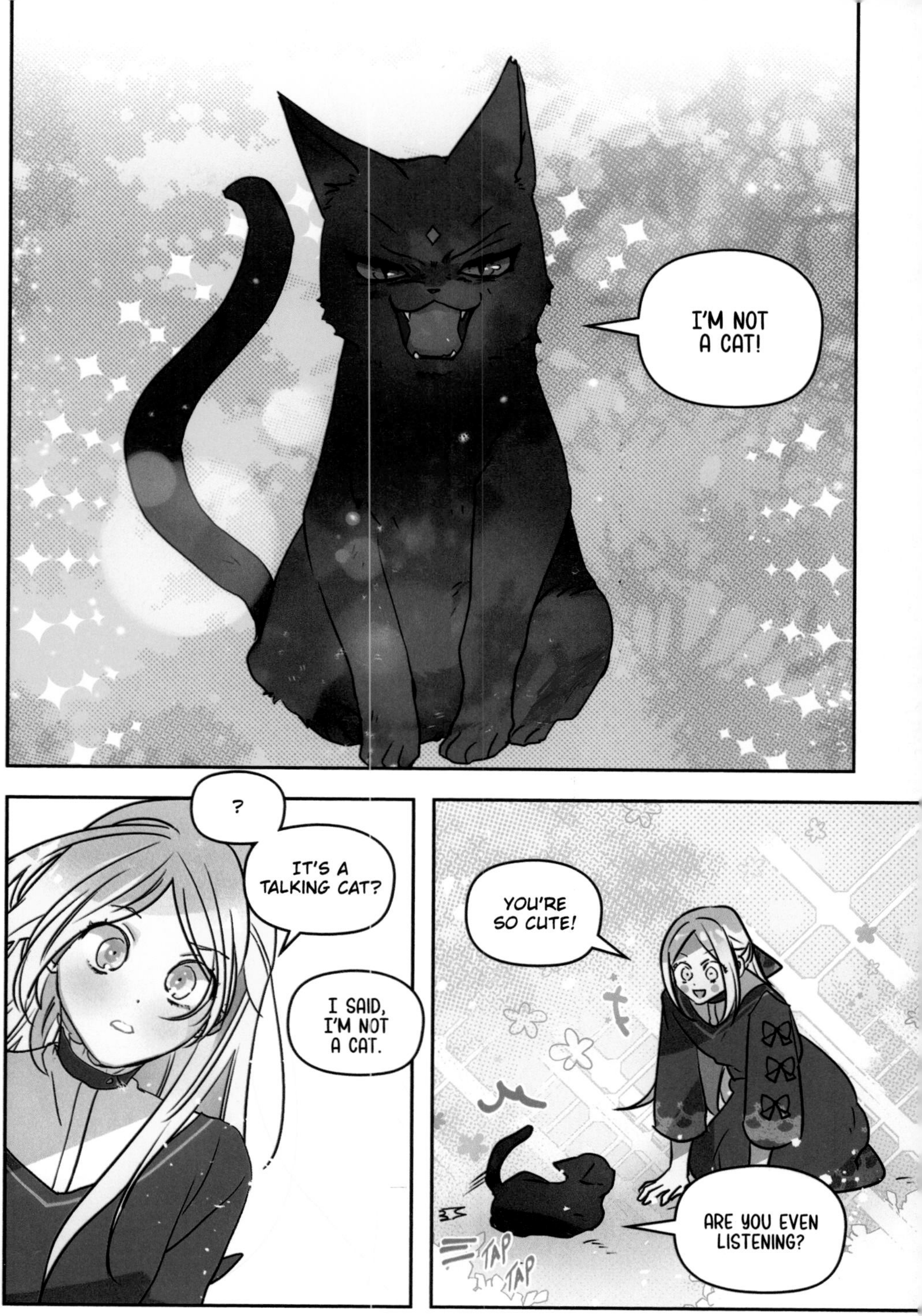
I'M NOT A CAT!
?
IT'S A TALKING CAT?
I SAID, I'M NOT A CAT.
YOU'RE SO CUTE!
ARE YOU EVEN LISTENING?
TAP TAP

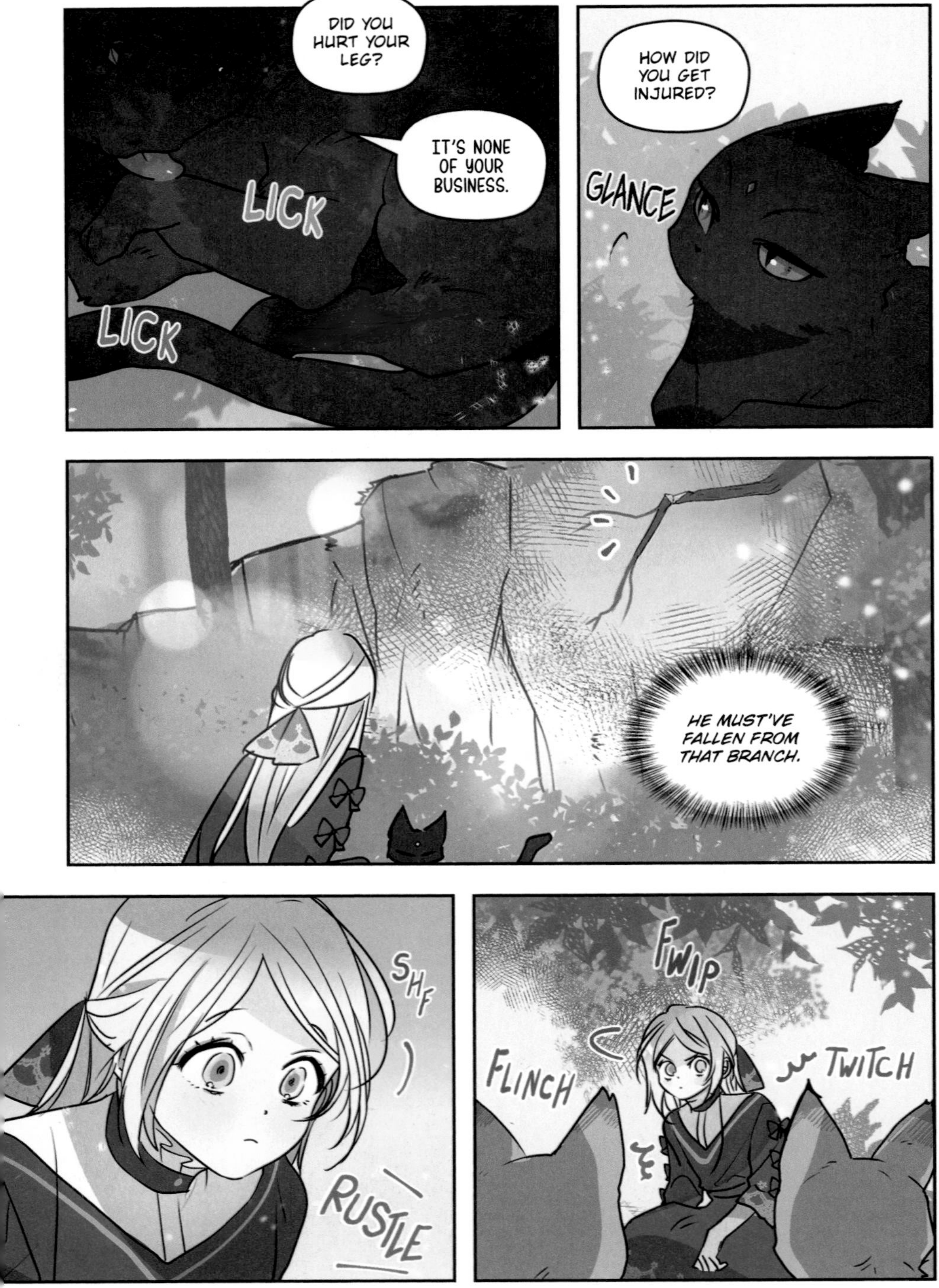
DID YOU HURT YOUR LEG?
IT'S NONE OF YOUR BUSINESS.
LICK
LICK
HOW DID YOU GET INJURED?
GLANCE
HE MUST'VE FALLEN FROM THAT BRANCH.
SHF
RUSTLE
FWIP
FLINCH
TWITCH

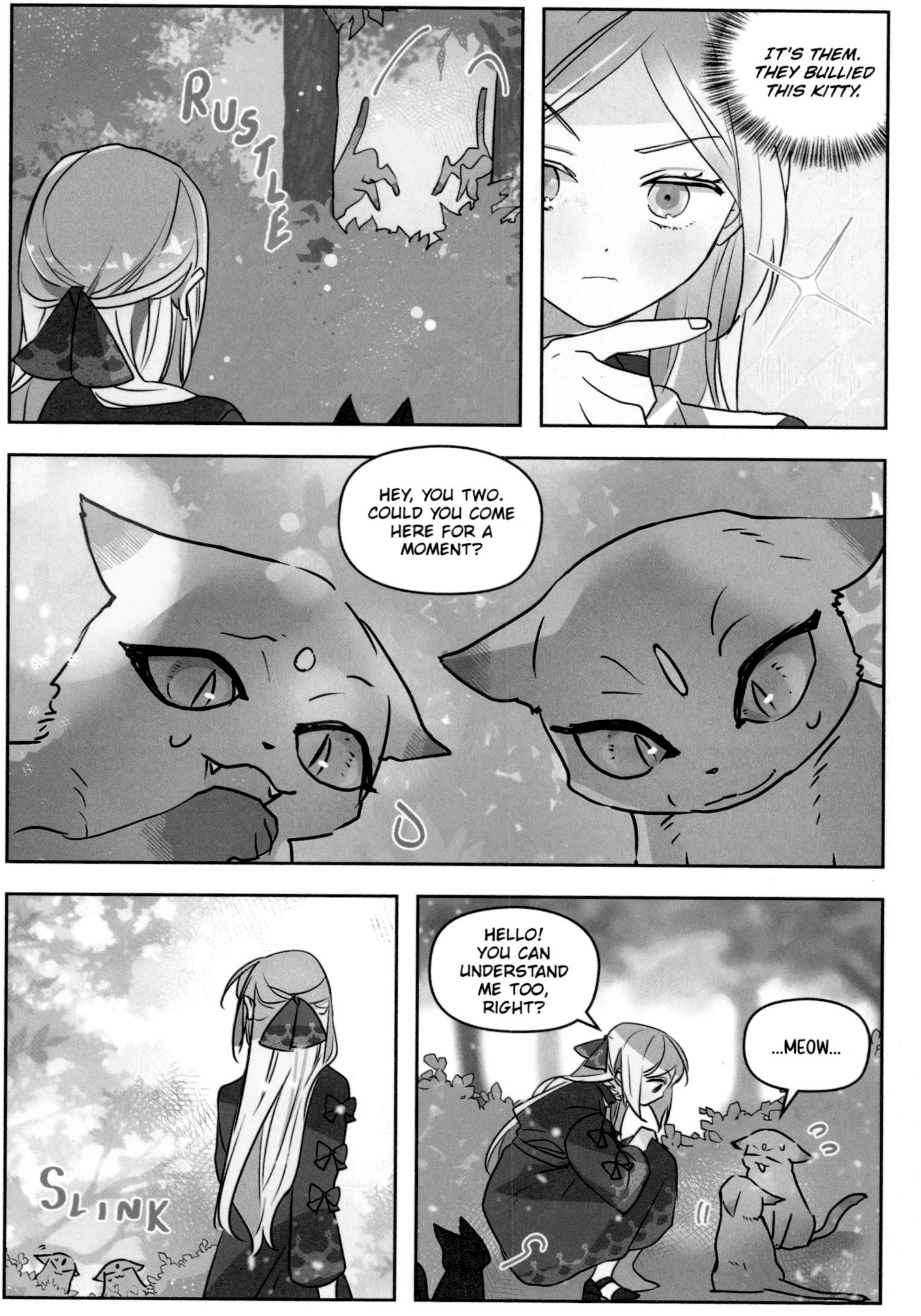
RUSTLE
IT'S THEM. THEY BULLIED THIS KITTY.
HEY, YOU TWO. COULD YOU COME HERE FOR A MOMENT?
SLINK
HELLO! YOU CAN UNDERSTAND ME TOO, RIGHT?
...MEOW...

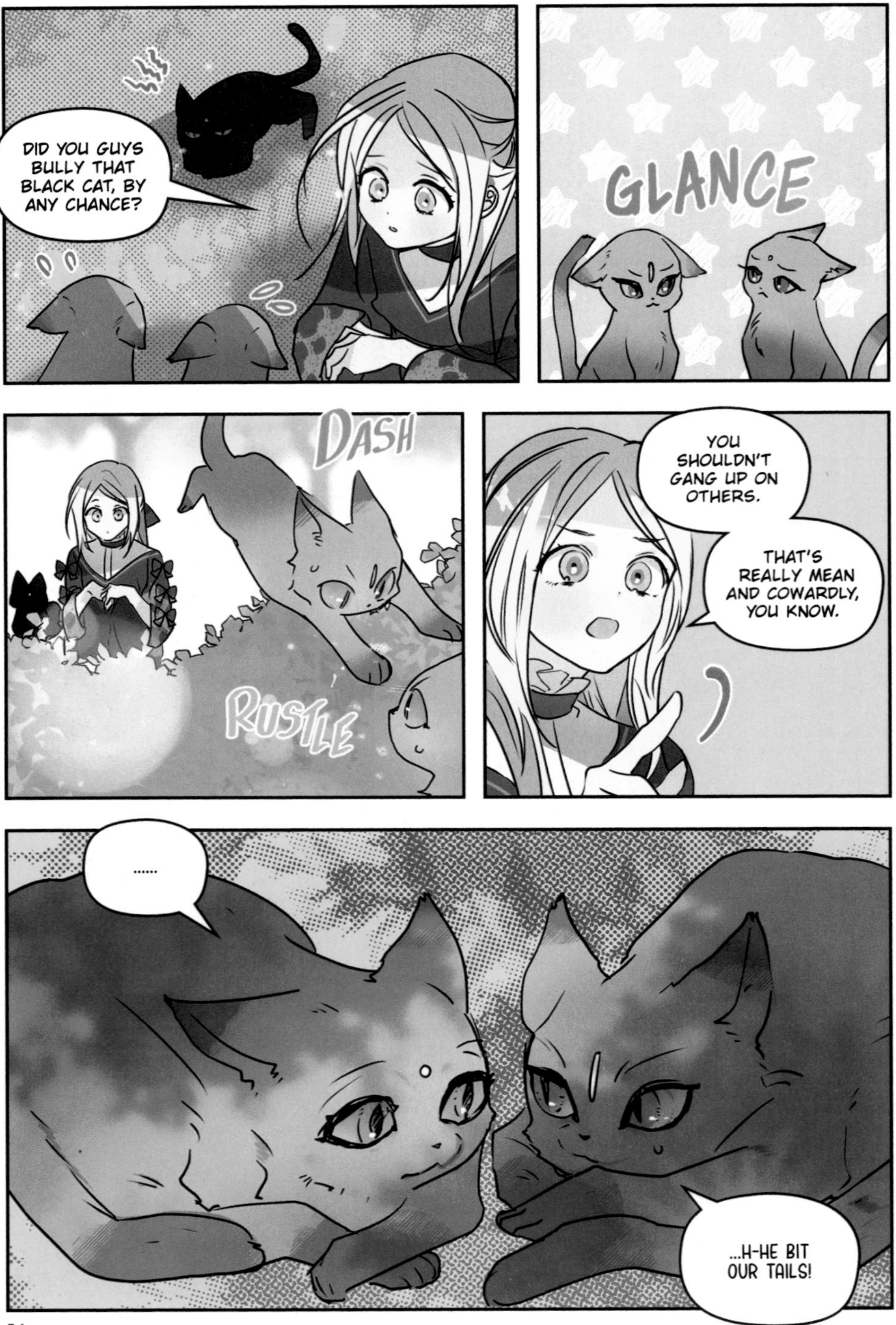
DID YOU GUYS BULLY THAT BLACK CAT, BY ANY CHANCE?
GLANCE
DASH
RUSTLE
YOU SHOULDN'T GANG UP ON OTHERS.
THAT'S REALLY MEAN AND COWARDLY, YOU KNOW.
......
...H-HE BIT OUR TAILS!

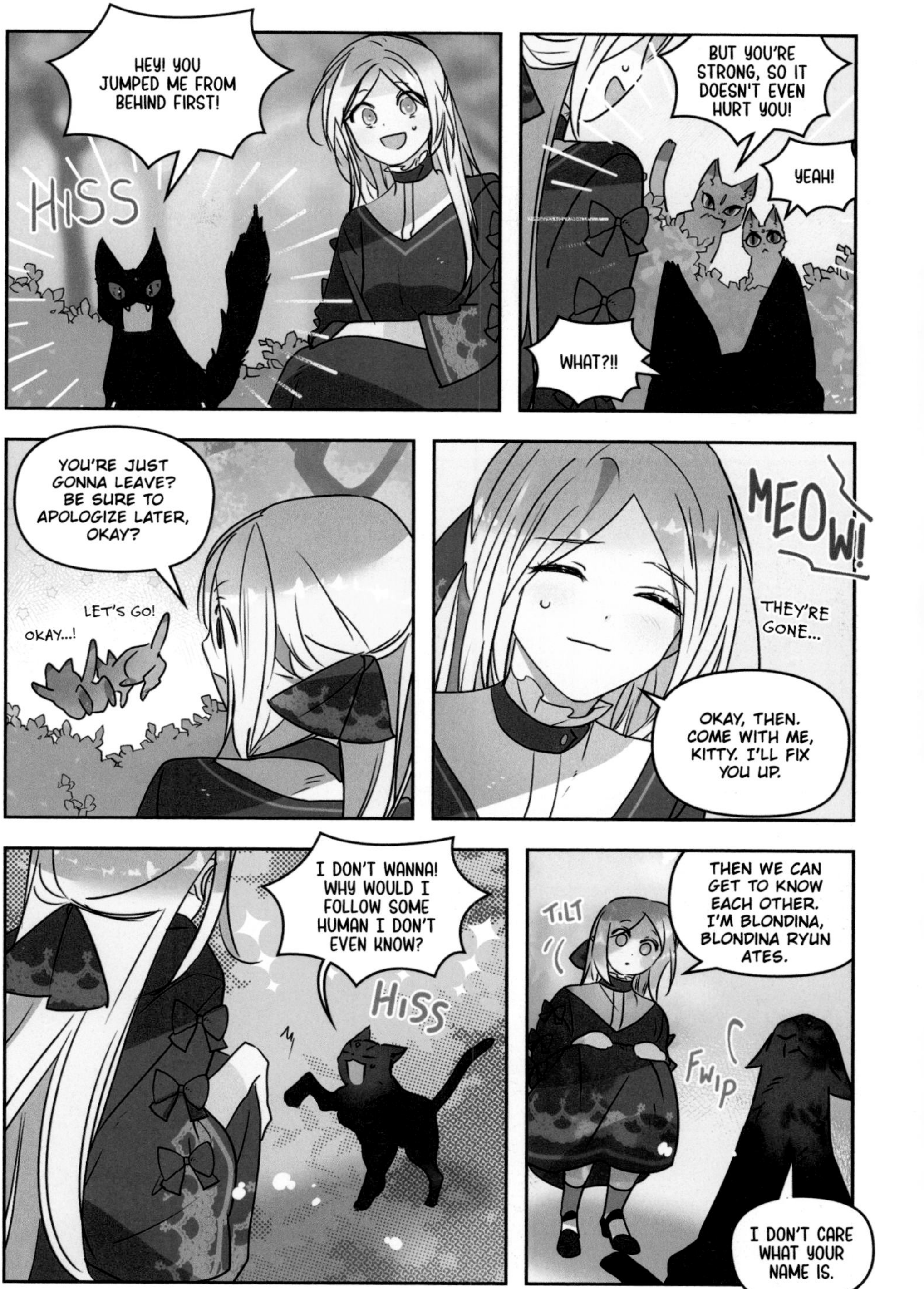
HEY! YOU JUMPED ME FROM BEHIND FIRST!
HISS
BUT YOU'RE STRONG, SO IT DOESN'T EVEN HURT YOU!
YEAH!
WHAT?!!
YOU'RE JUST GONNA LEAVE? BE SURE TO APOLOGIZE LATER, OKAY?
LET'S GO!
OKAY...!
MEOW!
THEY'RE GONE...
OKAY, THEN. COME WITH ME, KITTY. I'LL FIX YOU UP.
I DON'T WANNA! WHY WOULD I FOLLOW SOME HUMAN I DON'T EVEN KNOW?
HISS
TILT
THEN WE CAN GET TO KNOW EACH OTHER. I'M BLONDINA, BLONDINA RYUN ATES.
FWIP
I DON'T CARE WHAT YOUR NAME IS.

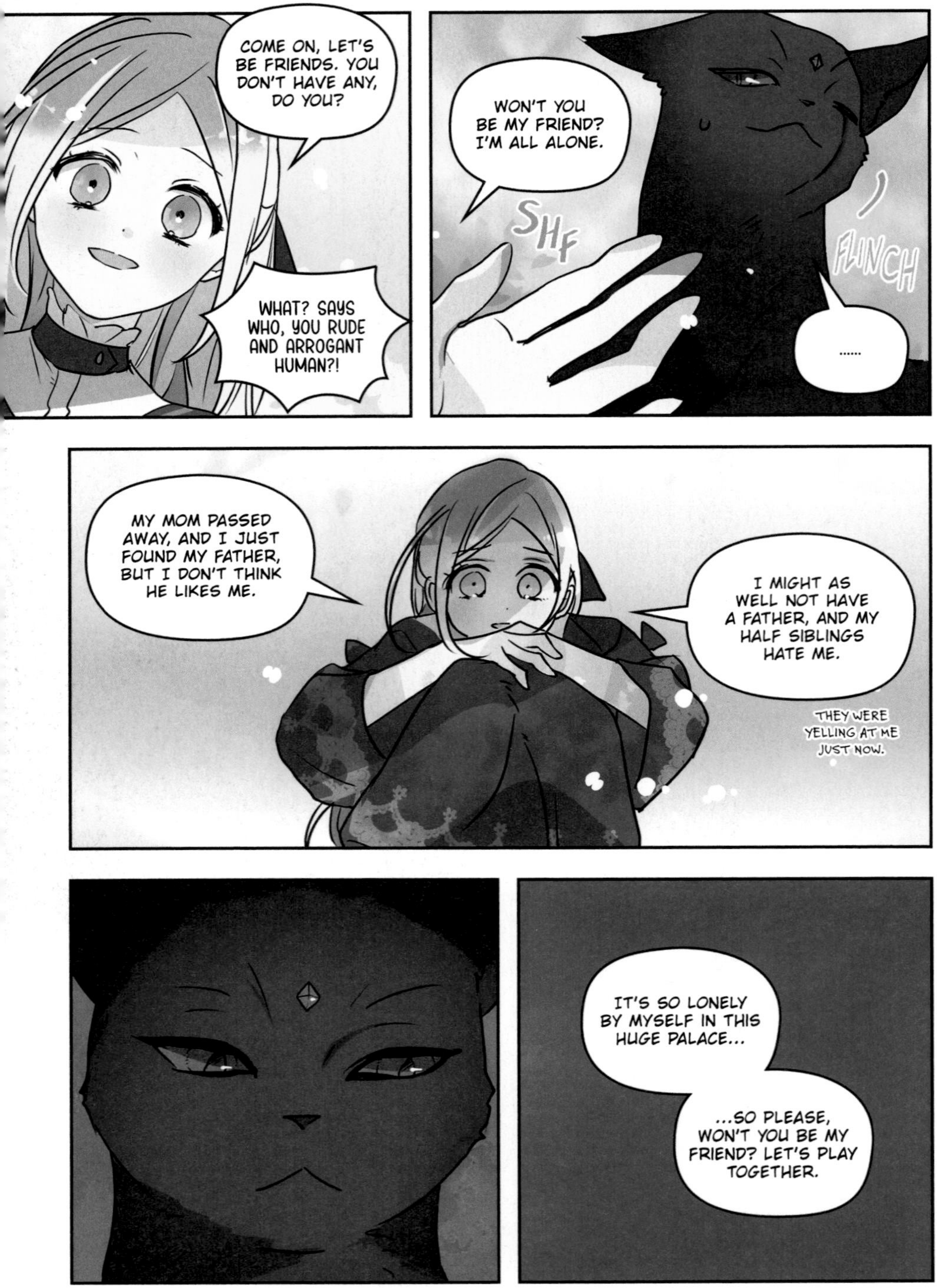
COME ON, LET'S BE FRIENDS. YOU DON'T HAVE ANY, DO YOU?
WHAT? SAYS WHO, YOU RUDE AND ARROGANT HUMAN?!
WON'T YOU BE MY FRIEND? I'M ALL ALONE.
SHF
FLINCH
......
MY MOM PASSED AWAY, AND I JUST FOUND MY FATHER, BUT I DON'T THINK HE LIKES ME.
I MIGHT AS WELL NOT HAVE A FATHER, AND MY HALF SIBLINGS HATE ME.
THEY WERE YELLING AT ME JUST NOW.
IT'S SO LONELY BY MYSELF IN THIS HUGE PALACE...
...SO PLEASE, WON'T YOU BE MY FRIEND? LET'S PLAY TOGETHER.

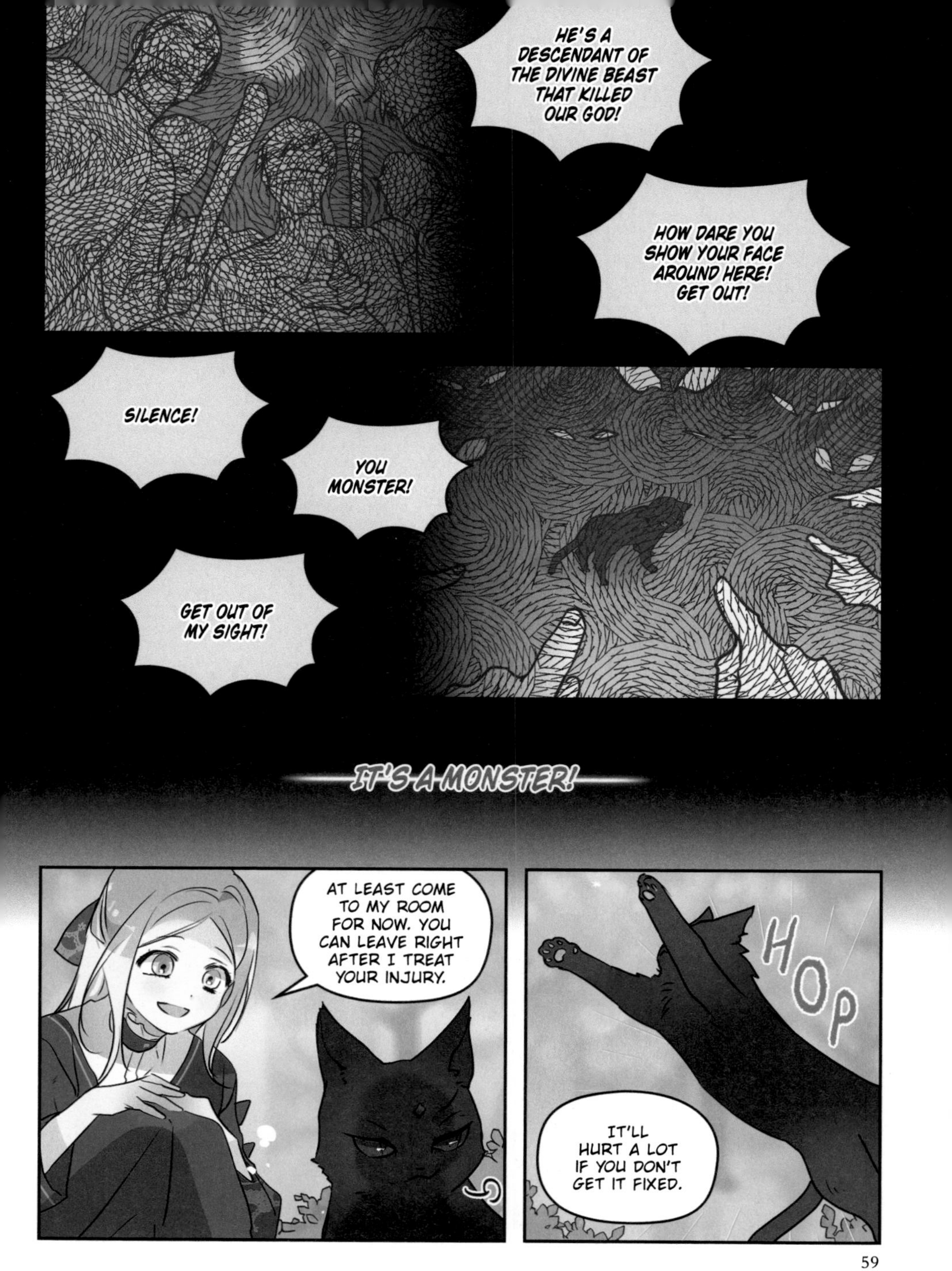
HE'S A DESCENDANT OF THE DIVINE BEAST THAT KILLED OUR GOD!
HOW DARE YOU SHOW YOUR FACE AROUND HERE! GET OUT!
SILENCE!
YOU MONSTER!
GET OUT OF MY SIGHT!
IT'S A MONSTER!
AT LEAST COME TO MY ROOM FOR NOW. YOU CAN LEAVE RIGHT AFTER I TREAT YOUR INJURY.
HOP
IT'LL HURT A LOT IF YOU DON'T GET IT FIXED.

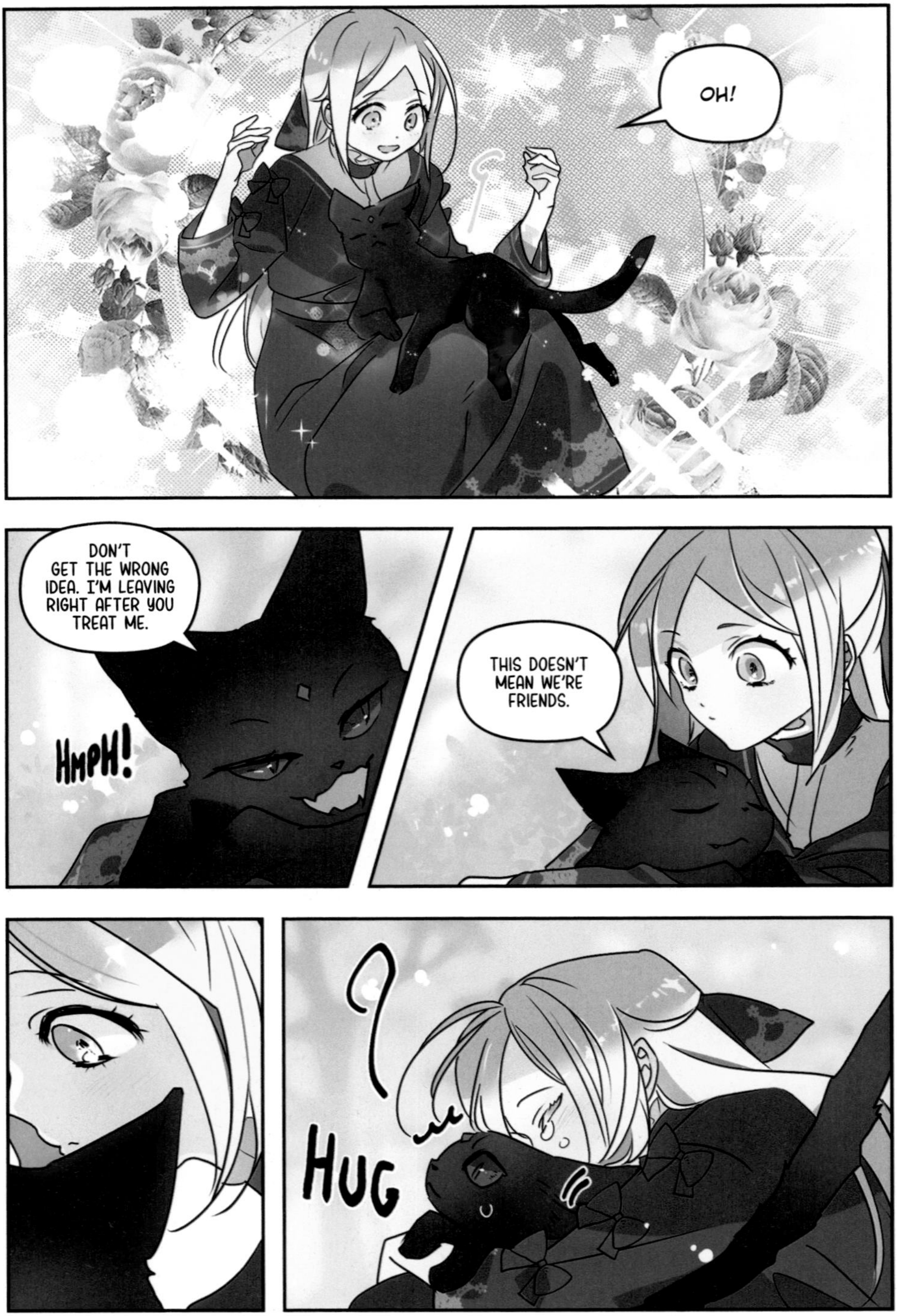
OH!
DON'T GET THE WRONG IDEA. I'M LEAVING RIGHT AFTER YOU TREAT ME.
HMPH!
THIS DOESN'T MEAN WE'RE FRIENDS.
?
HUG

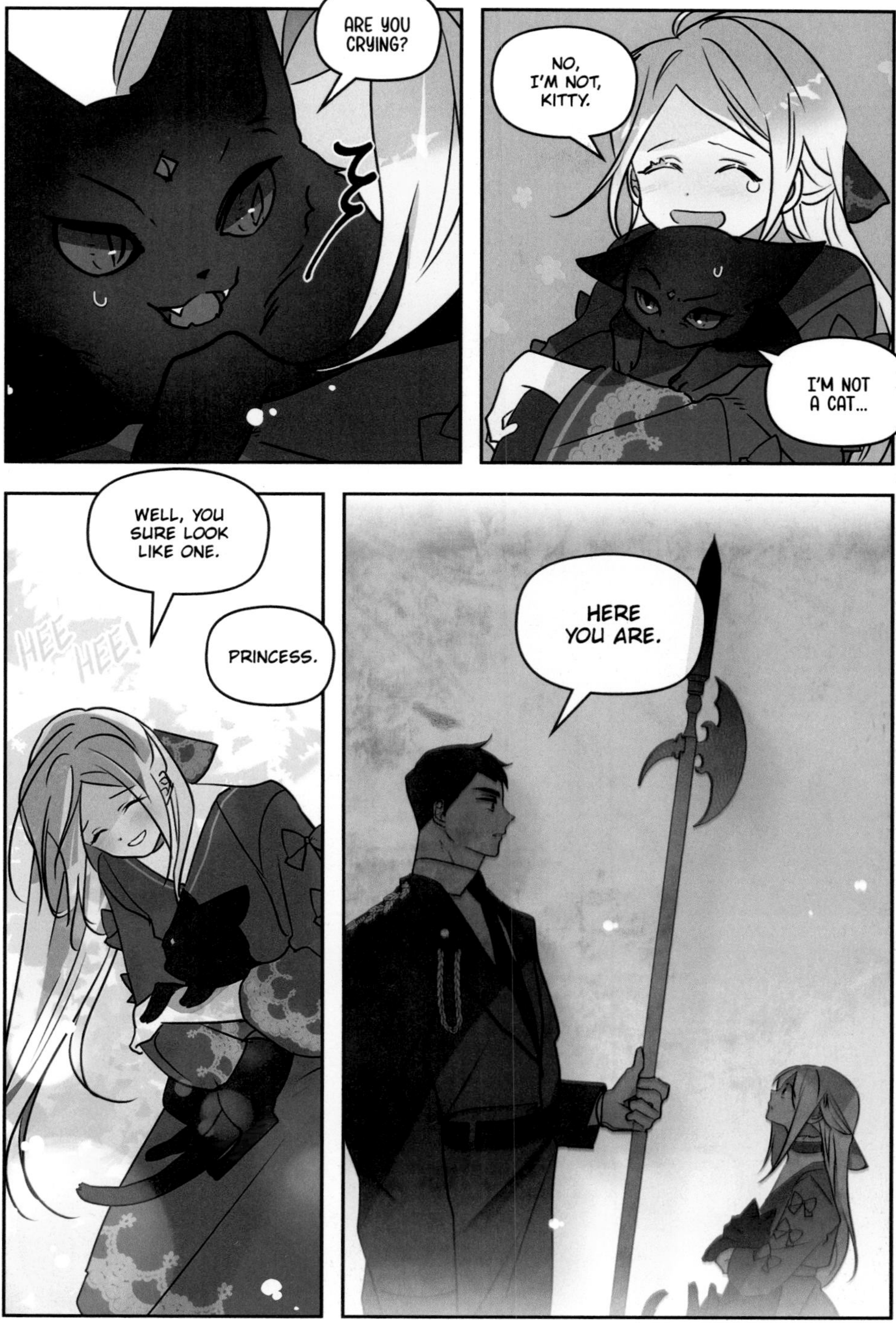
ARE YOU CRYING?
NO, I'M NOT, KITTY.
I'M NOT A CAT...
WELL, YOU SURE LOOK LIKE ONE.
HEE HEE!
PRINCESS.
HERE YOU ARE.

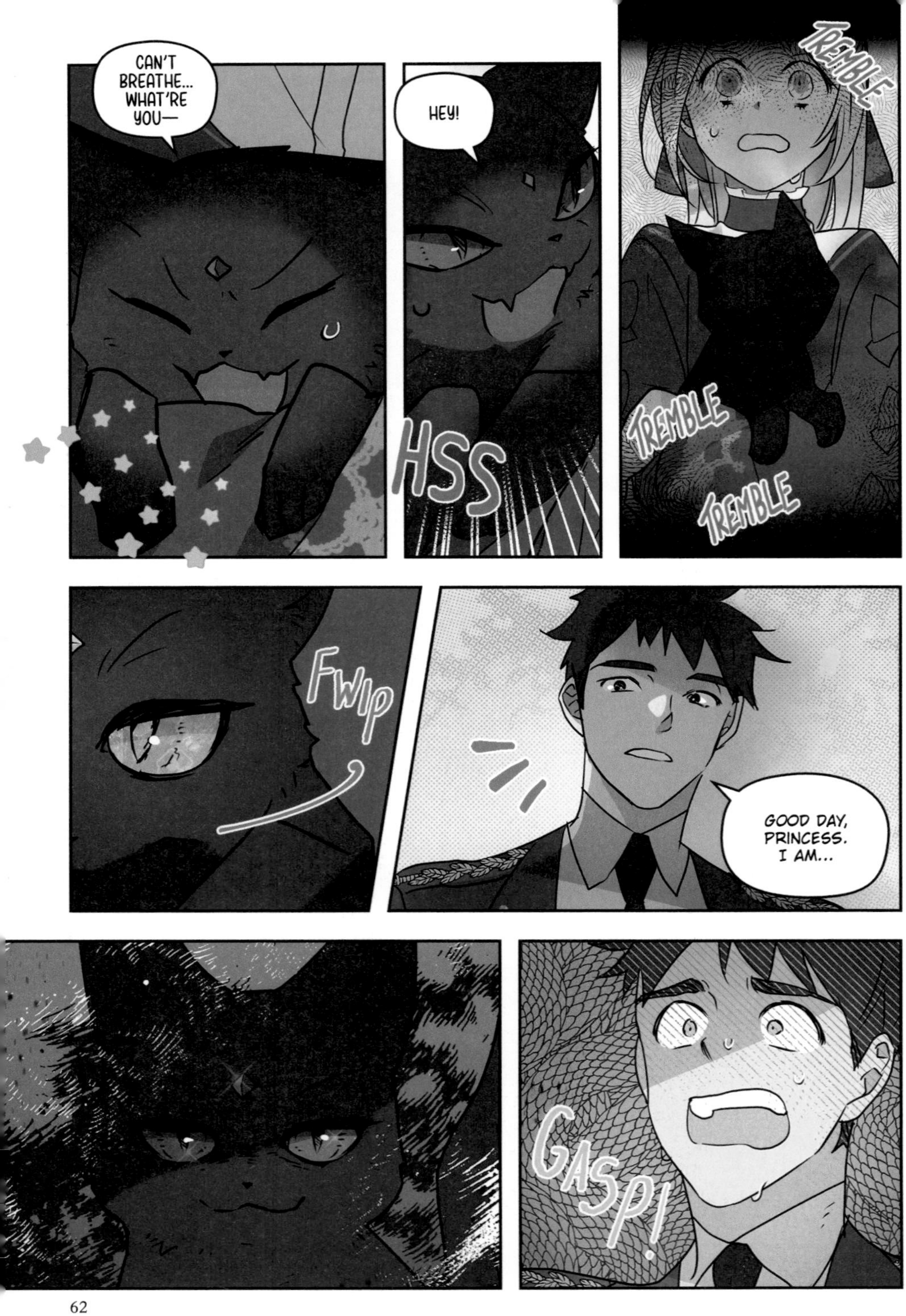

CAN'T BREATHE... WHAT'RE YOU—
HEY!
HSS
TREMBLE
TREMBLE
TREMBLE
FWIP
GOOD DAY, PRINCESS. I AM...
GASP!

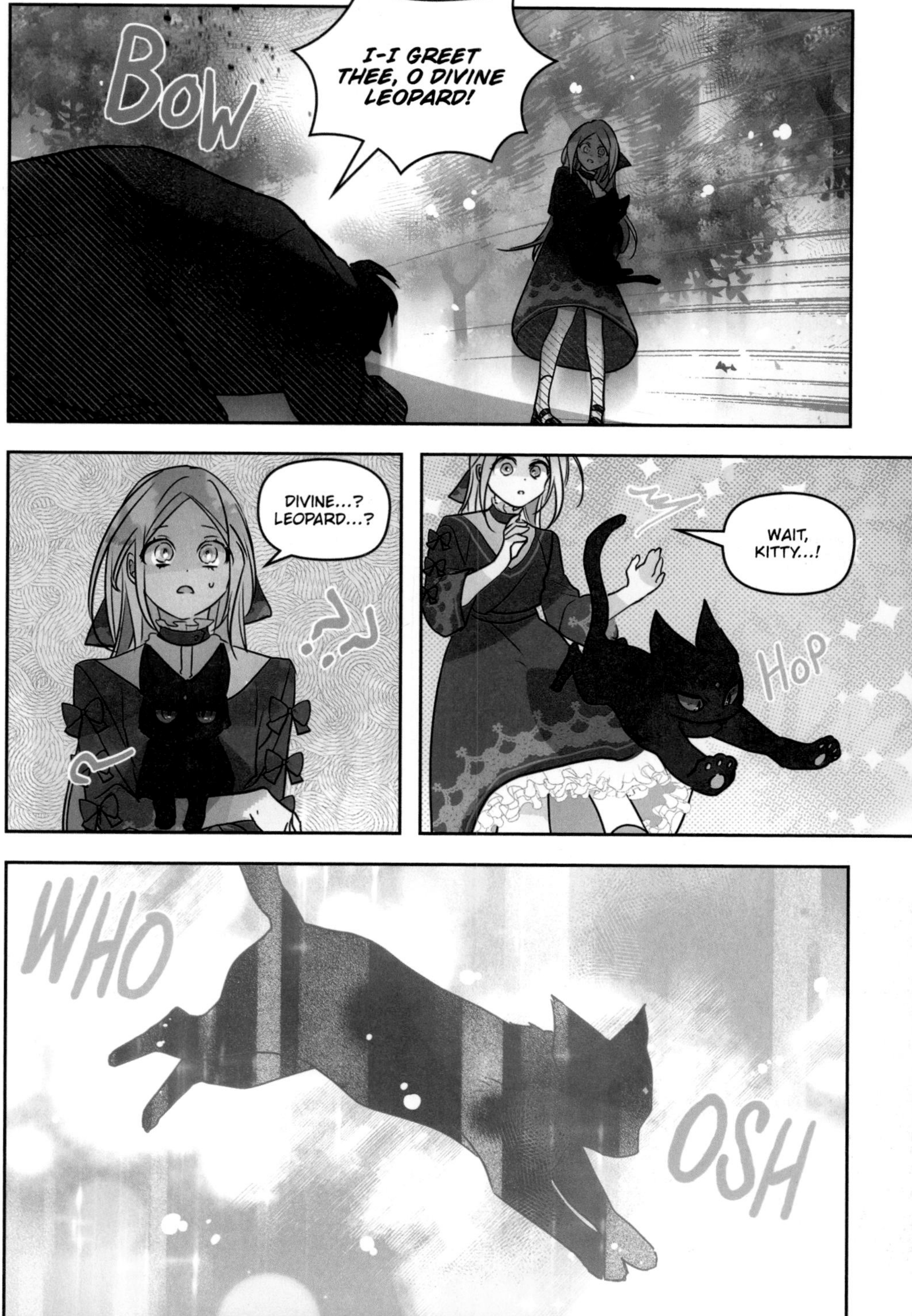
BOW
I-I GREET THEE, O DIVINE LEOPARD!
DIVINE...? LEOPARD...?
WAIT, KITTY...!
HOP
WHOOSH

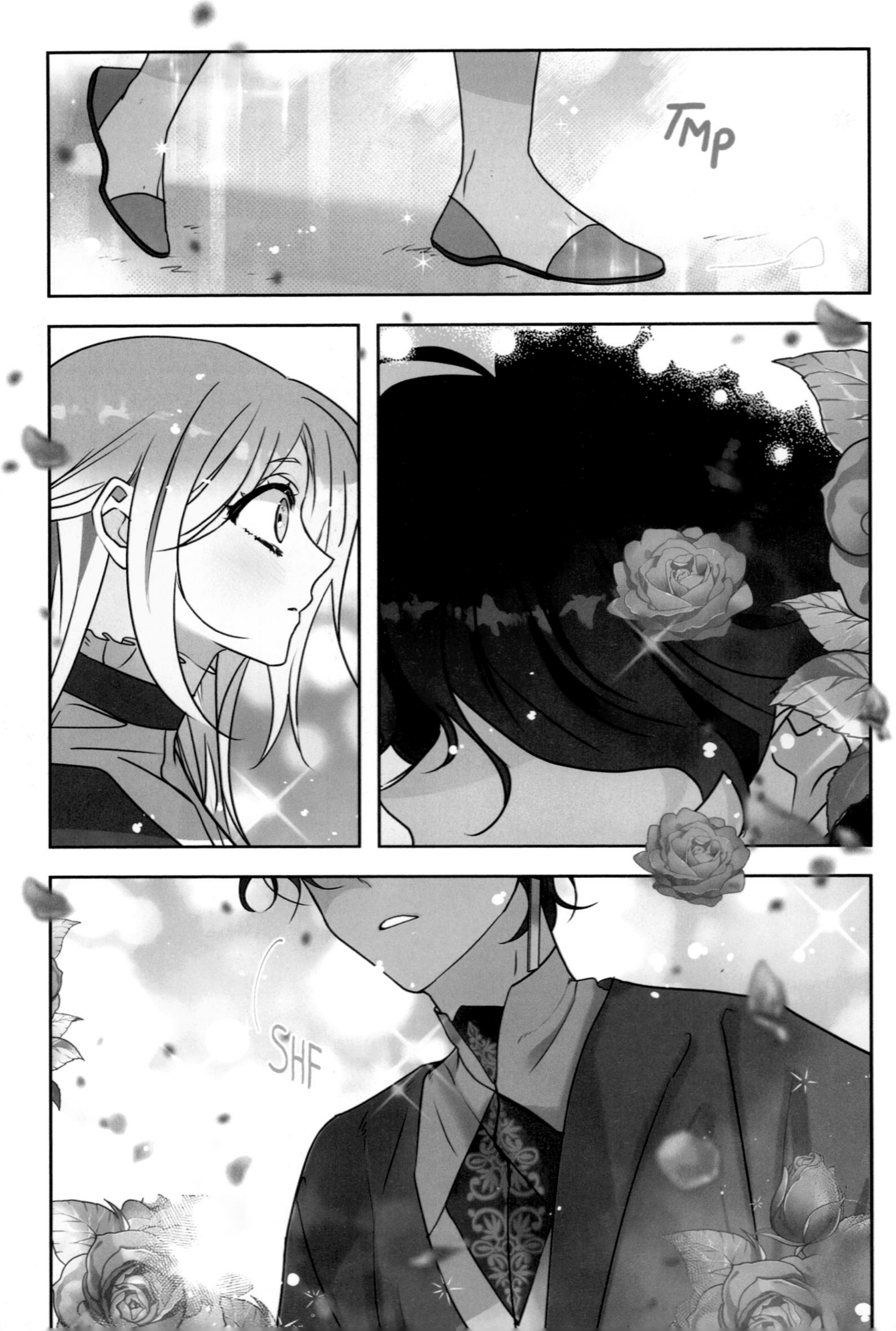
TMP
SHF

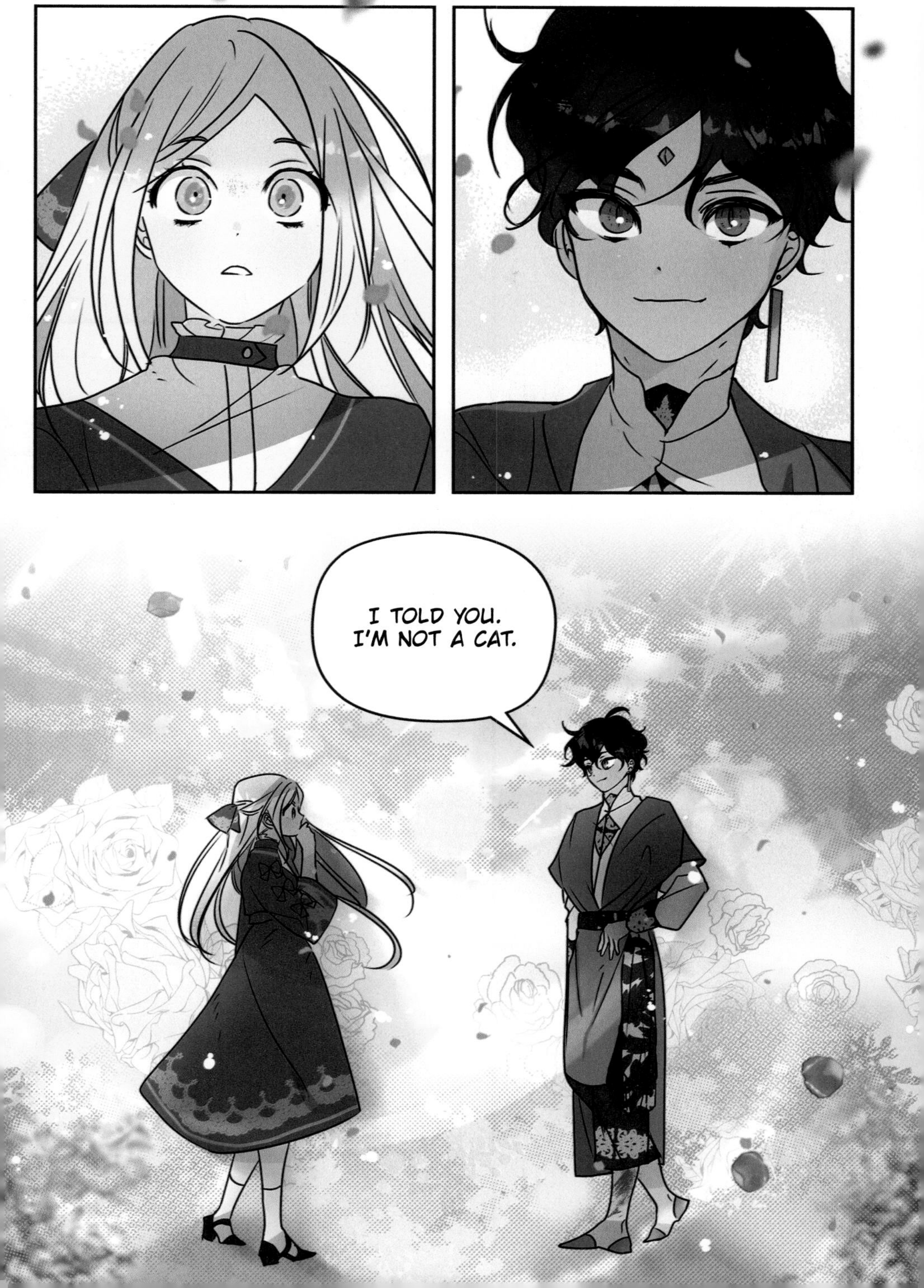
I TOLD YOU.
I'M NOT A CAT.

My
Gently
Raised
Beast

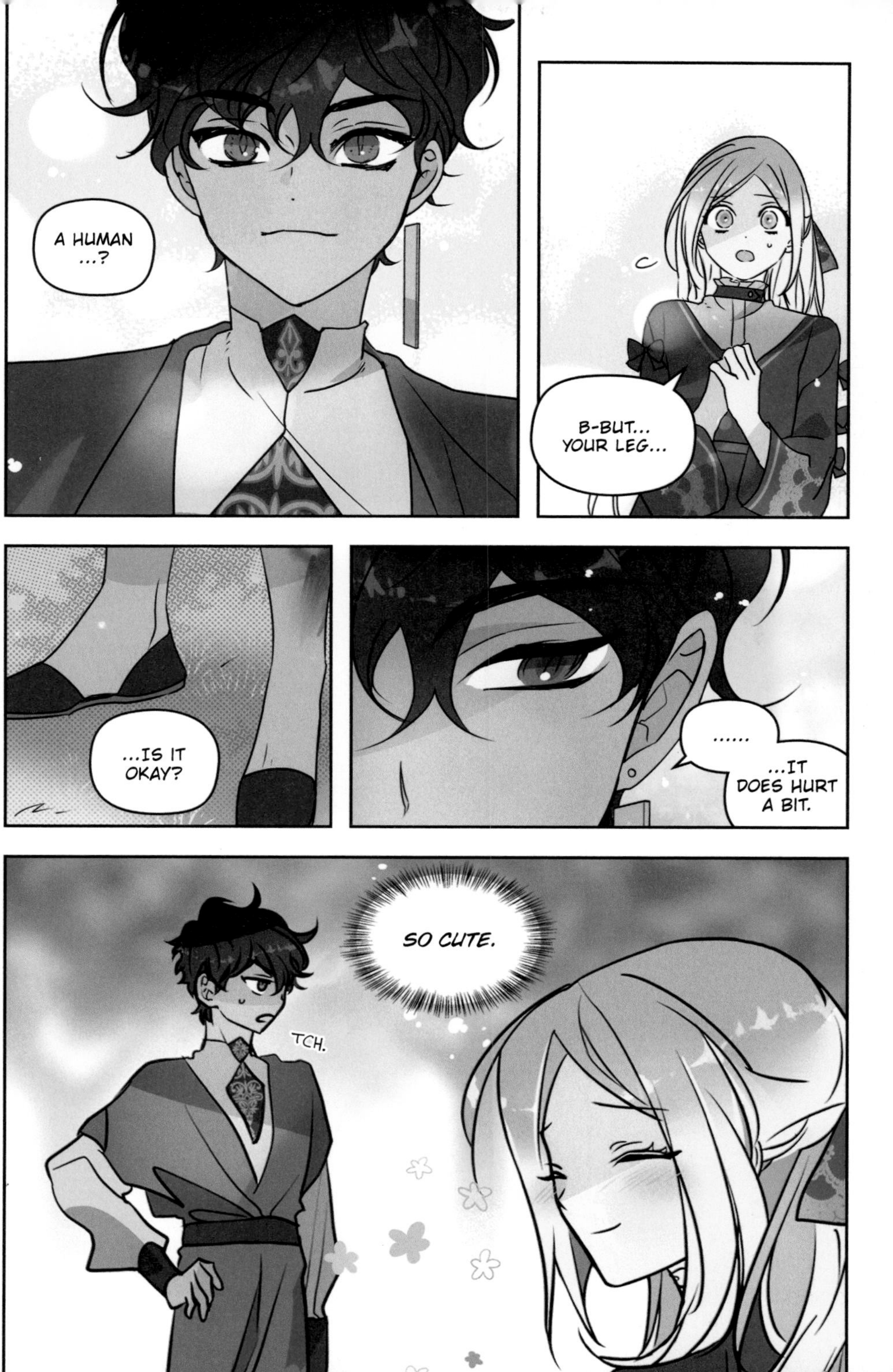
A HUMAN ...?
B-BUT... YOUR LEG...
...IS IT OKAY?
......
...IT DOES HURT A BIT.
SO CUTE.
TCH.

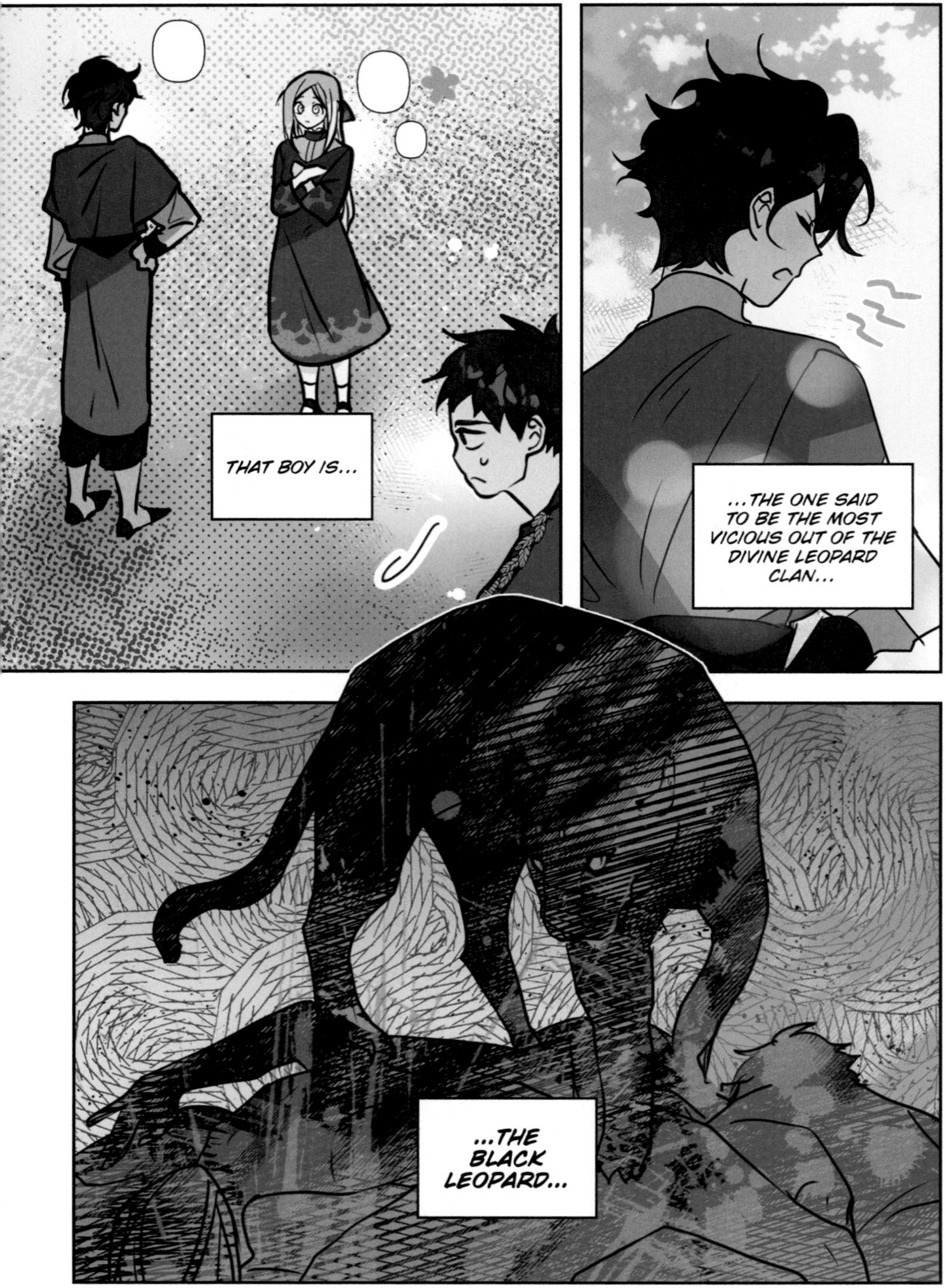

THAT BOY IS...
...THE ONE SAID TO BE THE MOST VICIOUS OUT OF THE DIVINE LEOPARD CLAN...
...THE BLACK LEOPARD...

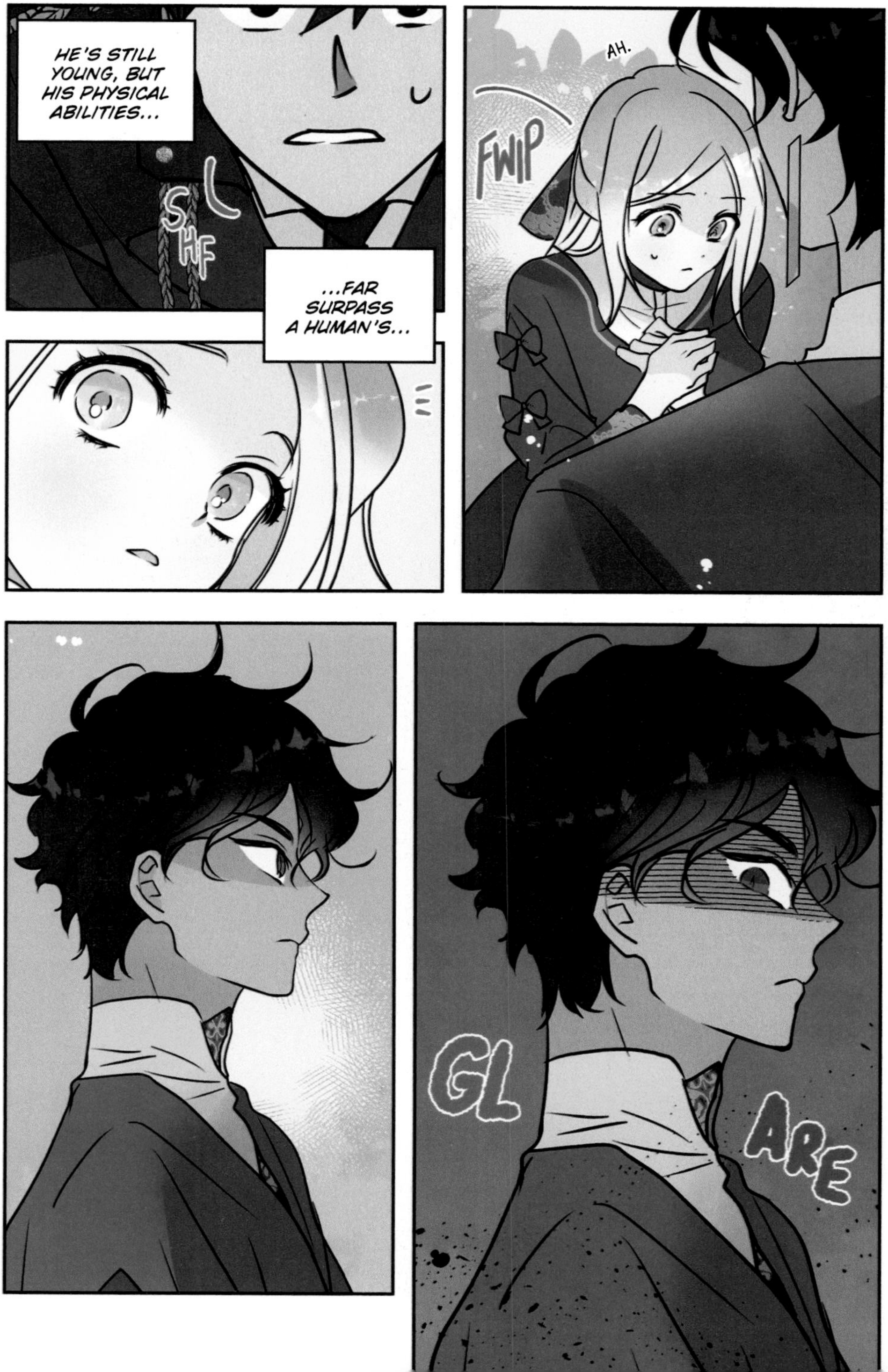
HE'S STILL YOUNG, BUT HIS PHYSICAL ABILITIES...
SHF
...FAR SURPASS A HUMAN'S...
AH.
FWIP
GLARE

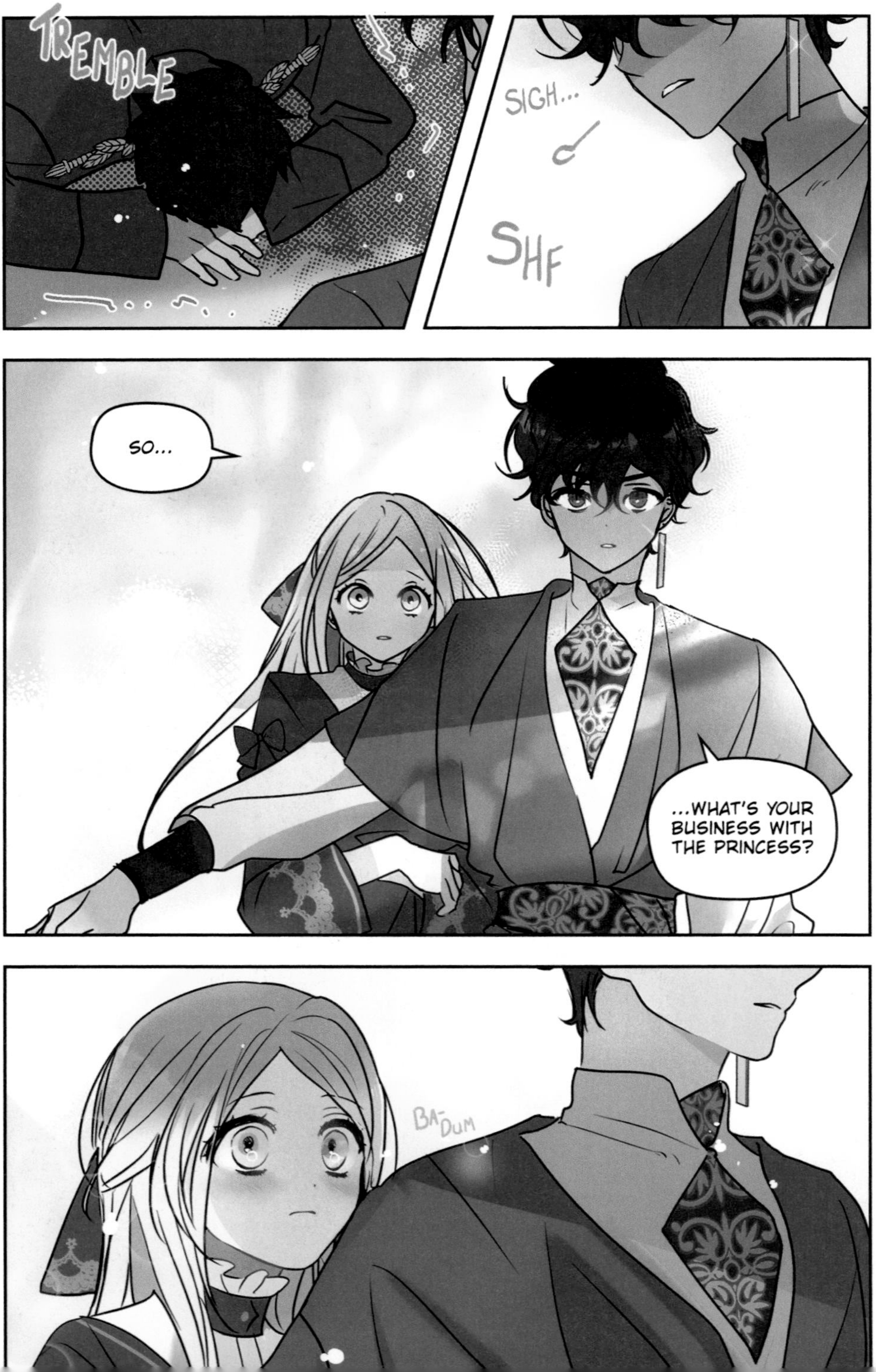

TREMBLE
SIGH...
SHF
SO...
...WHAT'S YOUR BUSINESS WITH THE PRINCESS?
BA-DUM

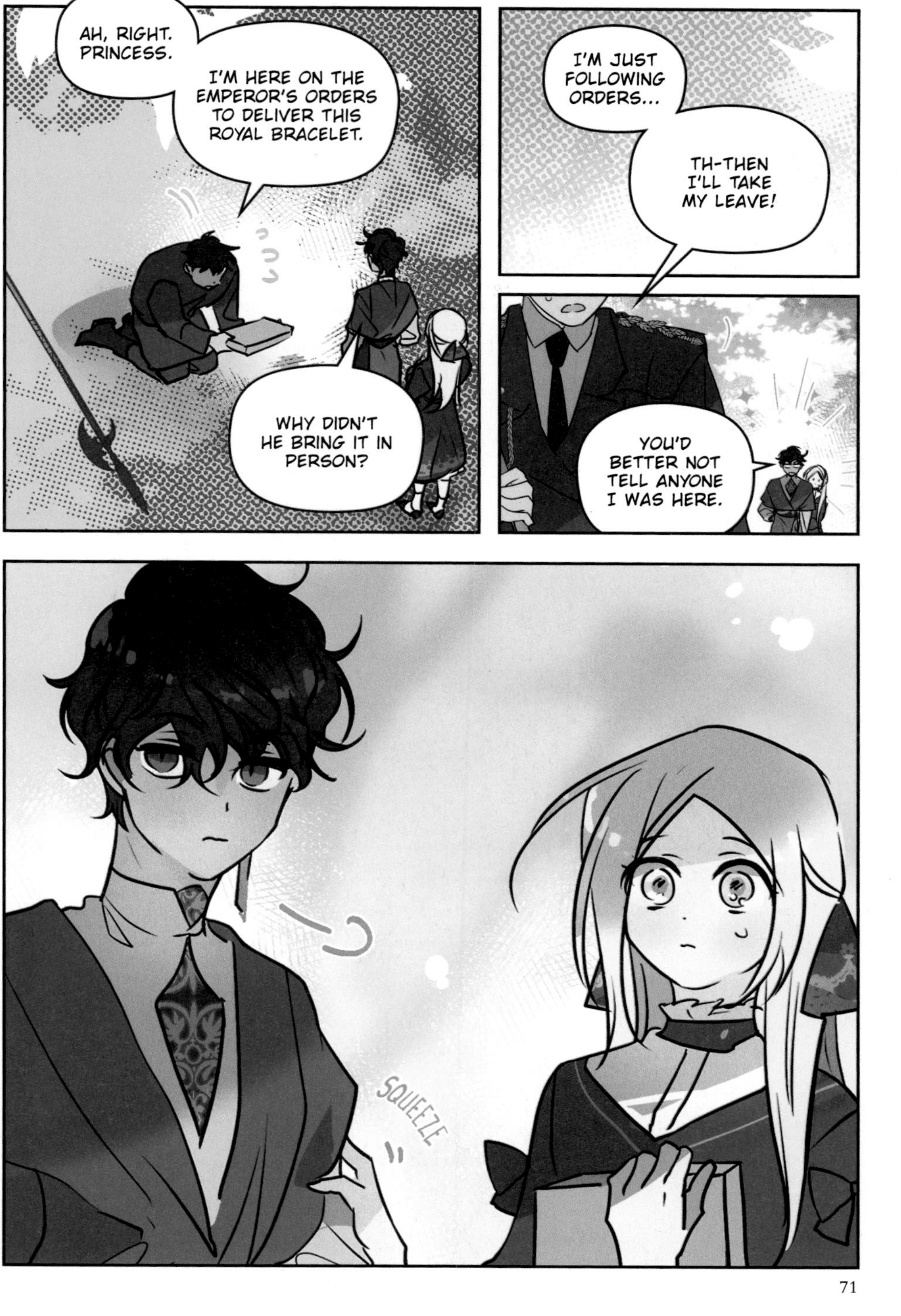
AH, RIGHT. PRINCESS.
I'M HERE ON THE EMPEROR'S ORDERS TO DELIVER THIS ROYAL BRACELET.
WHY DIDN'T HE BRING IT IN PERSON?
I'M JUST FOLLOWING ORDERS...
TH-THEN I'LL TAKE MY LEAVE!
YOU'D BETTER NOT TELL ANYONE I WAS HERE.
SQUEEZE

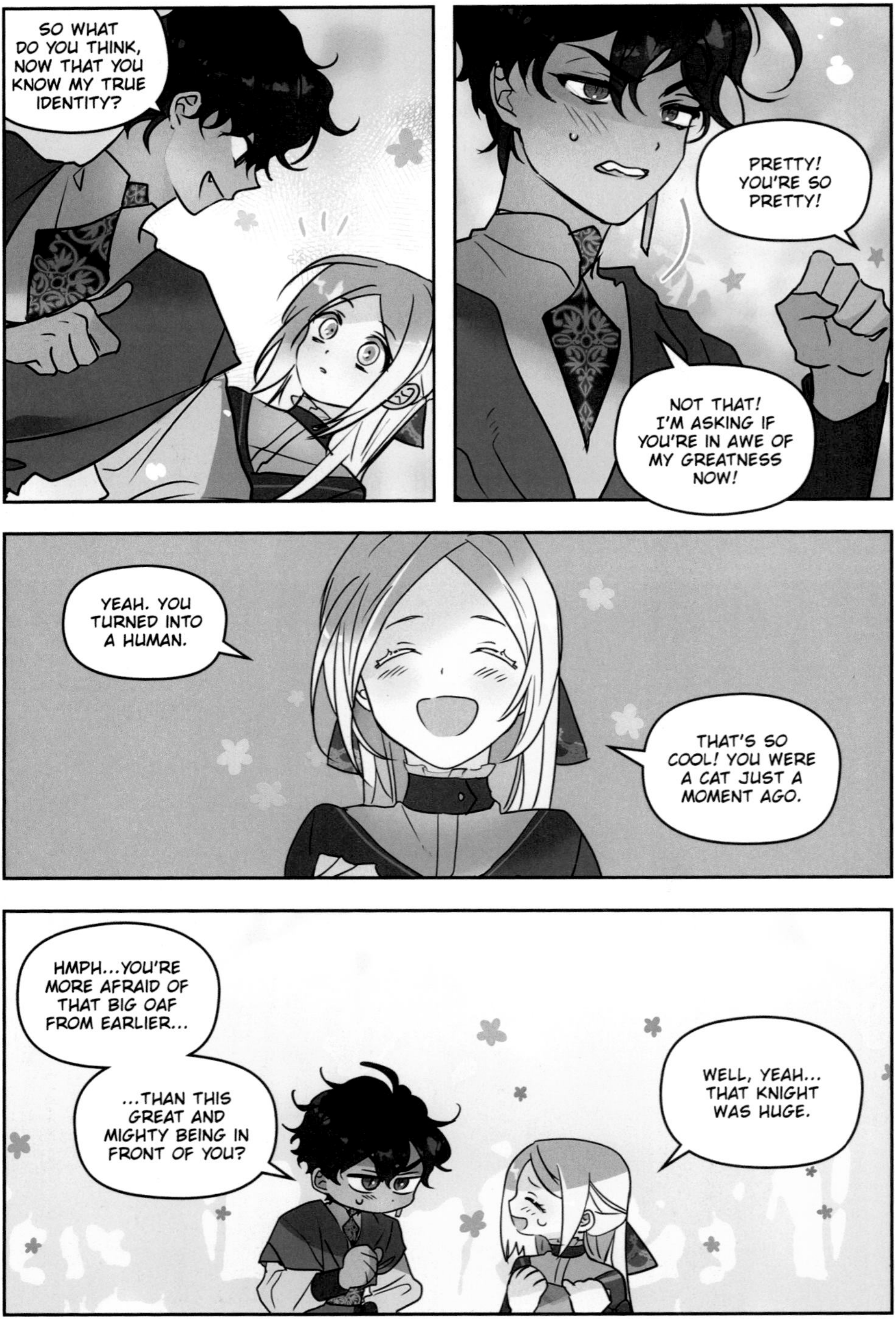
SO WHAT DO YOU THINK, NOW THAT YOU KNOW MY TRUE IDENTITY?
PRETTY! YOU'RE SO PRETTY!
NOT THAT! I'M ASKING IF YOU'RE IN AWE OF MY GREATNESS NOW!
YEAH. YOU TURNED INTO A HUMAN.
THAT'S SO COOL! YOU WERE A CAT JUST A MOMENT AGO.
HMPH...YOU'RE MORE AFRAID OF THAT BIG OAF FROM EARLIER...
...THAN THIS GREAT AND MIGHTY BEING IN FRONT OF YOU?
WELL, YEAH... THAT KNIGHT WAS HUGE.

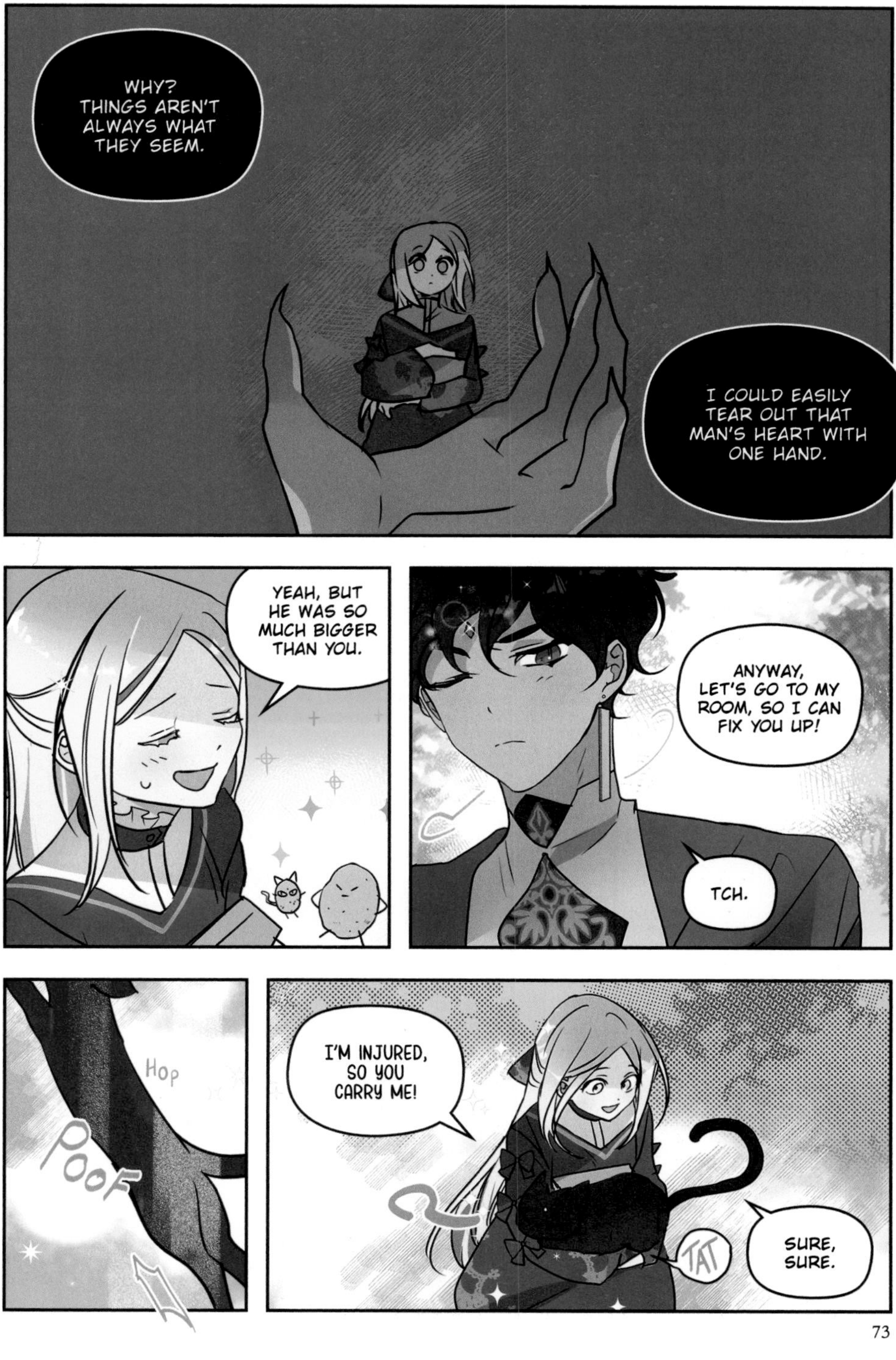
WHY? THINGS AREN'T ALWAYS WHAT THEY SEEM.
I COULD EASILY TEAR OUT THAT MAN'S HEART WITH ONE HAND.
YEAH, BUT HE WAS SO MUCH BIGGER THAN YOU.
ANYWAY, LET'S GO TO MY ROOM, SO I CAN FIX YOU UP!
TCH.
Hop
POOF
I'M INJURED, SO YOU CARRY ME!
TAT
SURE, SURE.

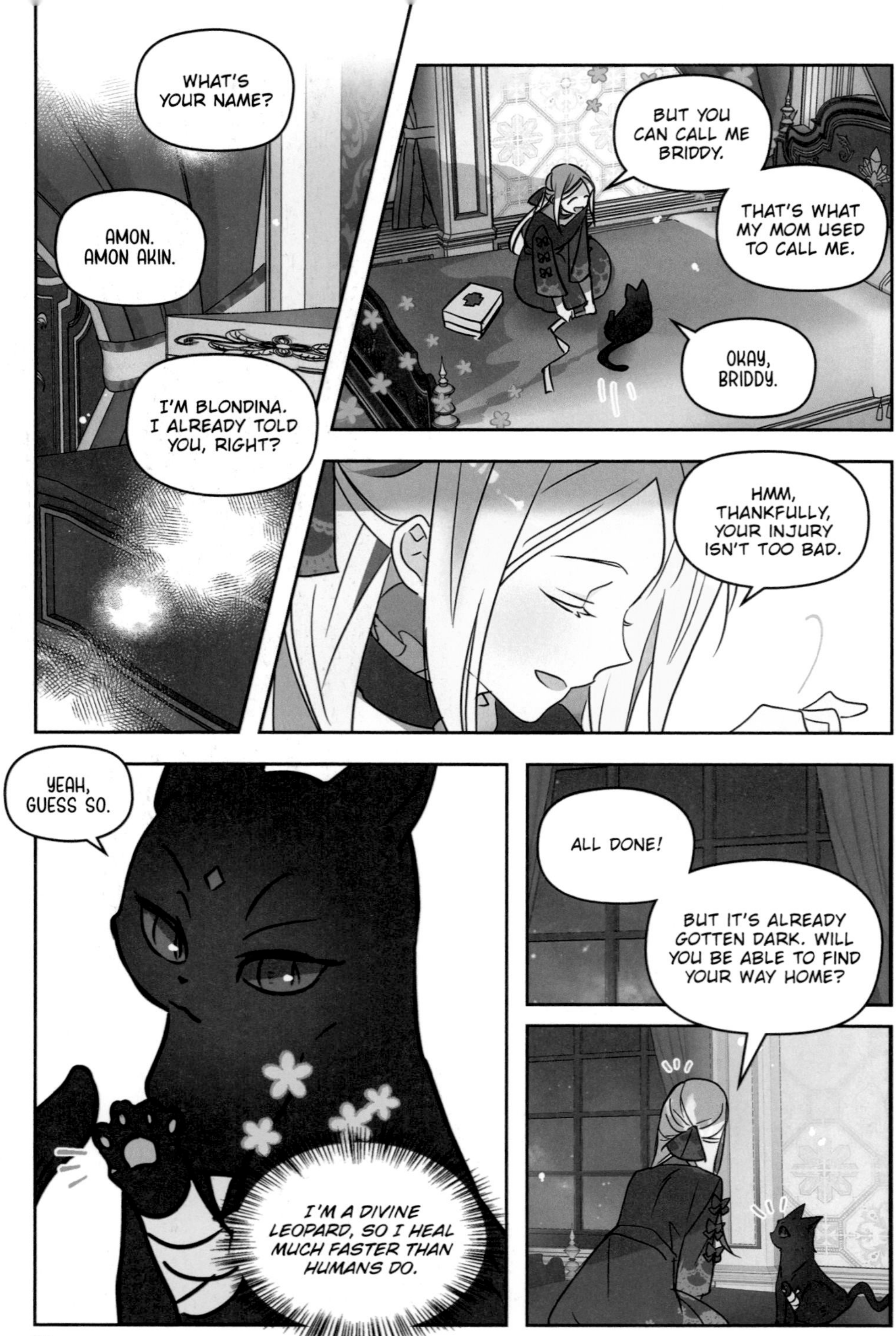
WHAT'S YOUR NAME?
AMON. AMON AKIN.
I'M BLONDINA. I ALREADY TOLD YOU, RIGHT?
BUT YOU CAN CALL ME BRIDDY.
THAT'S WHAT MY MOM USED TO CALL ME.
OKAY, BRIDDY.
HMM, THANKFULLY, YOUR INJURY ISN'T TOO BAD.
YEAH, GUESS SO.
I'M A DIVINE LEOPARD, SO I HEAL MUCH FASTER THAN HUMANS DO.
ALL DONE!
BUT IT'S ALREADY GOTTEN DARK. WILL YOU BE ABLE TO FIND YOUR WAY HOME?

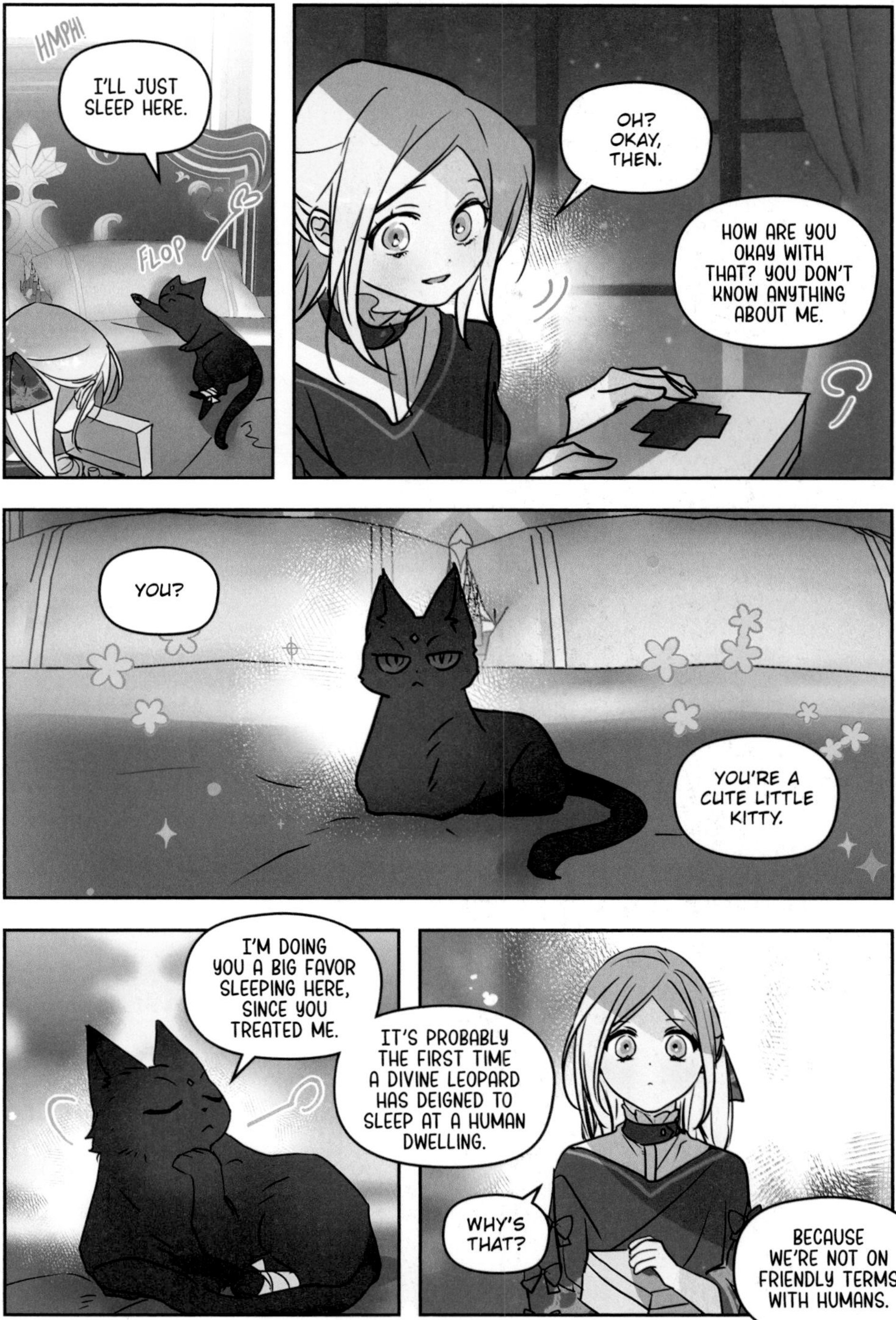
HMPH!
I'LL JUST SLEEP HERE.
FLOP
OH? OKAY, THEN.
HOW ARE YOU OKAY WITH THAT? YOU DON'T KNOW ANYTHING ABOUT ME.
YOU?
YOU'RE A CUTE LITTLE KITTY.
I'M DOING YOU A BIG FAVOR SLEEPING HERE, SINCE YOU TREATED ME.
IT'S PROBABLY THE FIRST TIME A DIVINE LEOPARD HAS DEIGNED TO SLEEP AT A HUMAN DWELLING.
WHY'S THAT?
BECAUSE WE'RE NOT ON FRIENDLY TERMS WITH HUMANS.

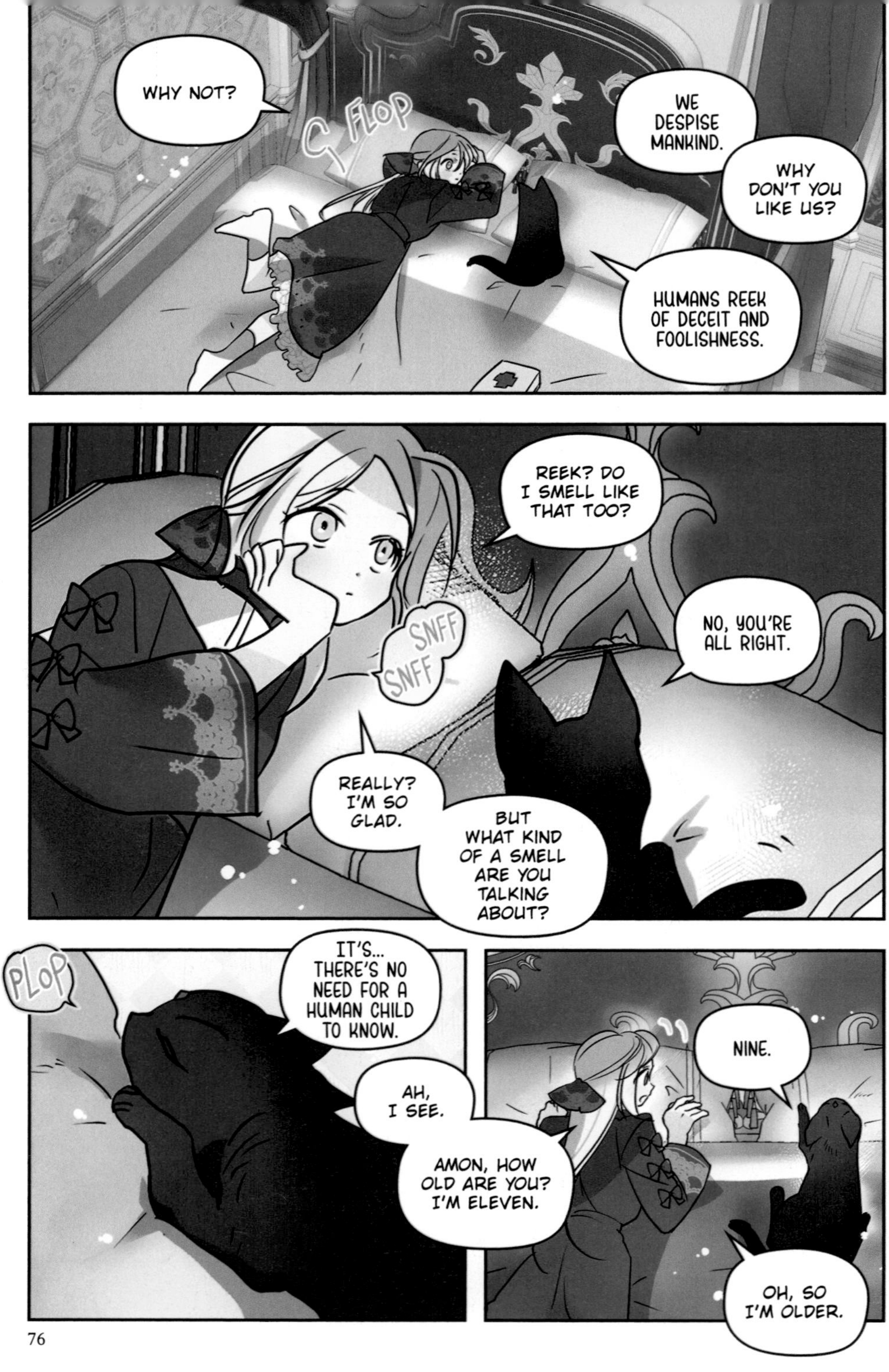
WHY NOT?
FLOP
WE DESPISE MANKIND.
WHY DON'T YOU LIKE US?
HUMANS REEK OF DECEIT AND FOOLISHNESS.
REEK? DO I SMELL LIKE THAT TOO?
SNFF SNFF
NO, YOU'RE ALL RIGHT.
REALLY? I'M SO GLAD.
BUT WHAT KIND OF A SMELL ARE YOU TALKING ABOUT?
PLOP
IT'S... THERE'S NO NEED FOR A HUMAN CHILD TO KNOW.
AH, I SEE.
AMON, HOW OLD ARE YOU? I'M ELEVEN.
NINE.
OH, SO I'M OLDER.

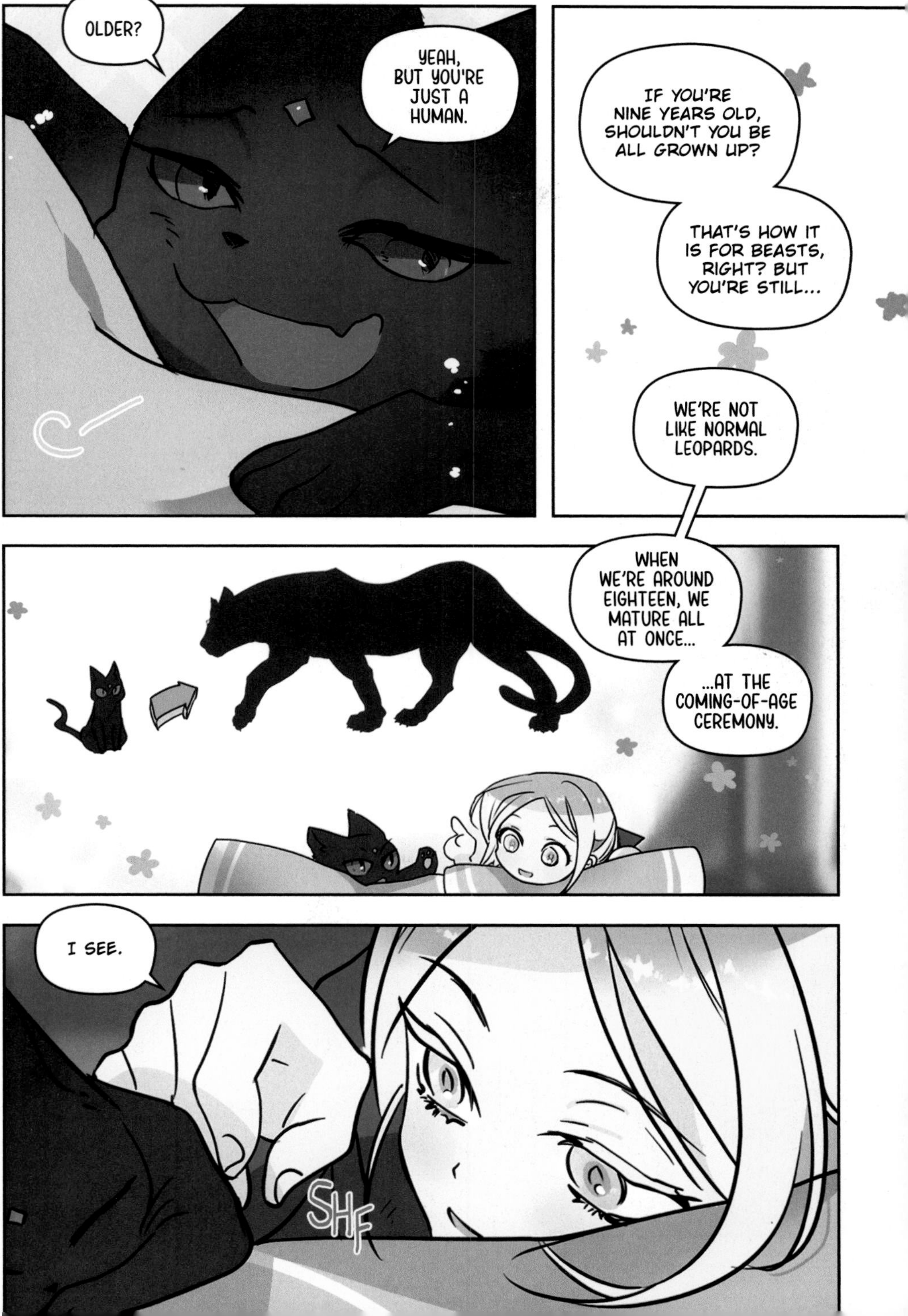
OLDER?
YEAH, BUT YOU'RE JUST A HUMAN.
IF YOU'RE NINE YEARS OLD, SHOULDN'T YOU BE ALL GROWN UP?
THAT'S HOW IT IS FOR BEASTS, RIGHT? BUT YOU'RE STILL...
WE'RE NOT LIKE NORMAL LEOPARDS.
WHEN WE'RE AROUND EIGHTEEN, WE MATURE ALL AT ONCE...
...AT THE COMING-OF-AGE CEREMONY.
I SEE.
SHF

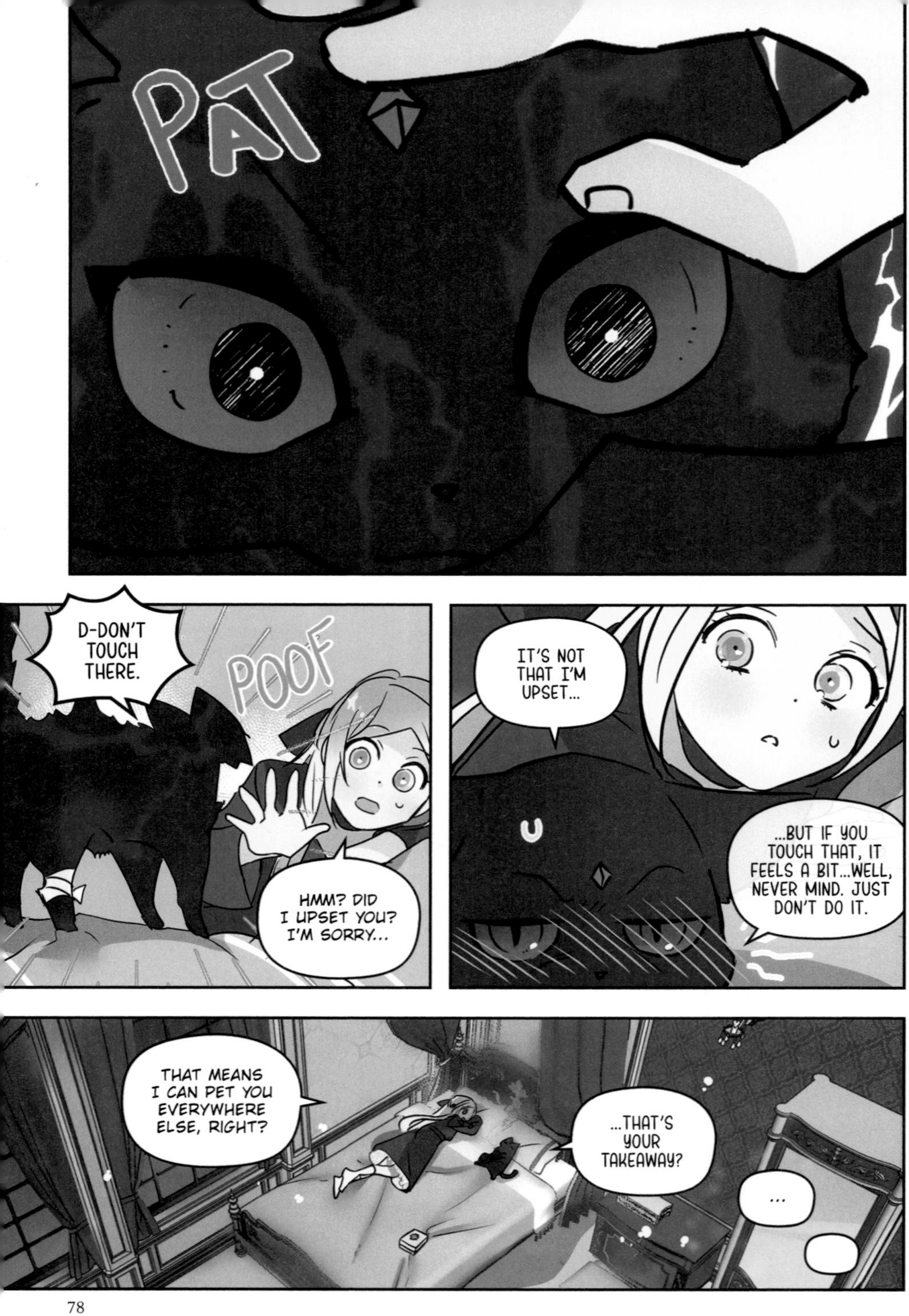
PAT
D-DON'T TOUCH THERE.
POOF
HMM? DID I UPSET YOU? I'M SORRY...
IT'S NOT THAT I'M UPSET...
...BUT IF YOU TOUCH THAT, IT FEELS A BIT...WELL, NEVER MIND. JUST DON'T DO IT.
THAT MEANS I CAN PET YOU EVERYWHERE ELSE, RIGHT?
...THAT'S YOUR TAKEAWAY?
...

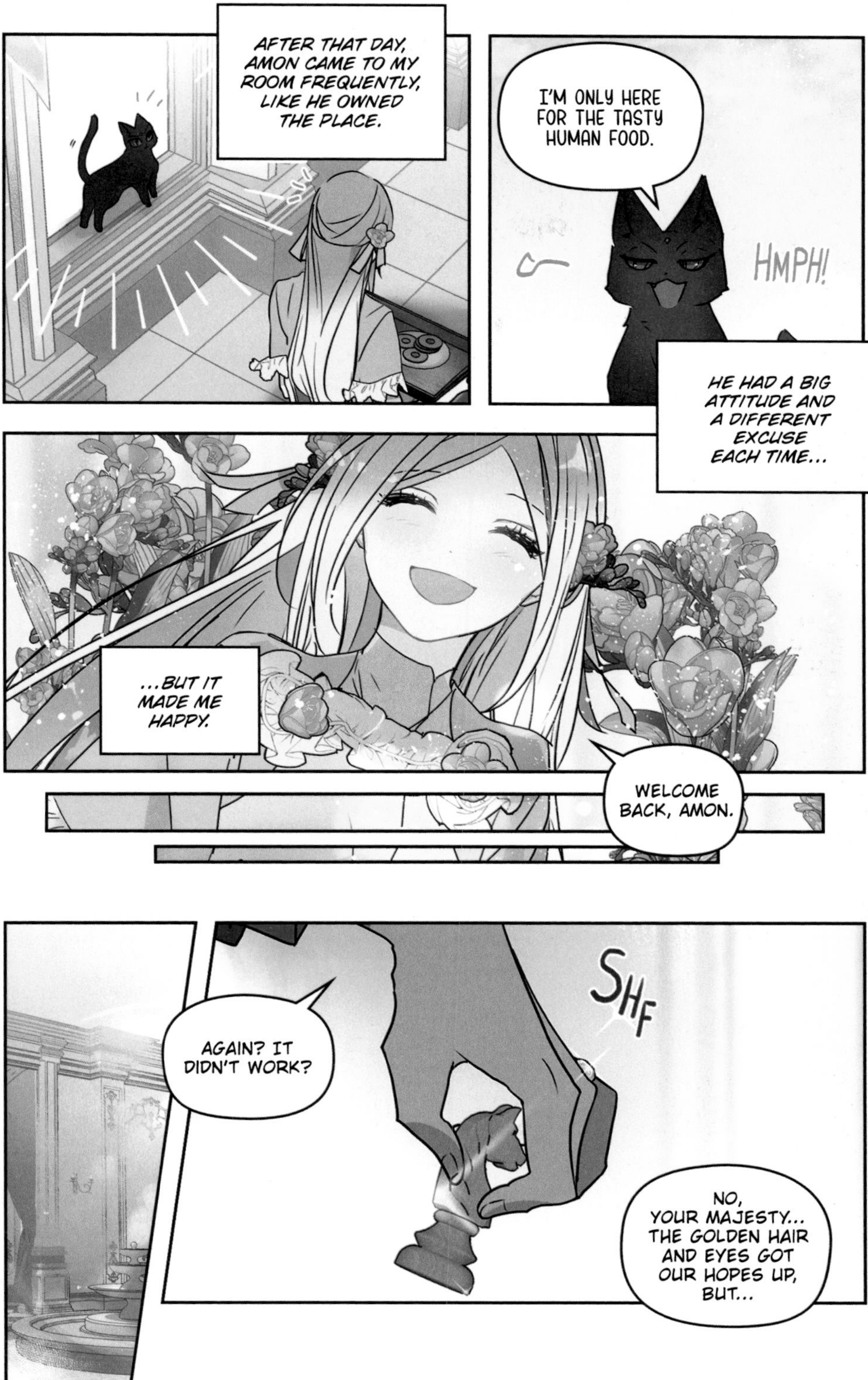

AFTER THAT DAY, AMON CAME TO MY ROOM FREQUENTLY, LIKE HE OWNED THE PLACE.
I'M ONLY HERE FOR THE TASTY HUMAN FOOD.
HMPH!
HE HAD A BIG ATTITUDE AND A DIFFERENT EXCUSE EACH TIME...
...BUT IT MADE ME HAPPY.
WELCOME BACK, AMON.
SHF
AGAIN? IT DIDN'T WORK?
NO, YOUR MAJESTY... THE GOLDEN HAIR AND EYES GOT OUR HOPES UP, BUT...

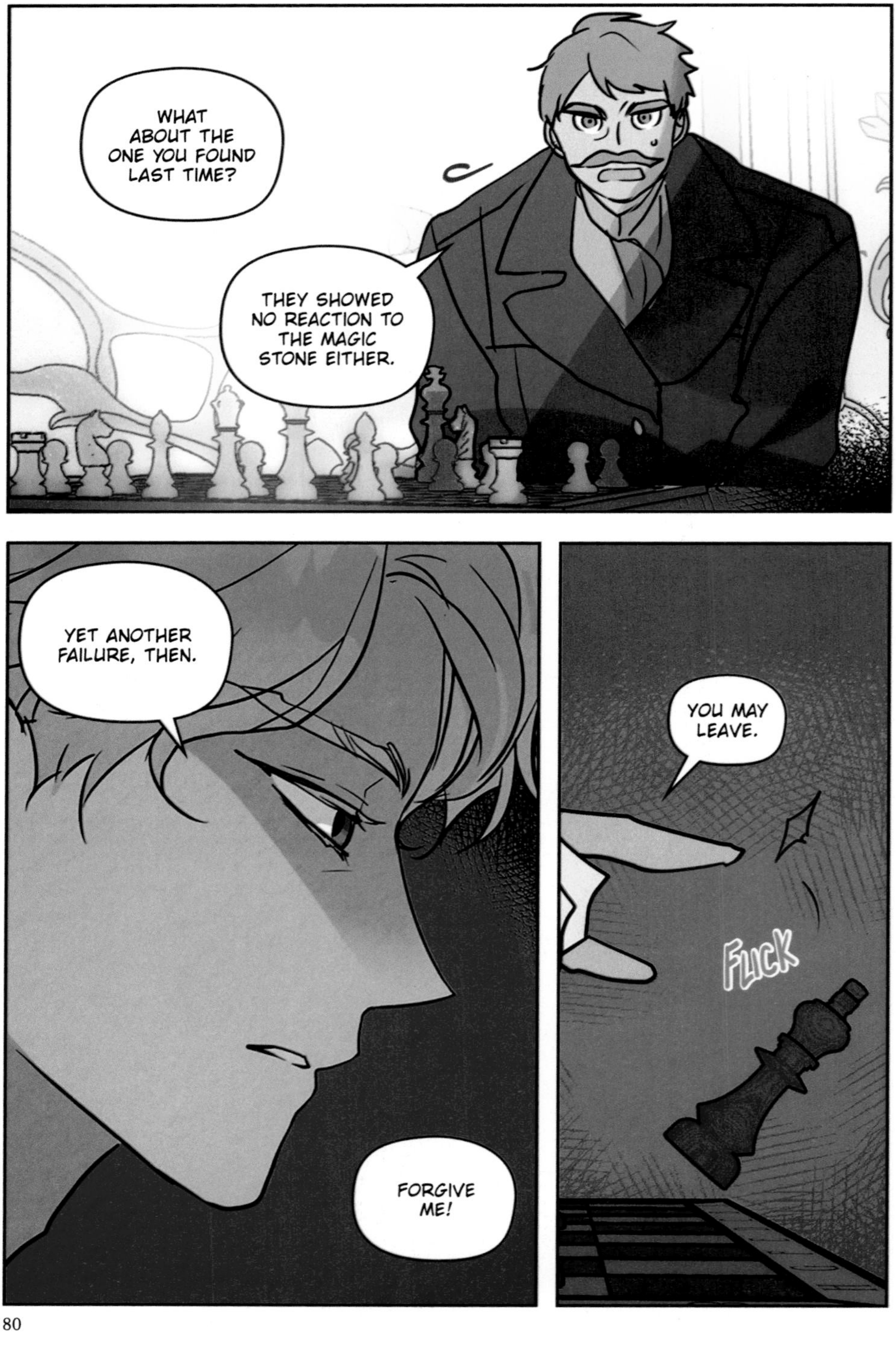
WHAT ABOUT THE ONE YOU FOUND LAST TIME?
THEY SHOWED NO REACTION TO THE MAGIC STONE EITHER.
YET ANOTHER FAILURE, THEN.
FORGIVE ME!
YOU MAY LEAVE.
FLICK

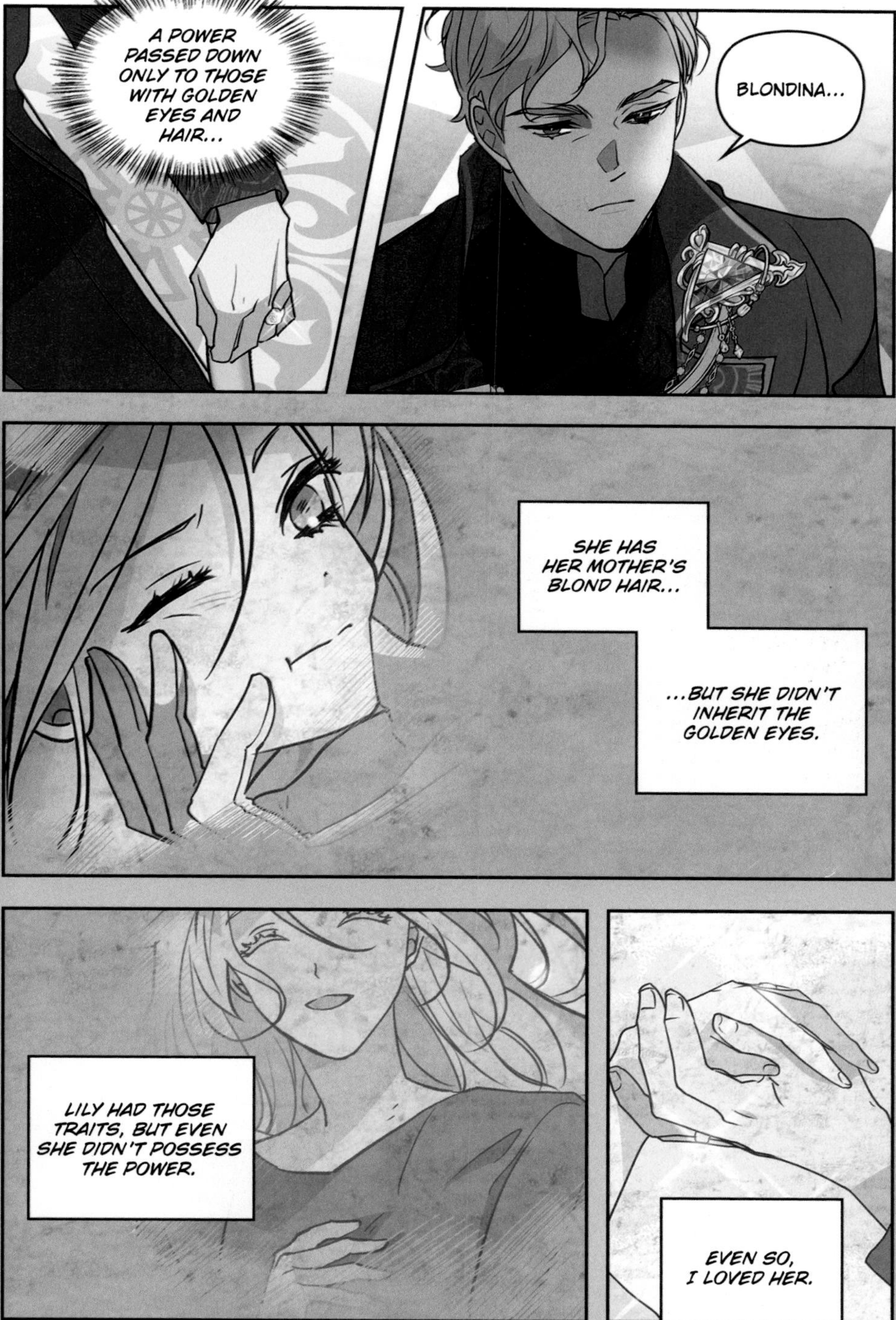
A POWER PASSED DOWN ONLY TO THOSE WITH GOLDEN EYES AND HAIR...
BLONDINA...
SHE HAS HER MOTHER'S BLOND HAIR...
...BUT SHE DIDN'T INHERIT THE GOLDEN EYES.
LILY HAD THOSE TRAITS, BUT EVEN SHE DIDN'T POSSESS THE POWER.
EVEN SO, I LOVED HER.

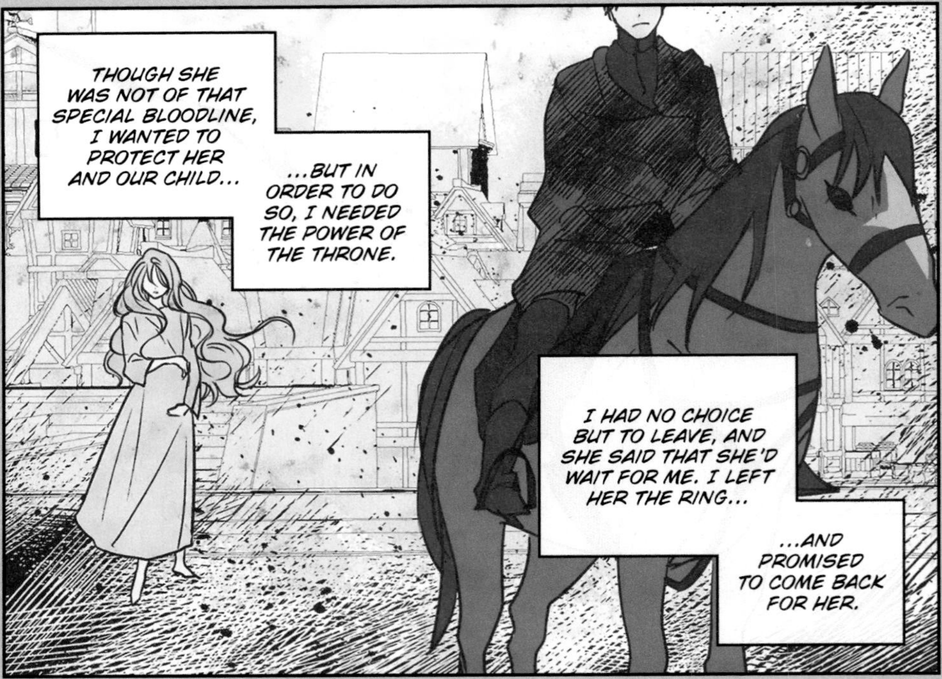
THOUGH SHE WAS NOT OF THAT SPECIAL BLOODLINE, I WANTED TO PROTECT HER AND OUR CHILD...
...BUT IN ORDER TO DO SO, I NEEDED THE POWER OF THE THRONE.
I HAD NO CHOICE BUT TO LEAVE, AND SHE SAID THAT SHE'D WAIT FOR ME. I LEFT HER THE RING...
...AND PROMISED TO COME BACK FOR HER.

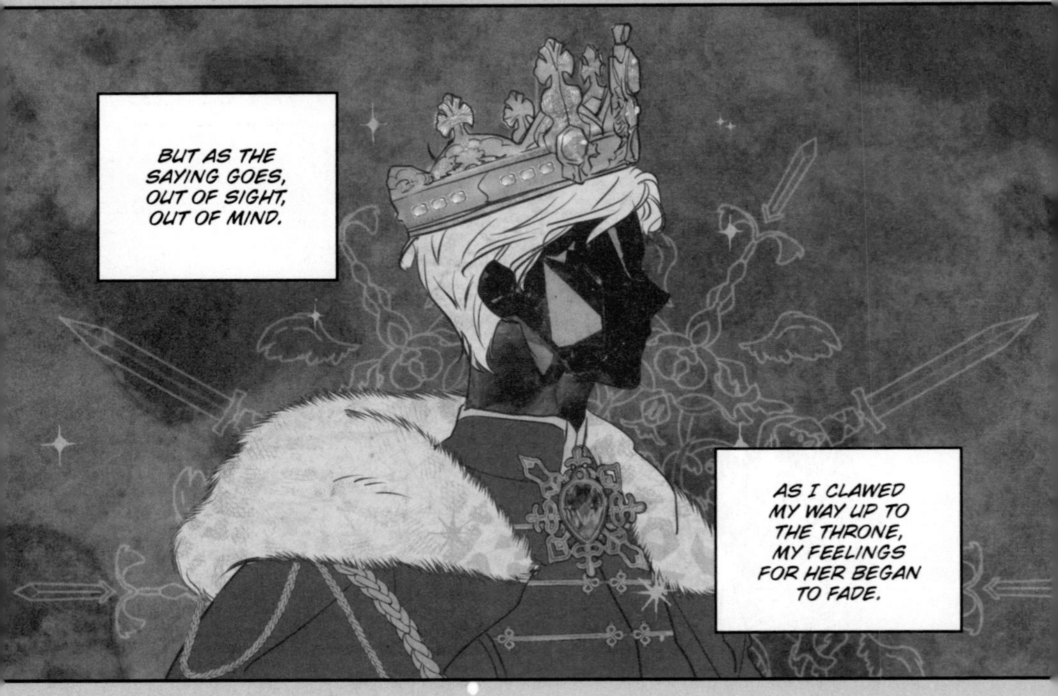
BUT AS THE SAYING GOES, OUT OF SIGHT, OUT OF MIND.
AS I CLAWED MY WAY UP TO THE THRONE, MY FEELINGS FOR HER BEGAN TO FADE.

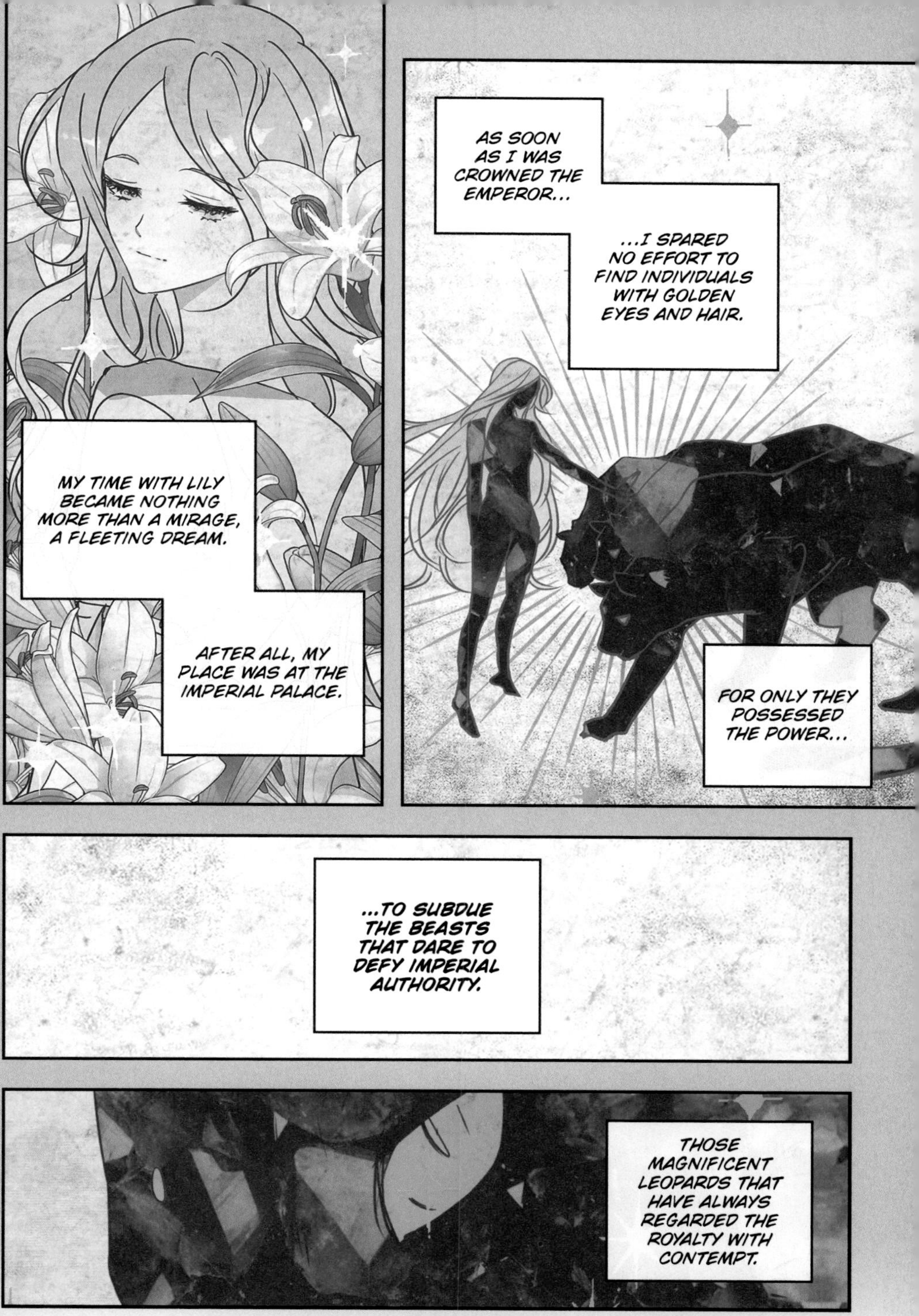
MY TIME WITH LILY BECAME NOTHING MORE THAN A MIRAGE, A FLEETING DREAM.
AFTER ALL, MY PLACE WAS AT THE IMPERIAL PALACE.
AS SOON AS I WAS CROWNED THE EMPEROR...
...I SPARED NO EFFORT TO FIND INDIVIDUALS WITH GOLDEN EYES AND HAIR.
FOR ONLY THEY POSSESSED THE POWER...
...TO SUBDUE THE BEASTS THAT DARE TO DEFY IMPERIAL AUTHORITY.
THOSE MAGNIFICENT LEOPARDS THAT HAVE ALWAYS REGARDED THE ROYALTY WITH CONTEMPT.

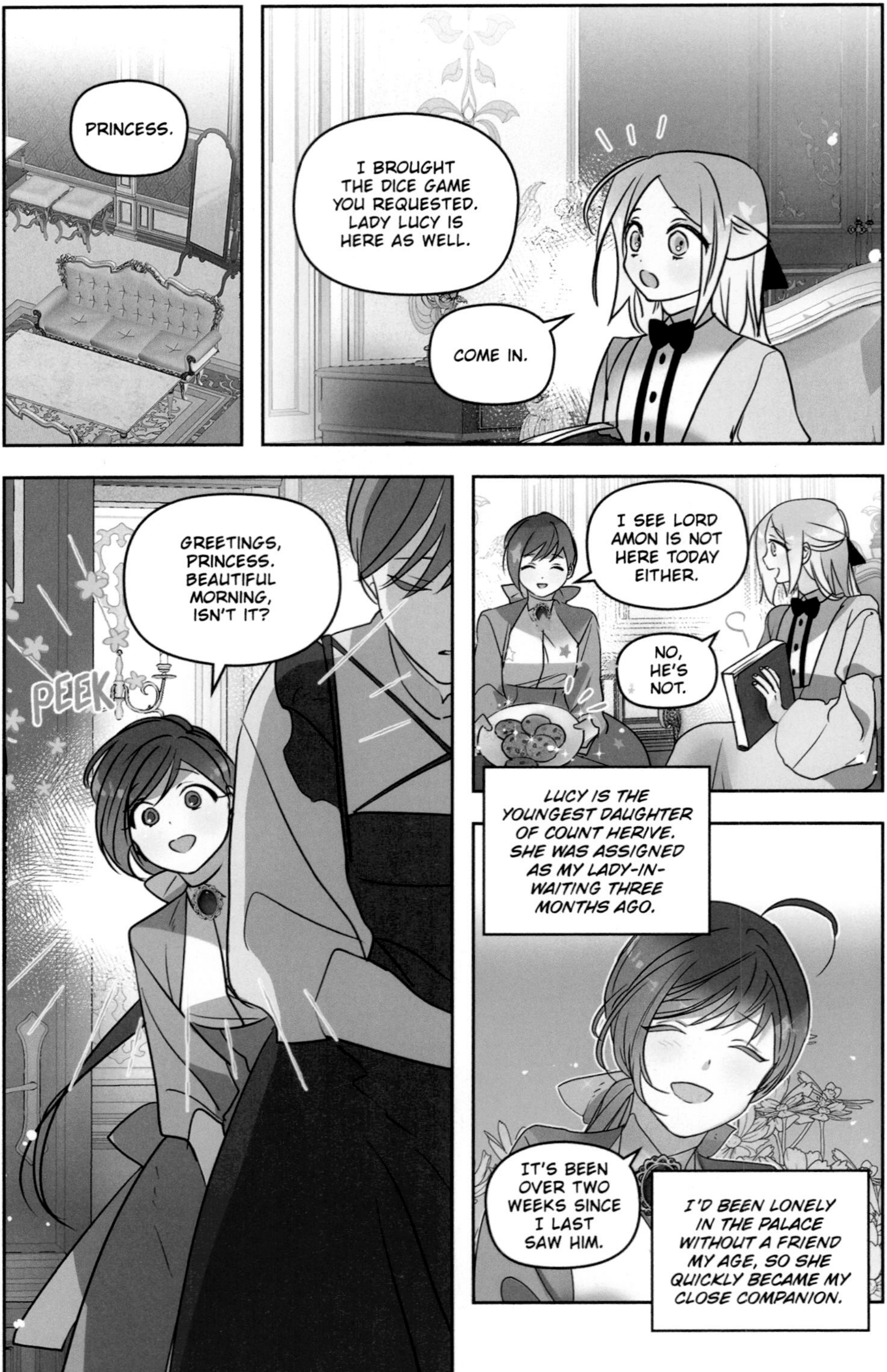
PRINCESS.
I BROUGHT THE DICE GAME YOU REQUESTED. LADY LUCY IS HERE AS WELL.
COME IN.
GREETINGS, PRINCESS. BEAUTIFUL MORNING, ISN'T IT?
PEEK
I SEE LORD AMON IS NOT HERE TODAY EITHER.
NO, HE'S NOT.
LUCY IS THE YOUNGEST DAUGHTER OF COUNT HERIVE. SHE WAS ASSIGNED AS MY LADY-IN-WAITING THREE MONTHS AGO.
IT'S BEEN OVER TWO WEEKS SINCE I LAST SAW HIM.
I'D BEEN LONELY IN THE PALACE WITHOUT A FRIEND MY AGE, SO SHE QUICKLY BECAME MY CLOSE COMPANION.

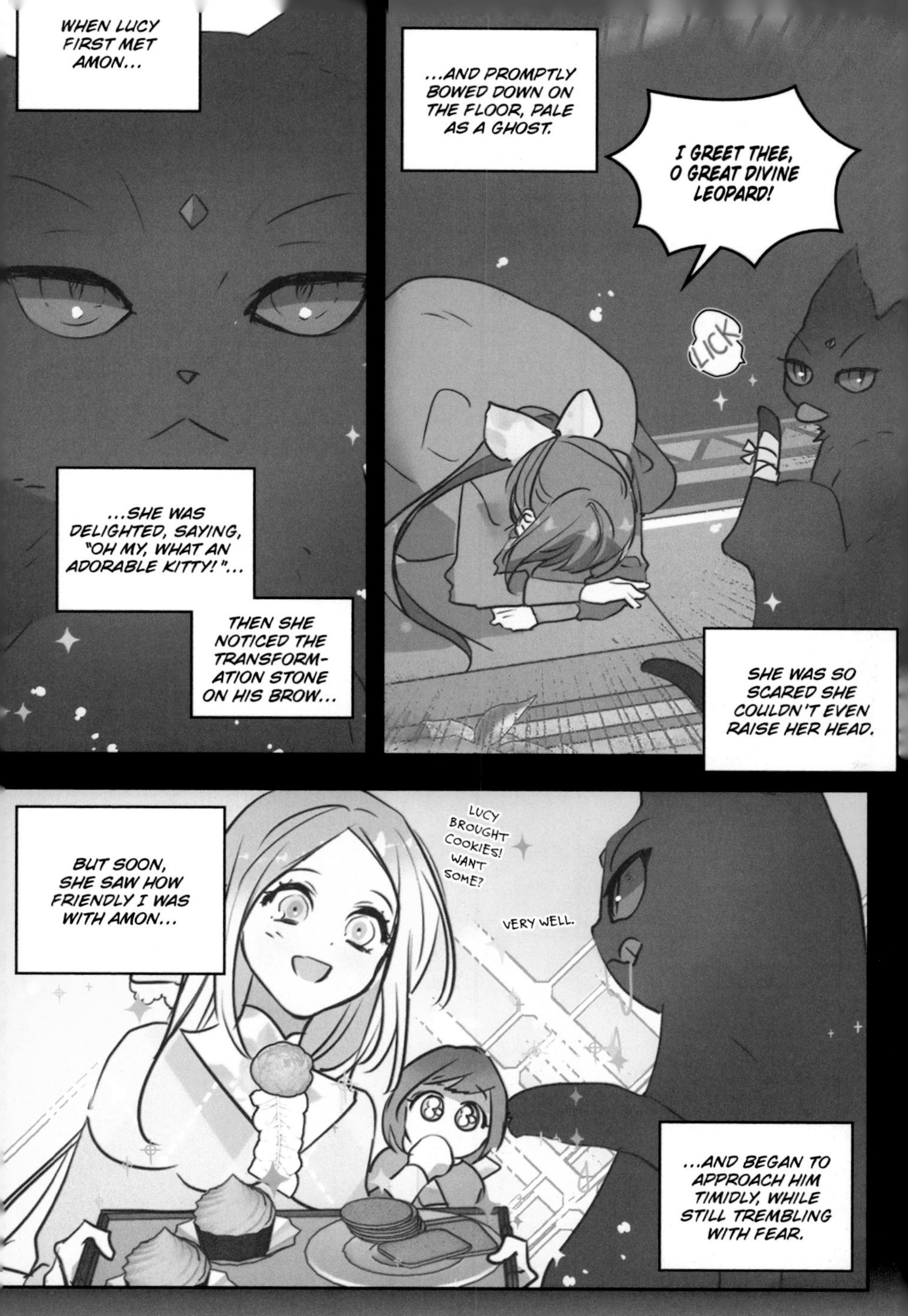
WHEN LUCY FIRST MET AMON...
...SHE WAS DELIGHTED, SAYING, "OH MY, WHAT AN ADORABLE KITTY!"...
THEN SHE NOTICED THE TRANSFORM-ATION STONE ON HIS BROW...
...AND PROMPTLY BOWED DOWN ON THE FLOOR, PALE AS A GHOST.
I GREET THEE, O GREAT DIVINE LEOPARD!
LICK
SHE WAS SO SCARED SHE COULDN'T EVEN RAISE HER HEAD.
BUT SOON, SHE SAW HOW FRIENDLY I WAS WITH AMON...
LUCY BROUGHT COOKIES! WANT SOME?
VERY WELL.
...AND BEGAN TO APPROACH HIM TIMIDLY, WHILE STILL TREMBLING WITH FEAR.

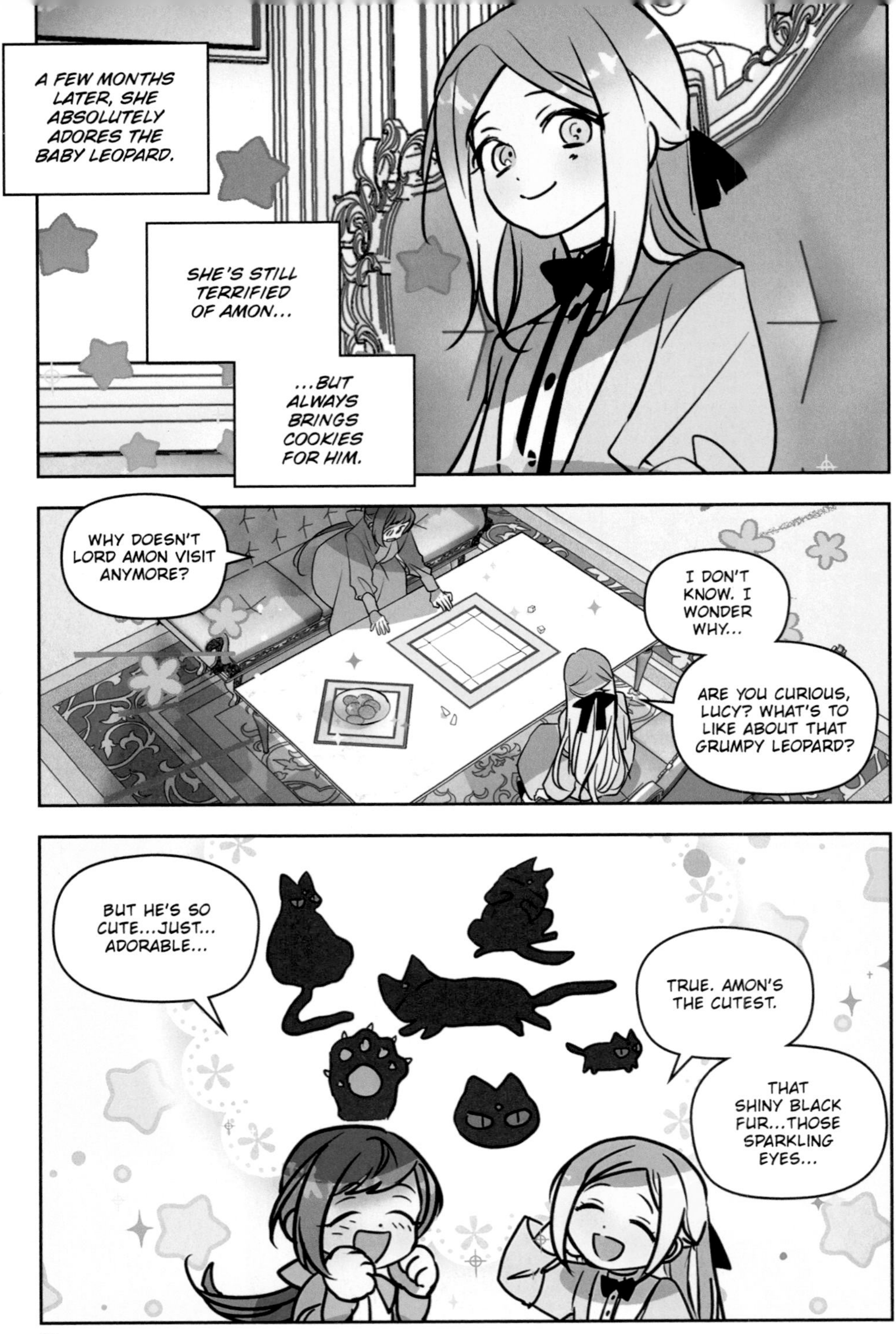
A FEW MONTHS LATER, SHE ABSOLUTELY ADORES THE BABY LEOPARD.
SHE'S STILL TERRIFIED OF AMON...
...BUT ALWAYS BRINGS COOKIES FOR HIM.
WHY DOESN'T LORD AMON VISIT ANYMORE?
I DON'T KNOW. I WONDER WHY...
ARE YOU CURIOUS, LUCY? WHAT'S TO LIKE ABOUT THAT GRUMPY LEOPARD?
BUT HE'S SO CUTE...JUST... ADORABLE...
TRUE. AMON'S THE CUTEST.
THAT SHINY BLACK FUR...THOSE SPARKLING EYES...

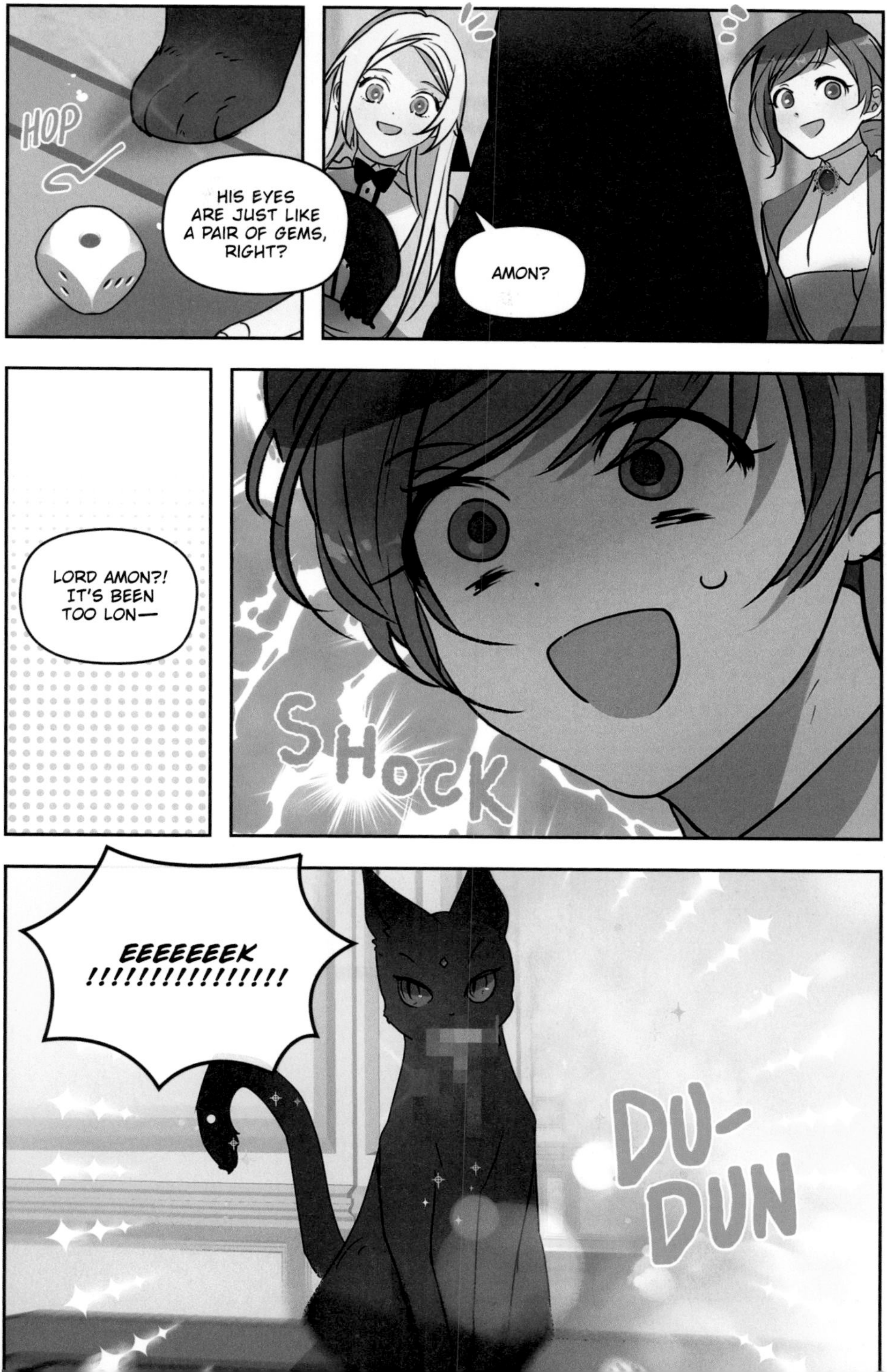
HOP
HIS EYES ARE JUST LIKE A PAIR OF GEMS, RIGHT?
AMON?
LORD AMON?! IT'S BEEN TOO LON—
SHOCK
EEEEEEEK !!!!!!!!!!!!!!!!!
DU-DUN

My Gently Raised Beast

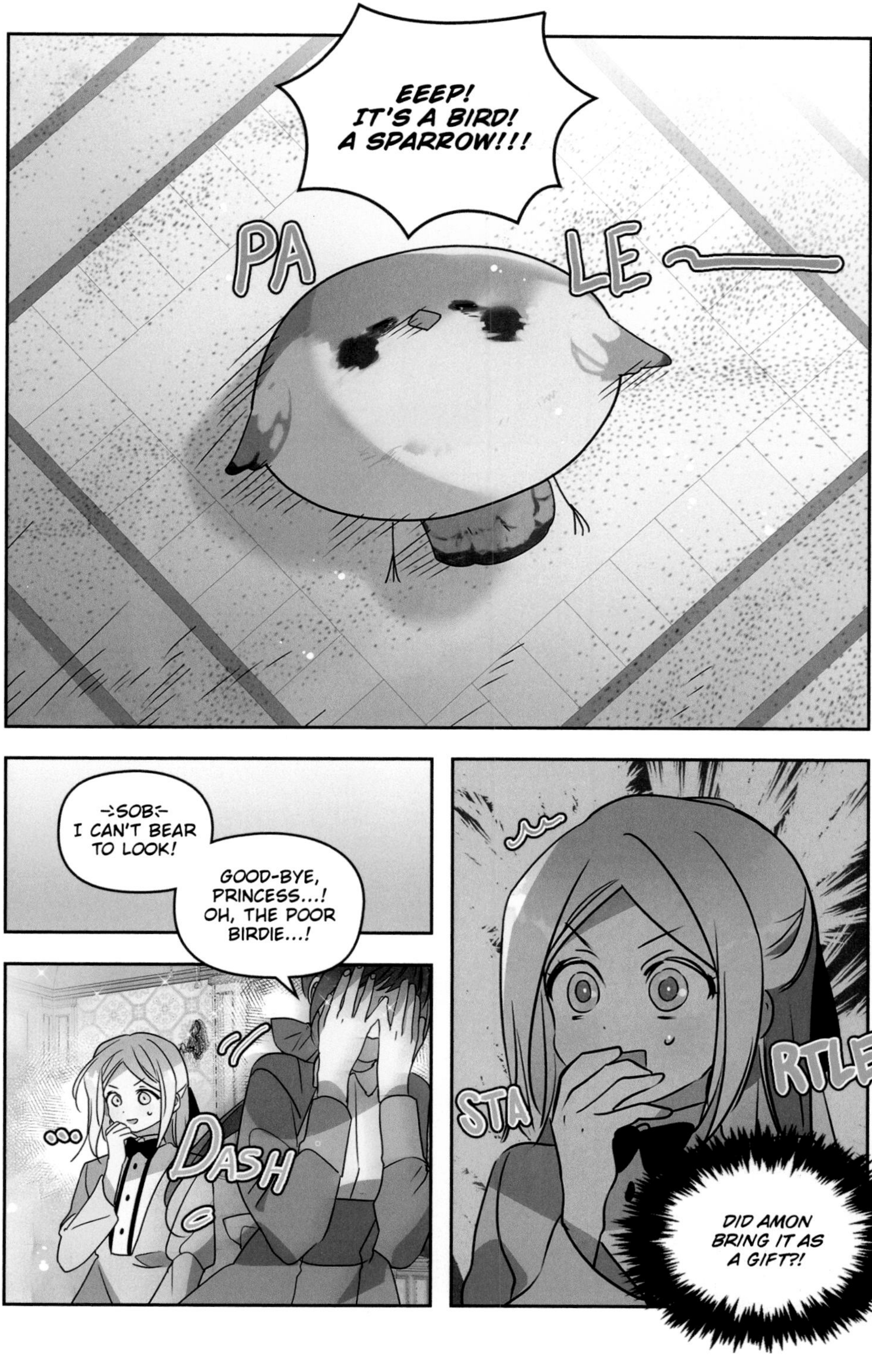
EEEP! IT'S A BIRD! A SPARROW!!!
PALE~
SOB
I CAN'T BEAR TO LOOK!
GOOD-BYE, PRINCESS...! OH, THE POOR BIRDIE...!
DASH
...
STARTLE
DID AMON BRING IT AS A GIFT?!

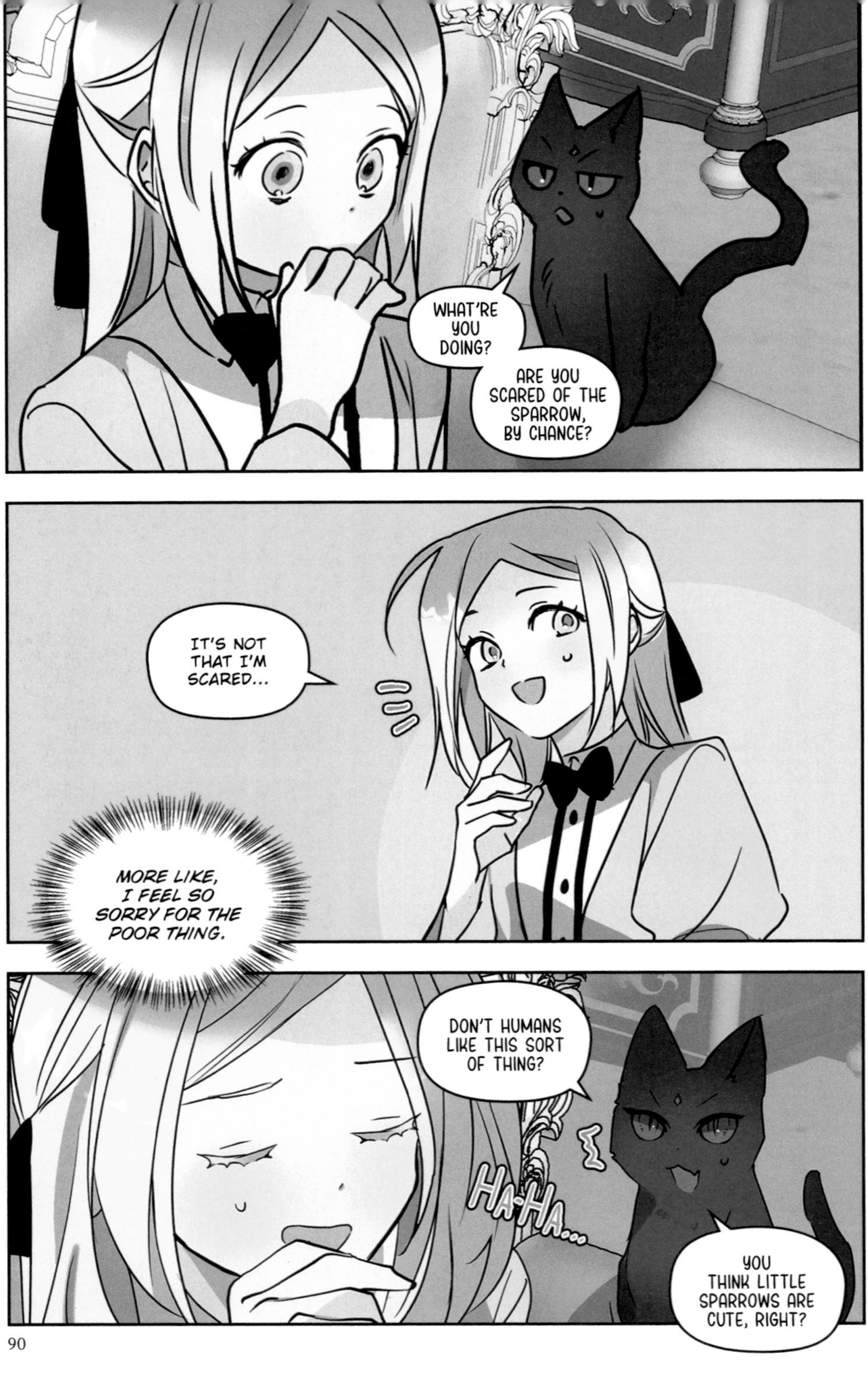
WHAT'RE YOU DOING?
ARE YOU SCARED OF THE SPARROW, BY CHANCE?
IT'S NOT THAT I'M SCARED...
MORE LIKE, I FEEL SO SORRY FOR THE POOR THING.
DON'T HUMANS LIKE THIS SORT OF THING?
HA-HA...
YOU THINK LITTLE SPARROWS ARE CUTE, RIGHT?

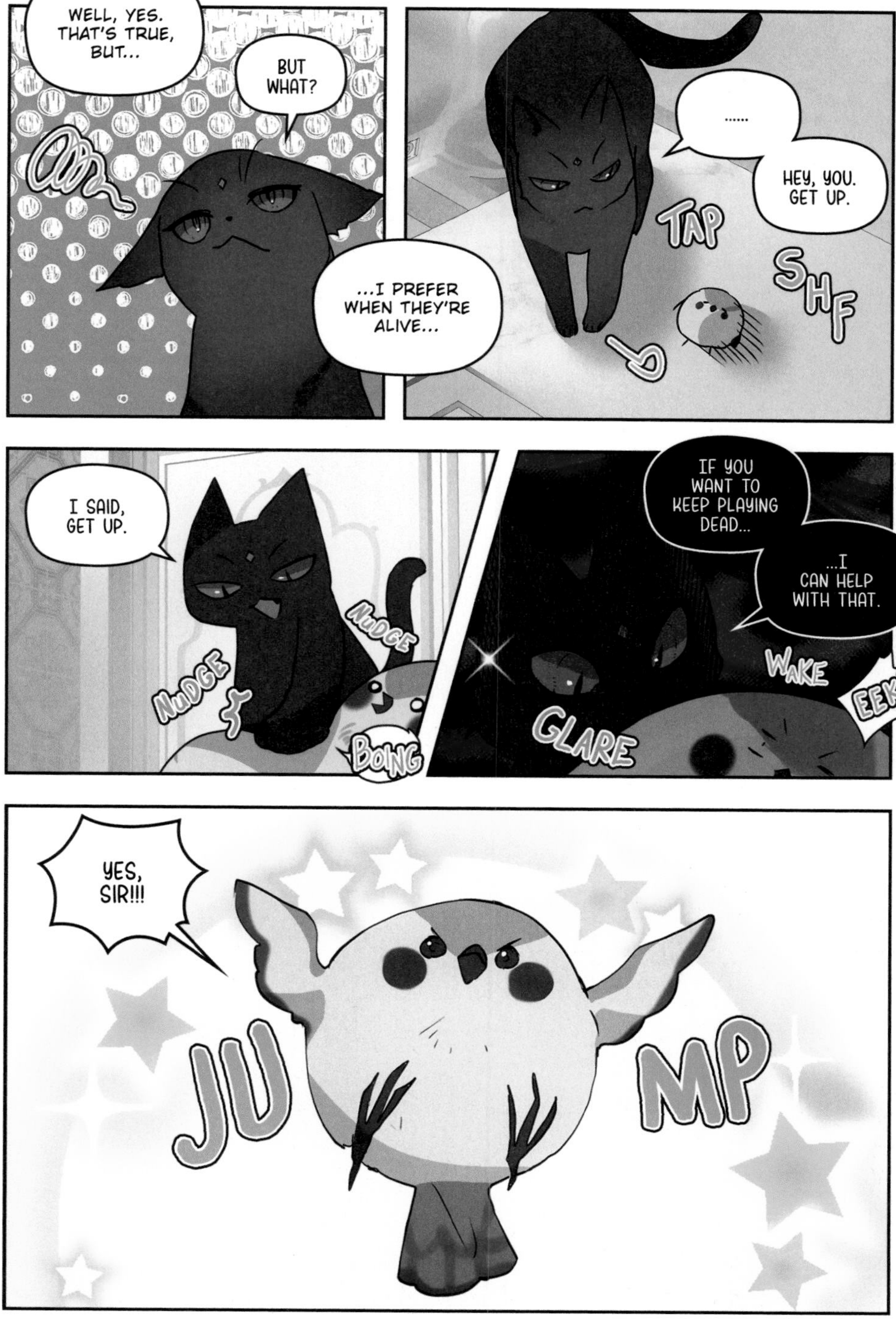
WELL, YES. THAT'S TRUE, BUT...
BUT WHAT?
...I PREFER WHEN THEY'RE ALIVE...
......
HEY, YOU. GET UP.
TAP
SHF
I SAID, GET UP.
NUDGE
NUDGE
BOING
IF YOU WANT TO KEEP PLAYING DEAD...
...I CAN HELP WITH THAT.
WAKE
EEK!
GLARE
YES, SIR!!!
JU
MP

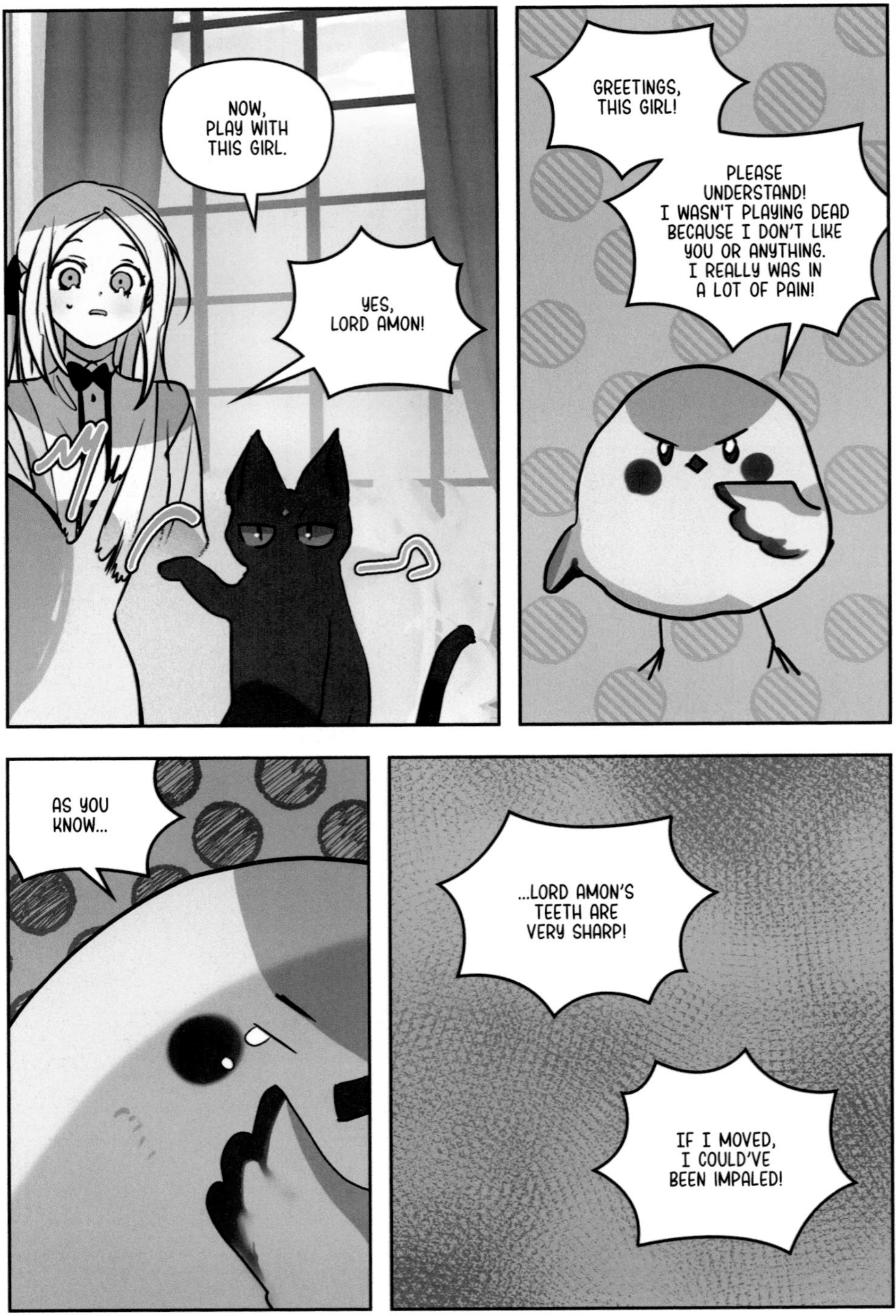
NOW, PLAY WITH THIS GIRL.
YES, LORD AMON!
GREETINGS, THIS GIRL!
PLEASE UNDERSTAND! I WASN'T PLAYING DEAD BECAUSE I DON'T LIKE YOU OR ANYTHING. I REALLY WAS IN A LOT OF PAIN!
AS YOU KNOW...
...LORD AMON'S TEETH ARE VERY SHARP!
IF I MOVED, I COULD'VE BEEN IMPALED!

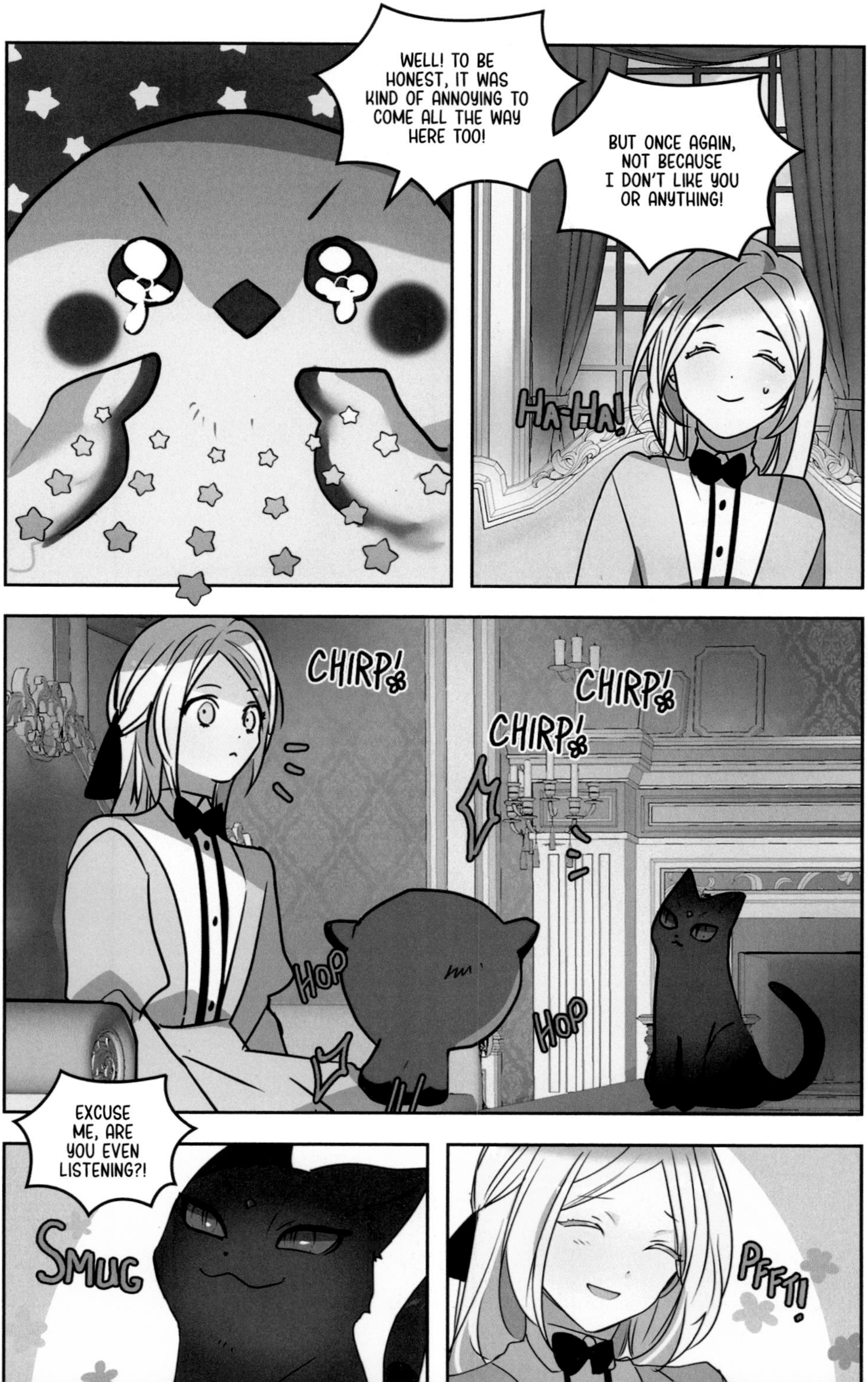
WELL! TO BE HONEST, IT WAS KIND OF ANNOYING TO COME ALL THE WAY HERE TOO!
BUT ONCE AGAIN, NOT BECAUSE I DON'T LIKE YOU OR ANYTHING!
HA-HA!
CHIRP!
CHIRP!
CHIRP!
HOP
HOP
EXCUSE ME, ARE YOU EVEN LISTENING?!
SMUG
PFFT!

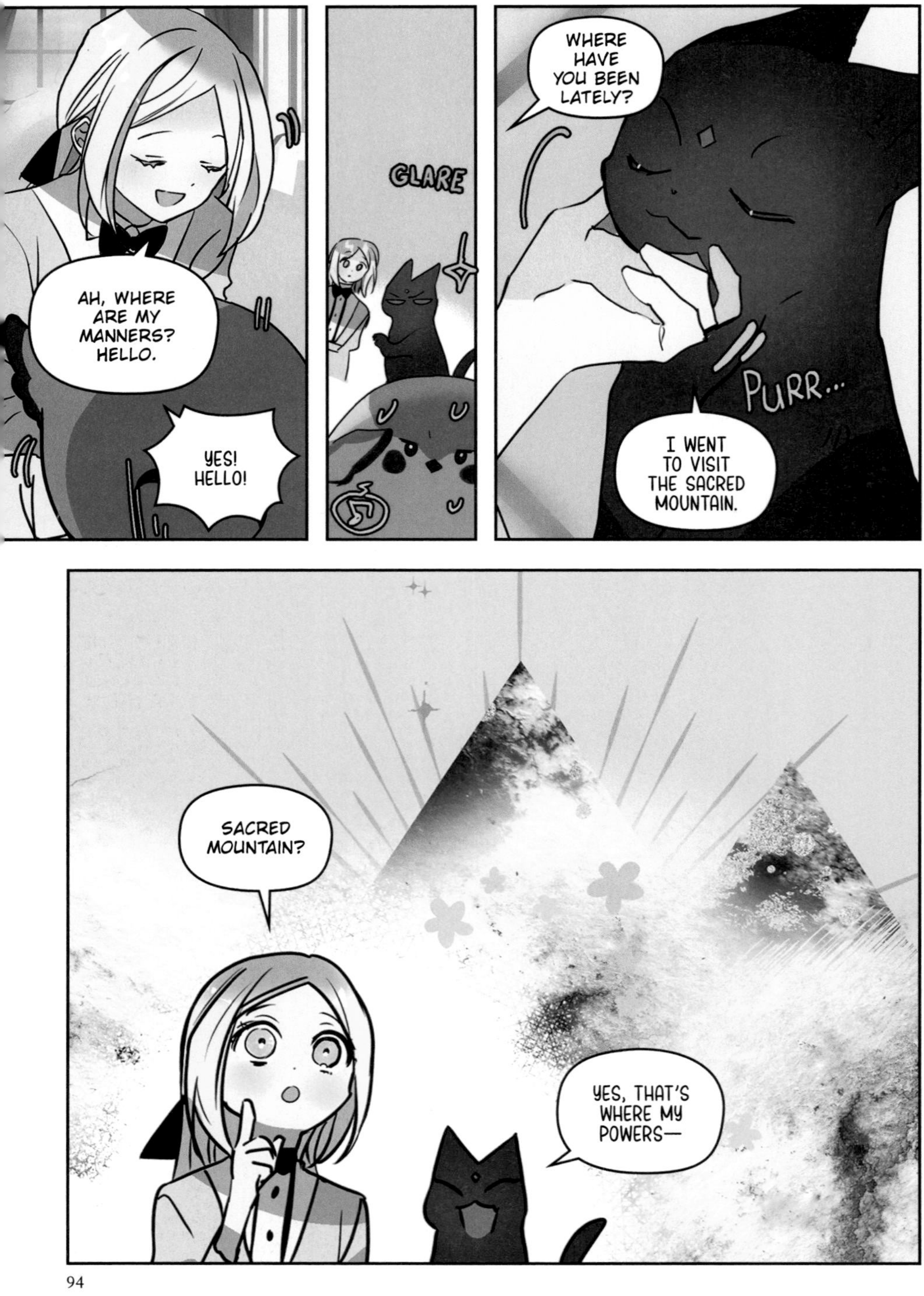
AH, WHERE ARE MY MANNERS? HELLO.
YES! HELLO!
GLARE
WHERE HAVE YOU BEEN LATELY?
PURR...
I WENT TO VISIT THE SACRED MOUNTAIN.
SACRED MOUNTAIN?
YES, THAT'S WHERE MY POWERS—

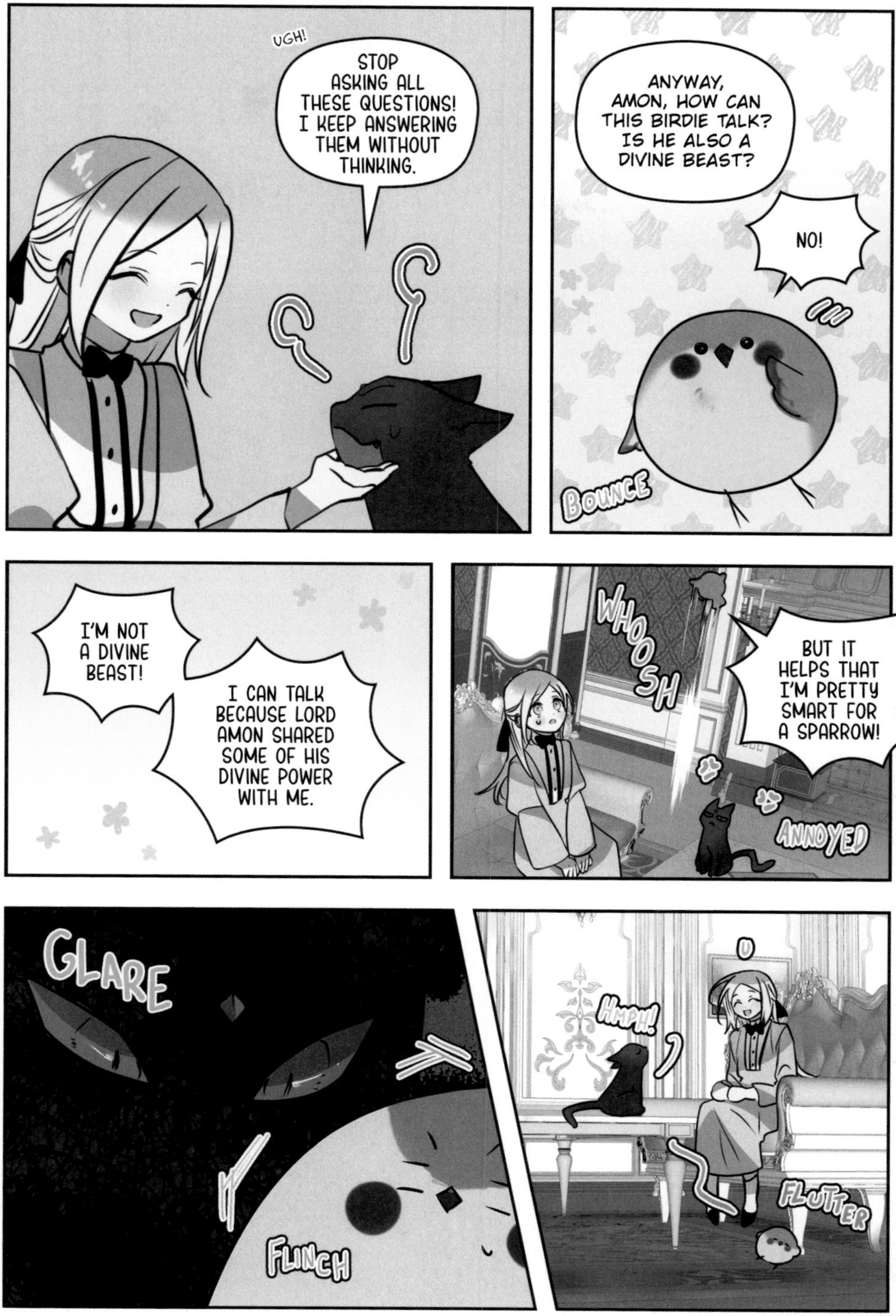
UGH!
STOP ASKING ALL THESE QUESTIONS! I KEEP ANSWERING THEM WITHOUT THINKING.
ANYWAY, AMON, HOW CAN THIS BIRDIE TALK? IS HE ALSO A DIVINE BEAST?
NO!
BOUNCE
I'M NOT A DIVINE BEAST!
I CAN TALK BECAUSE LORD AMON SHARED SOME OF HIS DIVINE POWER WITH ME.
WHOOSH
BUT IT HELPS THAT I'M PRETTY SMART FOR A SPARROW!
ANNOYED
GLARE
FLINCH
HMPH!
FLUTTER

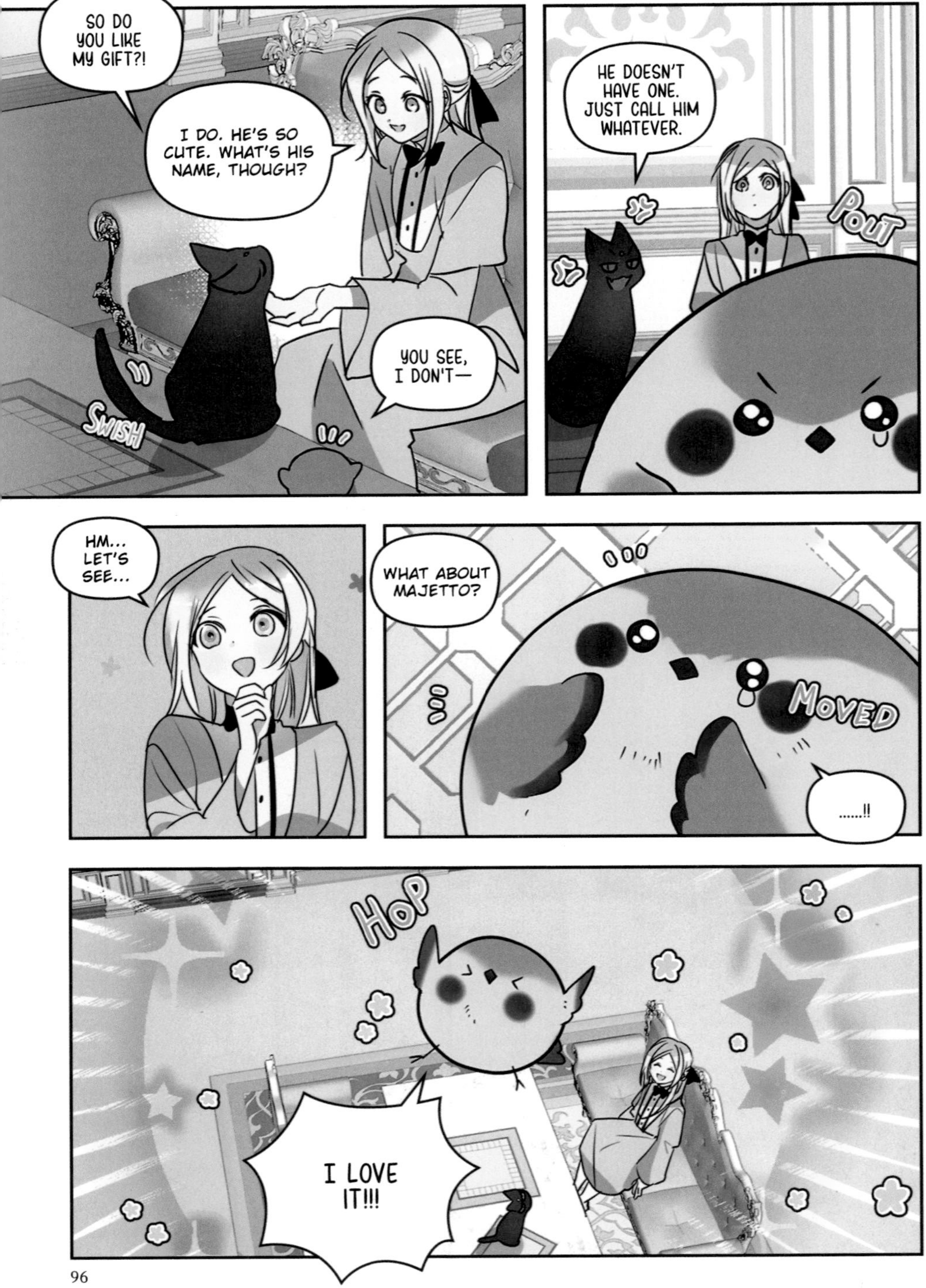
SO DO YOU LIKE MY GIFT?!
I DO. HE'S SO CUTE. WHAT'S HIS NAME, THOUGH?
SWISH
YOU SEE, I DON'T—
HE DOESN'T HAVE ONE. JUST CALL HIM WHATEVER.
POUT
HM... LET'S SEE...
WHAT ABOUT MAJETTO?
MOVED
......!!
HOP
I LOVE IT!!!

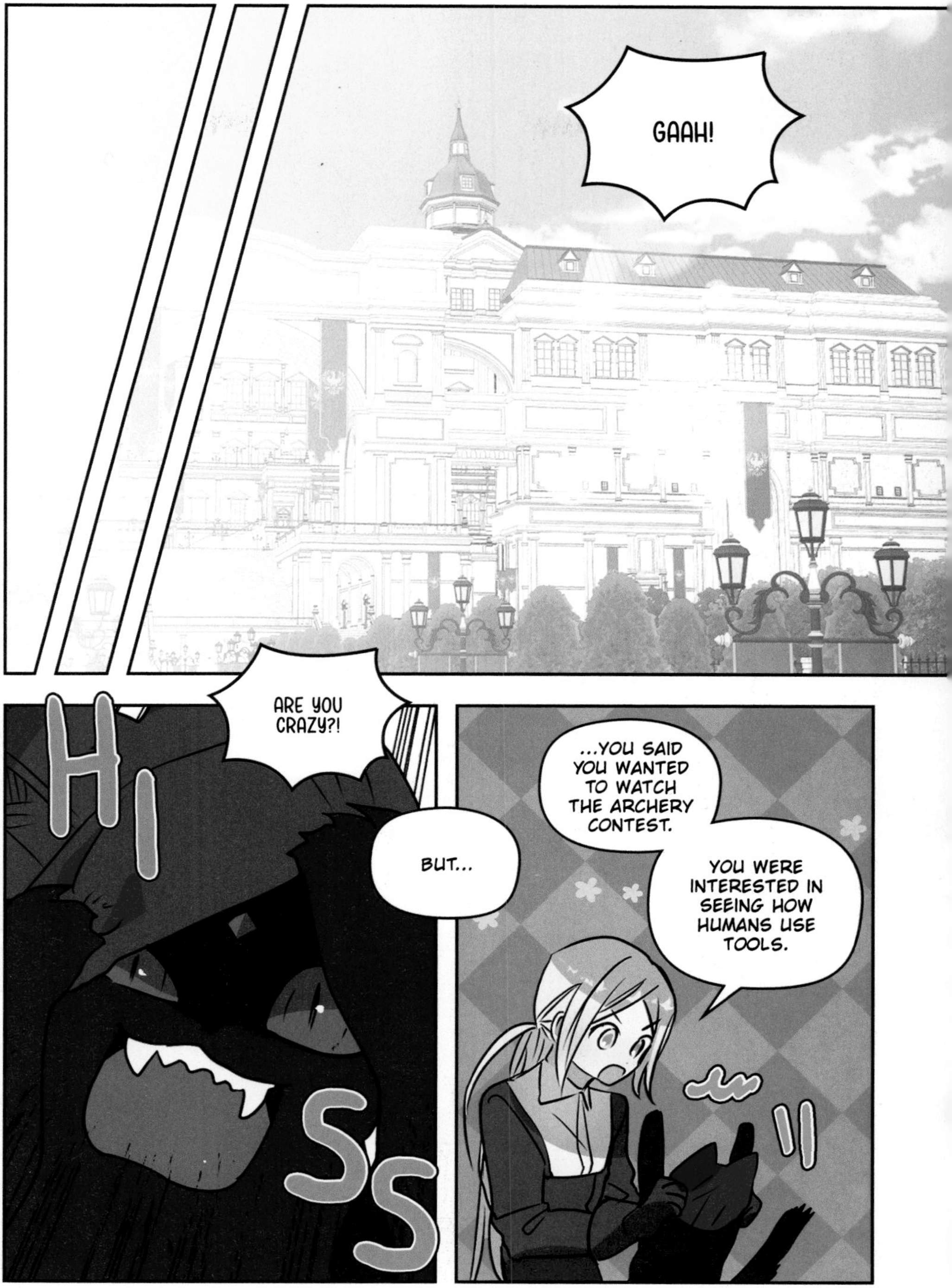
GAAH!
ARE YOU CRAZY?!
HISS
BUT...
...YOU SAID YOU WANTED TO WATCH THE ARCHERY CONTEST.
YOU WERE INTERESTED IN SEEING HOW HUMANS USE TOOLS.

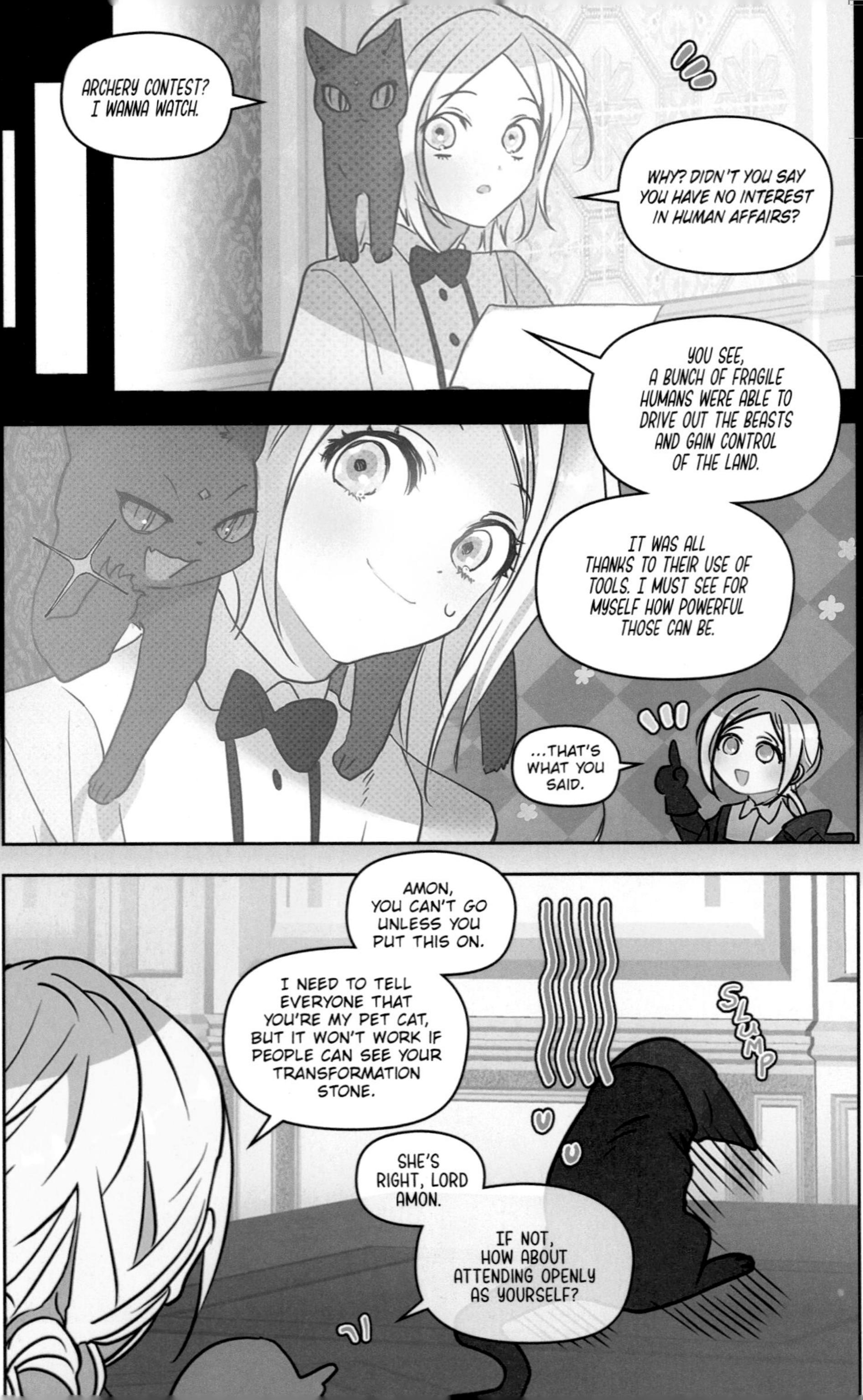
ARCHERY CONTEST? I WANNA WATCH.
WHY? DIDN'T YOU SAY YOU HAVE NO INTEREST IN HUMAN AFFAIRS?
YOU SEE, A BUNCH OF FRAGILE HUMANS WERE ABLE TO DRIVE OUT THE BEASTS AND GAIN CONTROL OF THE LAND.
IT WAS ALL THANKS TO THEIR USE OF TOOLS. I MUST SEE FOR MYSELF HOW POWERFUL THOSE CAN BE.
...THAT'S WHAT YOU SAID.
AMON, YOU CAN'T GO UNLESS YOU PUT THIS ON.
I NEED TO TELL EVERYONE THAT YOU'RE MY PET CAT, BUT IT WON'T WORK IF PEOPLE CAN SEE YOUR TRANSFORMATION STONE.
SLUMP
SHE'S RIGHT, LORD AMON.
IF NOT, HOW ABOUT ATTENDING OPENLY AS YOURSELF?

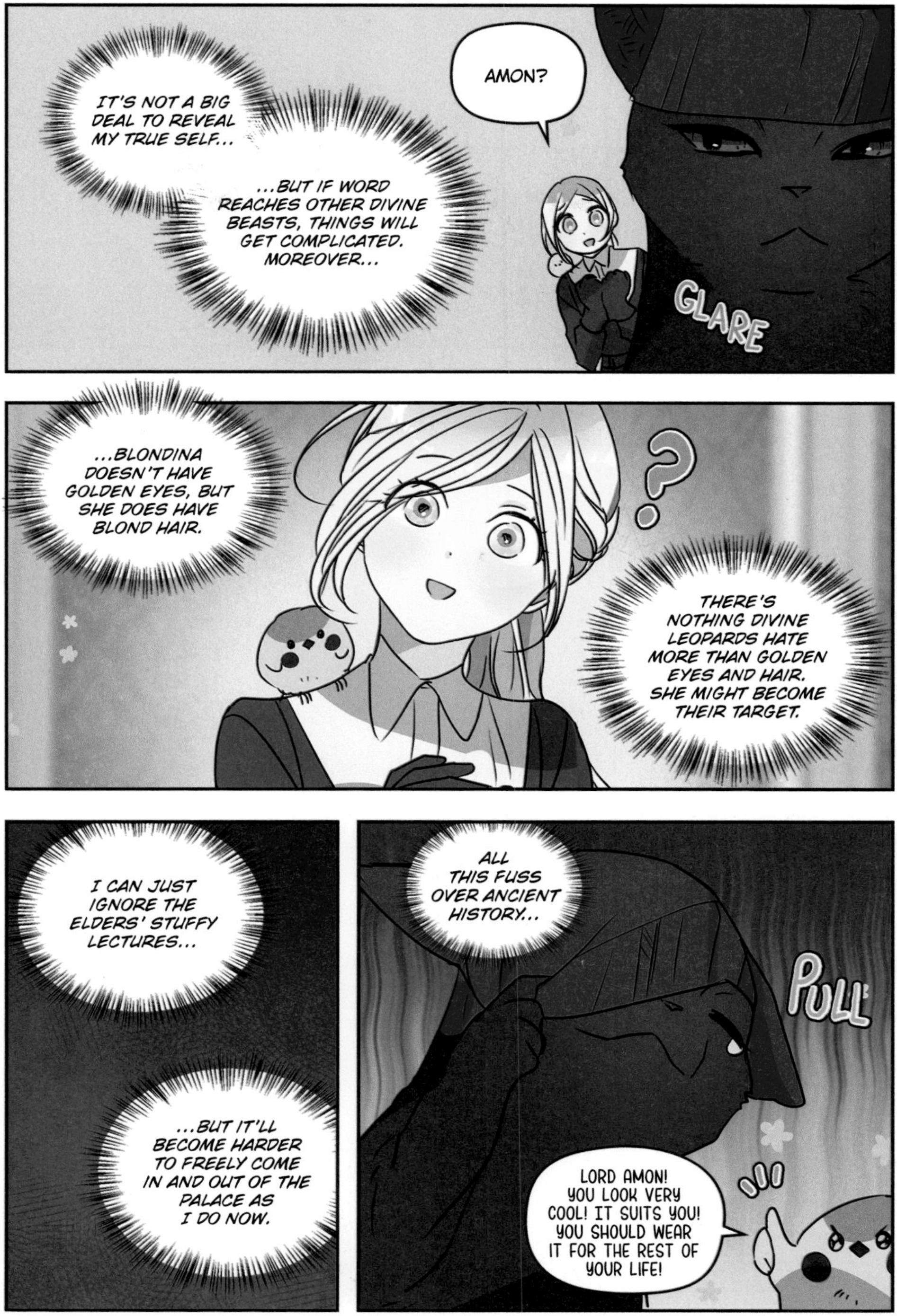
IT'S NOT A BIG DEAL TO REVEAL MY TRUE SELF...
...BUT IF WORD REACHES OTHER DIVINE BEASTS, THINGS WILL GET COMPLICATED. MOREOVER...
AMON?
GLARE
...BLONDINA DOESN'T HAVE GOLDEN EYES, BUT SHE DOES HAVE BLOND HAIR.
?
THERE'S NOTHING DIVINE LEOPARDS HATE MORE THAN GOLDEN EYES AND HAIR. SHE MIGHT BECOME THEIR TARGET.
I CAN JUST IGNORE THE ELDERS' STUFFY LECTURES...
...BUT IT'LL BECOME HARDER TO FREELY COME IN AND OUT OF THE PALACE AS I DO NOW.
ALL THIS FUSS OVER ANCIENT HISTORY...
PULL
LORD AMON! YOU LOOK VERY COOL! IT SUITS YOU! YOU SHOULD WEAR IT FOR THE REST OF YOUR LIFE!

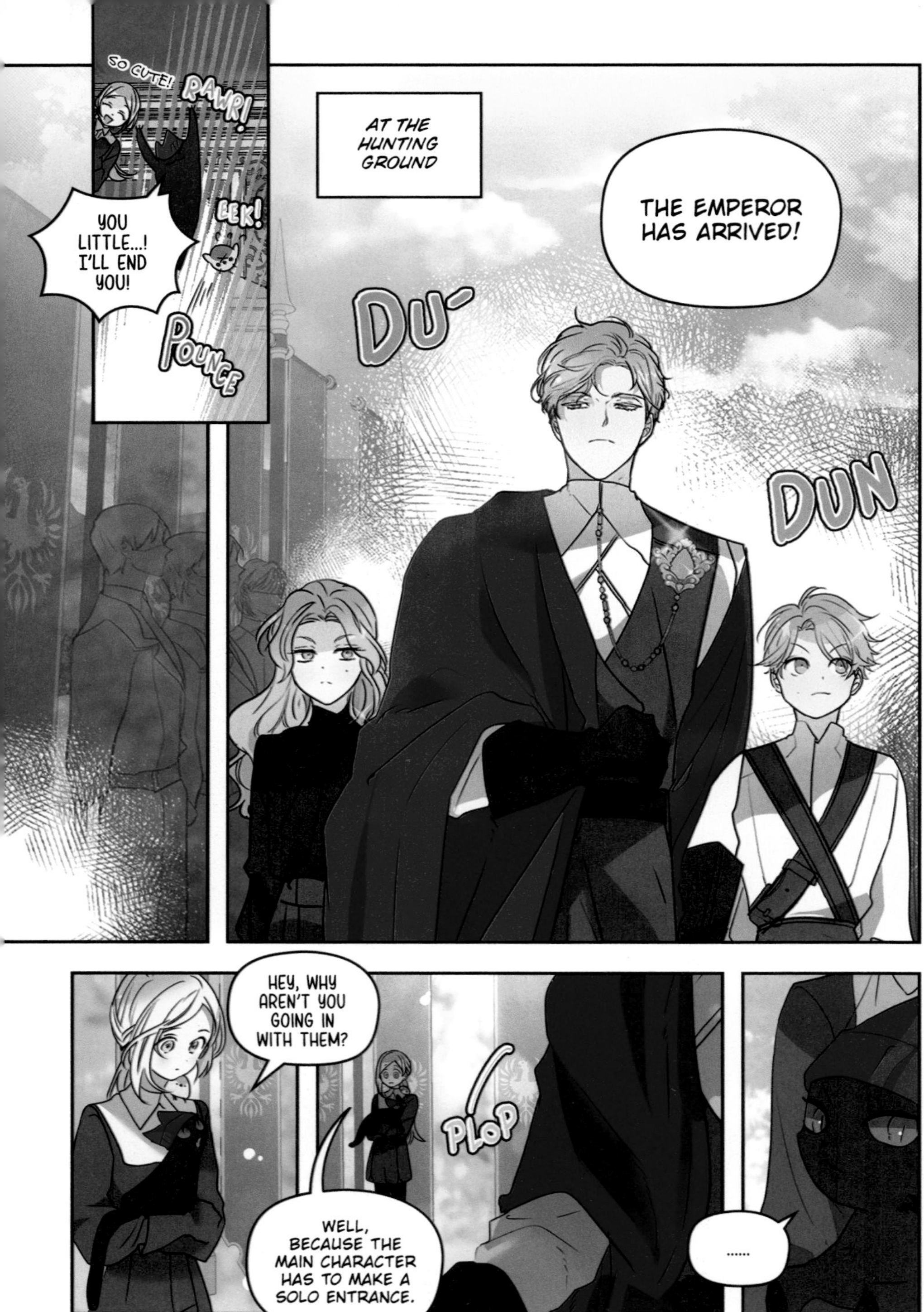
SO CUTE!
RAWR!
EEK!
YOU LITTLE...! I'LL END YOU!
POUNCE
AT THE HUNTING GROUND
THE EMPEROR HAS ARRIVED!
DU-
DUN
HEY, WHY AREN'T YOU GOING IN WITH THEM?
PLOP
WELL, BECAUSE THE MAIN CHARACTER HAS TO MAKE A SOLO ENTRANCE.
......

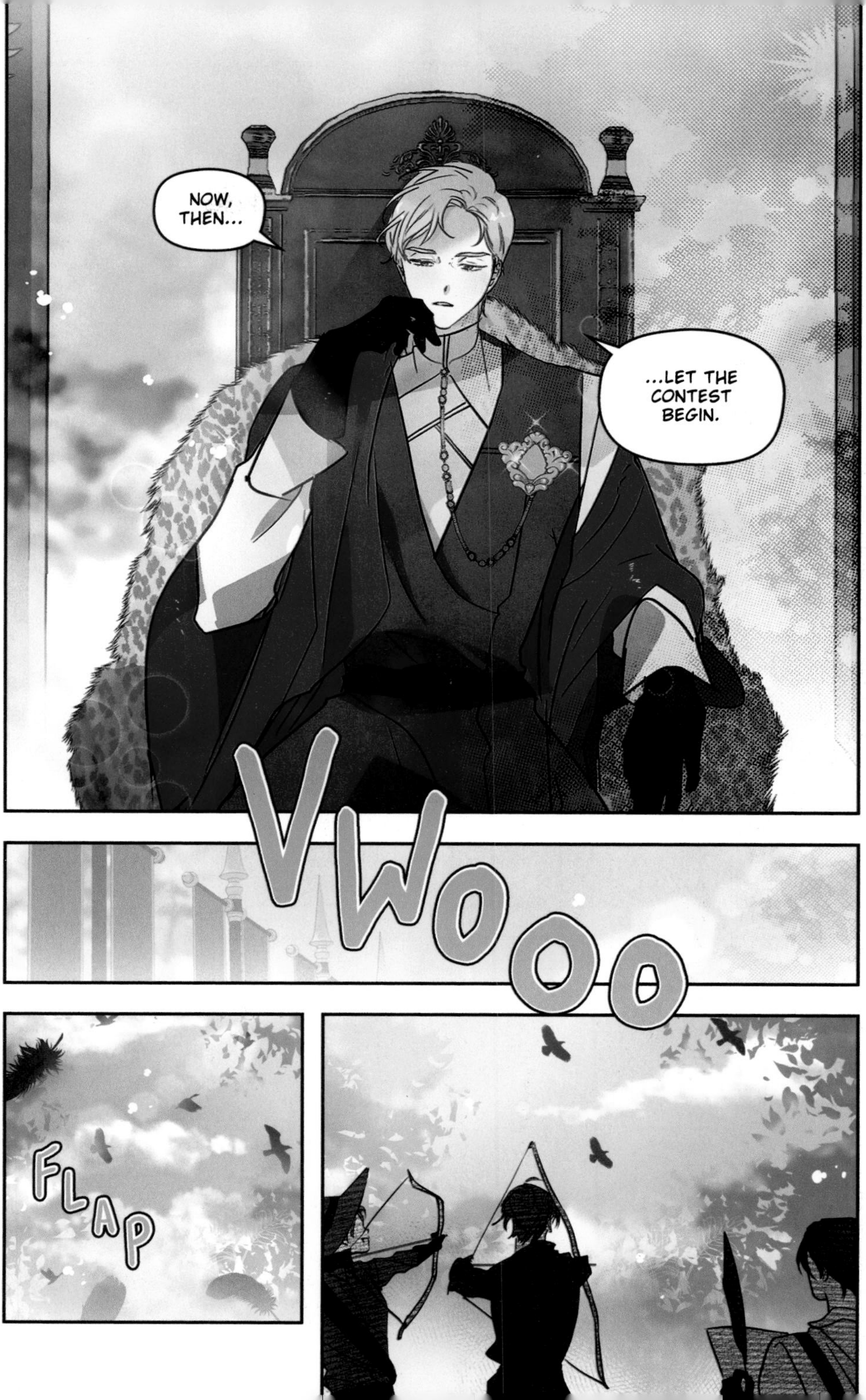
NOW, THEN...
...LET THE CONTEST BEGIN.
VWOOO
FLAP

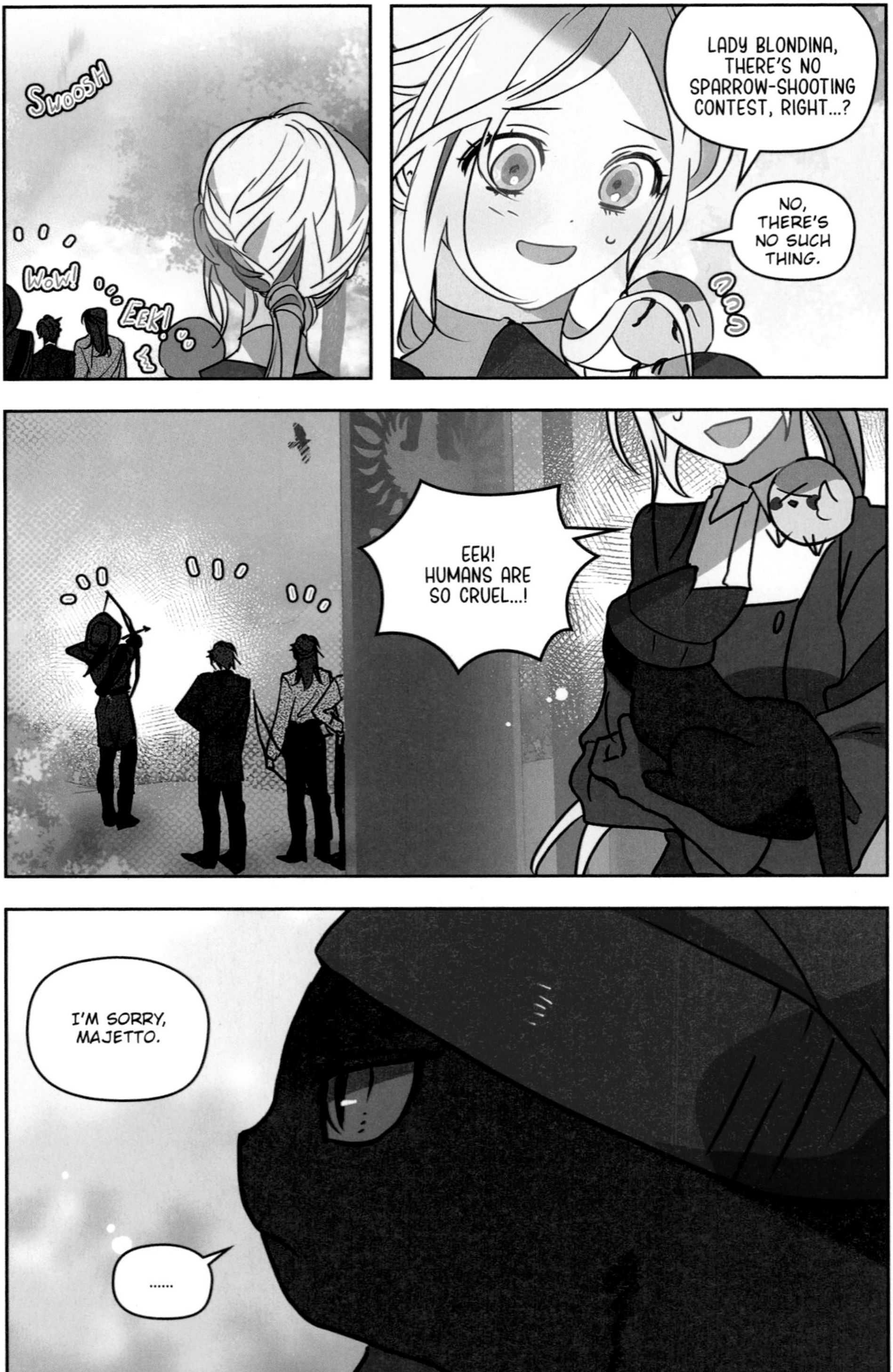
SWOOSH
WOW!
EEK!
LADY BLONDINA, THERE'S NO SPARROW-SHOOTING CONTEST, RIGHT...?
NO, THERE'S NO SUCH THING.
EEK! HUMANS ARE SO CRUEL...!
I'M SORRY, MAJETTO.
......

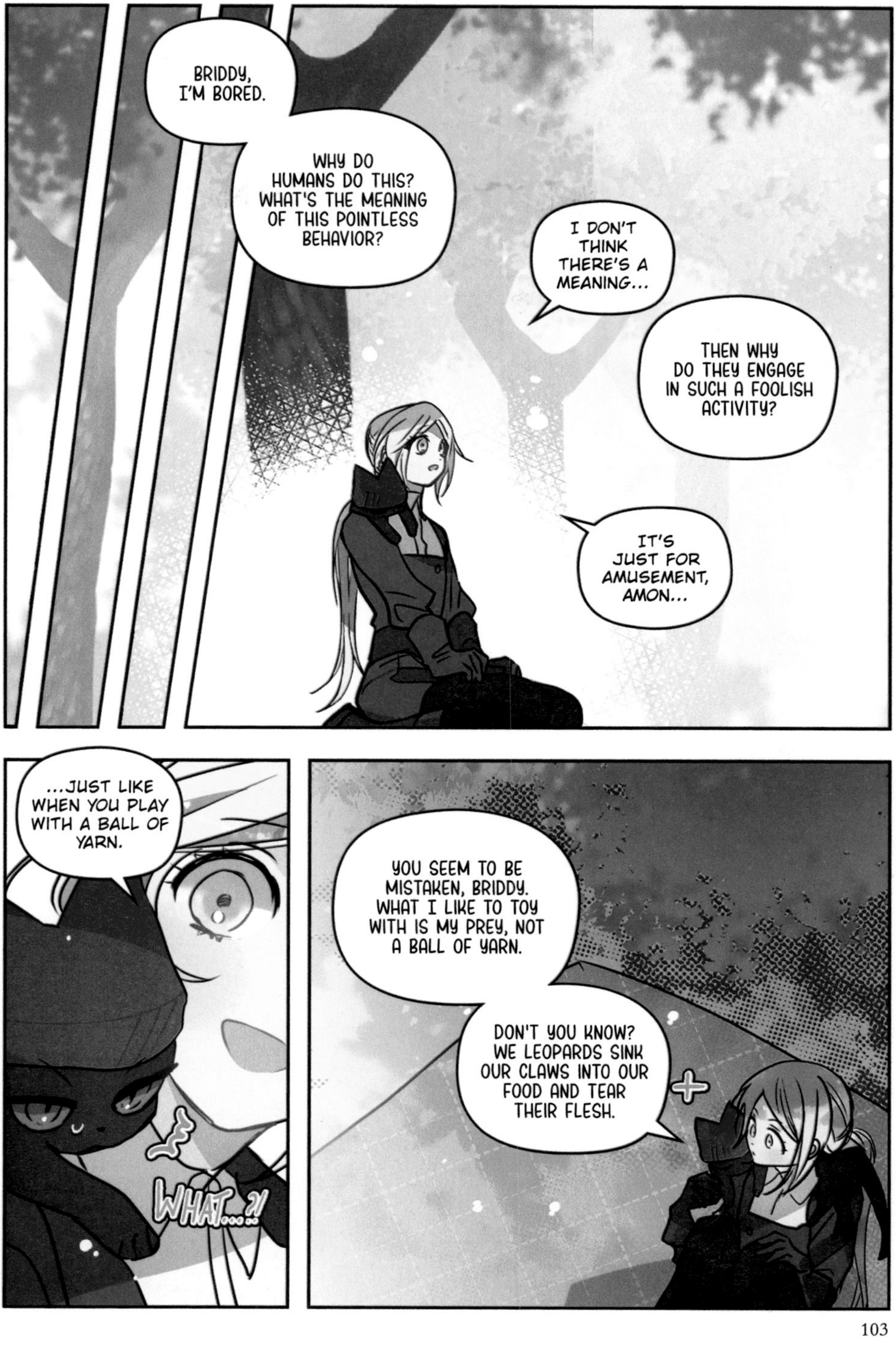
BRIDDY, I'M BORED.
WHY DO HUMANS DO THIS? WHAT'S THE MEANING OF THIS POINTLESS BEHAVIOR?
I DON'T THINK THERE'S A MEANING...
THEN WHY DO THEY ENGAGE IN SUCH A FOOLISH ACTIVITY?
IT'S JUST FOR AMUSEMENT, AMON...
...JUST LIKE WHEN YOU PLAY WITH A BALL OF YARN.
WHAT...?!
YOU SEEM TO BE MISTAKEN, BRIDDY. WHAT I LIKE TO TOY WITH IS MY PREY, NOT A BALL OF YARN.
DON'T YOU KNOW? WE LEOPARDS SINK OUR CLAWS INTO OUR FOOD AND TEAR THEIR FLESH.

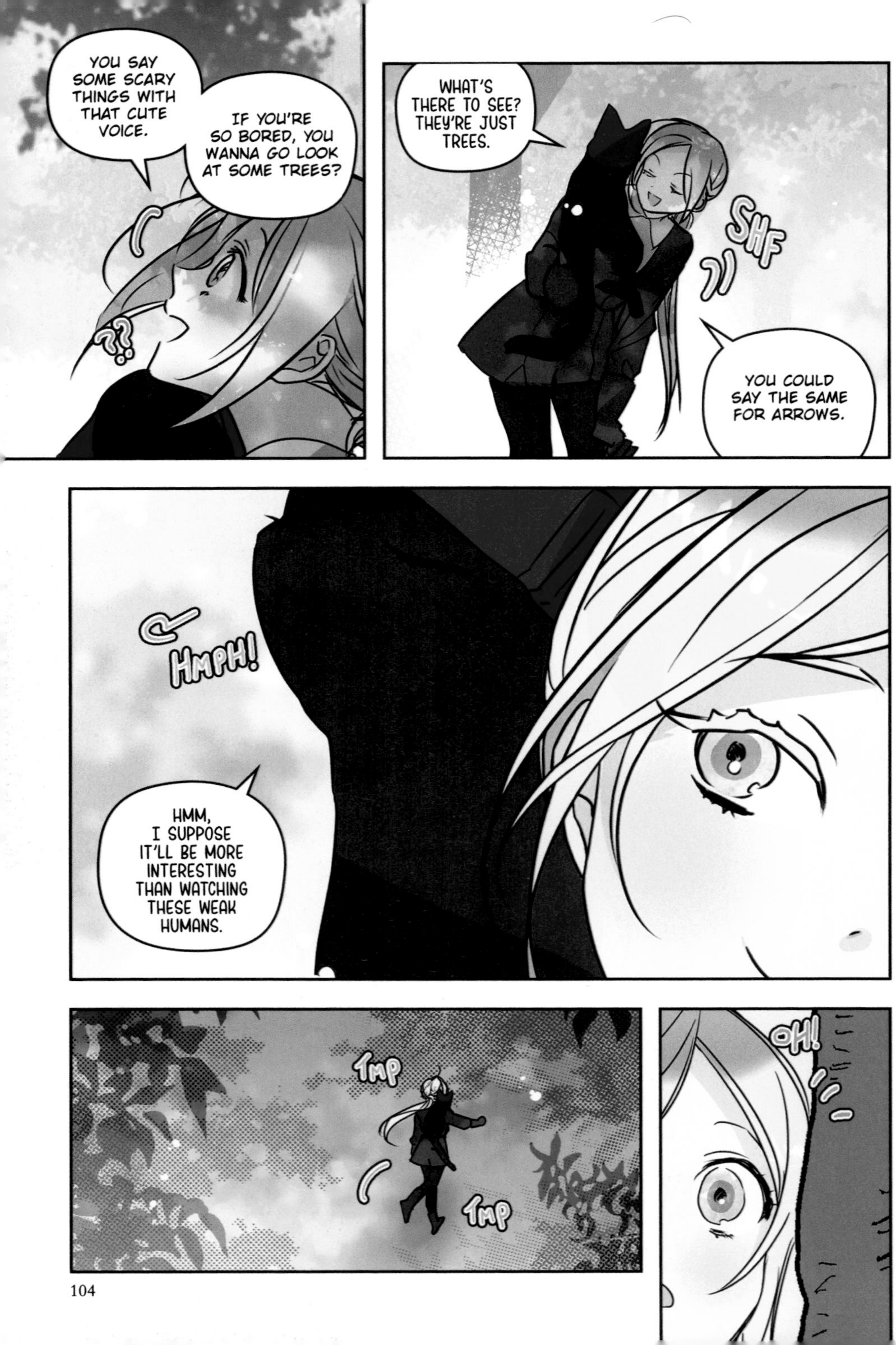
YOU SAY SOME SCARY THINGS WITH THAT CUTE VOICE.
IF YOU'RE SO BORED, YOU WANNA GO LOOK AT SOME TREES?
??
WHAT'S THERE TO SEE? THEY'RE JUST TREES.
SHF
YOU COULD SAY THE SAME FOR ARROWS.
HMPH!
HMM, I SUPPOSE IT'LL BE MORE INTERESTING THAN WATCHING THESE WEAK HUMANS.
TMP
TMP
OH!

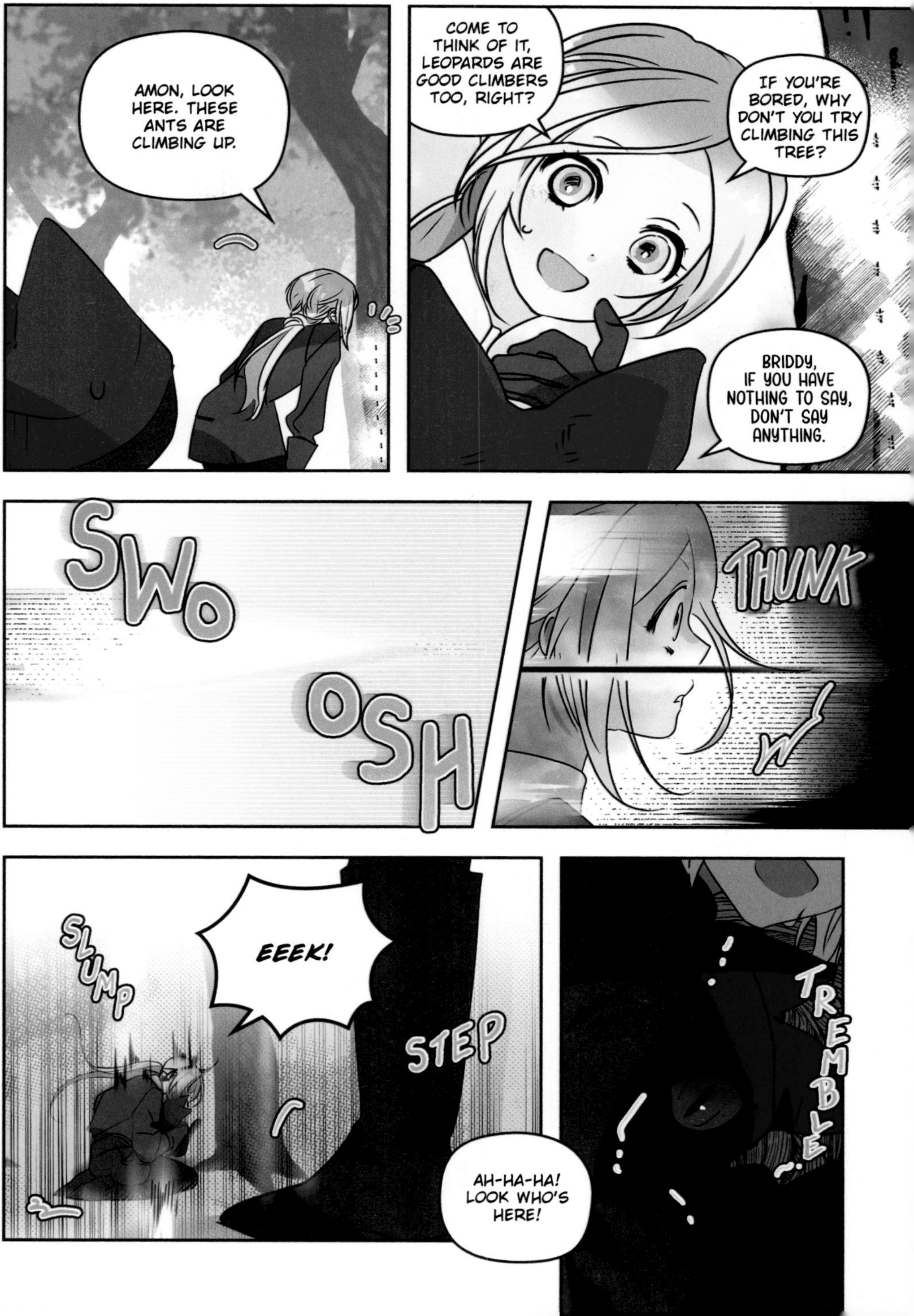
AMON, LOOK HERE. THESE ANTS ARE CLIMBING UP.
COME TO THINK OF IT, LEOPARDS ARE GOOD CLIMBERS TOO, RIGHT?
IF YOU'RE BORED, WHY DON'T YOU TRY CLIMBING THIS TREE?
BRIDDY, IF YOU HAVE NOTHING TO SAY, DON'T SAY ANYTHING.
SWOOSH
THUNK
EEEK!
SLUMP
STEP
TREMBLE
AH-HA-HA! LOOK WHO'S HERE!

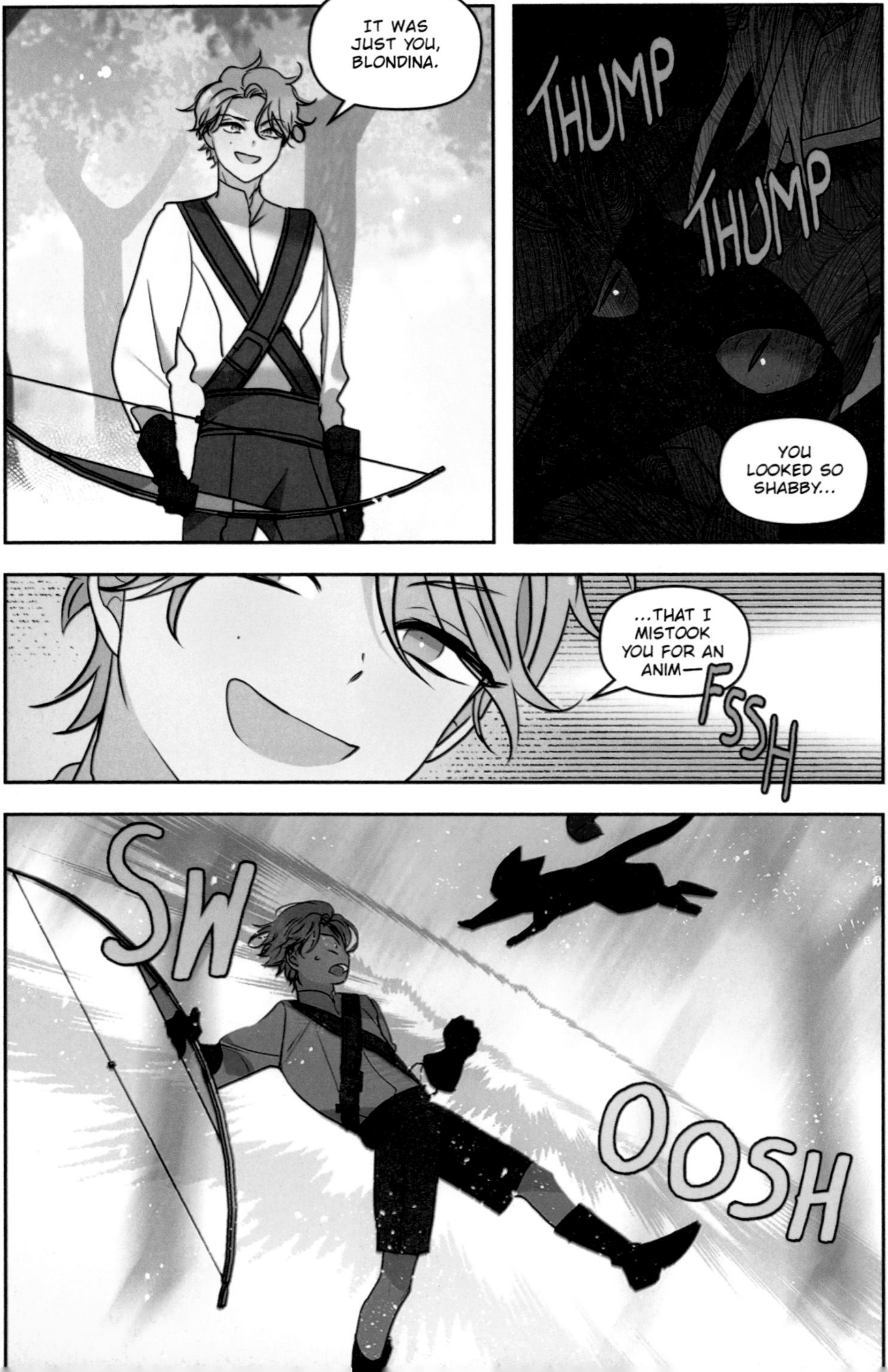
IT WAS JUST YOU, BLONDINA.
THUMP
THUMP
YOU LOOKED SO SHABBY...
...THAT I MISTOOK YOU FOR AN ANIM—
FSSH
SW
OOSH

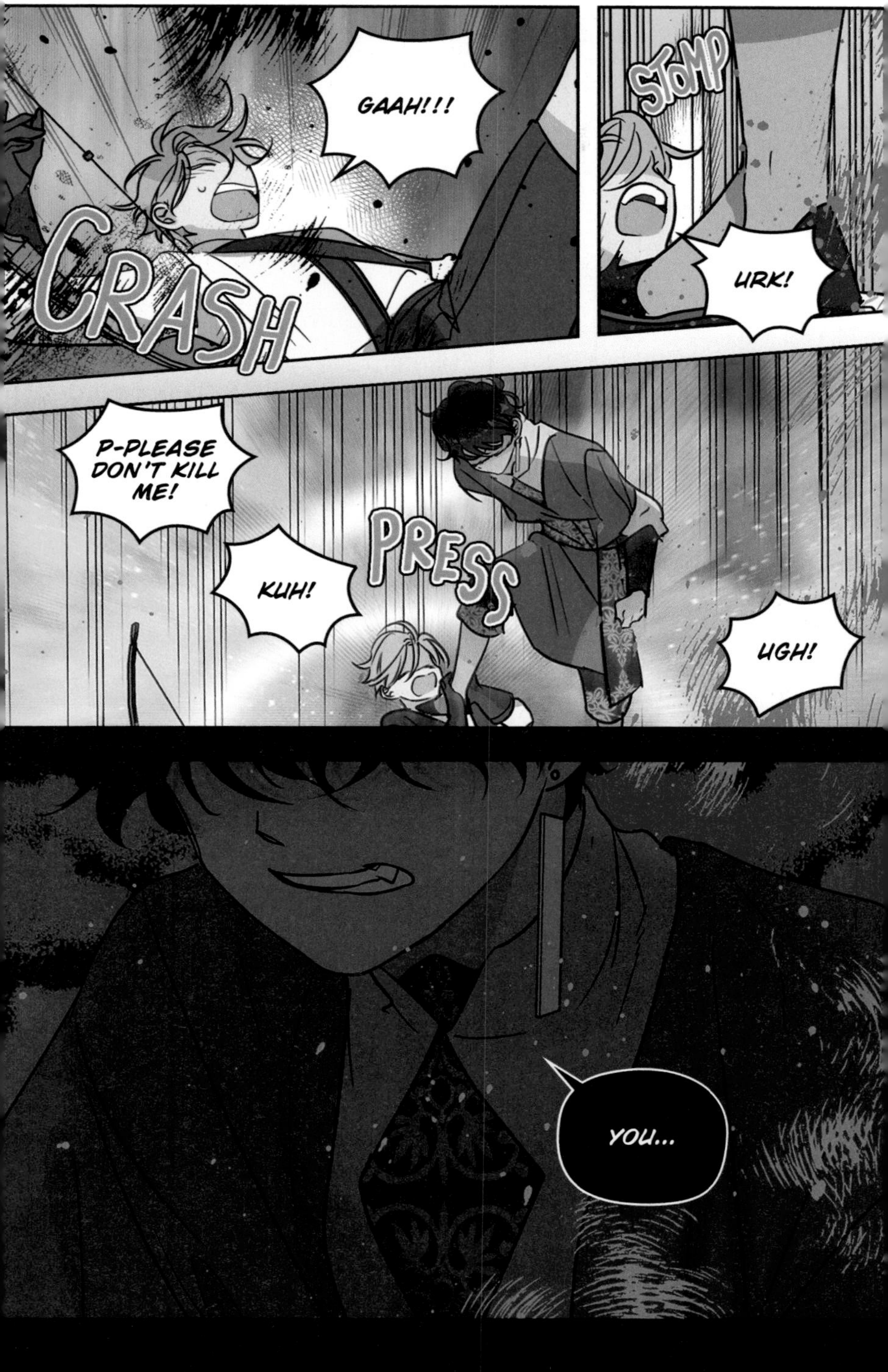
GAAH!!!
CRASH
STOMP
URK!
P-PLEASE DON'T KILL ME!
KUH!
PRESS
UGH!
YOU...

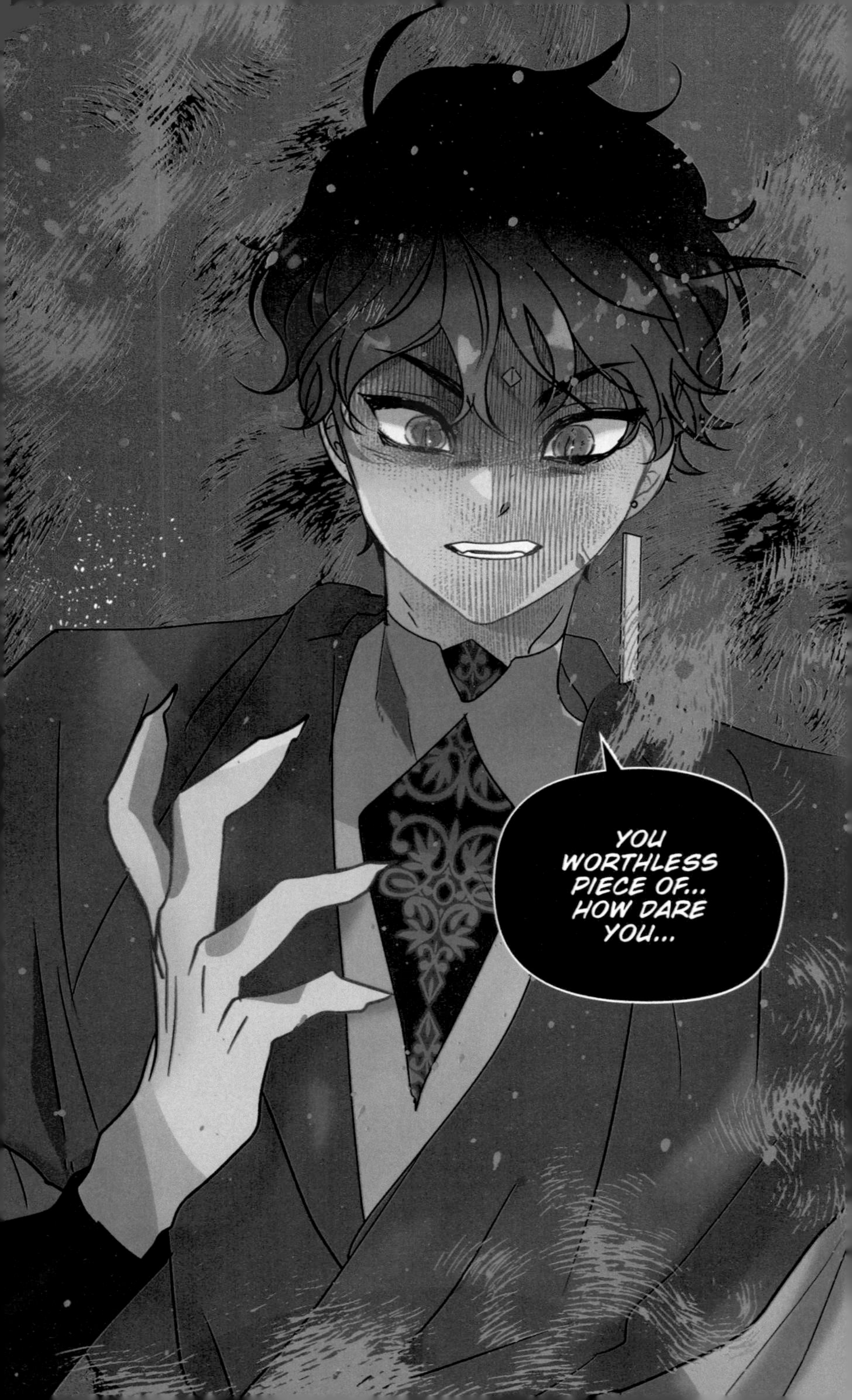
YOU WORTHLESS PIECE OF... HOW DARE YOU...

PART
2

My Gently Raised Beast

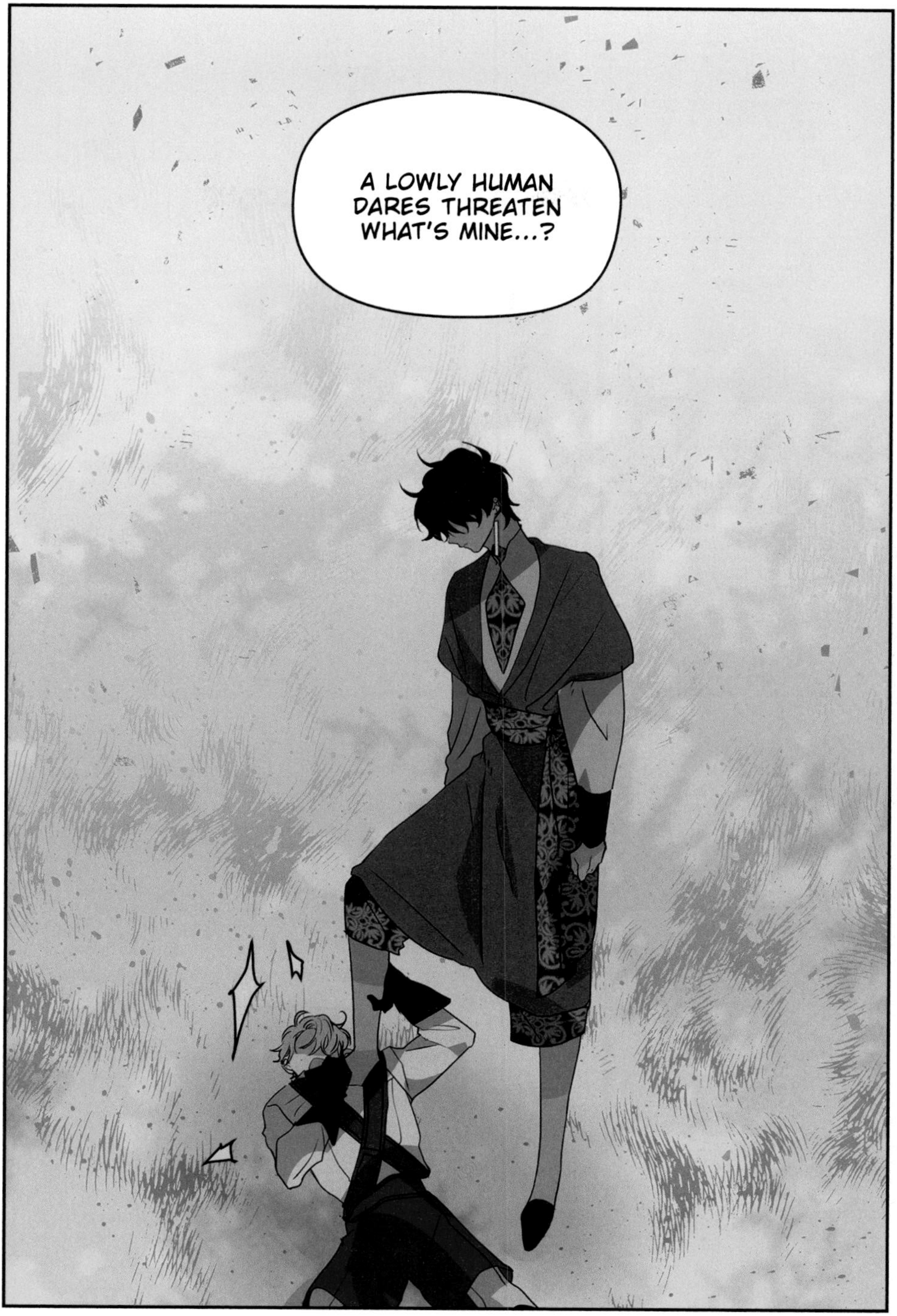
A LOWLY HUMAN DARES THREATEN WHAT'S MINE...?

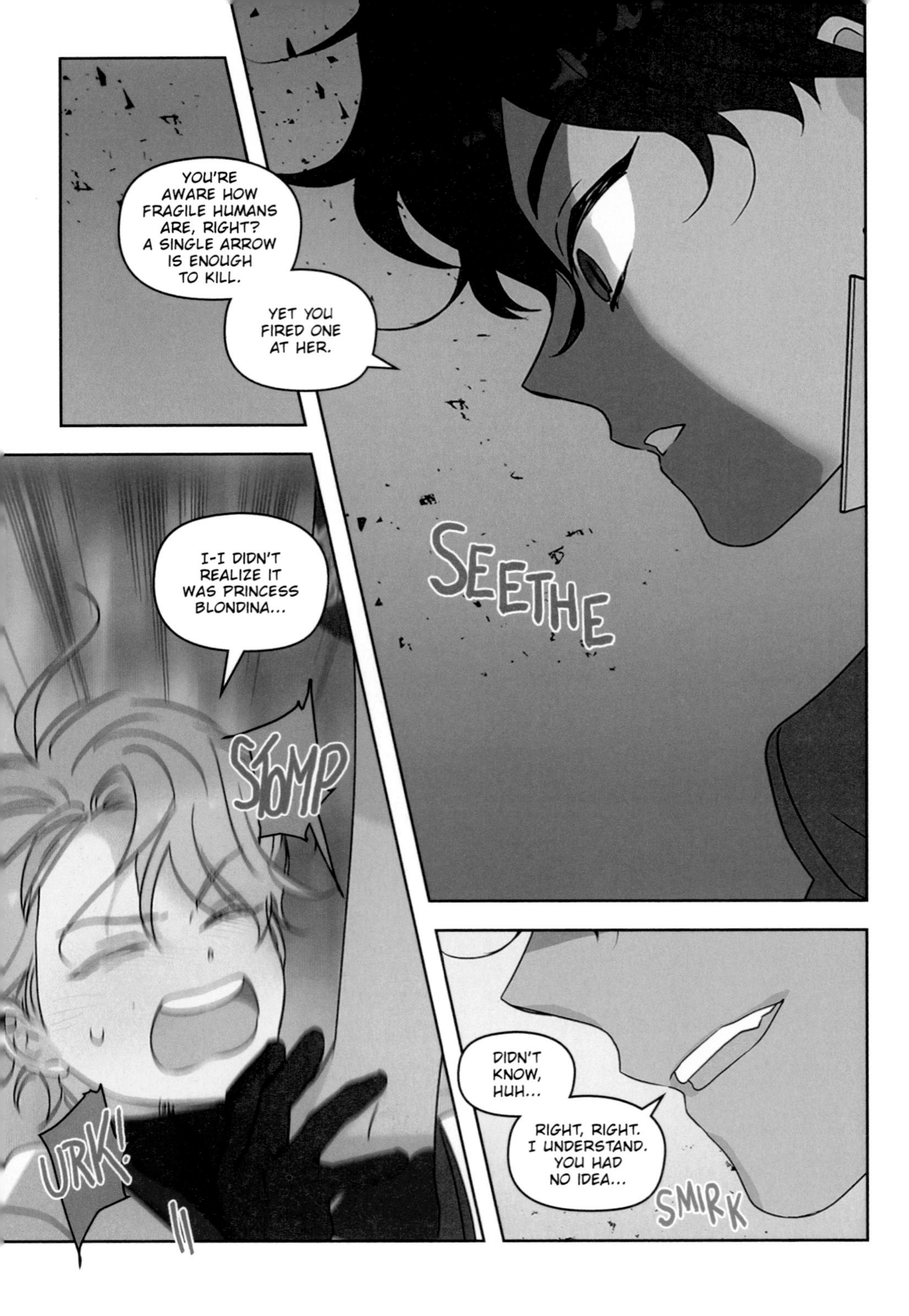
YOU'RE AWARE HOW FRAGILE HUMANS ARE, RIGHT? A SINGLE ARROW IS ENOUGH TO KILL.
YET YOU FIRED ONE AT HER.
SEETHE
I-I DIDN'T REALIZE IT WAS PRINCESS BLONDINA...
STOMP
URK!
DIDN'T KNOW, HUH...
RIGHT, RIGHT. I UNDERSTAND. YOU HAD NO IDEA...
SMIRK

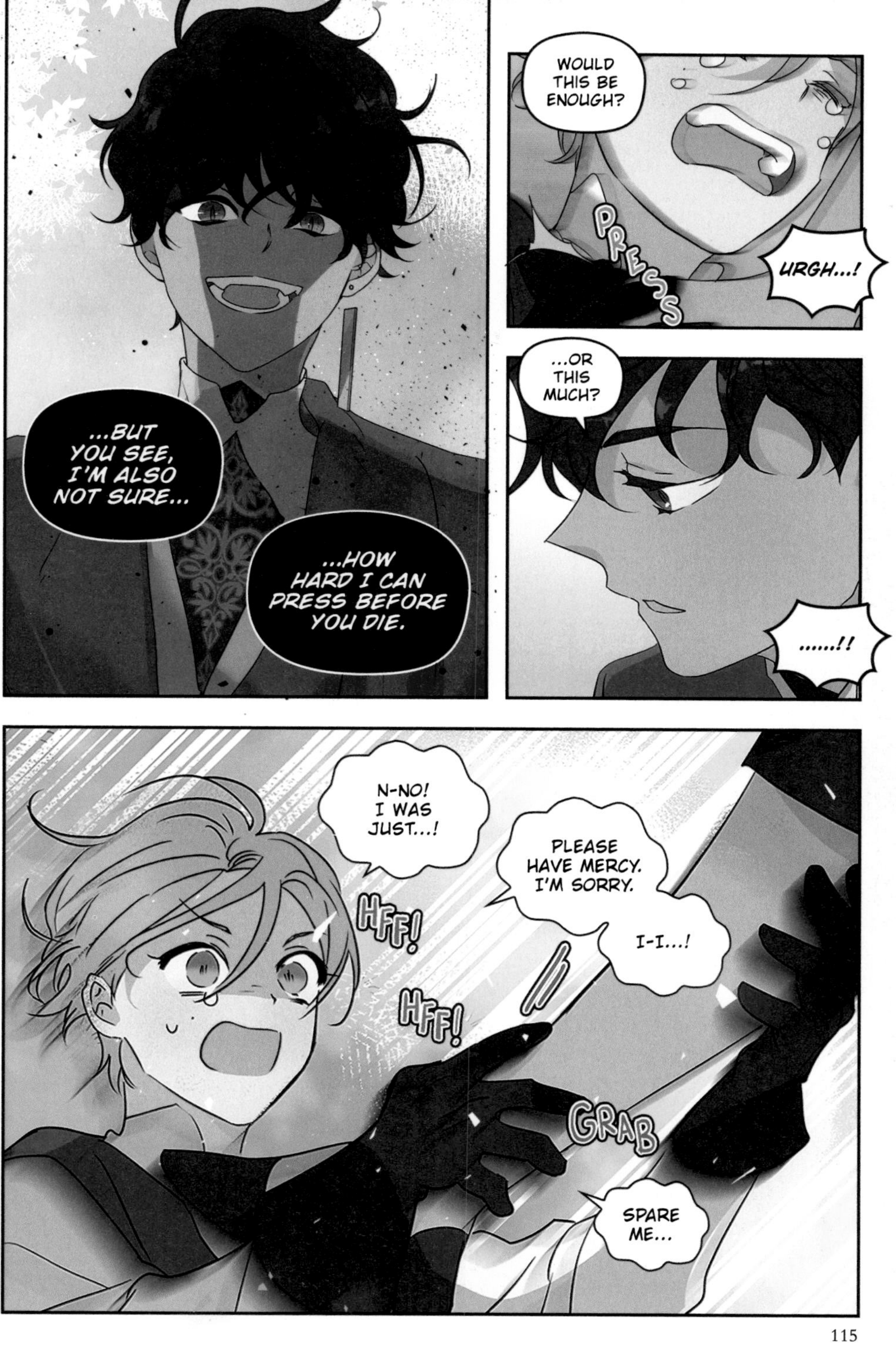
...BUT YOU SEE, I'M ALSO NOT SURE...
...HOW HARD I CAN PRESS BEFORE YOU DIE.
WOULD THIS BE ENOUGH?
PRESS
URGH...!
...OR THIS MUCH?
......!!
N-NO! I WAS JUST...!
PLEASE HAVE MERCY. I'M SORRY.
I-I...!
HFF!
HFF!
GRAB
SPARE ME...

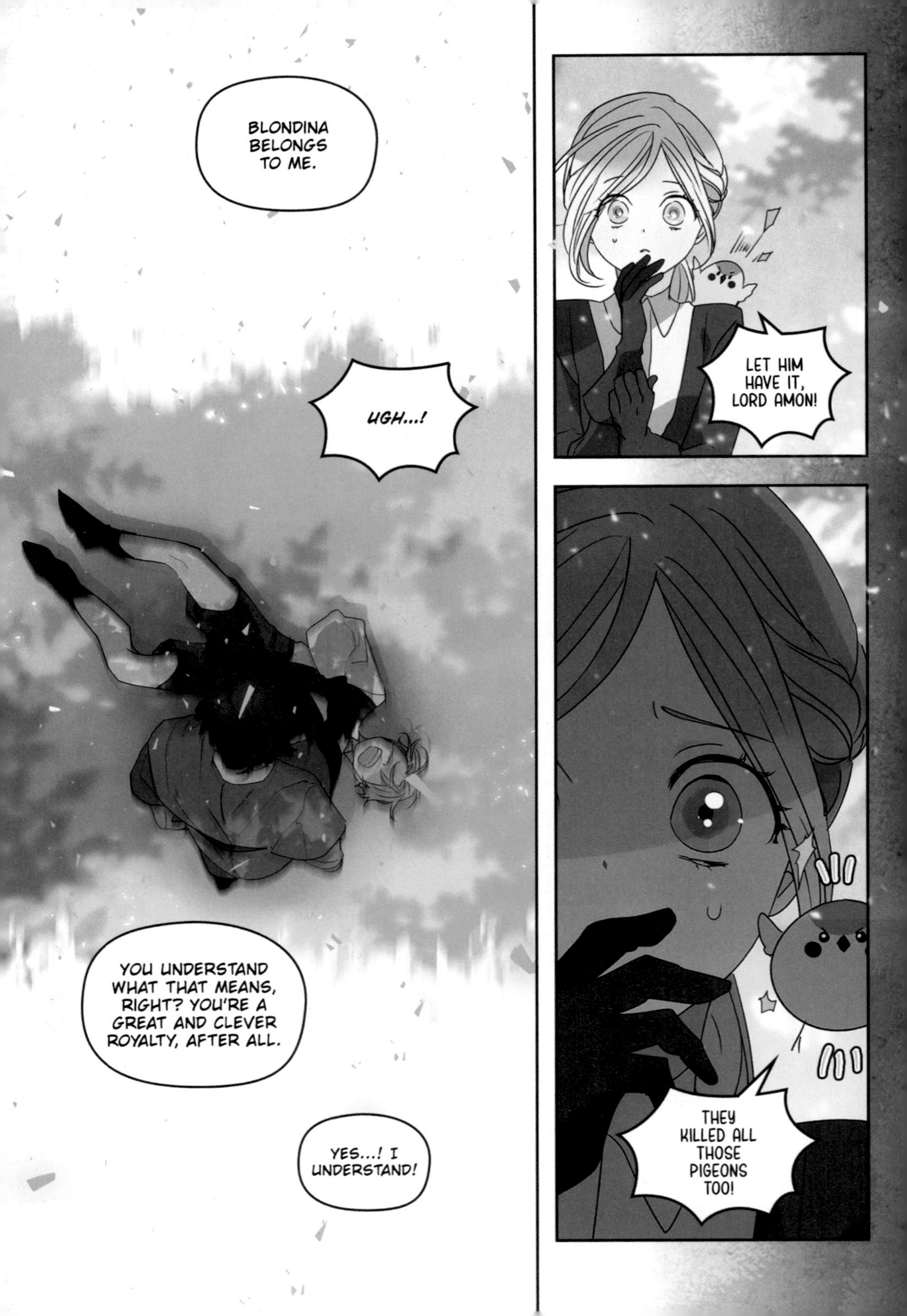
BLONDINA BELONGS TO ME.
UGH...!
YOU UNDERSTAND WHAT THAT MEANS, RIGHT? YOU'RE A GREAT AND CLEVER ROYALTY, AFTER ALL.
YES...! I UNDERSTAND!
LET HIM HAVE IT, LORD AMON!
THEY KILLED ALL THOSE PIGEONS TOO!

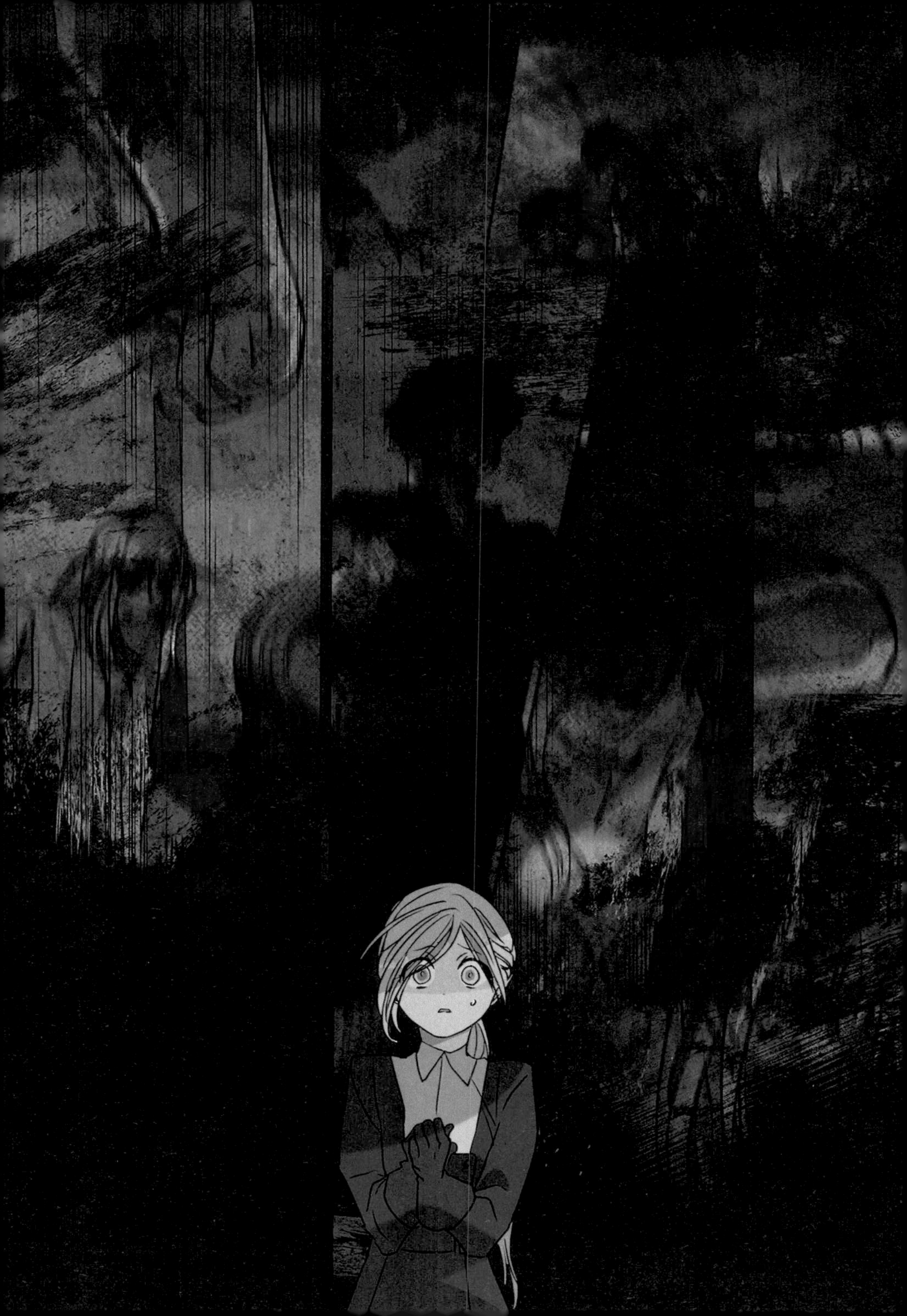

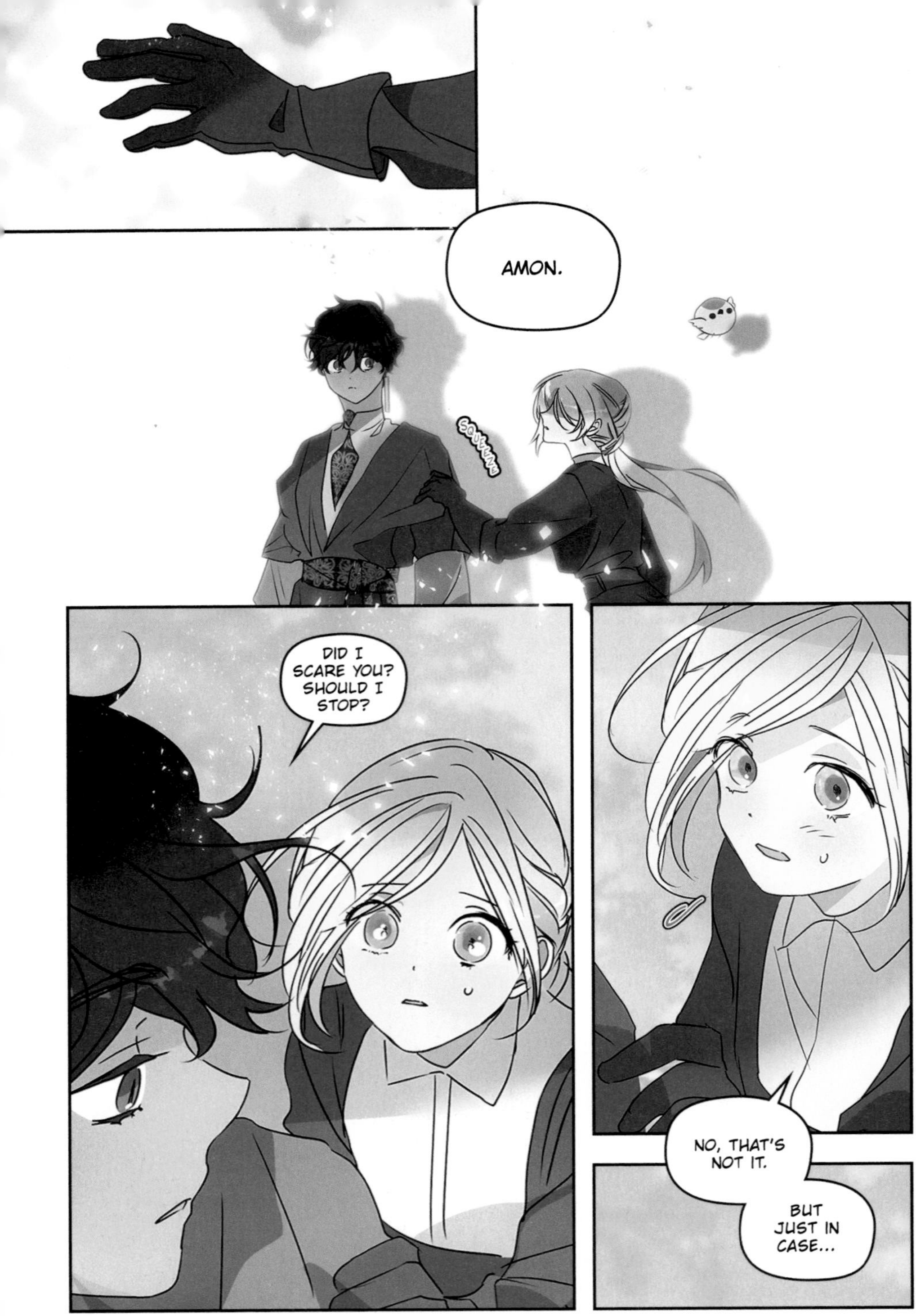
AMON.
SQUEEZE
DID I SCARE YOU? SHOULD I STOP?
NO, THAT'S NOT IT.
BUT JUST IN CASE...

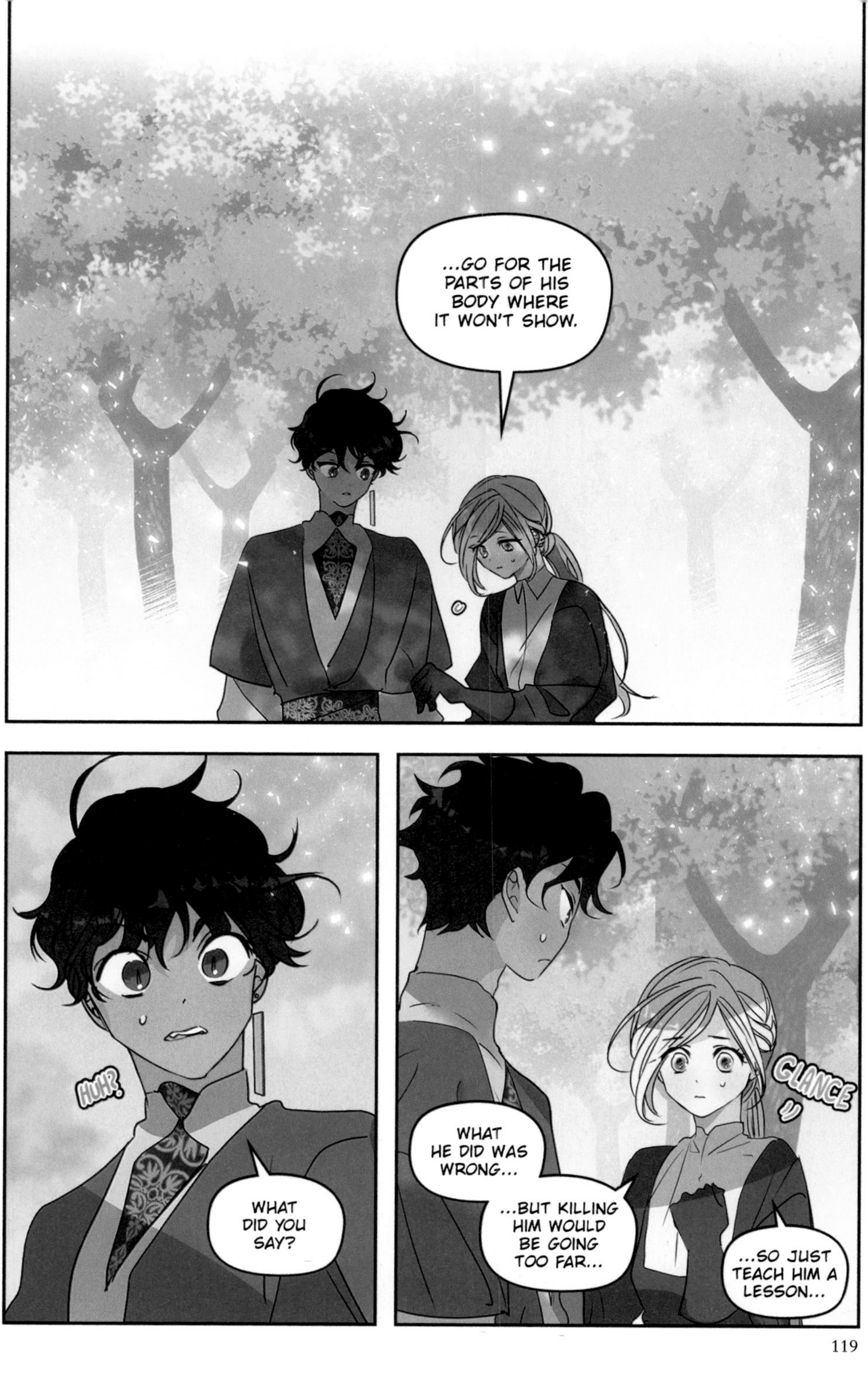
...GO FOR THE PARTS OF HIS BODY WHERE IT WON'T SHOW.
HUH?
WHAT DID YOU SAY?
GLANCE
WHAT HE DID WAS WRONG...
...BUT KILLING HIM WOULD BE GOING TOO FAR...
...SO JUST TEACH HIM A LESSON...

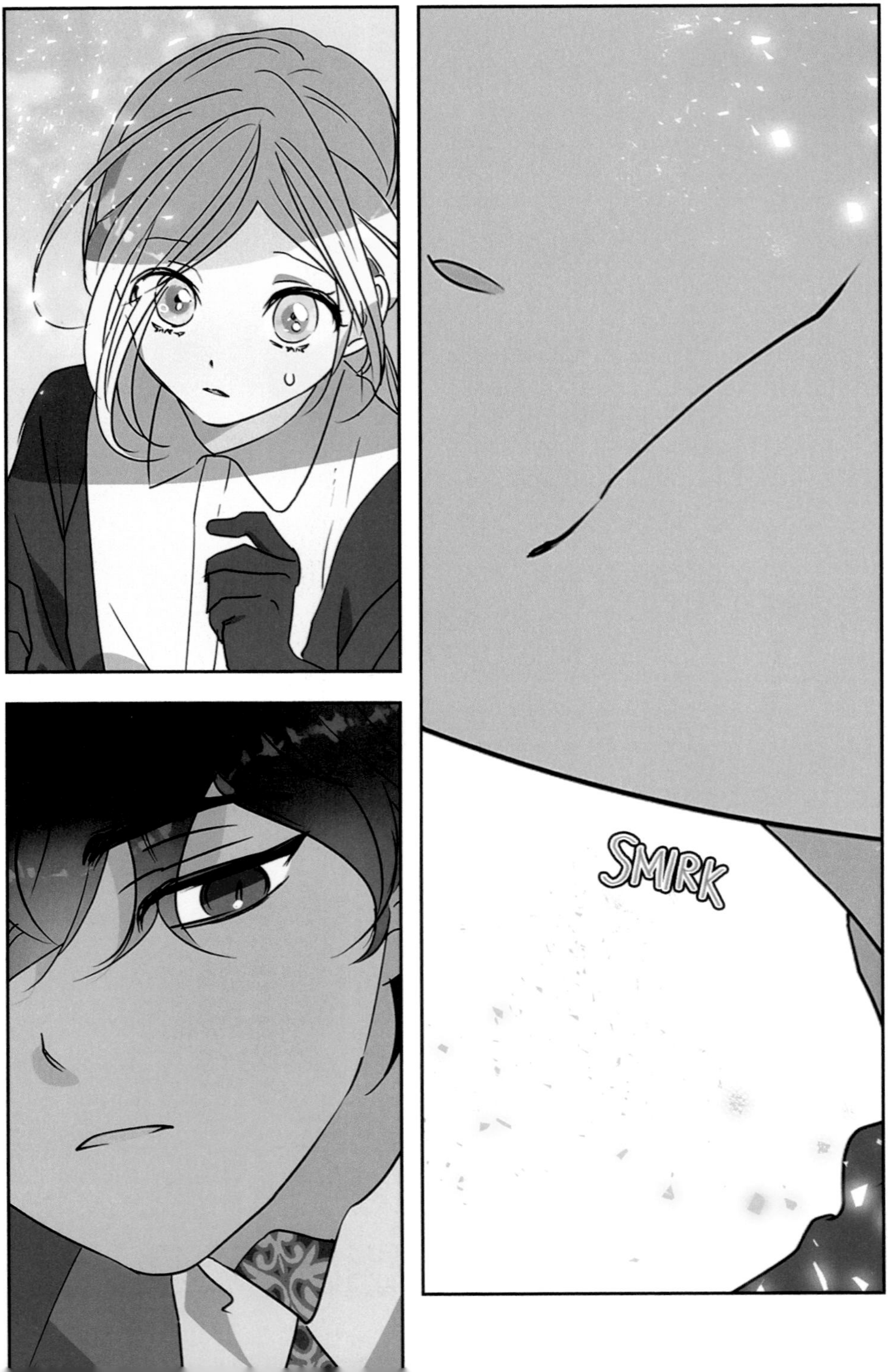
SMIRK

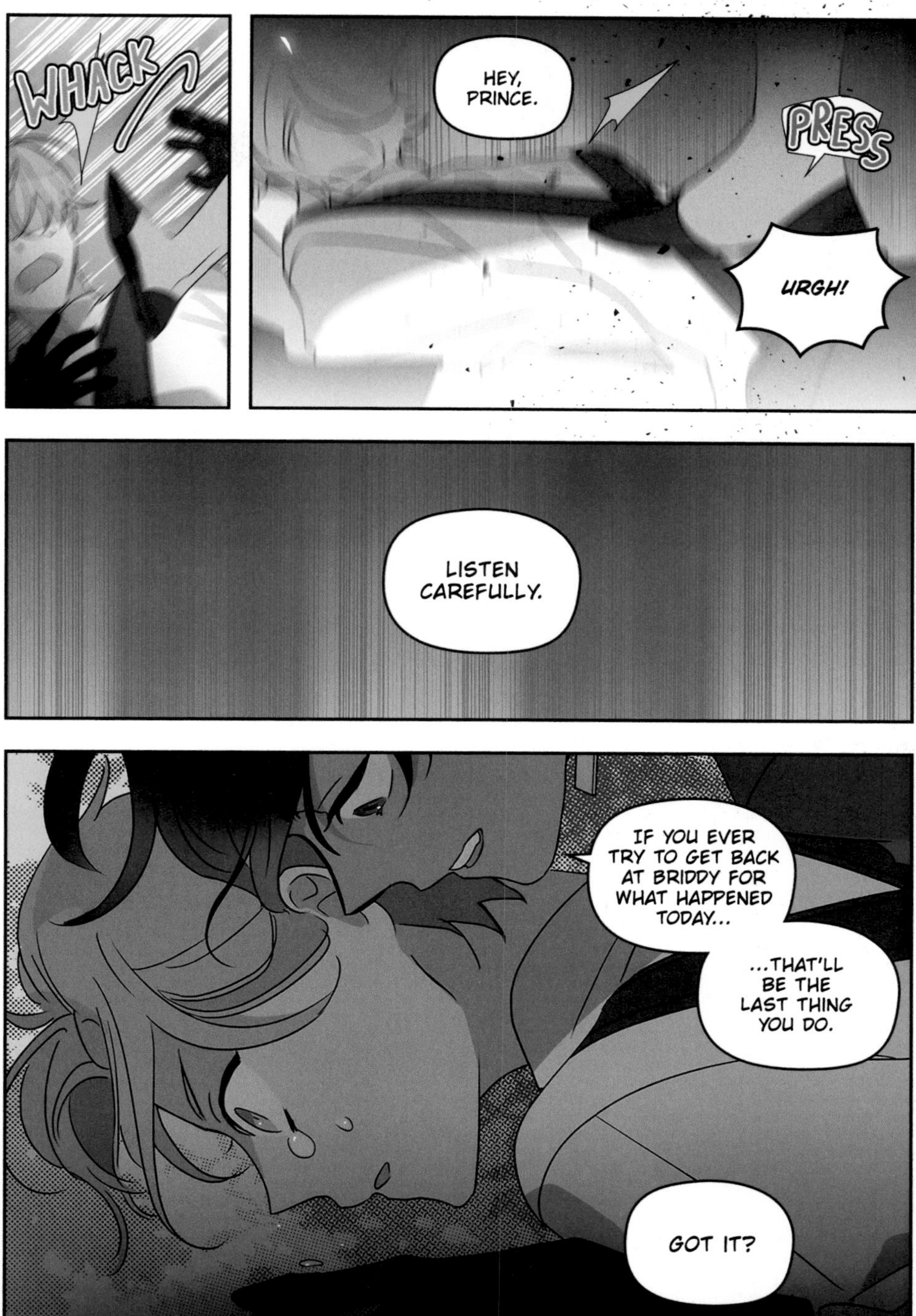
WHACK
HEY, PRINCE.
PRESS
URGH!
LISTEN CAREFULLY.
IF YOU EVER TRY TO GET BACK AT BRIDDY FOR WHAT HAPPENED TODAY...
...THAT'LL BE THE LAST THING YOU DO.
GOT IT?

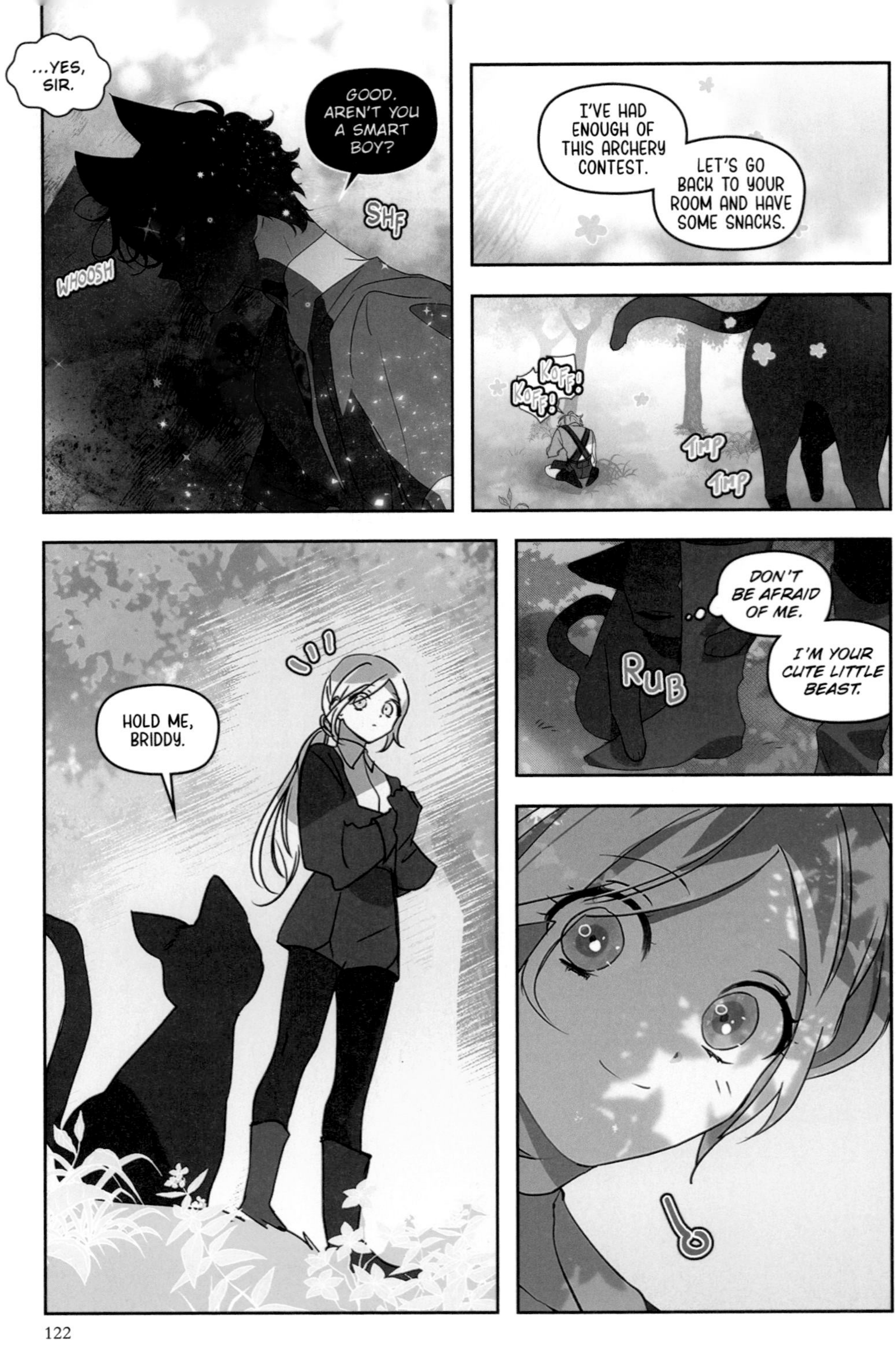
...YES, SIR.
GOOD. AREN'T YOU A SMART BOY?
SHF
WHOOSH
I'VE HAD ENOUGH OF THIS ARCHERY CONTEST.
LET'S GO BACK TO YOUR ROOM AND HAVE SOME SNACKS.
KOFF! KOFF!
TMP TMP
HOLD ME, BRIDDY.
DON'T BE AFRAID OF ME.
I'M YOUR CUTE LITTLE BEAST.
RUB

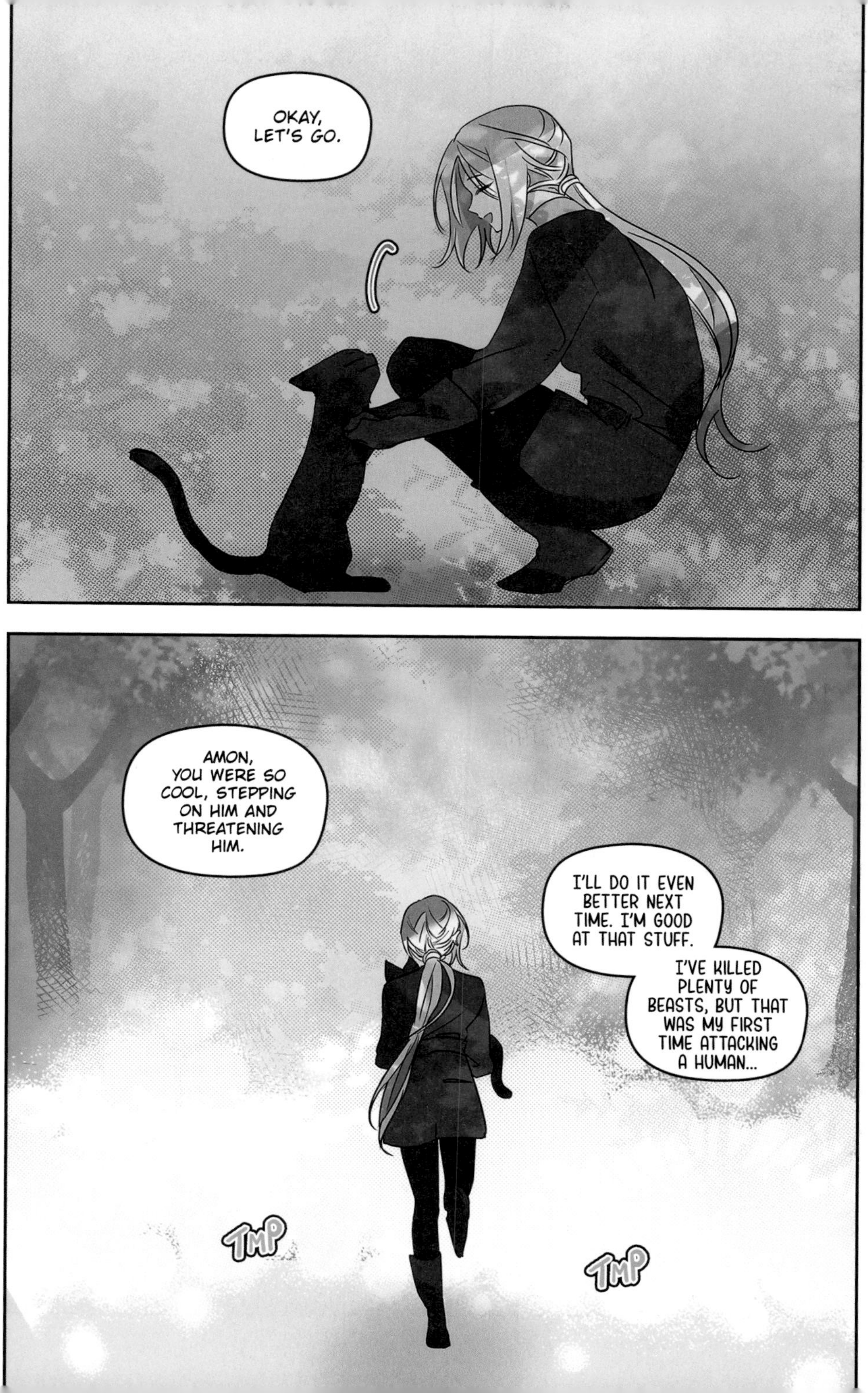
OKAY, LET'S GO.
AMON, YOU WERE SO COOL, STEPPING ON HIM AND THREATENING HIM.
I'LL DO IT EVEN BETTER NEXT TIME. I'M GOOD AT THAT STUFF.
I'VE KILLED PLENTY OF BEASTS, BUT THAT WAS MY FIRST TIME ATTACKING A HUMAN...
TMP
TMP

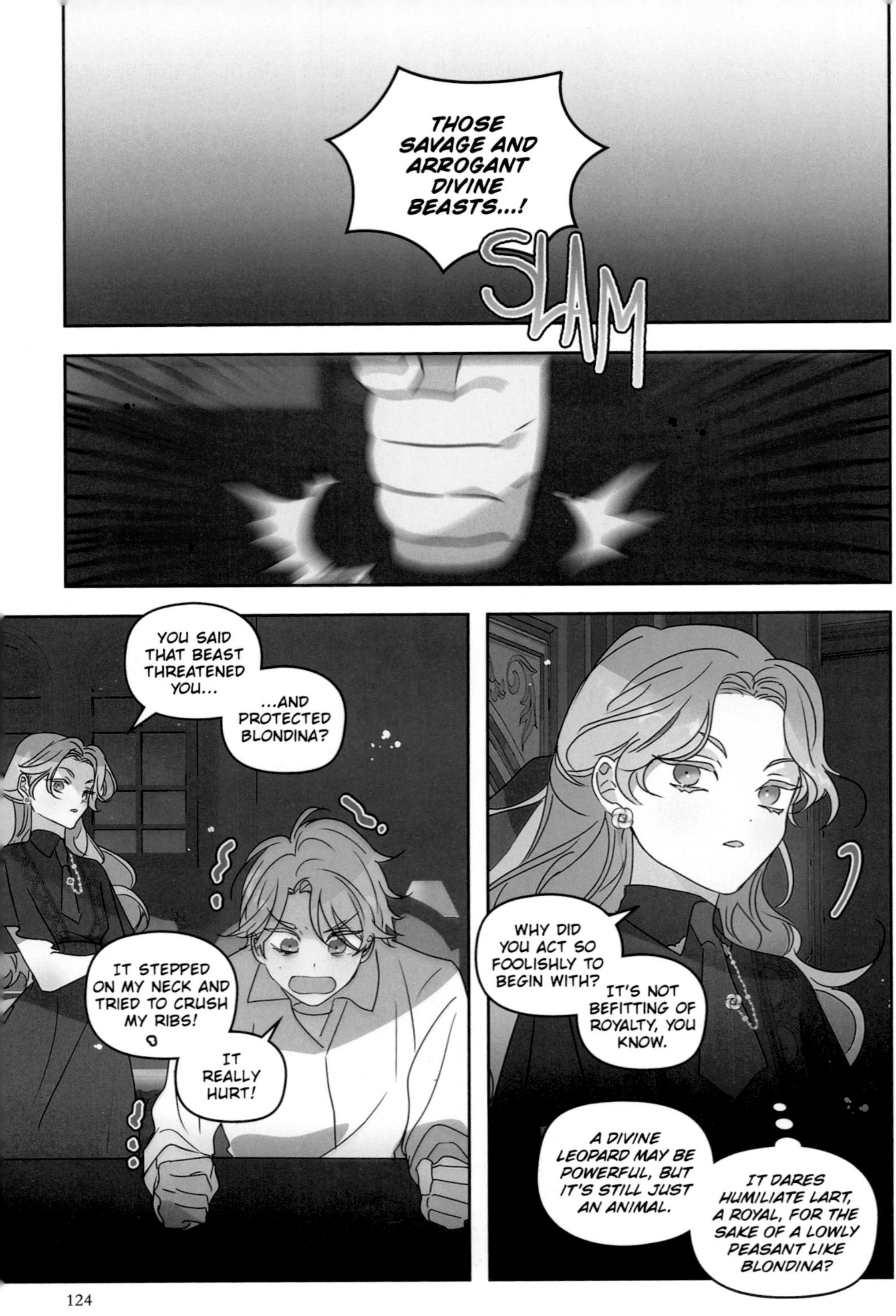
THOSE SAVAGE AND ARROGANT DIVINE BEASTS...!
SLAM
YOU SAID THAT BEAST THREATENED YOU...
...AND PROTECTED BLONDINA?
IT STEPPED ON MY NECK AND TRIED TO CRUSH MY RIBS!
IT REALLY HURT!
WHY DID YOU ACT SO FOOLISHLY TO BEGIN WITH?
IT'S NOT BEFITTING OF ROYALTY, YOU KNOW.
A DIVINE LEOPARD MAY BE POWERFUL, BUT IT'S STILL JUST AN ANIMAL.
IT DARES HUMILIATE LART, A ROYAL, FOR THE SAKE OF A LOWLY PEASANT LIKE BLONDINA?

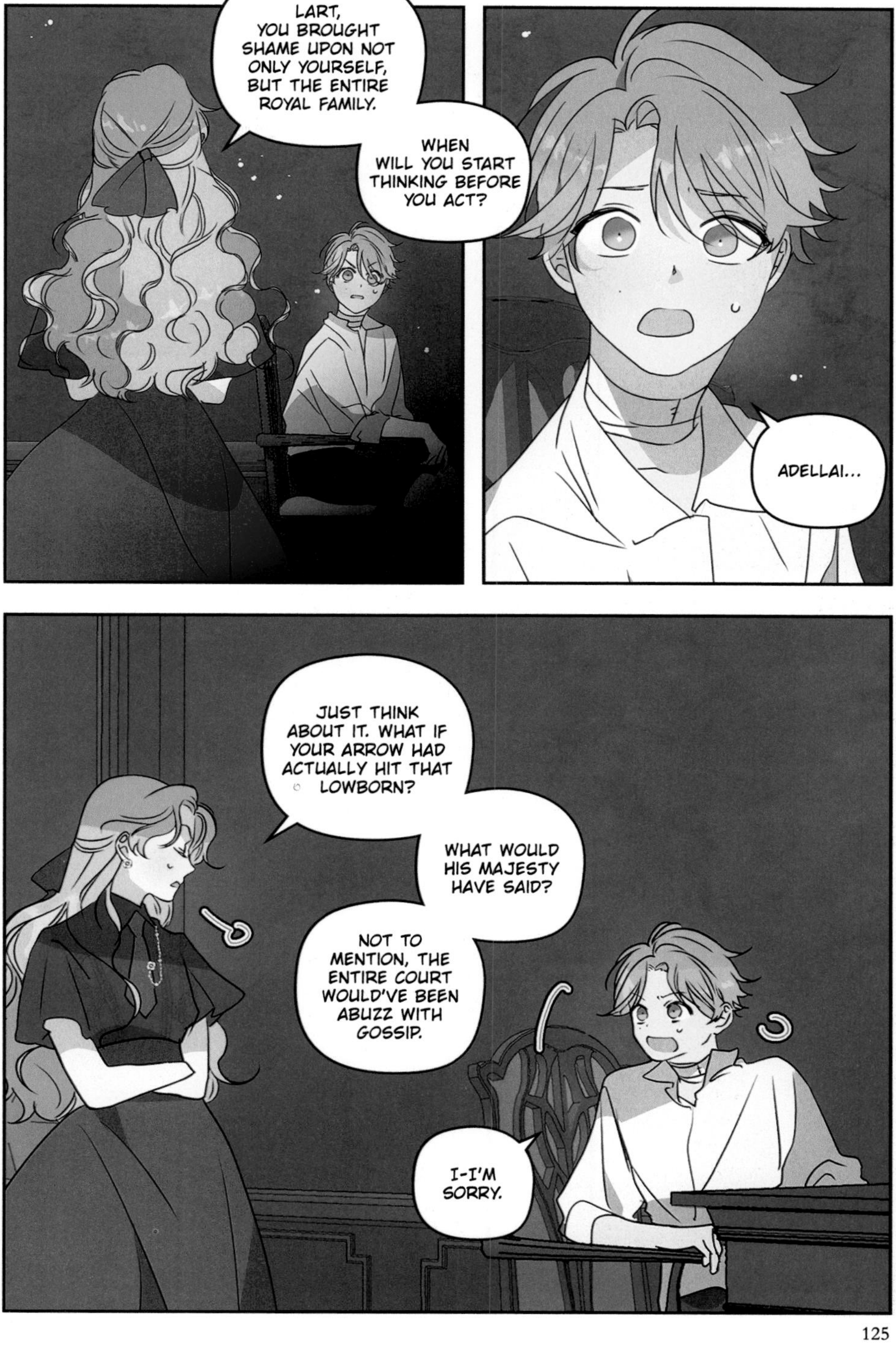
LART, YOU BROUGHT SHAME UPON NOT ONLY YOURSELF, BUT THE ENTIRE ROYAL FAMILY.
WHEN WILL YOU START THINKING BEFORE YOU ACT?
ADELLAI...
JUST THINK ABOUT IT. WHAT IF YOUR ARROW HAD ACTUALLY HIT THAT LOWBORN?
WHAT WOULD HIS MAJESTY HAVE SAID?
NOT TO MENTION, THE ENTIRE COURT WOULD'VE BEEN ABUZZ WITH GOSSIP.
I-I'M SORRY.

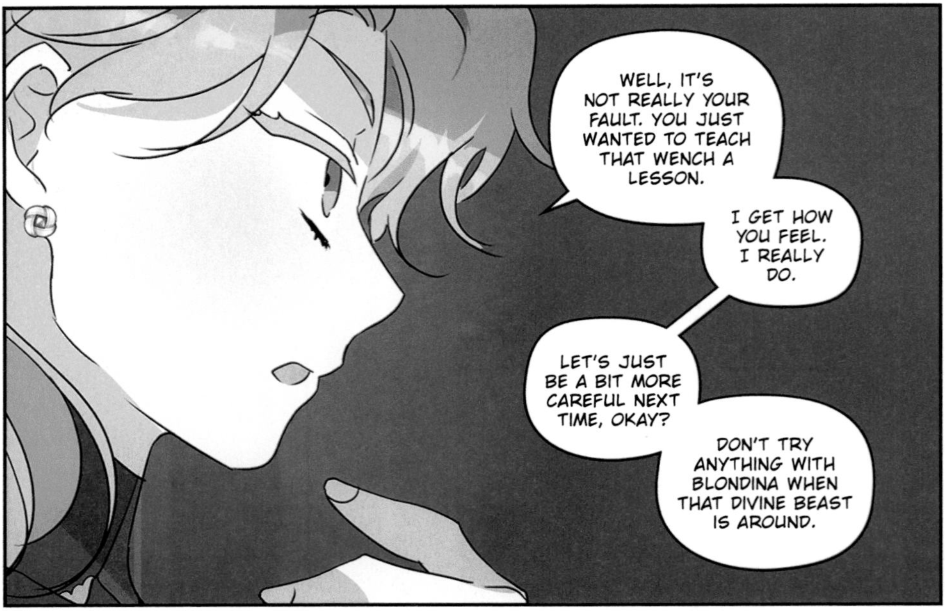
WELL, IT'S NOT REALLY YOUR FAULT. YOU JUST WANTED TO TEACH THAT WENCH A LESSON.
I GET HOW YOU FEEL. I REALLY DO.
LET'S JUST BE A BIT MORE CAREFUL NEXT TIME, OKAY?
DON'T TRY ANYTHING WITH BLONDINA WHEN THAT DIVINE BEAST IS AROUND.

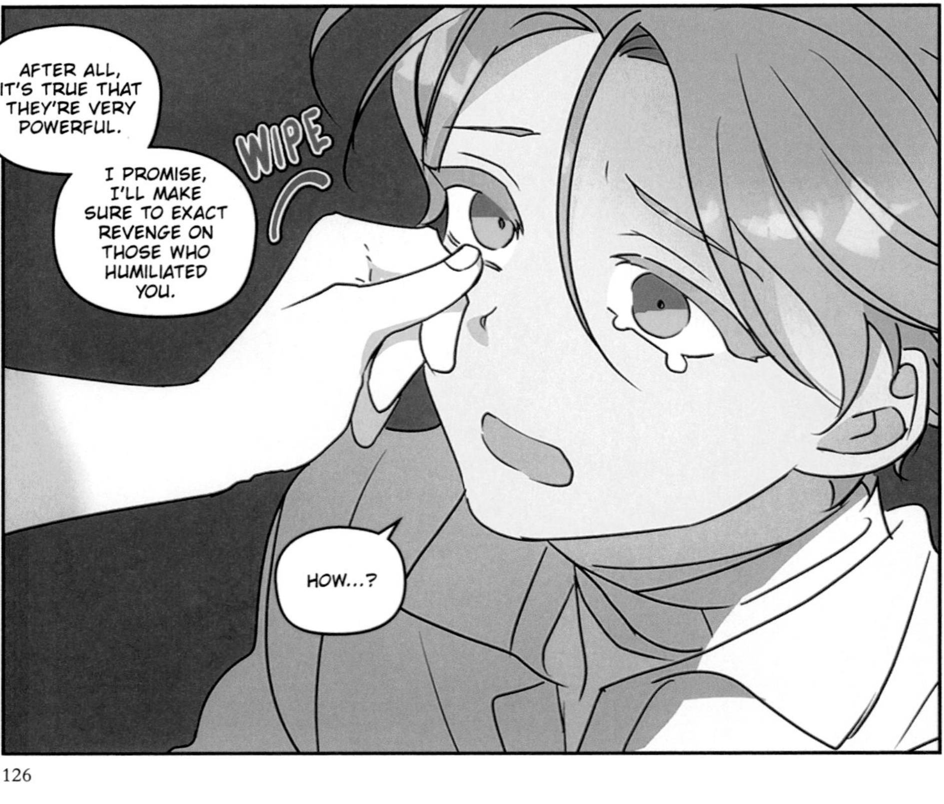
AFTER ALL, IT'S TRUE THAT THEY'RE VERY POWERFUL.
I PROMISE, I'LL MAKE SURE TO EXACT REVENGE ON THOSE WHO HUMILIATED YOU.
WIPE
HOW...?

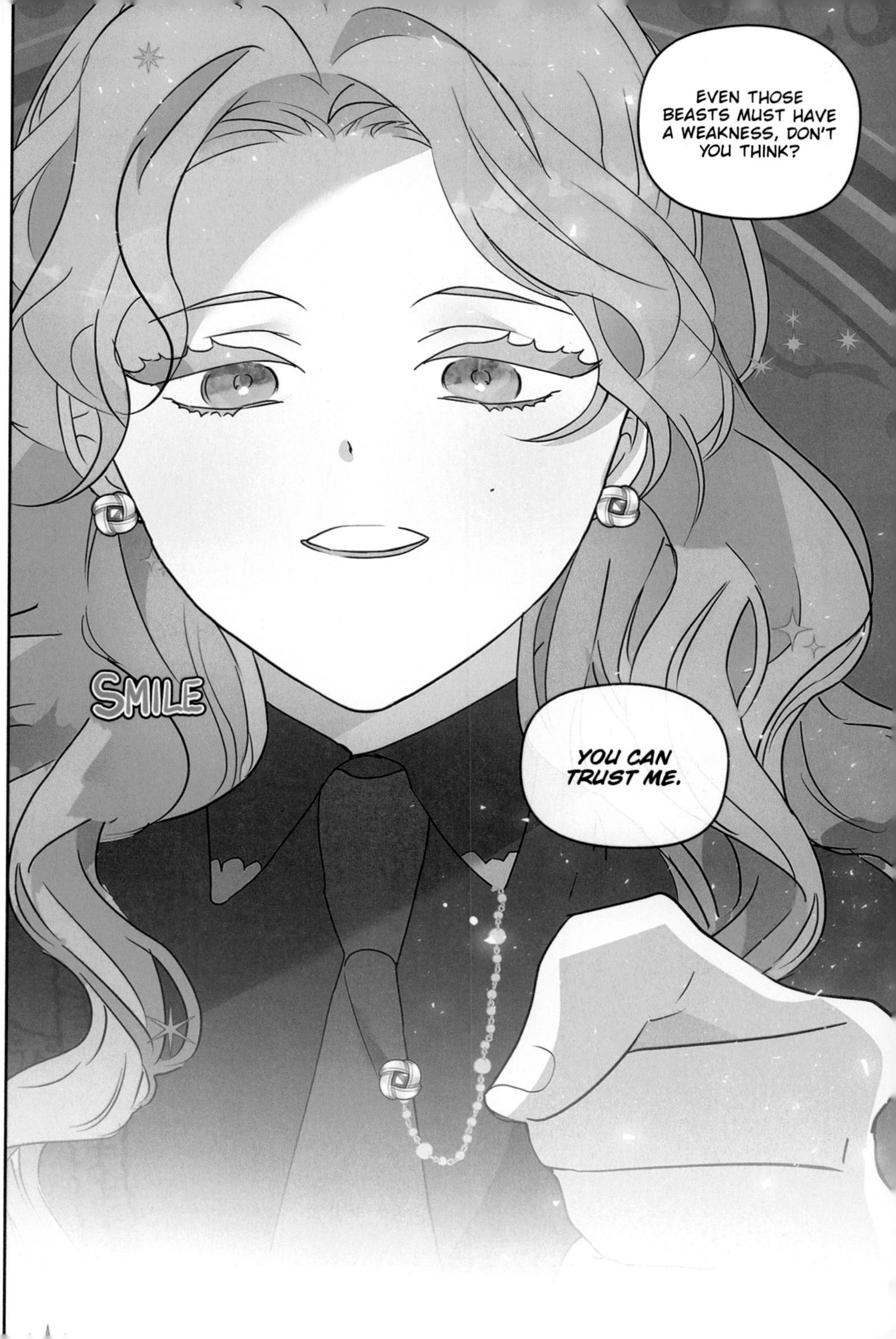
EVEN THOSE BEASTS MUST HAVE A WEAKNESS, DON'T YOU THINK?
SMILE
YOU CAN TRUST ME.

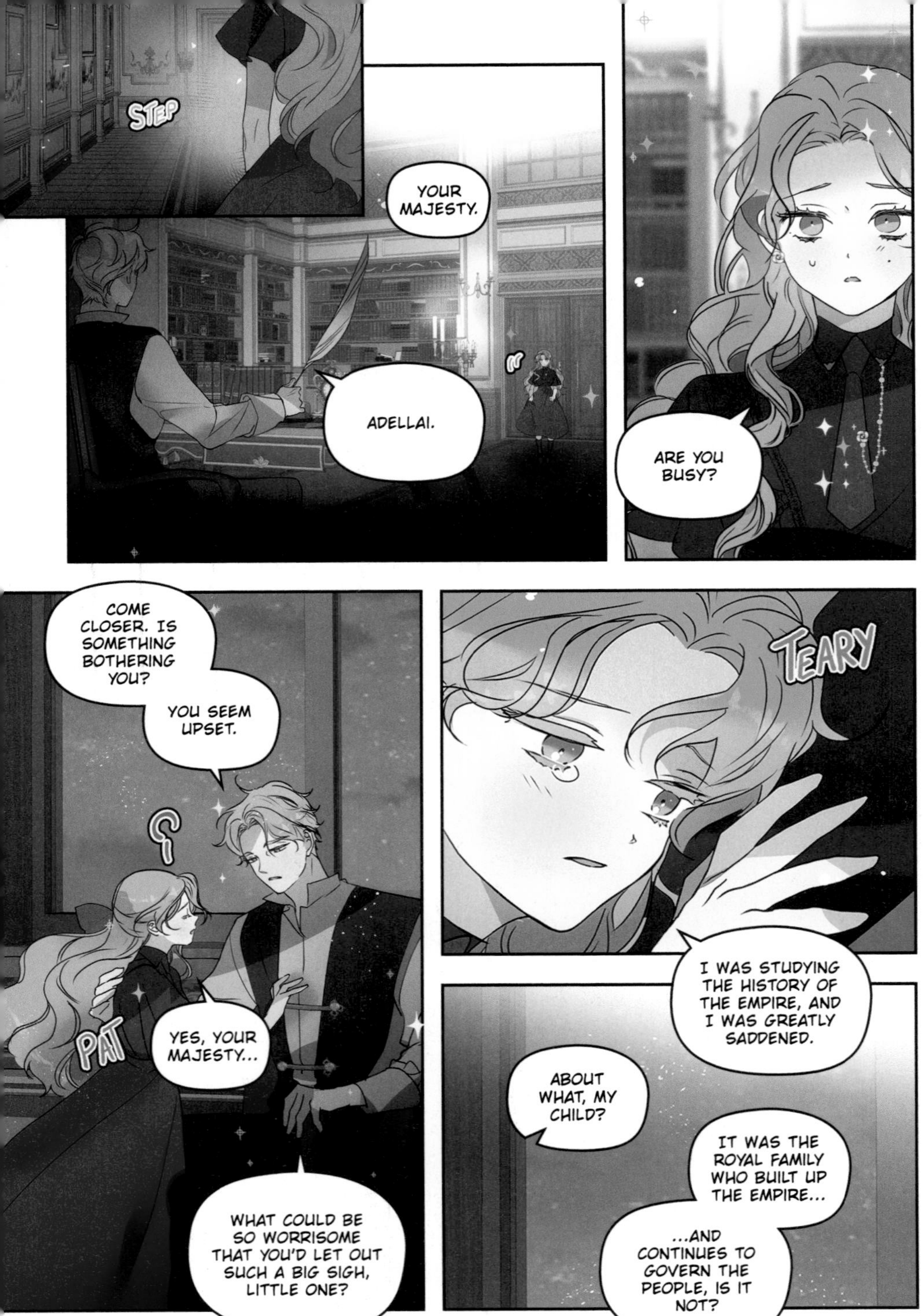
STEP
YOUR MAJESTY.
ADELLAI.
ARE YOU BUSY?
COME CLOSER. IS SOMETHING BOTHERING YOU?
YOU SEEM UPSET.
?
YES, YOUR MAJESTY...
PAT
WHAT COULD BE SO WORRISOME THAT YOU'D LET OUT SUCH A BIG SIGH, LITTLE ONE?
TEARY
I WAS STUDYING THE HISTORY OF THE EMPIRE, AND I WAS GREATLY SADDENED.
ABOUT WHAT, MY CHILD?
IT WAS THE ROYAL FAMILY WHO BUILT UP THE EMPIRE...
...AND CONTINUES TO GOVERN THE PEOPLE, IS IT NOT?

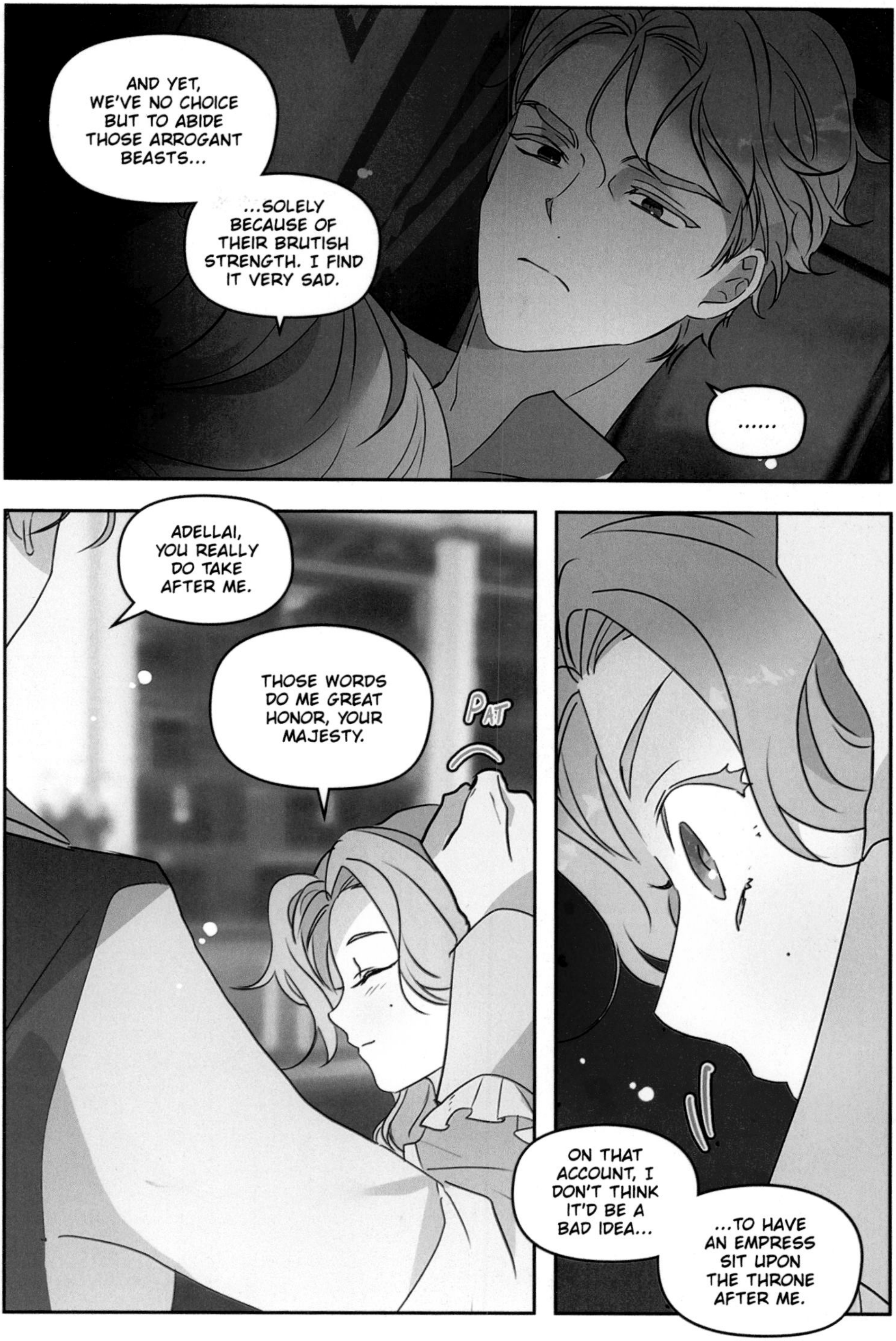
AND YET, WE'VE NO CHOICE BUT TO ABIDE THOSE ARROGANT BEASTS...
...SOLELY BECAUSE OF THEIR BRUTISH STRENGTH. I FIND IT VERY SAD.
......
ADELLAI, YOU REALLY DO TAKE AFTER ME.
THOSE WORDS DO ME GREAT HONOR, YOUR MAJESTY.
PAT
ON THAT ACCOUNT, I DON'T THINK IT'D BE A BAD IDEA...
...TO HAVE AN EMPRESS SIT UPON THE THRONE AFTER ME.

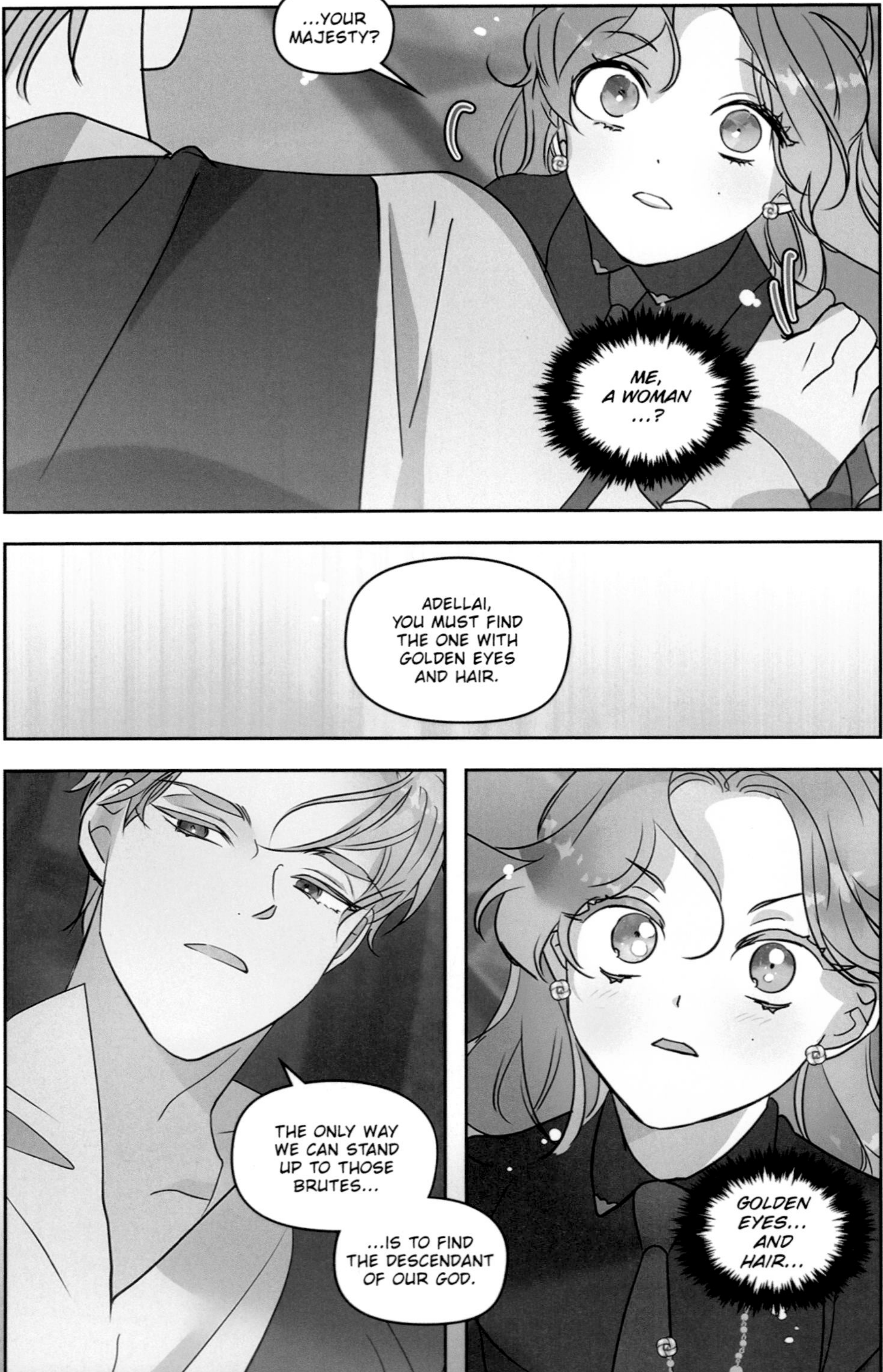
...YOUR MAJESTY?
ME, A WOMAN ...?
ADELLAI, YOU MUST FIND THE ONE WITH GOLDEN EYES AND HAIR.
THE ONLY WAY WE CAN STAND UP TO THOSE BRUTES...
...IS TO FIND THE DESCENDANT OF OUR GOD.
GOLDEN EYES... AND HAIR...

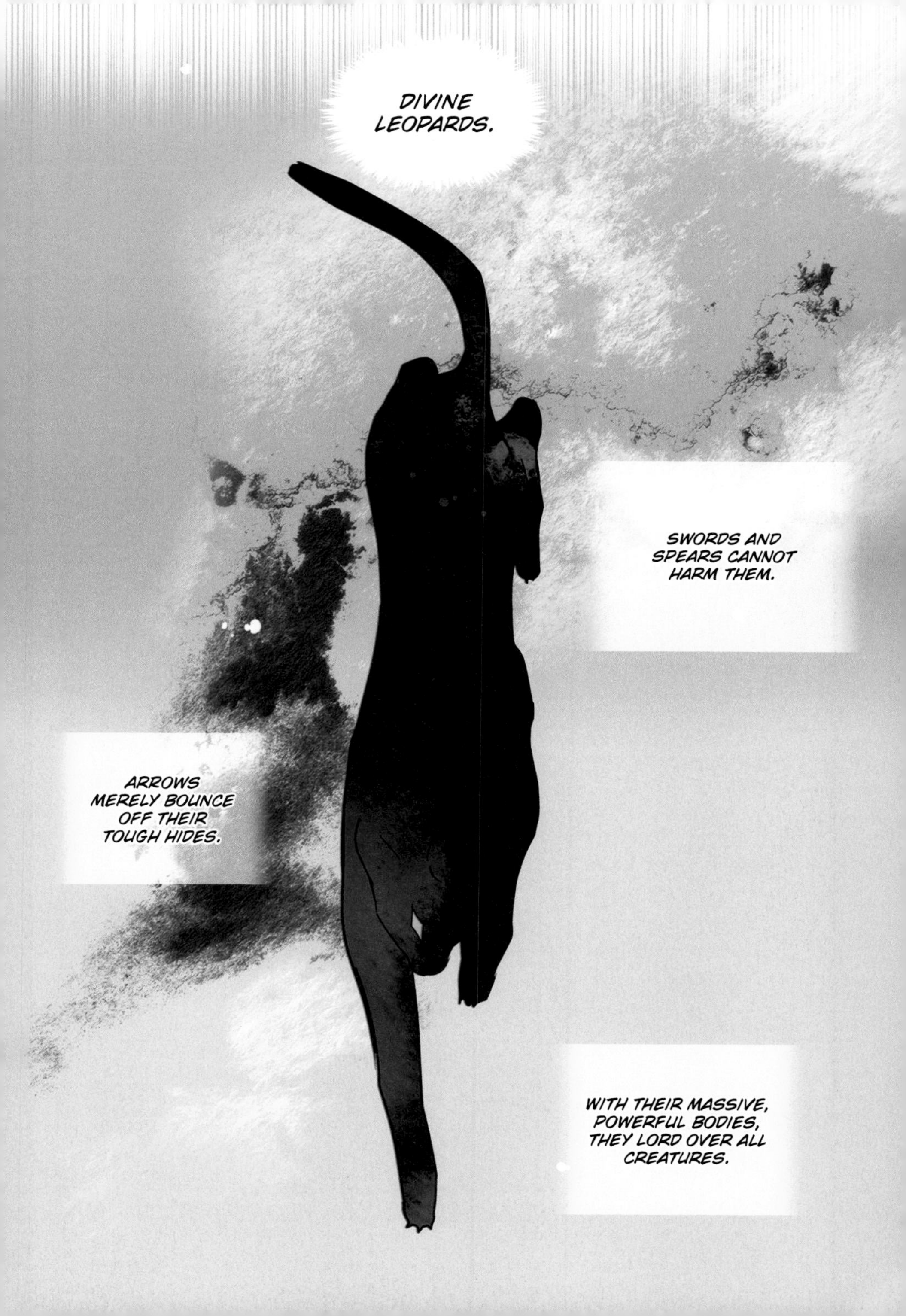
DIVINE LEOPARDS.
SWORDS AND SPEARS CANNOT HARM THEM.
ARROWS MERELY BOUNCE OFF THEIR TOUGH HIDES.
WITH THEIR MASSIVE, POWERFUL BODIES, THEY LORD OVER ALL CREATURES.

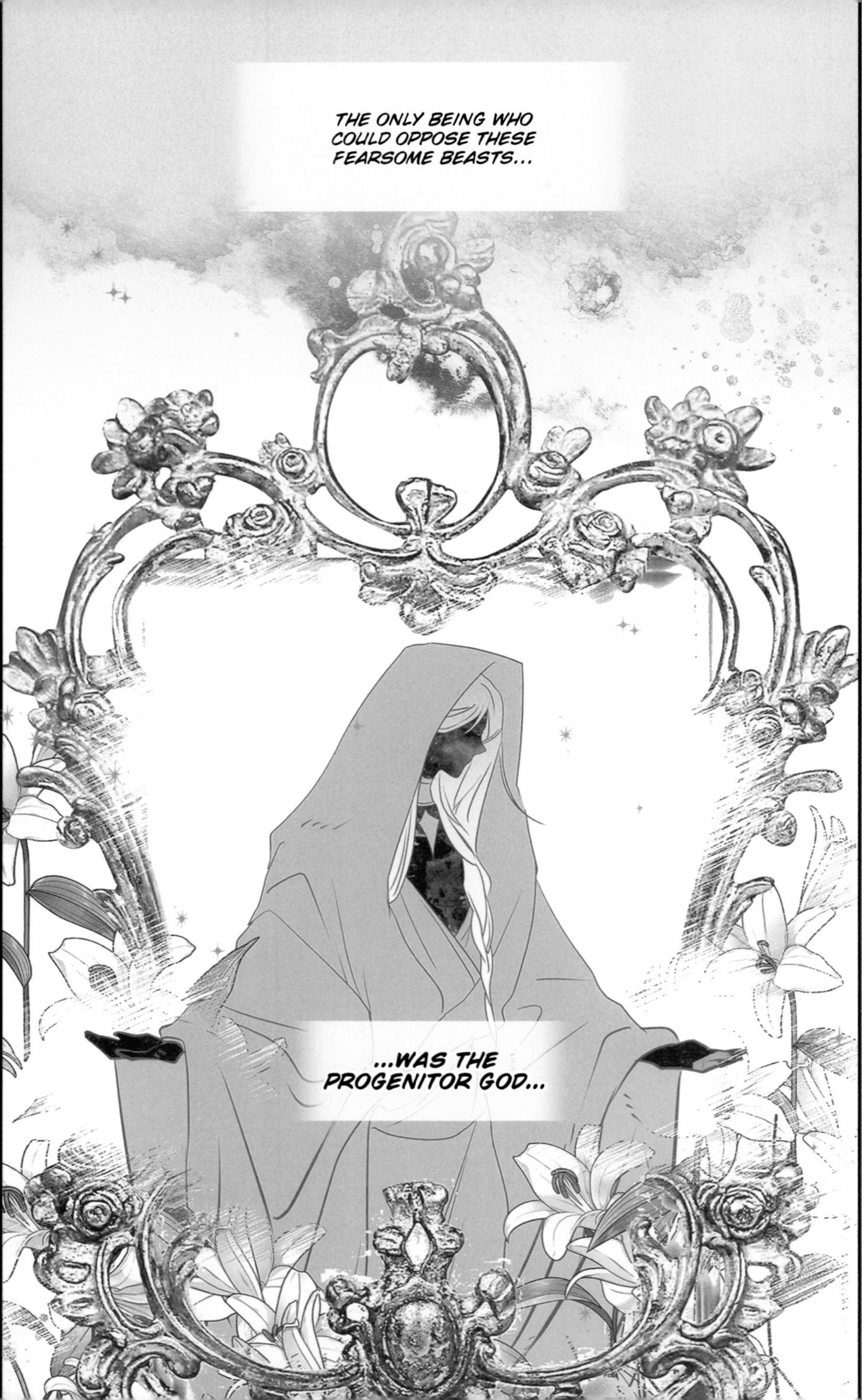
THE ONLY BEING WHO COULD OPPOSE THESE FEARSOME BEASTS...
...WAS THE PROGENITOR GOD...

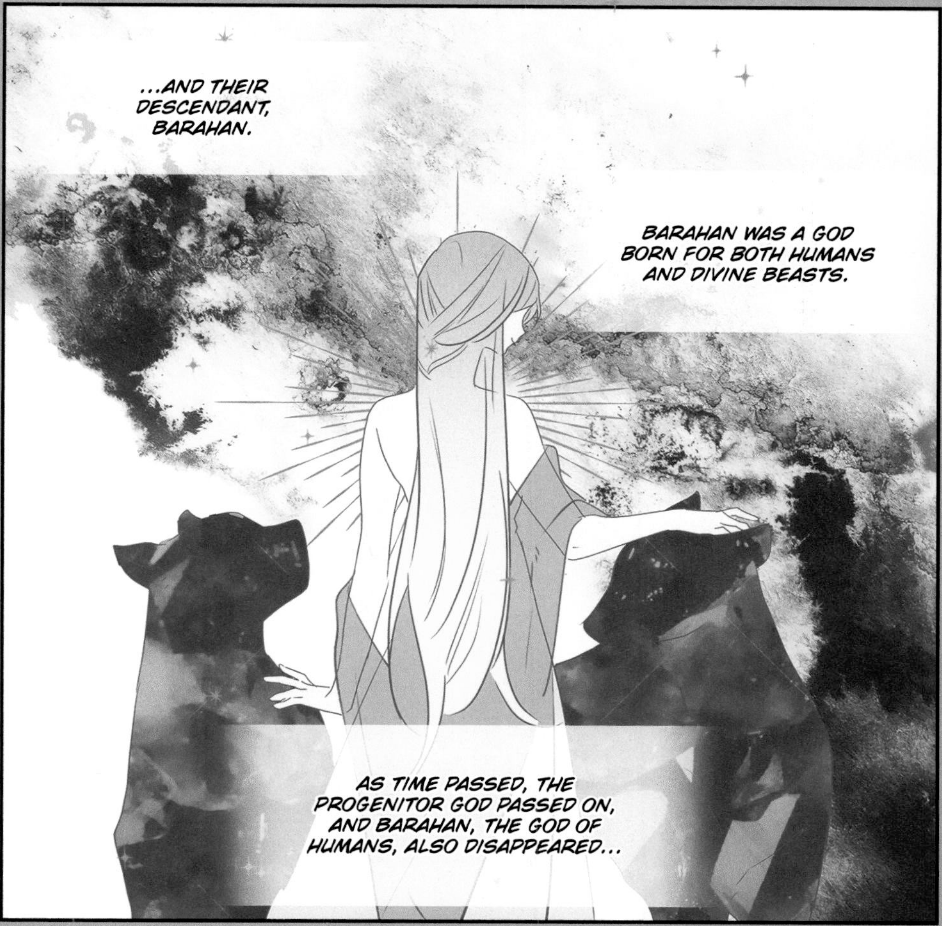
...AND THEIR DESCENDANT, BARAHAN.
BARAHAN WAS A GOD BORN FOR BOTH HUMANS AND DIVINE BEASTS.
AS TIME PASSED, THE PROGENITOR GOD PASSED ON, AND BARAHAN, THE GOD OF HUMANS, ALSO DISAPPEARED...

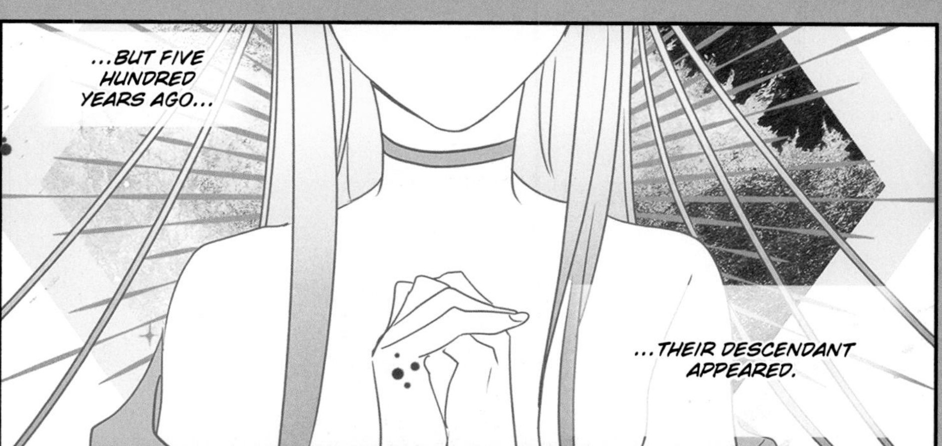
...BUT FIVE HUNDRED YEARS AGO...
...THEIR DESCENDANT APPEARED.

ALTHOUGH THEY WERE KILLED BY A BLACK DIVINE LEOPARD...

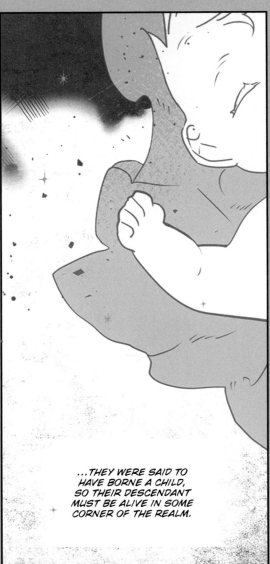

...THEY WERE SAID TO HAVE BORNE A CHILD, SO THEIR DESCENDANT MUST BE ALIVE IN SOME CORNER OF THE REALM.

ONCE THIS PERSON IS FOUND, HUMANS WILL AGAIN HOLD DOMINION OVER THE LAND.

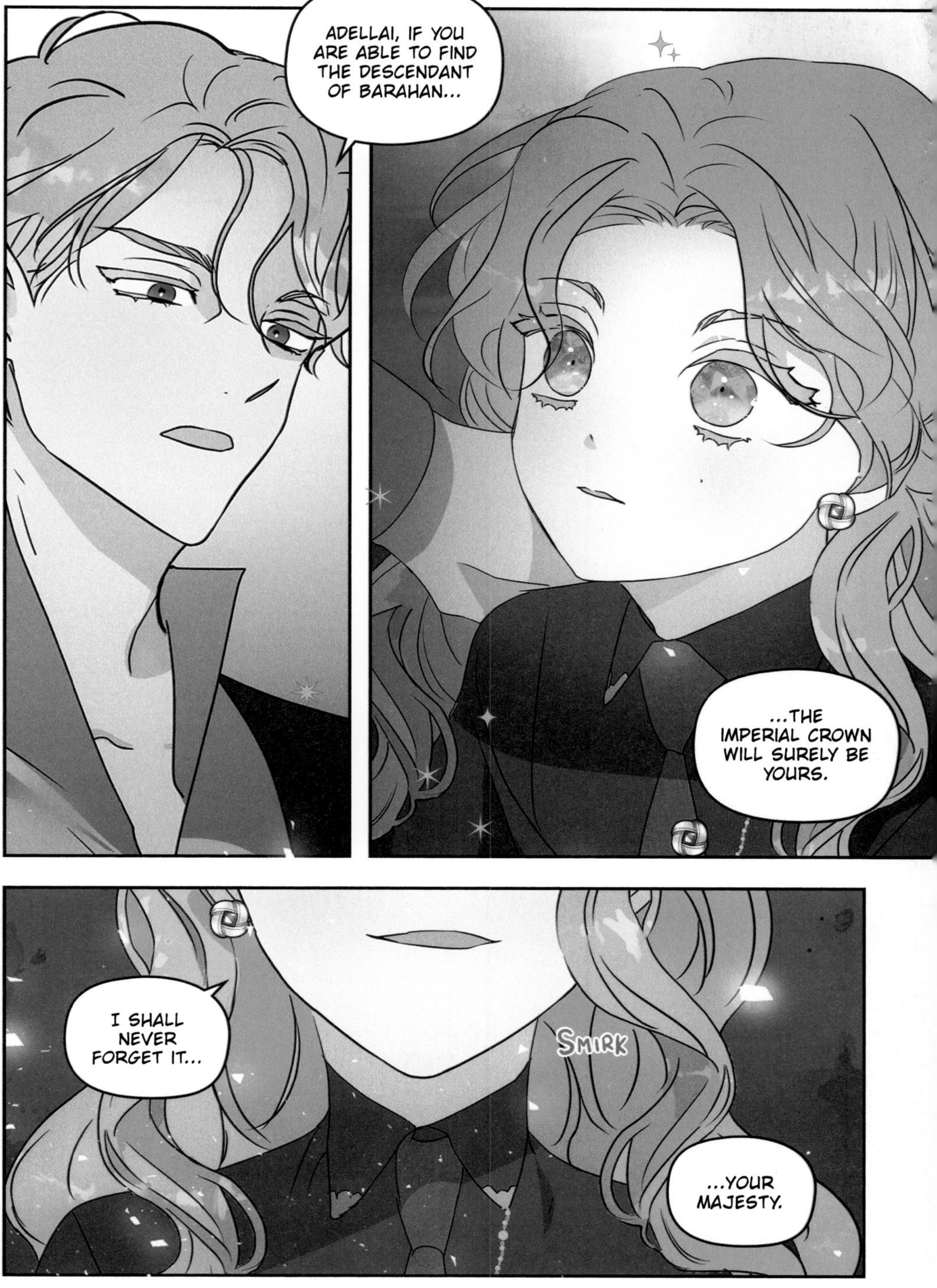
ADELLAI, IF YOU ARE ABLE TO FIND THE DESCENDANT OF BARAHAN...
...THE IMPERIAL CROWN WILL SURELY BE YOURS.
I SHALL NEVER FORGET IT...
SMIRK
...YOUR MAJESTY.

My
Gently
Raised
Beast

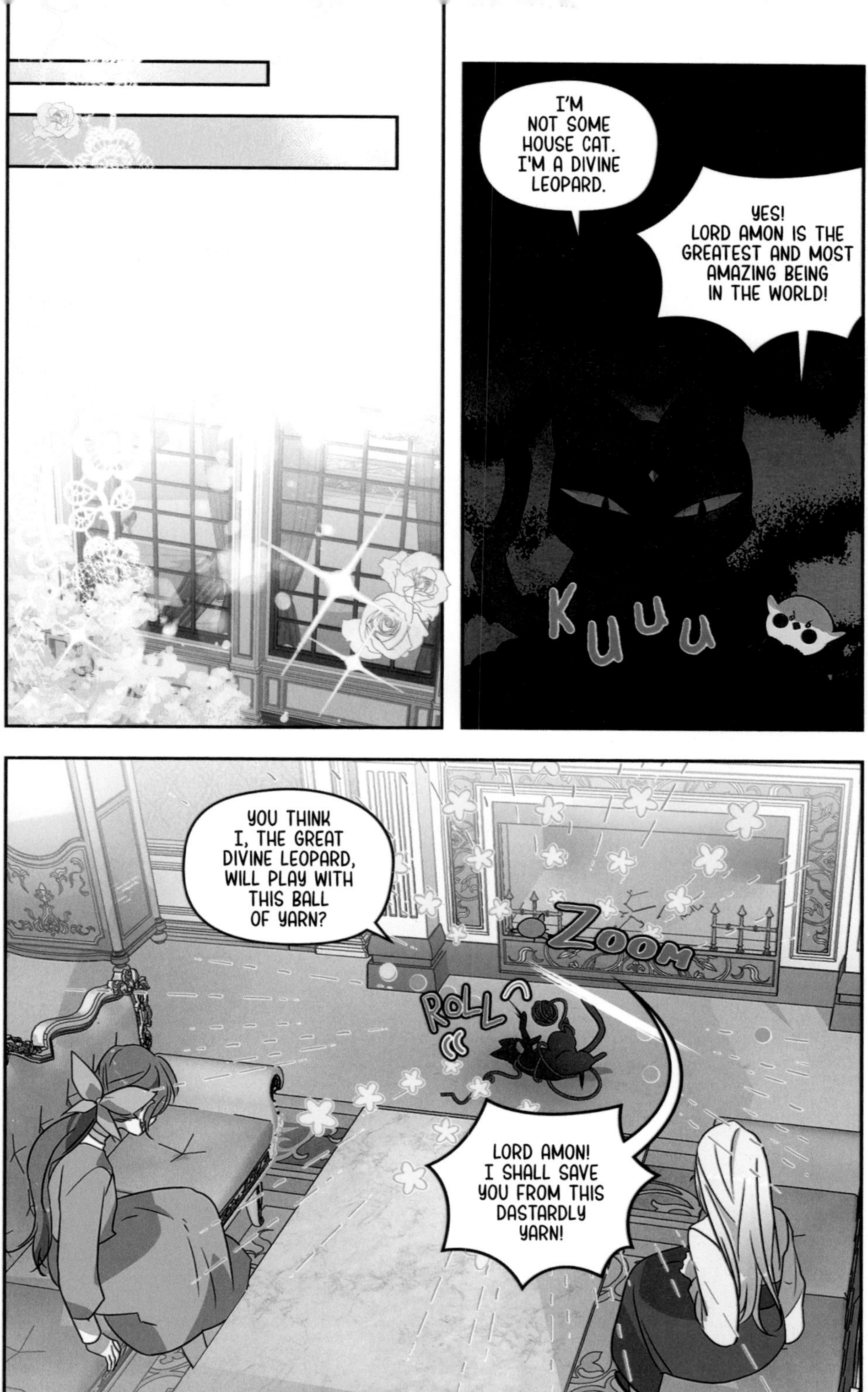
I'M NOT SOME HOUSE CAT. I'M A DIVINE LEOPARD.
YES! LORD AMON IS THE GREATEST AND MOST AMAZING BEING IN THE WORLD!
KUUU
YOU THINK I, THE GREAT DIVINE LEOPARD, WILL PLAY WITH THIS BALL OF YARN?
ZOOM
ROLL
LORD AMON! I SHALL SAVE YOU FROM THIS DASTARDLY YARN!

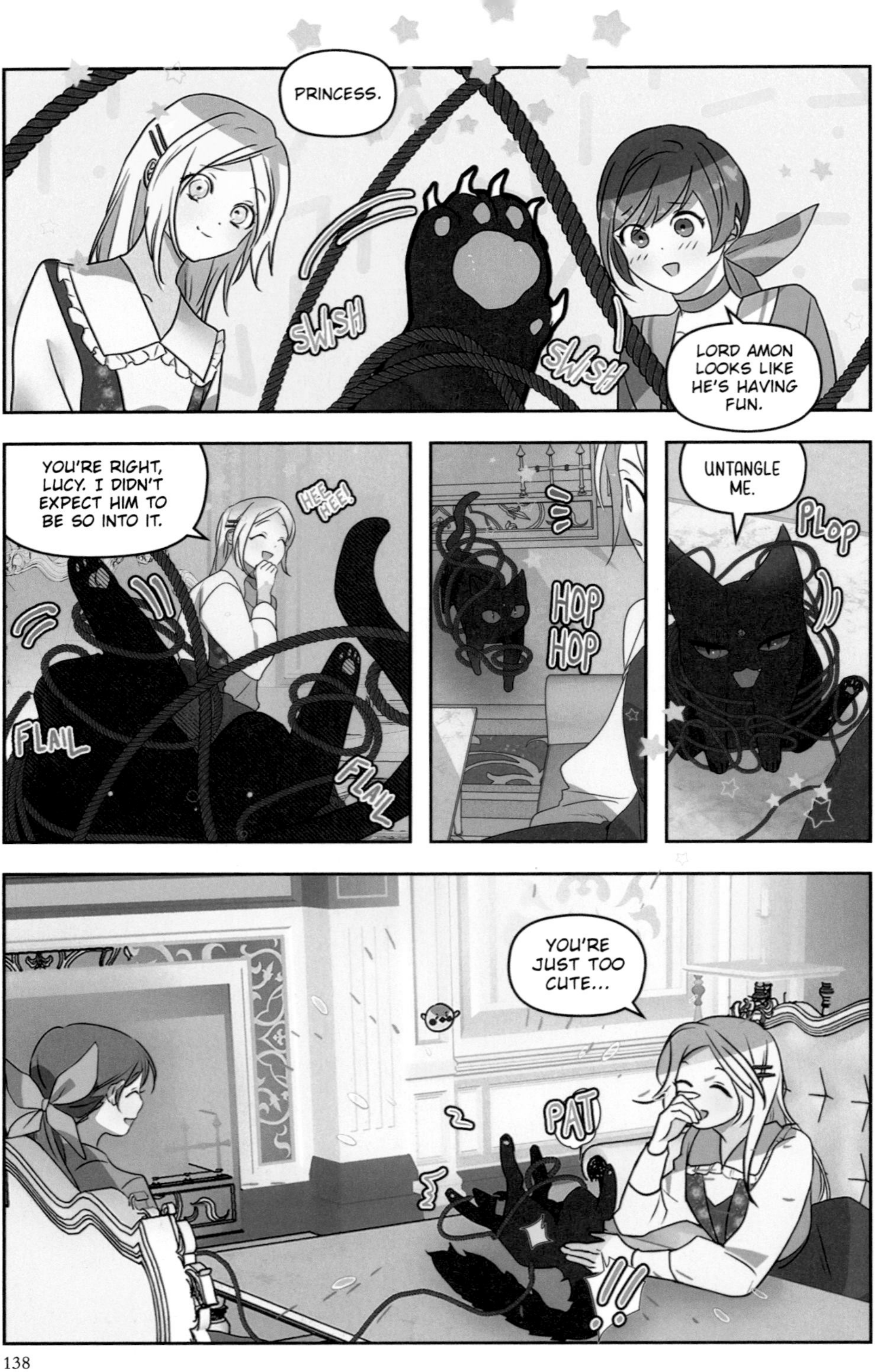
PRINCESS.
SWISH
SWISH
LORD AMON LOOKS LIKE HE'S HAVING FUN.
YOU'RE RIGHT, LUCY. I DIDN'T EXPECT HIM TO BE SO INTO IT.
HEE HEE!
FLAIL
FLAIL
HOP HOP
UNTANGLE ME.
PLOP
YOU'RE JUST TOO CUTE...
PAT

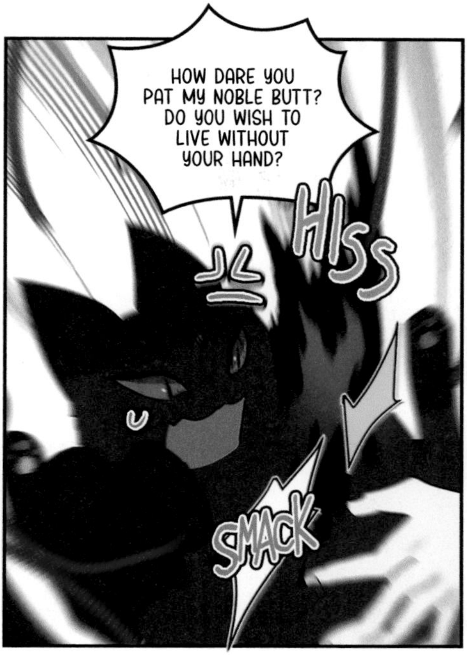
HOW DARE YOU PAT MY NOBLE BUTT? DO YOU WISH TO LIVE WITHOUT YOUR HAND?
HISS
SMACK

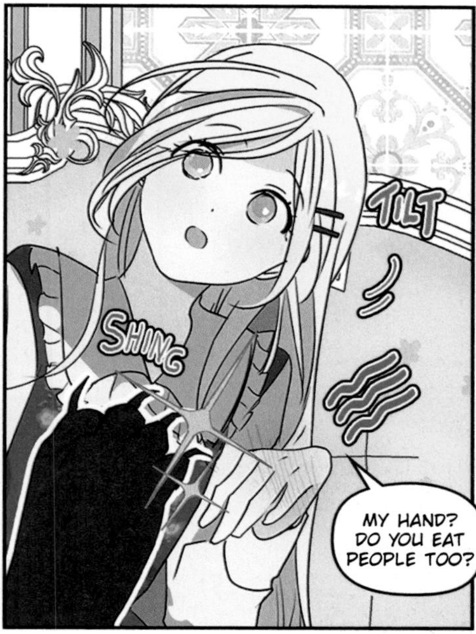
TILT
SHING
MY HAND? DO YOU EAT PEOPLE TOO?

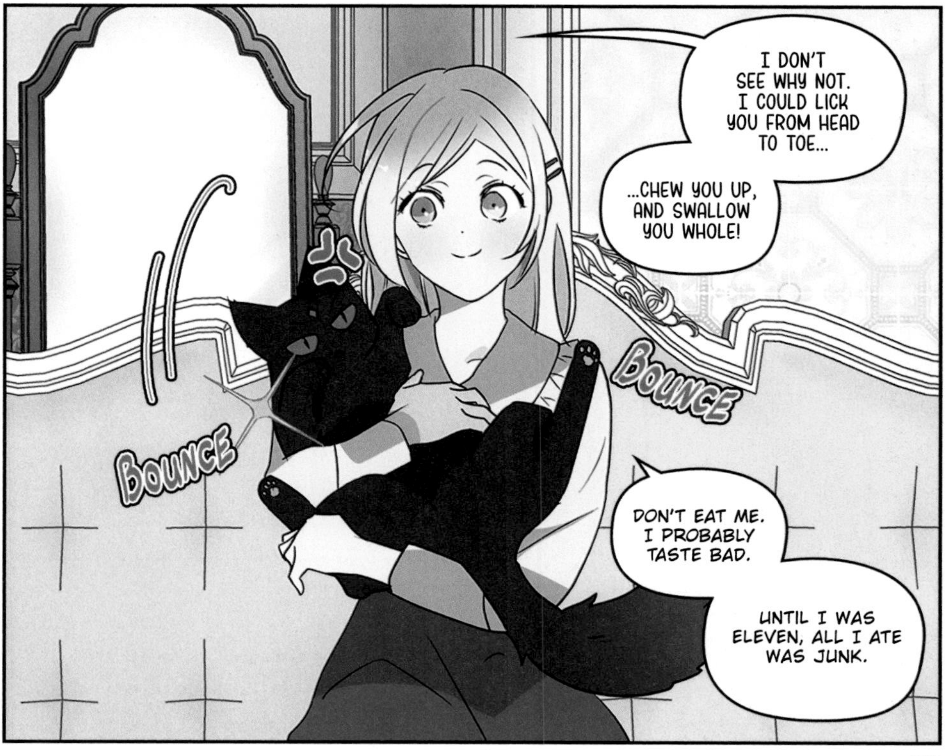
I DON'T SEE WHY NOT. I COULD LICK YOU FROM HEAD TO TOE...
...CHEW YOU UP, AND SWALLOW YOU WHOLE!
BOUNCE
BOUNCE
DON'T EAT ME. I PROBABLY TASTE BAD.
UNTIL I WAS ELEVEN, ALL I ATE WAS JUNK.

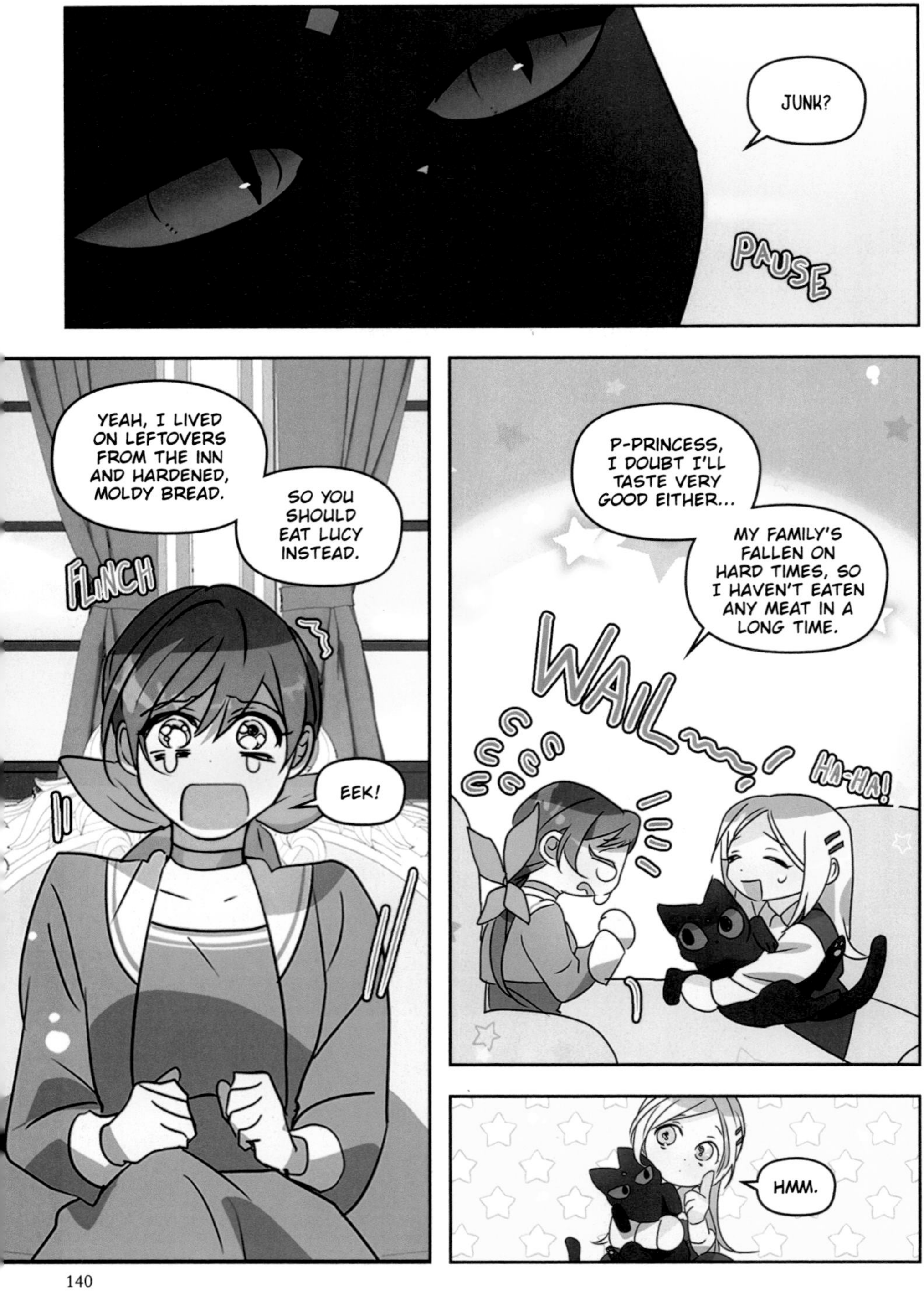
JUNK?
PAUSE
YEAH, I LIVED ON LEFTOVERS FROM THE INN AND HARDENED, MOLDY BREAD.
SO YOU SHOULD EAT LUCY INSTEAD.
FLINCH
EEK!
P-PRINCESS, I DOUBT I'LL TASTE VERY GOOD EITHER...
MY FAMILY'S FALLEN ON HARD TIMES, SO I HAVEN'T EATEN ANY MEAT IN A LONG TIME.
WAIL
HA-HA!
HMM.

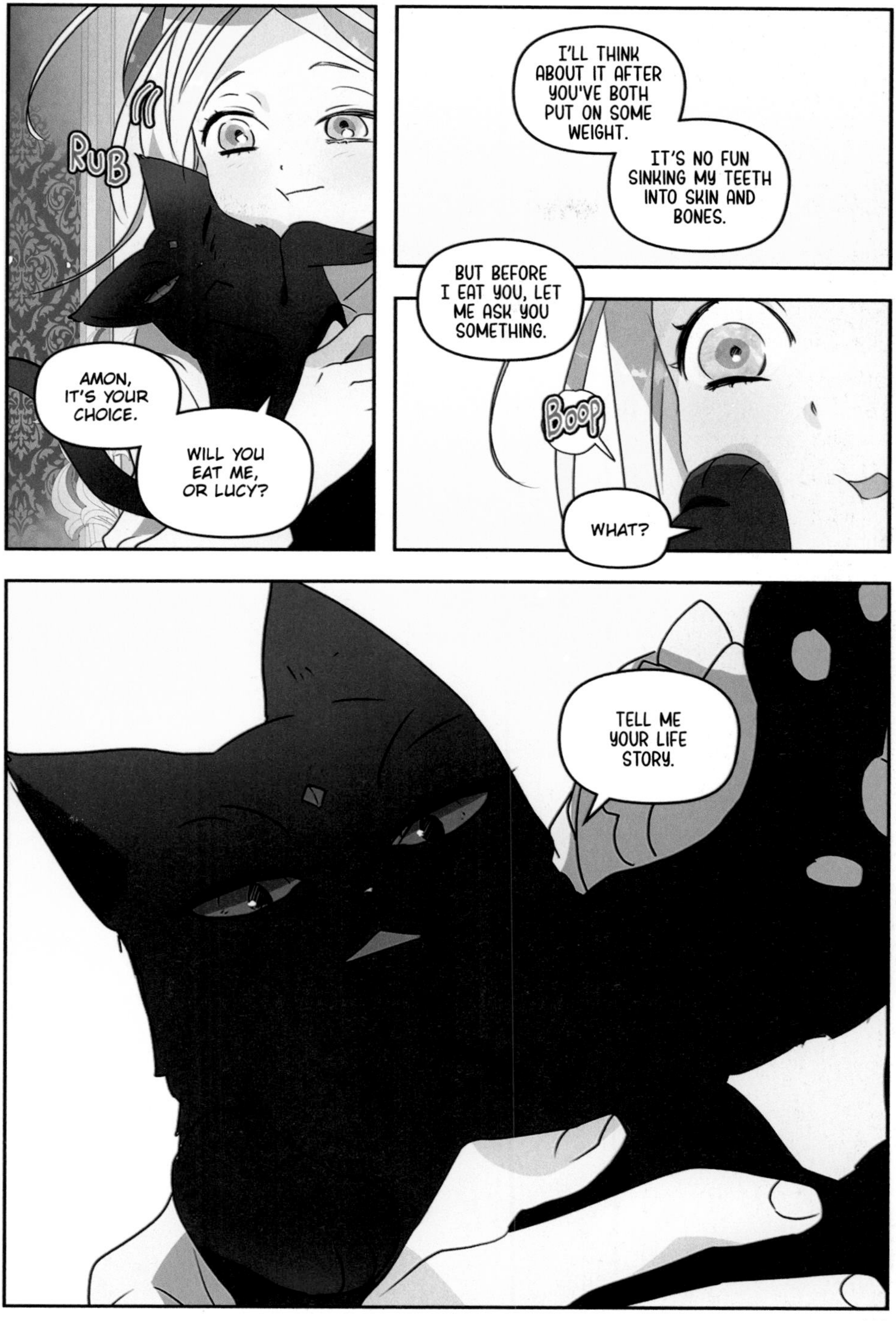
RUB
AMON, IT'S YOUR CHOICE.
WILL YOU EAT ME, OR LUCY?
I'LL THINK ABOUT IT AFTER YOU'VE BOTH PUT ON SOME WEIGHT.
IT'S NO FUN SINKING MY TEETH INTO SKIN AND BONES.
BUT BEFORE I EAT YOU, LET ME ASK YOU SOMETHING.
BOOP
WHAT?
TELL ME YOUR LIFE STORY.

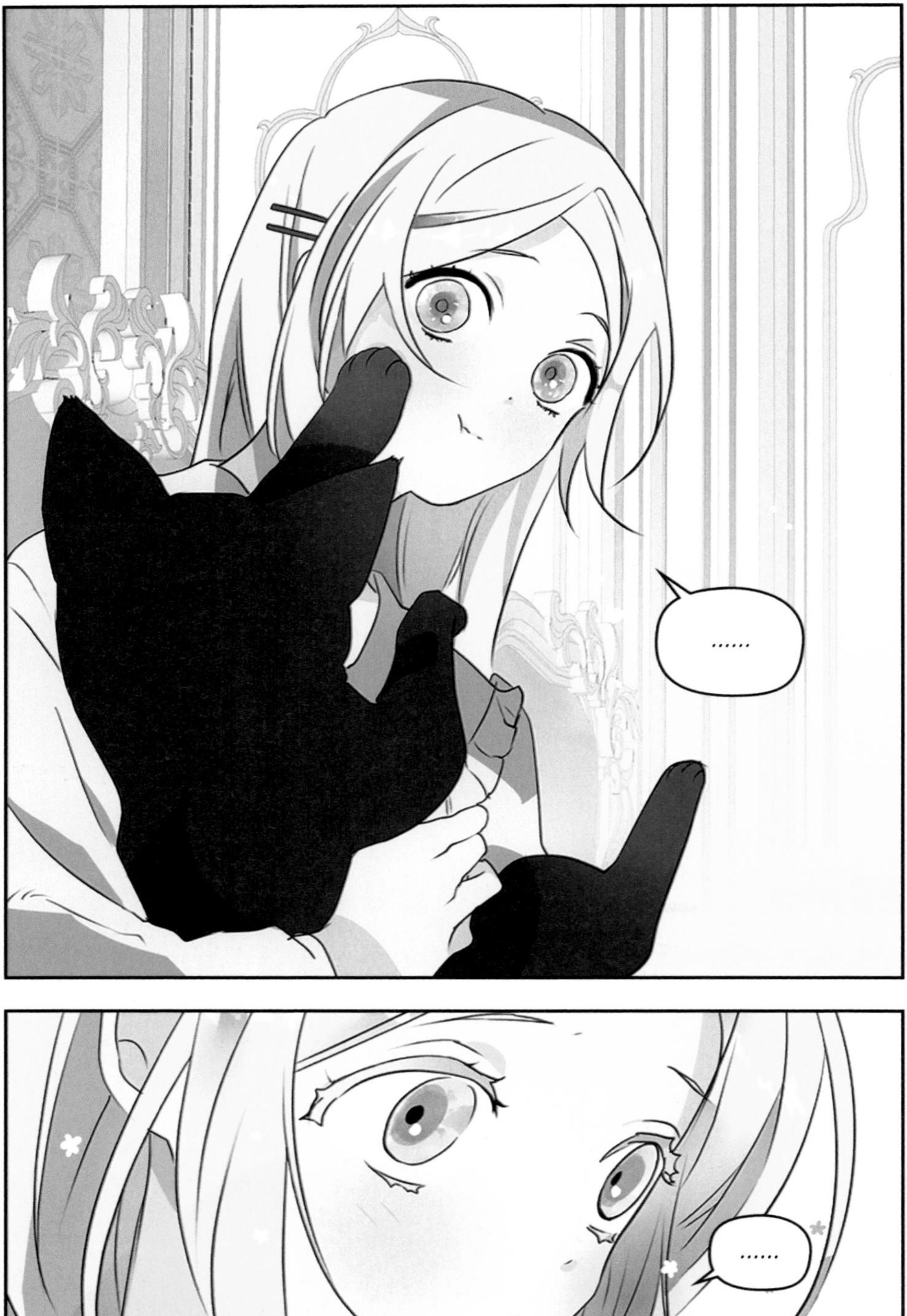
......
......

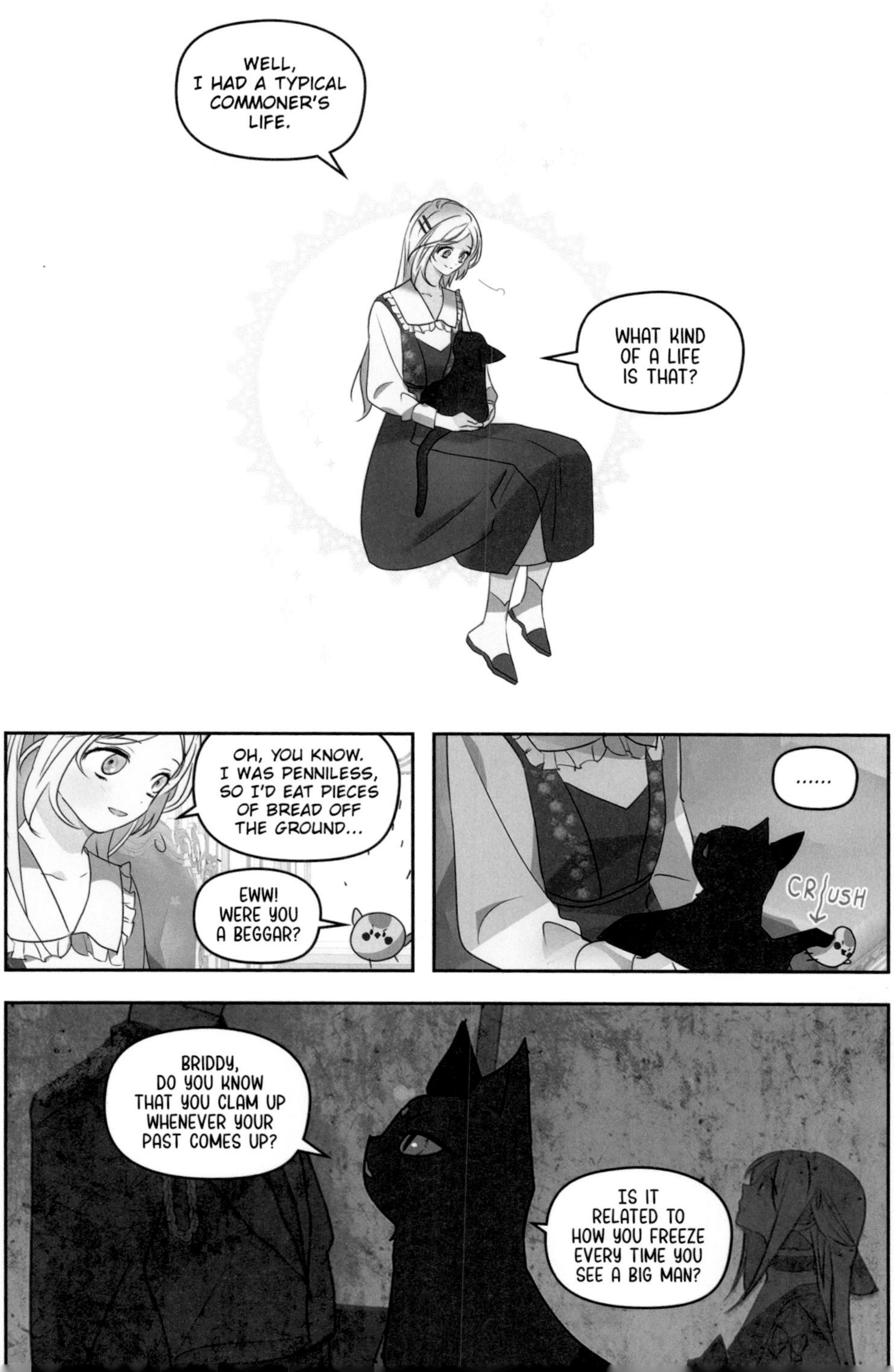

WELL, I HAD A TYPICAL COMMONER'S LIFE.
WHAT KIND OF A LIFE IS THAT?
OH, YOU KNOW. I WAS PENNILESS, SO I'D EAT PIECES OF BREAD OFF THE GROUND...
EWW! WERE YOU A BEGGAR?
......
CRUSH
BRIDDY, DO YOU KNOW THAT YOU CLAM UP WHENEVER YOUR PAST COMES UP?
IS IT RELATED TO HOW YOU FREEZE EVERY TIME YOU SEE A BIG MAN?

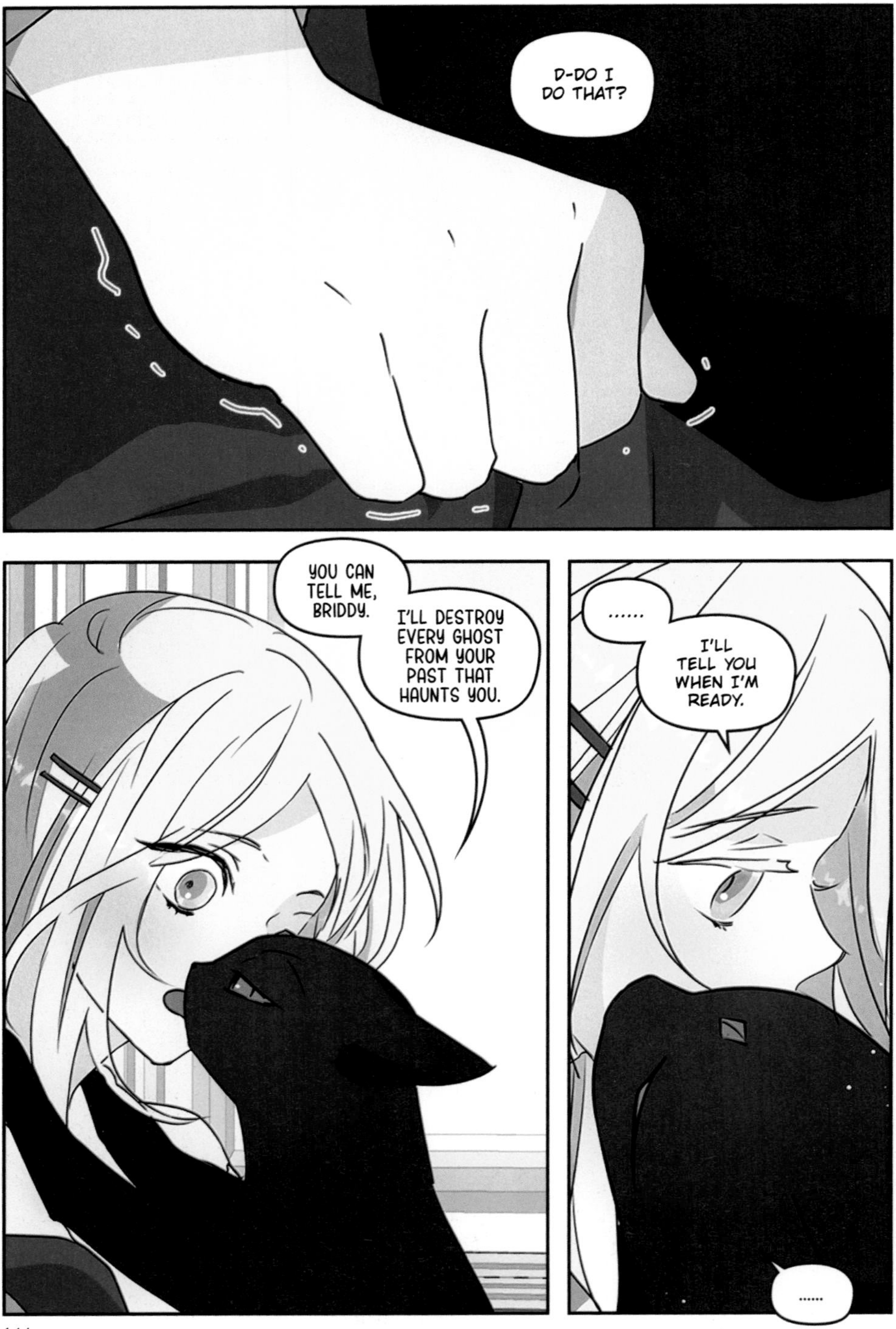

D-DO I DO THAT?
YOU CAN TELL ME, BRIDDY.
I'LL DESTROY EVERY GHOST FROM YOUR PAST THAT HAUNTS YOU.
......
I'LL TELL YOU WHEN I'M READY.
......

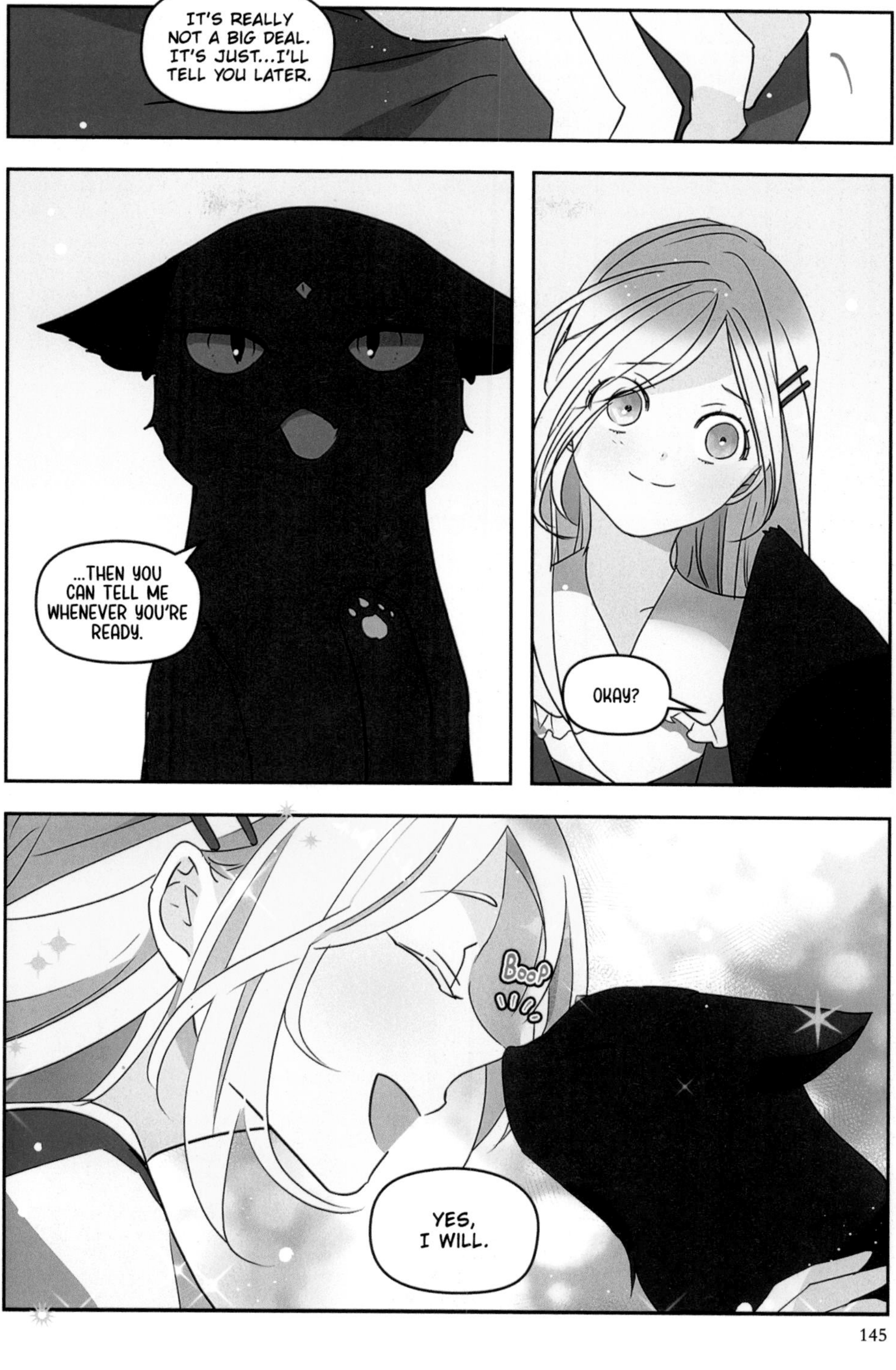
IT'S REALLY NOT A BIG DEAL. IT'S JUST...I'LL TELL YOU LATER.
...THEN YOU CAN TELL ME WHENEVER YOU'RE READY.
OKAY?
BOOP
YES, I WILL.

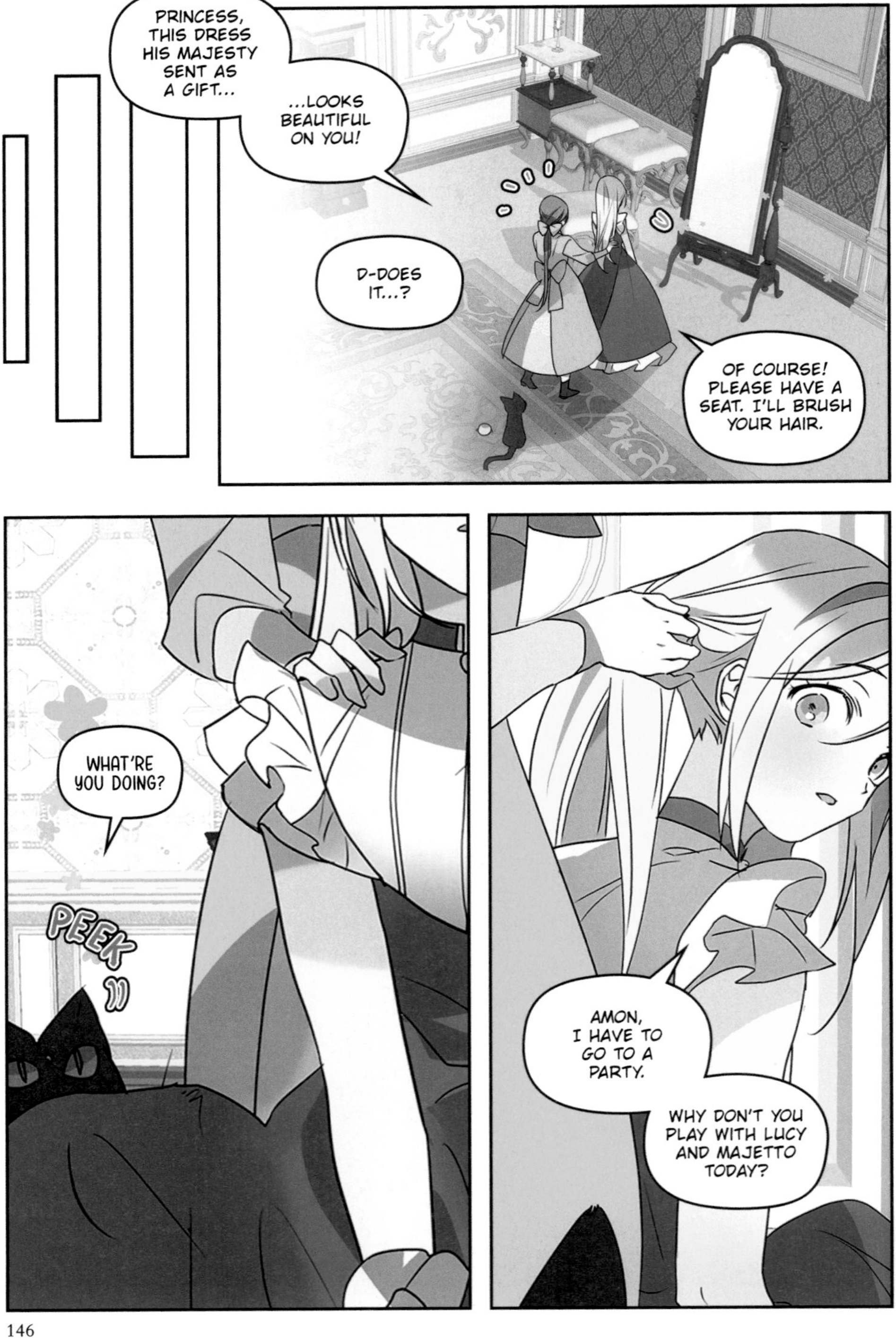
PRINCESS, THIS DRESS HIS MAJESTY SENT AS A GIFT...
...LOOKS BEAUTIFUL ON YOU!
D-DOES IT...?
OF COURSE! PLEASE HAVE A SEAT. I'LL BRUSH YOUR HAIR.
WHAT'RE YOU DOING?
PEEK
AMON, I HAVE TO GO TO A PARTY.
WHY DON'T YOU PLAY WITH LUCY AND MAJETTO TODAY?

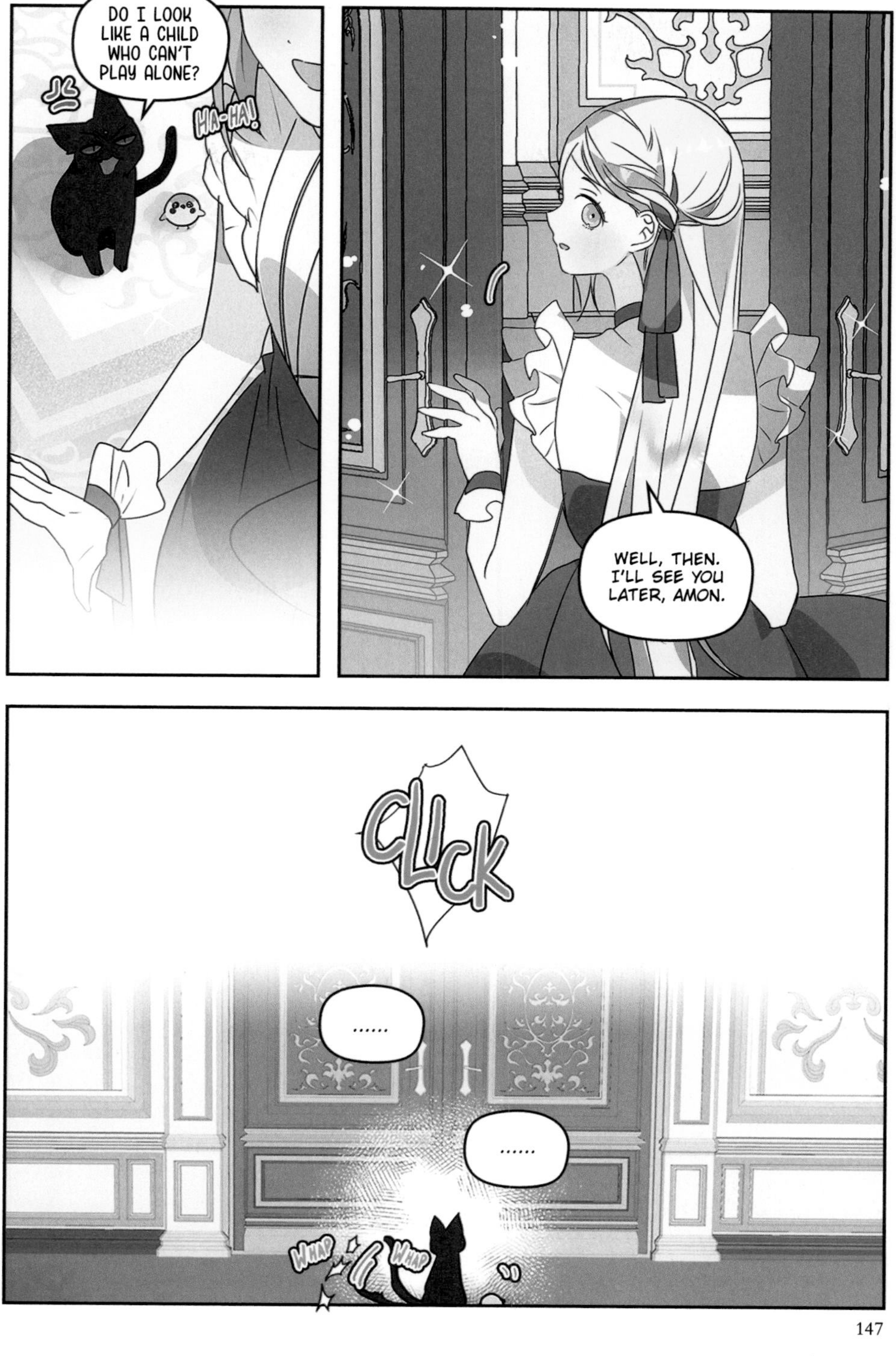
DO I LOOK LIKE A CHILD WHO CAN'T PLAY ALONE?
HA-HA!
WELL, THEN. I'LL SEE YOU LATER, AMON.
CLICK
......
......
WHAP
WHAP

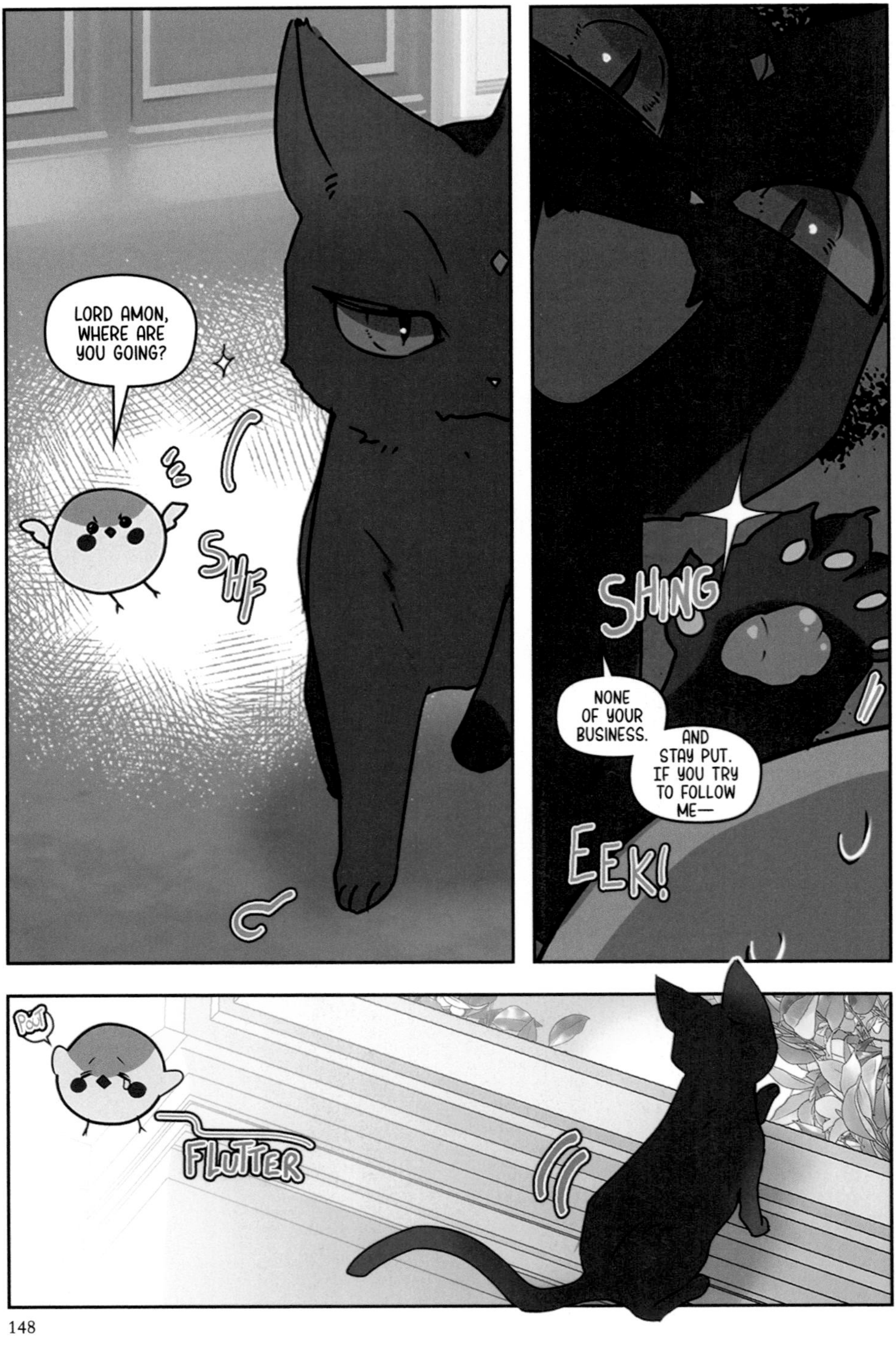

LORD AMON, WHERE ARE YOU GOING?
SHF
SHING
NONE OF YOUR BUSINESS.
AND STAY PUT. IF YOU TRY TO FOLLOW ME—
EEK!
POUT
FLUTTER

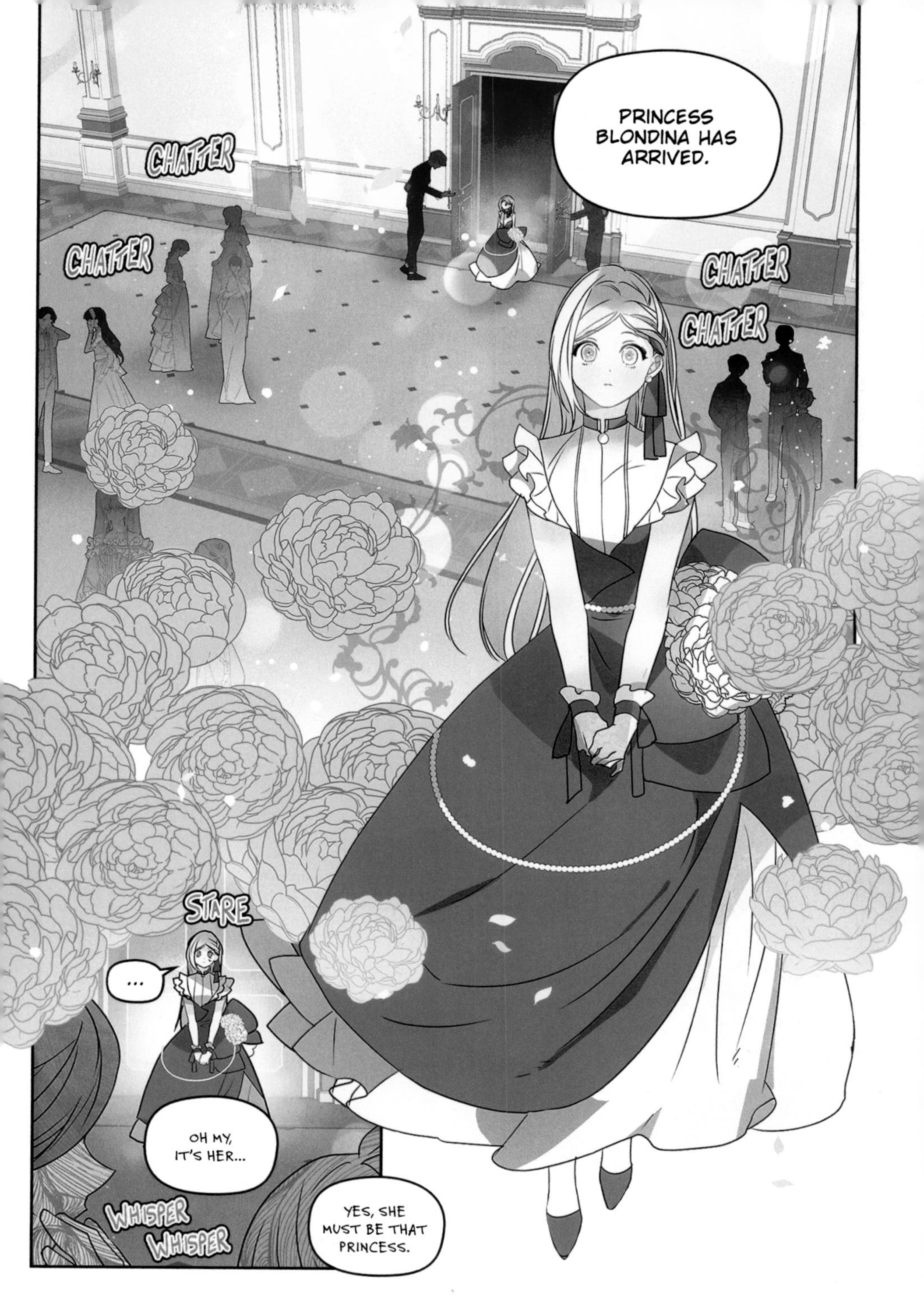
PRINCESS BLONDINA HAS ARRIVED.
CHATTER
CHATTER
CHATTER
CHATTER
STARE
...
OH MY, IT'S HER...
WHISPER WHISPER
YES, SHE MUST BE THAT PRINCESS.

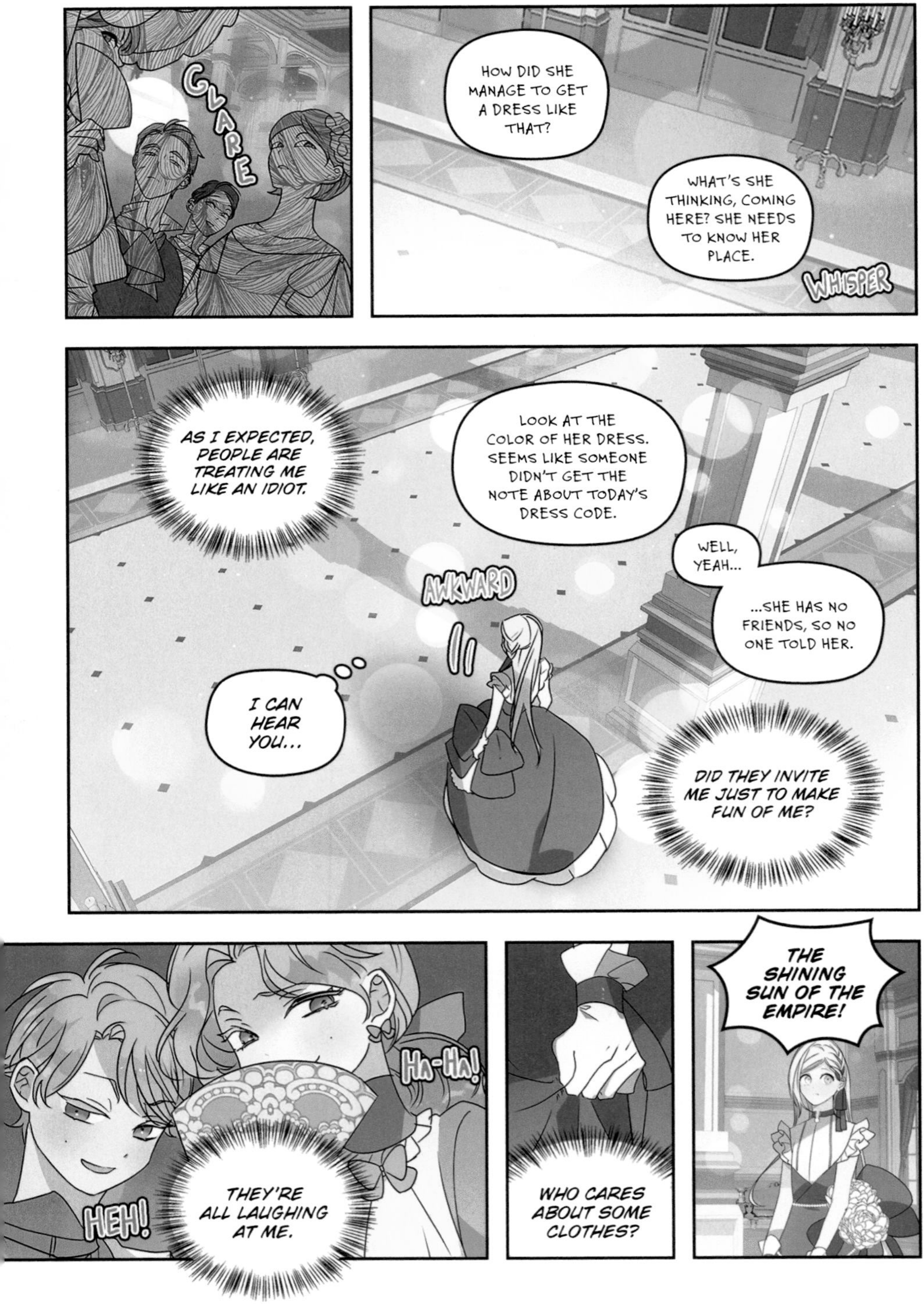
GLARE
HOW DID SHE MANAGE TO GET A DRESS LIKE THAT?
WHAT'S SHE THINKING, COMING HERE? SHE NEEDS TO KNOW HER PLACE.
WHISPER
AS I EXPECTED, PEOPLE ARE TREATING ME LIKE AN IDIOT.
LOOK AT THE COLOR OF HER DRESS. SEEMS LIKE SOMEONE DIDN'T GET THE NOTE ABOUT TODAY'S DRESS CODE.
WELL, YEAH...
...SHE HAS NO FRIENDS, SO NO ONE TOLD HER.
AWKWARD
I CAN HEAR YOU...
DID THEY INVITE ME JUST TO MAKE FUN OF ME?
HA-HA!
HEH!
THEY'RE ALL LAUGHING AT ME.
WHO CARES ABOUT SOME CLOTHES?
THE SHINING SUN OF THE EMPIRE!

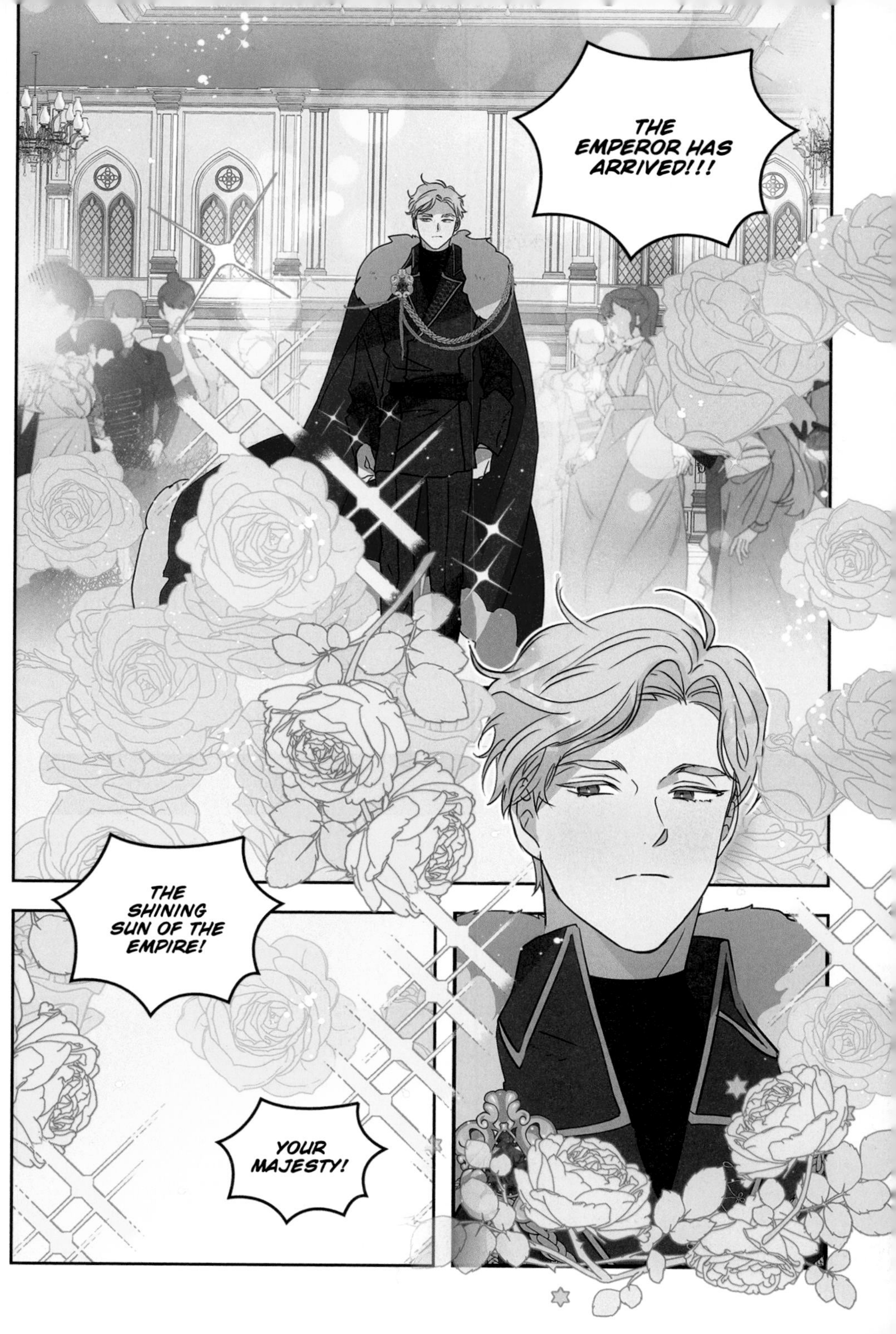
THE EMPEROR HAS ARRIVED!!!
THE SHINING SUN OF THE EMPIRE!
YOUR MAJESTY!

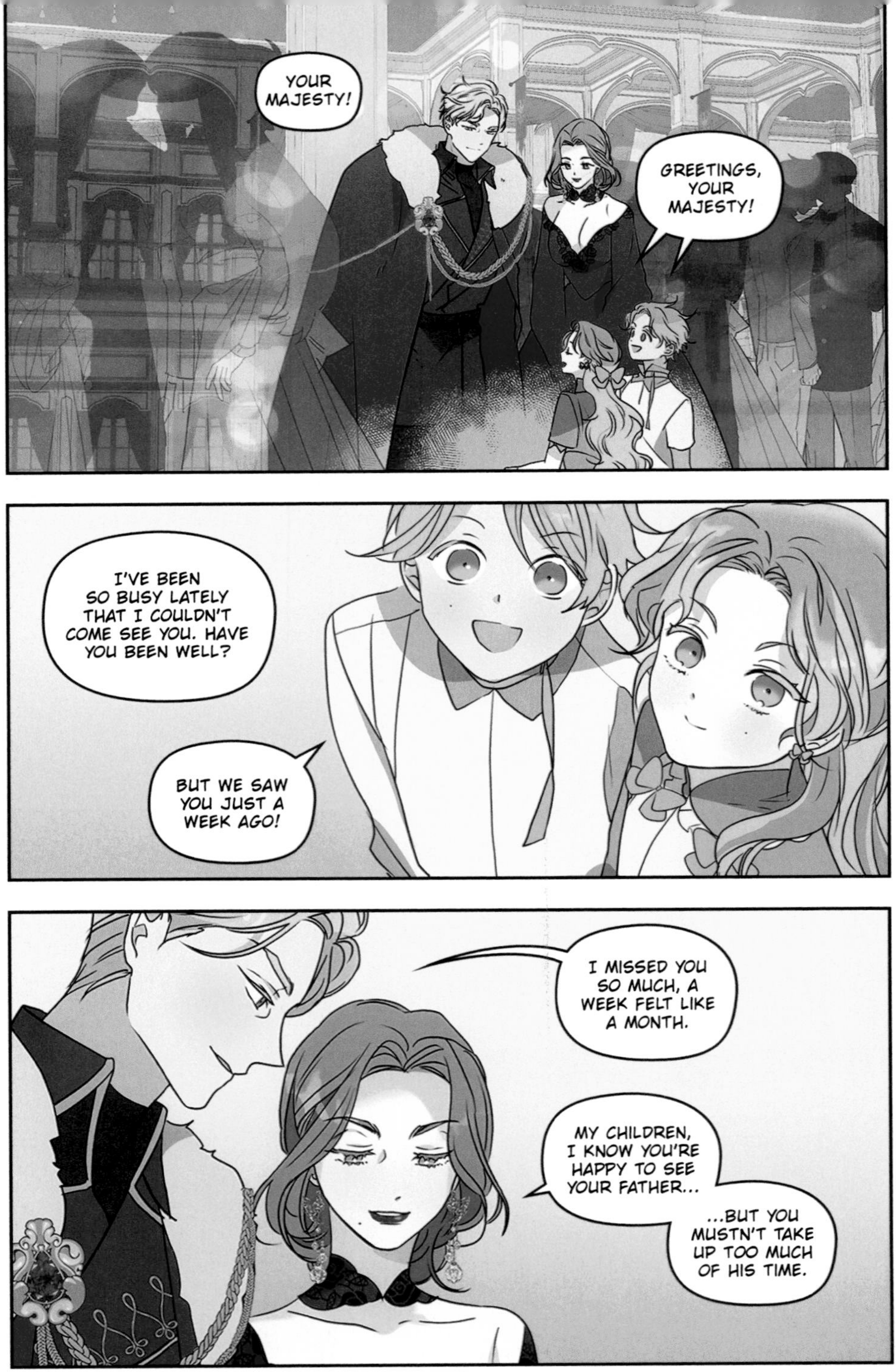
YOUR MAJESTY!
GREETINGS, YOUR MAJESTY!
I'VE BEEN SO BUSY LATELY THAT I COULDN'T COME SEE YOU. HAVE YOU BEEN WELL?
BUT WE SAW YOU JUST A WEEK AGO!
I MISSED YOU SO MUCH, A WEEK FELT LIKE A MONTH.
MY CHILDREN, I KNOW YOU'RE HAPPY TO SEE YOUR FATHER...
...BUT YOU MUSTN'T TAKE UP TOO MUCH OF HIS TIME.

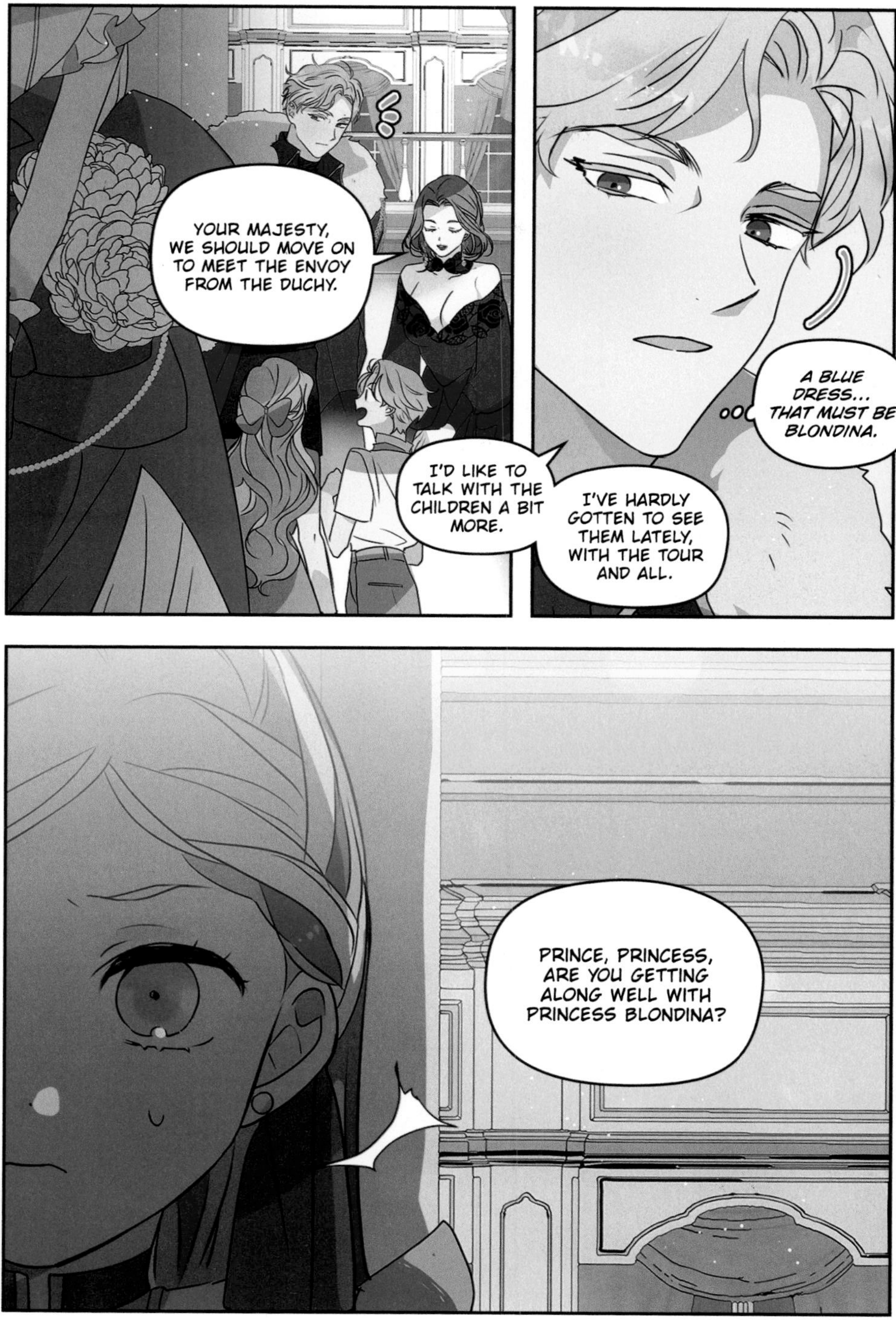
YOUR MAJESTY, WE SHOULD MOVE ON TO MEET THE ENVOY FROM THE DUCHY.
I'D LIKE TO TALK WITH THE CHILDREN A BIT MORE.
I'VE HARDLY GOTTEN TO SEE THEM LATELY, WITH THE TOUR AND ALL.
A BLUE DRESS... THAT MUST BE BLONDINA.
PRINCE, PRINCESS, ARE YOU GETTING ALONG WELL WITH PRINCESS BLONDINA?

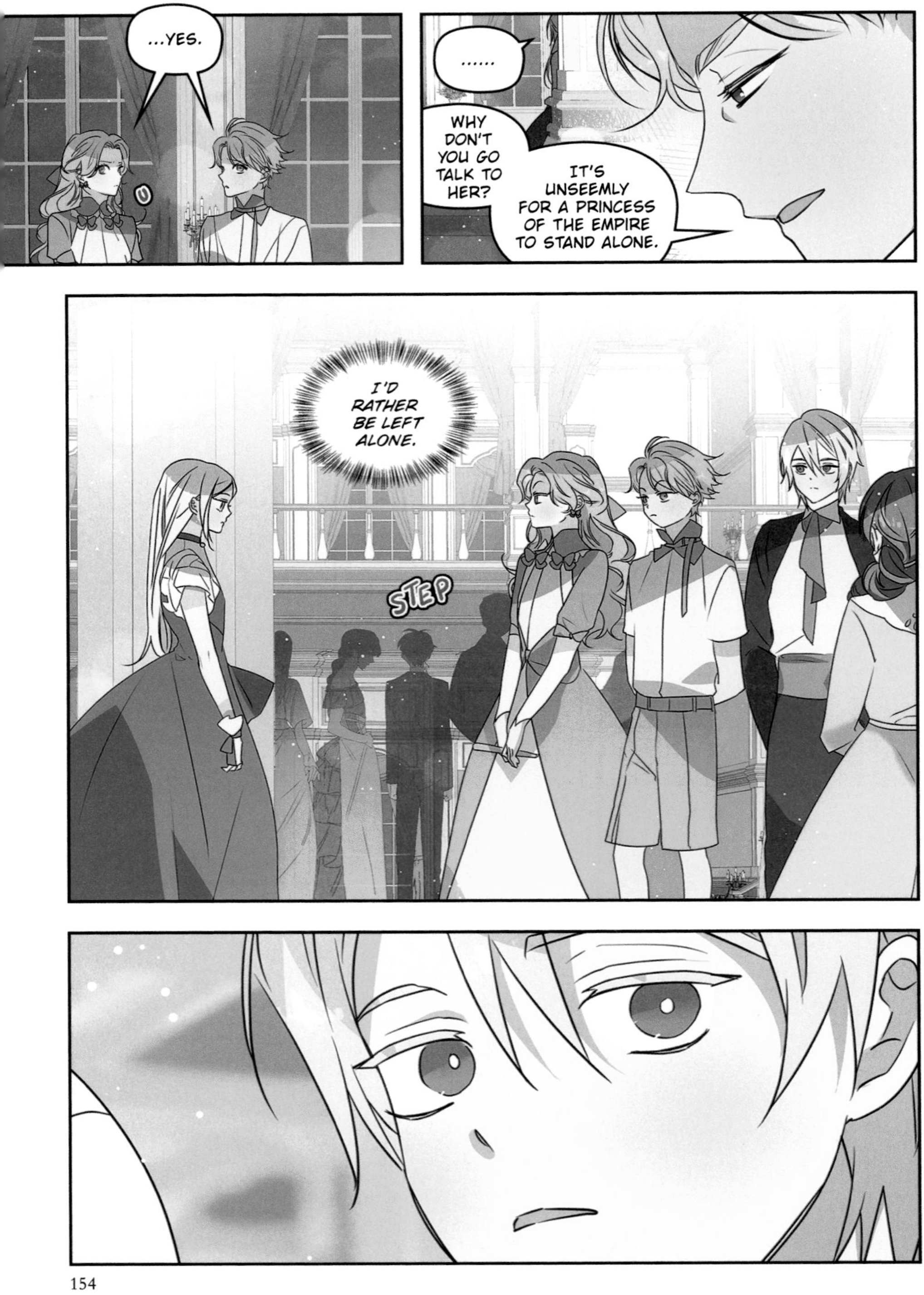

...YES.
U
......
WHY DON'T YOU GO TALK TO HER?
IT'S UNSEEMLY FOR A PRINCESS OF THE EMPIRE TO STAND ALONE.
I'D RATHER BE LEFT ALONE.
STEP

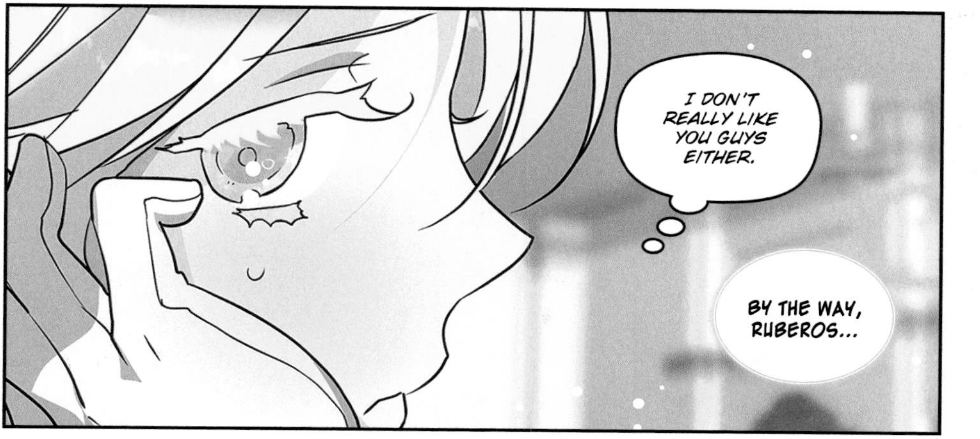
I DON'T REALLY LIKE YOU GUYS EITHER.
BY THE WAY, RUBEROS...

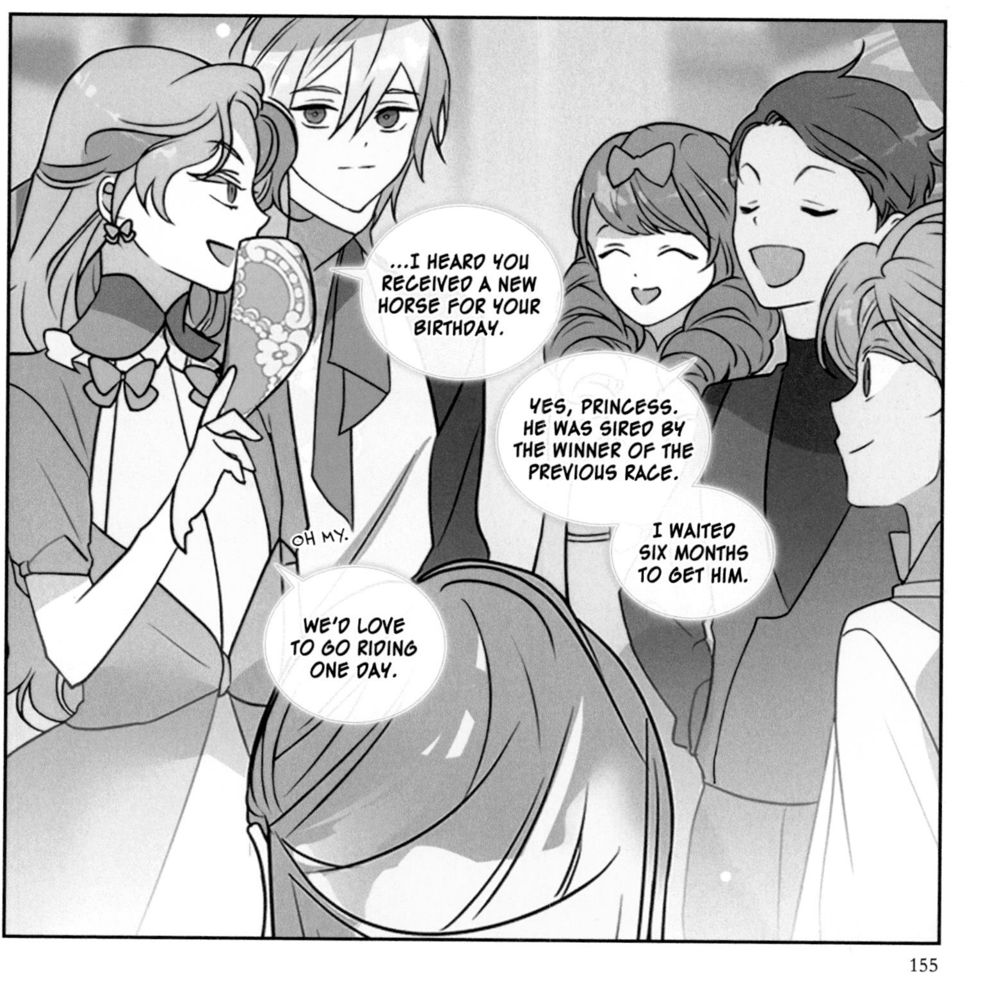
...I HEARD YOU RECEIVED A NEW HORSE FOR YOUR BIRTHDAY.
YES, PRINCESS. HE WAS SIRED BY THE WINNER OF THE PREVIOUS RACE.
I WAITED SIX MONTHS TO GET HIM.
OH MY.
WE'D LOVE TO GO RIDING ONE DAY.

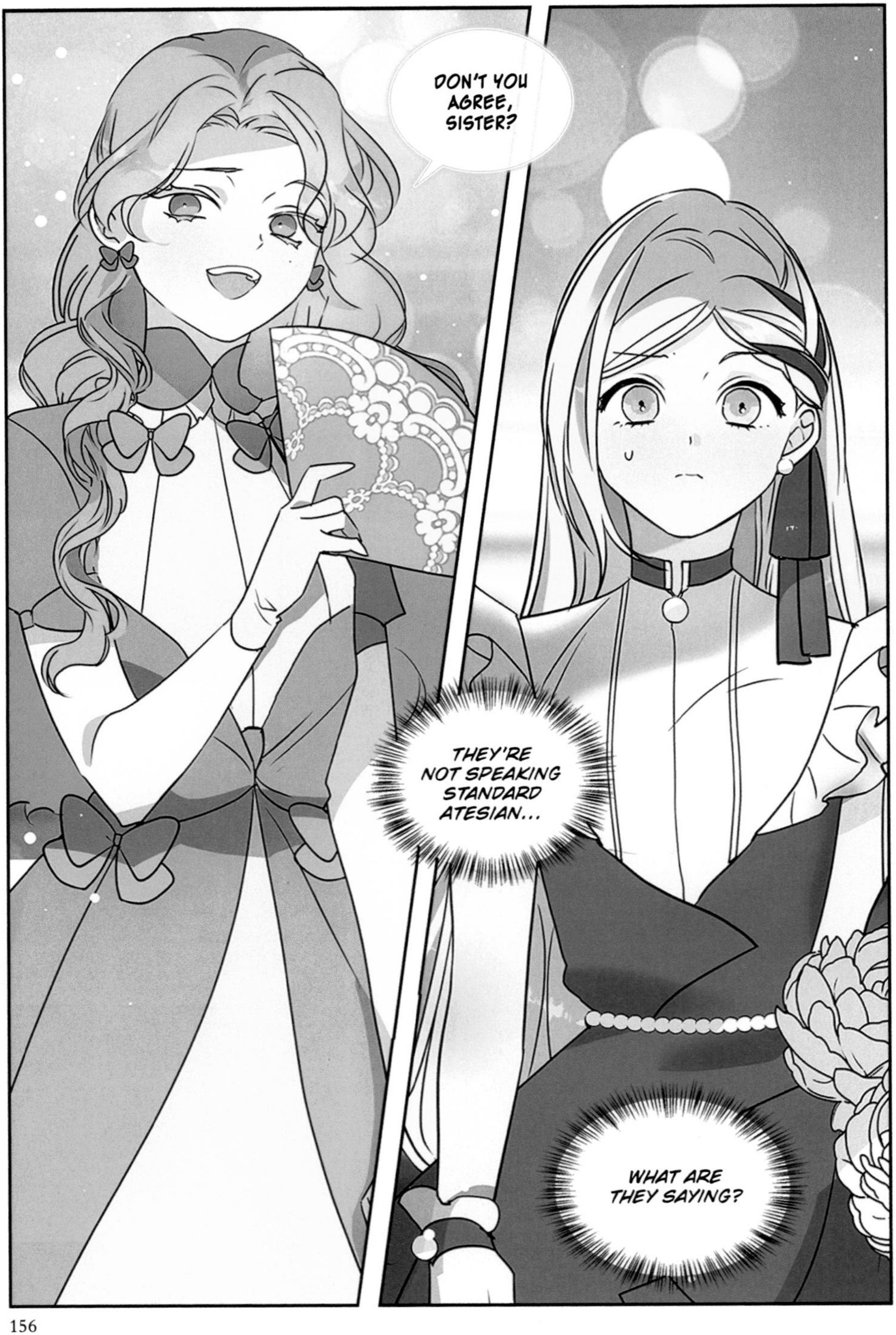

DON'T YOU AGREE, SISTER?
THEY'RE NOT SPEAKING STANDARD ATESIAN...
WHAT ARE THEY SAYING?

My Gently Raised Beast

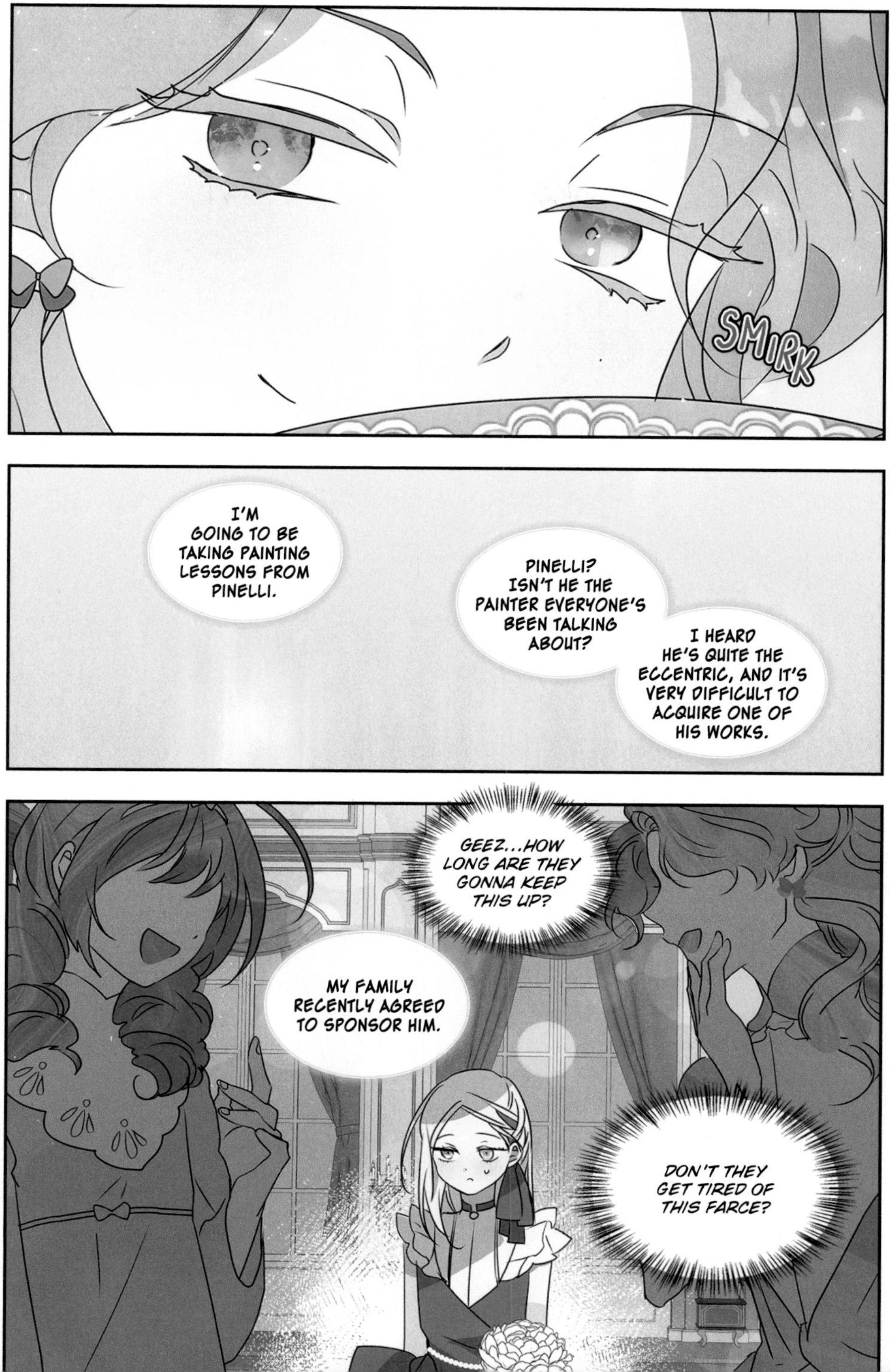
SMIRK
I'M GOING TO BE TAKING PAINTING LESSONS FROM PINELLI.
PINELLI? ISN'T HE THE PAINTER EVERYONE'S BEEN TALKING ABOUT?
I HEARD HE'S QUITE THE ECCENTRIC, AND IT'S VERY DIFFICULT TO ACQUIRE ONE OF HIS WORKS.
GEEZ...HOW LONG ARE THEY GONNA KEEP THIS UP?
MY FAMILY RECENTLY AGREED TO SPONSOR HIM.
DON'T THEY GET TIRED OF THIS FARCE?

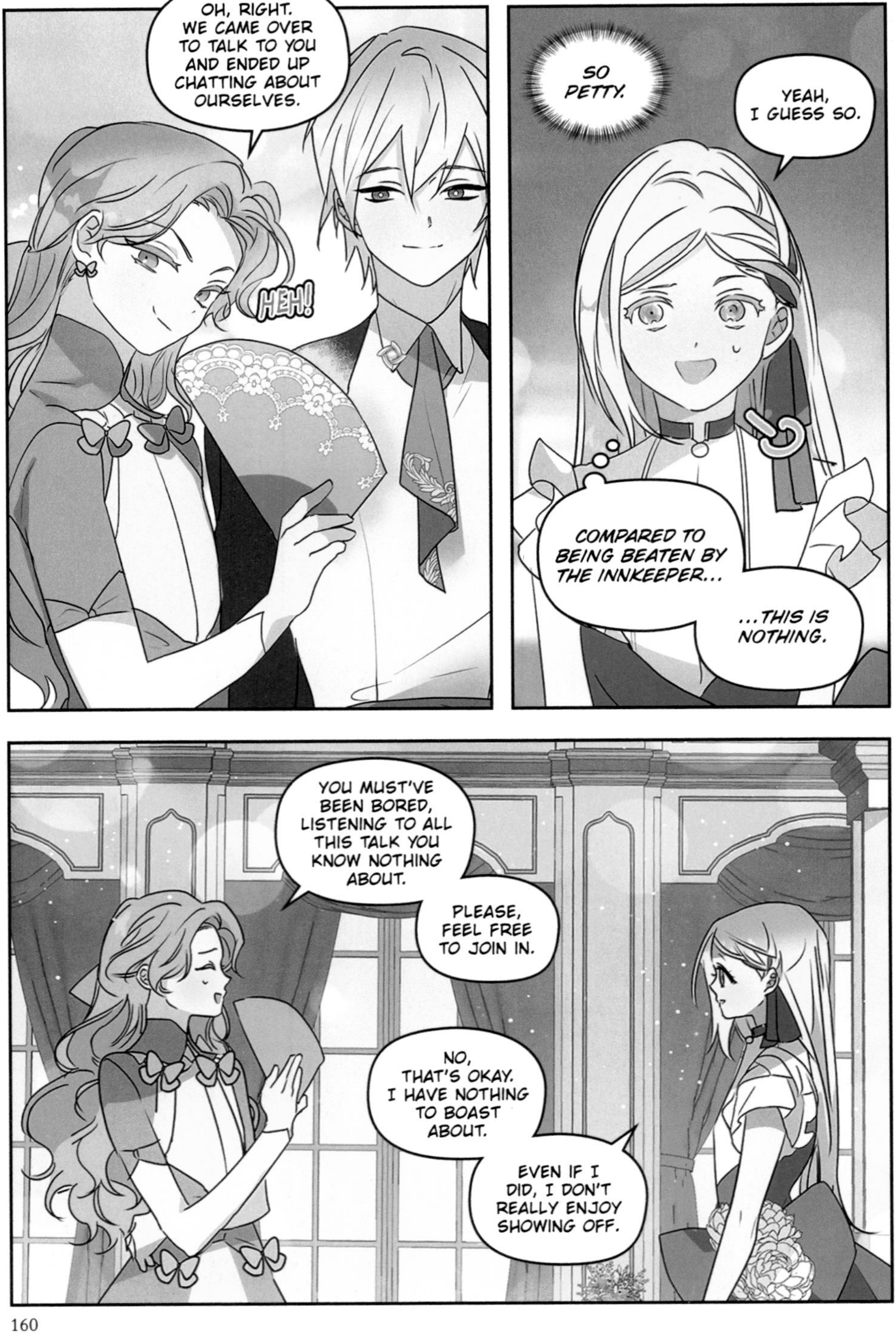
OH, RIGHT. WE CAME OVER TO TALK TO YOU AND ENDED UP CHATTING ABOUT OURSELVES.
HEH!
SO PETTY.
YEAH, I GUESS SO.
COMPARED TO BEING BEATEN BY THE INNKEEPER...
...THIS IS NOTHING.
YOU MUST'VE BEEN BORED, LISTENING TO ALL THIS TALK YOU KNOW NOTHING ABOUT.
PLEASE, FEEL FREE TO JOIN IN.
NO, THAT'S OKAY. I HAVE NOTHING TO BOAST ABOUT.
EVEN IF I DID, I DON'T REALLY ENJOY SHOWING OFF.

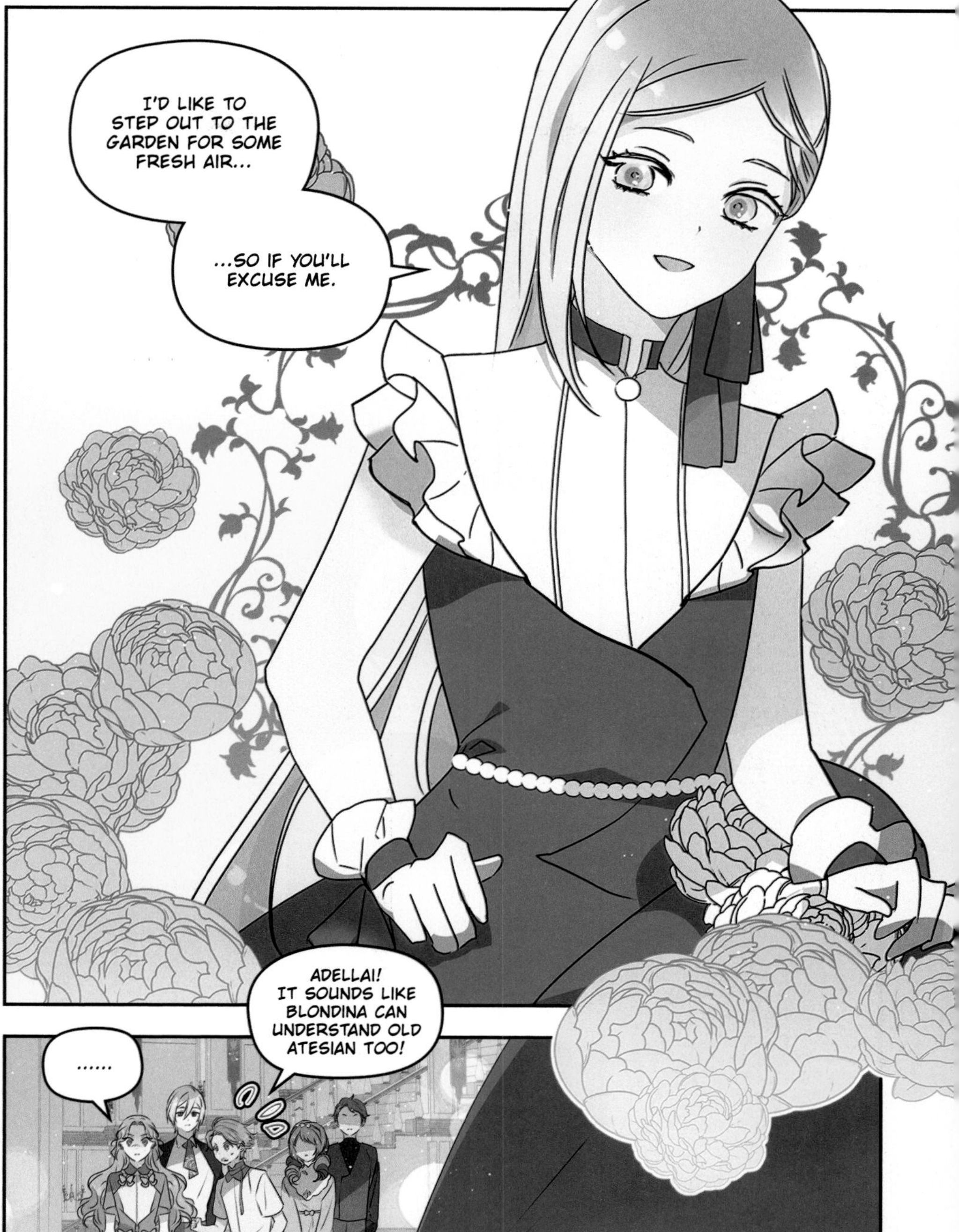

I'D LIKE TO STEP OUT TO THE GARDEN FOR SOME FRESH AIR...
...SO IF YOU'LL EXCUSE ME.
ADELLAI! IT SOUNDS LIKE BLONDINA CAN UNDERSTAND OLD ATESIAN TOO!
......

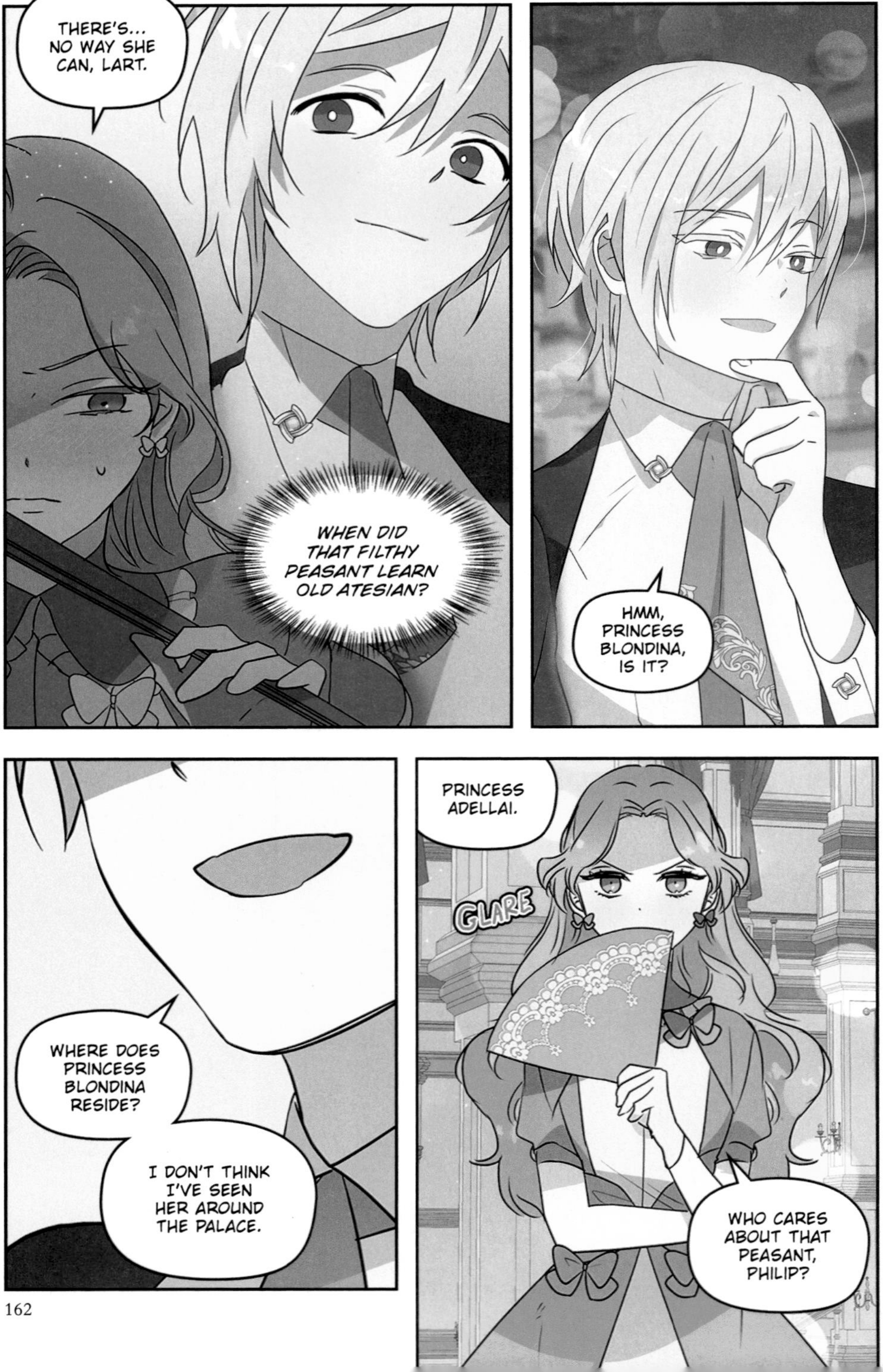
THERE'S... NO WAY SHE CAN, LART.
WHEN DID THAT FILTHY PEASANT LEARN OLD ATESIAN?
HMM, PRINCESS BLONDINA, IS IT?
WHERE DOES PRINCESS BLONDINA RESIDE?
I DON'T THINK I'VE SEEN HER AROUND THE PALACE.
PRINCESS ADELLAI.
GLARE
WHO CARES ABOUT THAT PEASANT, PHILIP?

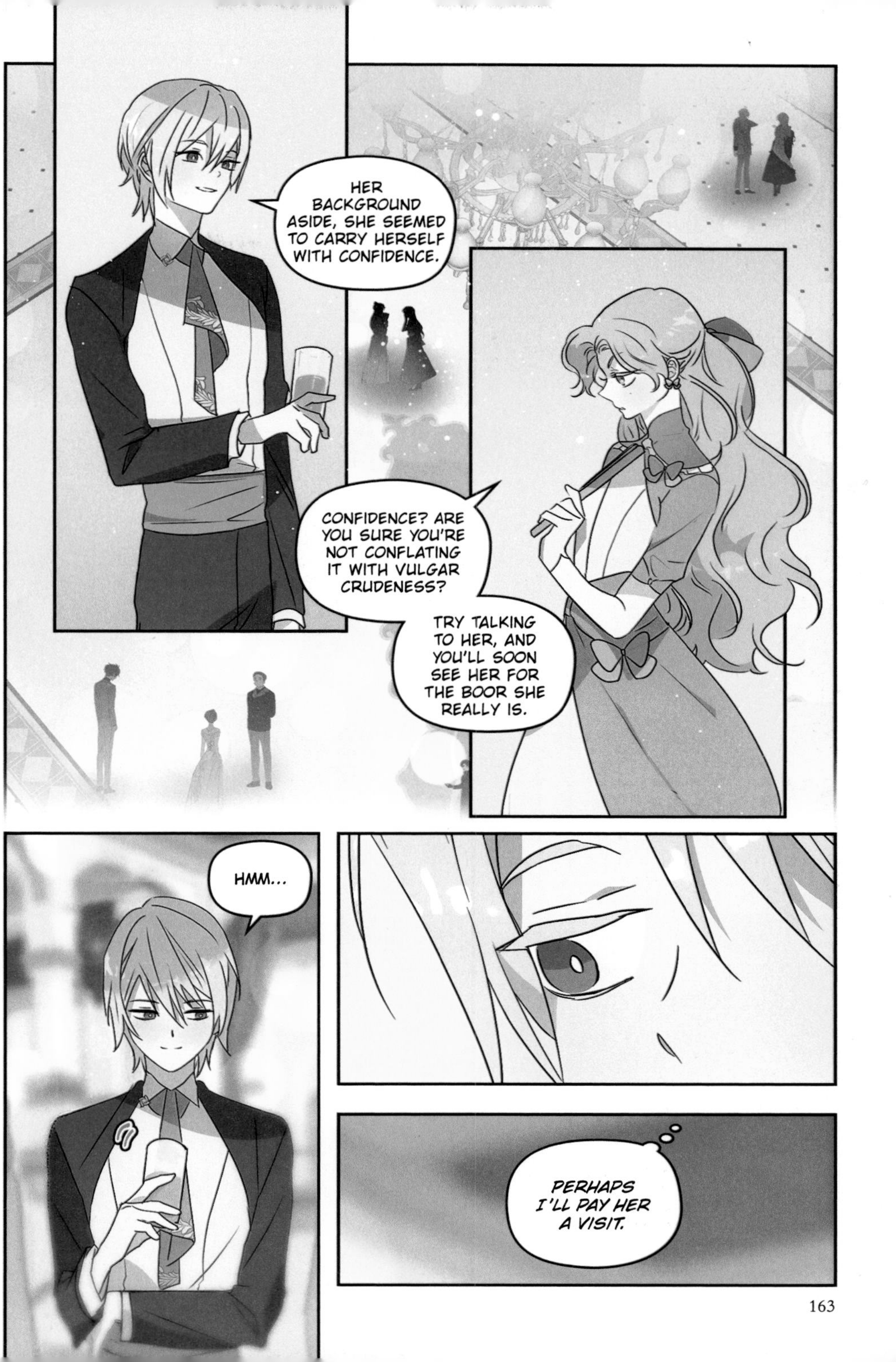
HER BACKGROUND ASIDE, SHE SEEMED TO CARRY HERSELF WITH CONFIDENCE.
CONFIDENCE? ARE YOU SURE YOU'RE NOT CONFLATING IT WITH VULGAR CRUDENESS?
TRY TALKING TO HER, AND YOU'LL SOON SEE HER FOR THE BOOR SHE REALLY IS.
HMM...
PERHAPS I'LL PAY HER A VISIT.

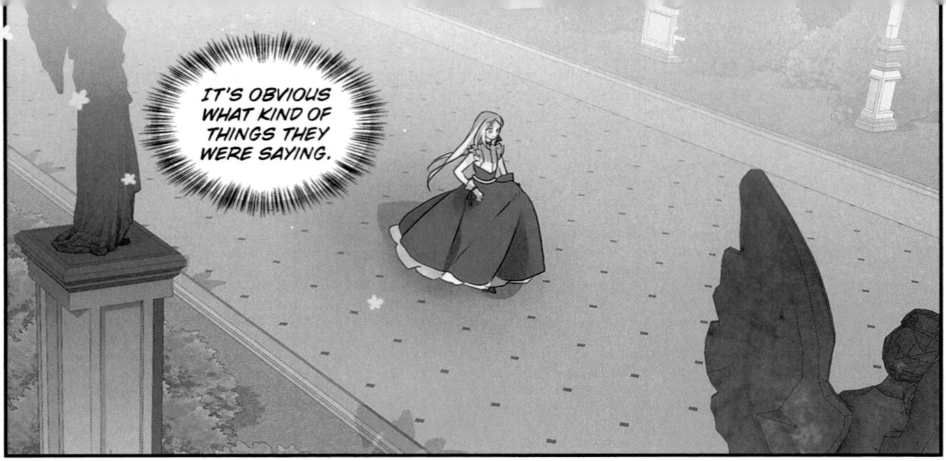
IT'S OBVIOUS WHAT KIND OF THINGS THEY WERE SAYING.

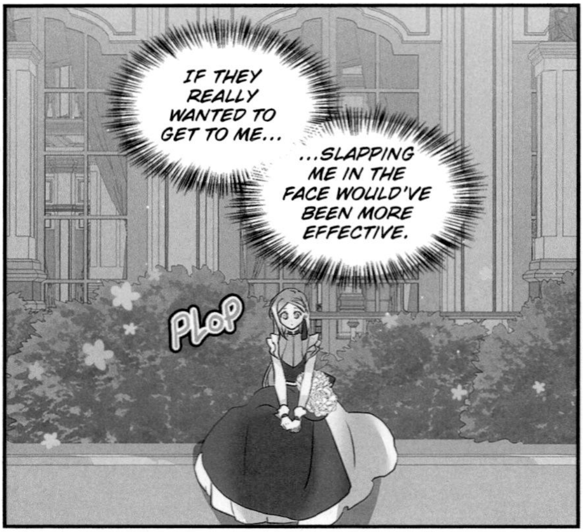
IF THEY REALLY WANTED TO GET TO ME...
...SLAPPING ME IN THE FACE WOULD'VE BEEN MORE EFFECTIVE.
PLOP

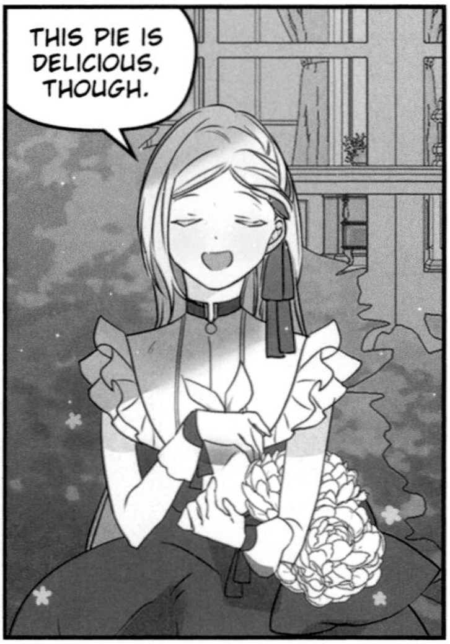
THIS PIE IS DELICIOUS, THOUGH.

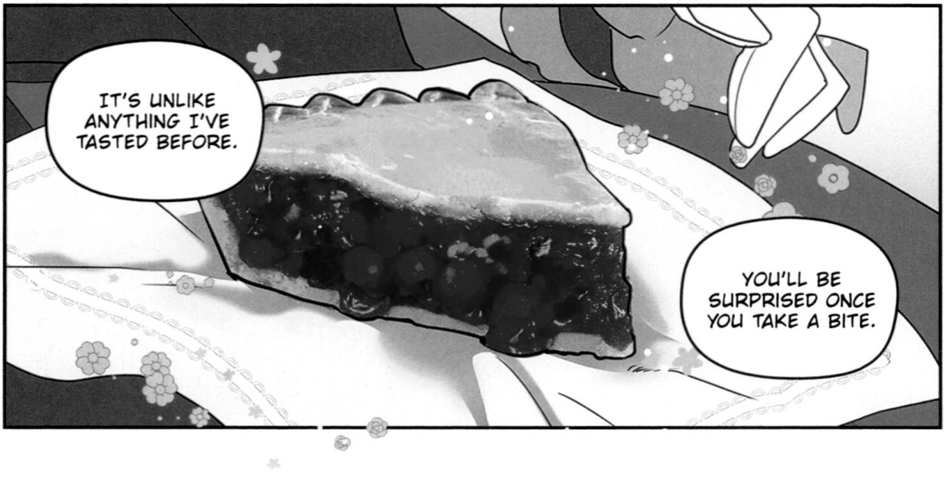
IT'S UNLIKE ANYTHING I'VE TASTED BEFORE.
YOU'LL BE SURPRISED ONCE YOU TAKE A BITE.

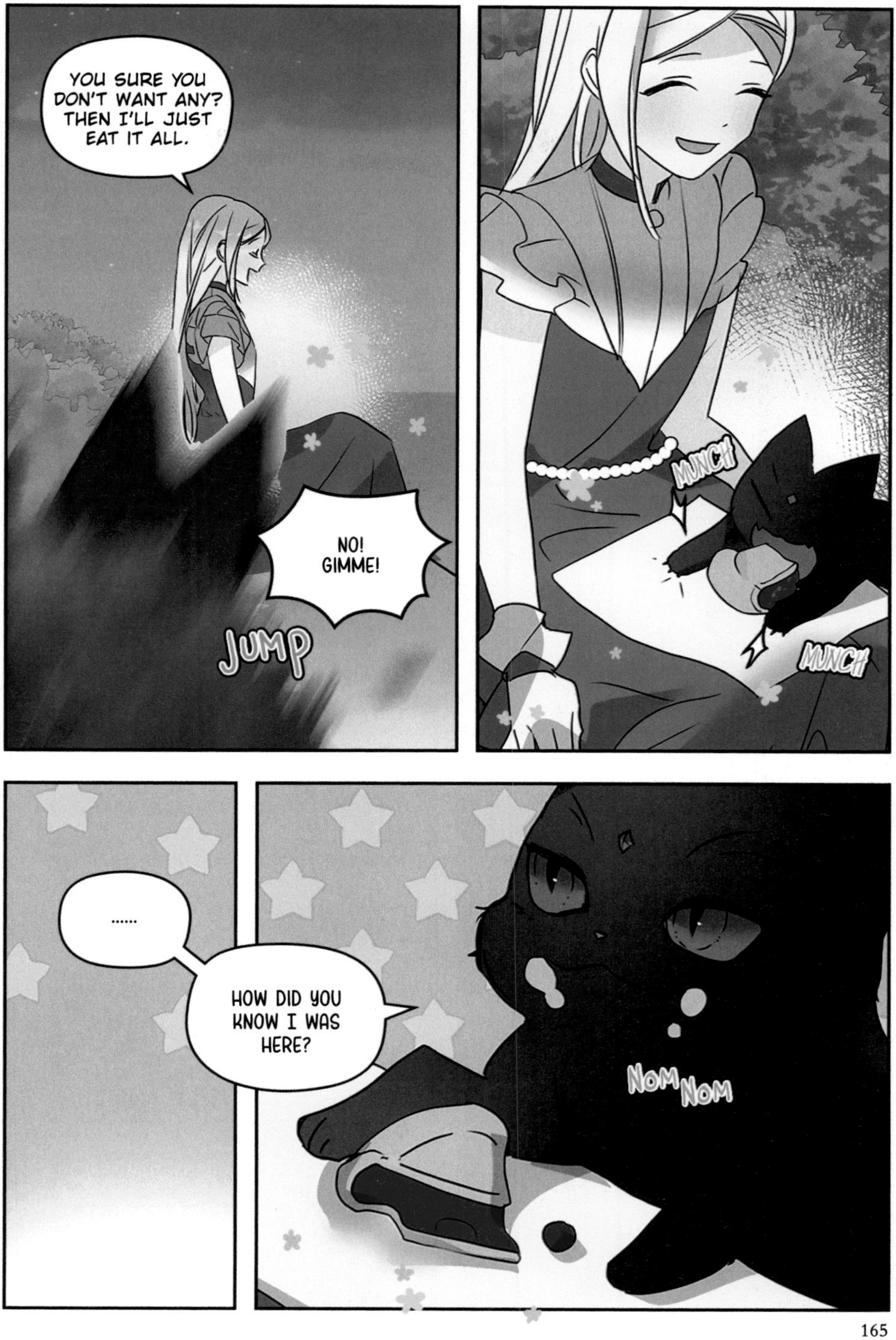
YOU SURE YOU DON'T WANT ANY? THEN I'LL JUST EAT IT ALL.
NO! GIMME!
JUMP
MUNCH
MUNCH
......
HOW DID YOU KNOW I WAS HERE?
NOM NOM

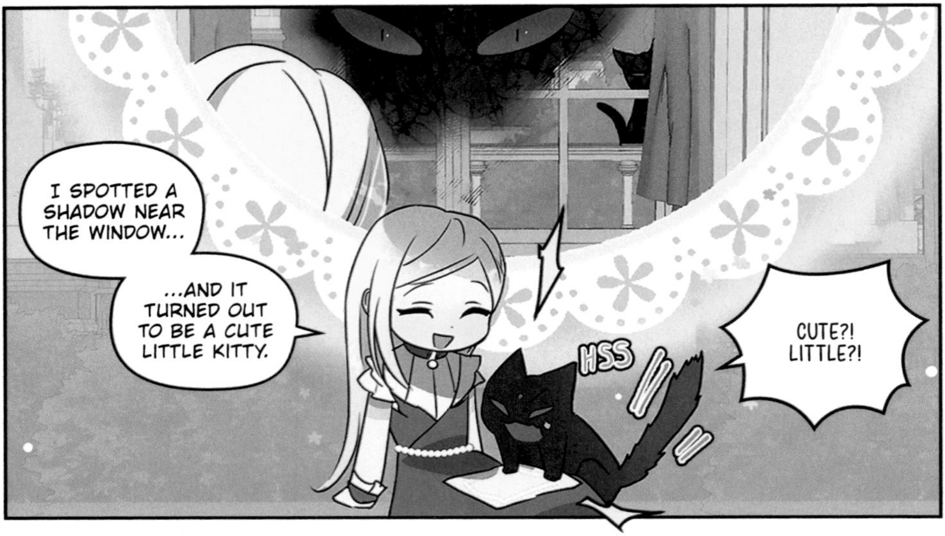
I SPOTTED A SHADOW NEAR THE WINDOW...
...AND IT TURNED OUT TO BE A CUTE LITTLE KITTY.
HSS
CUTE?! LITTLE?!

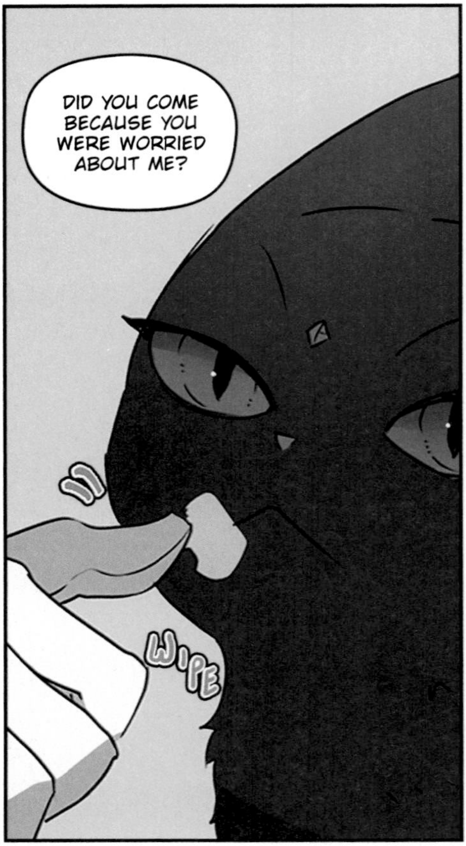
DID YOU COME BECAUSE YOU WERE WORRIED ABOUT ME?
WIPE

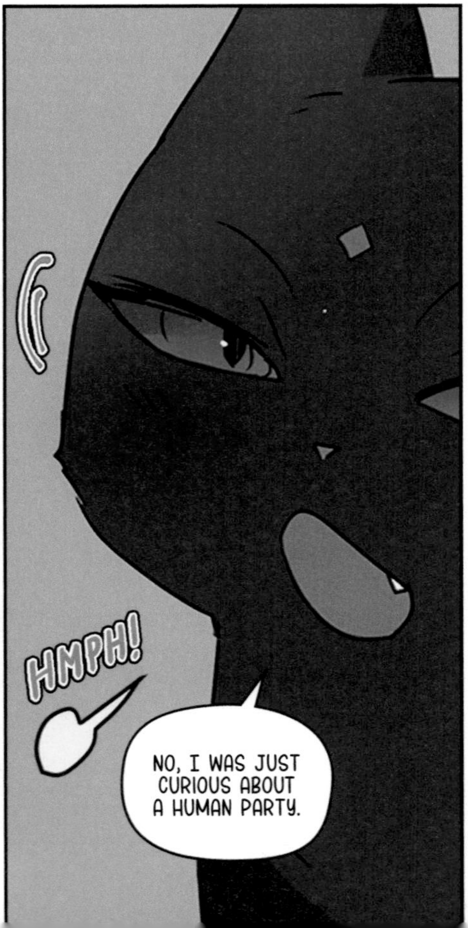
HMPH!
NO, I WAS JUST CURIOUS ABOUT A HUMAN PARTY.

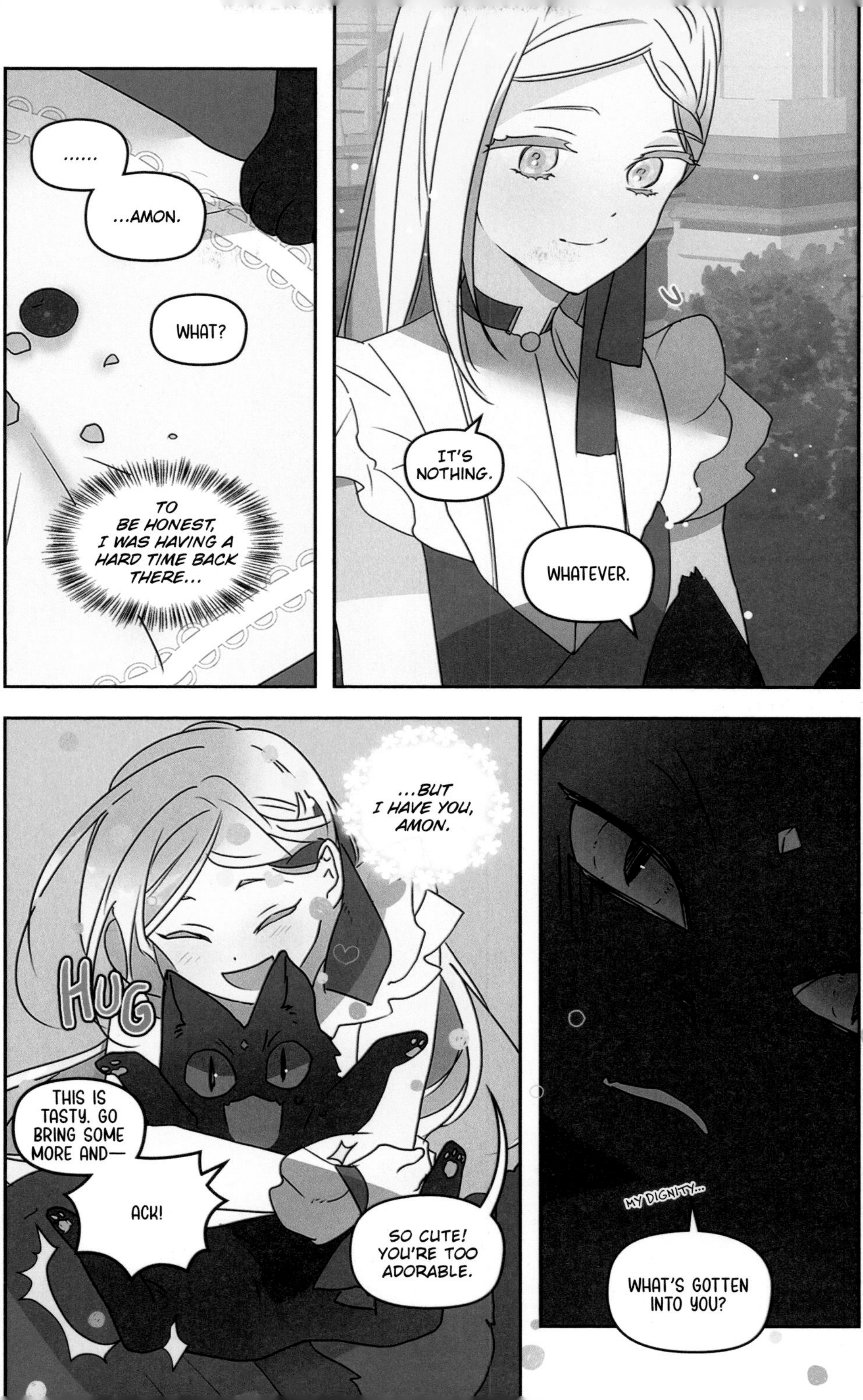
......
...AMON.
WHAT?
TO BE HONEST, I WAS HAVING A HARD TIME BACK THERE...
IT'S NOTHING.
WHATEVER.
...BUT I HAVE YOU, AMON.
HUG
THIS IS TASTY. GO BRING SOME MORE AND—
ACK!
SO CUTE! YOU'RE TOO ADORABLE.
MY DIGNITY...
WHAT'S GOTTEN INTO YOU?

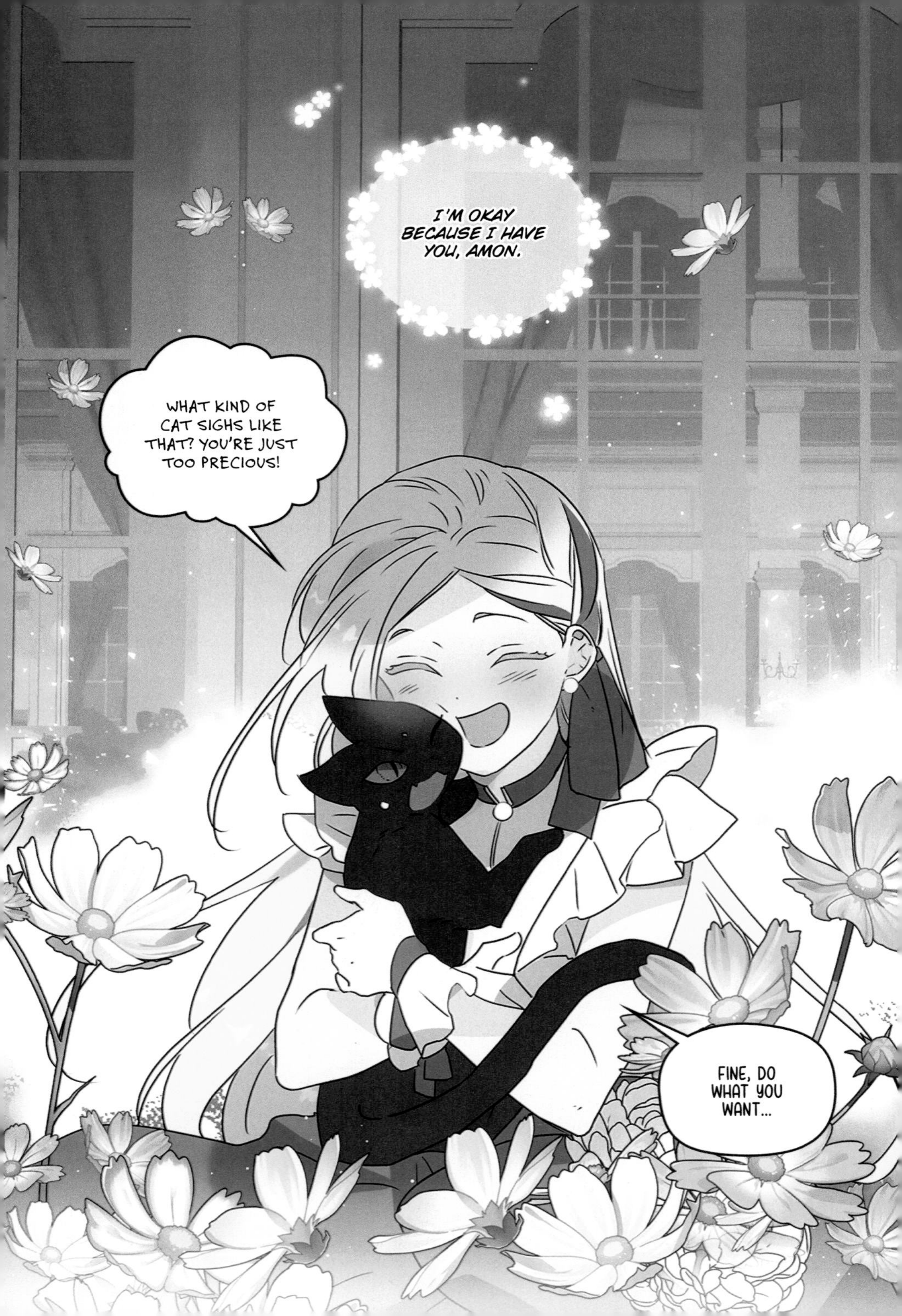
I'M OKAY BECAUSE I HAVE YOU, AMON.
WHAT KIND OF CAT SIGHS LIKE THAT? YOU'RE JUST TOO PRECIOUS!
FINE, DO WHAT YOU WANT...

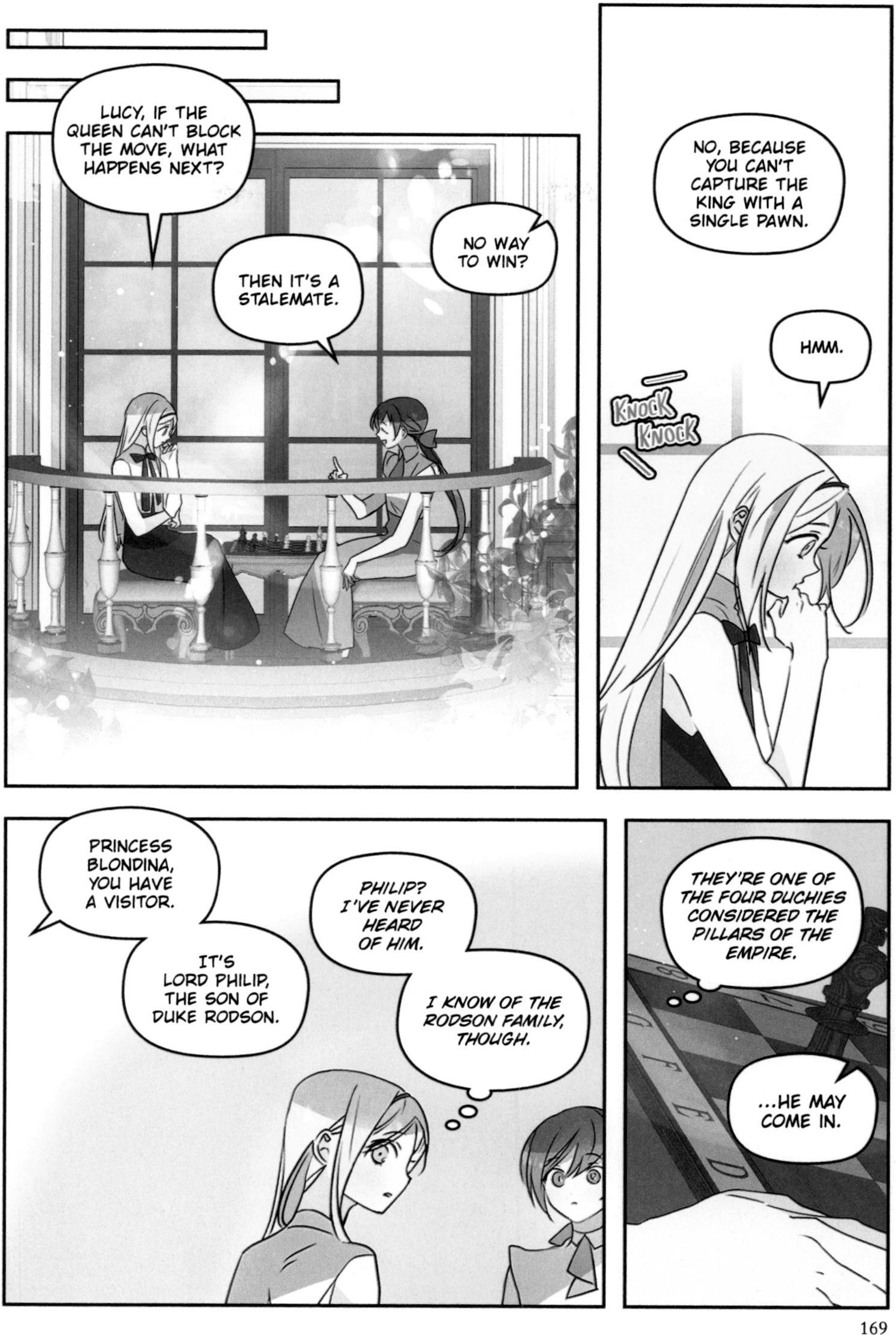
LUCY, IF THE QUEEN CAN'T BLOCK THE MOVE, WHAT HAPPENS NEXT?
THEN IT'S A STALEMATE.
NO WAY TO WIN?
NO, BECAUSE YOU CAN'T CAPTURE THE KING WITH A SINGLE PAWN.
HMM.
KNOCK KNOCK
PRINCESS BLONDINA, YOU HAVE A VISITOR.
IT'S LORD PHILIP, THE SON OF DUKE RODSON.
PHILIP? I'VE NEVER HEARD OF HIM.
I KNOW OF THE RODSON FAMILY, THOUGH.
THEY'RE ONE OF THE FOUR DUCHIES CONSIDERED THE PILLARS OF THE EMPIRE.
...HE MAY COME IN.

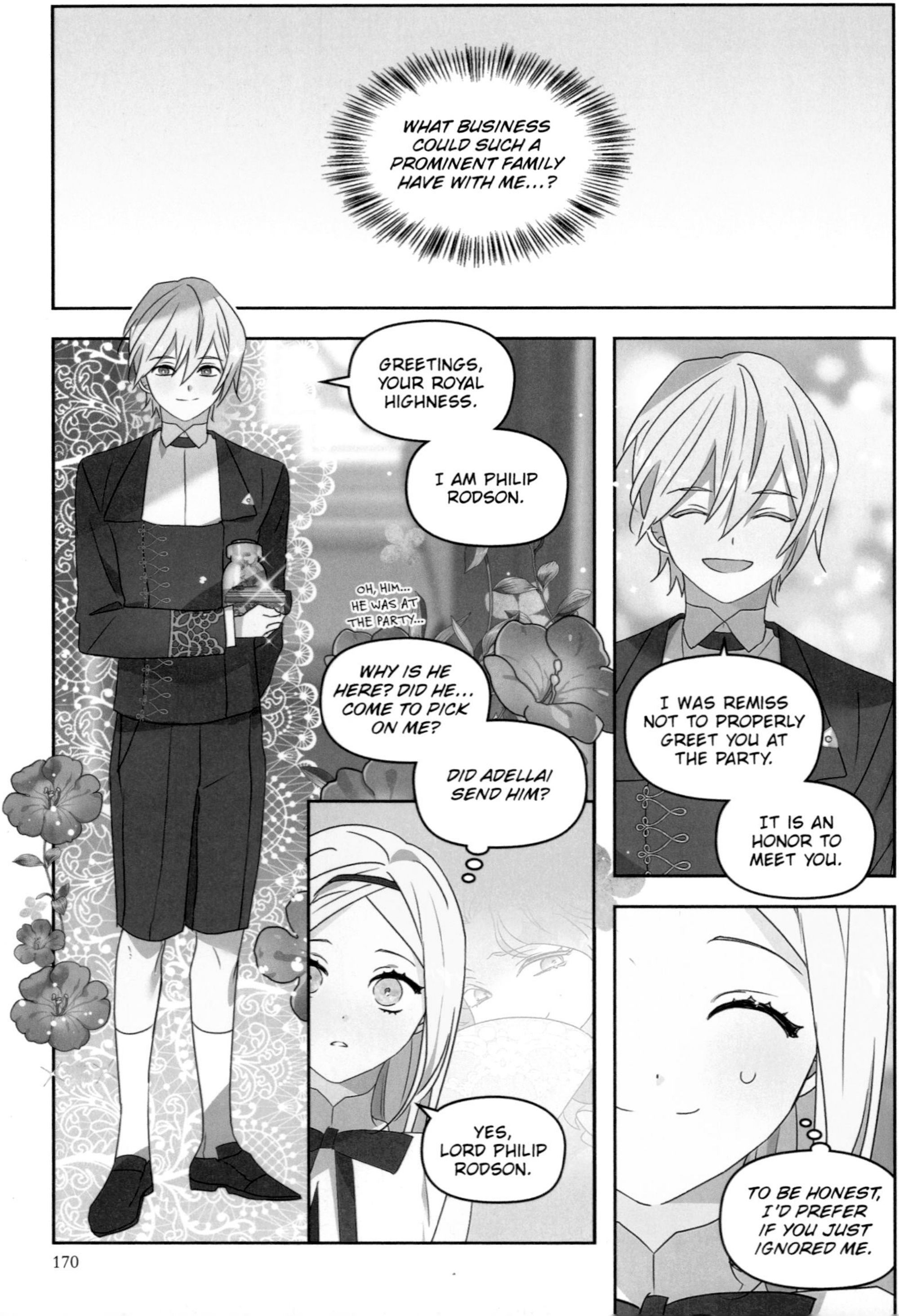

WHAT BUSINESS COULD SUCH A PROMINENT FAMILY HAVE WITH ME...?
GREETINGS, YOUR ROYAL HIGHNESS.
I AM PHILIP RODSON.
I WAS REMISS NOT TO PROPERLY GREET YOU AT THE PARTY.
IT IS AN HONOR TO MEET YOU.
OH, HIM... HE WAS AT THE PARTY...
WHY IS HE HERE? DID HE... COME TO PICK ON ME?
DID ADELLAI SEND HIM?
YES, LORD PHILIP RODSON.
TO BE HONEST, I'D PREFER IF YOU JUST IGNORED ME.

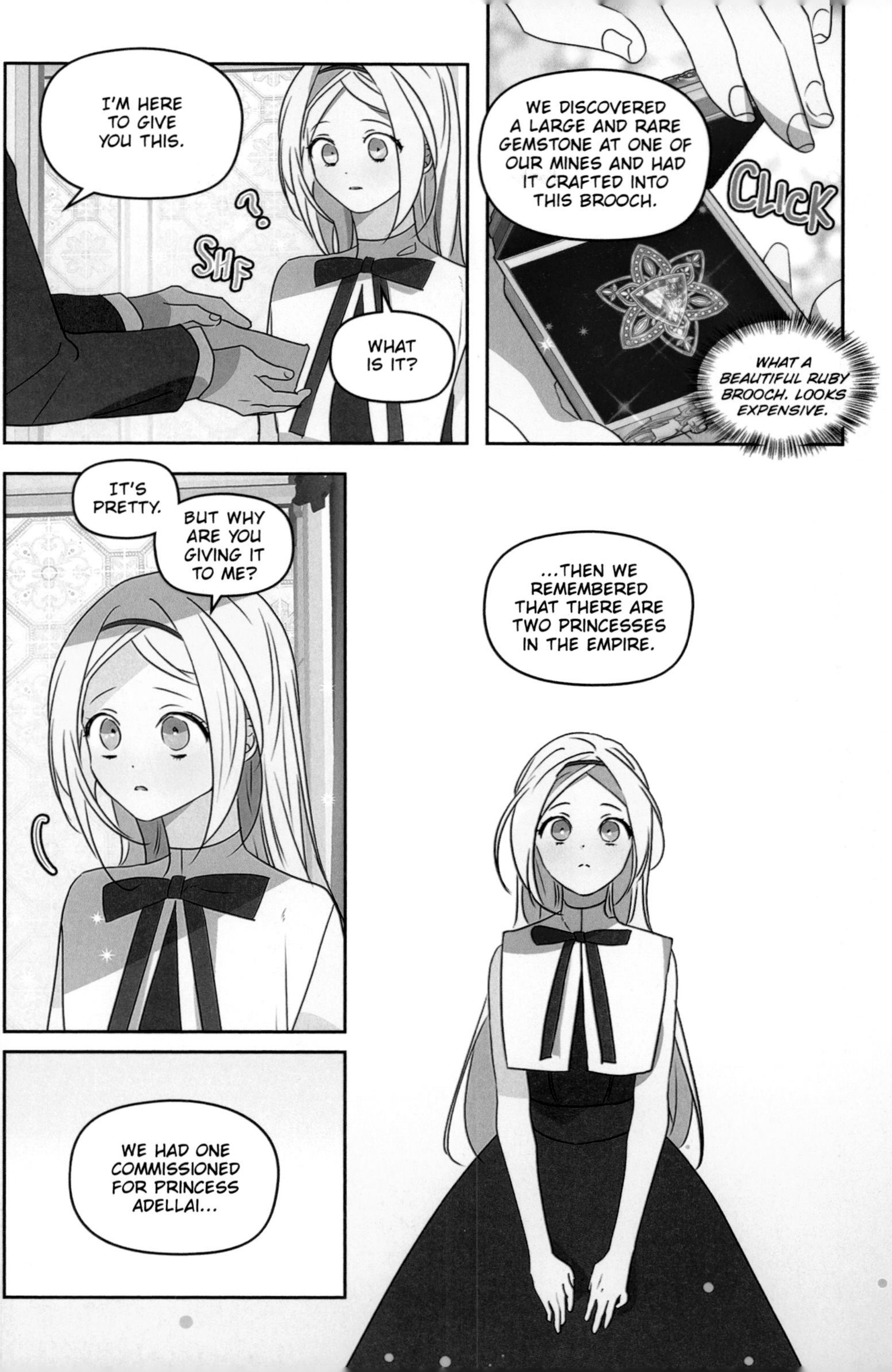

I'M HERE TO GIVE YOU THIS.
?
SHF
WHAT IS IT?
WE DISCOVERED A LARGE AND RARE GEMSTONE AT ONE OF OUR MINES AND HAD IT CRAFTED INTO THIS BROOCH.
CLICK
WHAT A BEAUTIFUL RUBY BROOCH. LOOKS EXPENSIVE.
IT'S PRETTY.
BUT WHY ARE YOU GIVING IT TO ME?
WE HAD ONE COMMISSIONED FOR PRINCESS ADELLAI...
...THEN WE REMEMBERED THAT THERE ARE TWO PRINCESSES IN THE EMPIRE.

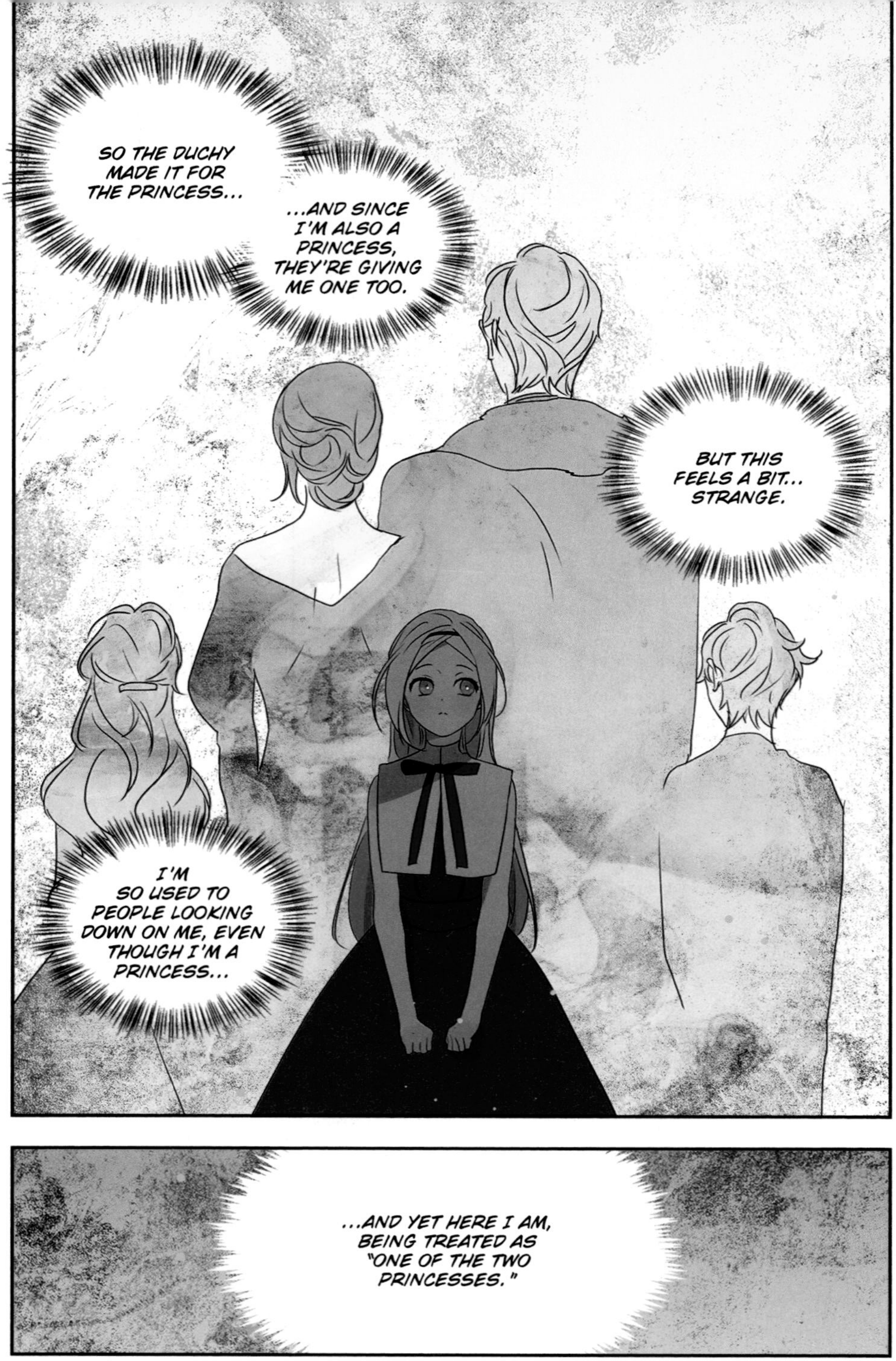
SO THE DUCHY MADE IT FOR THE PRINCESS...
...AND SINCE I'M ALSO A PRINCESS, THEY'RE GIVING ME ONE TOO.
BUT THIS FEELS A BIT... STRANGE.
I'M SO USED TO PEOPLE LOOKING DOWN ON ME, EVEN THOUGH I'M A PRINCESS...
...AND YET HERE I AM, BEING TREATED AS "ONE OF THE TWO PRINCESSES."

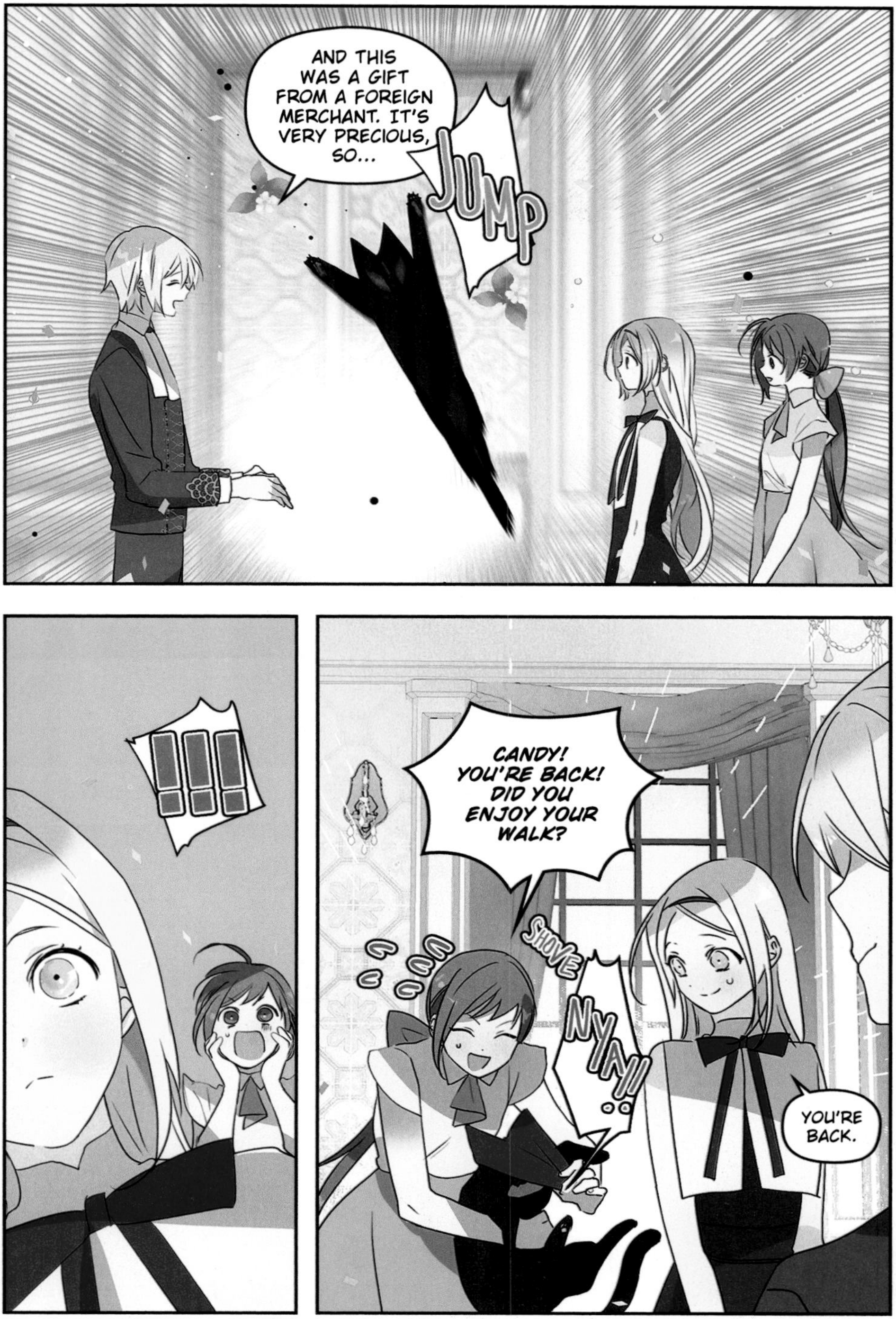
AND THIS WAS A GIFT FROM A FOREIGN MERCHANT. IT'S VERY PRECIOUS, SO...
JUMP
!!!
CANDY! YOU'RE BACK! DID YOU ENJOY YOUR WALK?
SHOVE
NYA!!..
YOU'RE BACK.

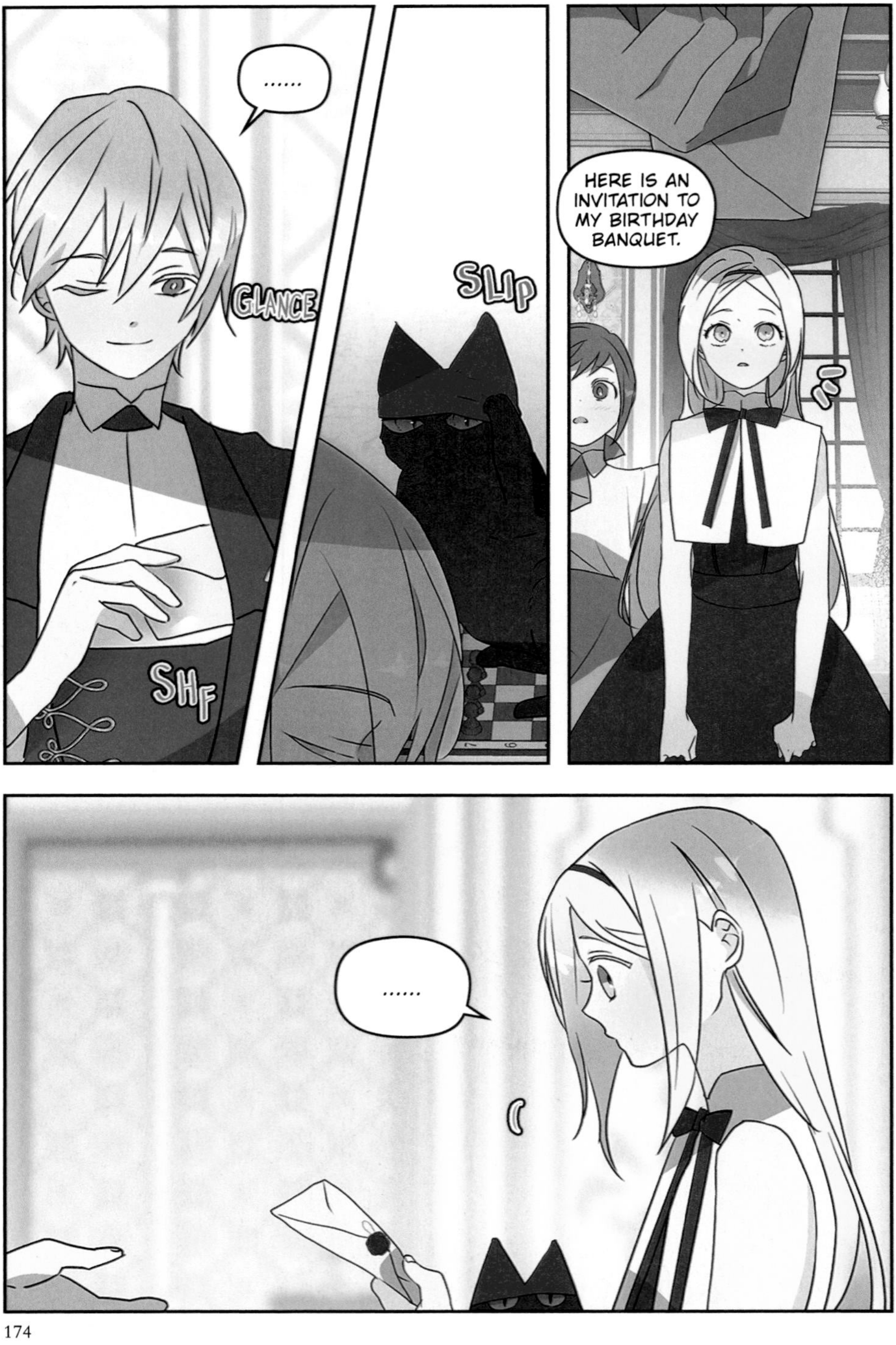
......
GLANCE
SHF
SLIP
HERE IS AN INVITATION TO MY BIRTHDAY BANQUET.
......

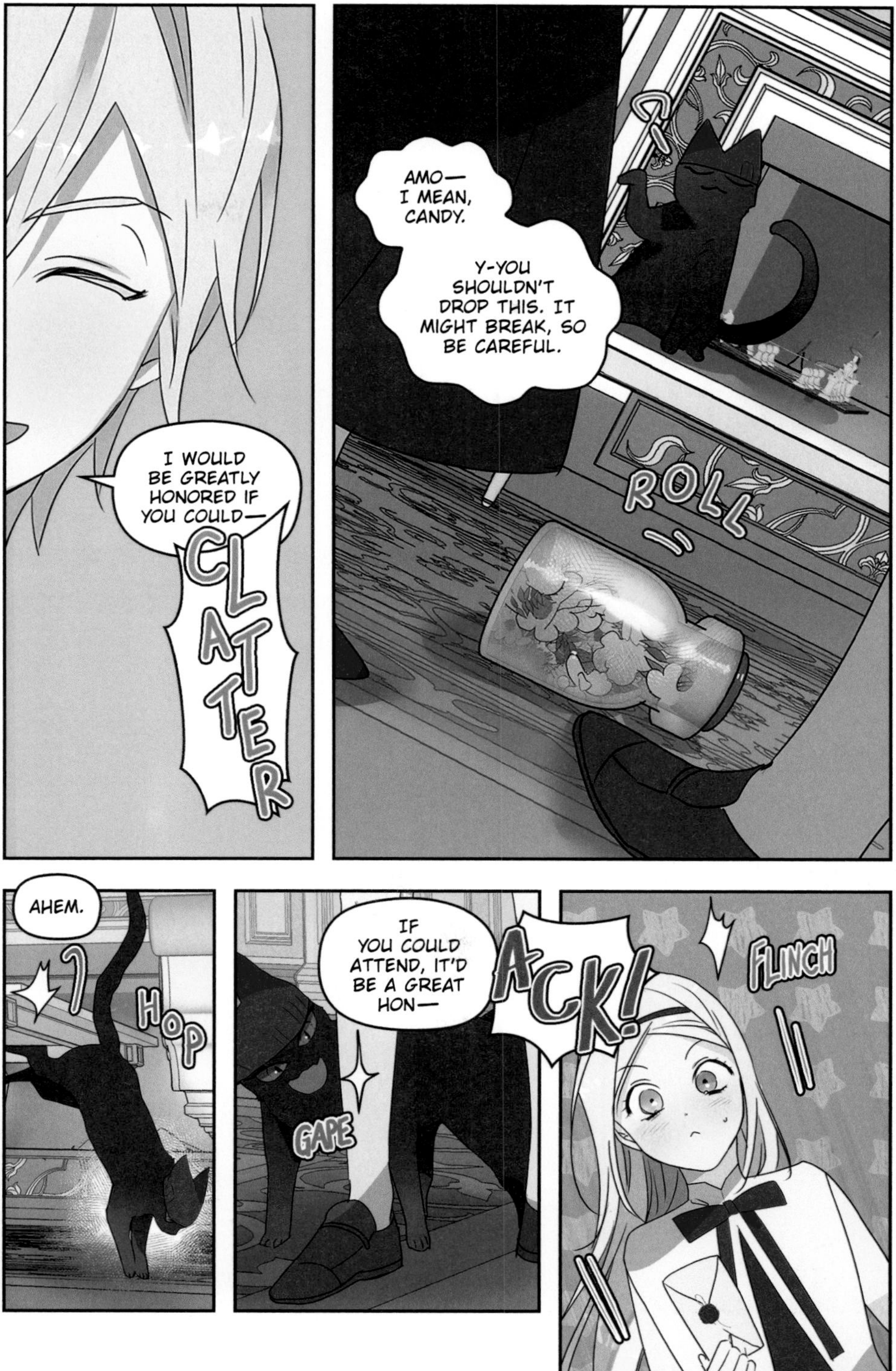
I WOULD BE GREATLY HONORED IF YOU COULD—
CLATTER
AMO— I MEAN, CANDY.
Y-YOU SHOULDN'T DROP THIS. IT MIGHT BREAK, SO BE CAREFUL.
ROLL
AHEM.
HOP
IF YOU COULD ATTEND, IT'D BE A GREAT HON—
GAPE
ACK!
FLINCH

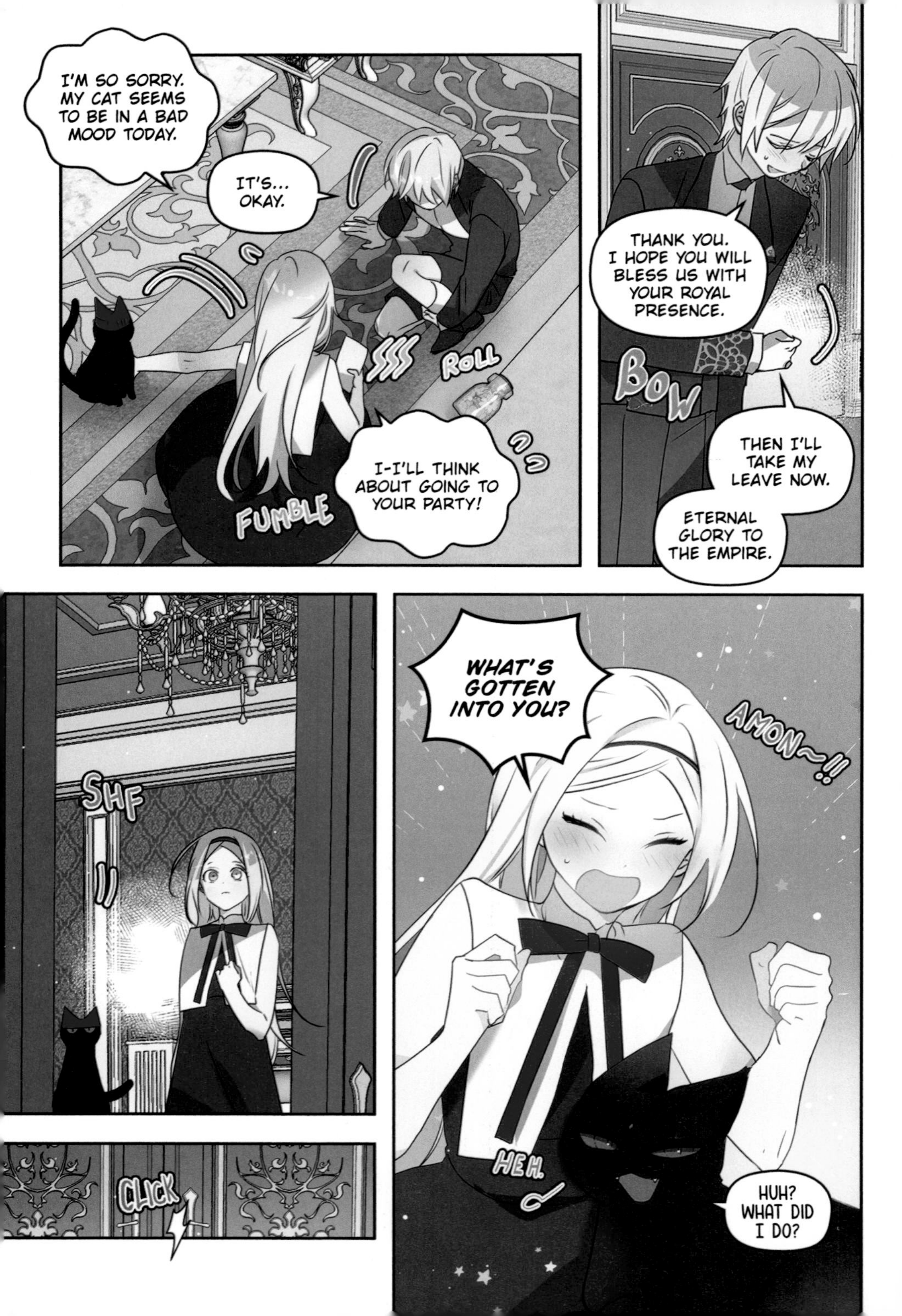
I'M SO SORRY. MY CAT SEEMS TO BE IN A BAD MOOD TODAY.
IT'S... OKAY.
SSS
ROLL
I-I'LL THINK ABOUT GOING TO YOUR PARTY!
FUMBLE
THANK YOU. I HOPE YOU WILL BLESS US WITH YOUR ROYAL PRESENCE.
BOW
THEN I'LL TAKE MY LEAVE NOW.
ETERNAL GLORY TO THE EMPIRE.
SHF
CLICK
WHAT'S GOTTEN INTO YOU?
AMON~!!
HEH.
HUH? WHAT DID I DO?

My Gently Raised Beast

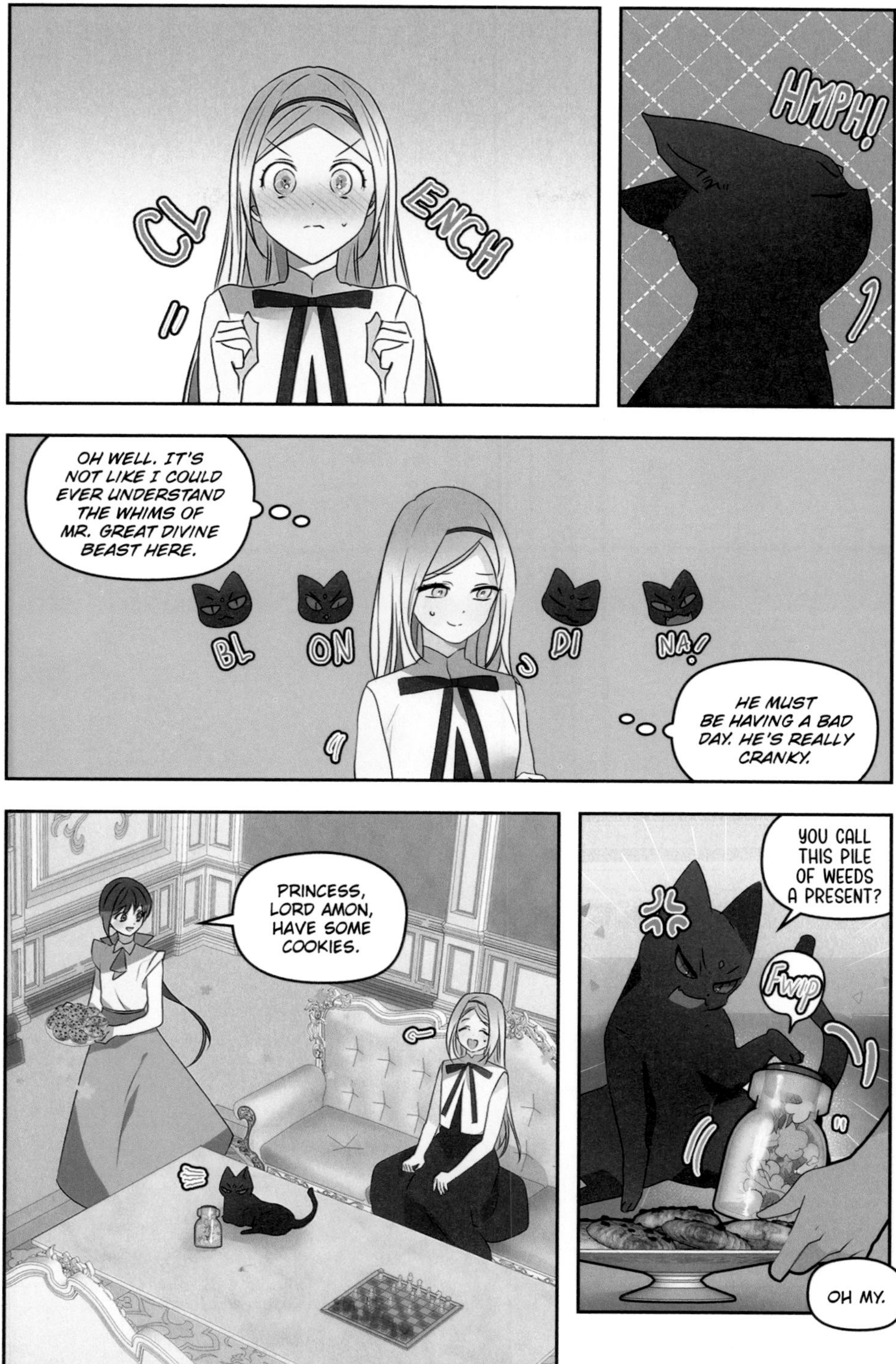
CL
ENCH
HMPH!
OH WELL. IT'S NOT LIKE I COULD EVER UNDERSTAND THE WHIMS OF MR. GREAT DIVINE BEAST HERE.
BL
ON
DI
NA!
HE MUST BE HAVING A BAD DAY. HE'S REALLY CRANKY.
PRINCESS, LORD AMON, HAVE SOME COOKIES.
YOU CALL THIS PILE OF WEEDS A PRESENT?
Fwip
OH MY.

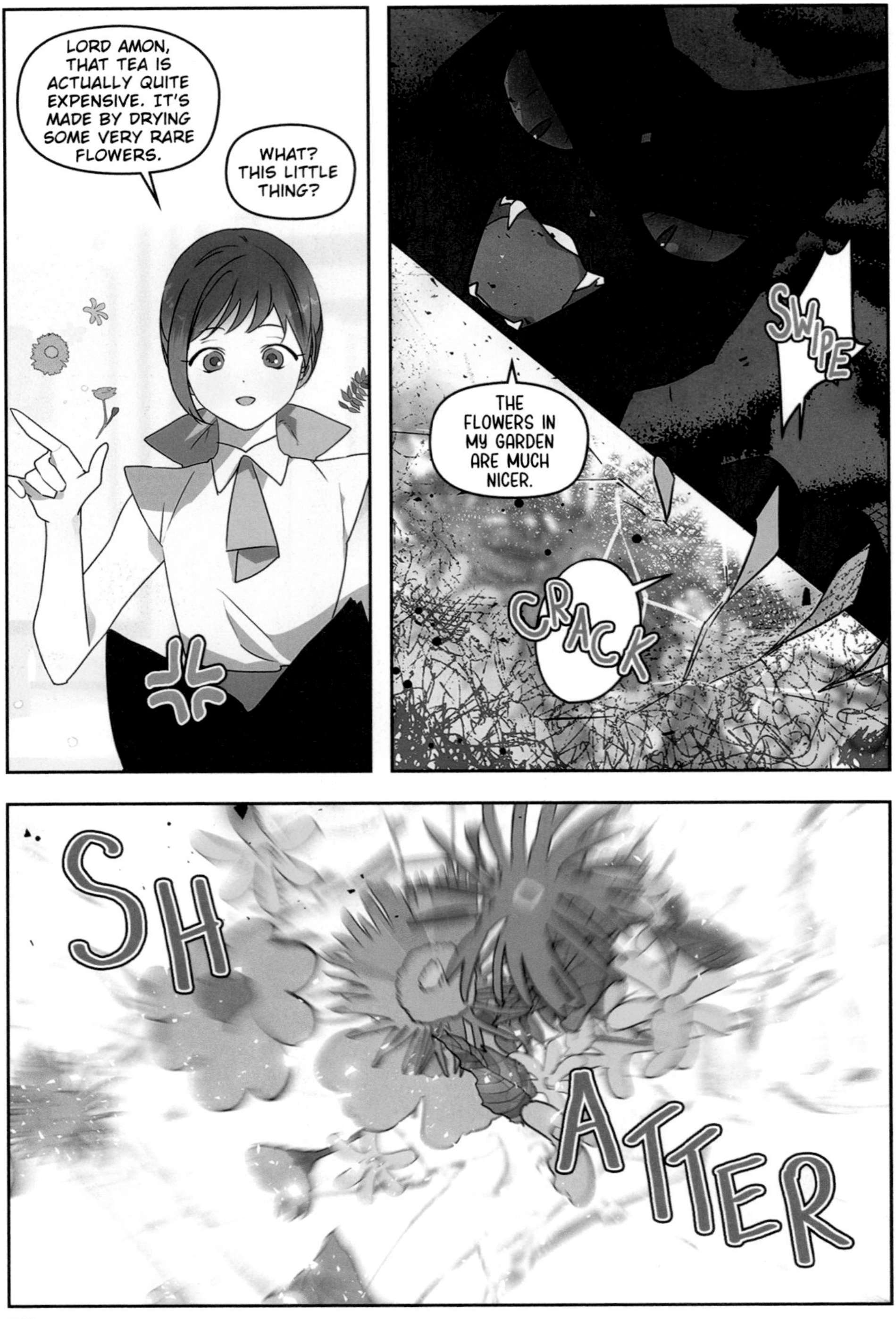
LORD AMON, THAT TEA IS ACTUALLY QUITE EXPENSIVE. IT'S MADE BY DRYING SOME VERY RARE FLOWERS.
WHAT? THIS LITTLE THING?
SWIPE
THE FLOWERS IN MY GARDEN ARE MUCH NICER.
CRACK
SHATTER

AMON!

STAND

SWIPE

FLINCH

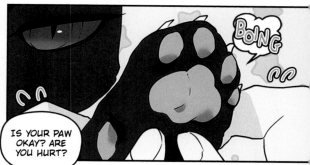

BOING

IS YOUR PAW OKAY? ARE YOU HURT?

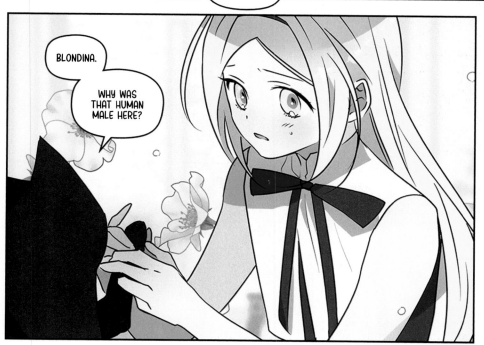

BLONDINA.

WHY WAS THAT HUMAN MALE HERE?

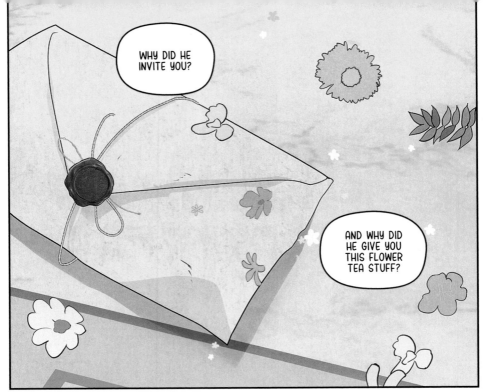

WHY DID HE INVITE YOU?

AND WHY DID HE GIVE YOU THIS FLOWER TEA STUFF?

......

FLUSTERED

LORD AMON, YOU SHOULD ASK ONE QUESTION AT A TIME...

...SO THE PRINCESS CAN ANSWER.

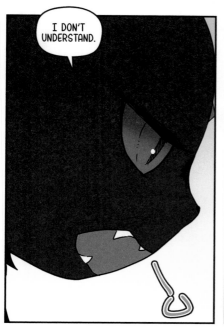

I DON'T UNDERSTAND.

DO HUMANS USUALLY GIVE OUT INVITATIONS IN PERSON?

I'M NOT SURE. MAYBE HE WAS BEING EXTRA COURTEOUS BECAUSE I'M A PRINCESS?

AND WHAT ABOUT THE FLOWER TEA?!

JUST BEING NICE, I GUESS?

IF I MENTION THE BROOCH, HE MIGHT TRY TO BREAK THAT TOO...

HE COULD'VE JUST HAD ANOTHER HUMAN DELIVER IT!

WELL...

HOW WOULD I KNOW WHAT HE'S THINKING?

GRIT

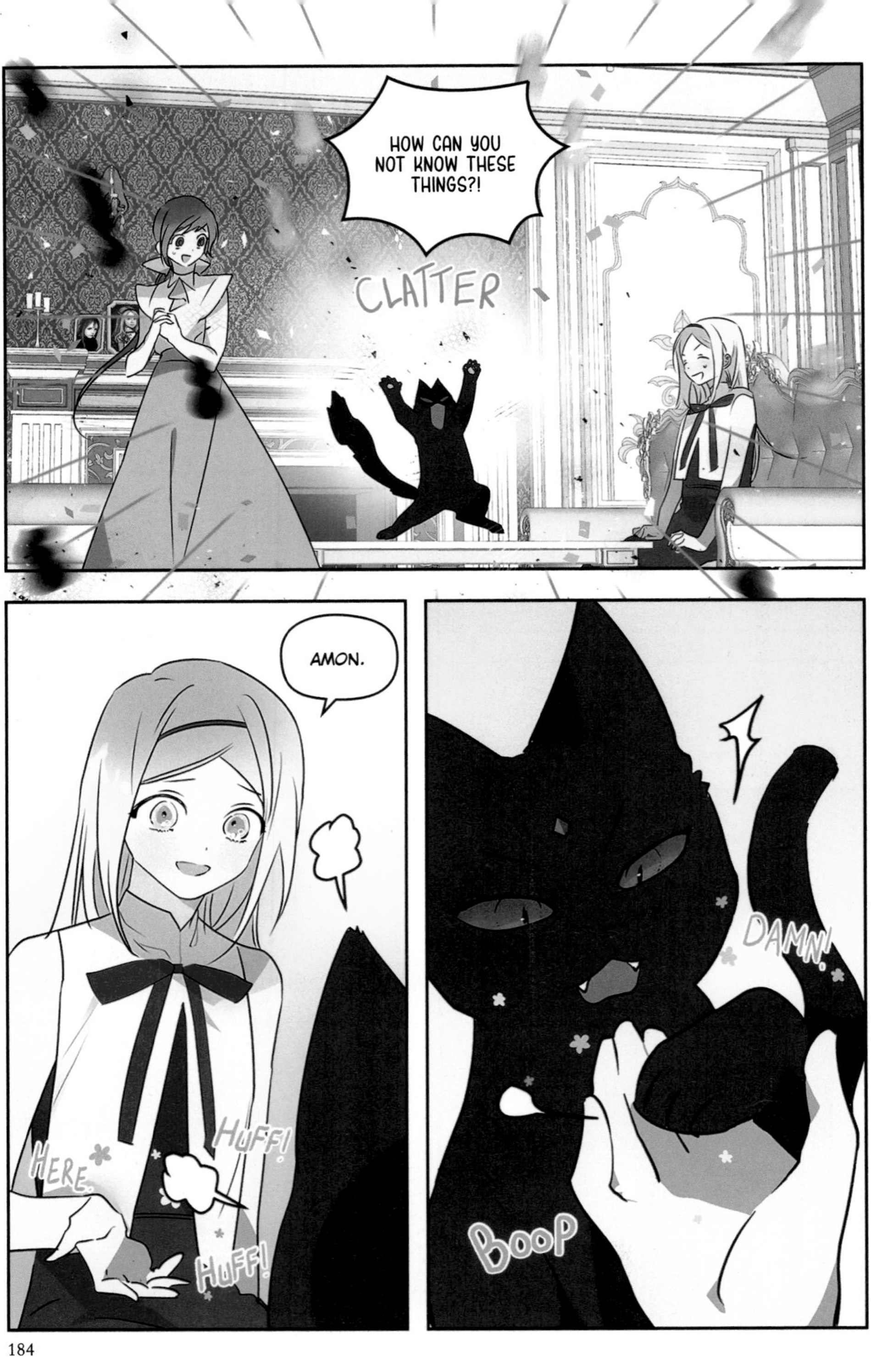
HOW CAN YOU NOT KNOW THESE THINGS?!
CLATTER
AMON.
HERE.
HUFF!
HUFF!
DAMN!
BOOP

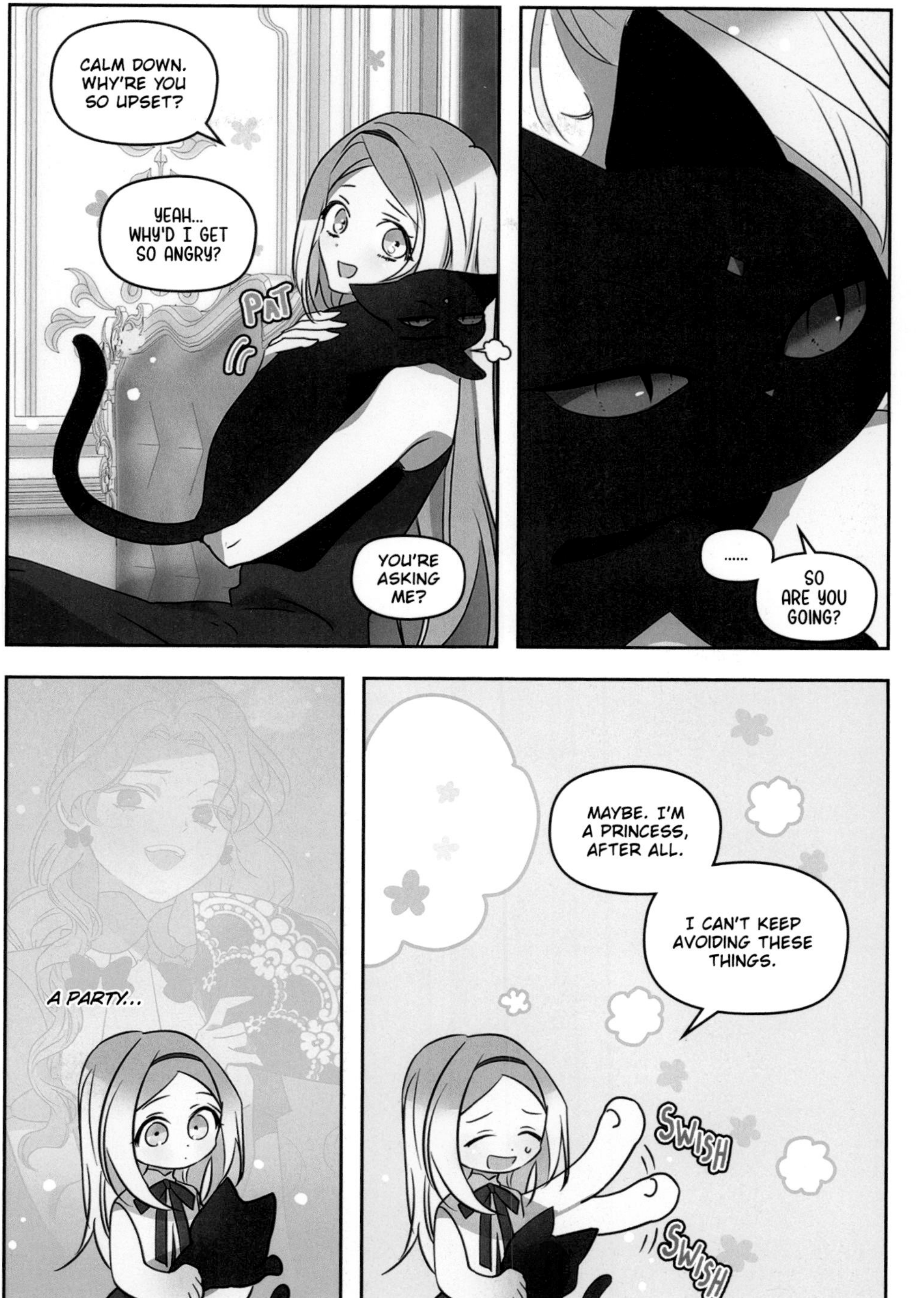
CALM DOWN. WHY'RE YOU SO UPSET?
YEAH... WHY'D I GET SO ANGRY?
PAT
YOU'RE ASKING ME?
......
SO ARE YOU GOING?
A PARTY...
MAYBE. I'M A PRINCESS, AFTER ALL.
I CAN'T KEEP AVOIDING THESE THINGS.
SWISH
SWISH

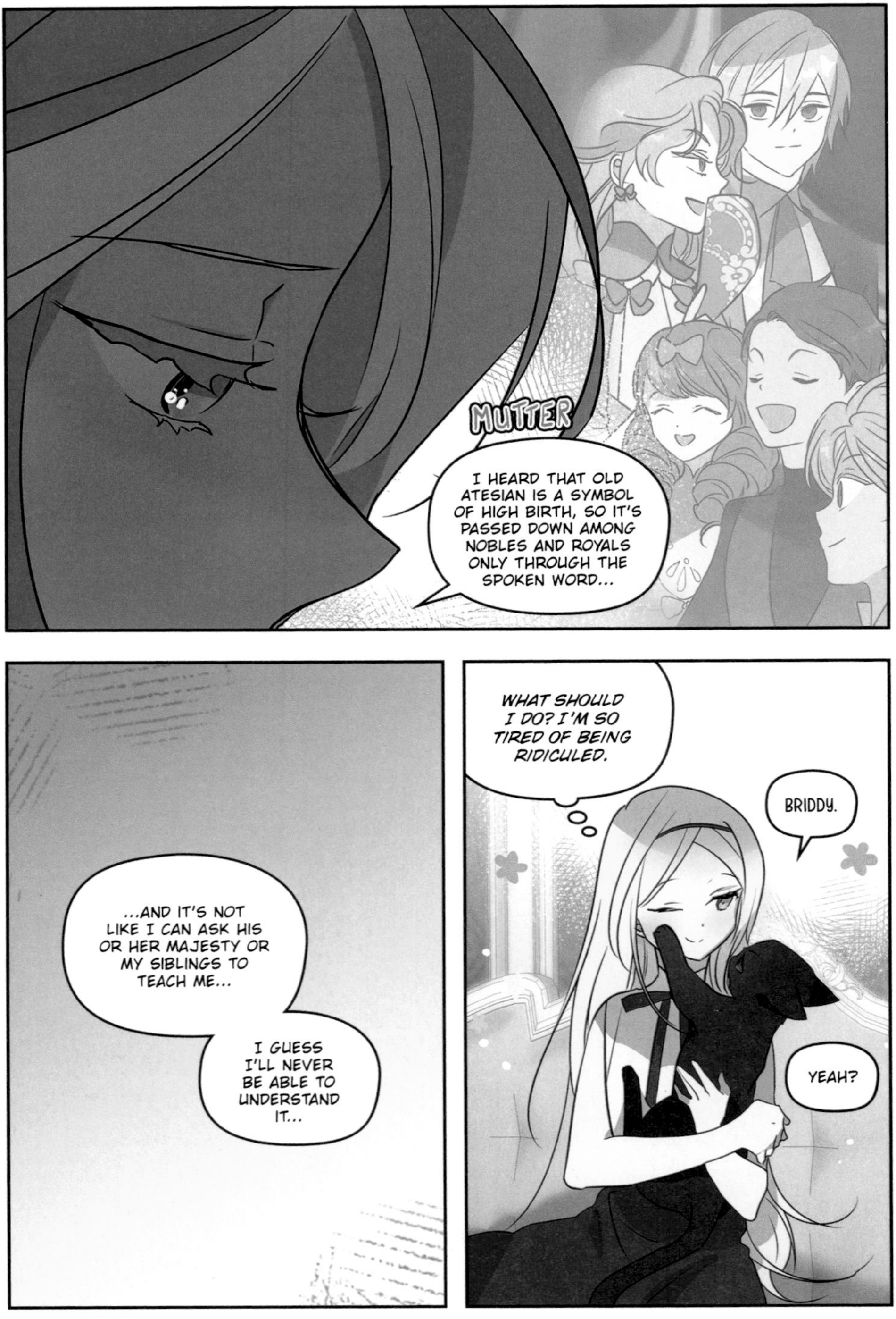
MUTTER
I HEARD THAT OLD ATESIAN IS A SYMBOL OF HIGH BIRTH, SO IT'S PASSED DOWN AMONG NOBLES AND ROYALS ONLY THROUGH THE SPOKEN WORD...
...AND IT'S NOT LIKE I CAN ASK HIS OR HER MAJESTY OR MY SIBLINGS TO TEACH ME...
I GUESS I'LL NEVER BE ABLE TO UNDERSTAND IT...
WHAT SHOULD I DO? I'M SO TIRED OF BEING RIDICULED.
BRIDDY.
YEAH?

DO YOU WANT TO LEARN IT?

WHAT? OLD ATESIAN?

BUT I HEARD THAT YOU CAN'T STUDY IT, EVEN IF YOU WANTED TO.

EVEN THE LIBRARY DOESN'T HAVE ANY BOOKS ON IT...

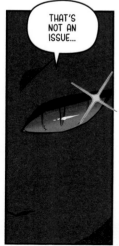

THAT'S NOT AN ISSUE...

...BECAUSE I CAN TEACH YOU.

TA-

REALLY?!

DAA

WOW!!

AMON, YOU KNOW OLD ATESIAN?

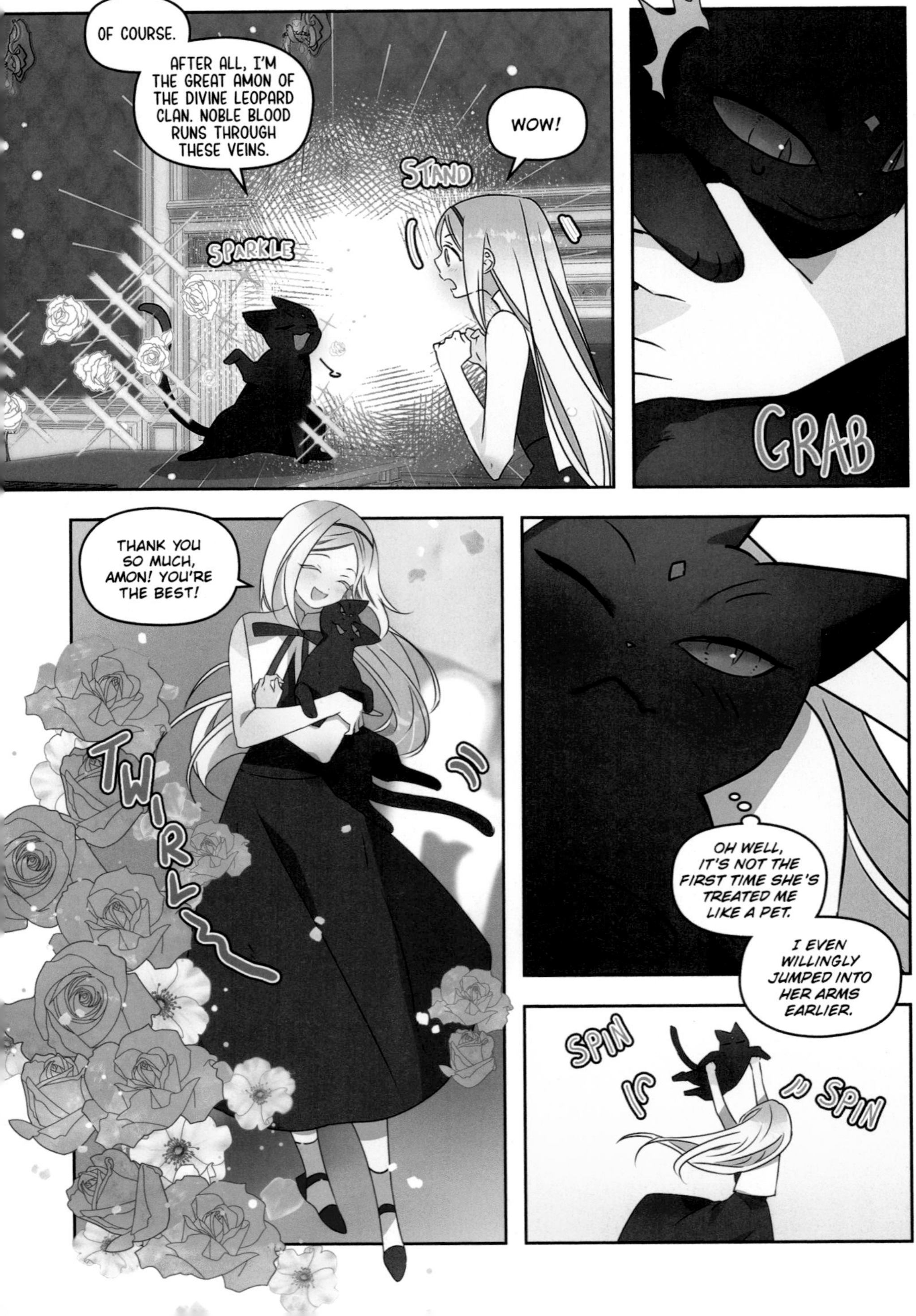
OF COURSE.
AFTER ALL, I'M THE GREAT AMON OF THE DIVINE LEOPARD CLAN. NOBLE BLOOD RUNS THROUGH THESE VEINS.
SPARKLE
STAND
WOW!
GRAB
THANK YOU SO MUCH, AMON! YOU'RE THE BEST!
TWIRL~
OH WELL, IT'S NOT THE FIRST TIME SHE'S TREATED ME LIKE A PET.
I EVEN WILLINGLY JUMPED INTO HER ARMS EARLIER.
SPIN
SPIN

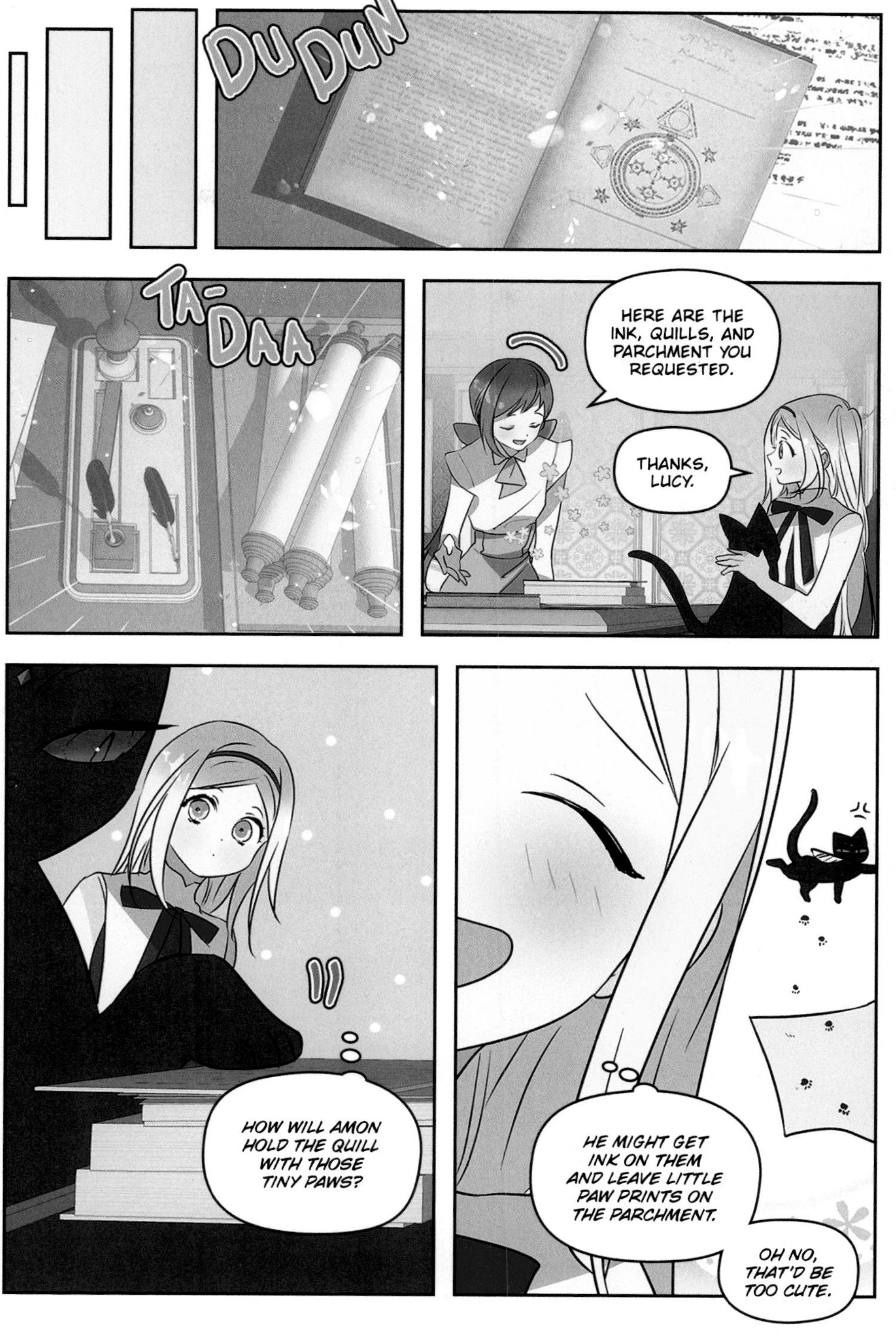
DU DUN
TA-DAA
HERE ARE THE INK, QUILLS, AND PARCHMENT YOU REQUESTED.
THANKS, LUCY.
HOW WILL AMON HOLD THE QUILL WITH THOSE TINY PAWS?
HE MIGHT GET INK ON THEM AND LEAVE LITTLE PAW PRINTS ON THE PARCHMENT.
OH NO, THAT'D BE TOO CUTE.

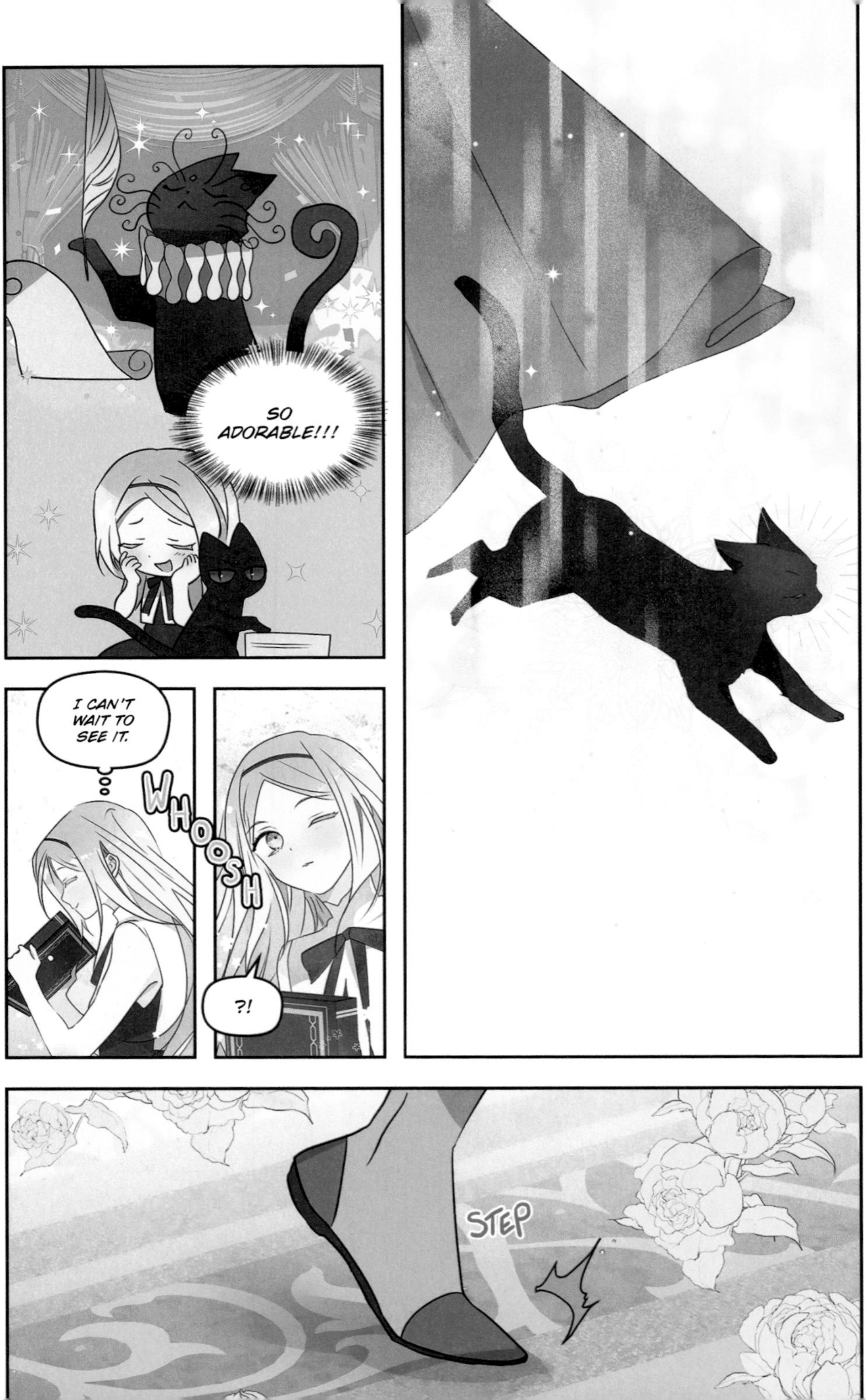
SO ADORABLE!!!
I CAN'T WAIT TO SEE IT.
WHOOSH
?!
STEP

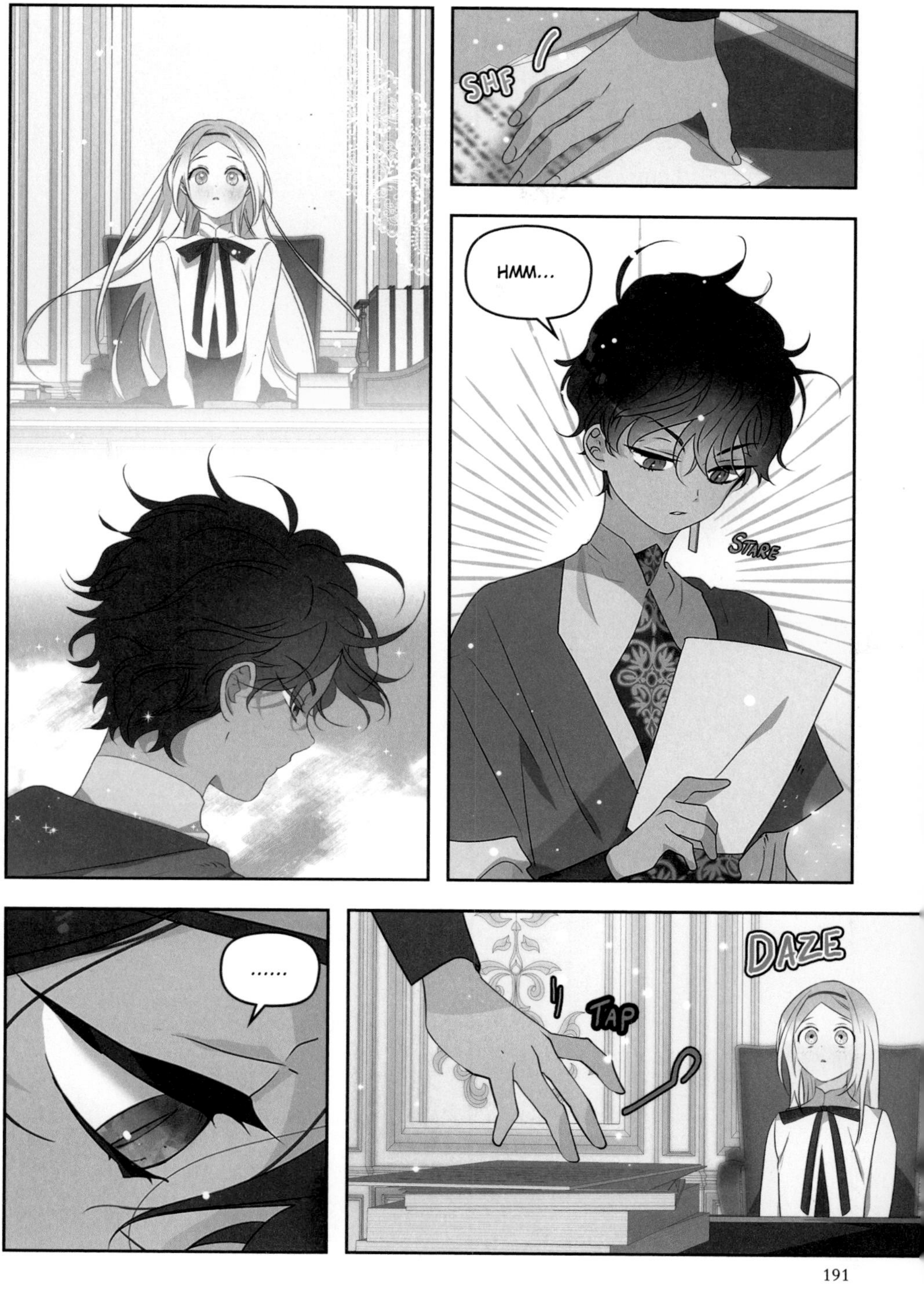
SHF
HMM...
STARE
......
DAZE
TAP

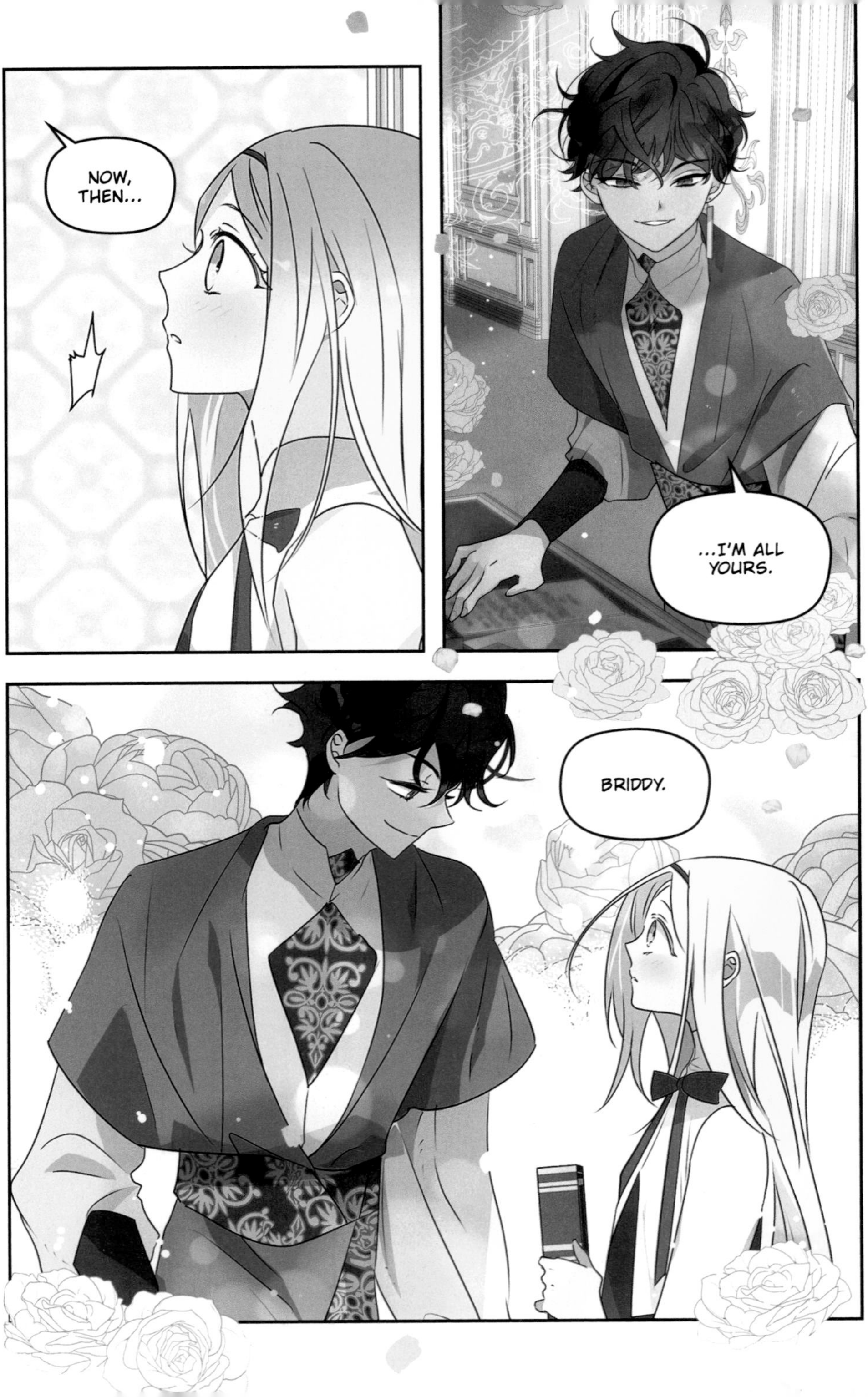
NOW, THEN...
...I'M ALL YOURS.
BRIDDY.

My Gently Raised Beast

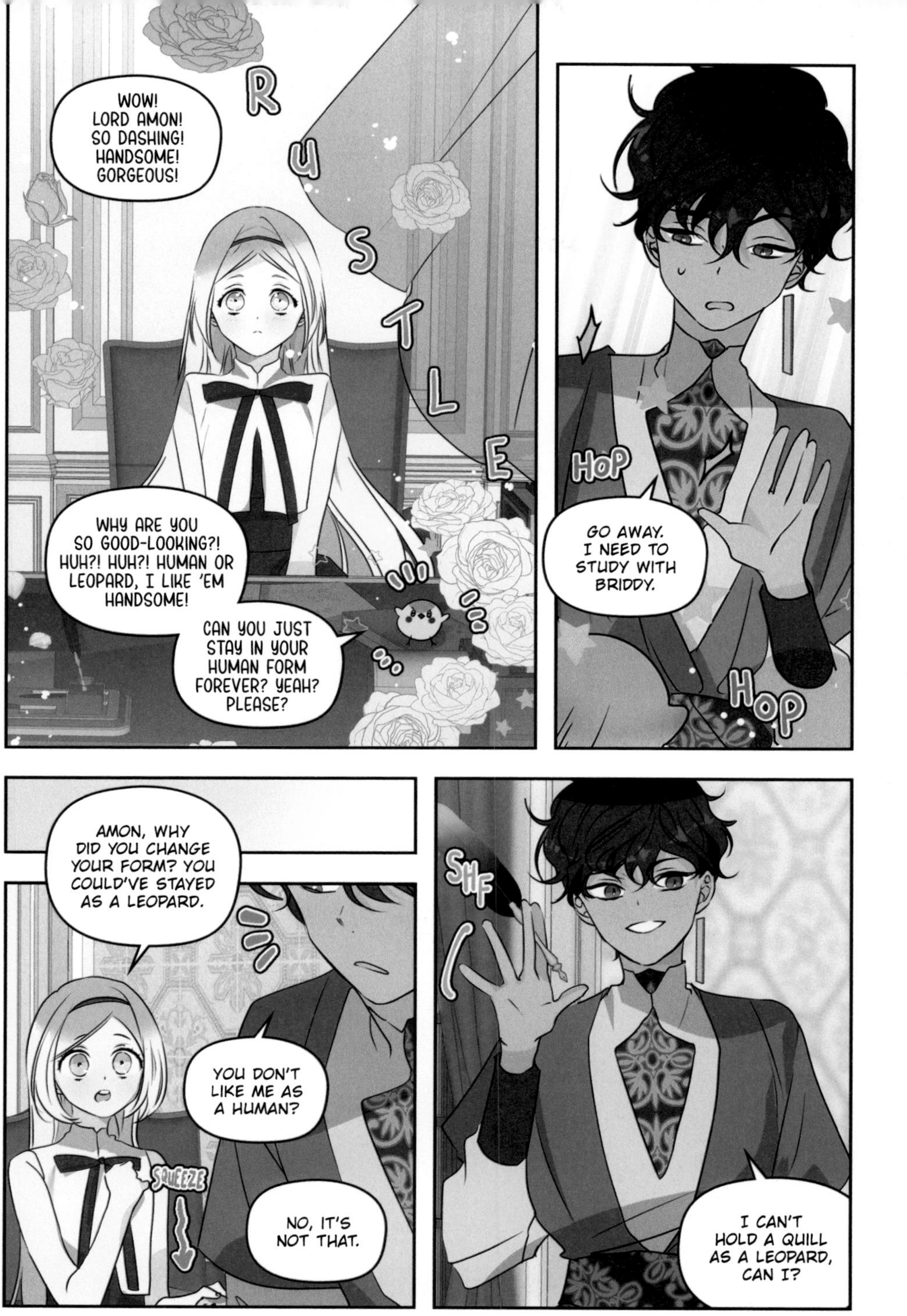
WOW! LORD AMON! SO DASHING! HANDSOME! GORGEOUS!
RUSTLE
WHY ARE YOU SO GOOD-LOOKING?! HUH?! HUH?! HUMAN OR LEOPARD, I LIKE 'EM HANDSOME!
CAN YOU JUST STAY IN YOUR HUMAN FORM FOREVER? YEAH? PLEASE?
HOP
GO AWAY. I NEED TO STUDY WITH BRIDDY.
HOP
AMON, WHY DID YOU CHANGE YOUR FORM? YOU COULD'VE STAYED AS A LEOPARD.
YOU DON'T LIKE ME AS A HUMAN?
SQUEEZE
NO, IT'S NOT THAT.
SHF
I CAN'T HOLD A QUILL AS A LEOPARD, CAN I?

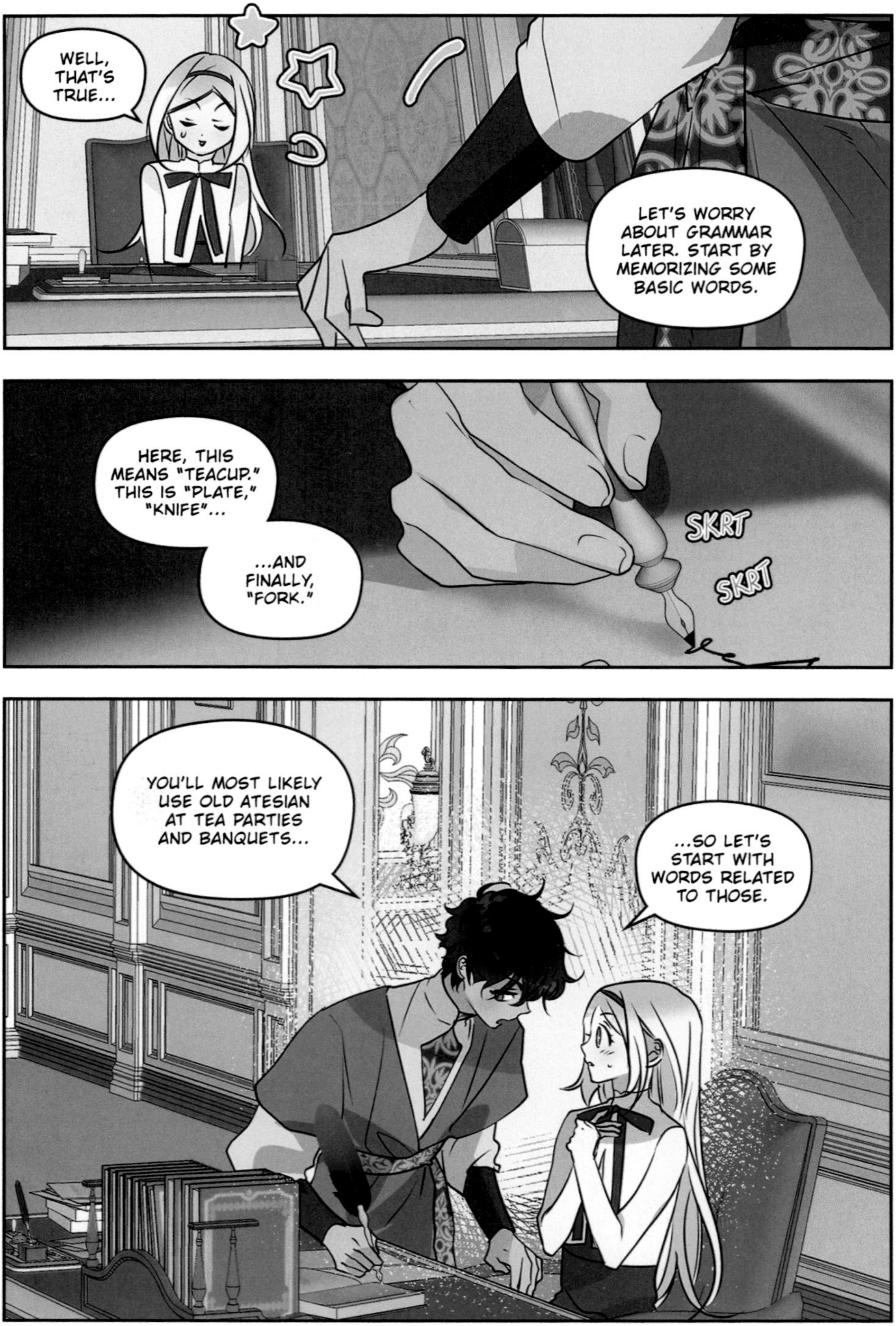
WELL, THAT'S TRUE...
LET'S WORRY ABOUT GRAMMAR LATER. START BY MEMORIZING SOME BASIC WORDS.
HERE, THIS MEANS "TEACUP." THIS IS "PLATE," "KNIFE"...
...AND FINALLY, "FORK."
SKRT
SKRT
YOU'LL MOST LIKELY USE OLD ATESIAN AT TEA PARTIES AND BANQUETS...
...SO LET'S START WITH WORDS RELATED TO THOSE.

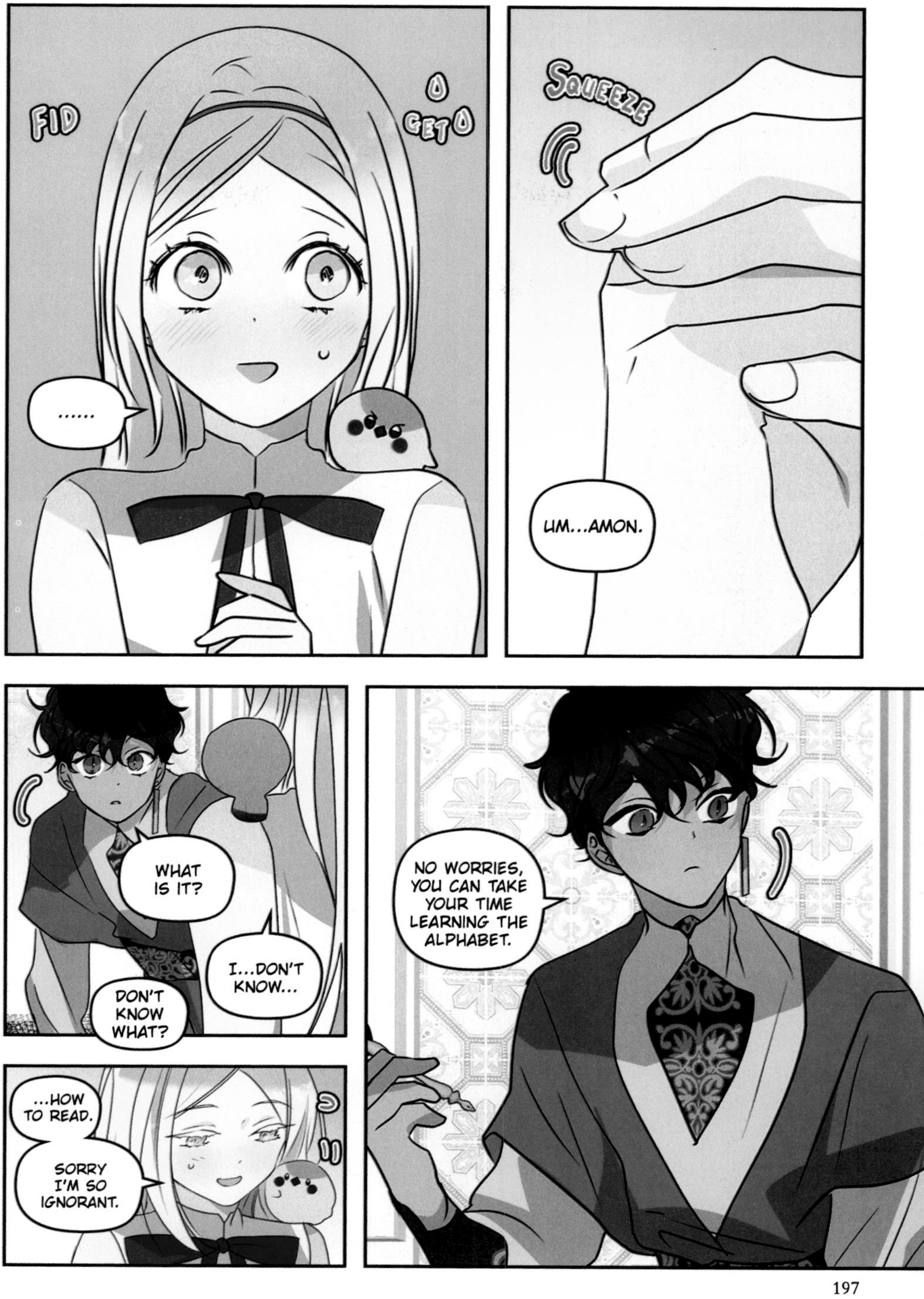
FID
GET
......
SQUEEZE
UM...AMON.
WHAT IS IT?
I...DON'T KNOW...
DON'T KNOW WHAT?
NO WORRIES, YOU CAN TAKE YOUR TIME LEARNING THE ALPHABET.
...HOW TO READ.
SORRY I'M SO IGNORANT.

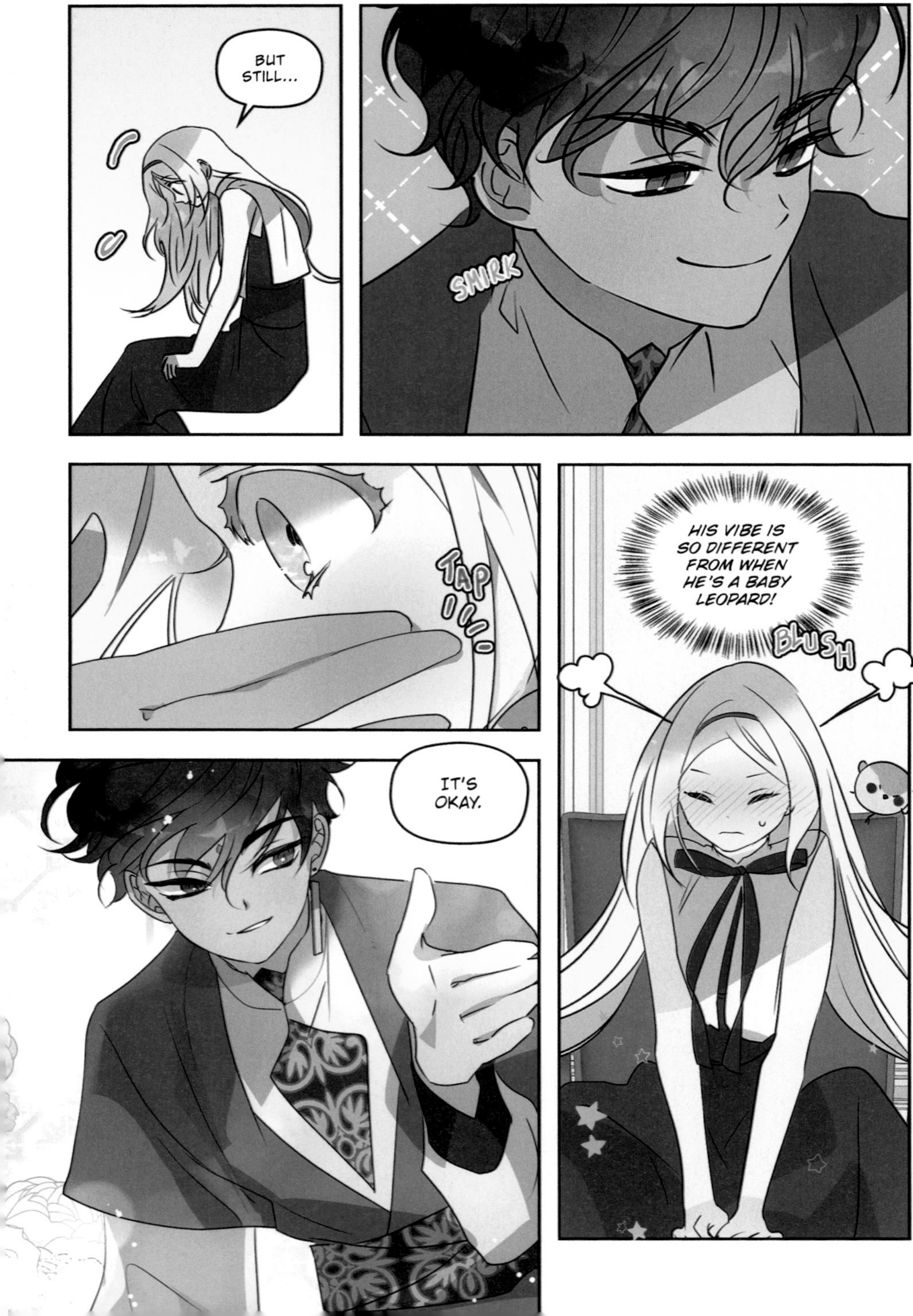
BUT STILL...
SMIRK
TAP
HIS VIBE IS SO DIFFERENT FROM WHEN HE'S A BABY LEOPARD!
BLUSH
IT'S OKAY.

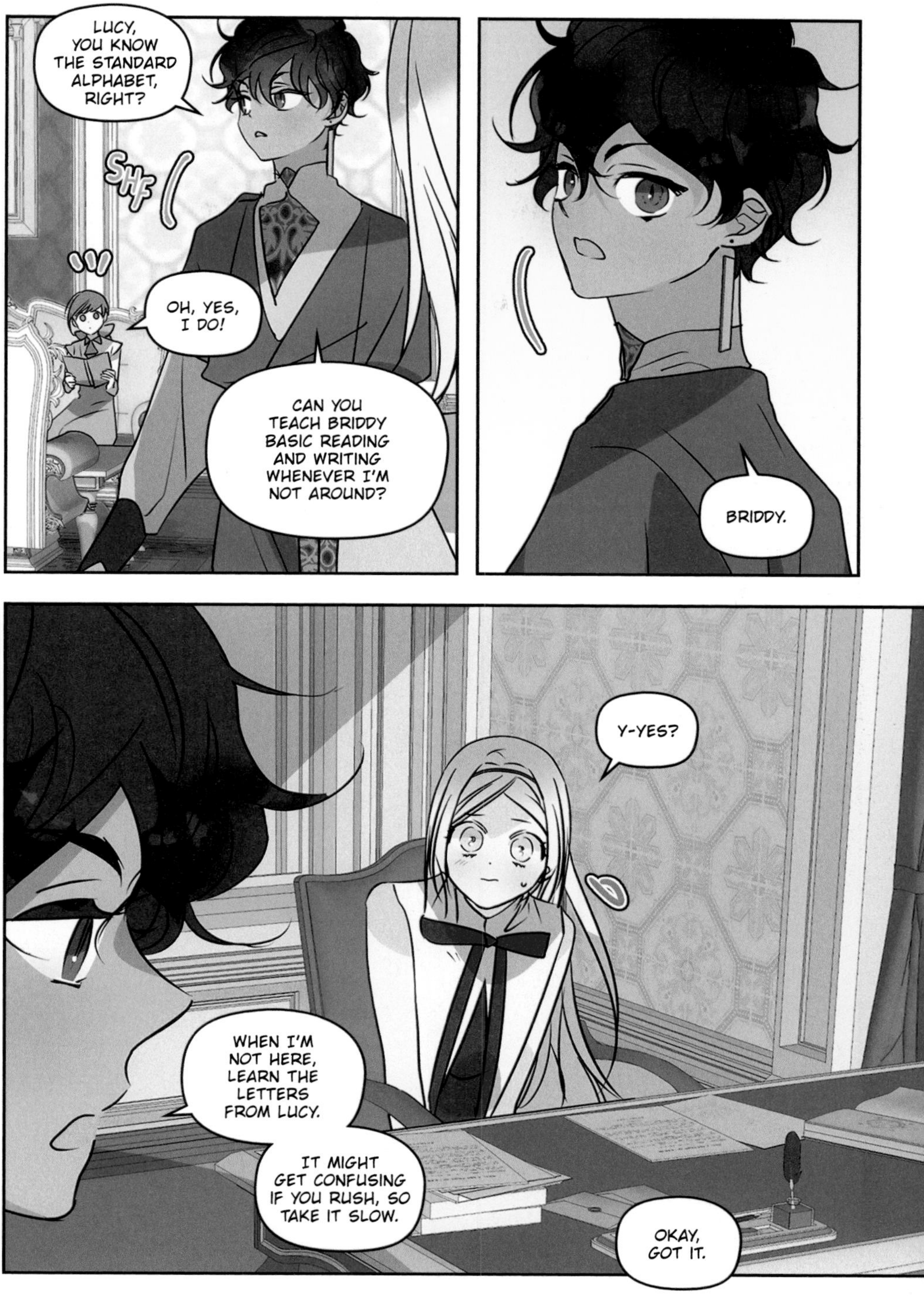
LUCY, YOU KNOW THE STANDARD ALPHABET, RIGHT?
SHF
OH, YES, I DO!
CAN YOU TEACH BRIDDY BASIC READING AND WRITING WHENEVER I'M NOT AROUND?
BRIDDY.
Y-YES?
WHEN I'M NOT HERE, LEARN THE LETTERS FROM LUCY.
IT MIGHT GET CONFUSING IF YOU RUSH, SO TAKE IT SLOW.
OKAY, GOT IT.

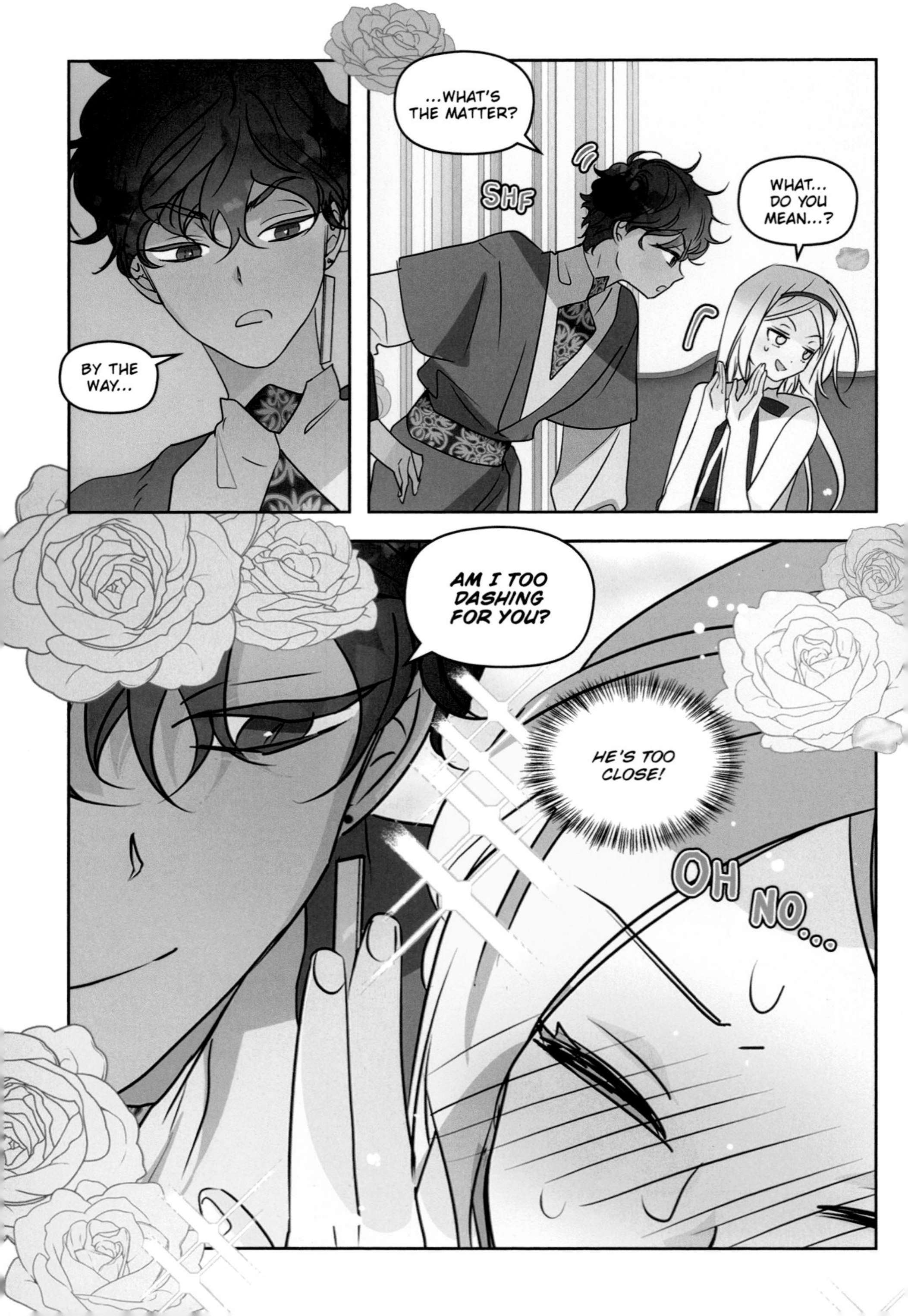
BY THE WAY...
...WHAT'S THE MATTER?
SHF
WHAT... DO YOU MEAN...?
AM I TOO DASHING FOR YOU?
HE'S TOO CLOSE!
OH NO...

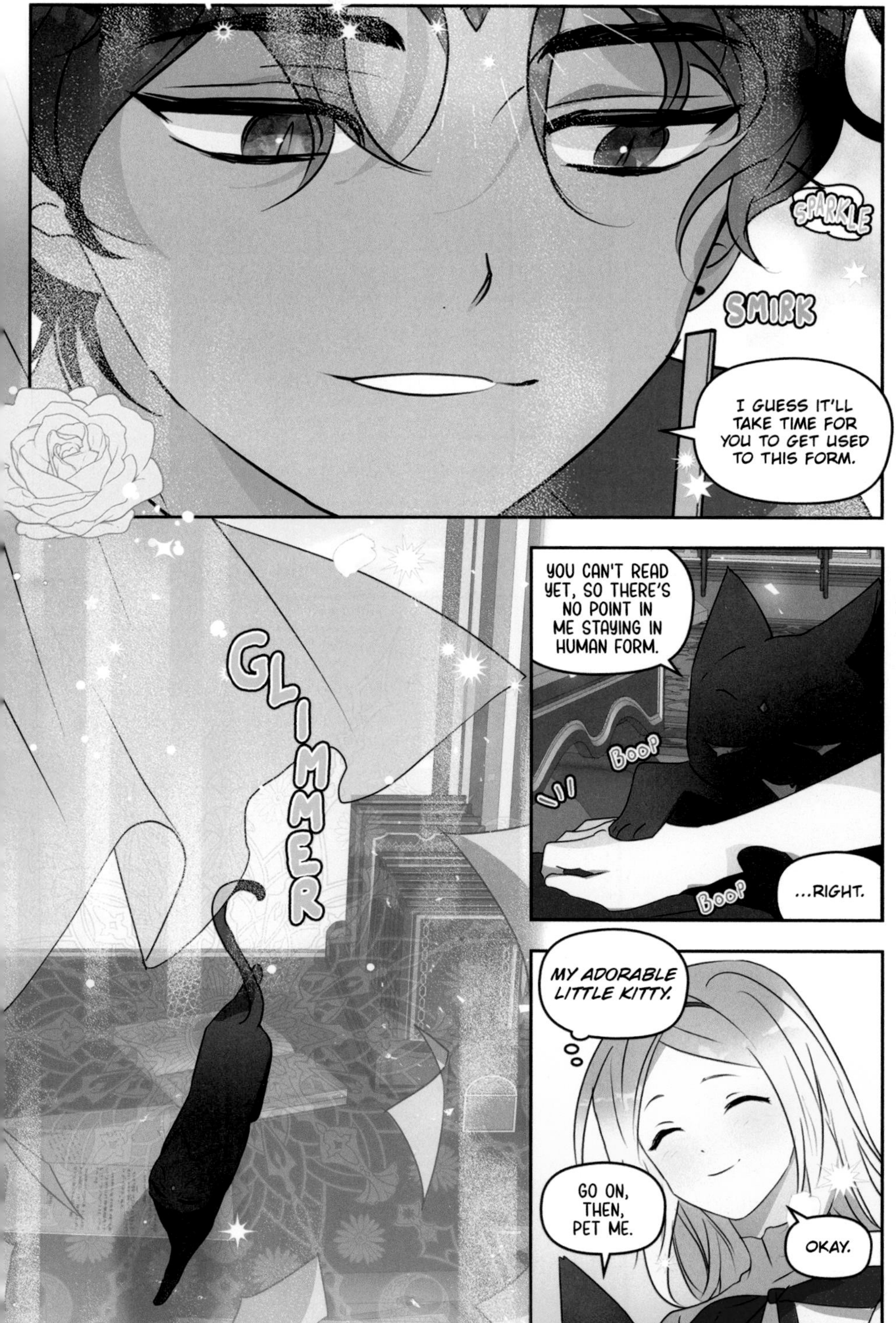
SPARKLE
SMIRK
I GUESS IT'LL TAKE TIME FOR YOU TO GET USED TO THIS FORM.
GLIMMER
YOU CAN'T READ YET, SO THERE'S NO POINT IN ME STAYING IN HUMAN FORM.
BOOP
BOOP
...RIGHT.
MY ADORABLE LITTLE KITTY.
GO ON, THEN, PET ME.
OKAY.

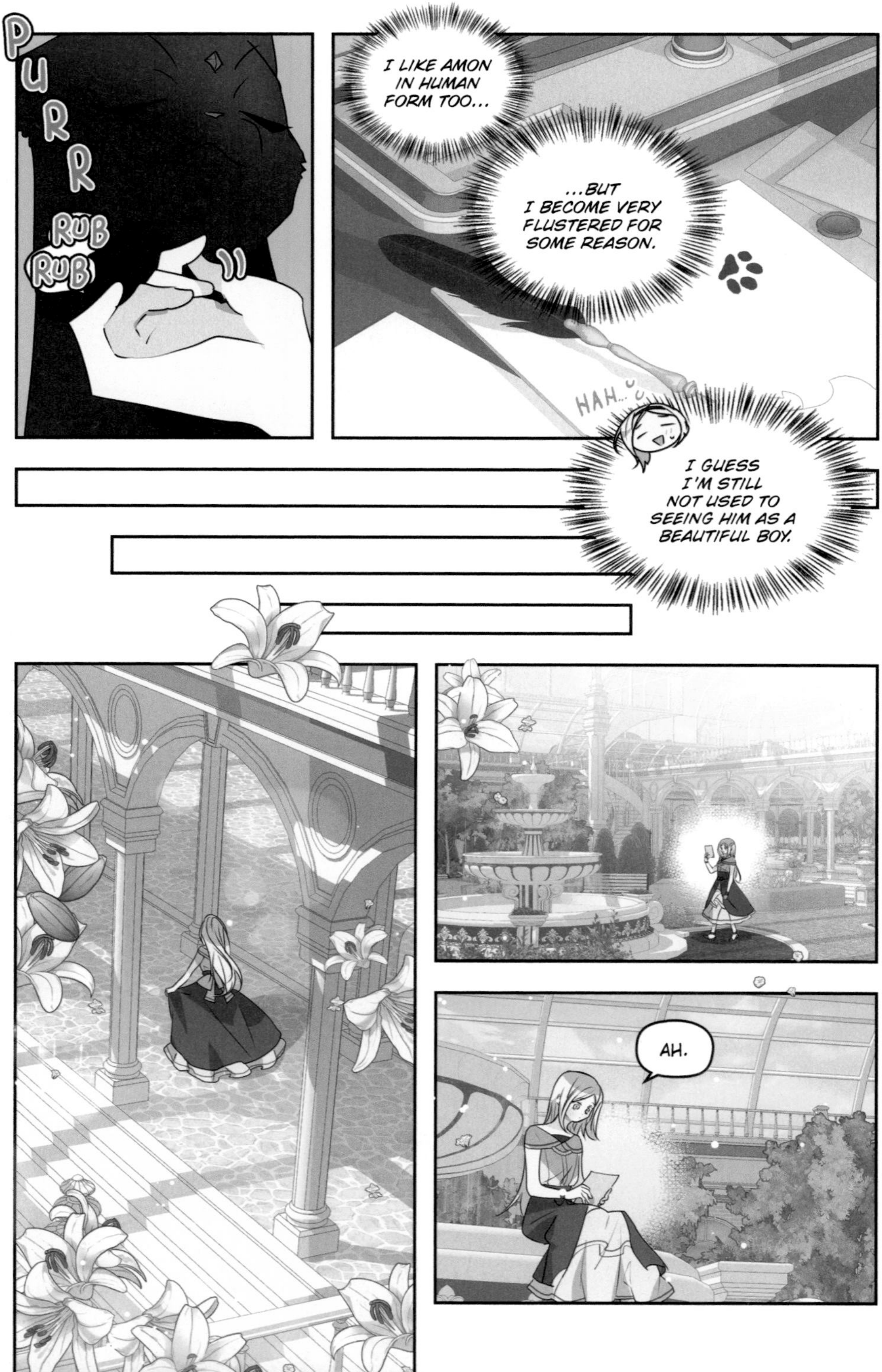
PURR
RUB
RUB
I LIKE AMON IN HUMAN FORM TOO...
...BUT I BECOME VERY FLUSTERED FOR SOME REASON.
HAH...
I GUESS I'M STILL NOT USED TO SEEING HIM AS A BEAUTIFUL BOY.
AH.

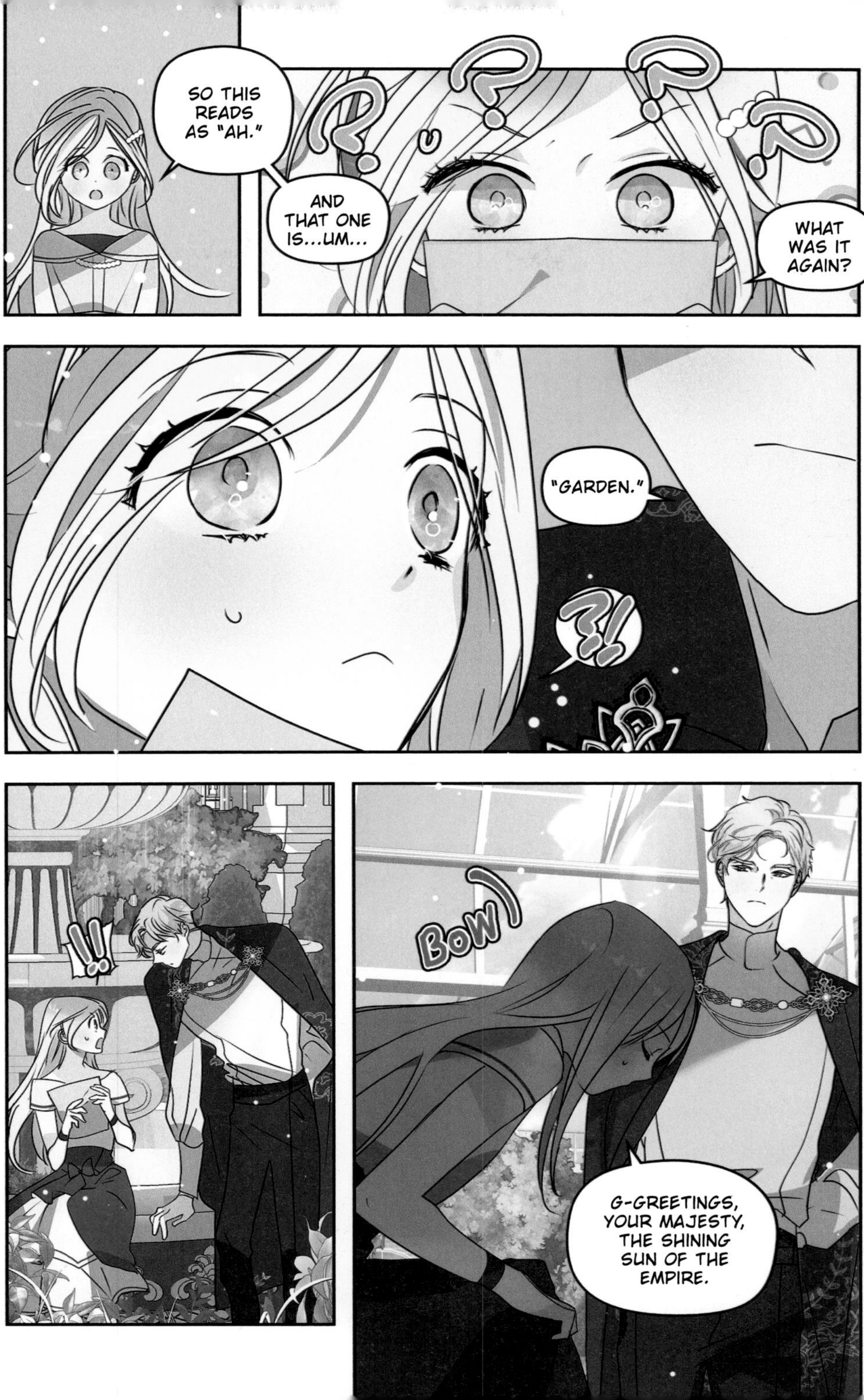

SO THIS READS AS "AH."
AND THAT ONE IS...UM...
WHAT WAS IT AGAIN?
"GARDEN."
?!
!!
BOW
G-GREETINGS, YOUR MAJESTY, THE SHINING SUN OF THE EMPIRE.

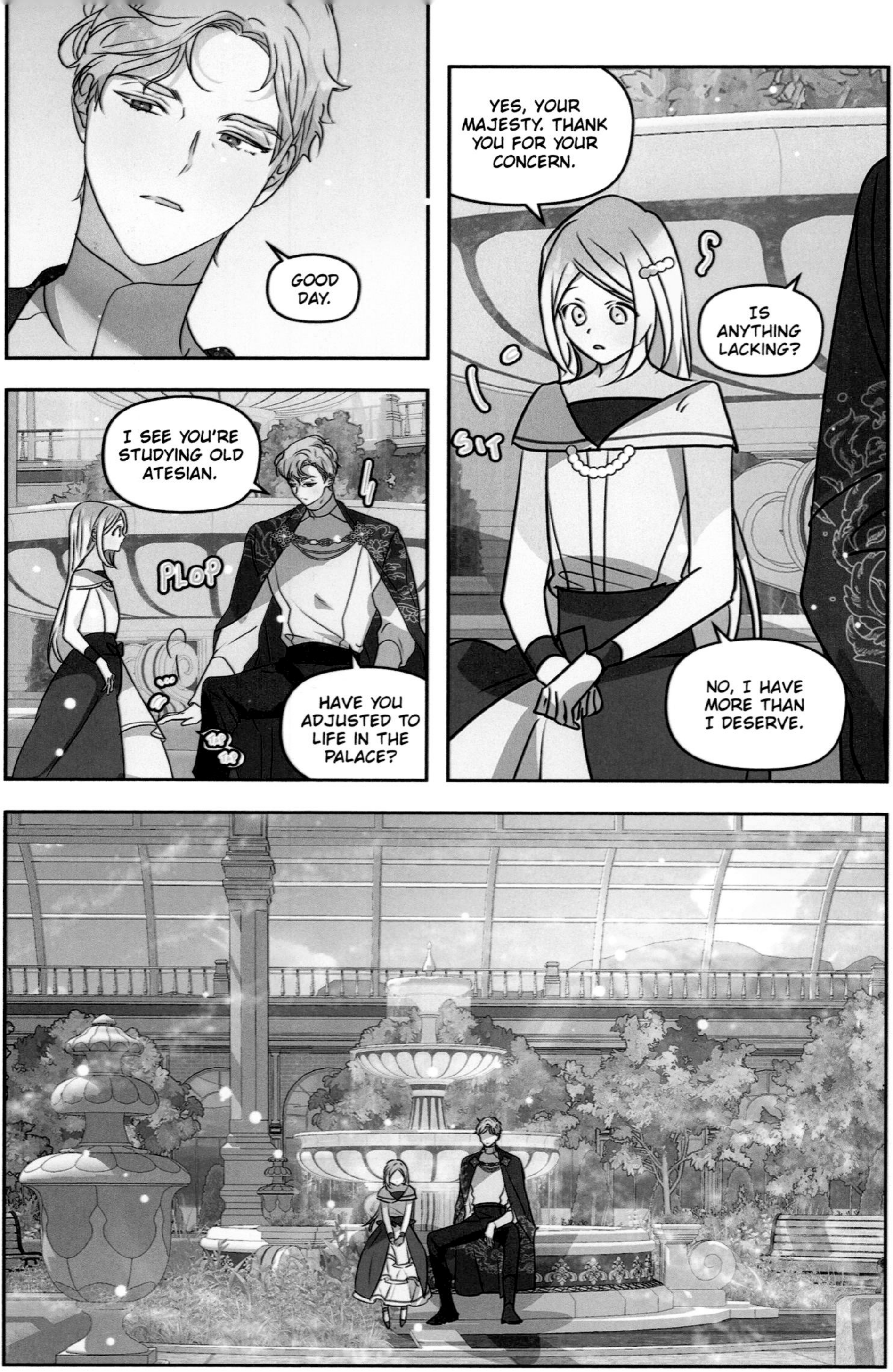
GOOD DAY.
I SEE YOU'RE STUDYING OLD ATESIAN.
PLOP
HAVE YOU ADJUSTED TO LIFE IN THE PALACE?
YES, YOUR MAJESTY. THANK YOU FOR YOUR CONCERN.
SIT
IS ANYTHING LACKING?
NO, I HAVE MORE THAN I DESERVE.

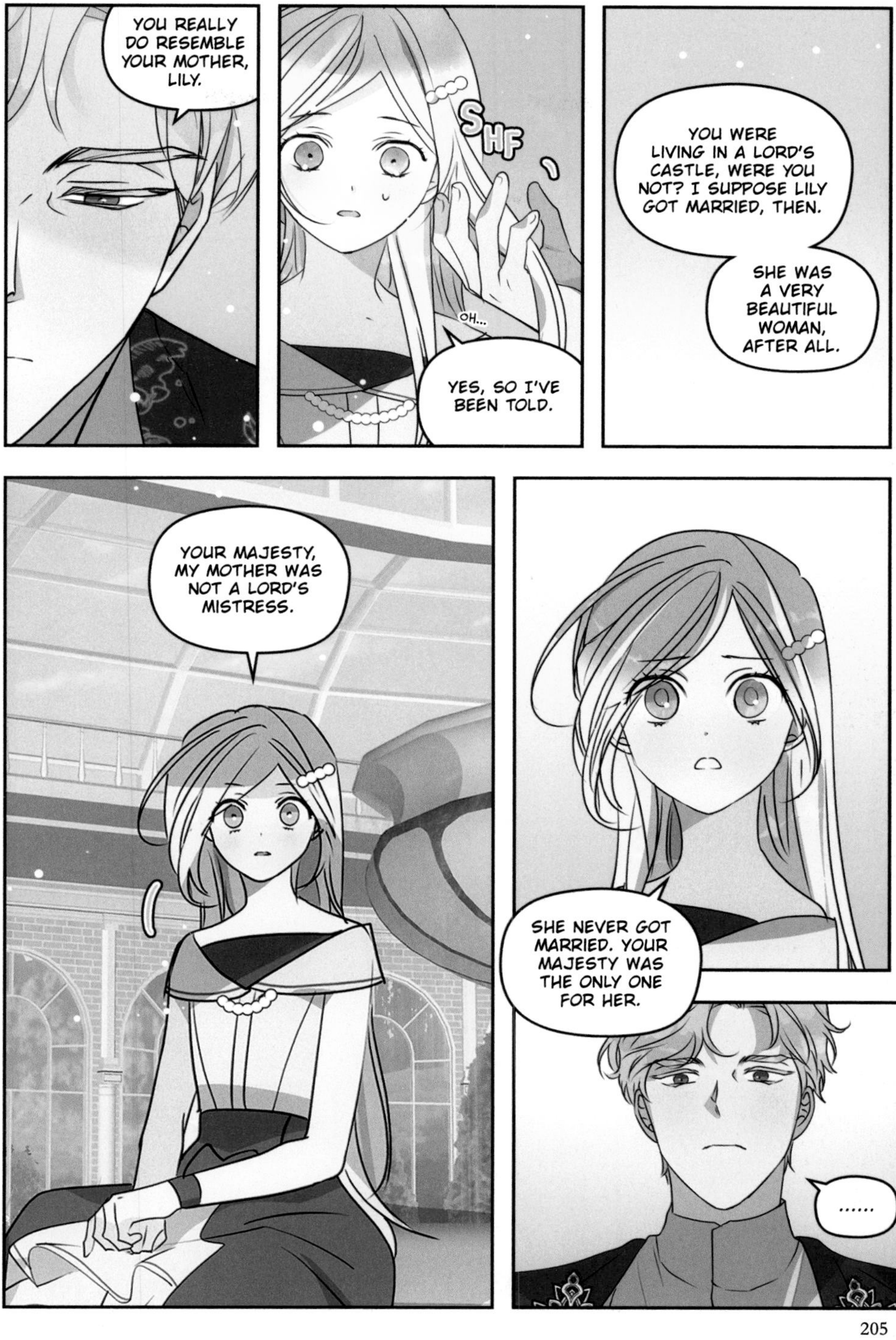
YOU REALLY DO RESEMBLE YOUR MOTHER, LILY.
SHF
OH...
YES, SO I'VE BEEN TOLD.
YOU WERE LIVING IN A LORD'S CASTLE, WERE YOU NOT? I SUPPOSE LILY GOT MARRIED, THEN.
SHE WAS A VERY BEAUTIFUL WOMAN, AFTER ALL.
YOUR MAJESTY, MY MOTHER WAS NOT A LORD'S MISTRESS.
SHE NEVER GOT MARRIED. YOUR MAJESTY WAS THE ONLY ONE FOR HER.
......

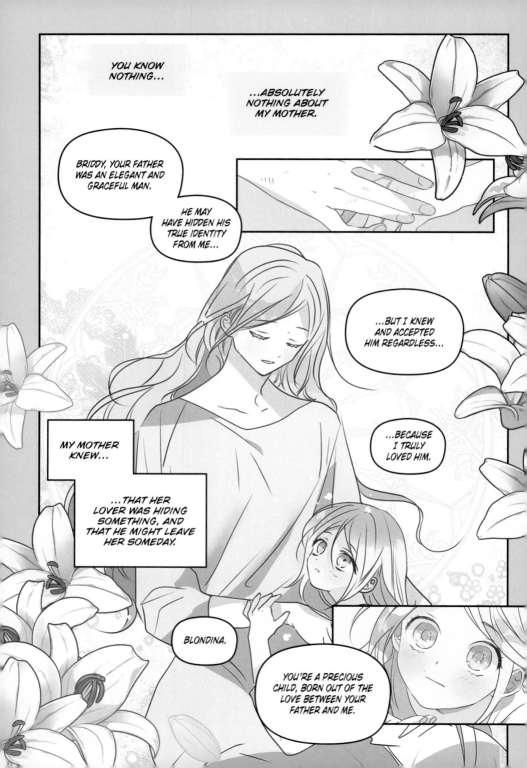

YOU KNOW NOTHING...

...ABSOLUTELY NOTHING ABOUT MY MOTHER.

BRIDDY, YOUR FATHER WAS AN ELEGANT AND GRACEFUL MAN.

HE MAY HAVE HIDDEN HIS TRUE IDENTITY FROM ME...

...BUT I KNEW AND ACCEPTED HIM REGARDLESS...

...BECAUSE I TRULY LOVED HIM.

MY MOTHER KNEW...

...THAT HER LOVER WAS HIDING SOMETHING, AND THAT HE MIGHT LEAVE HER SOMEDAY.

BLONDINA.

YOU'RE A PRECIOUS CHILD, BORN OUT OF THE LOVE BETWEEN YOUR FATHER AND ME.

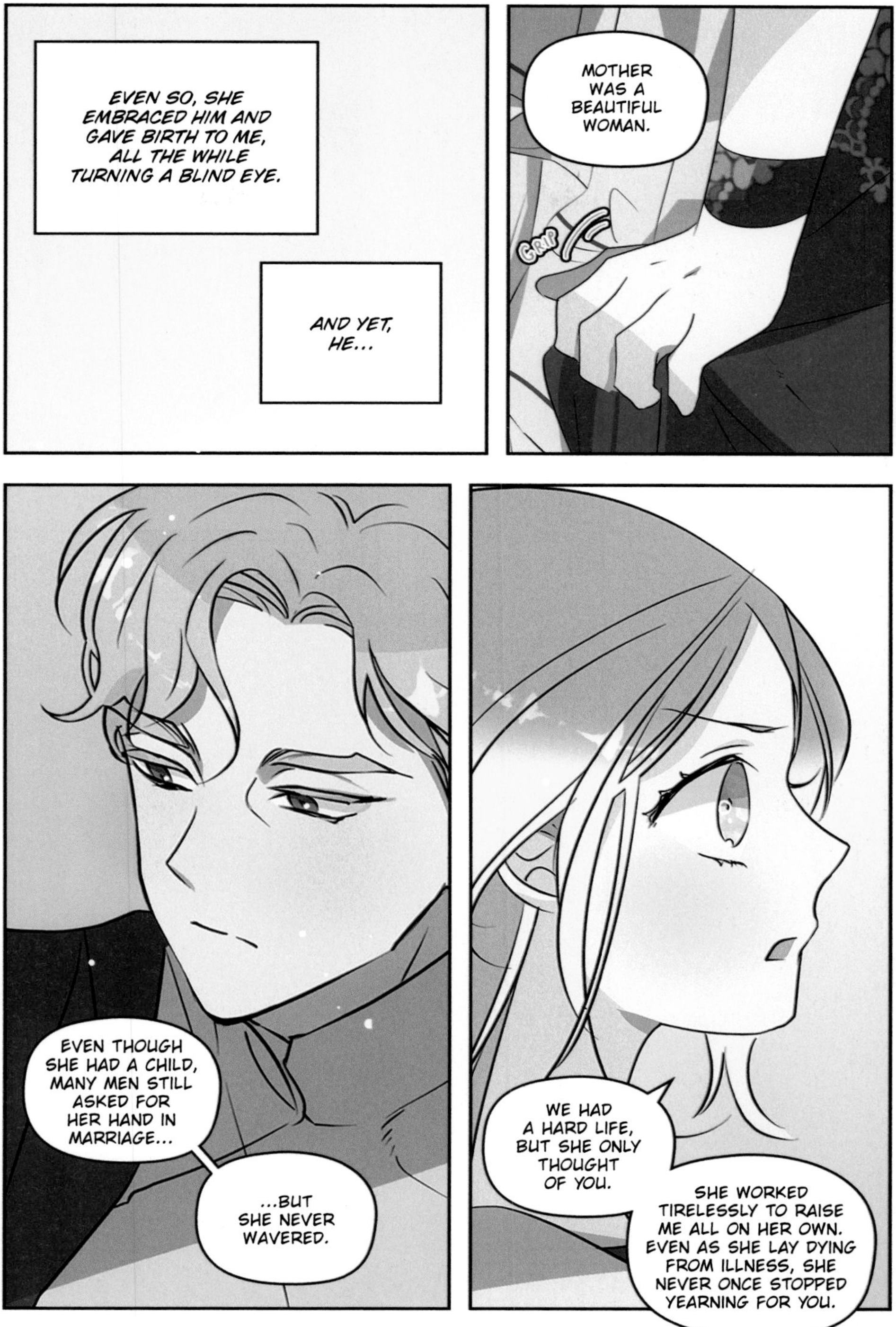
EVEN SO, SHE EMBRACED HIM AND GAVE BIRTH TO ME, ALL THE WHILE TURNING A BLIND EYE.
AND YET, HE...
MOTHER WAS A BEAUTIFUL WOMAN.
GRIP
EVEN THOUGH SHE HAD A CHILD, MANY MEN STILL ASKED FOR HER HAND IN MARRIAGE...
...BUT SHE NEVER WAVERED.
WE HAD A HARD LIFE, BUT SHE ONLY THOUGHT OF YOU.
SHE WORKED TIRELESSLY TO RAISE ME ALL ON HER OWN. EVEN AS SHE LAY DYING FROM ILLNESS, SHE NEVER ONCE STOPPED YEARNING FOR YOU.

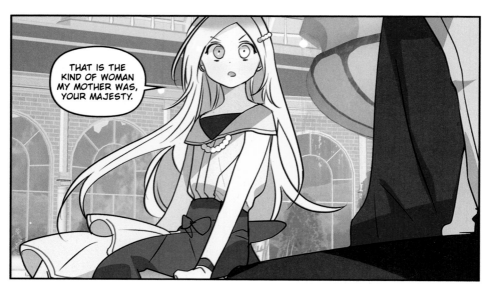

THAT IS THE KIND OF WOMAN MY MOTHER WAS, YOUR MAJESTY.

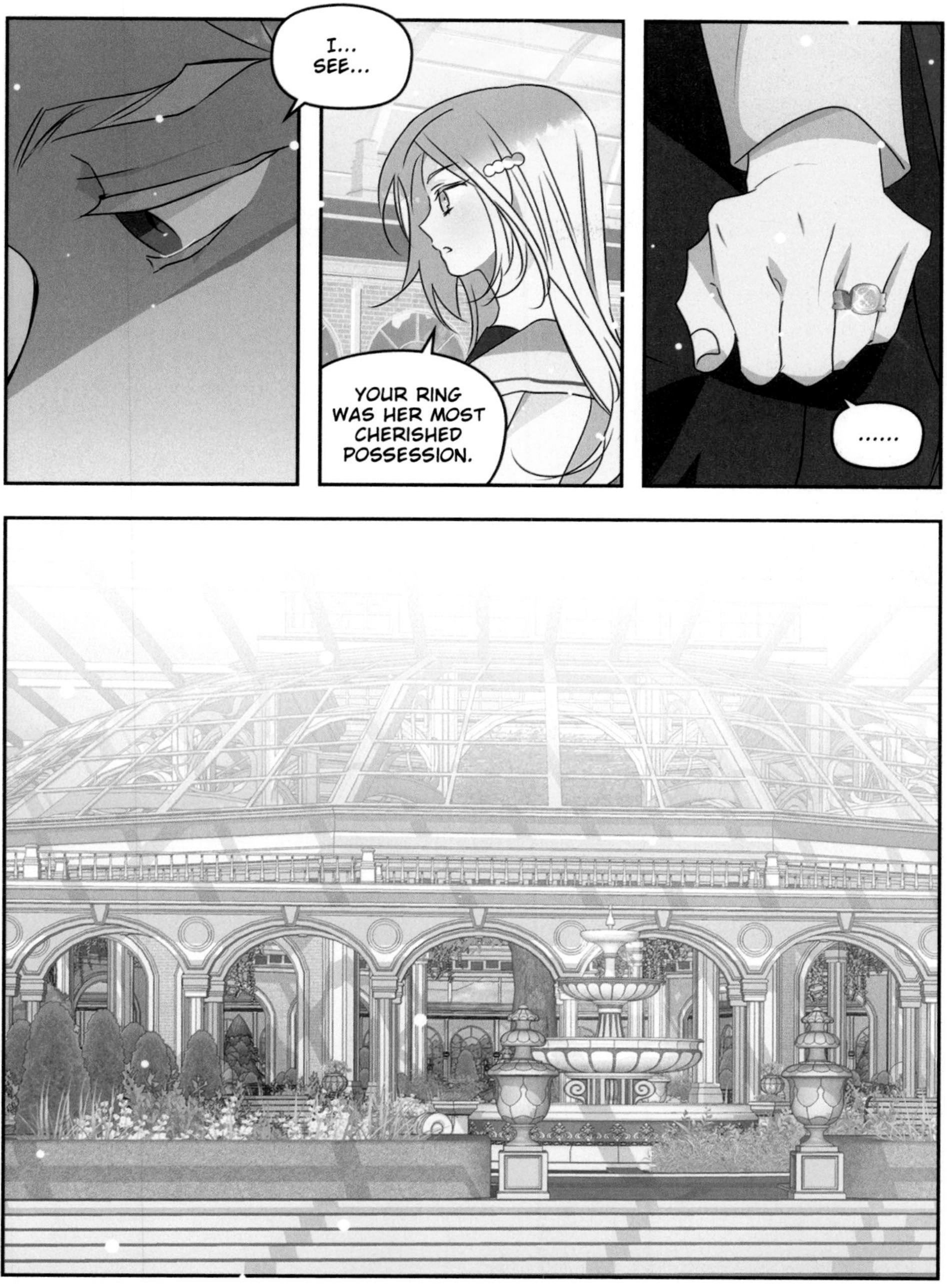
I... SEE...
YOUR RING WAS HER MOST CHERISHED POSSESSION.
......

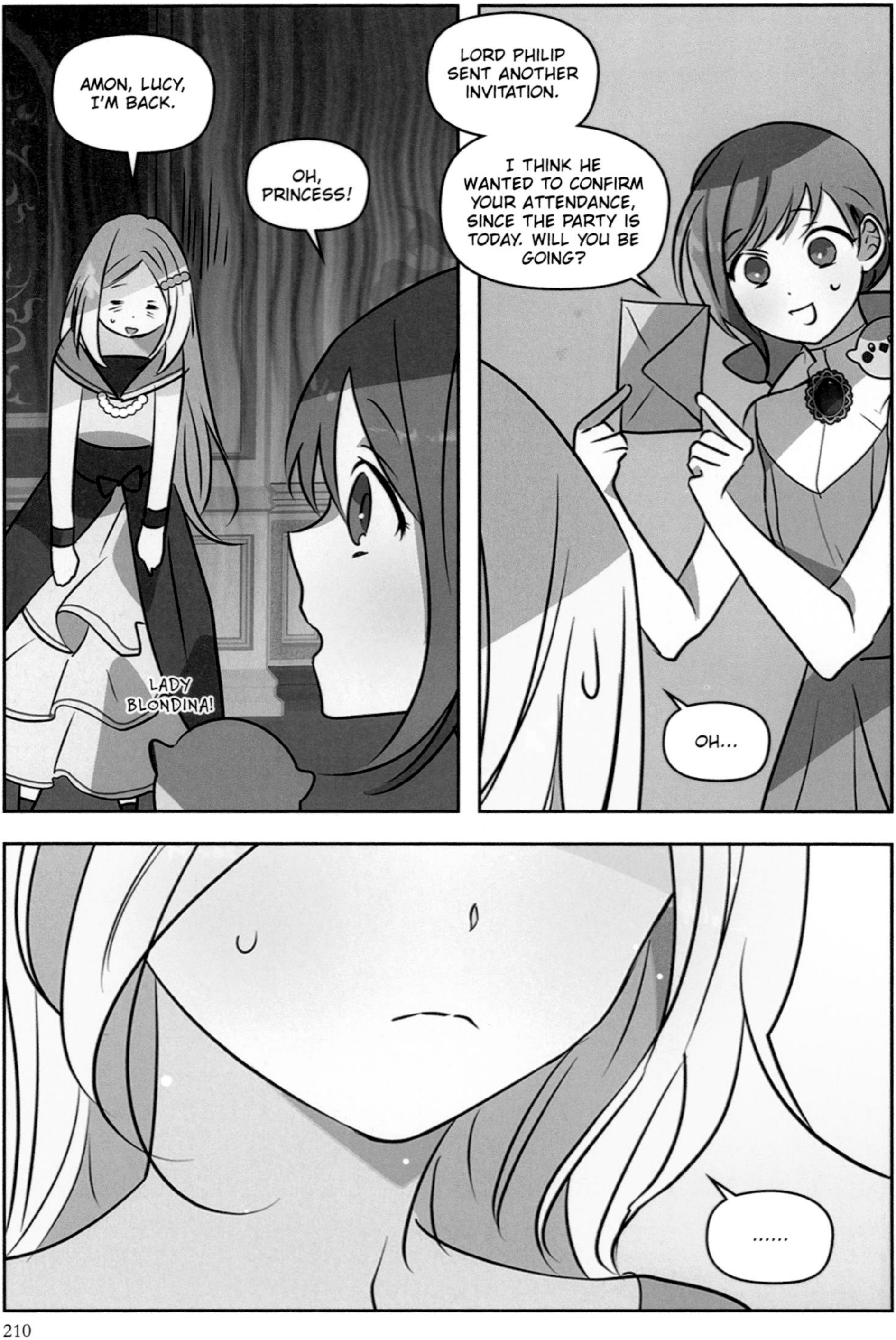
AMON, LUCY, I'M BACK.
OH, PRINCESS!
LADY BLONDINA!
LORD PHILIP SENT ANOTHER INVITATION.
I THINK HE WANTED TO CONFIRM YOUR ATTENDANCE, SINCE THE PARTY IS TODAY. WILL YOU BE GOING?
OH...
......

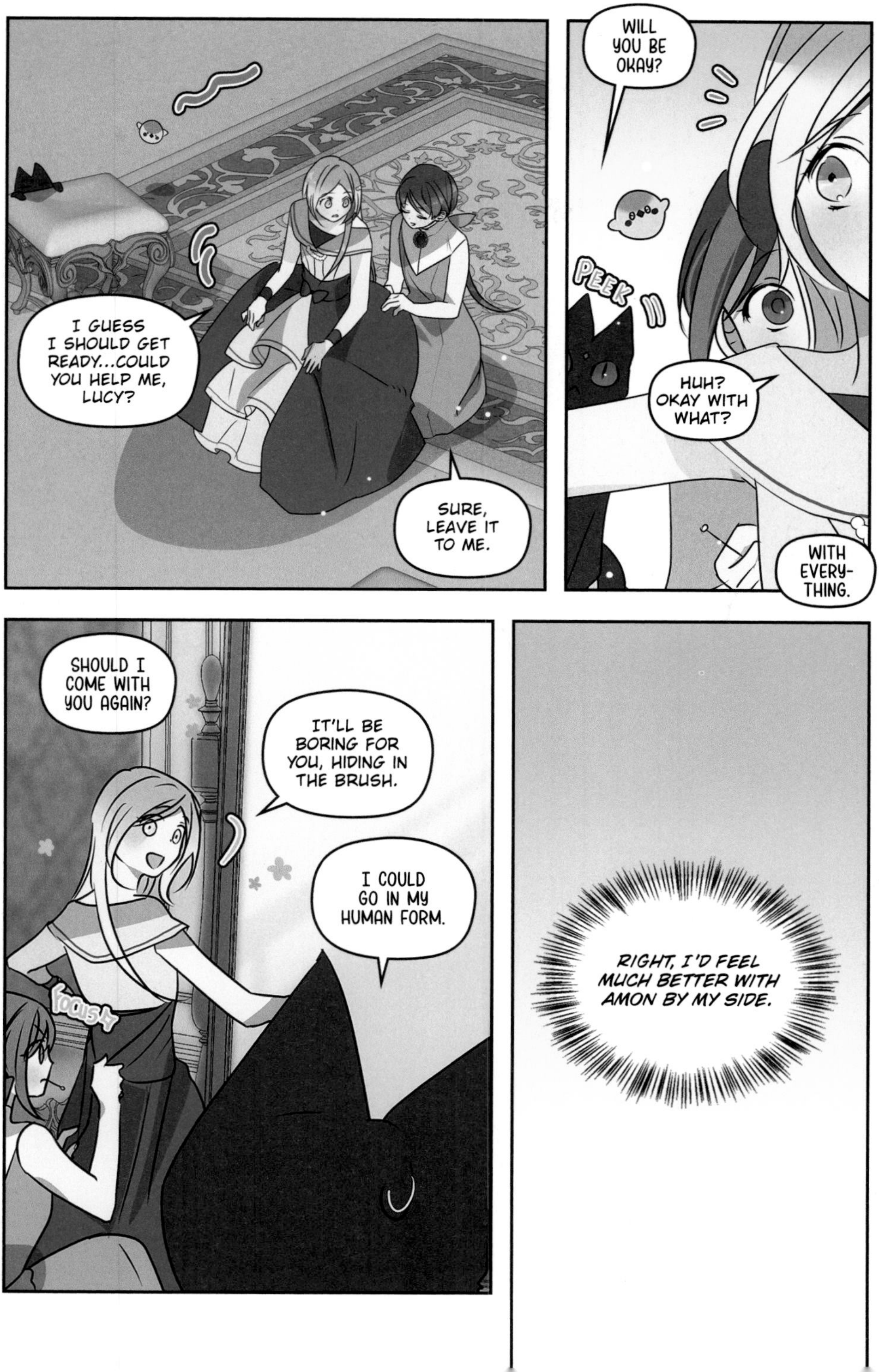
I GUESS I SHOULD GET READY...COULD YOU HELP ME, LUCY?
SURE, LEAVE IT TO ME.
WILL YOU BE OKAY?
PEEK
HUH? OKAY WITH WHAT?
WITH EVERY-THING.
SHOULD I COME WITH YOU AGAIN?
IT'LL BE BORING FOR YOU, HIDING IN THE BRUSH.
I COULD GO IN MY HUMAN FORM.
RIGHT, I'D FEEL MUCH BETTER WITH AMON BY MY SIDE.

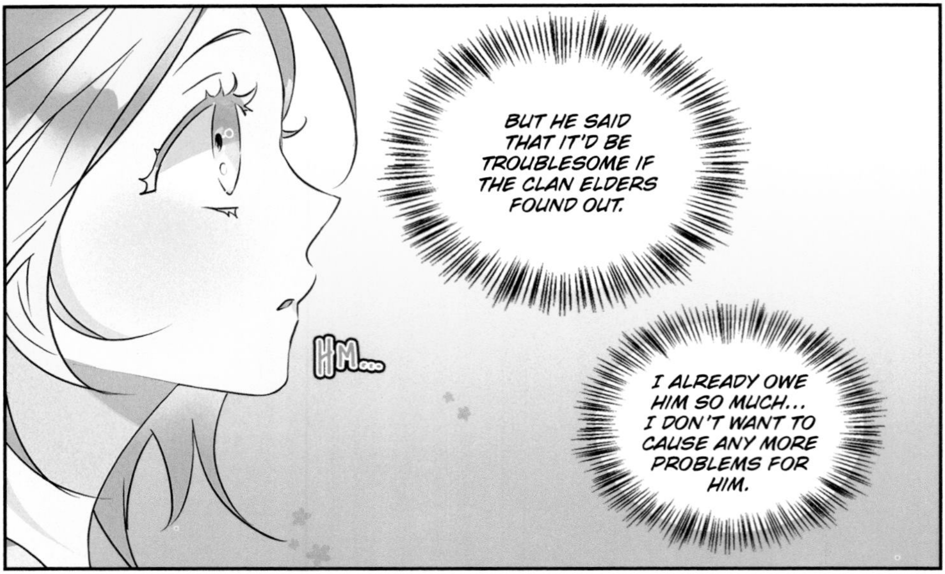
BUT HE SAID THAT IT'D BE TROUBLESOME IF THE CLAN ELDERS FOUND OUT.
HM...
I ALREADY OWE HIM SO MUCH... I DON'T WANT TO CAUSE ANY MORE PROBLEMS FOR HIM.

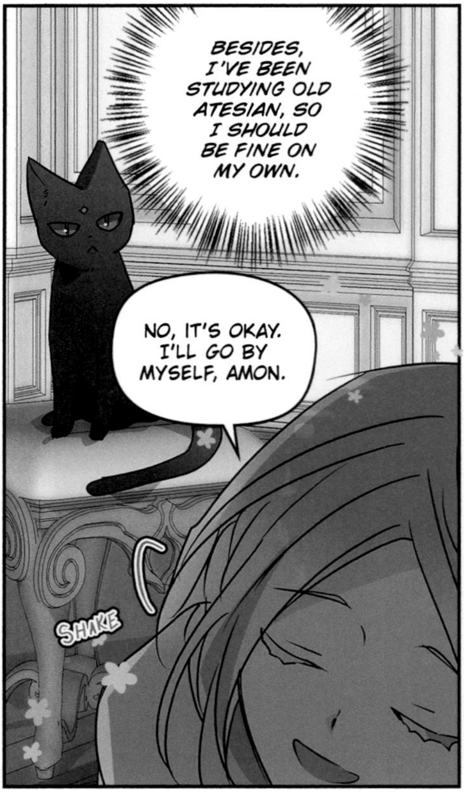
BESIDES, I'VE BEEN STUDYING OLD ATESIAN, SO I SHOULD BE FINE ON MY OWN.
NO, IT'S OKAY. I'LL GO BY MYSELF, AMON.
SHAKE

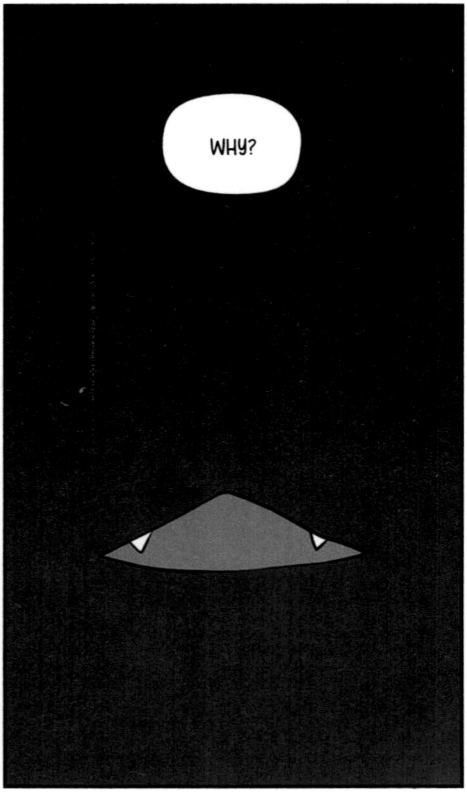
WHY?

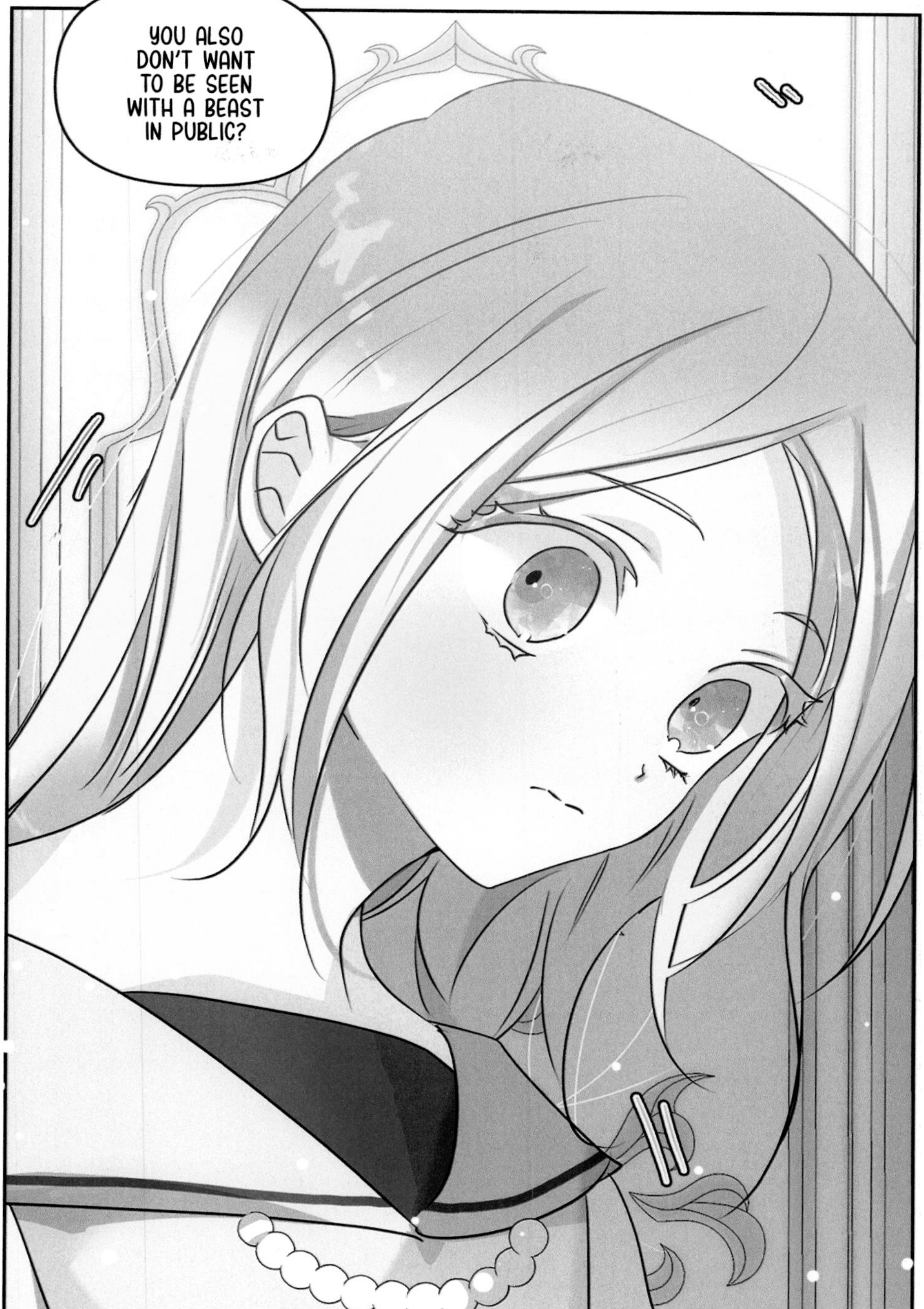
YOU ALSO DON'T WANT TO BE SEEN WITH A BEAST IN PUBLIC?

PART
3

My Gently Raised Beast

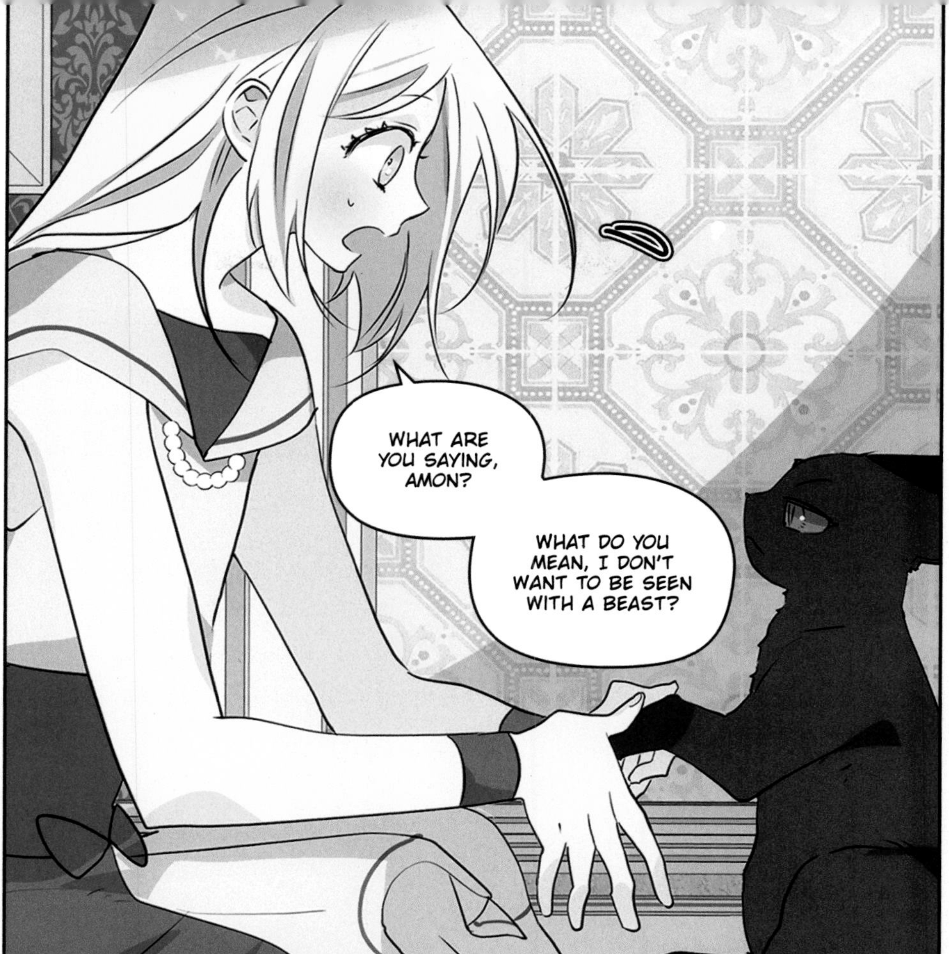
WHAT ARE YOU SAYING, AMON?
WHAT DO YOU MEAN, I DON'T WANT TO BE SEEN WITH A BEAST?

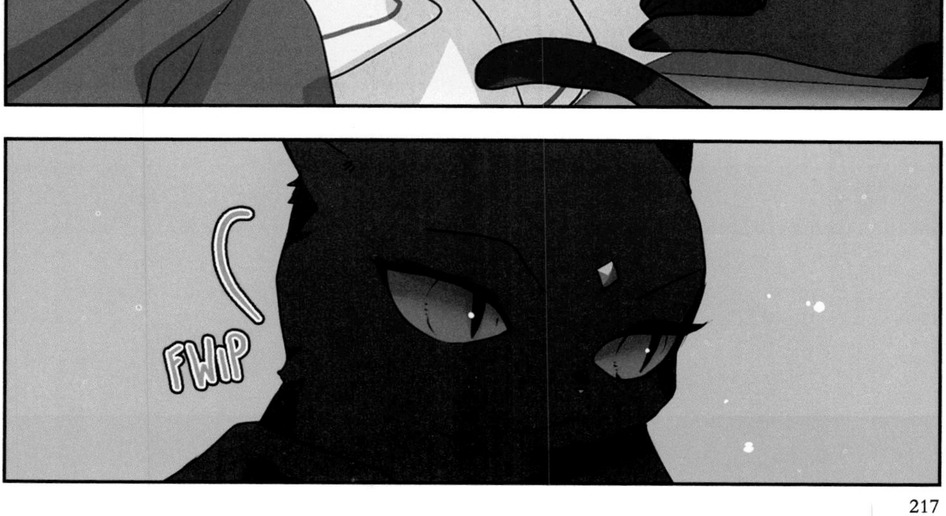
FWIP

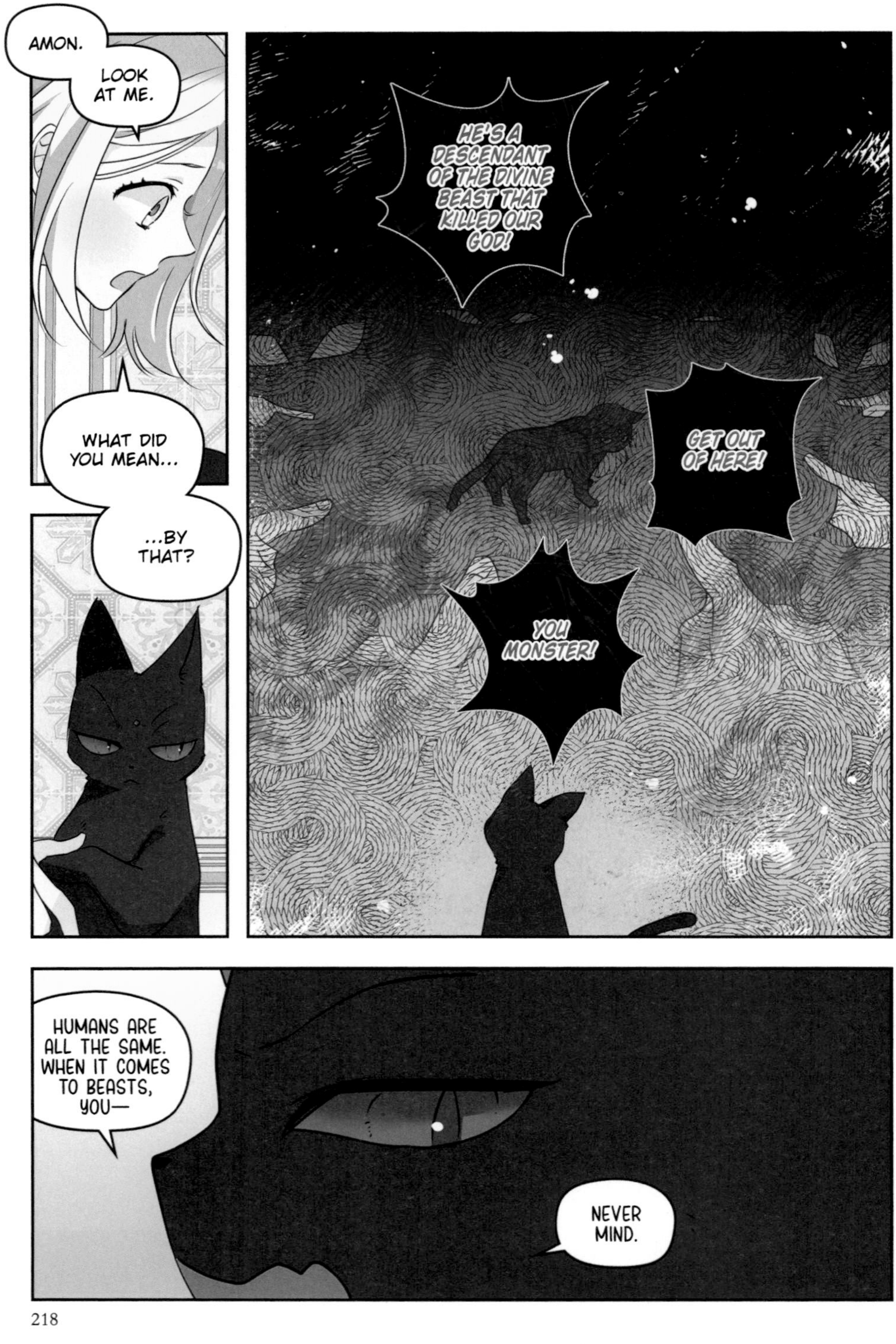
AMON.
LOOK AT ME.
WHAT DID YOU MEAN...
...BY THAT?
HE'S A DESCENDANT OF THE DIVINE BEAST THAT KILLED OUR GOD!
GET OUT OF HERE!
YOU MONSTER!
HUMANS ARE ALL THE SAME. WHEN IT COMES TO BEASTS, YOU—
NEVER MIND.

HUH?

ANYWAY, IF ANYONE BOTHERS YOU, JUST BITE THEM. HUMANS HAVE TEETH TOO, RIGHT? OR YOU COULD SCRATCH THEM WITH YOUR NAILS.

OKAY, I WILL. I'M SORRY I HAVE TO LEAVE, EVEN THOUGH THIS IS YOUR FIRST VISIT IN A WHILE.

PLAY WITH LUCY FOR TODAY, OKAY?

PLAY WITH HER? DO I LOOK LIKE A CHILD?

JU

MP

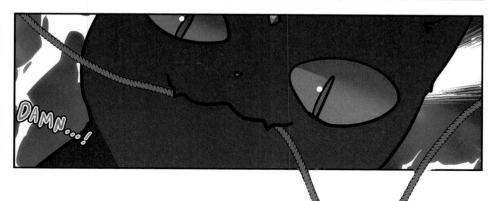

DAMN...!

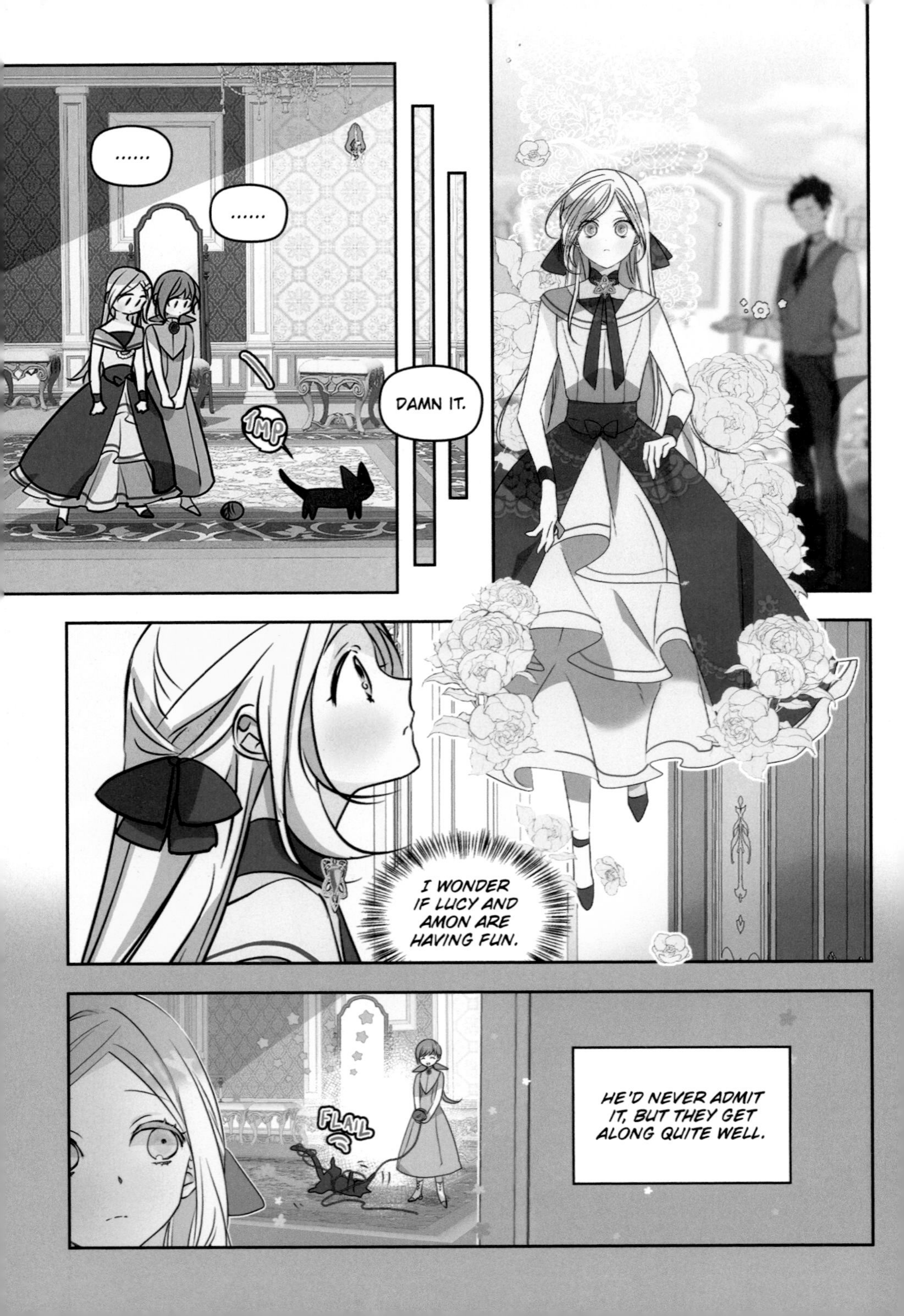

......
......
TMP
DAMN IT.
I WONDER IF LUCY AND AMON ARE HAVING FUN.
FLAIL
HE'D NEVER ADMIT IT, BUT THEY GET ALONG QUITE WELL.

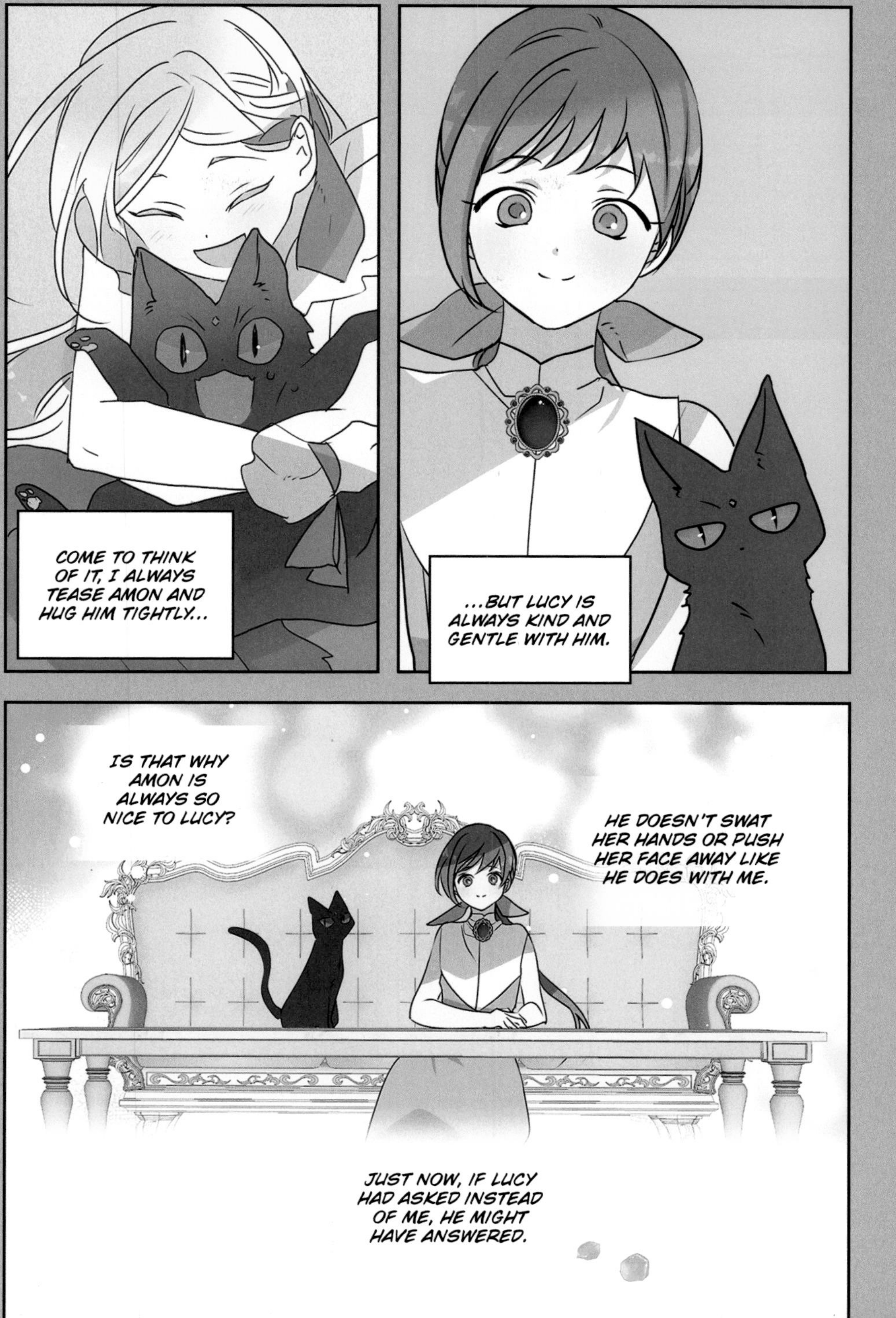
COME TO THINK OF IT, I ALWAYS TEASE AMON AND HUG HIM TIGHTLY...
...BUT LUCY IS ALWAYS KIND AND GENTLE WITH HIM.
IS THAT WHY AMON IS ALWAYS SO NICE TO LUCY?
HE DOESN'T SWAT HER HANDS OR PUSH HER FACE AWAY LIKE HE DOES WITH ME.
JUST NOW, IF LUCY HAD ASKED INSTEAD OF ME, HE MIGHT HAVE ANSWERED.

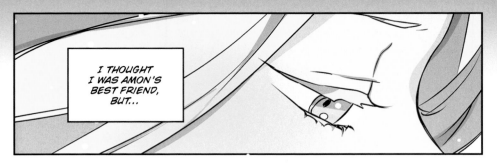

I THOUGHT I WAS AMON'S BEST FRIEND, BUT...

CLACK
CLACK

PRINCESS BLONDINA RYUN ATES HAS ARRIVED!

...AM I JUST BEING SELFISH?

YOU MADE IT, PRINCESS.

YES, SINCE YOU WERE KIND ENOUGH TO INVITE ME PERSONALLY.

OH...

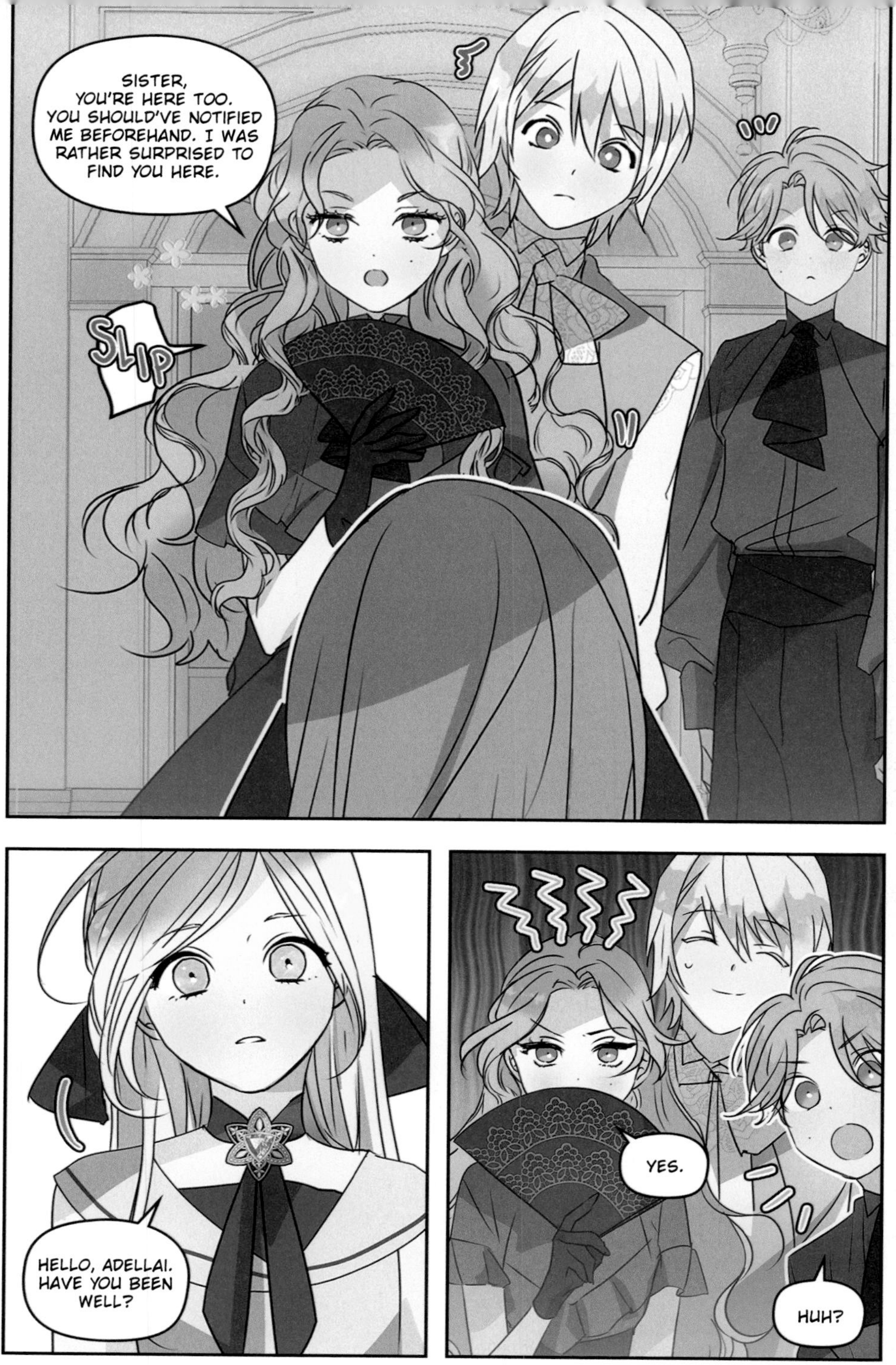
SISTER, YOU'RE HERE TOO. YOU SHOULD'VE NOTIFIED ME BEFOREHAND. I WAS RATHER SURPRISED TO FIND YOU HERE.
SLIP
HELLO, ADELLAI. HAVE YOU BEEN WELL?
YES.
HUH?

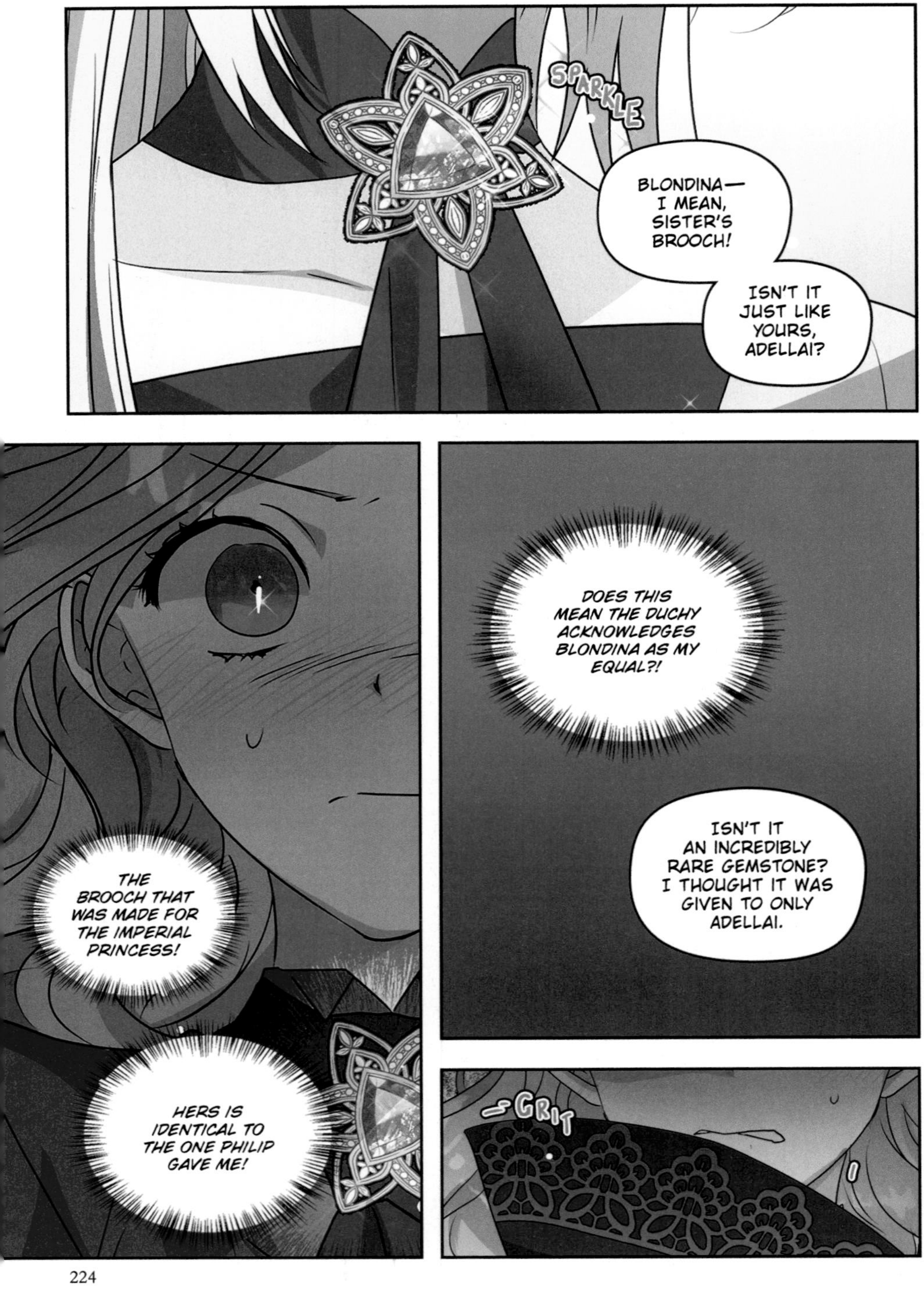
SPARKLE
BLONDINA— I MEAN, SISTER'S BROOCH!
ISN'T IT JUST LIKE YOURS, ADELLAI?
THE BROOCH THAT WAS MADE FOR THE IMPERIAL PRINCESS!
HERS IS IDENTICAL TO THE ONE PHILIP GAVE ME!
DOES THIS MEAN THE DUCHY ACKNOWLEDGES BLONDINA AS MY EQUAL?!
ISN'T IT AN INCREDIBLY RARE GEMSTONE? I THOUGHT IT WAS GIVEN TO ONLY ADELLAI.
GRIT

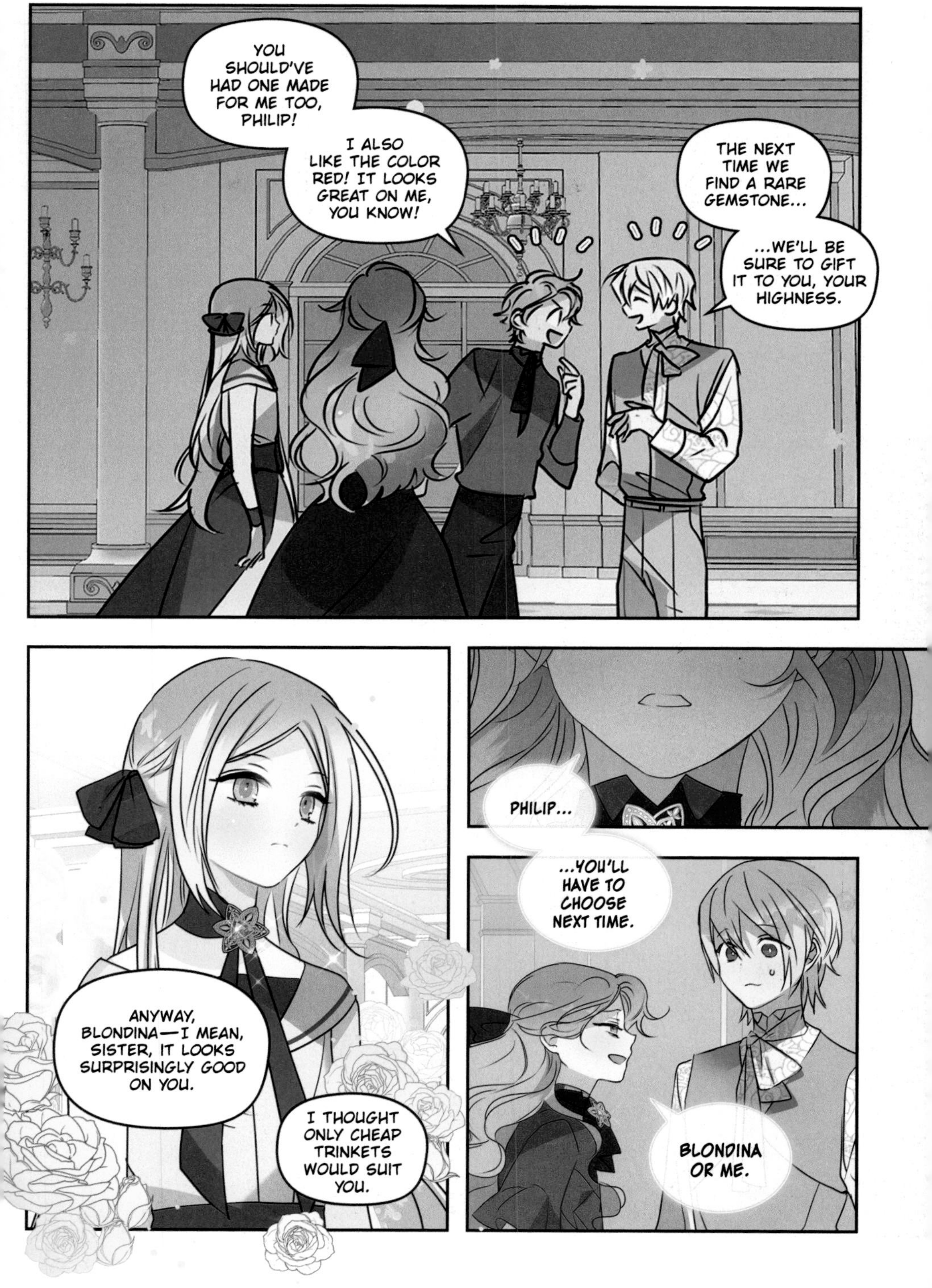
YOU SHOULD'VE HAD ONE MADE FOR ME TOO, PHILIP!
I ALSO LIKE THE COLOR RED! IT LOOKS GREAT ON ME, YOU KNOW!
THE NEXT TIME WE FIND A RARE GEMSTONE...
...WE'LL BE SURE TO GIFT IT TO YOU, YOUR HIGHNESS.
ANYWAY, BLONDINA—I MEAN, SISTER, IT LOOKS SURPRISINGLY GOOD ON YOU.
I THOUGHT ONLY CHEAP TRINKETS WOULD SUIT YOU.
PHILIP...
...YOU'LL HAVE TO CHOOSE NEXT TIME.
BLONDINA OR ME.

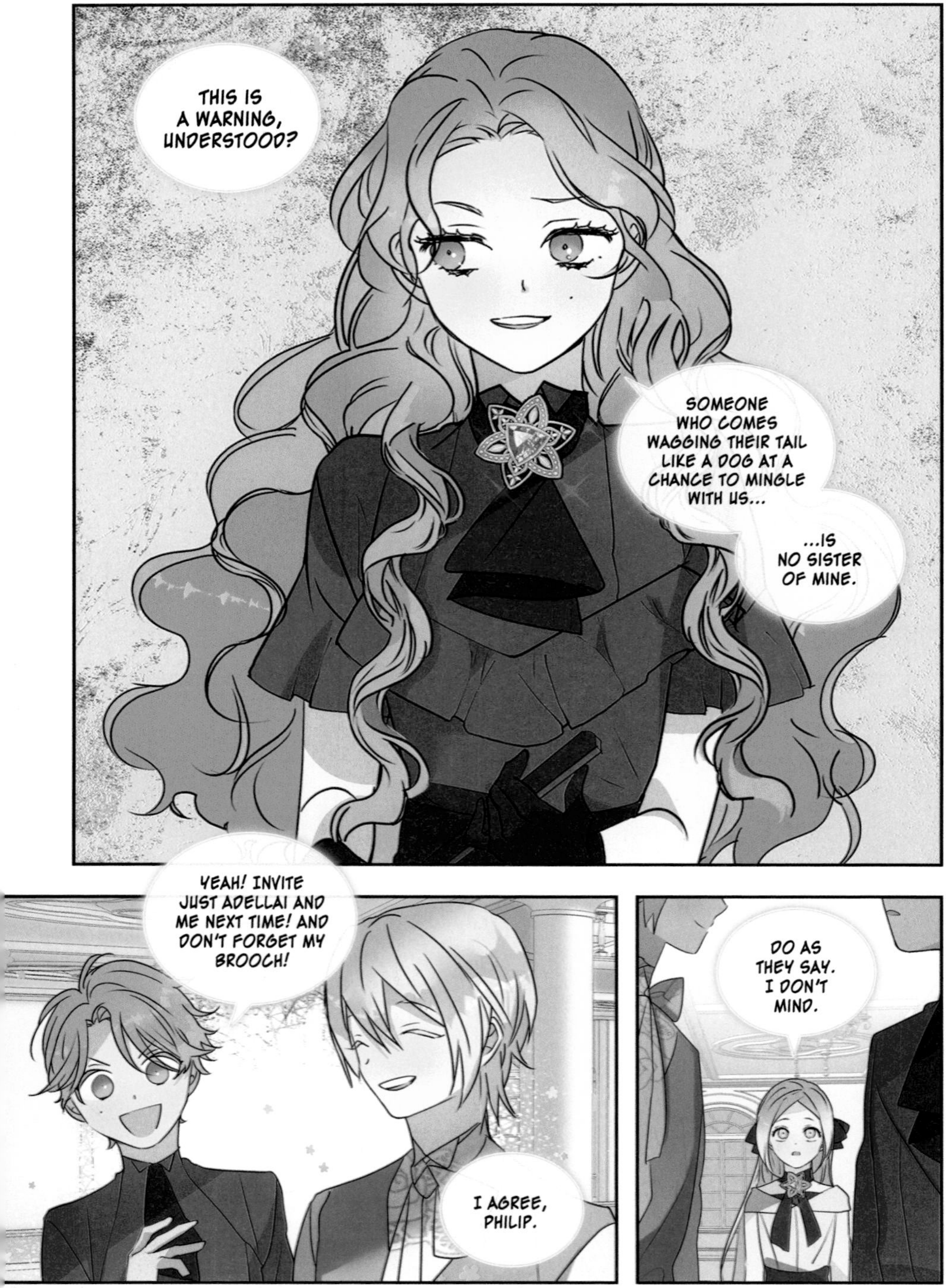
THIS IS A WARNING, UNDERSTOOD?
SOMEONE WHO COMES WAGGING THEIR TAIL LIKE A DOG AT A CHANCE TO MINGLE WITH US...
...IS NO SISTER OF MINE.
YEAH! INVITE JUST ADELLAI AND ME NEXT TIME! AND DON'T FORGET MY BROOCH!
I AGREE, PHILIP.
DO AS THEY SAY. I DON'T MIND.

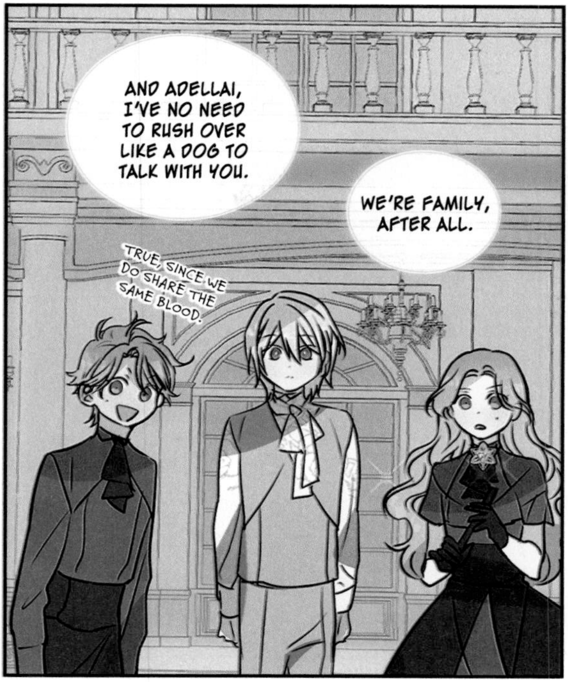
AND ADELLAI, I'VE NO NEED TO RUSH OVER LIKE A DOG TO TALK WITH YOU.
WE'RE FAMILY, AFTER ALL.
TRUE, SINCE WE DO SHARE THE SAME BLOOD.

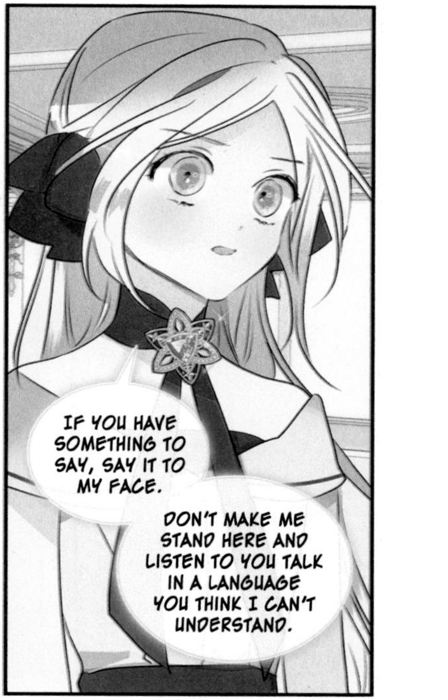
IF YOU HAVE SOMETHING TO SAY, SAY IT TO MY FACE.
DON'T MAKE ME STAND HERE AND LISTEN TO YOU TALK IN A LANGUAGE YOU THINK I CAN'T UNDERSTAND.

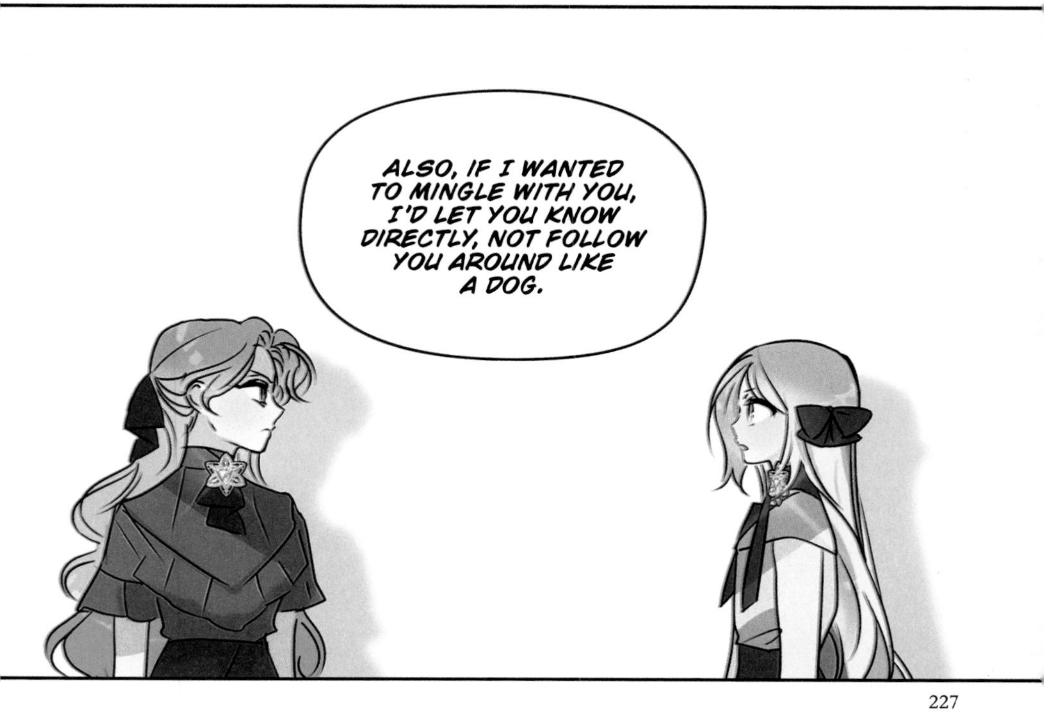
ALSO, IF I WANTED TO MINGLE WITH YOU, I'D LET YOU KNOW DIRECTLY, NOT FOLLOW YOU AROUND LIKE A DOG.

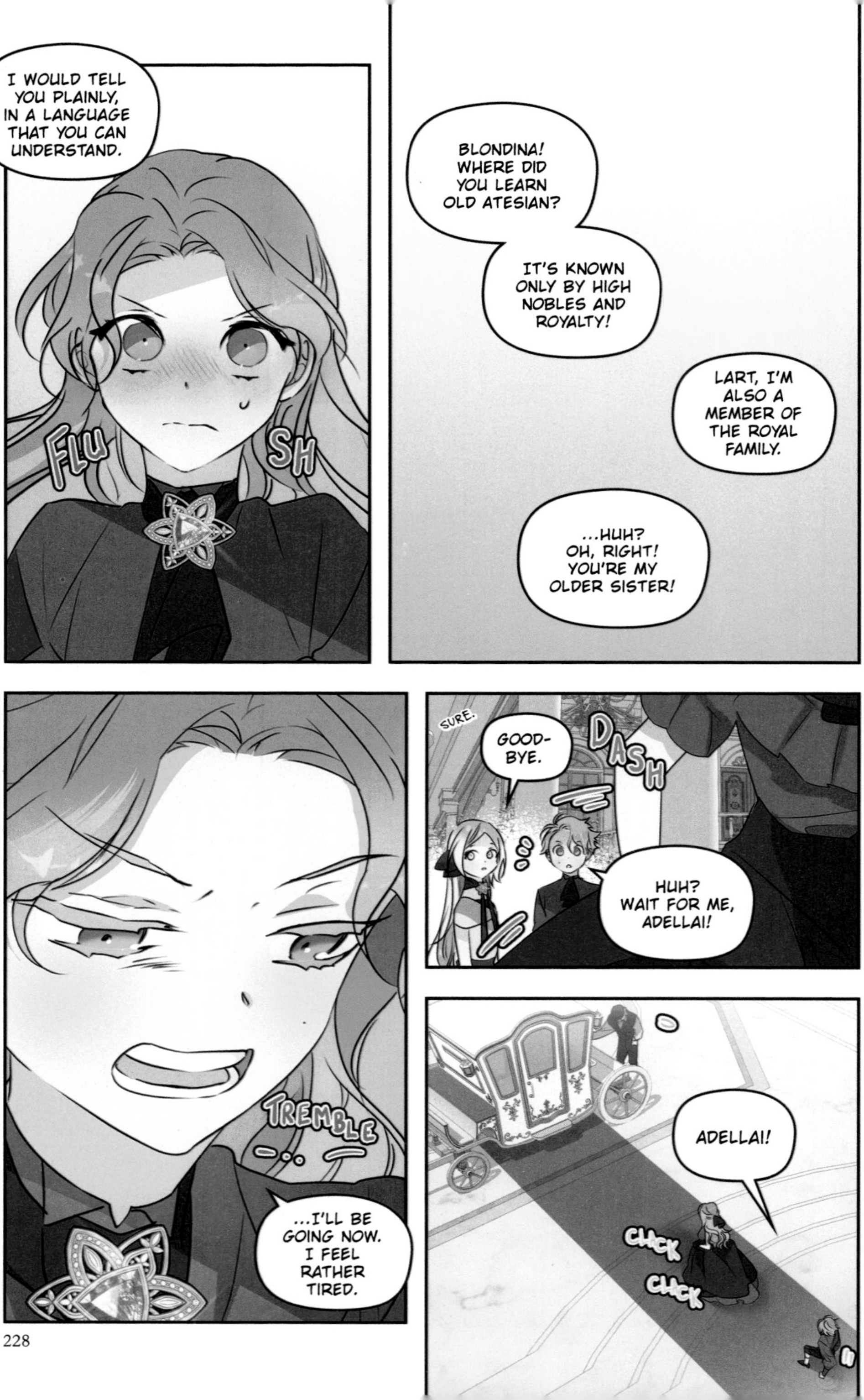
I WOULD TELL YOU PLAINLY, IN A LANGUAGE THAT YOU CAN UNDERSTAND.
FLUSH
BLONDINA! WHERE DID YOU LEARN OLD ATESIAN?
IT'S KNOWN ONLY BY HIGH NOBLES AND ROYALTY!
LART, I'M ALSO A MEMBER OF THE ROYAL FAMILY.
...HUH? OH, RIGHT! YOU'RE MY OLDER SISTER!
TREMBLE
...I'LL BE GOING NOW. I FEEL RATHER TIRED.
SURE.
GOOD-BYE.
DASH
HUH? WAIT FOR ME, ADELLAI!
ADELLAI!
CLACK
CLACK

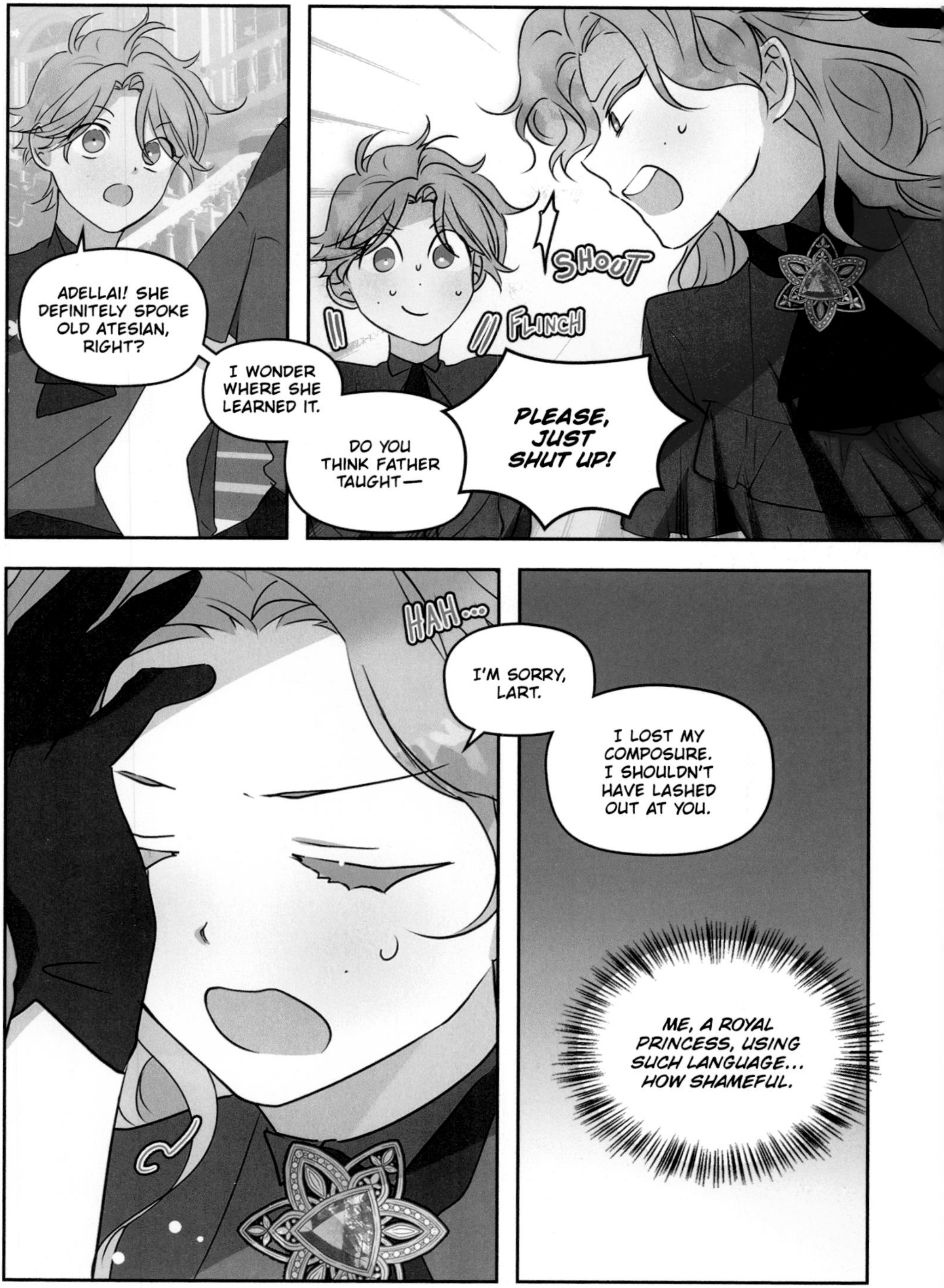
ADELLAI! SHE DEFINITELY SPOKE OLD ATESIAN, RIGHT?
I WONDER WHERE SHE LEARNED IT.
DO YOU THINK FATHER TAUGHT—
SHOUT
FLINCH
PLEASE, JUST SHUT UP!
HAH...
I'M SORRY, LART.
I LOST MY COMPOSURE. I SHOULDN'T HAVE LASHED OUT AT YOU.
ME, A ROYAL PRINCESS, USING SUCH LANGUAGE... HOW SHAMEFUL.

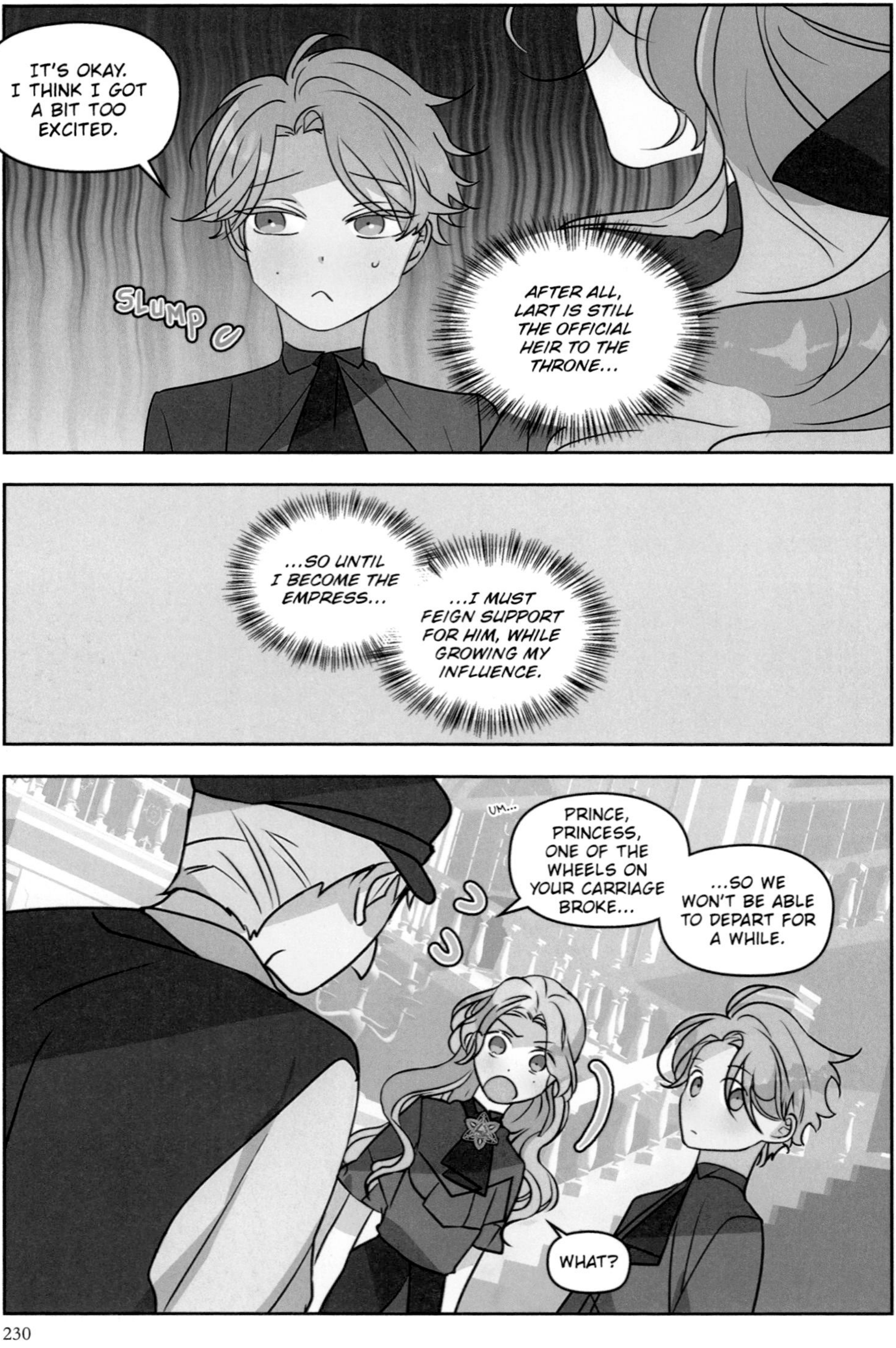
IT'S OKAY. I THINK I GOT A BIT TOO EXCITED.
SLUMP
AFTER ALL, LART IS STILL THE OFFICIAL HEIR TO THE THRONE...
...SO UNTIL I BECOME THE EMPRESS...
...I MUST FEIGN SUPPORT FOR HIM, WHILE GROWING MY INFLUENCE.
UM...
PRINCE, PRINCESS, ONE OF THE WHEELS ON YOUR CARRIAGE BROKE...
...SO WE WON'T BE ABLE TO DEPART FOR A WHILE.
WHAT?

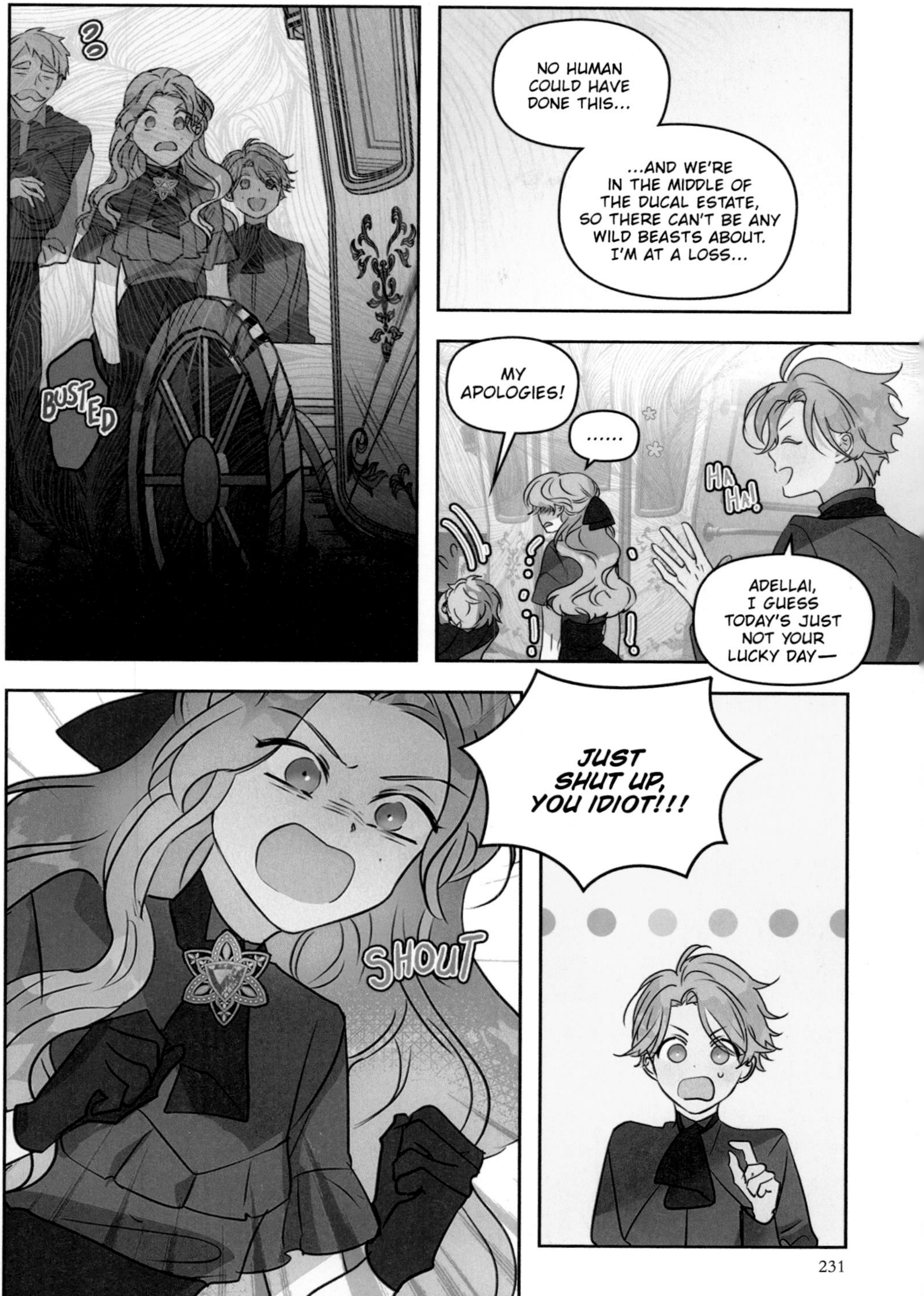
BUSTED
NO HUMAN COULD HAVE DONE THIS...
...AND WE'RE IN THE MIDDLE OF THE DUCAL ESTATE, SO THERE CAN'T BE ANY WILD BEASTS ABOUT. I'M AT A LOSS...
MY APOLOGIES!
......
HA HA!
ADELLAI, I GUESS TODAY'S JUST NOT YOUR LUCKY DAY—
JUST SHUT UP, YOU IDIOT!!!
SHOUT

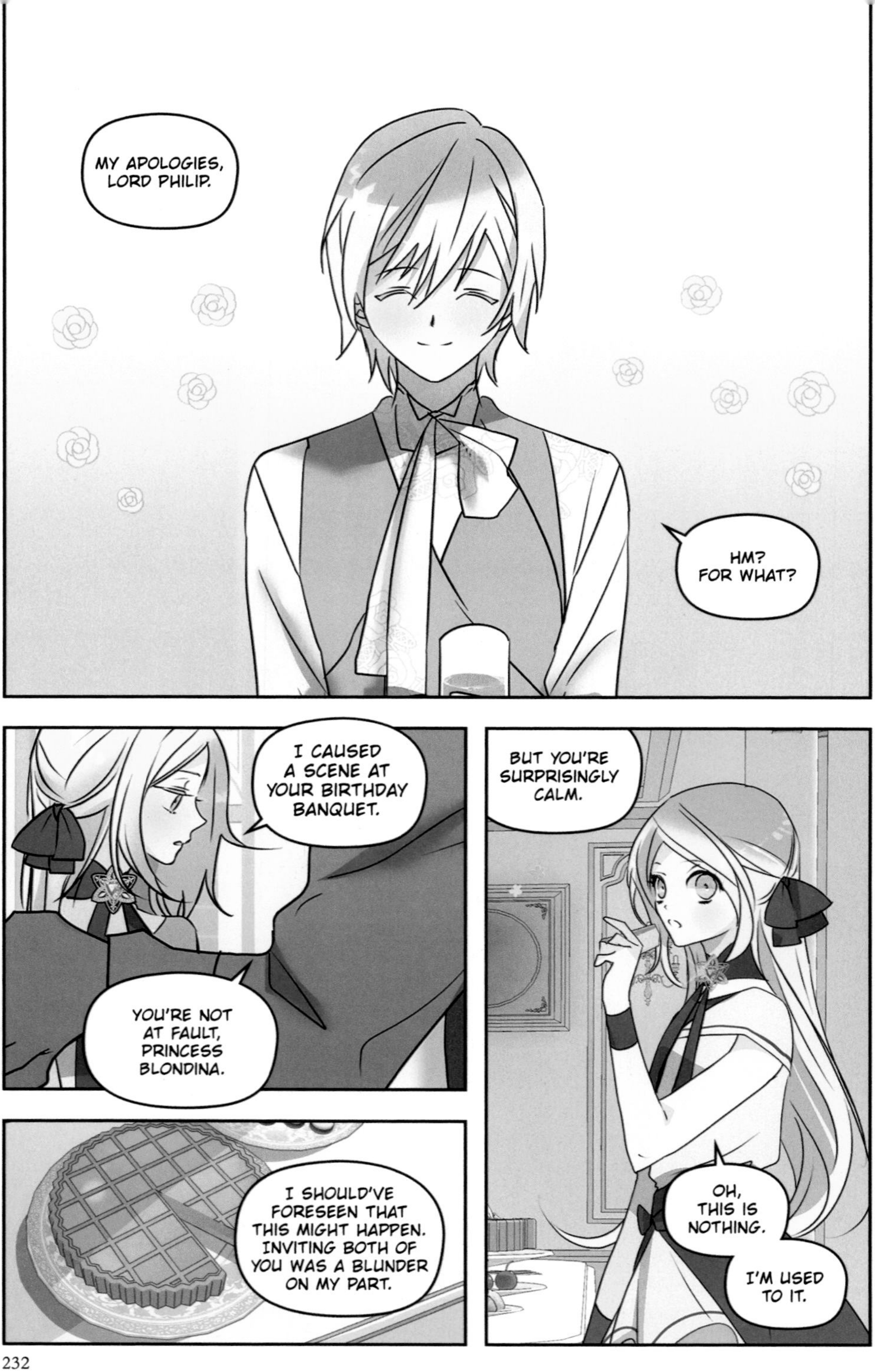
MY APOLOGIES, LORD PHILIP.
HM? FOR WHAT?
I CAUSED A SCENE AT YOUR BIRTHDAY BANQUET.
YOU'RE NOT AT FAULT, PRINCESS BLONDINA.
I SHOULD'VE FORESEEN THAT THIS MIGHT HAPPEN. INVITING BOTH OF YOU WAS A BLUNDER ON MY PART.
BUT YOU'RE SURPRISINGLY CALM.
OH, THIS IS NOTHING.
I'M USED TO IT.

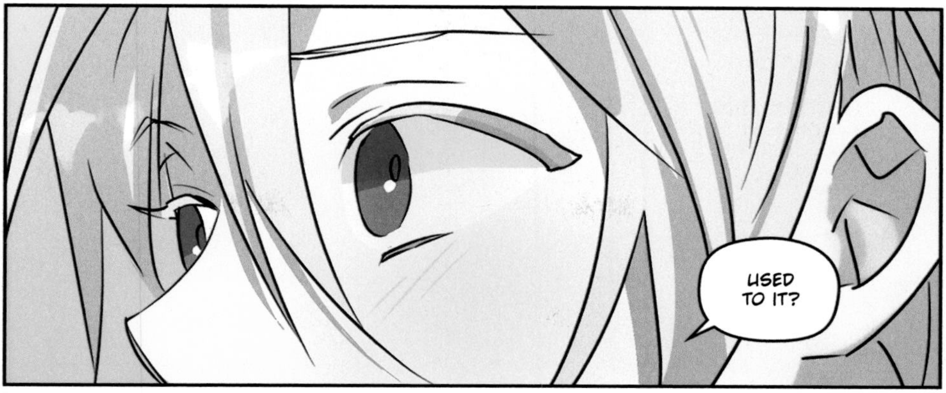
USED TO IT?

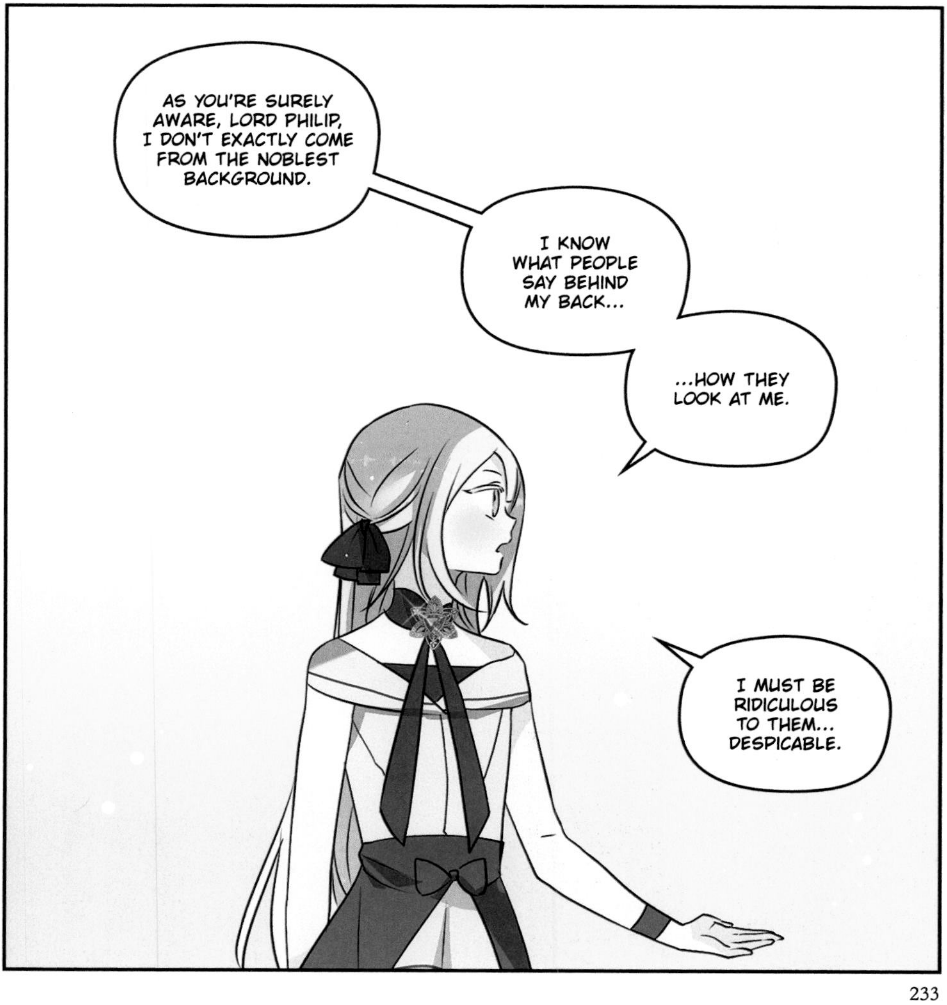
AS YOU'RE SURELY AWARE, LORD PHILIP, I DON'T EXACTLY COME FROM THE NOBLEST BACKGROUND.
I KNOW WHAT PEOPLE SAY BEHIND MY BACK...
...HOW THEY LOOK AT ME.
I MUST BE RIDICULOUS TO THEM... DESPICABLE.

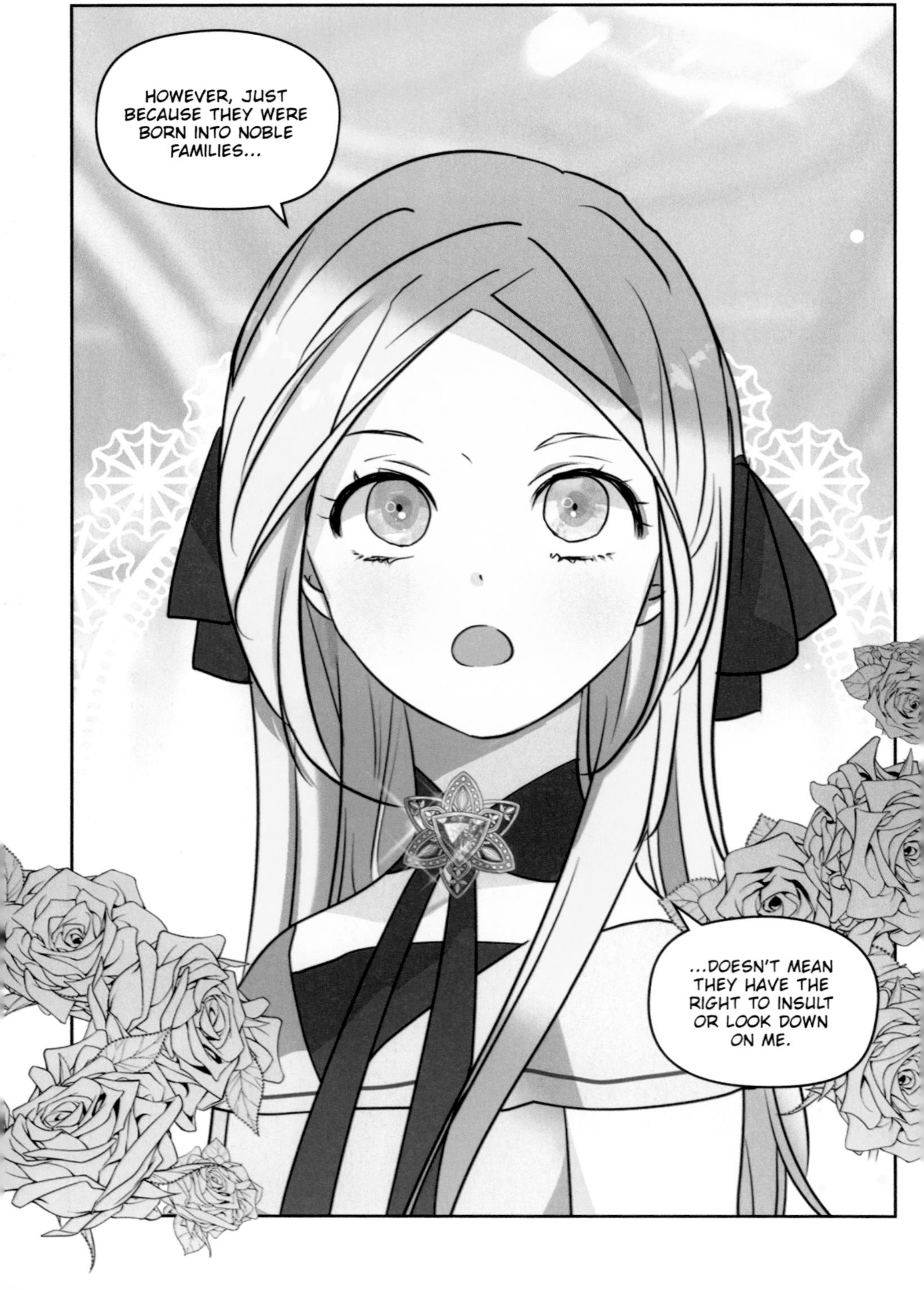
HOWEVER, JUST BECAUSE THEY WERE BORN INTO NOBLE FAMILIES...
...DOESN'T MEAN THEY HAVE THE RIGHT TO INSULT OR LOOK DOWN ON ME.

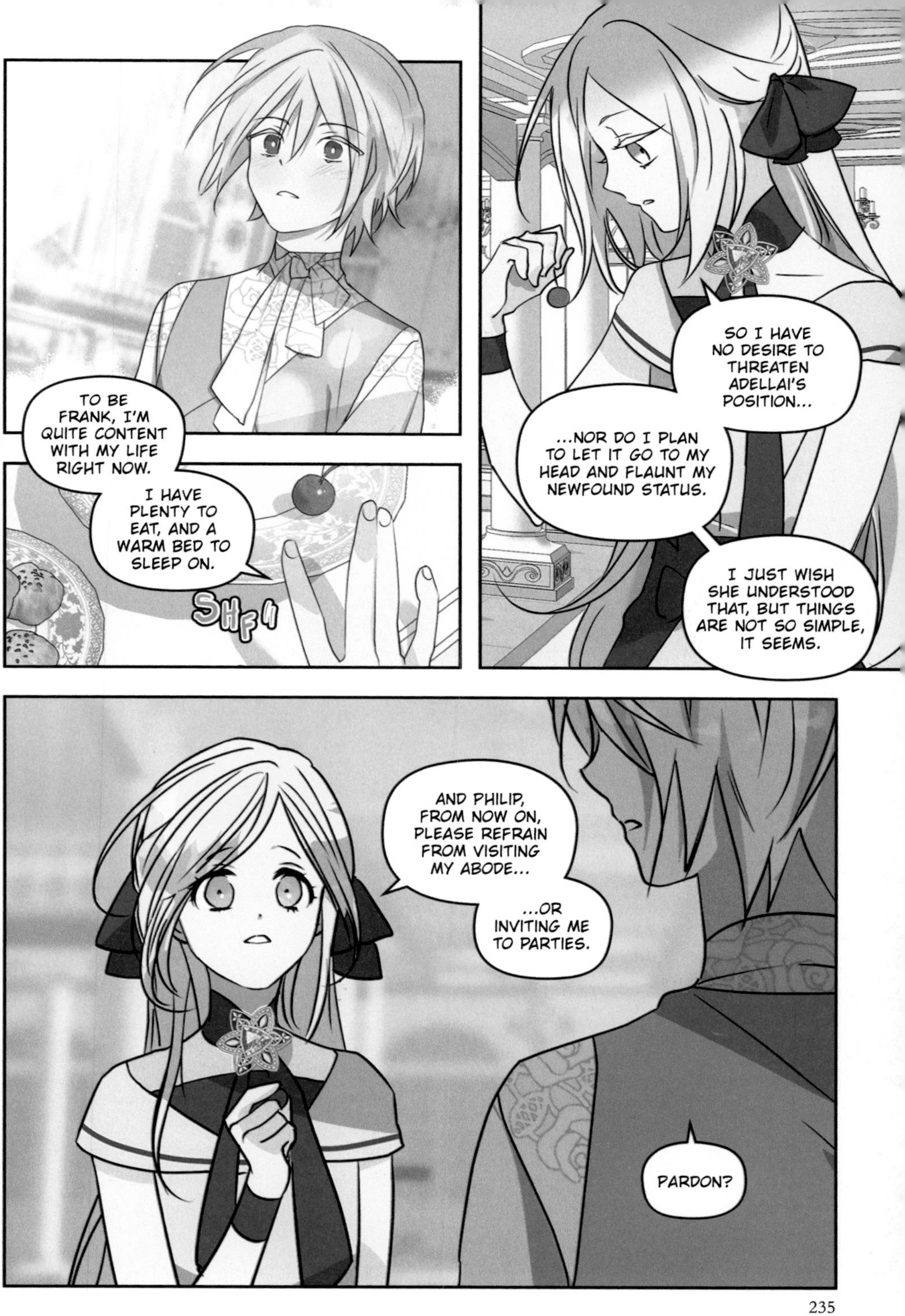
TO BE FRANK, I'M QUITE CONTENT WITH MY LIFE RIGHT NOW.
I HAVE PLENTY TO EAT, AND A WARM BED TO SLEEP ON.
SHF
SO I HAVE NO DESIRE TO THREATEN ADELLAI'S POSITION...
...NOR DO I PLAN TO LET IT GO TO MY HEAD AND FLAUNT MY NEWFOUND STATUS.
I JUST WISH SHE UNDERSTOOD THAT, BUT THINGS ARE NOT SO SIMPLE, IT SEEMS.
AND PHILIP, FROM NOW ON, PLEASE REFRAIN FROM VISITING MY ABODE...
...OR INVITING ME TO PARTIES.
PARDON?

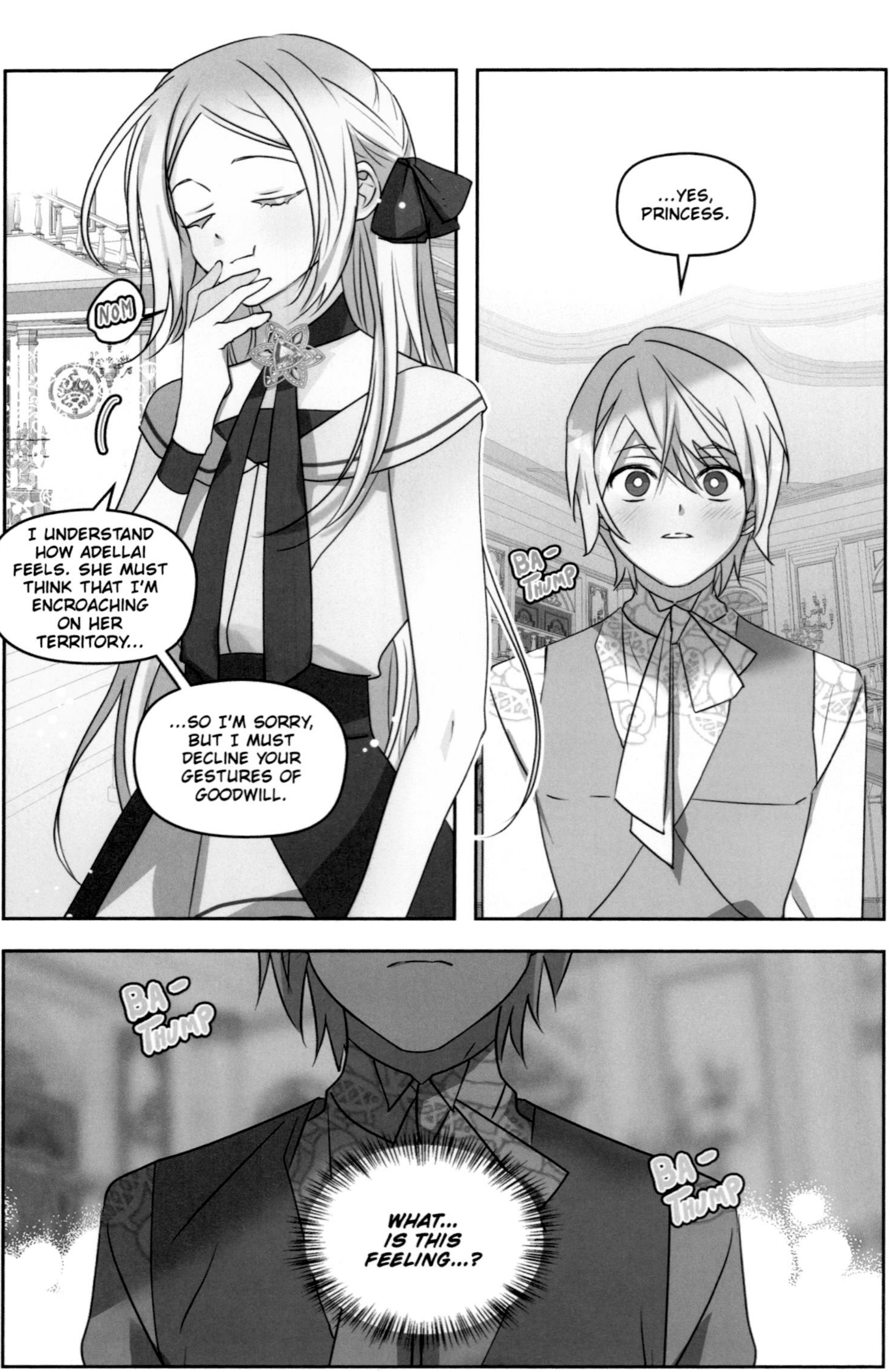
NOM
I UNDERSTAND HOW ADELLAI FEELS. SHE MUST THINK THAT I'M ENCROACHING ON HER TERRITORY...
...SO I'M SORRY, BUT I MUST DECLINE YOUR GESTURES OF GOODWILL.
...YES, PRINCESS.
BA-THUMP
BA-THUMP
BA-THUMP
WHAT... IS THIS FEELING...?

My Gently Raised Beast

SO, THE OTHER DAY, LORD AMON WAS SMELLING THE FLOWERS, AND HIS EARS STARTED TWITCHING...

...AND HIS TAIL WAS SWINGING BACK AND FORTH. IT WAS SO CUTE, I WANTED TO REACH OUT AND GRAB IT.

REALLY? THEN WHY DIDN'T YOU?

WHAT?

HOW COULD I DARE TO GRAB A GREAT DIVINE BEAST'S...

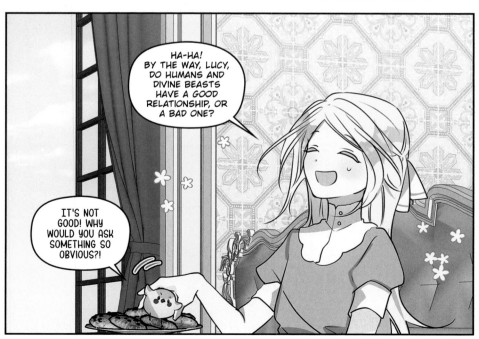

HA-HA! BY THE WAY, LUCY, DO HUMANS AND DIVINE BEASTS HAVE A GOOD RELATIONSHIP, OR A BAD ONE?

IT'S NOT GOOD! WHY WOULD YOU ASK SOMETHING SO OBVIOUS?!

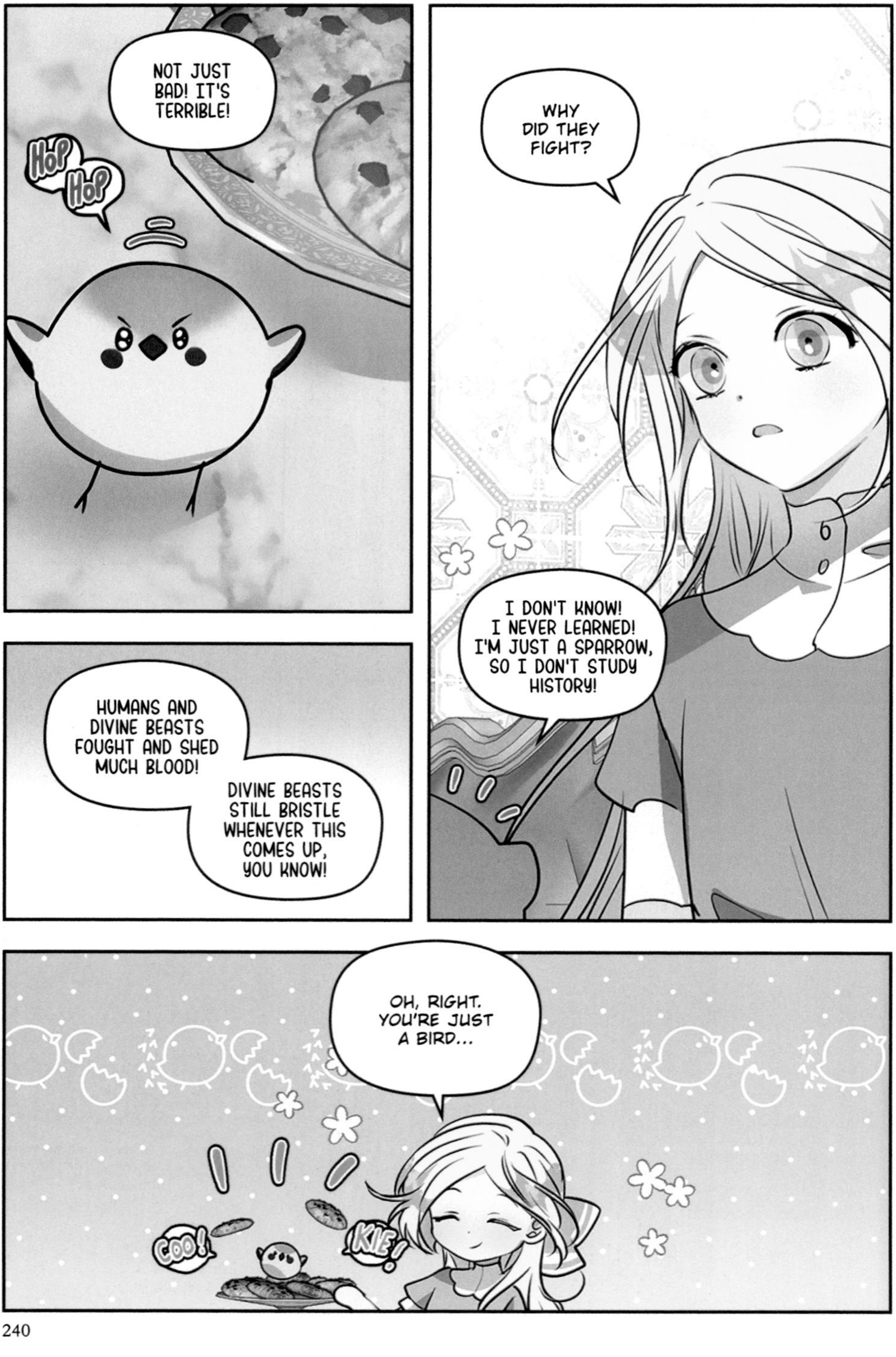
NOT JUST BAD! IT'S TERRIBLE!
HOP HOP
WHY DID THEY FIGHT?
HUMANS AND DIVINE BEASTS FOUGHT AND SHED MUCH BLOOD!
DIVINE BEASTS STILL BRISTLE WHENEVER THIS COMES UP, YOU KNOW!
I DON'T KNOW! I NEVER LEARNED! I'M JUST A SPARROW, SO I DON'T STUDY HISTORY!
OH, RIGHT. YOU'RE JUST A BIRD...
COO!
KIE!

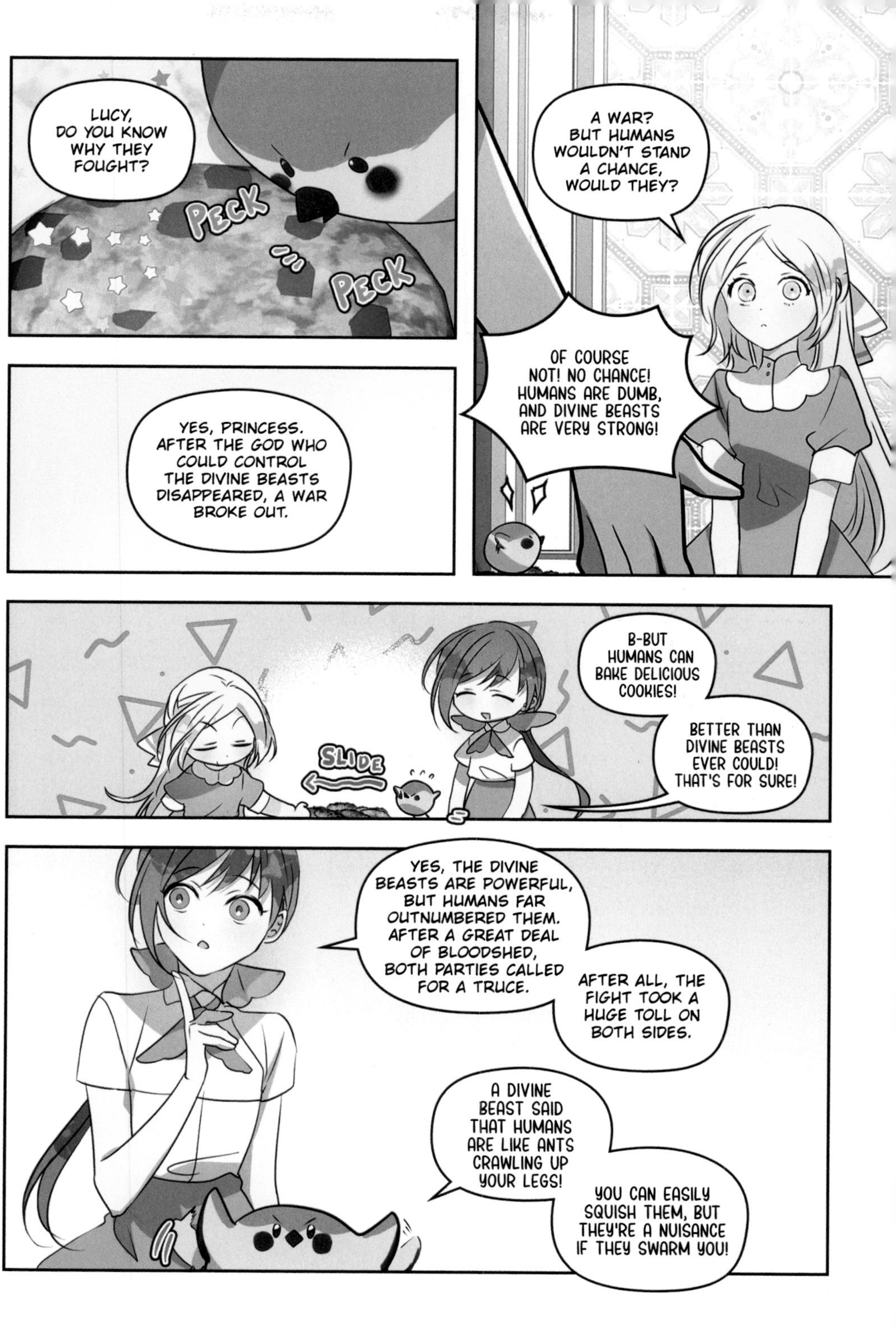
LUCY, DO YOU KNOW WHY THEY FOUGHT?
PECK
PECK
A WAR? BUT HUMANS WOULDN'T STAND A CHANCE, WOULD THEY?
YES, PRINCESS. AFTER THE GOD WHO COULD CONTROL THE DIVINE BEASTS DISAPPEARED, A WAR BROKE OUT.
OF COURSE NOT! NO CHANCE! HUMANS ARE DUMB, AND DIVINE BEASTS ARE VERY STRONG!
B-BUT HUMANS CAN BAKE DELICIOUS COOKIES!
BETTER THAN DIVINE BEASTS EVER COULD! THAT'S FOR SURE!
SLIDE
YES, THE DIVINE BEASTS ARE POWERFUL, BUT HUMANS FAR OUTNUMBERED THEM. AFTER A GREAT DEAL OF BLOODSHED, BOTH PARTIES CALLED FOR A TRUCE.
AFTER ALL, THE FIGHT TOOK A HUGE TOLL ON BOTH SIDES.
A DIVINE BEAST SAID THAT HUMANS ARE LIKE ANTS CRAWLING UP YOUR LEGS!
YOU CAN EASILY SQUISH THEM, BUT THEY'RE A NUISANCE IF THEY SWARM YOU!

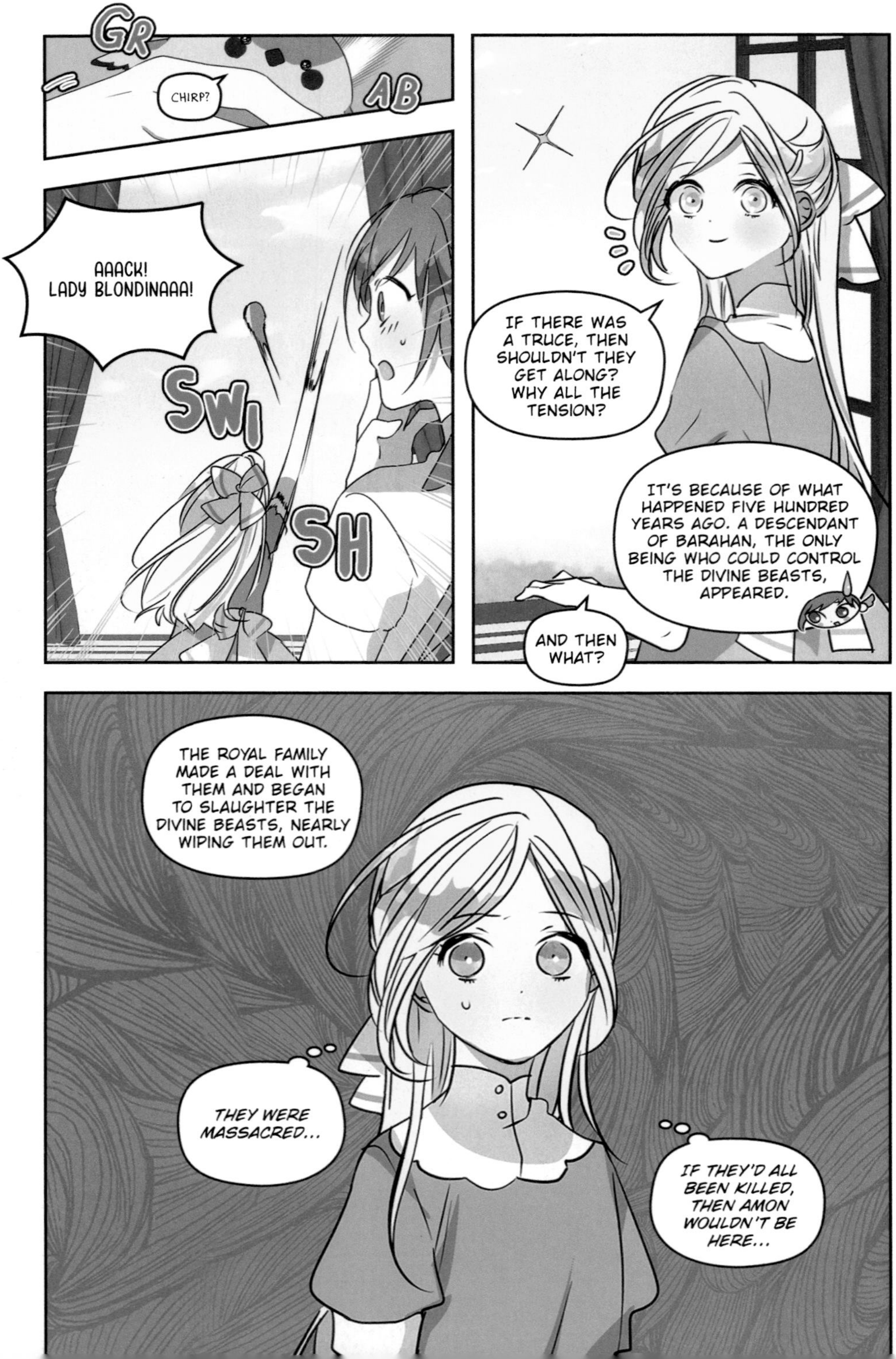
GR
CHIRP?
AB
AAACK! LADY BLONDINAAA!
SWI
SH
IF THERE WAS A TRUCE, THEN SHOULDN'T THEY GET ALONG? WHY ALL THE TENSION?
IT'S BECAUSE OF WHAT HAPPENED FIVE HUNDRED YEARS AGO. A DESCENDANT OF BARAHAN, THE ONLY BEING WHO COULD CONTROL THE DIVINE BEASTS, APPEARED.
AND THEN WHAT?
THE ROYAL FAMILY MADE A DEAL WITH THEM AND BEGAN TO SLAUGHTER THE DIVINE BEASTS, NEARLY WIPING THEM OUT.
THEY WERE MASSACRED...
IF THEY'D ALL BEEN KILLED, THEN AMON WOULDN'T BE HERE...

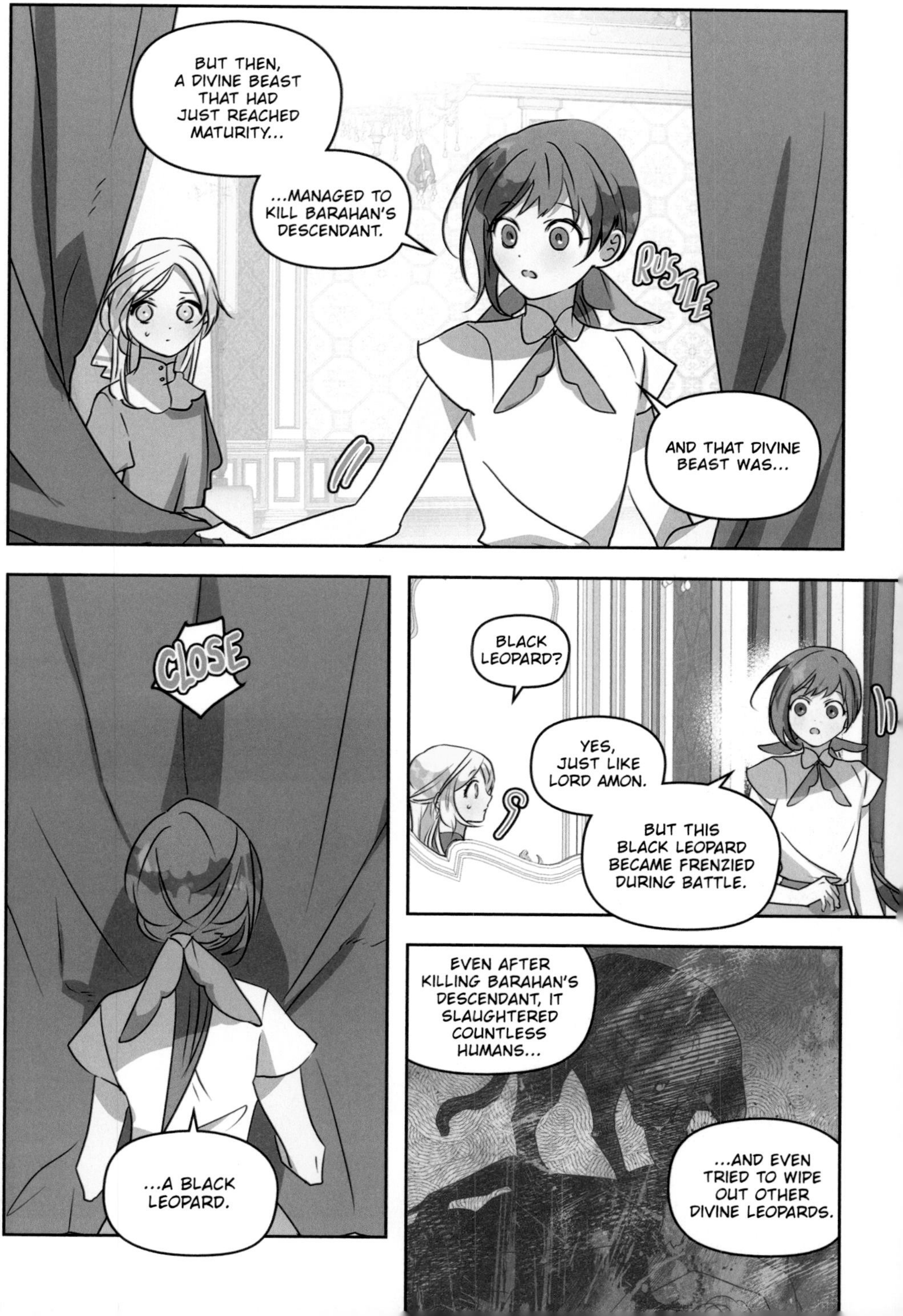
BUT THEN, A DIVINE BEAST THAT HAD JUST REACHED MATURITY...
...MANAGED TO KILL BARAHAN'S DESCENDANT.
RUSTLE
AND THAT DIVINE BEAST WAS...
CLOSE
...A BLACK LEOPARD.
BLACK LEOPARD?
YES, JUST LIKE LORD AMON.
BUT THIS BLACK LEOPARD BECAME FRENZIED DURING BATTLE.
EVEN AFTER KILLING BARAHAN'S DESCENDANT, IT SLAUGHTERED COUNTLESS HUMANS...
...AND EVEN TRIED TO WIPE OUT OTHER DIVINE LEOPARDS.

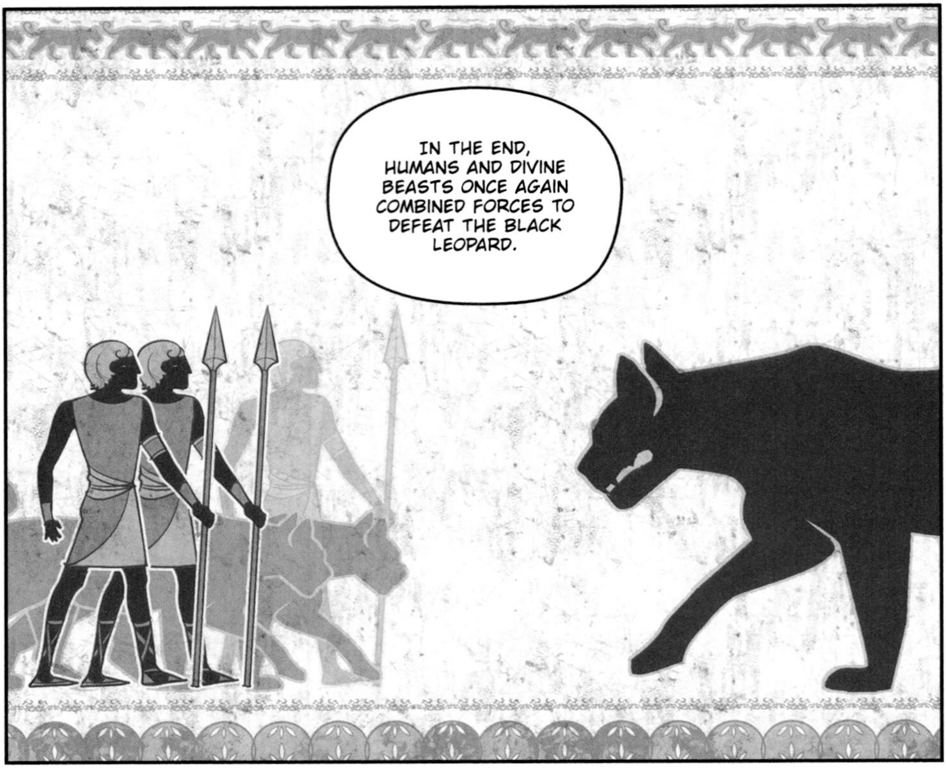
IN THE END, HUMANS AND DIVINE BEASTS ONCE AGAIN COMBINED FORCES TO DEFEAT THE BLACK LEOPARD.

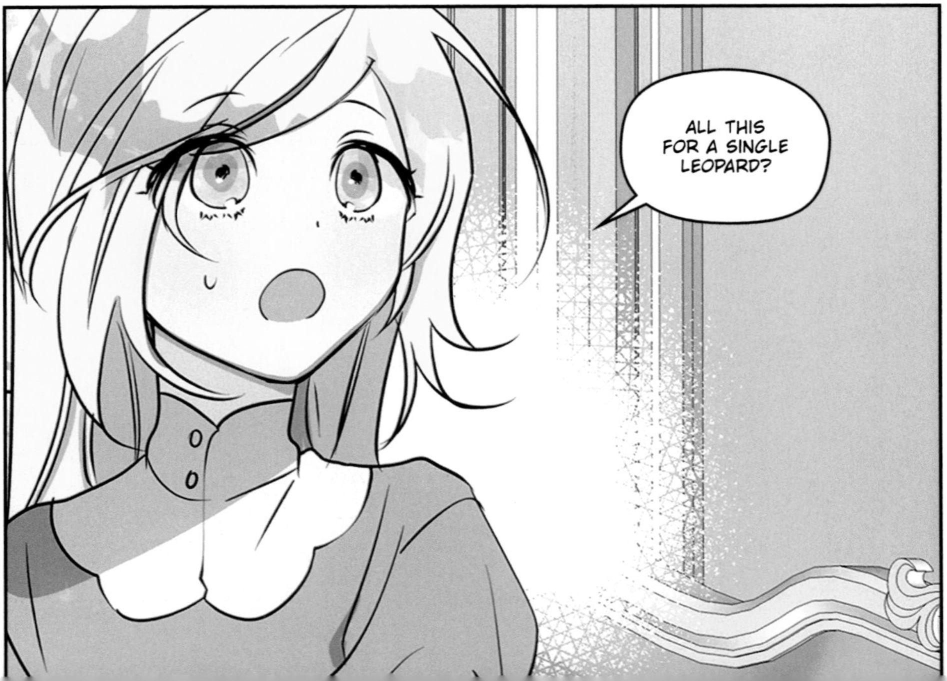
ALL THIS FOR A SINGLE LEOPARD?

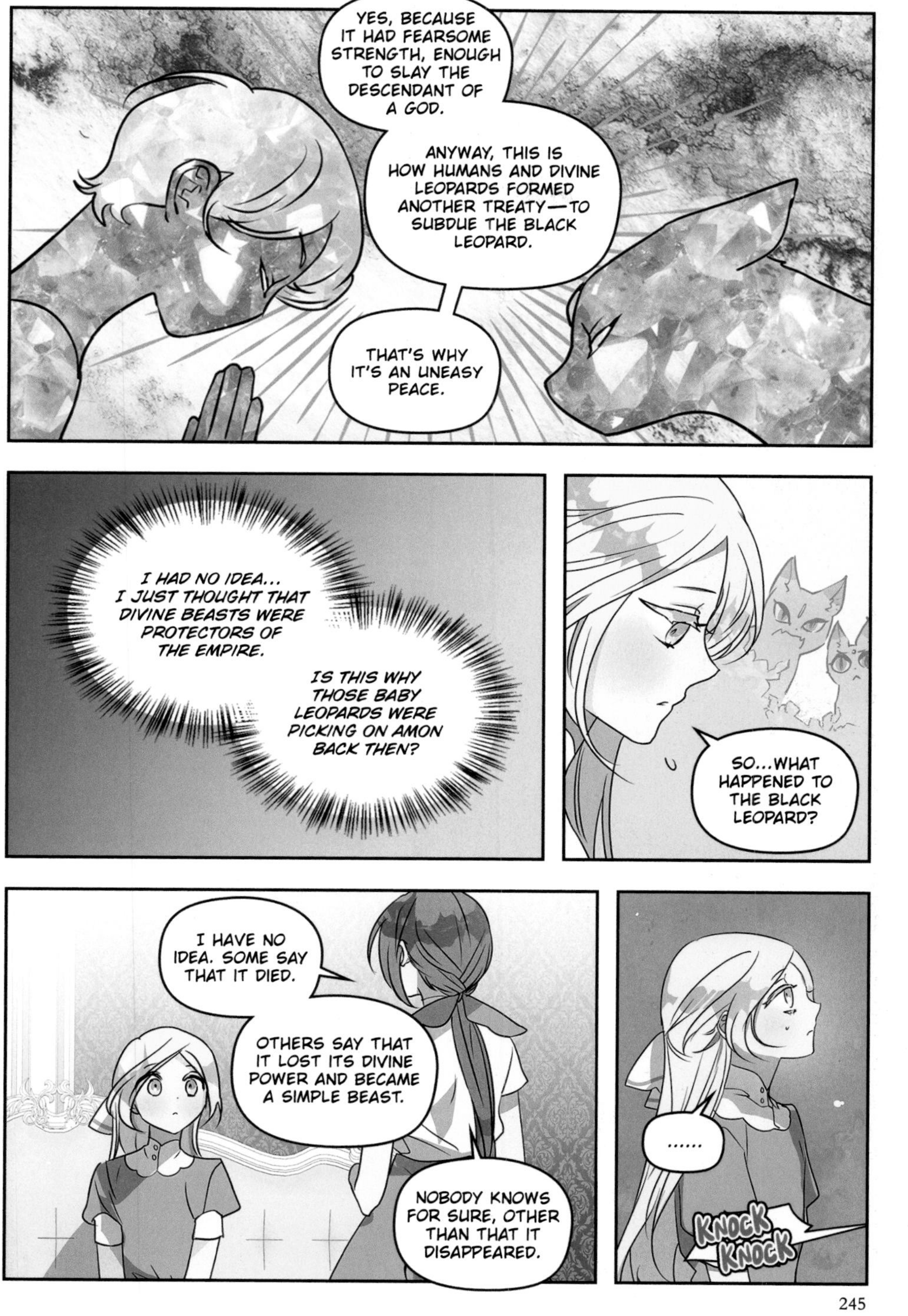
YES, BECAUSE IT HAD FEARSOME STRENGTH, ENOUGH TO SLAY THE DESCENDANT OF A GOD.
ANYWAY, THIS IS HOW HUMANS AND DIVINE LEOPARDS FORMED ANOTHER TREATY—TO SUBDUE THE BLACK LEOPARD.
THAT'S WHY IT'S AN UNEASY PEACE.
I HAD NO IDEA... I JUST THOUGHT THAT DIVINE BEASTS WERE PROTECTORS OF THE EMPIRE.
IS THIS WHY THOSE BABY LEOPARDS WERE PICKING ON AMON BACK THEN?
SO...WHAT HAPPENED TO THE BLACK LEOPARD?
I HAVE NO IDEA. SOME SAY THAT IT DIED.
OTHERS SAY THAT IT LOST ITS DIVINE POWER AND BECAME A SIMPLE BEAST.
NOBODY KNOWS FOR SURE, OTHER THAN THAT IT DISAPPEARED.
......
KNOCK KNOCK

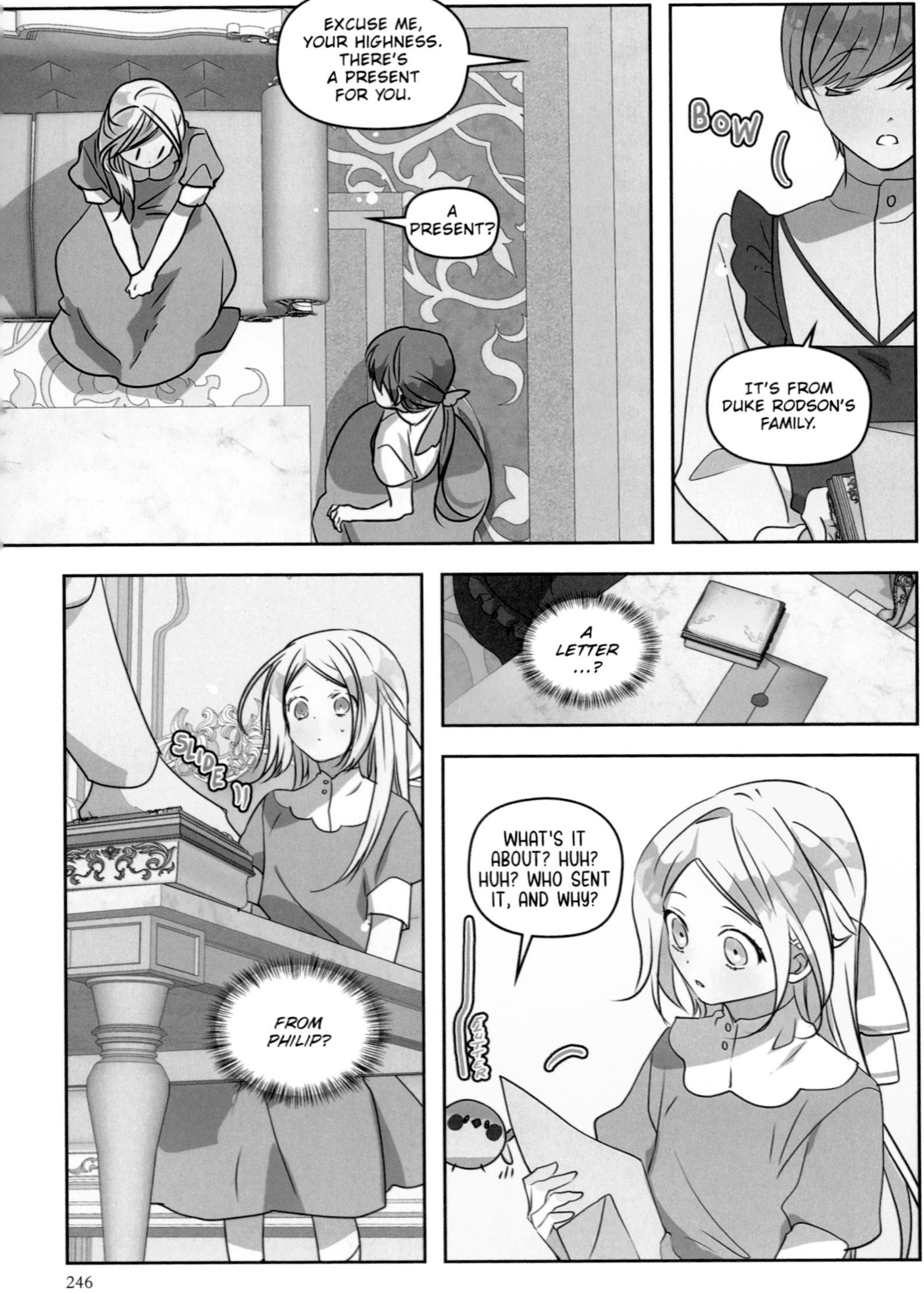
EXCUSE ME, YOUR HIGHNESS. THERE'S A PRESENT FOR YOU.
A PRESENT?
BOW
IT'S FROM DUKE RODSON'S FAMILY.
SLIDE
A LETTER ...?
FROM PHILIP?
WHAT'S IT ABOUT? HUH? HUH? WHO SENT IT, AND WHY?

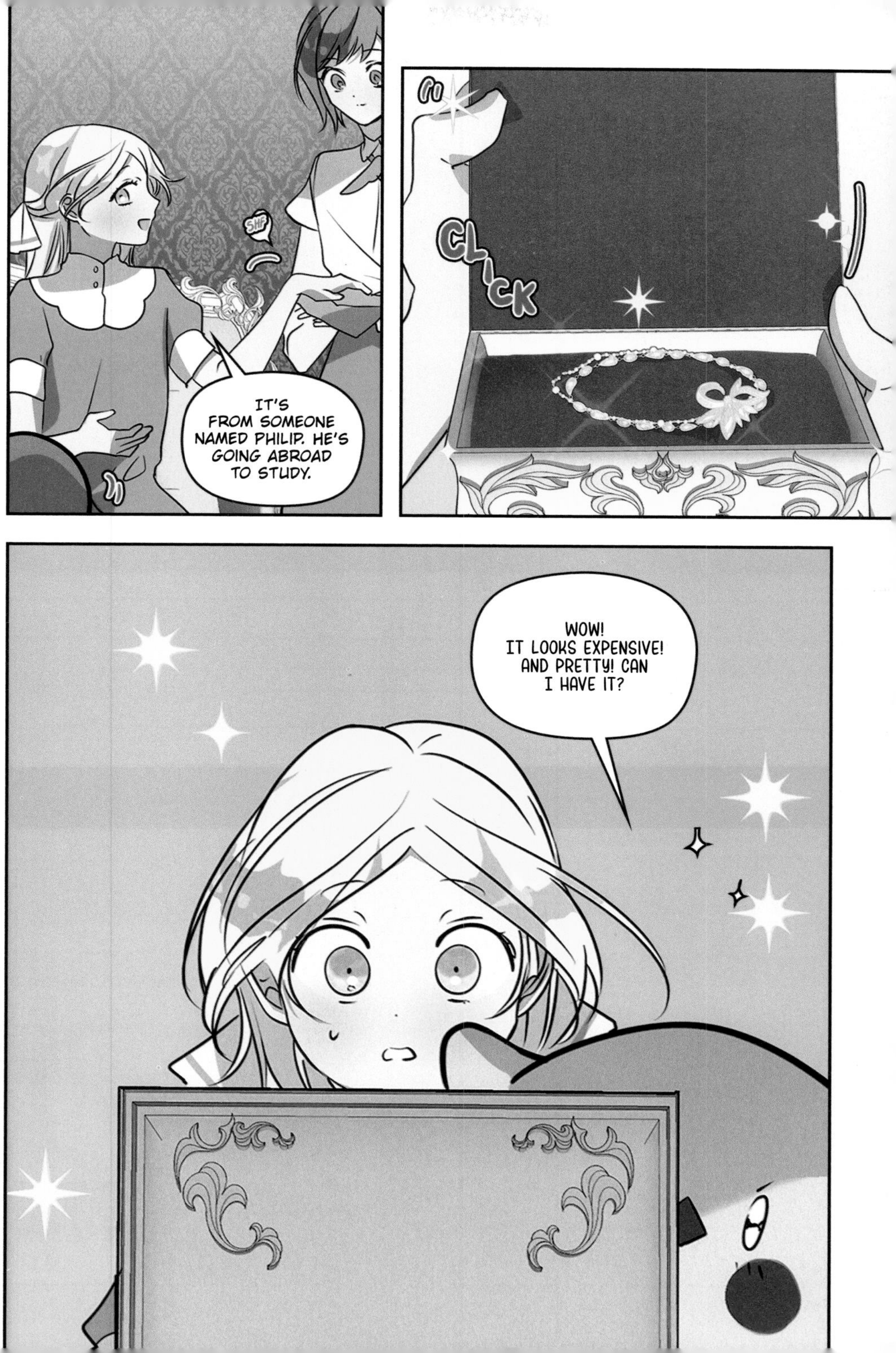
SHF
IT'S FROM SOMEONE NAMED PHILIP. HE'S GOING ABROAD TO STUDY.
CLICK
WOW! IT LOOKS EXPENSIVE! AND PRETTY! CAN I HAVE IT?

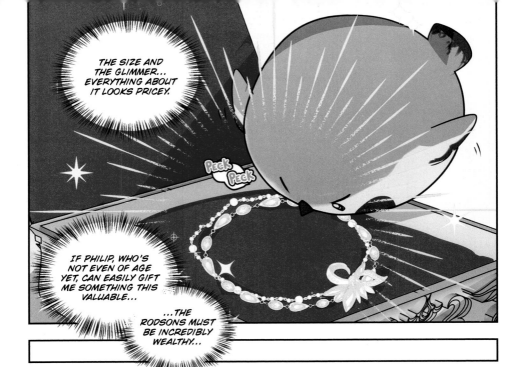

THE SIZE AND THE GLIMMER... EVERYTHING ABOUT IT LOOKS PRICEY.

PECK PECK

IF PHILIP, WHO'S NOT EVEN OF AGE YET, CAN EASILY GIFT ME SOMETHING THIS VALUABLE...

...THE RODSONS MUST BE INCREDIBLY WEALTHY...

CLOP

CLOP

SHE SHOULD'VE RECEIVED IT BY NOW.

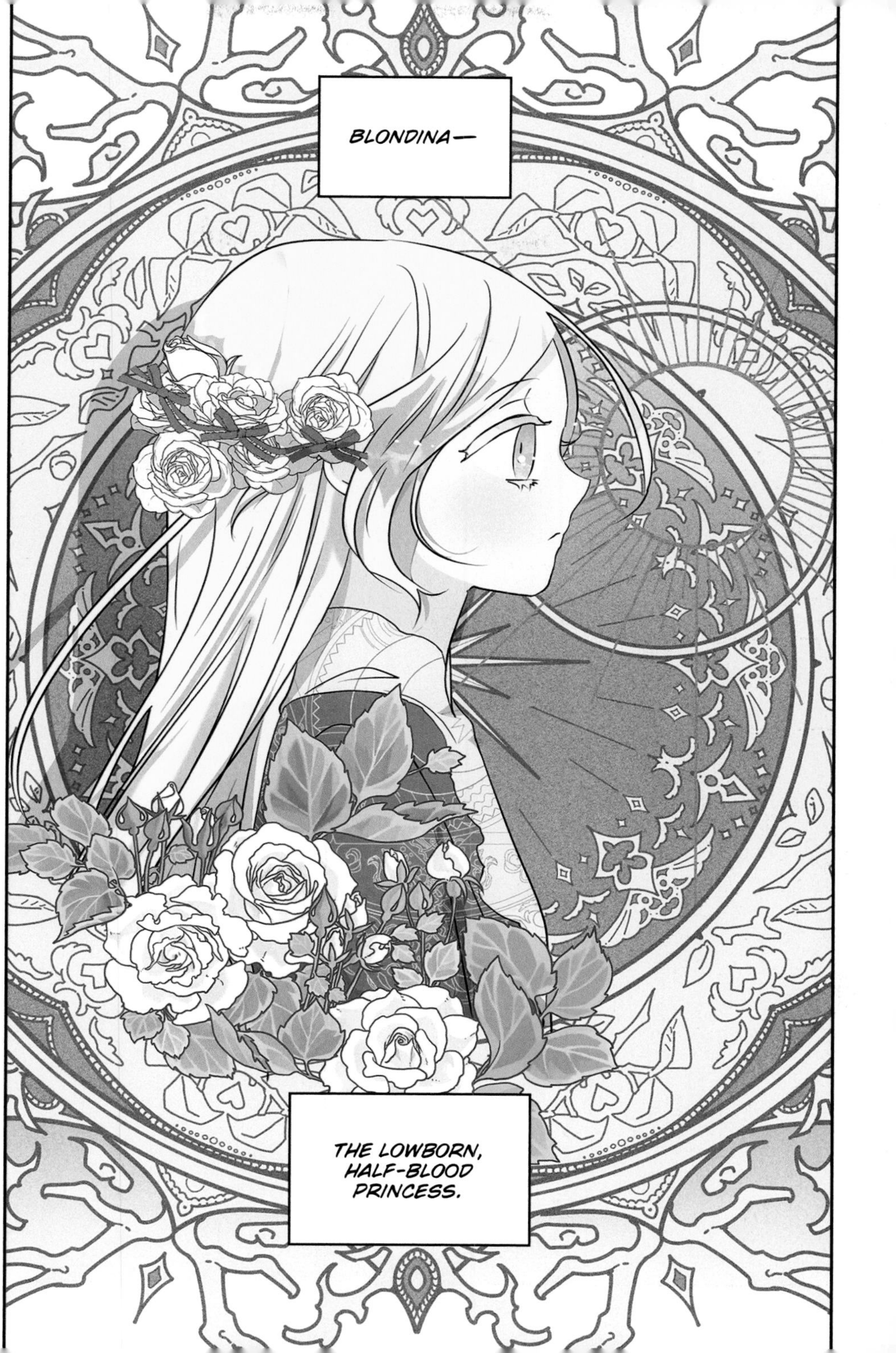
BLONDINA—
THE LOWBORN, HALF-BLOOD PRINCESS.

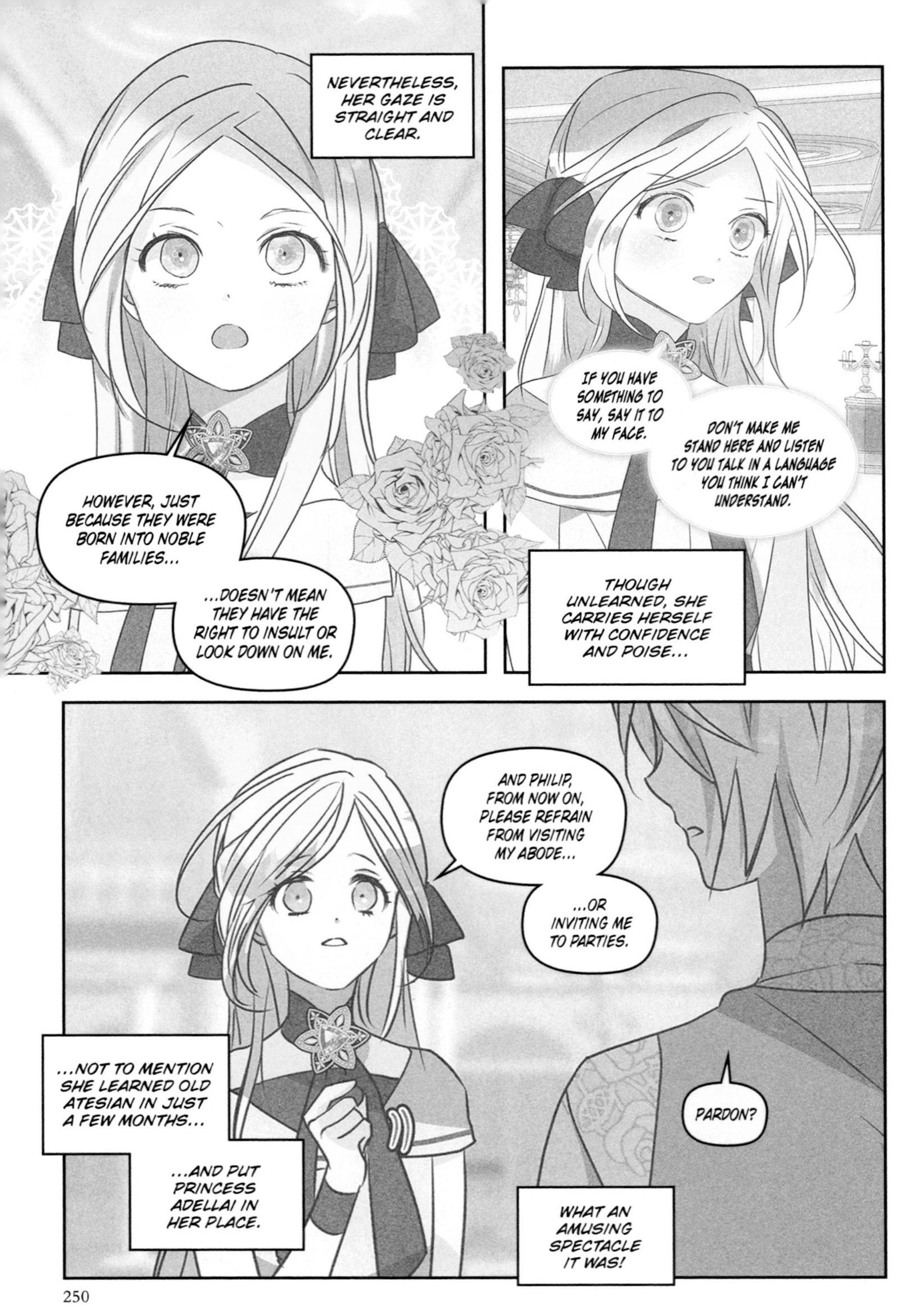
NEVERTHELESS, HER GAZE IS STRAIGHT AND CLEAR.
HOWEVER, JUST BECAUSE THEY WERE BORN INTO NOBLE FAMILIES...
...DOESN'T MEAN THEY HAVE THE RIGHT TO INSULT OR LOOK DOWN ON ME.
IF YOU HAVE SOMETHING TO SAY, SAY IT TO MY FACE.
DON'T MAKE ME STAND HERE AND LISTEN TO YOU TALK IN A LANGUAGE YOU THINK I CAN'T UNDERSTAND.
THOUGH UNLEARNED, SHE CARRIES HERSELF WITH CONFIDENCE AND POISE...
AND PHILIP, FROM NOW ON, PLEASE REFRAIN FROM VISITING MY ABODE...
...OR INVITING ME TO PARTIES.
...NOT TO MENTION SHE LEARNED OLD ATESIAN IN JUST A FEW MONTHS...
...AND PUT PRINCESS ADELLAI IN HER PLACE.
PARDON?
WHAT AN AMUSING SPECTACLE IT WAS!

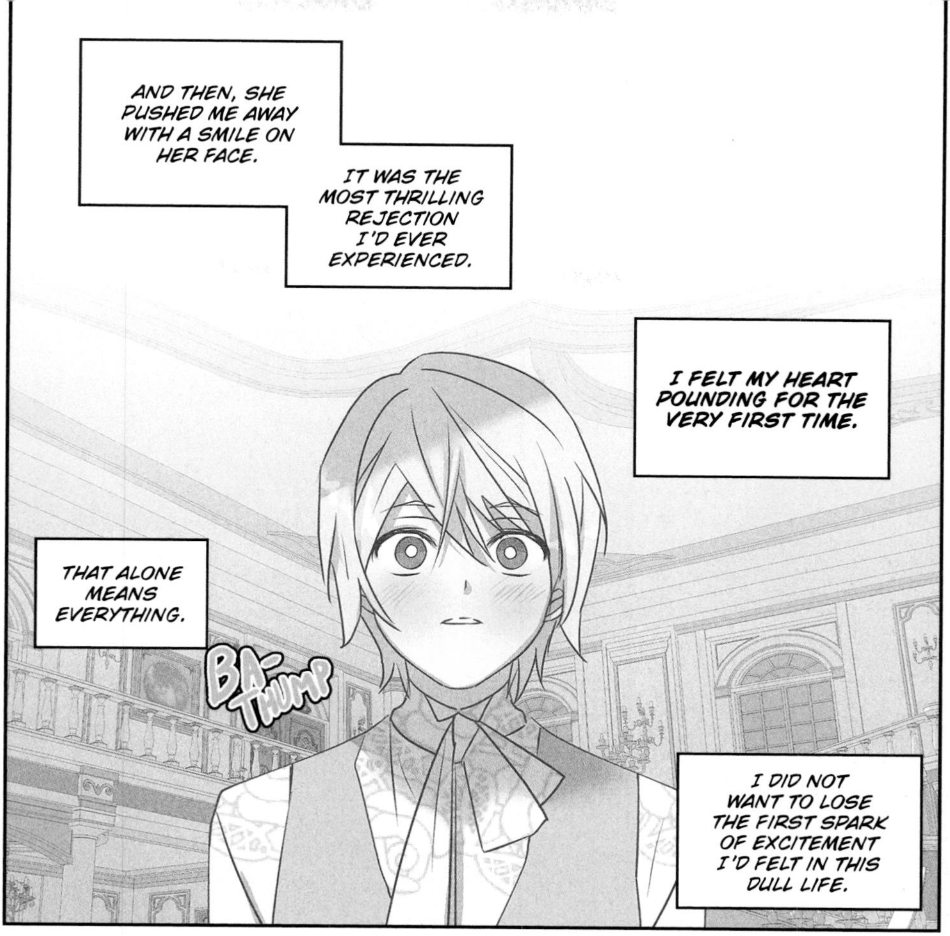
AND THEN, SHE PUSHED ME AWAY WITH A SMILE ON HER FACE.
IT WAS THE MOST THRILLING REJECTION I'D EVER EXPERIENCED.
I FELT MY HEART POUNDING FOR THE VERY FIRST TIME.
THAT ALONE MEANS EVERYTHING.
BA-THUMP
I DID NOT WANT TO LOSE THE FIRST SPARK OF EXCITEMENT I'D FELT IN THIS DULL LIFE.

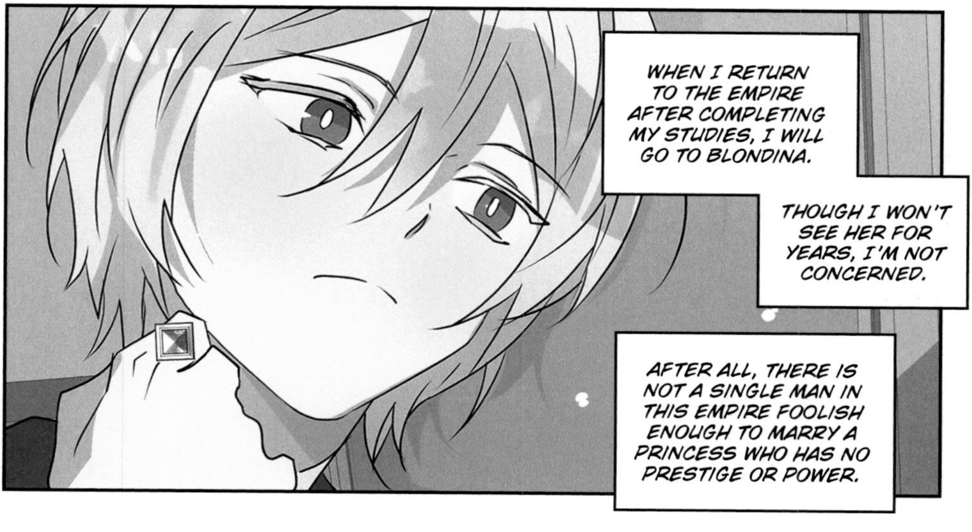
WHEN I RETURN TO THE EMPIRE AFTER COMPLETING MY STUDIES, I WILL GO TO BLONDINA.
THOUGH I WON'T SEE HER FOR YEARS, I'M NOT CONCERNED.
AFTER ALL, THERE IS NOT A SINGLE MAN IN THIS EMPIRE FOOLISH ENOUGH TO MARRY A PRINCESS WHO HAS NO PRESTIGE OR POWER.

THE HIGH NOBLES WON'T TOUCH HER BECAUSE OF HER BLOODLINE...

...AND THE EMPEROR WILL REJECT ANYONE OF LOWER RANK, FOR THE SAKE OF ROYAL PRIDE.

IN THE END, SHE IS FATED TO LIVE OUT A LONELY LIFE, TUCKED AWAY IN A REMOTE CORNER OF THE PALACE.

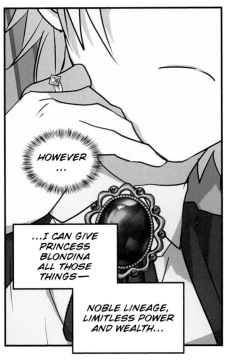

HOWEVER ...

...I CAN GIVE PRINCESS BLONDINA ALL THOSE THINGS—

NOBLE LINEAGE, LIMITLESS POWER AND WEALTH...

THE PRINCESS, ABANDONED BY HER FATHER AND RIDICULED BY HER FAMILY...

...WILL BE ABLE TO LIVE HAPPILY BY MY SIDE...

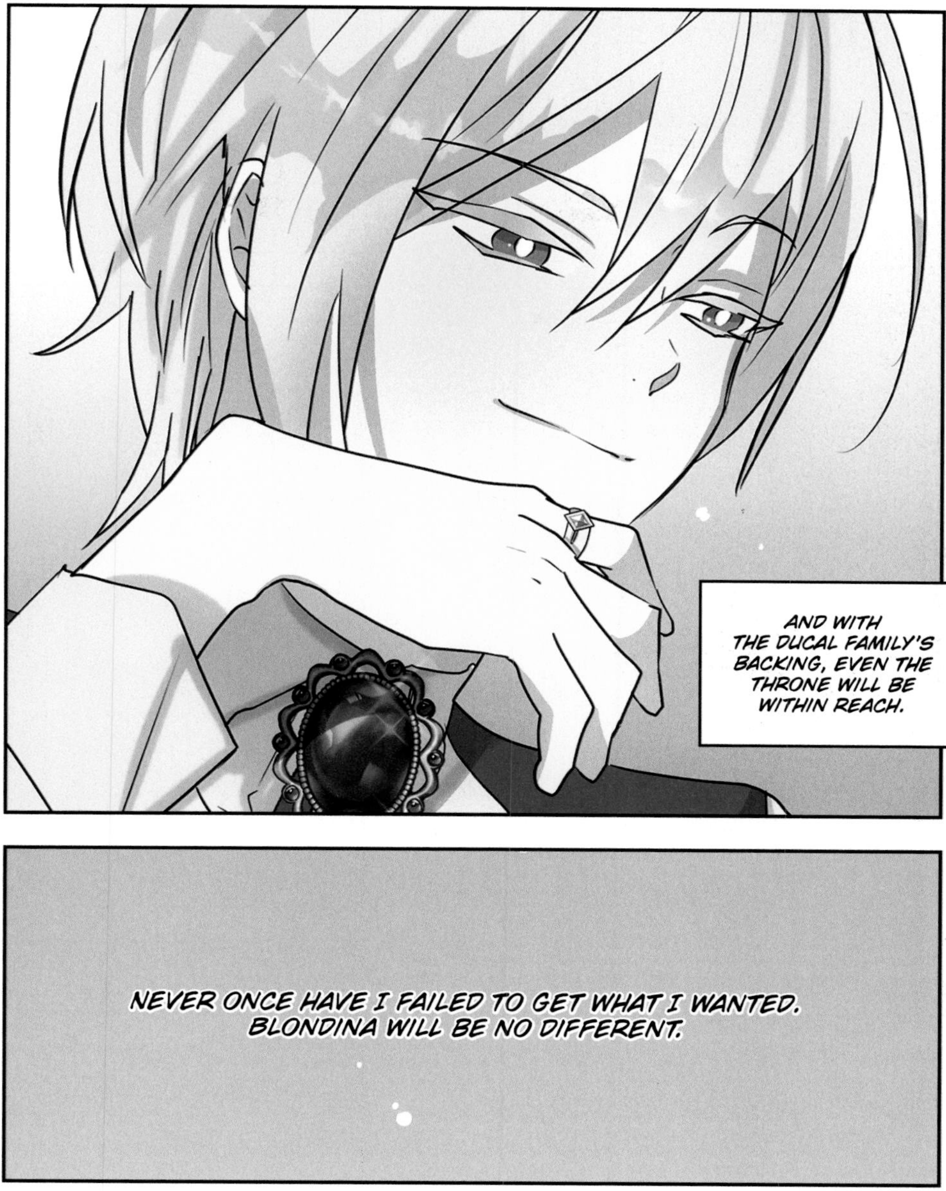
AND WITH THE DUCAL FAMILY'S BACKING, EVEN THE THRONE WILL BE WITHIN REACH.
NEVER ONCE HAVE I FAILED TO GET WHAT I WANTED. BLONDINA WILL BE NO DIFFERENT.

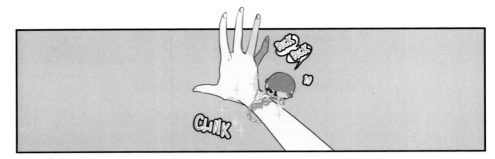

PECK
PECK
CLINK
HM...
WHAT IS LIFE?
WHAT'S THAT SHINY TRINKET?
PECK
PECK
PECK
EEK! YOU SCARED ME!
ZOOM
AMON! YOU'VE BEEN VISITING OFTEN THESE DAYS!
I SAID, WHAT IS THAT THING?
A GIFT.
......

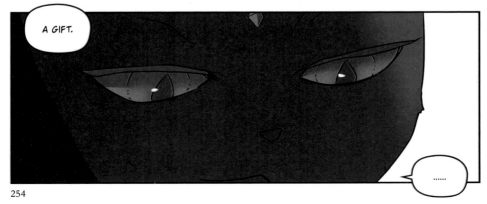

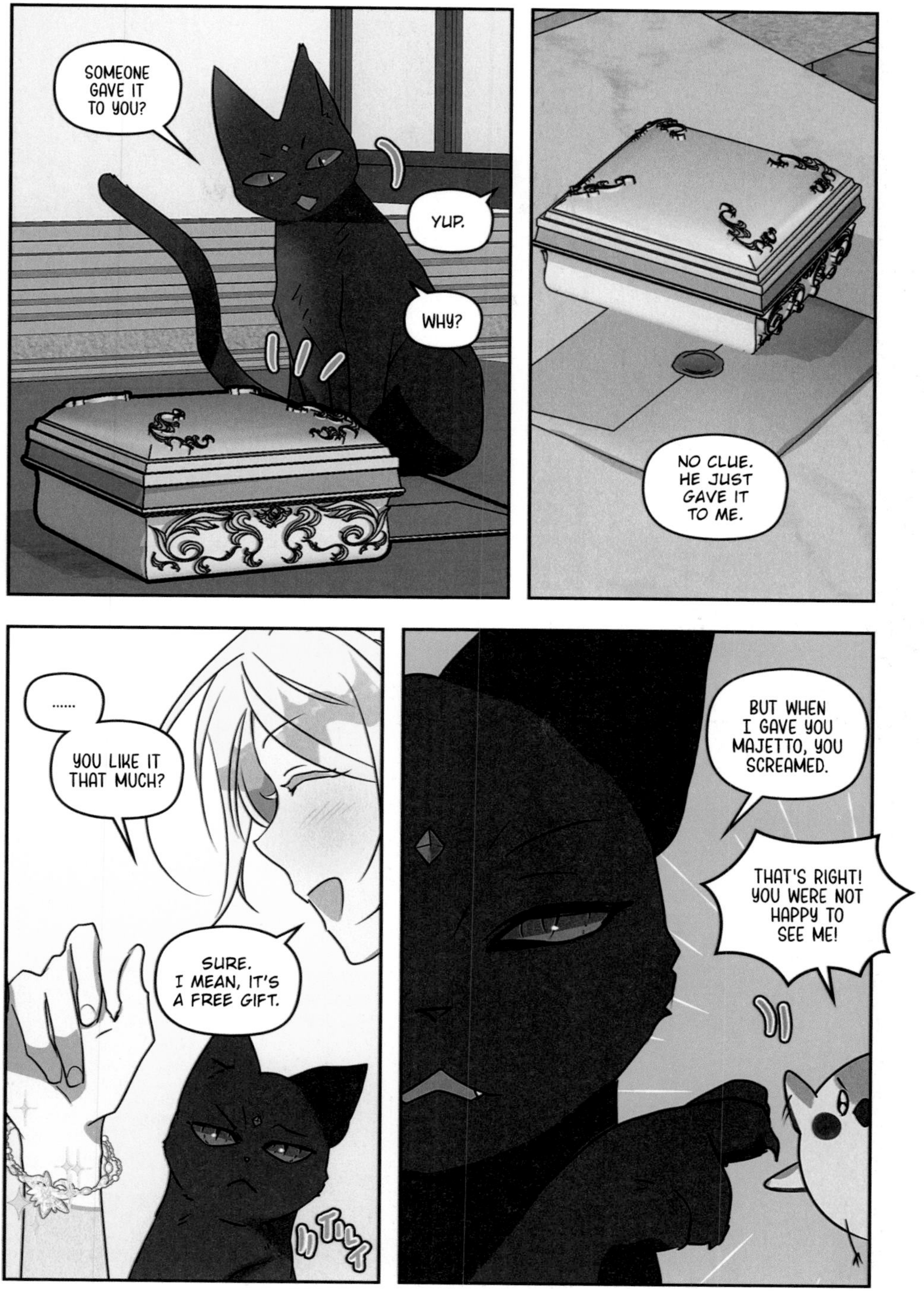
SOMEONE GAVE IT TO YOU?
YUP.
WHY?
NO CLUE. HE JUST GAVE IT TO ME.
......
YOU LIKE IT THAT MUCH?
SURE. I MEAN, IT'S A FREE GIFT.
TILT
BUT WHEN I GAVE YOU MAJETTO, YOU SCREAMED.
THAT'S RIGHT! YOU WERE NOT HAPPY TO SEE ME!

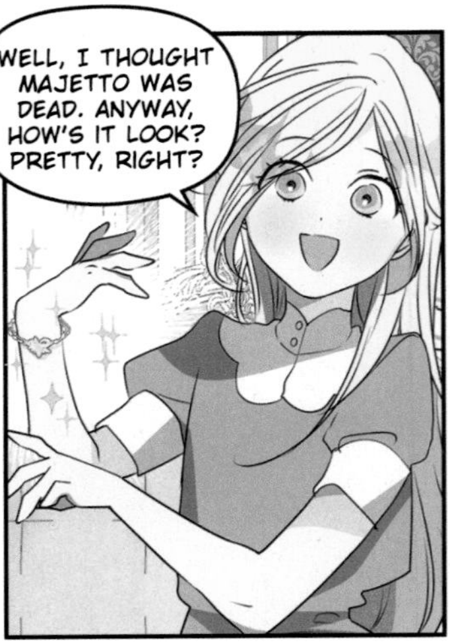
WELL, I THOUGHT MAJETTO WAS DEAD. ANYWAY, HOW'S IT LOOK? PRETTY, RIGHT?

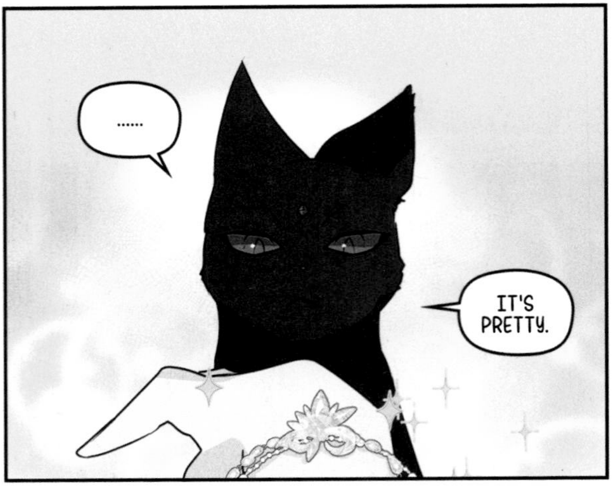
......
IT'S PRETTY.

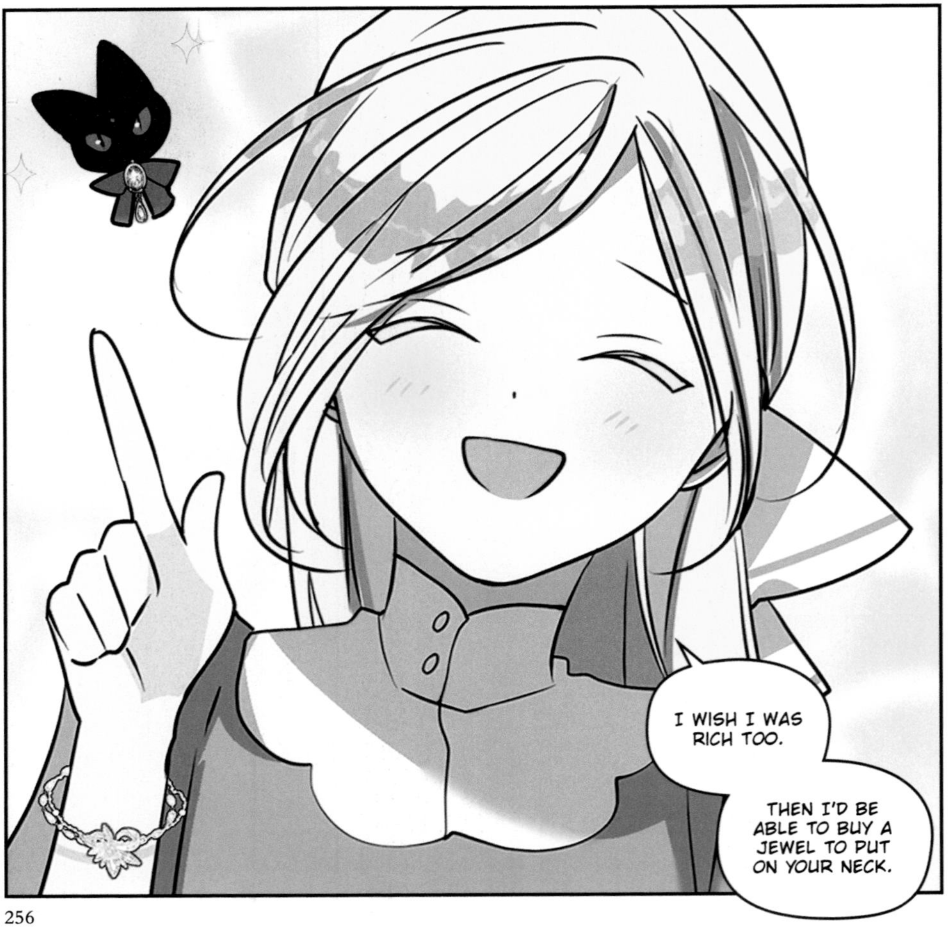
I WISH I WAS RICH TOO.
THEN I'D BE ABLE TO BUY A JEWEL TO PUT ON YOUR NECK.

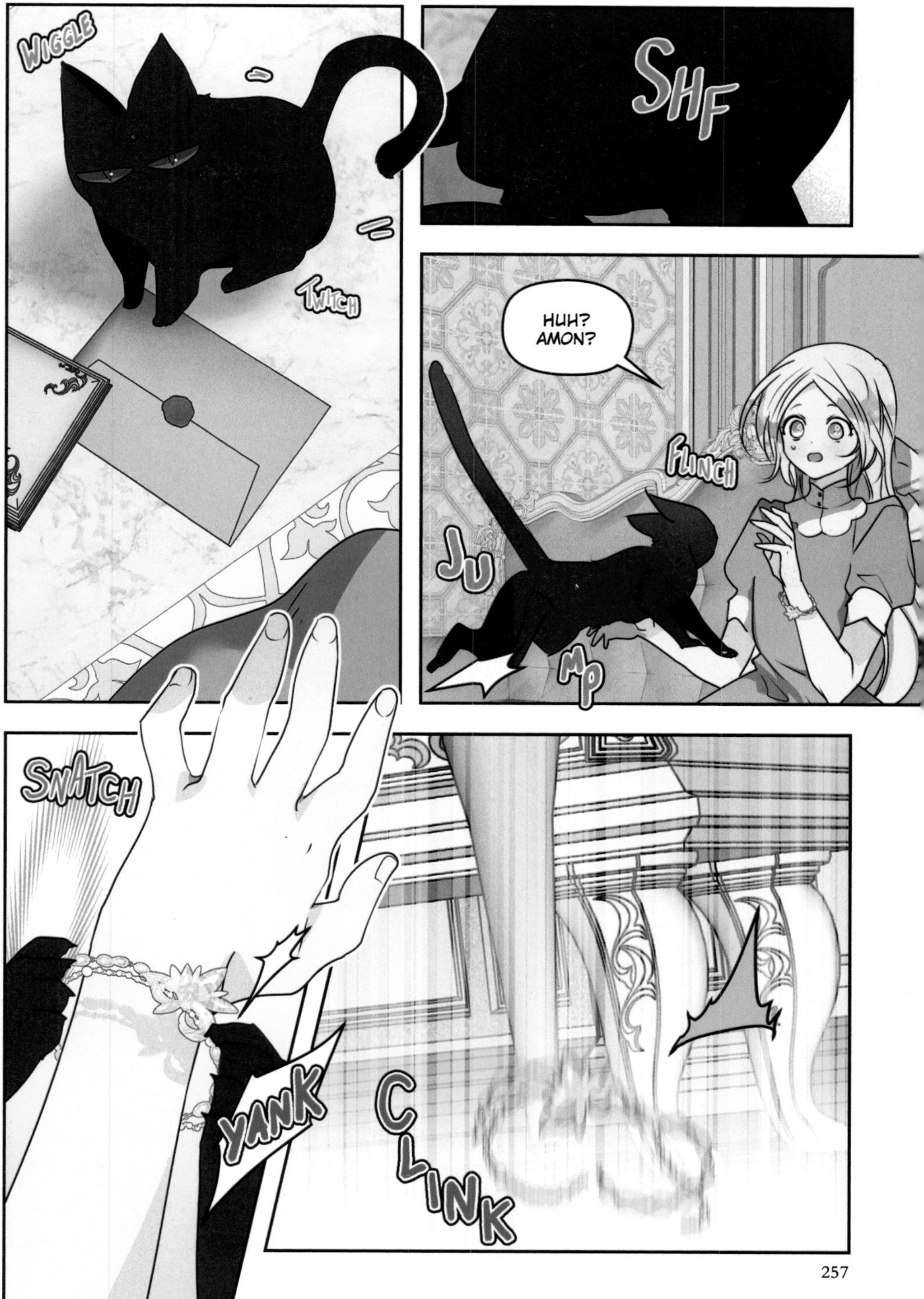

WIGGLE
TWITCH
SHF
HUH? AMON?
FLINCH
JU
MP
SNATCH
YANK
CLINK

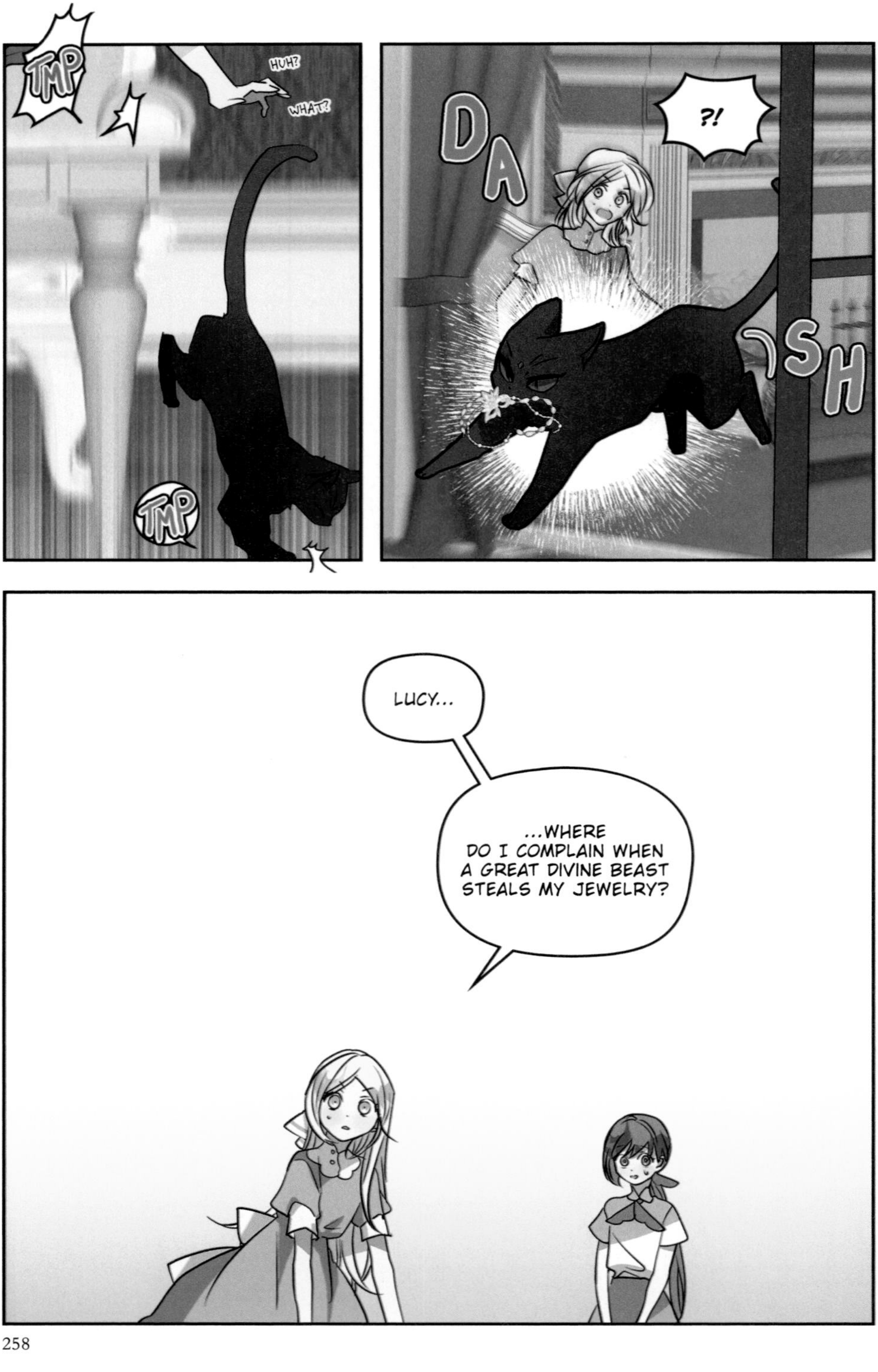
TMP
HUH?
WHAT?
TMP
DA
?!
SH
LUCY...
...WHERE DO I COMPLAIN WHEN A GREAT DIVINE BEAST STEALS MY JEWELRY?

My
Gently
Raised
Beast

IT'S BEEN A WEEK SINCE AMON RAN OFF WITH MY BRACELET...

I WONDER WHY HE DID IT.

DID HE WANT THE BRACELET FOR HIMSELF?

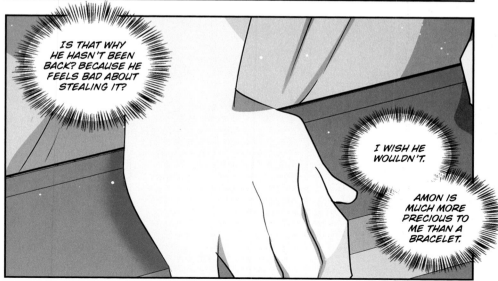

IS THAT WHY HE HASN'T BEEN BACK? BECAUSE HE FEELS BAD ABOUT STEALING IT?

I WISH HE WOULDN'T.

AMON IS MUCH MORE PRECIOUS TO ME THAN A BRACELET.

REALLY, THOUGH. WHY DID HE STEAL IT...?

GREED! AVARICE! MATERIALISM!

I'LL BE HEADING BACK NOW, PRINCESS.

BYE!

MAJETTO IS GOING TOO!

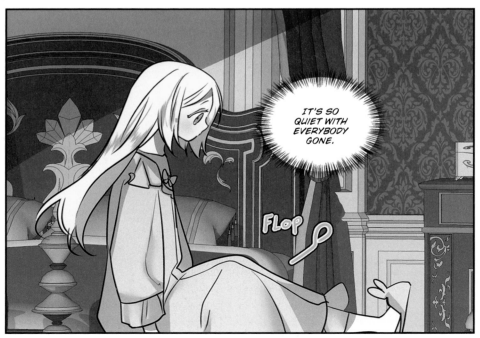

IT'S SO QUIET WITH EVERYBODY GONE.

FLOP

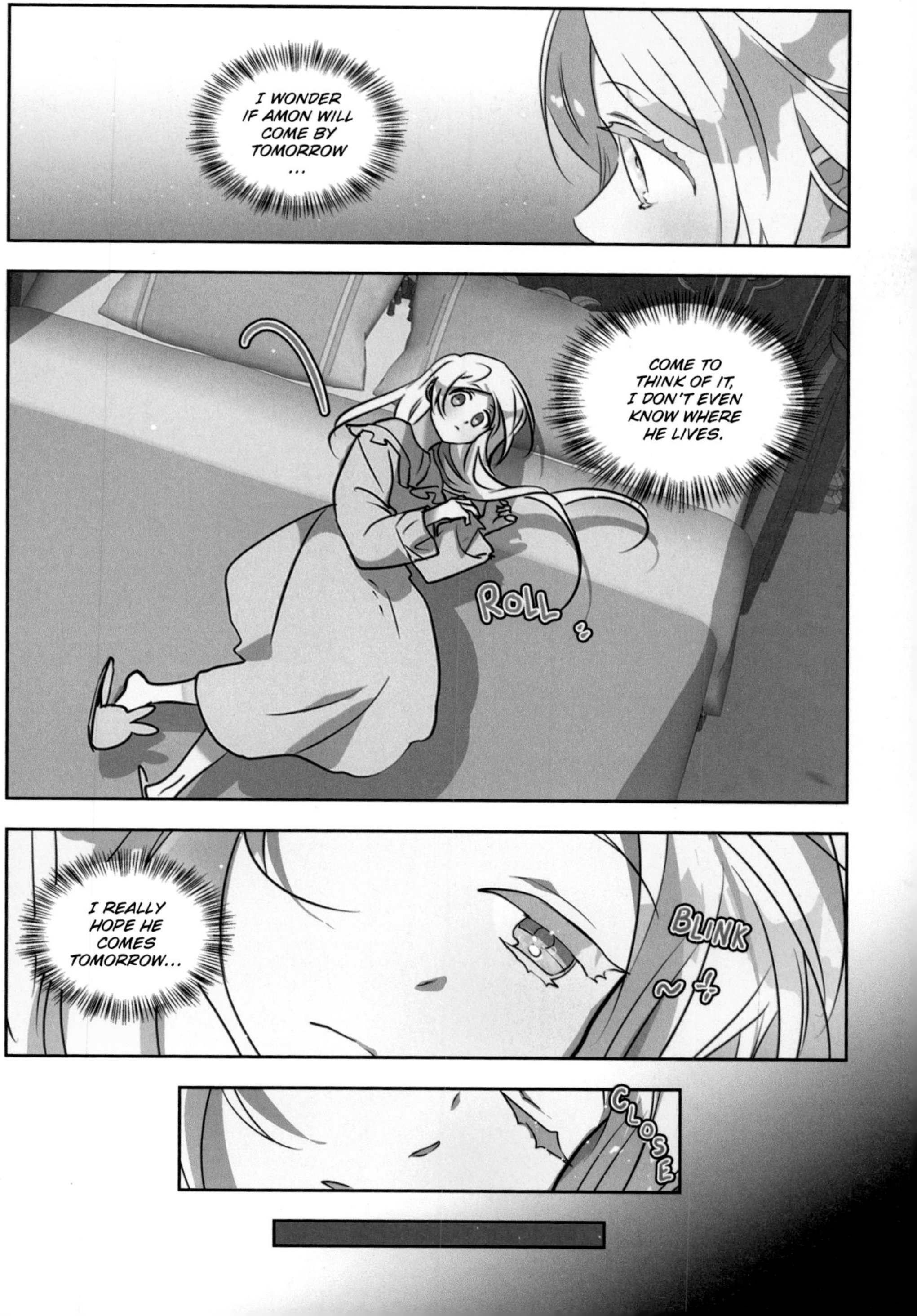
I WONDER IF AMON WILL COME BY TOMORROW ...
COME TO THINK OF IT, I DON'T EVEN KNOW WHERE HE LIVES.
ROLL
I REALLY HOPE HE COMES TOMORROW...
BLINK
CLOSE

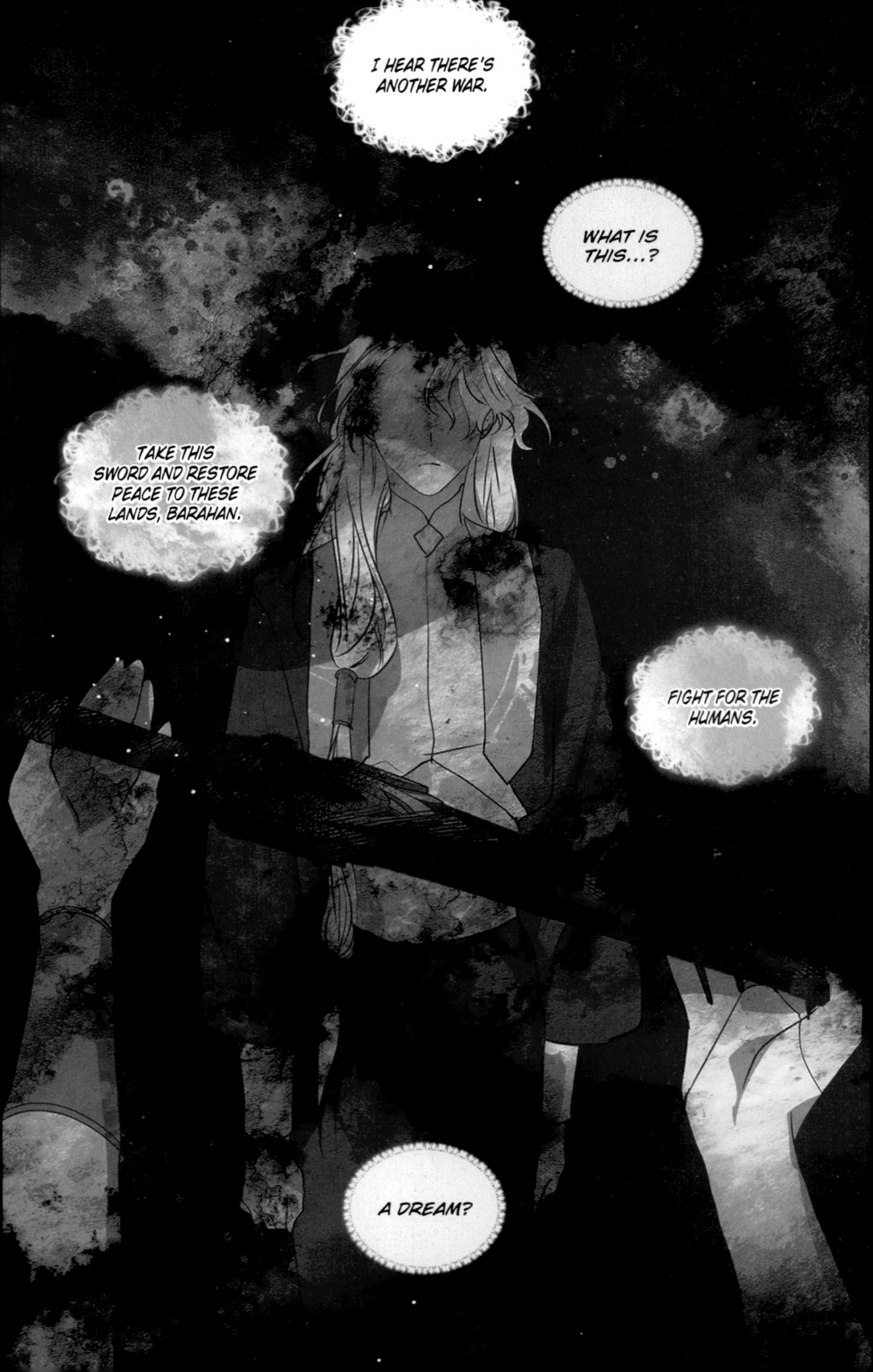
I HEAR THERE'S ANOTHER WAR.
WHAT IS THIS...?
TAKE THIS SWORD AND RESTORE PEACE TO THESE LANDS, BARAHAN.
FIGHT FOR THE HUMANS.
A DREAM?

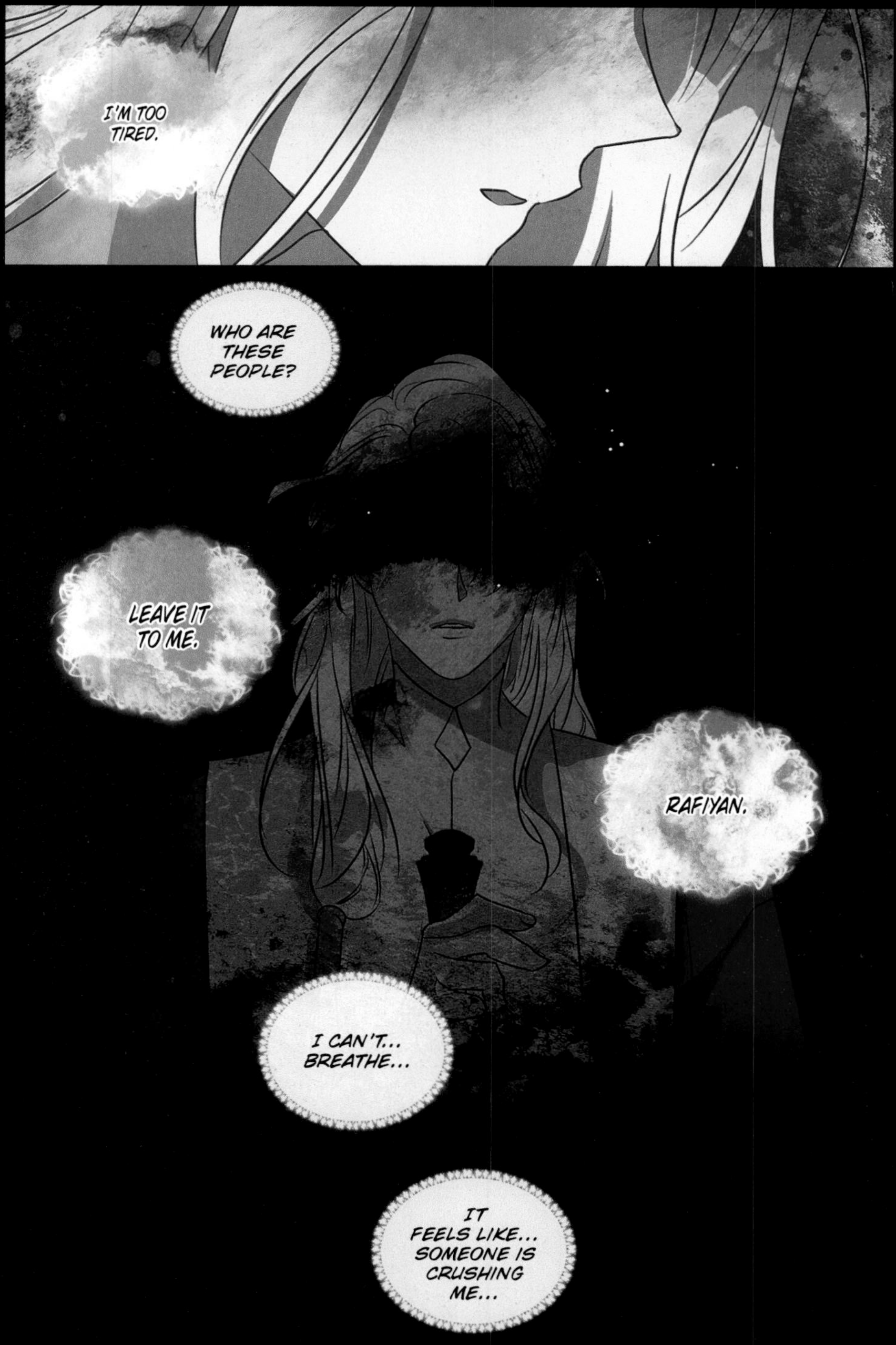
I'M TOO TIRED.
WHO ARE THESE PEOPLE?
LEAVE IT TO ME.
RAFIYAN.
I CAN'T... BREATHE...
IT FEELS LIKE... SOMEONE IS CRUSHING ME...

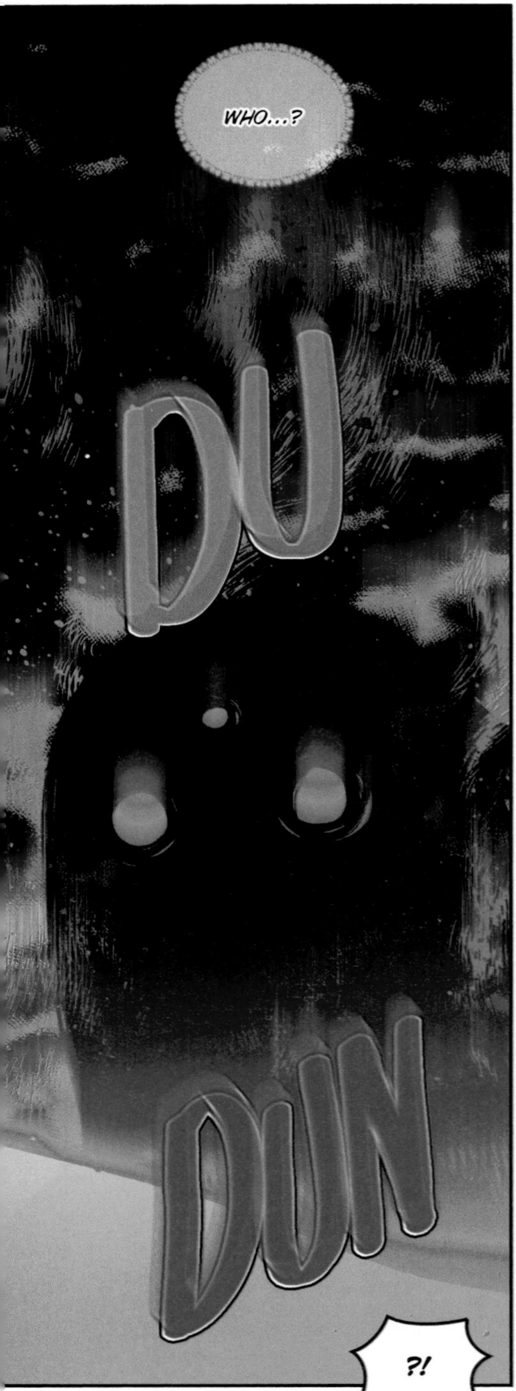
WHO...?
DU
DUN
?!

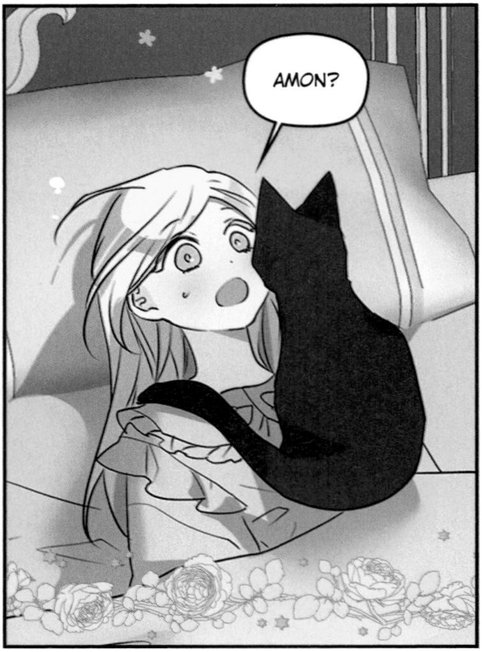
AMON?

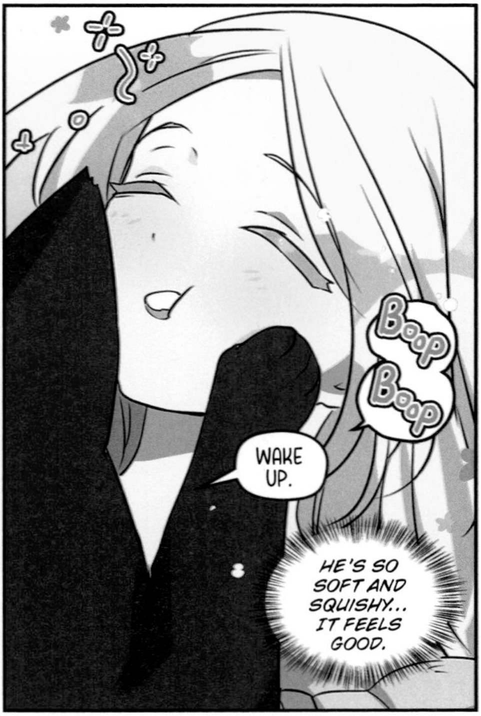
BOOP
BOOP
WAKE UP.
HE'S SO SOFT AND SQUISHY... IT FEELS GOOD.

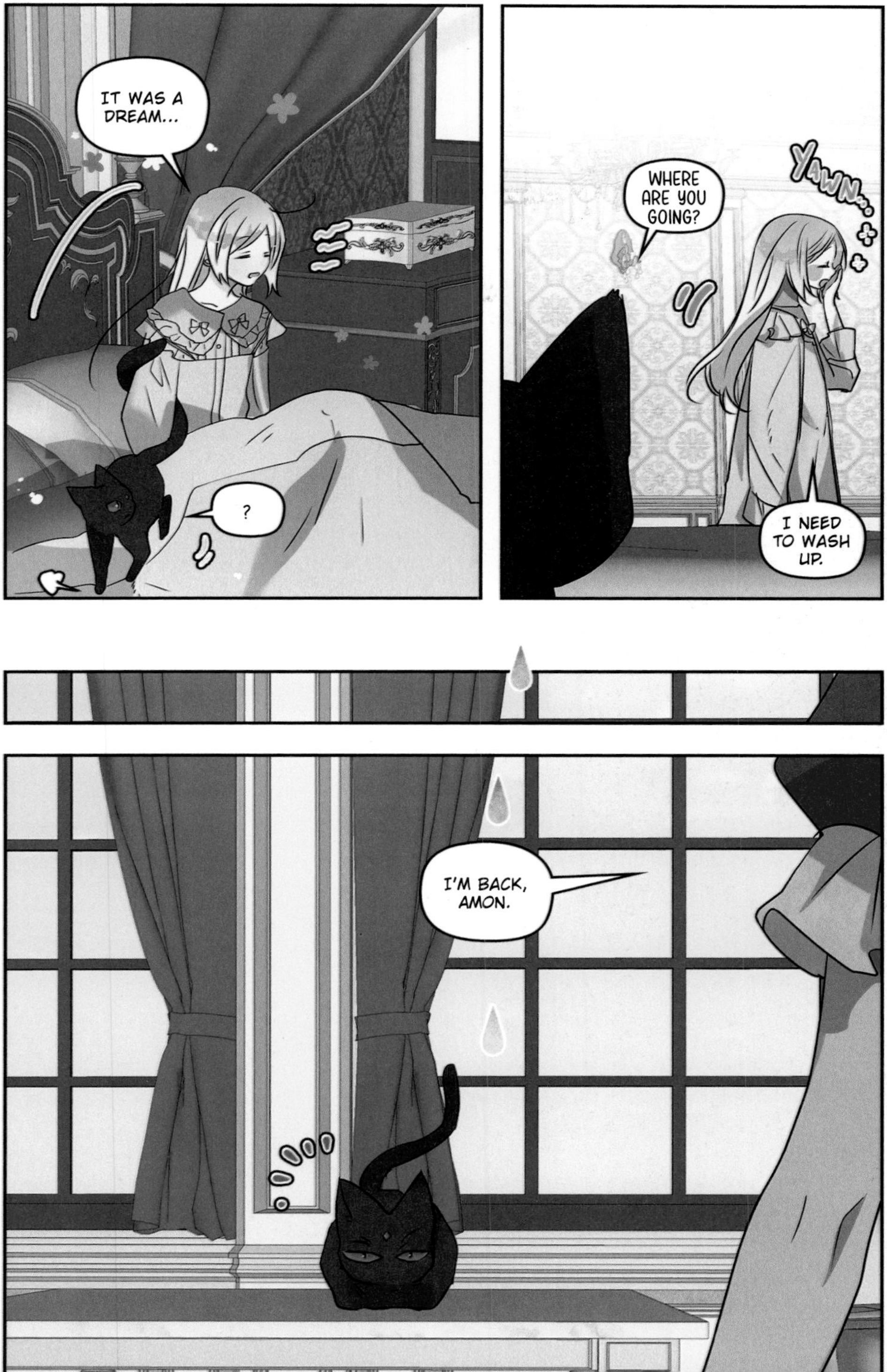
IT WAS A DREAM...
?
WHERE ARE YOU GOING?
YAWN...
I NEED TO WASH UP.
I'M BACK, AMON.

LONG TIME NO SEE!

YEAH.

SHF

PATTER PATTER

HUH? WHAT'S THAT?

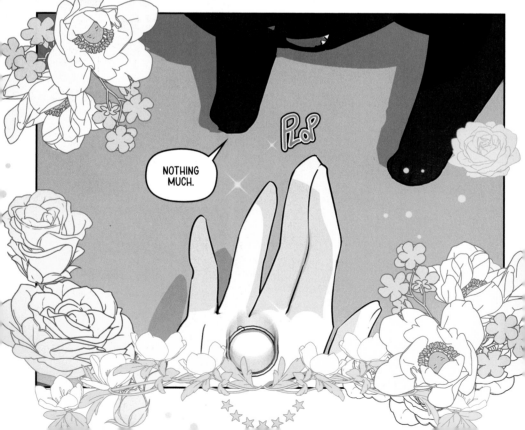

NOTHING MUCH.

PLOP

A RING??

IS IT FOR ME?

WELL...

WHERE DID YOU GET THIS? YOU DIDN'T STEAL IT, DID YOU?

YOU DARE ACCUSE ME, A DIVINE BEAST, OF THEFT?

NYA!!

WELL, YOU DID TOTALLY STEAL MY BRACELET.

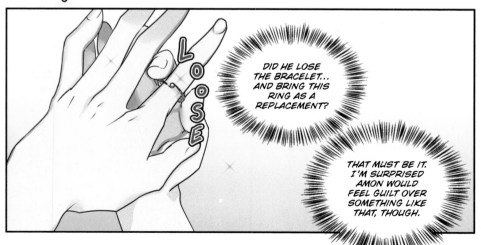

LOOSE

DID HE LOSE THE BRACELET... AND BRING THIS RING AS A REPLACEMENT?

THAT MUST BE IT. I'M SURPRISED AMON WOULD FEEL GUILT OVER SOMETHING LIKE THAT, THOUGH.

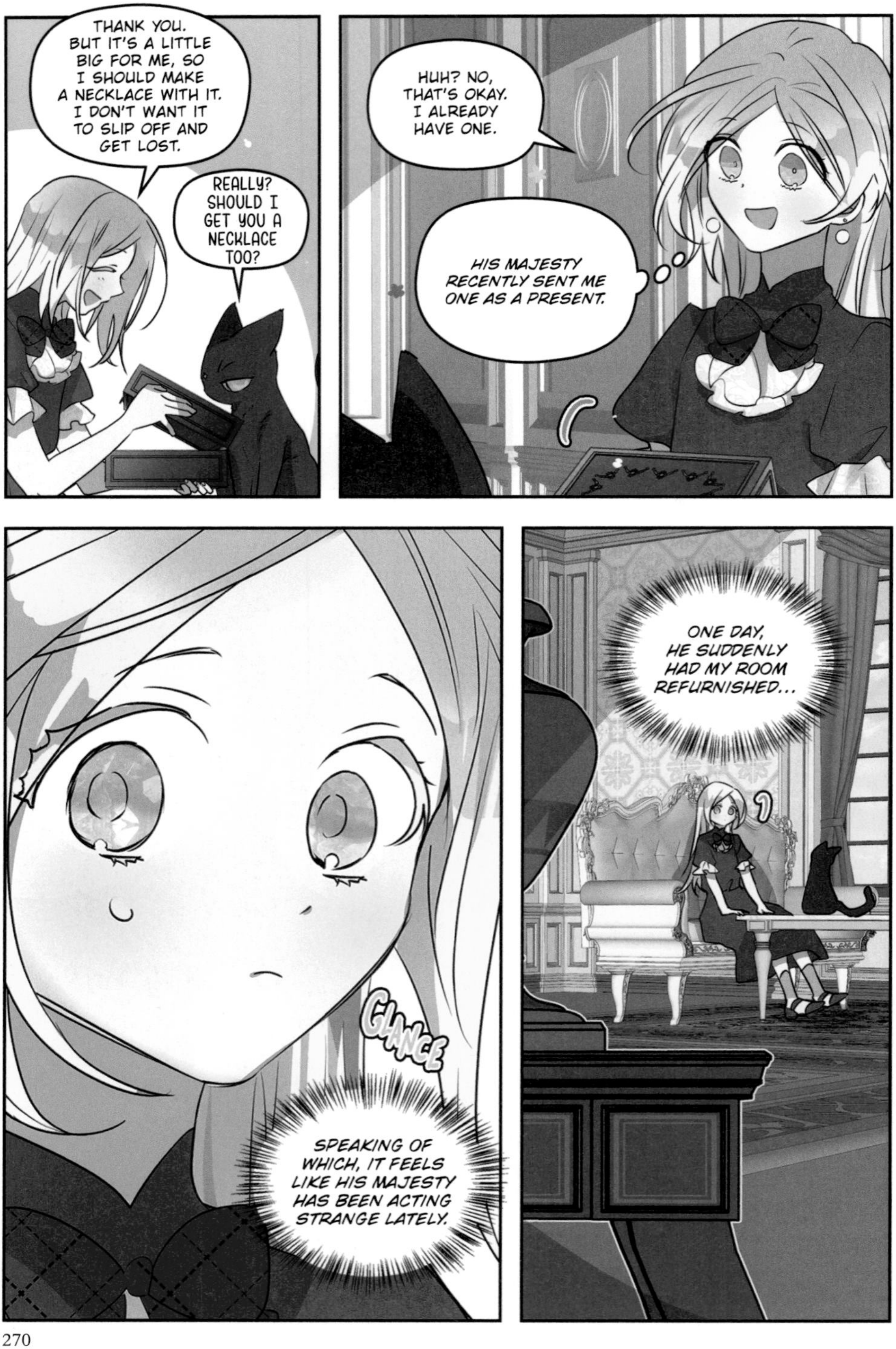
THANK YOU. BUT IT'S A LITTLE BIG FOR ME, SO I SHOULD MAKE A NECKLACE WITH IT. I DON'T WANT IT TO SLIP OFF AND GET LOST.
REALLY? SHOULD I GET YOU A NECKLACE TOO?
HUH? NO, THAT'S OKAY. I ALREADY HAVE ONE.
HIS MAJESTY RECENTLY SENT ME ONE AS A PRESENT.
GLANCE
SPEAKING OF WHICH, IT FEELS LIKE HIS MAJESTY HAS BEEN ACTING STRANGE LATELY.
ONE DAY, HE SUDDENLY HAD MY ROOM REFURNISHED...

...AND THE OTHER DAY, HE SUDDENLY GIFTED ME THIS NECKLACE.

SHUT

I THINK IT STARTED AFTER WE HAD THAT TALK IN THE GARDEN...

SUDDENLY GIVING ME SOME ATTENTION CHANGES NOTHING, THOUGH.

IN FACT, I'D PREFER IF HE JUST IGNORED ME...

DON'T MEET WITH HIM ANYMORE.

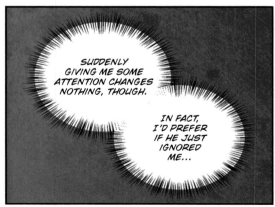

TAP
TAP

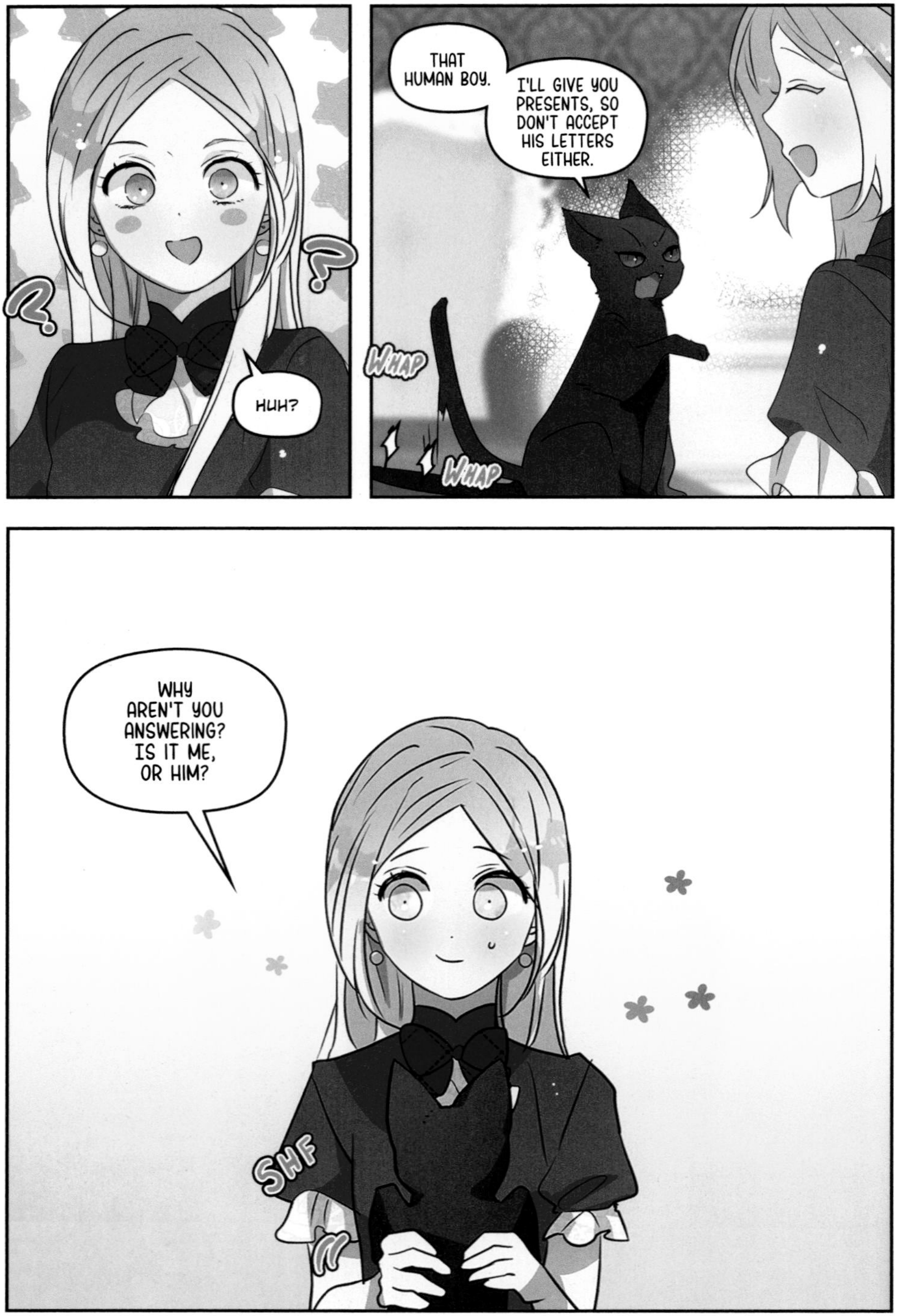
HUH?
THAT HUMAN BOY.
I'LL GIVE YOU PRESENTS, SO DON'T ACCEPT HIS LETTERS EITHER.
WHAP
WHAP
WHY AREN'T YOU ANSWERING? IS IT ME, OR HIM?
SHF

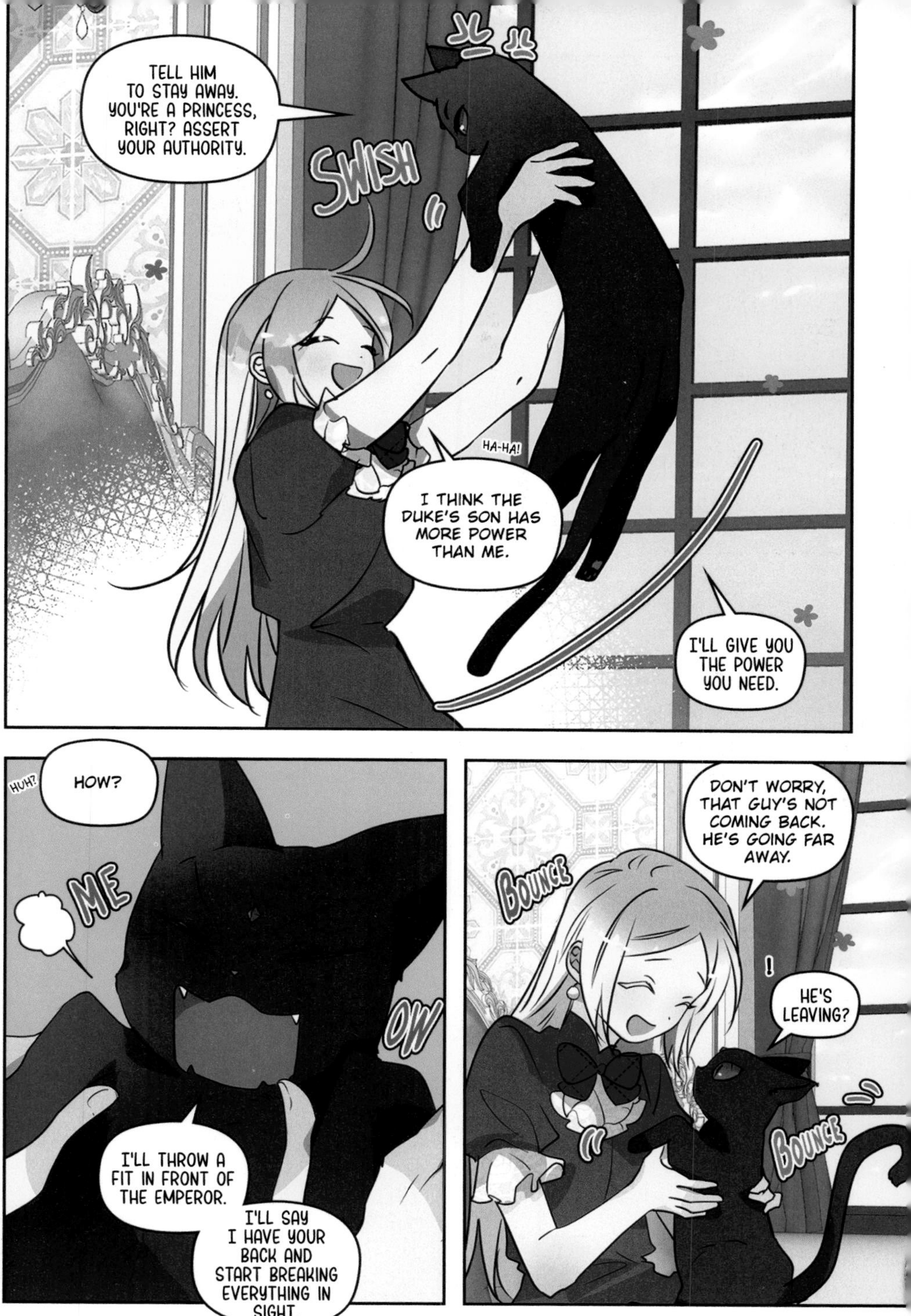
TELL HIM TO STAY AWAY. YOU'RE A PRINCESS, RIGHT? ASSERT YOUR AUTHORITY.
SWISH
HA-HA!
I THINK THE DUKE'S SON HAS MORE POWER THAN ME.
I'LL GIVE YOU THE POWER YOU NEED.
HUH?
HOW?
ME
OW
I'LL THROW A FIT IN FRONT OF THE EMPEROR.
I'LL SAY I HAVE YOUR BACK AND START BREAKING EVERYTHING IN SIGHT.
DON'T WORRY, THAT GUY'S NOT COMING BACK. HE'S GOING FAR AWAY.
BOUNCE
!
HE'S LEAVING?
BOUNCE

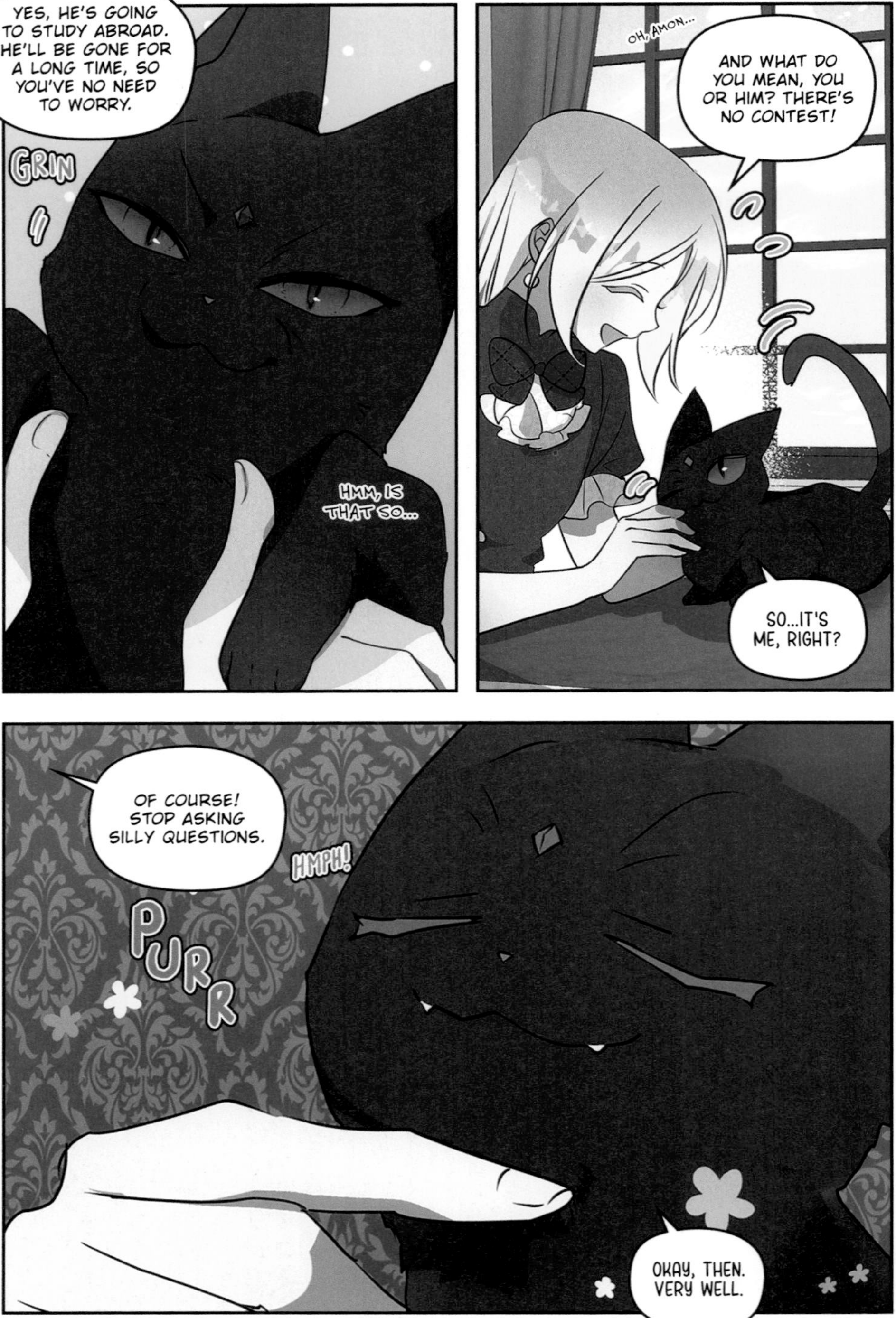
YES, HE'S GOING TO STUDY ABROAD. HE'LL BE GONE FOR A LONG TIME, SO YOU'VE NO NEED TO WORRY.
GRIN
HMM, IS THAT SO...
OH, AMON...
AND WHAT DO YOU MEAN, YOU OR HIM? THERE'S NO CONTEST!
SO...IT'S ME, RIGHT?
OF COURSE! STOP ASKING SILLY QUESTIONS.
HMPH!
PURR
OKAY, THEN. VERY WELL.

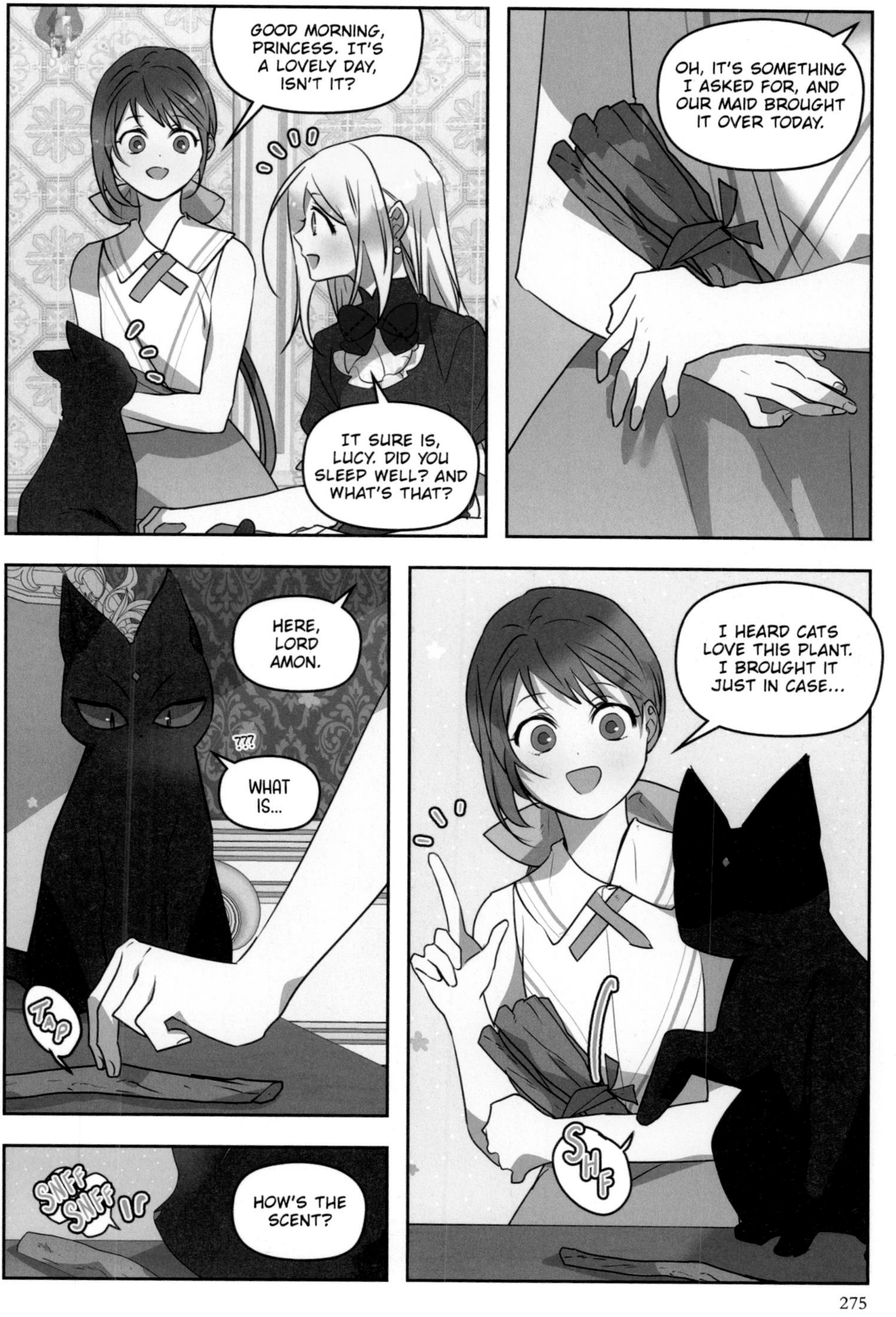
GOOD MORNING, PRINCESS. IT'S A LOVELY DAY, ISN'T IT?
IT SURE IS, LUCY. DID YOU SLEEP WELL? AND WHAT'S THAT?
OH, IT'S SOMETHING I ASKED FOR, AND OUR MAID BROUGHT IT OVER TODAY.
HERE, LORD AMON.
???
WHAT IS...
TAP
I HEARD CATS LOVE THIS PLANT. I BROUGHT IT JUST IN CASE...
SHF
SNFF SNFF
HOW'S THE SCENT?

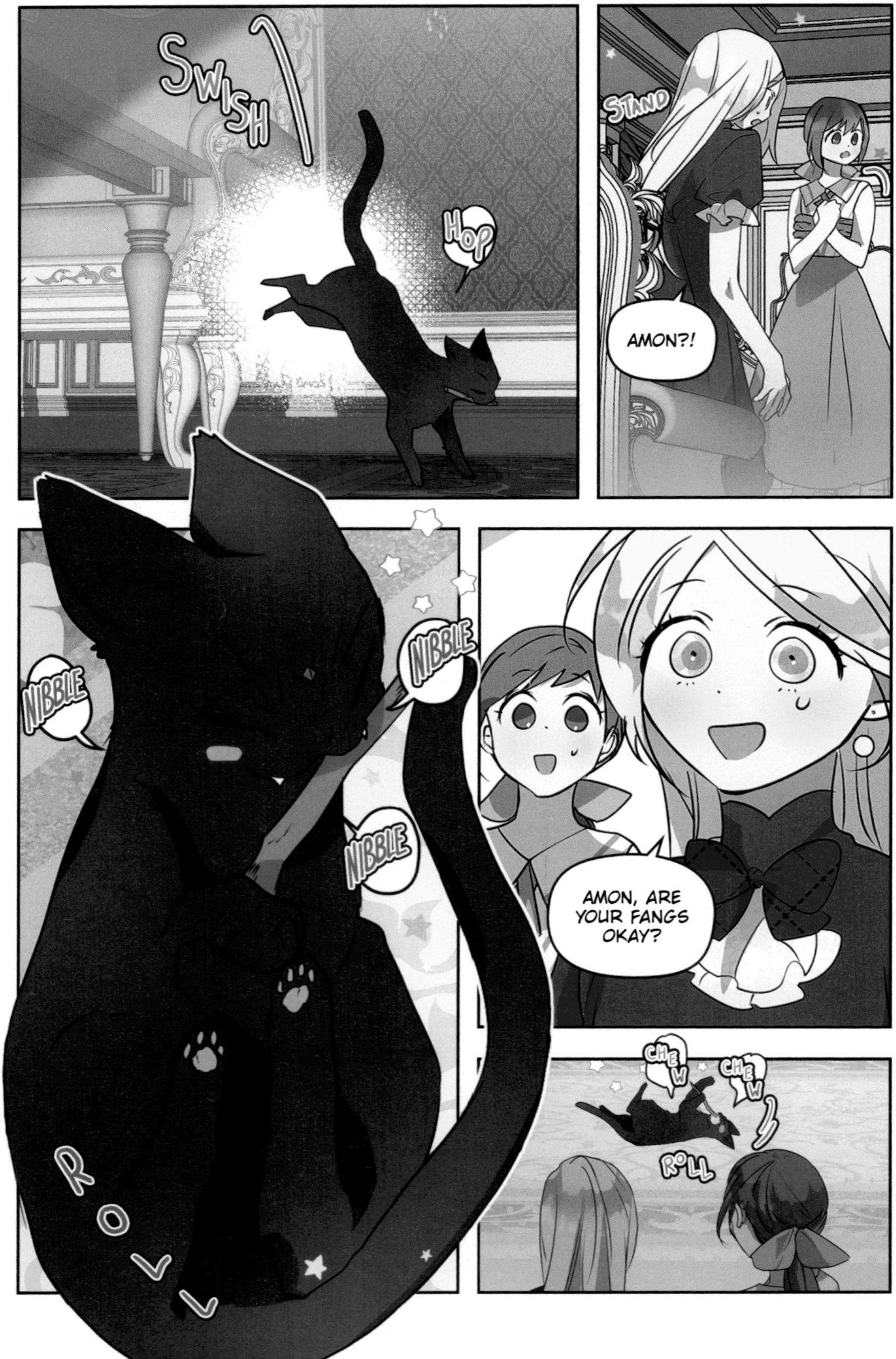
SWISH
HOP
STAND
AMON?!
NIBBLE
NIBBLE
NIBBLE
AMON, ARE YOUR FANGS OKAY?
ROLL
CHEW
CHEW
ROLL

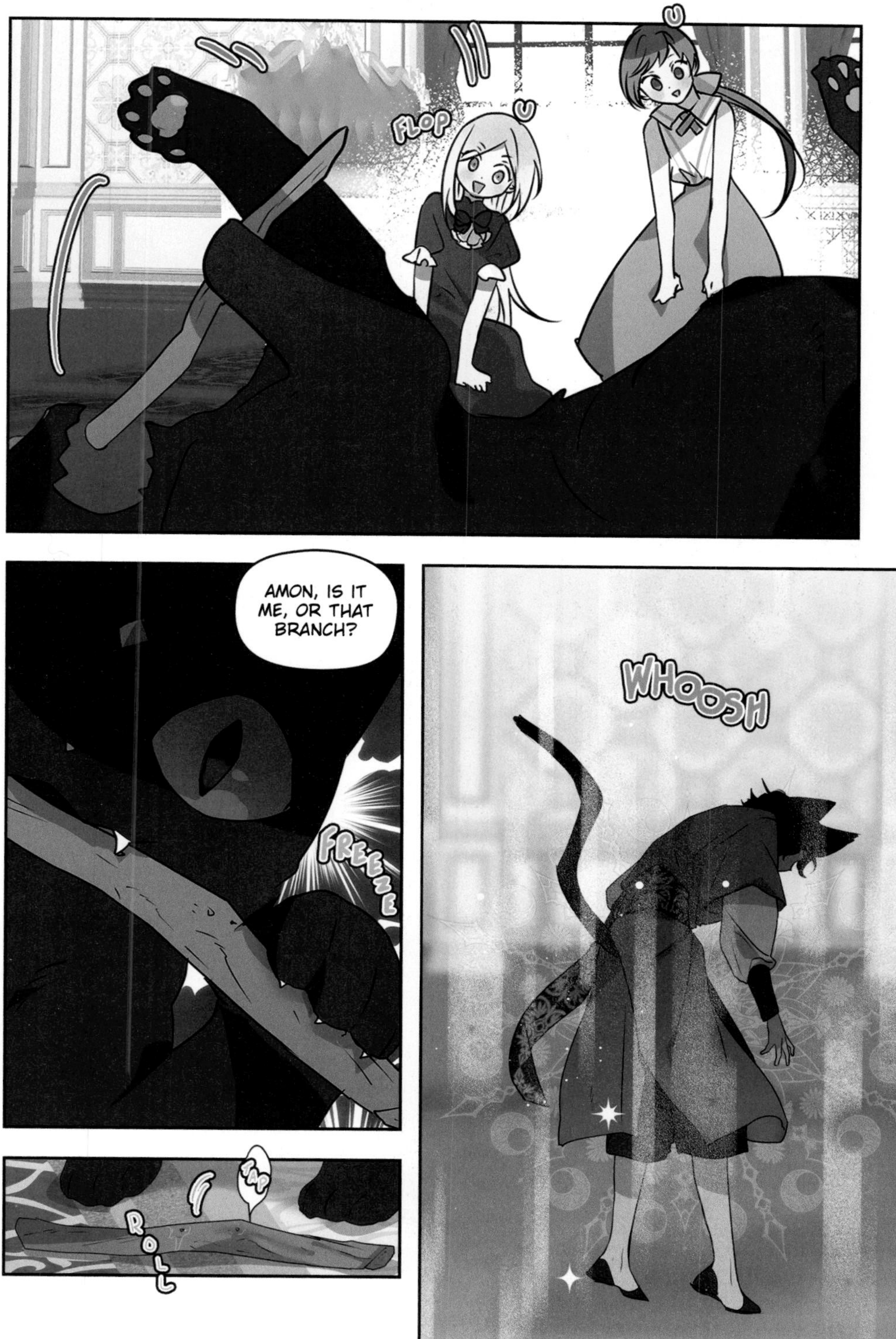
FLOP
AMON, IS IT ME, OR THAT BRANCH?
FREEZE
WHOOSH
TAP
ROLL

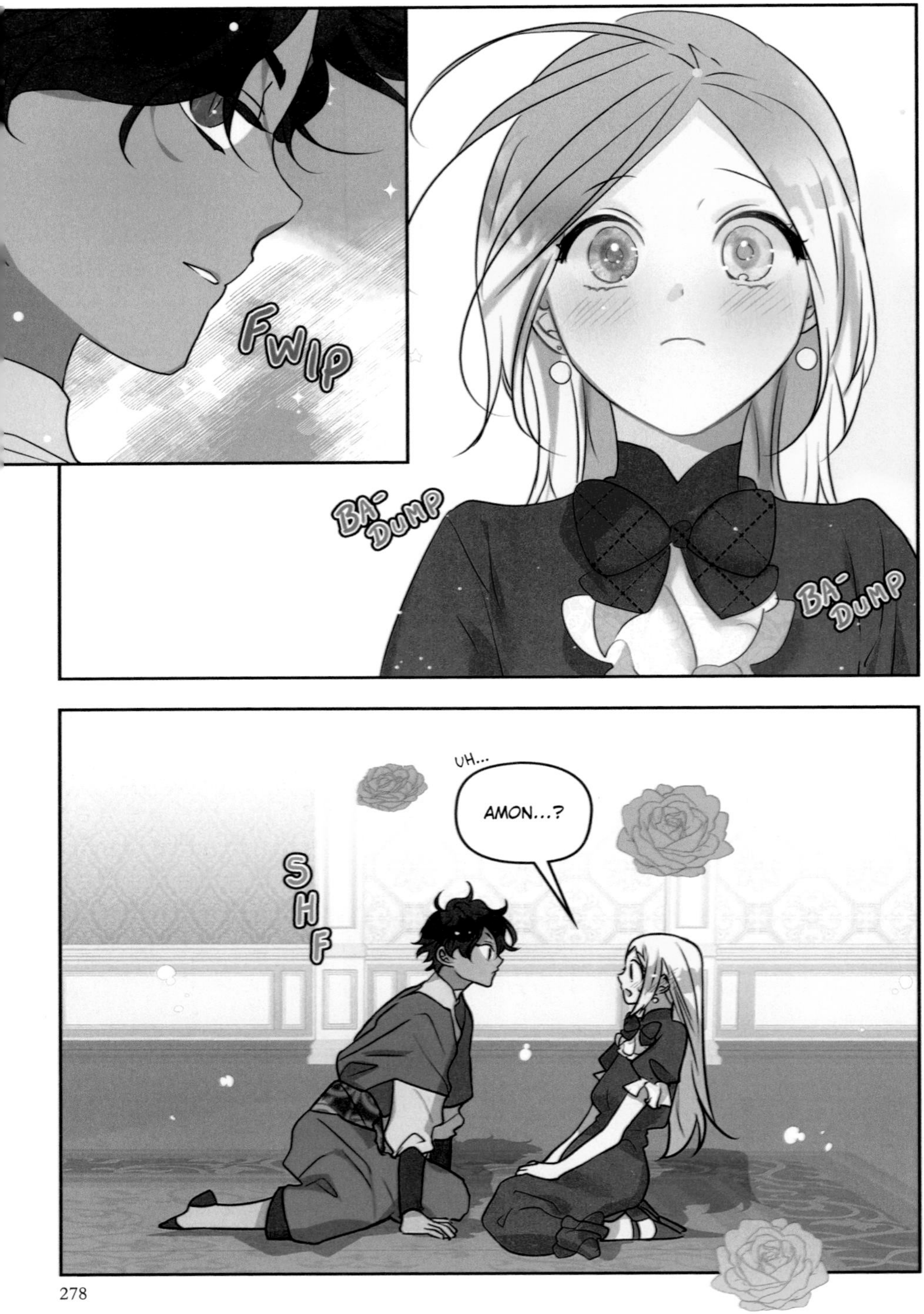
FWIP
BA-DUMP
BA-DUMP
UH...
AMON...?
SHF

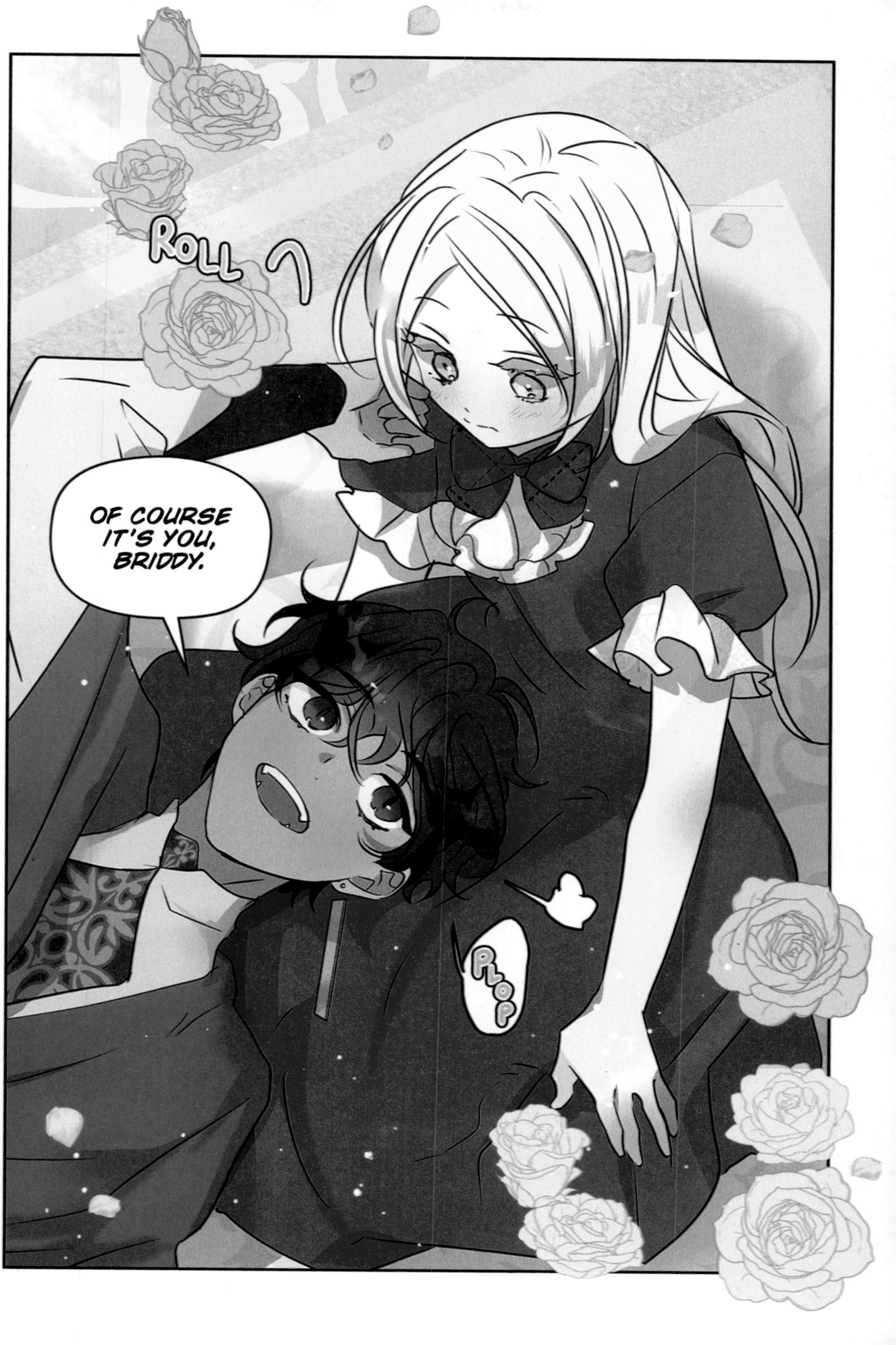
ROLL
OF COURSE IT'S YOU, BRIDDY.
PLOP

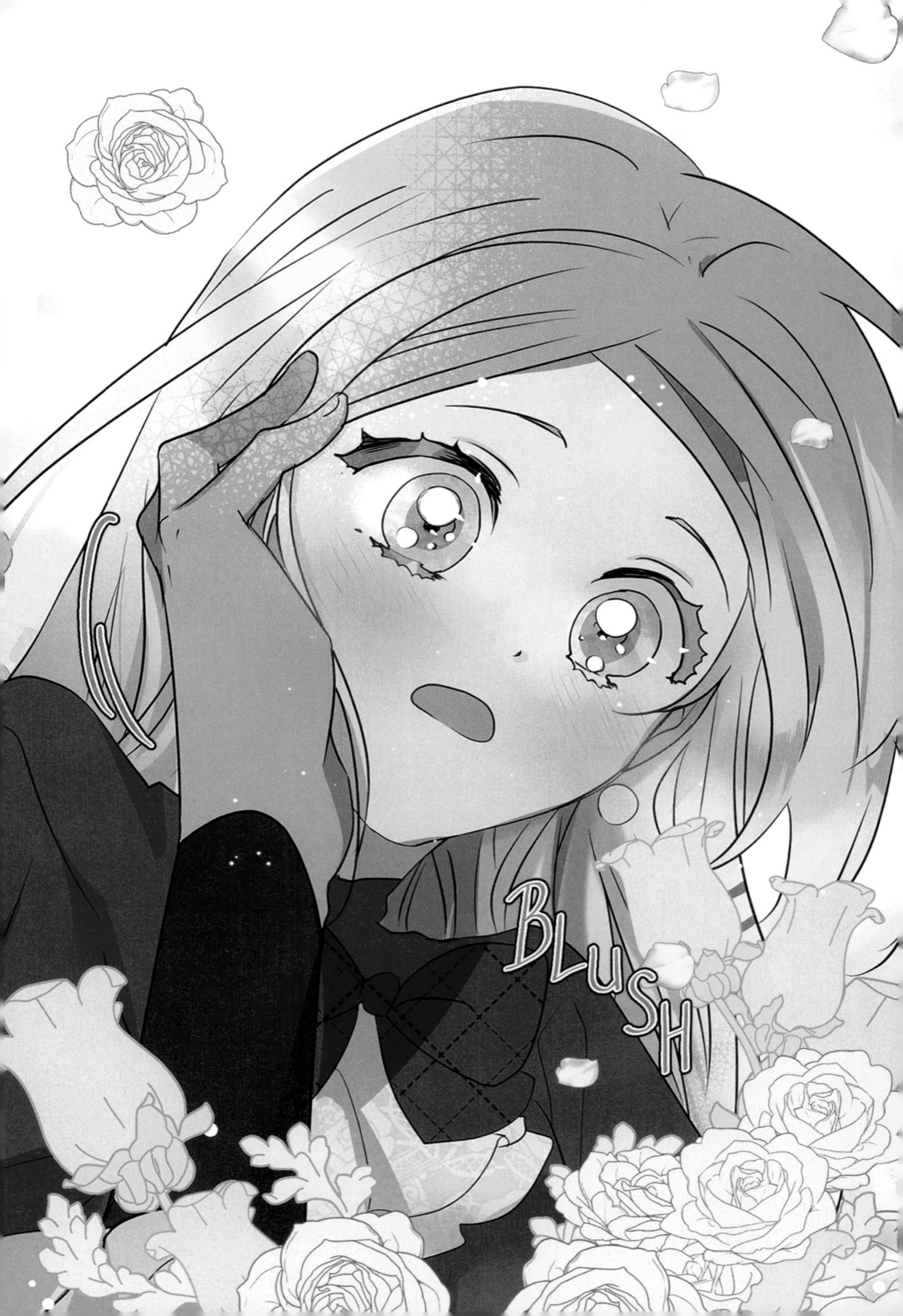
BLUSH

My
Gently
Raised
Beast

To be continued in Volume 2...

Blondina Ryun Ates

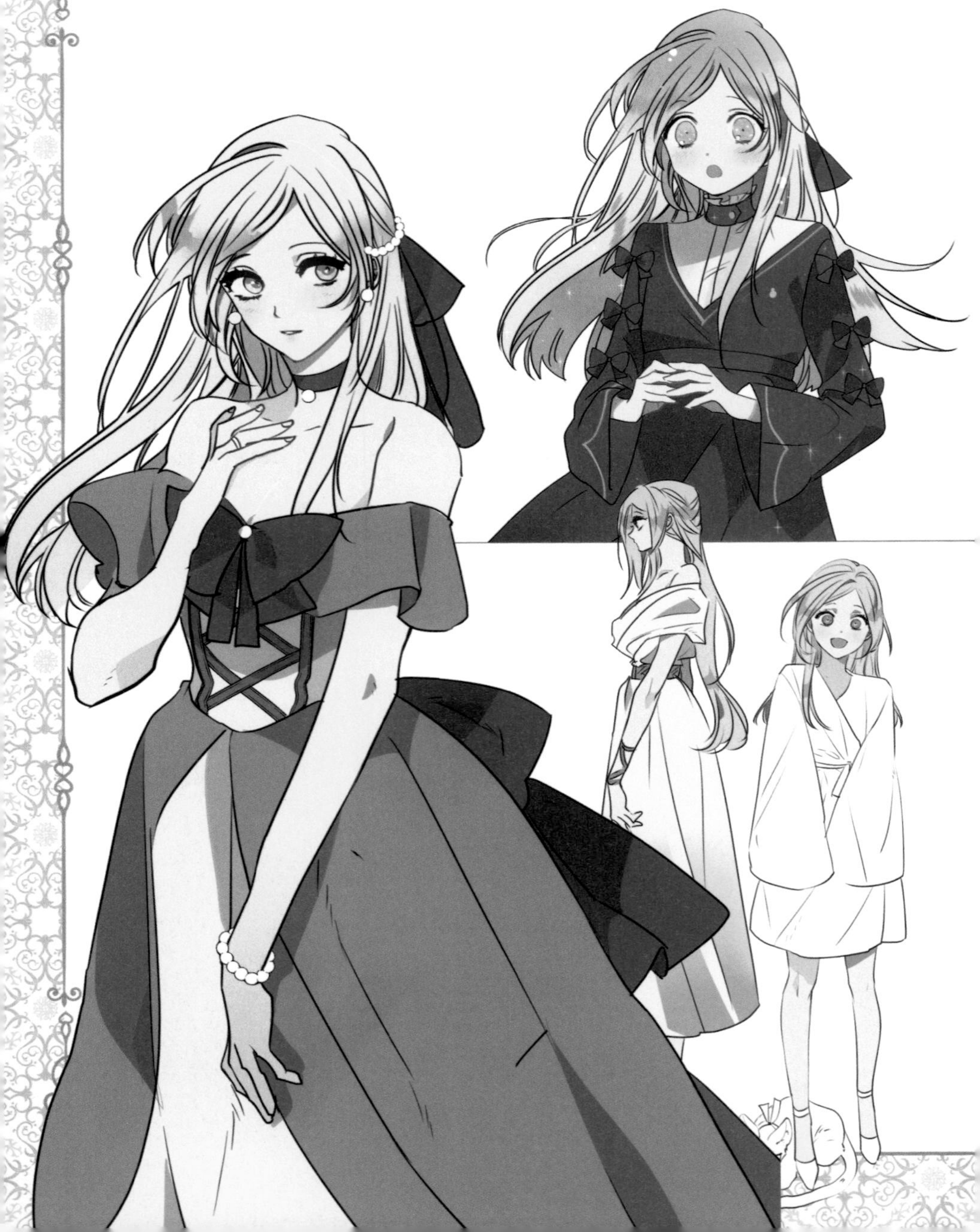

THE FIRST PRINCESS OF THE EMPIRE OF ATES

Nickname	**Briddy**
Height	Child: 4' 6" / Adult: 5' 7"
Age	Child: 11 / Adult: 20
Hairstyle	Blond, straight and soft
Eye Color	Silver
Costume Concept	As an adult: often wears off-the-shoulder dresses.

CHARACTER DESIGN BACKSTORY

As a member of the royal family, Blondina has golden hair. Unlike the other royals, however, she was designed with platinum blond hair to emphasize her status as an outsider who did not grow up in the imperial palace, as well as to set her apart from the rest of the royal family who seek to oppress the Divine Beasts.

Amon Akin

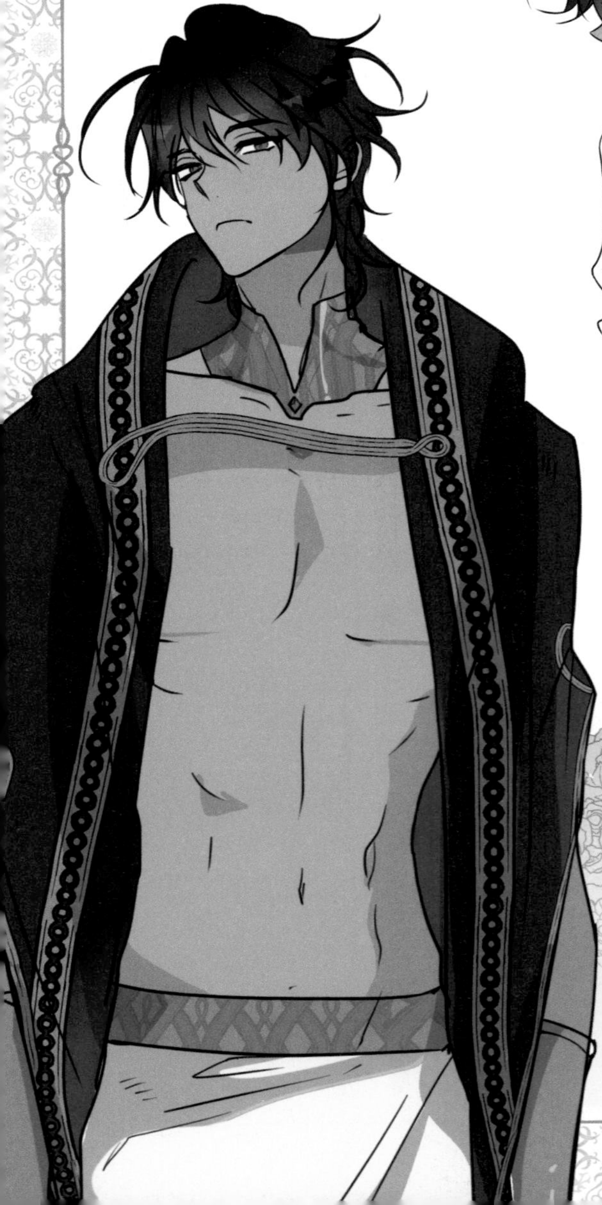

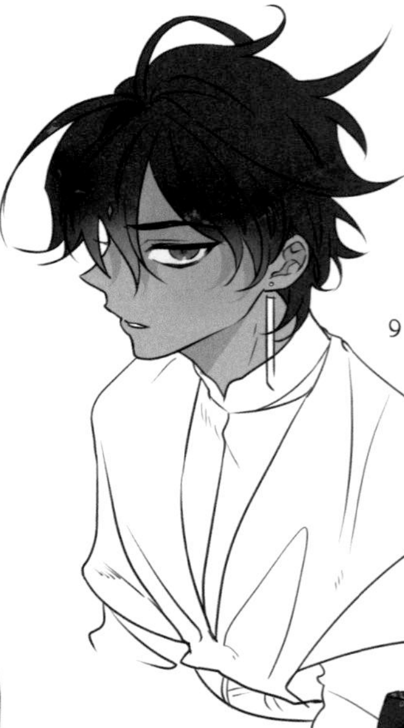

9 Year-Old Ver.

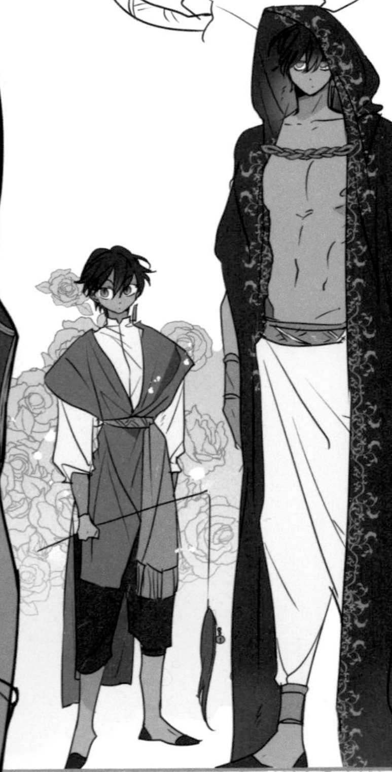

Leader of the Divine Beasts

Nickname	Amon
Height	Child: 4' 11" / Adult: 6' 3"
Age	Child: 9 / Adult: 18
Hairstyle	Black, messy and unkempt
Eye Color	Purple
Costume Concept	As an adult: a priestly robe with an open torso

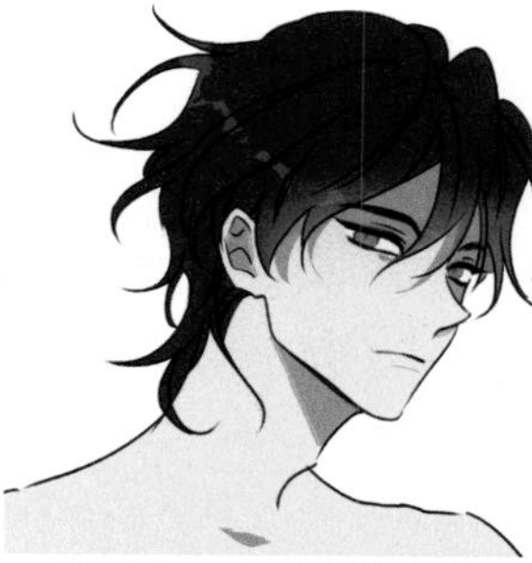

Character Design Backstory

Amon's darker skin tone was not in the original novel, but the comics artist Yeoseulki came up with the idea to accentuate his sexiness!

Divine Beast Form

The earlier designs of Amon's leopard form included elaborate patterns to reflect his status as the leader of the Divine Beasts. However, they were omitted in the final version because it was determined that he is not the type of person who would prefer ornate costumes or decorative patterns.

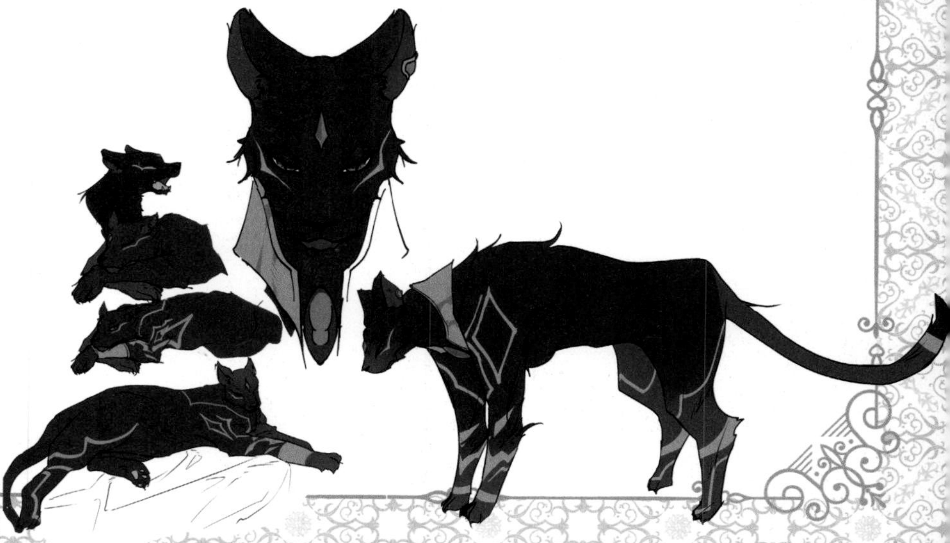

❦ VOLUME 2 PREVIEW ❦

Kind words from the emperor...

Prince Lart and...Lucy?

What is Princess Adellai scheming...?

Amon meets with the clan elder...

The little girl becomes a young lady, but what about—?

My Gently Raised Beast

❋Volume 2 Coming 2023!❋

I

My Gently Raised Beast

Art by: Yeoseulki ❧ Adapted by: Teava ❧ Original story by: Early Flower

Translation: WEBTOON ❧ Lettering: Chana Conley

This book is a work of fiction. Names, characters, places, and incidents are the product of the author's imagination or are used fictitiously. Any resemblance to actual events, locales, or persons, living or dead, is coincidental.

My Gently Raised Beast, Volume 1
©Yeoseulki, Teava, Early Flower 2022 /
C&C Revolution Inc.
All rights reserved.
English edition published by arrangement with
C&C Revolution Inc. through RIVERSE Inc.

English translation © 2021 WEBTOON
English edition © 2022 Ize Press

Ize Press
150 West 30th Street
19th Floor
New York, NY 10001

Visit us at izepress.com
facebook.com/izepress
twitter.com/izepress
instagram.com/izepress

First Ize Press Edition: December 2022
Edited by Ize Press Editorial:
Stephen Kim, JuYoun Lee
Designed by Ize Press Design:
Wendy Chan

The publisher is not responsible for websites (or their content) that are not owned by the publisher.

Library of Congress Control Number:
2022943359

ISBN: 979-8-4009-0009-9

10 9 8 7 6 5 4 3 2 1

WOR

Printed in the United States of America